P9-AOQ-069

INTRODUCTION TO THE ODYSSEY SURVEYS OF AMERICAN WRITING

The Odyssey Surveys of American Writing consist of four books which, taken in chronological order, present the best and most representative American writing from its beginning to the 1960's. The series has been planned by a general editor, who has established the time limits and appropriate authors for each of the four surveys, determined the kinds of editorial apparatus used, and set general policies for texts and footnotes. These editorial policies are designed to create a consistent approach throughout the series, to present authoritative texts, to give the minimum in annotation, to supply factual rather than interpretative editorial materials, and to present through introductions and occasional headnotes the historical context within which the works originally appeared.

Each of the surveys has been edited by an expert in the area covered by the volume. Thus each volume represents the judgment of a specialist editor about the age which it covers. Within the broad editorial policies of the entire series, the editors of individual surveys have been given complete freedom for selections, types of approach, historical statements, critical attitudes, and texts. The result is that each survey reflects the best informed current attitudes toward the period it covers, and that each survey is different in method and critical assumptions. The general editor has seen as his primary duty the organization of these necessarily varied points of view and methods of approach into four volumes which maintain their distinctiveness and at the same time reflect the unique assumptions and ideals of their particular ages.

C. Hugh Holman

THE ODYSSEY SURVEYS OF AMERICAN WRITING

General Editor: C. Hugh Holman

Colonial and Federalist American Writing (1607-1830)
Edited by George F. Horner and Robert A. Bain

The Romantic Movement in American Writing (1830-1865)
Edited by Richard Harter Fogle

The Realistic Movement in American Writing (1865-1900)
Edited by Bruce R. McElderry, Jr.

Twentieth Century American Writing (1900-1960's)
Edited by William T. Stafford

TWENTIETH CENTURY AMERICAN WRITING

By WILLIAM T. STAFFORD

THE ODYSSEY PRESS · INC
The Bobbs-Merrill Company, Inc., Publishers
Indianapolis · New York

COPYRIGHT © 1965 BY THE ODYSSEY PRESS, INC.

1970 THE ODYSSEY PRESS
A Division of the Bobbs-Merrill Company, Inc.
PRINTED IN THE UNITED STATES OF AMERICA
Library of Congress Catalog Card Number: 65-19411
ISBN 0-672-63130-x (pbk)
ISBN 0-672-63211-x
Seventh Printing

ACKNOWLEDGMENTS

APPLETON-CENTURY. For "The Flower-Fed Buffaloes" from *Going to the Stars* by Vachel Lindsay. Copyright 1926 by D. Appleton & Company; copyright renewed 1954. Reprinted by permission of Appleton-Century.

BEACON PRESS. For pp. 1-18 of *No! In Thunder: Essays on Myth and Literature* by Leslie Fiedler, © 1960 by Leslie Fiedler, and pp. 159-175 of *Stranger in the Village* by James Baldwin, copyright © 1955 by James Baldwin. Reprinted by permission of the Beacon Press.

DODD, MEAD & COMPANY. For "The Factory and the Attic" from *A Bed of Neuroses* by Wolcott Gibbs, copyright 1933 by Wolcott Gibbs. Reprinted by permission of Dodd, Mead & Company.

DOUBLEDAY & COMPANY, INC. For "Dolor" and "Night Crow," copyright 1947 by Theodore Roethke, and "Old Florist," copyright 1946 by Harper & Row, Publishers; all from *Lost Son and Other Poems* by Theodore Roethke. For "The Valiant Woman," from *The Prince of Darkness and Other Stories* by J. F. Powers, copyright 1947 by J. F. Powers. All of these selections reprinted by permission of Doubleday & Company, Inc.

FARRAR, STRAUS & COMPANY, INC. For "Words for Hart Crane" from *Life Studies* by Robert Lowell; copyright © 1956, 1959 by Robert Lowell. Reprinted by permission of Farrar, Straus & Company, Inc.

SAMUEL FRENCH, INC. For "The Adding Machine" by Elmer L. Rice, copyright 1922, 1929 by Elmer L. Rice; copyright 1923 by Doubleday, Page & Company; copyright 1949 (In Renewal) by Elmer L. Rice; copyright 1950, 1956 (In Renewal) by Elmer L. Rice. All Rights Reserved. CAUTION: Professionals and amateurs are hereby warned that "The Adding Machine," being fully protected under the copyright laws of the United States of America, the British Empire, including the Dominion of Canada, and all other countries of the Copyright Union, is subject to a royalty. All rights, including professional, amateur, motion pictures, recitation, public reading, radio and television broadcasting and the rights of translation into foreign languages are strictly reserved. Amateurs may give stage production of this play upon payment of a royalty of Fifty Dollars for each performance one week before the play is to be given to Samuel French, Inc., at 25 West 45th Street, New York 36, New York, or 7623 Sunset Blvd., Hollywood 46, California, or if in Canada to Samuel French (Canada), Ltd., at 27 Grenville Street, Toronto, Ontario.

HARCOURT, BRACE & WORLD, INC. For "The Function of Criticism" from *Selected Essays of T. S. Eliot*, copyright 1932, 1936, 1950 by Harcourt, Brace & World, Inc.; © 1960, 1964 by T. S. Eliot; and for "The Love Song of J. Alfred Prufrock," "The Hippopotamus," "The Waste Land," "The Hollow Men," and "Ash-Wednesday," all from *Collected Poems 1909-1962* by T. S. Eliot, copyright 1936 by Harcourt, Brace & World, Inc.; © 1963, 1964 by T. S. Eliot. All of these selections reprinted by permission of Harcourt, Brace & World, Inc., and Faber & Faber, Ltd. For "Broken-face Gargoyles" and "Accomplished Facts" from *Smoke and Steel* by Carl Sandburg, copyright 1920 by Harcourt, Brace & World, Inc. For "Flowers Tell Months" from *Good Morning, America* by Carl Sandburg, copyright 1928, 1956 by Carl Sandburg. For "The People Will Live On" from *The People, Yes* by Carl Sandburg, copyright 1936 by Harcourt, Brace & World, Inc. For "Public Letter to Emily Dickinson" and excerpt from "Notes for a Preface" from *Complete Poems,* copyright 1950 by Carl Sandburg. For "when god lets my body be," "in Just-," "Buffalo Bill's," copyright 1923, 1951 by E. E. Cummings; foreword to *Is 5,* copyright 1926 by Horace Liveright, renewed 1954 by E. E. Cummings; "i sing of Olaf glad and big," copyright 1931, 1959 by E. E. Cummings; "anyone lived in a pretty how town," copyright 1940 by E. E. Cummings; "pity this busy monster, manunkind," "one's not half two. It's two are halves of one:" copyright 1944 by E. E. Cummings; "what if a much of a which of a wind," copyright by E. E. Cummings; all reprinted from *Poems 1923-1954* by E. E. Cummings. For excerpt from *The Man Who Knew Coolidge* by Sinclair Lewis, copyright 1928 by Harcourt, Brace & World, Inc., renewed 1956 by Michael Lewis. For "Letter to T. S. Eliot" from *Letters of Ezra Pound 1907-1941* edited by D. D. Paige, copyright 1950 by Harcourt, Brace & World, Inc. For "Flowering Judas" from *Flowering Judas and Other Stories,* copyright 1930, 1935, 1958 by Katherine Anne Porter. For "O K*A*P*L*A*N, MY K*A*P*L*A*N" from *The Education of Hyman Kaplan* by Leonard Q. Ross [Leo Rosten], copyright 1937 by Harcourt, Brace & World, Inc. For "Mr. Edwards and the Spider" and "After the Surprising Conversions" from *Lord Weary's Castle,* copyright 1944, 1946 by Robert Lowell. For "The Orient Express" from *The Seven-League Crutches* by Randall Jarrell, copyright 1951 by Harcourt, Brace & World, Inc. For "Museum Piece" and "Juggler" from *Ceremony and Other Poems,* copyright 1948, 1949, 1950 by Richard Wilbur. For "Exeunt," copyright 1952 by The New Yorker Magazine, Inc. (first published under the title "Exodus"); reprinted from *Things of This World* by Richard Wilbur. For "Blackberry Winter" from *The Circus in the Attic and Other Stories,* copyright 1947 by Robert Penn Warren. All of these selections reprinted by permission of Harcourt, Brace & World, Inc.

HARPER & ROW, PUBLISHERS. For "Walden" (June 1939) from *One Man's Meat* by E. B. White, copyright 1939 by E. B. White. Reprinted with the permission of Harper & Row, Publishers, Incorporated. For "Renascence," copyright 1912-1940 by Edna St. Vincent Millay; "Euclid Alone Has Looked on Beauty Bare," copyright 1917-1945 by Edna St. Vincent Millay; "If I should Learn, in Some Quite Casual Way," copyright 1923-1951 by Edna St. Vincent Millay and Norma Millay Ellis; all of these poems are from *Collected Poems* by Harper & Brothers, and are reprinted by permission of Norma Millay Ellis.

HARVARD UNIVERSITY PRESS. For pp. 278-280 from Ostram's *Untriangulated Stars: Letters of Edwin Arlington Robinson to Harry de Forest Smith: 1890-1905,* published in 1947 by Harvard University Press. Reprinted by permission of Harvard University Press.

HOLT, RINEHART AND WINSTON, INC. For "Forgive, O Lord" and "Lines Written in Dejection on the Eve of Great Success" from *In the Clearing* by Robert Frost, copyright 1942, © 1962 by Robert Frost. For "The Figure a Poem Makes," "Mowing," "The Tuft of Flowers," "Mending Wall," "The Mountain," "Home Burial," "After Apple-Picking," "The Wood-Pile," "Birches," "'Out, Out—'," "Fire and Ice," "Stopping by Woods on a Snowy Evening," "West-Running Brook," "A Soldier," "What Fifty Said," "The Bear," "Design," "The Silken Tent," "The Subverted Flower," "Our Hold on the Planet," and "The Secret Sits," all from *Complete Poems of Robert Frost,* copyright 1916, 1921, 1923, 1928, 1930, 1934, 1939 by Holt, Rinehart and Winston, Inc.; copyright 1936, 1942, 1949 by Robert Frost; copyright renewed 1944, 1951, © 1956, 1962 by Robert Frost. For "Chicago," "Under a Hat Rim," "Flux," "Monotone," "Nocturne in a Deserted Brickyard," "I Am the People, the Mob" from *Chicago Poems* by Carl Sandburg, copyright 1916 by Holt, Rinehart and Winston, Inc.; copyright renewed 1944 by Carl Sandburg. All of these selections reprinted by permission of Holt, Rinehart and Winston, Inc.

HOUGHTON MIFFLIN COMPANY. For pp. v-vii, the prefatory note, from *U.S.A.,* published by Houghton Mifflin Company, copyright by John Dos Passos, and "Newsreel XXXIV," "The House of Morgan," "Newsreel XXXV," and "The Camera Eye (39)" from *1919,* copyright by John Dos Passos. All of these selections reprinted by permission of John Dos Passos. For "Patterns" by Amy Lowell from *The Complete Poetic Works of Amy Lowell* (Boston: Houghton Mifflin Company, 1955). For "Ars Poetica," "You, Andrew Marvell," "Immortal Autumn," "Not Marble nor the Gilded Monuments," and "Empire Builders" from *Collected Poems of Archibald MacLeish.* All of these selections reprinted by permission of Houghton Mifflin Company.

RANDALL JARRELL. For "The Death of the Ball Turret Gunner," copyright by Randall Jarrell. Reprinted by permission of Randall Jarrell.

ALFRED A. KNOPF, INC. For "A & P" from *Pigeon Feathers and Other Stories* by John Updike, copyright 1961 © 1962 by John Updike. "A & P" originally appeared in *The New Yorker*. For "Bells for John Whiteside's Daughter" and "Here Lies a Lady," copyright 1924 by Alfred A. Knopf, Inc., renewed 1952 by John Crowe Ransom; also for "Blue Girls," copyright 1927 by Alfred A. Knopf, Inc., renewed 1955 by John Crowe Ransom; all of these poems are from *Selected Poems* by John Crowe Ransom. For "Preface to The Best Stories of Sarah Orne Jewett" from *Willa Cather on Writing,* copyright 1925 by Alfred A. Knopf, Inc. For "The Sculptor's Funeral" from *Youth and the Bright Medusa* by Willa Cather, copyright 1904, 1932 by Willa Cather. For "The Plot Against the Giant," "Floral Decorations for Bananas," "A High-Toned Old Christian Woman," "The Emperor of Ice-Cream," "Disillusionment of Ten O'Clock," "Anecdote of the Jar," all with copyright 1923, 1951 by Wallace Stevens; also for "The Idea of Order at Key West," copyright 1936 by Wallace Stevens, "Study of Two Pears," copyright 1942 by Wallace Stevens, "Of Modern Poetry," copyright 1942 by Wallace Stevens, and "The Ultimate Poem Is Abstract," copyright 1947 by Wallace Stevens; all of these poems from *The Collected Poems of Wallace Stevens.* For pp. 235-238 of *Opus Posthumous* by Wallace Stevens, copyright 1957 by Elsie Stevens and Holly Stevens. For "The Husbandman," from *A Mencken Chrestomathy* by H. L. Mencken, copyright 1924 by Alfred A. Knopf, Inc. All of these selections reprinted by permission of Alfred A. Knopf, Inc.

LIVERIGHT PUBLISHING CORPORATION. For "Chaplinesque," "Proem to Brooklyn Bridge," "Van Winkle," and "The River" from *The Collected Poems of Hart Crane,* copyright © R-1961 by Liveright Publishing Corporation. Reprinted by permission of Liveright, Publishers, New York.

THE MACMILLAN COMPANY. For "Poetry," "To a Steam Roller," "To a Snail," and "The Mind Is an Enchanting Thing" by Marianne Moore from *Collected Poems,* copyright 1935 by The Macmillan Company. For "A Net to Snare the Moonlight" and "General William Booth Enters into Heaven," copyright 1913 by The Macmillan Company; "Abraham Lincoln Walks at Midnight," copyright 1914 by The Macmillan Company, renewed 1942 by Elizabeth C. Lindsay; all of these poems are from *Collected Poems* by Vachel Lindsay. For "Dedication and Preface" of *A Handy Guide for Beggars* by Vachel Lindsay, copyright 1916. For "Flammonde," "Cassandra," "Eros Turannos," "Bewick Finzer," and "The Man Against the Sky" from *Man Against the Sky* by E. A. Robinson, copyright 1916 by The Macmillan Company, renewed 1944 by Ruth Nivison. For "New England" by E. A. Robinson from *Dionysus in Doubt,* copyright 1925 by The Macmillan Company, renewed 1953 by Ruth Nivison and Barbara R. Holt. For "The Rat" by E. A. Robinson from *The Three Taverns,* copyright 1920 by The Macmillan Company, renewed 1948 by Ruth Nivison. For "Book I" from *Tristram* by E. A. Robinson, copyright 1927 by The Macmillan Company, renewed 1955 by Ruth Nivison and Barbara R. Holt. For Robert Frost's "Introduction" to *King Jasper* by E. A. Robinson, copyright 1935 by The Macmillan Company. For pp. 101-104 from *Selected Letters* by E. A. Robinson, copyright 1940 by The Macmillan Company. All of these selections reprinted by permission of The Macmillan Company. For "The Hill," "Cassius Hueffer," "Knowlt Hoheimer," "Lydia Puckett," "Margaret Fuller Slack," "Editor Whedon." "Daisy Fraser," "Mrs. Kessler," "Harry Wilmans," "Godwin James," and "Lucinda Matlock," all from *Spoon River Anthology* (New York: The Macmillan Company, 1914, 1915, 1942), copyright by Edgar Lee Masters. Reprinted by permission of Mrs. Ellen C. Masters.

NEW DIRECTIONS. For "Danse Russe," "Tract," "The Red Wheelbarrow," and "This Is Just to Say" from *The Collected Earlier Poems of William Carlos Williams,* copyright 1938, 1951 by William Carlos Williams. For pp. 69-70 of *The Crack-Up* by F. Scott Fitzgerald, ed. by Edmund Wilson, copyright 1945 by New Directions. For excerpt from "A Retrospect" from *The Literary Essays of Ezra Pound,* all rights reserved. For "A Virginal," "The Rest," "A Pact," "The Beautiful Toilet," "The Jewel Stairs' Grievance," and "Hugh Selwyn Mauberley: Stanzas I-V, Envoi," all from *Personae: The Collected Poems of Ezra Pound,* copyright 1926, 1954 by Ezra Pound. All of these selections reprinted by permission of New Directions.

OXFORD UNIVERSITY PRESS, INC. For "The Groundhog" from *Collected Poems: 1930-1960* by Richard Eberhart, © Richard Eberhart 1960. Reprinted by permission of Oxford University Press, Inc., and Chatto & Windus, Ltd.

RANDOM HOUSE, INC. For "The Glass Menagerie" by Tennessee Williams, copyright 1945 by Tennessee Williams and Edwina D. Williams. Reprinted from *Six Modern*

American Plays. For "Desire Under the Elms" by Eugene O'Neill, copyright 1924 and renewed 1952 by Eugene O'Neill. Reprinted from *Nine Plays by Eugene O'Neill.* For "Winter Is Another Country" by Archibald MacLeish, copyright 1948 by Archibald MacLeish. Reprinted from *Act Five and Other Poems* by Archibald MacLeish. For "Shine, Perishing Republic," "Boats in a Fog," and "Joy," copyright 1925 and renewed 1953 by Robinson Jeffers. Reprinted from *The Selected Poetry of Robinson Jeffers.* For "Fire on the Hills," copyright 1932 and renewed 1959 by Robinson Jeffers; reprinted from *The Selected Poetry of Robinson Jeffers.* For "The Purse-Seine," copyright 1937 by Random House, Inc.; reprinted from *The Selected Poetry of Robinson Jeffers.* For "The Bloody Sire," copyright 1941 by Robinson Jeffers; reprinted from *Be Angry at the Sun and Other Poems* by Robinson Jeffers. For "A Rose for Emily," copyright 1930 and renewed 1957 by William Faulkner; reprinted from *Collected Stories of William Faulkner.* For The Stockholm Address from *The Faulkner Reader,* copyright 1954 by William Faulkner (Random House, Inc.). For pp. 261-271 from *The Autobiography of Alice B. Toklas* by Gertrude Stein, copyright 1933 and renewed 1960 by Alice B. Toklas. For "Introduction" to *Flowering Judas and Other Stories* by Katherine Anne Porter, copyright 1930, 1935 by Katherine Anne Porter. For "Auto Wreck" and "Drug Store," copyright 1941 by Karl Shapiro; reprinted from *Poems 1940-1953* by Karl Shapiro. All of these selections reprinted by permission of Random House, Inc.

SATURDAY REVIEW. For "G.B.S. Enters Heaven(?)" by Joseph Wood Krutch, from Saturday Review, May 24, 1952; reprinted in the *Saturday Review Reader No. 2* (New York, 1953). Reprinted by permission of *Saturday Review* and Joseph Wood Krutch.

CHARLES SCRIBNER'S SONS. For Chapter 7 from *Look Homeward, Angel* by Thomas Wolfe, copyright 1929 by Charles Scribner's Sons, renewal copyright © 1957 by Edward C. Aswell and/or Fred W. Wolfe. For pp. 49-53 from *Thomas Wolfe's Letters to His Mother* edited by John Skelly Terry, copyright 1943 by Charles Scribner's Sons. For "Crazy Sunday," copyright 1932 by American Mercury, Inc., renewal copyright © 1960 by Frances Scott Fitzgerald Lanahan; reprinted from *Taps at Reveille* by F. Scott Fitzgerald. For "Big Two-Hearted River," from *In Our Time* by Ernest Hemingway, copyright 1925 by Charles Scribner's Sons, renewal copyright 1953 by Ernest Hemingway. For pp. 19-28 and 69-73 of *Green Hills of Africa* by Ernest Hemingway, copyright 1935 by Charles Scribner's Sons. For "Miniver Cheevy" (copyright 1907 by Charles Scribner's Sons; renewal copyright 1935) from *Town Down the River* by Edwin Arlington Robinson. All of these selections reprinted by permission of Charles Scribner's Sons.

THE VIKING PRESS, INC. For "A Father-to-Be" from *Seize the Day* by Saul Bellow, copyright © 1955 by Saul Bellow. First appeared in *The New Yorker.* For "Reality in America" from *The Liberal Imagination* by Lionel Trilling, copyright 1940, 1946 by Lionel Trilling. For Chapters 7 and 8 from *The Grapes of Wrath* by John Steinbeck, copyright © 1939 by John Steinbeck. For "The Book of the Grotesque" and "Sophistication" from *Winesburg, Ohio* by Sherwood Anderson, copyright 1919 by B. W. Huebsch, 1947 by Eleanor Copenhaver Anderson. All of these selections reprinted by permission of The Viking Press, Inc.

THE WORLD PUBLISHING COMPANY. For pp. 1-18 from *Hey, Rub-a-Dub-Dub!* by Theodore Dreiser, copyright 1920 by Boni and Liveright, copyright 1947 by Mrs. Theodore Dreiser. Reprinted by permission of The World Publishing Company.

for two memorable teachers

ROBERTA M. CARTER

and

MARGARET GRAMLING

PREFACE

The first American writer represented in this anthology is Edwin Arlington Robinson, who published his first book of verse in 1896; the last is John Updike, who was born in 1932 and had published seven books by 1963. Close though we are to all of the American literature written between these two publication dates, we have only a few hesitances about calling it the richest of our literary periods. Certainly its literature has been the most varied to have come from any half century of writing in America, and with the emergence of our nation as one of the world's major political and economic powers, its literature has been more widely influential than ever before. These last two contentions, however, do not necessarily support the first; for variety and influence are not necessarily one with quality. The quality of literature is always difficult to measure, even with the aid of a good deal more time than that afforded by the nearness to us of the literature of our own century. Yet modern American literature, it will be maintained, *is* rich, *is* powerful, *is*, perhaps, the most salient and inclusive single representation of whatever modern American life is, but ultimate support (or lack of it) for this final contention is probably more the responsibility of student and teacher, of posterity, than it is of an editor.

The wide range of literature written in modern America is available to all, and we can easily enough witness its emergence, trace its new developments and their demises, and follow its various schools and movements. We can give emphasis to those writers the age itself appears to have considered its "major" ones, and we can explore the eddies and backwaters, the contributory figures and influences, and see their relations to the whole as well as their faces to the world as things in themselves.

The general Introduction and the thirteen section Introductions under which the literature in this anthology is gathered are intended to serve just that purpose: to show the rise of the new poetry (in Robinson and

Frost, the Chicago school, the Imagists, and others), the new fiction (in Dreiser, in Willa Cather, and Sinclair Lewis), and the new drama; the flowering in the 1920's of each of those genres, in the poetry of Pound, Eliot, and Stevens, in the fiction of Anderson, Fitzgerald, and Hemingway, in the plays of Rice and O'Neill. Various kinds of poetic experimentation are also represented, both from the 1920's and from the 1930's, experiments by Amy Lowell and Edna St. Vincent Millay, by Hart Crane, Archibald MacLeish, Robinson Jeffers, and E. E. Cummings. Excerpts are given from major novels by Wolfe, by Dos Passos, and by Steinbeck. These novelists, with the addition of the poets Marianne Moore, William Carlos Williams, and John Crowe Ransom, move us through the 1930's. At the center of the anthology are ten essays, by writers as "old" and various as H. L. Mencken and Joseph Wood Krutch and those as "new" and various as Peter De Vries and James Baldwin. Robert Penn Warren, Katherine Anne Porter, and William Faulkner represent the Southern Renaissance, and Tennessee Williams, recent drama. The last two sections sample recent American poetry—and even more recent American fiction. A selected bibliography is provided for the period as a whole, and individual bibliographies and chronologies (or biographies) accompany each writer represented. Initial publication dates are given at the end of each selection.

Literary criticism in this volume is restricted to prefaces and essays, letters and diaries, proclamations and manifestoes, by writers who also have justifications other than their criticism alone. The omission here of any kind of critical interpretation upon the literature itself is intentional. Perhaps for any literature, but certainly for modern, the student should be at liberty to respond, the teacher to teach, without the interference of interpretative dogma. Hence no footnotes (except those which T. S. Eliot himself supplied for "The Waste Land") are given. Students and teachers are thus invited to approach this body of writing directly, and not through an editorial map or mask.

A Personal Note:

I perhaps owe much more than I should to more people than I should for various kinds of aid given me while completing this volume. To the general editor of this series, for example, Dean C. Hugh Holman of the University of North Carolina, my debt is great indeed. He not only first persuaded me to undertake the task; he also, step by step, gave unstintingly of his time, his sage counsel, his broad tolerance. Many friends and colleagues at Purdue University also provided invaluable help. Professor Russell Cosper, Dean M. B. Ogle, President Frederick L. Hovde, and the Board of Trustees made possible a sabbatical during the 1963-64 academic year in order for me to complete this job. Professor Maurice Beebe, my good friend and fellow editor of *Modern Fiction Studies*, kept a steady stream of research aids flowing through the mails to me while I was in Finland and thus made possible the completion of the volume while I was there. For various other kindnesses I wish to thank Professors William Braswell, Richard Crowder, Robert Lowe, Allen Hayman, Barriss Mills and Harold Watts as well as the staff of the Purdue University Libraries.

Working conditions and facilities for completing the book were much more convenient than they had to be because of my cooperative colleagues at the *Åbo Akademi* and *Turun Yliopisto* in Turku, Finland, where I was Fulbright Lecturer in American Literature during 1963-64. I especially wish to thank Professor Nils Erik Enkvist of the *Akademi* and Dr. Inna Koskenniemi and Fil. Lis. Kalevi Wiik of the *Yliopisto.*

But it is my wife, Fran Stafford, to whom I owe the most. She complained no more than was absolutely necessary about the multitude of day-to-day demands I invariably made on her and thus provided me with my most desperate need: free time. She deserves my special thanks.

W. T. S.

CONTENTS

Introduction

New Directions

New Consolidations

At Mid-Century

Twentieth Century American Writing

INTRODUCTION

The rise of modern American literature, concomitant with the emergence of the nation as a world power during the early years of this century, is easily traced. World War I stimulated its beginnings and heralded its triumphs in the 1920's. The depression-ridden 1930's, with the Wall Street crash of 1929 at one end and the beginnings of World War II at the other, reflect its continuous rise, as do the two decades since the end of the Second World War. Modern American literature does seem truly to reflect this pattern. The spiritual and social problems it reflects, its violence and upheavals, its imaginative curiosity and mystical hungerings, all have political, philosophical, and economic parallels. Like its non-literary counterparts, the definable emergence of modern American literature, say, between 1900 and World War I, maintains its ties to the past.

Poetry was the most variously vibrant genre of the revival. Although the new poetry is often conveniently dated with the founding of Harriet Monroe's *Poetry* in Chicago in 1912, it actually extended both backward and forward. Emerson, Whitman, and Emily Dickinson—Edward Taylor had not yet been discovered—constituted the traditions it was to follow. With the exception of a few poems by Stephen Crane, even fewer by Moody, it was to start as if new. Robinson had published three volumes before 1912, the same year Frost first sailed to England and a full year before his first book in 1913, but the first three volumes of *Poetry* also contained works by Pound, Hilda Doolittle, Lindsay, Amy Lowell, Williams, Fletcher, Sandburg, Edna St. Vincent Millay, Wallace Stevens, Masters, and Marianne Moore. There was an almost simultaneous development in England. *The Little Review*, founded (like *Poetry*) in Chicago, significantly moved East, first to New York and then to Europe. Pound was already in England, active with T. E. Hulme (and others) among not only the Georgians but also the Imagists, before his leadership was usurped by Amy Lowell and he moved to Paris. Eliot had also moved to England (in 1915); Frost, in the meantime, returned to America. And by the end of World War I, the lines were clearly drawn, although there was intermittent interaction between the two groups. The Midwest group —notably Lindsay, Masters, and Sandburg—had stayed home; Robinson had never left; and Frost had returned. The expatriate group, led by Pound and Eliot but also attracting many others, in effect made its permanent home in Europe.

The new fiction moved somewhat less rapidly—and only a little later. It also had nineteenth-century roots, and the change from old to new was less radically apparent. The fiction of James, of Edith Wharton, of Stephen Crane presaged one development—in their carefully mannered styles, in their concern for form, in their dedication to "art." The other was in the work of the new realists and naturalists, in Twain and Howells, on the one hand, and such naturalists as Norris, Jack London, and Upton Sinclair and the "Muckrakers" on the other. Willa Cather capped one movement as Dreiser did the other. Sinclair Lewis straddled many; he revolted from the village as Masters had done, detested American complacency, like Dreiser, and half loved the Midwest, like Cather. But the movement was not to reach its finest fruition until the 1920's and the catalyst of the First World War.

The development of modern American drama is somewhat more complicated—its achievement in America more revolutionary, its ties to the American past more tenuous. There was no Melville or Henry James of the American drama before O'Neill, no Whitman or Emily Dickinson. The reasons for this condition are many, varied, and more the province of nineteenth-century literary history than of this. The economics of the American theater, the star system, the absence of any national theater, or of experimental or "art" theaters in the country—all no doubt played their part. But there were new dramatic stirrings around the beginning of the new century. Late nineteenth-century realists such as James A. Herne and William Vaughn Moody were tentatively exploring realistic drama for the first time on the American stage. Eugene Walter and Percy MacKaye conducted some tentative dramatic experimentation, but the most important new emphasis seems to have come from abroad, from the naturalistic, symbolic, and critical drama of Europe. Experimental and progressive "little" theaters began to spring up over America. Plays by Ibsen, Strindberg, Hauptmann, Shaw, and Maeterlinck were performed. Such groups also welcomed new experimental drama by Americans. One such group moved from Provincetown, Massachusetts, to Greenwich Village in 1915 with Eugene O'Neill as one of its playwrights. The Washington Square Players developed into the famous Theatre Guild, the producers of Elmer Rice's *The Adding Machine*. O'Neill's first full-length Broadway play, *Beyond the Horizon*, was not produced until 1920, and most modern American playwrights of consequence came after him.

Even so, it was the first two decades of the twentieth century that established the patterns of modern American literature, and if that literature had a discernible continuity with the American past (and it did), it also began to have increasing intercourse with the rest of the intellectual world. Darwin, Marx, and Freud were the three great intellectual figures of the nineteenth century in Europe. Their multiple and radical impact in America almost precisely coincided with the beginnings of modern American literature. European popularizers of the new ideas, men such as Spencer and Huxley, soon began to be widely effective here; and among the new writers, so were Dostoevski and Turgenev; Zola, Balzac, and Flaubert; Hardy and Conrad; Yeats, Shaw, and Synge; Ibsen and Strindberg. After about 1920 American writers were to view Europe as much their intellectual home as their native land. Europe, moreover, at about the same time, first turned serious attention to American literature.

The flowering of modern American literature, however, occurred during the 1920's. The scene was multifarious: disenchantment brought about by the meaningless end of the world's first total war; the resulting materialistic boom and its following national extravagances, corruptions, and decadence; the hypocrisies of prohibition, the "Red scares," the witch-hunting; the spiritual bankruptcy, the blatant amorality. Eliot's most famous poem named it *The Waste Land.* Gertrude Stein told Ernest Hemingway, "You are all a lost generation." The American as American was named George Folansbee Babbitt; "Booboisie," said H. L. Mencken. And there was also a Jay Gatsby, a Clyde Griffiths, and "the Hairy Ape." The total result was to be more than a few figs from these thistles.

The poets, in the meantime, were turning toward or away from Eliot and Pound, who were still in Europe. Archibald MacLeish was there, and so was E. E. Cummings. William Carlos Williams had returned to America. Robinson and Frost in effect had not left and, like Sandburg, were still writing. But a host of new experimentalists had also flourished: Robinson Jeffers, from his solitary tower at Carmel, California; Wallace Stevens, from the executive suite of a Hartford Insurance Company in Connecticut; Hart Crane, from a cold-water walk-up in Manhattan; Marianne Moore, from her Brooklyn apartment; Allen Tate and John Crowe Ransom, from the groves of Academe in Nashville, Tennessee. The seeds of the new poetry created this harvest: various, vibrant, and dedicated.

The fiction of the decade was marked at the beginning with Sherwood Anderson's *Winesburg, Ohio* (in 1919) and at the end with Faulkner's first Yoknapatawpha novels (in 1929). In between is modern American fiction's most impressive achievement. Here appeared the first war novels of Cummings, Dos Passos, and Hemingway. Here too were F. Scott Fitzgerald's indelible definitions of the age—most impressively in *The Great Gatsby*, but also in his beautifully mannered short stories. The same year that saw *Gatsby* (1925) also, significantly enough, saw three novels representing an earlier generation's maturest work: Lewis's *Arrowsmith*, Dreiser's *An American Tragedy*, Cather's *The Professor's House.* This is the decade, after James, that first defined the possibilities of the modern American short story—by Anderson and Fitzgerald, by Hemingway and Katherine Anne Porter. The decade went out, if anything, as strong as it came in; for 1929 not only introduced Faulkner's best work, it also was the year of *A Farewell to Arms* and the first novel by Thomas Wolfe, *Look Homeward, Angel.* The decade, in addition, had witnessed fiction by James Branch Cabell and Ellen Glasgow, by Floyd Dell and Edith Wharton, by Thornton Wilder and Ring Lardner.

The drama of the 1920's had a matching grace. It too debunked the war—in Anderson and Stallings' *What Price Glory?* It damned mechanization (in *The Adding Machine*), and it satirized American complacency (in George Kelley's *The Show-Off*). It explored previously tabooed subject matter (in Sidney Howard's *They Knew What They Wanted*). It opened its arms and showered with praise the many experiments, as well as the sometimes excessive demands, and the unmistakable dramatic genius of Eugene O'Neill. His were the plays which dominated the American Theater of the 1920's.

This amazing decade thus encloses a great body of modern American literature—in poetry, in fiction, and in drama. It shattered conventional taboos; it pursued esthetic originality. It rebelled against the American past; it tried to embrace the world. It probed for spiritual understanding; it castigated fundamental institutions. It upheld the dissenting dignity of the individual; it saw the inevitable crush of heredity and environment. The age was an age of Mencken as well as an age of Eliot, of Van Wyck Brooks as well as of Edmund Wilson. There was a "new" criticism and a "new" humanism, and ultimately the age was to construct a new American past and prescribe a new American future. The 1920's enchant and puzzle, attract and repel, predict and retract. But whatever the ultimate definition of our age, it seems likely that the literature of the 1920's will somehow embed its center, somehow impale its core.

The 1930's, the depression years, the recovery under the New Deal, and the beginnings of World War II early in the '40's also encompass a rich area of modern American literature. Its various facets, moreover, are coming more and more to be seen as much more complex and contradictory than was previously thought.

Its most public image—that of widespread social protest—is still undeniably valid. The Wall Street Crash of 1929 did bring home many of the expatriates. MacLeish, Dos Passos, and Hemingway all returned. The Civil War in Spain evoked strong political loyalties, and there were undeniable consequences in the American literature of the period—most spectacularly perhaps in Hemingway's *For Whom the Bell Tolls.* And he had also written, it must be remembered, *To Have and Have Not.* The great social novels of the decade are also in this tradition—in James Farrell's *Studs Lonigan* trilogy, in Dos Passos's monumental *U.S.A.*, in Steinbeck's *In Dubious Battle* and *The Grapes of Wrath.* MacLeish's poetry of the period revealed unmistakable dialectical ends. And Sandburg wrote *The People, Yes.* In drama the impulse was equally apparent—in the federally sponsored National Theater Project no less than on Broadway. Maxwell Anderson, who had gotten his start in the '20's, along with O'Neill, won a Pulitzer Prize with his savage *Both Your Houses.* And his various plays in verse, mostly historical ones, well prepared him for his masterpiece, *Winterset,* and its moving social implications. Its ties with the Sacco-Vanzetti case no less than the ties of his *Key Largo* with the Spanish Civil War were symptomatic of the times. Clifford Odets' *Waiting for Lefty* and *Awake and Sing* also had strong social themes, as did the dramatization of Steinbeck's *Of Mice and Men,* which was given the Drama Critics Circle Award for 1937.

The depression years, however, were equally the age of other traditions, and some now see, even in the works of Dos Passos and Steinbeck, achievements of form and technique that surpass their achievements of protest. Eliot's *Ash Wednesday,* published in 1930, was to lead inevitably to his *Four Quartets,* begun in 1940. Fitzgerald's *Tender Is the Night* and Hemingway's most famous stories came in this period, and writers as various as John O'Hara, William Saroyan, James Gould Cozzens, and John P. Marquand (all of whom published some of their best early works during the 1930's) could not fairly be described as writers of social protest.

It was also in 1930 that the agrarian manifesto, *I'll Take My Stand,* appeared. The so-called Southern Renaissance most conveniently dates from that document. The poetry and criticism of Tate and Ransom were first to be widely felt during the 1930's. William Faulkner, probably the most praised of all modern American writers, published his richest books between 1929 and 1942, and every one of Thomas Wolfe's novels, except the first, was written during this decade, as was most of the best work of Katherine Anne Porter. Ellen Glasgow continued to write. There was Erskine Caldwell's *Tobacco Road* (of 1932), and there was Margaret Mitchell's *Gone With the Wind* (of 1936).

The literature of the 1930's is as vital to the achievement of modern American literature as that of the 1920's. And indeed, there is unmistakable continuity between them. The end of World War I and the beginning of World War II seemingly define an era stronger than that indicated by the turn of the century and the new beginnings or than that so conveniently dated between the '20's and the '30's. Literary achievement, however, is continuous; and dates, in one sense, are meaningless. Still, for the most part it is the American literature published between the two World Wars that our own century thus far honors most, and which constitutes the major part of the writing included in this anthology. But some trends are discernible since the end of World War II, some achievements definable; and this work too, at least tentatively, is a part of our modern literary heritage.

Recent American drama, for example, has clear peaks and dips. Very little of consequence developed from the war itself, but a major new playwright was discovered in Tennessee Williams who, since *The Glass*

Menagerie in 1945, has come as close as any, since O'Neill and Anderson, to dominating the American theater of his time. With contemporaries such as Arthur Miller and William Inge, Williams led an American theater that, at least for awhile, appeared both mature and vigorous. Verse drama got a modern hearing with plays by Eliot and MacLeish. Post-war doldrums, in short, seemed to be dispersing, but the frightful economies of production soon again became acute, and even vigorous off-Broadway experimentalism appeared unable to forestall a decline. In the early 1960's, however, with new imaginative plays by the young Edward Albee and Arthur Kopit—especially the mordant comedies of Albee—the modern American theater was very much alive.

Poetry also had many new voices, but innovation seemed less the rule than consolidation did. Poets such as Shapiro and Roethke, Robert Lowell and Richard Wilbur were clearly modern in their tones and diction, their techniques and strategy. In subject matter and themes they were different enough from one another and from the recent past, but there were no innovations of consequence, no clearly new directions. The noisy unrestraint of the Beats was never poetry enough to be meaningful and promised no more than the Dada movement of the 1920's. Rebellion has been an established pattern in the development of American poetry, but the direction of any meaningful rebellion in the 1950's and '60's was not clear.

Recent American fiction perhaps holds the richest promise for the future. The young writers of the most widely acclaimed war novels—Mailer, Jones, Shaw, Wouk—were almost all disappointing in subsequent works. The South, however, continued its tradition of rich talent, in Warren, of course, but also in Carson McCullers, Eudora Welty, Truman Capote, and William Styron, among others. James Gould Cozzens first began to receive the attention he deserved. With the rapidly emerging fiction of Wright Morris, Saul Bellow, J. D. Salinger, James Baldwin, John Cheever, J. F. Powers, and John Updike, American fiction seemed to be on the edge of a new renaissance.

Whether the promise would become the reality could not of course be predicted. The first decade of the century now seems weaker than the 1950's, but what ultimately follows will have to be another story.

NEW DIRECTIONS

CHAPTER ONE

THE NEW POETRY

Edwin Arlington Robinson and Robert Frost were significantly both parts of and not parts of the so-called new poetry movement, usually dated as beginning in 1912 with the founding, in Chicago, of Harriet Monroe's *Poetry, a Magazine of Verse* and, in London, of the first *Georgian Anthology*. To be sure, there were important stirrings both before and after this date. Ezra Pound's first *Personæ* had been published in 1909, and his edition of *Des Imagists* appeared in 1914, the same year as Amy Lowell's *Sword Blades and Poppy Seed*. Robinson's first volume of poems, *The Torrent and the Night Before*, had appeared in 1896; and although Frost's "My Butterfly" had appeared as early as 1894, his published output, when he sailed for England in 1912, was only fourteen poems (in unimportant periodicals). The fact, moreover, that Frost's move to England *was* in 1912 had only coincidental relevance to the activities of both the Georgian and Imagists poets there; for he had had little association with either of the poetic groups.

Both poets nevertheless had important ties with the new poetry movement. Although Robinson consistently wrote his poems in conventional forms, his was a strikingly new kind of verse in America. It was highly intellectualized in content, realistic in attitude, penetrating in its psychological observations, free of the conventional poetic diction of his day, and close—much closer than many critics realized—to the rhythms of actual speech. Robinson's practice was thus consistent enough with many of the aims of both the Imagists in England and those of the poets associated with Harriet Monroe in Chicago. Both groups were in reaction against what they considered the conventionalized romanticisms of the Victorians, the "sweetly smooth" of Tennyson no less than the "politely moral" of Longfellow. The new poets valued a simple concreteness over what they considered the old vagueness, a simple sincerity over eloquence and rhetoric, intensity and concentration over wordiness and diffuseness, the language of contemporary speech over handed-down poetic diction, the freedom to choose any subject matter over the restriction of the old "poetical order." So in practice did Robinson. Except for his avoidance of free verse—and perhaps his lack of ties with Whitman, the French Symbolists, the English metaphysicals, or Oriental poetry—he was thus squarely in the stream of the new poetry.

The accomplishments of the new poets undoubtedly contributed to the public acceptance of Robinson, and the warm critical reaction to the appearance of his *The Man Against the Sky* in 1916 would not have been possible without the "preparation" the new movement gave the public during the years immediately preceding it: This contention is supported by the comparative indifference of the public to the three volumes of poetry which preceded his 1916 volume. Even though Robinson had very limited personal relationships with the poets associated with the new movement, his "Eros Turannos" appeared in the same 1914 issue of *Poetry* that contained Sandburg's first Chicago poems.

Robinson was an isolated individual all of his life. His close friends and patrons—Josephine Preston Peabody and William Vaughn Moody, whom he had known at Harvard, and E. C. Stedman, Percy MacKaye, Herman Hagedorn, Ridgely Torrence, and Daniel Greogory Mason, the composer, who taught music at Columbia—were none of them important figures in the developing new poetry, even if one grudgingly made a specific exception of Moody. Robinson's summers at the MacDowell colony at Peterboro, New Hampshire, where after 1911 most of his poetry was written, were no exception. That retreat only provided him with a more comfortable kind of isolation.

The isolated individual thus appears everywhere in Robinson's poetry, first and last. "Credo" opens: "I cannot find my way. . . ." Luke Havergal is told to "Go to the *western* gate." Richard Cory "Went home and put a bullet through his head." Miniver Cheevy is "born too late." The man Flammonde is withheld "from the destinies/That came so near to being his" by "some small satanic sort of kink," and the unnamed protagonist of *The Man Against the Sky* is most memorably seen "As if he were the last god going home/Unto his last desire."

Robinson's sensibility is modern throughout, whether the subject matter is the New England rustics (of the Tilbury Town poems), the crass commercialism of his age (as in "Cassándra"), the anguished dilemmas of his medieval characters (in the Arthurian trilogy), or the subjects and characters of the classical age about whom he often wrote. The widespread public appeal of his Arthurian trilogy, especially in the third volume, *Tristram* (1927), which brought him his third Pulitzer prize and the monetary reward of having become the monthly selection of a large book club, was clearly the appeal of his viewpoint and treatment, not the appeal of his subject matter.

Robinson's world nevertheless remained—even in the late narratives such as *King Jasper* (1935)—a bleak world, void alike of any easy goals or certain successes. And yet, although strongly compelled by the naturalistic doctrines of his day, he never quite steps over into the absolute determinism and pessimism that became the predictable road of so many of his similarly inclined contemporaries. The bewilderments of Hardy and Zola, the realism of the eighteenth-century Crabbe, are tinctured in Robinson with the transcendentalist heritage of his own New England. Gleams of light, however uncertain, inevitably penetrate the dark and reveal a shadowed nobility that obstinately refuses to die. This obstinate belief in self, this insistence upon the value of the individual, he never quite lets go of. Although to exist for Robinson is never the splendid privilege it was for Emerson, there is always in his poems perpetual awe and wonder at man's determination to endure.

Robinson's poetic experimentation is almost exclusively in the use of common speech rhythms, not in stanzaic innovations. Free verse was as much an anathema to him as to Frost—"like playing tennis without a net." There is nonetheless considerable diversity of form, especially in the earlier work, in the sonnet, in the eight-line tetrameter, in the quatrain, in the sophisticated French forms and, perhaps most importantly, in the colloquial flow of his blank verse, which became his most commonly used meter after about 1916. In narrative, descriptive, and reflective poetry he has no modern equal. His language is unmistakably modern, and so is his temper.

Frost's ties with the new poetry were somewhat more direct than Robinson's, but he too was never permanently related to any of the various coteries related to the development. In England, after the publication of *A Boy's Will* (1913) and *North of Boston* (1914), he did make friends and find professional esteem with the Georgian group that included Walter de la Mare, John Masefield, W. H. Davies, Rupert Brooke, and, perhaps most importantly for Frost, the critic Edward Thomas. Moreover, soon after *A Boy's Will* appeared, he met Ezra Pound, whose favorable review of that collection appeared in *Poetry* in May of 1913. Pound, as a matter of fact, also favorably reviewed *North of Boston* in *Poetry* late in 1914 under the title of "Modern Georgics." But their friendship, as Louise Bogan has pointed out, was short-lived, although Frost joined in the demand for Pound's release from a federal hospital following World War Two.

With Frost's return to his homeland in 1915 and the publication of the American edition of *North of Boston,* his already significant English following was soon matched and exceeded by a growing American one. But once back in America Frost did not identify himself with any of the various wings of the new poetry movement; he returned instead to a New Hampshire farm to continue writing about country things.

As with Robinson, however, the new poetry played its part in the public acceptance of Frost's poetry. As we have seen, the beginning of that acceptance, unlike Robinson's case, was directly related to his association with the new poets in England. Frost's ties, moreover, with a specifically American tradition were clearly seen very early. His attitude toward the world and his technique put him squarely in the tradition of Emerson and Emily Dickinson, for all three explore the veil of natural fact for the spiritual truth it mirrors. This tradition plays its part in the rise of Frost in another way since the hard, imagistic patterns of these two nineteenth-century Americans were often pointed to by the new poets as a contrast to the rhetorical "softness" of their contemporaries.

Even so, actual influences on Frost's work are difficult to establish. We do know that he read and admired Robinson's *The Town Down the River* (1910), and his Introduction to *King Jasper* (1935) is warm with praise. Yet no one would mistake a Frost poem for a Robinson one. Robinson belonged to the tradition of the cultivated New England town, and his record of its dissolution, particularly in the Tilbury Town poems, reveals a series of outcasts, misfits, and failures—modern enough as representative aliens—who are far too highly intellectualized in conception ever to be mistaken for any of Frost's creations.

This is not to suggest that Frost's own poems are simple, unreflective, or easily optimistic—although they were perhaps thought so, by some at least, for a time. Even such early lyrics as "Mowing" and "The Tuft of Flowers" make of their rural subjects something cleanly and distinctly seen. The dramatic relationship between man and nature that such poems begin to set up in *A Boy's Will* move, in *North of Boston* (in "Mending Wall," say, or in "The Mountain"), to the depiction of character with the distance and detachment we more conventionally associate with the realistic novel than we do with "rural lyrics." In "After Apple-Picking" and "The Wood-Pile," both also in his second volume, there is no mistaking the profundity of vision, nor the mastery of technique, that makes of the rural subject a universal experience.

These virtues remained in many poems of the several collections that followed the first two—in "Birches," certainly, of *Mountain Interval* (1916), or "Stopping by Woods on a Snowy Evening" of *New Hampshire* (1923). The apothegmatic intensity of a relatively slight poem such as "Fire and Ice" had apparently also been with him from the first, and it was to continue to serve him well—when droll, as in "What Fifty Said"; when satiric, as in "The Bear"; or even when strange, as in the conventional sonnet form with uncharacteristic subject matter, as in "A Soldier" or "The Silken Tent." It was as late as the late 1950's that something of a cultural hubbub was started when J. Donald Adams in the New York *Times* took Lionel Trilling to task for calling Frost, on the occasion of his eighty-fifth birthday, a "Terrifying poet"; but close readers had seen man's capacity for the terrifying in Frost's poems for a long, long time. One has only to recall the early "'Out, Out—,'" or, somewhat later, "Design" or "The Subverted Flower."

Frost made remarkably few false starts. The volumes immediately preceding and during World War II—*A Further Range* (1936), *Witness Tree* (1942), and *Steeple Bush* (1947)—are perhaps more marred than most with preachments on things national and international, on collectivistic tendencies of modern man in time of economic depression and political chaos, on any pooling of individual resources that allows men to think individual responsibilities could thereby be lessened. "The New Deil" as Frost called it, or even the United Nations, too easily foster, he seems to have felt, people's desire to rely on somebody else. As a consequence, some of the poems in these volumes, as well as the two Biblical verse plays of the same period, *A Masque of Reason* and *A Masque of Mercy* (1945 and 1947), often seem to degenerate into the garrulous wise-cracks or topical conceits of the unimpressed rural conservative. There was also perhaps a deeper mellowness and a more stoical profundity in these same volumes. "Come In," "Two Tramps in Mud Time," and "The Wind and The Rain" were also of this period.

Frost's fame grew steadily during these years, reaching a kind of unprecedented apotheosis in his middle eighties. He had been awarded four Pulitzer Prizes by 1943. Honorary degrees were conferred on him by Oxford and Cambridge in 1957. Resolutions of the United States Senate honored his seventy-fifth and eighty-fifth birthdays. His magnificent recitation of "The Gift Outright" at the inauguration of John F. Kennedy in January of 1961 (after a merciless sunlight prohibited his reading the occasional poem written for the affair) effectively capped the position of unofficial poet-laureateship he had in fact held during the last decade or so of his life. Never before perhaps has a man of letters in America emerged so clearly as the ideal manifestation of American character. Not since Longfellow, at least, had there been in America so beneficent a relationship between a poet and the American public—a relationship which at the same time had the unquestioned and common approval of the literary, academic, and political communities.

Frost was more variedly successful than Robinson in fitting the cadences of common speech to regular verse patterns. His adaptations of the idioms, intonations, and rhythms of his native New England language constitute one of the major technical achievements of modern poetry. Partly because the adaptation is in terms of idiom rather than in terms of dialect, partly because natural New England speech patterns are at once terse and discursive, the result in Frost's poetry is as if the language were overheard, were cause and effect alike. Experimentation is also much more varied in Frost than in Robinson, and the list of forms he successfully practiced—the masque, the dramatic monologue and dialogue, the ode, the eclogue, the satire—as well as the variety of meters he employed—blank verse, heroic couplets, terza rima, ballad meters, and sonnet and sonnet variants—constitute, when considered with his free forms, a variety of poetic practice, however constant the "voice," probably unsurpassed by any other modern poet.

Because of a ready willingness always to talk about his work, and a consequent addiction both to the lecture platform and to the classroom, Frost left behind a large body of comment about his poetic intentions and practices, although none of it is very systematized. Robinson, comparatively, said very little about his work, content not only, as Frost said of him, "with the old way to be new," but content also to let his poetry speak for itself. What little memorable prose we have from Robinson is much more likely to be about his attitudes toward the world, as suggested by the two letters reprinted in this volume, than it is about his poetry. Frost, on the other hand, was not only willing but seemingly eager to talk and talk and talk about his own work. Much of that talk, to be sure, is very good talk indeed, as in his "The Figure a Poem Makes," which appeared as the Preface to a collection of his own poems. Even when his subject was the work of another, as in his Introduction to Robinson's *King Jasper,* its pertinence to his own poetry is likely to outweigh its pertinence to his ostensible subject.

Both Robinson and Frost, however, are significant for their poetry, not their criticism, for their poetic practice, not their poetic theories. In their practice, in the practical achievement of their collected poetical works, they both reside in the very center of most of what was best in the new poetry movement, however tenuous, intermittent, or indirect their *formal* and *active* relation to the movement. Robinson and Frost constitute in one of its phases the peak of the achievement of modern American literature.

Edwin Arlington Robinson

(1869-1935)

CHRONOLOGY:

1869 Born December 22, Head Tide, Maine.

1870 Moved to Gardiner, Maine, the "Tilbury Town" of his poems.

1891-93 Attended Harvard.

1896 *The Torrent and the Night Before,* at his own expense.

1897 Moved to New York City; was timekeeper for New York subway construction; *The Children of the Night,* a revision of his first volume, subsidized by friends.

1898 Moved to Harvard as clerk for a short time before returning to New York.

1902 *Captain Craig,* again backed by friends.

1905 Met Theodore Roosevelt; gained some public recognition; given position in New York Custom House (to 1909).

1910 *The Town Down the River.*

1911 Joined MacDowell Colony, Peterboro, New Hampshire, where he spent summers the rest of his life.

1914 *Van Zorn,* verse play.

1915 *The Porcupine,* verse play.

1916 *The Man Against the Sky,* warmly received.
1917 *Merlin,* the first of his Arthurian trilogy.
1920 *Lancelot; The Three Taverns.*
1921 *Avon's Harvest; Collected Poems* (won Pulitzer Prize, 1922).
1923 *Roman Bartholow.*
1924 *The Man Who Died Twice* (won Pulitzer Prize, 1925).
1925 *Dionysus in Doubt.*
1927 *Tristram* (won Pulitzer Prize, 1928, and most popular volume).
1928 *Sonnets, 1899-1927,*
1929 *Cavender's House.*
1930 *The Glory of the Nightingales.*
1931 *Matthias at the Door.*
1932 *Nicodemus.*
1933 *Talifer.*
1934 *Amaranth.*
1935 *King Jasper;* died April 6, in New York City.
1936 *Hannibal Brown: Posthumous Poems.*

BIBLIOGRAPHY:

The most important text is *Collected Poems of Edwin Arlington Robinson* (New York, 1942). Good selections are also in *Tilbury Town: Selected Poems of Edwin Arlington Robinson,* ed. Lawrance Thompson (New York, 1953) and *Selected Early Poems and Letters,* ed. C. T. Davis (New York, 1960). Important letters are in *Selected Letters,* ed. Ridgely Torrence (New York, 1940) and *Untriangulated Stars: Letters of Edwin Arlington Robinson to Harry de Forest Smith, 1890-1905,* ed. Denham Sutcliffe (Cambridge, Mass., 1947).

Standard biographical and critical studies are Hermann Hagedorn, *Edwin Arlington Robinson* (New York, 1938) and Emory Neff, *Edwin Arlington Robinson* (New York, 1947); Ellsworth Barnard, *Edwin Arlington Robinson: A Critical Study* (New York, 1952); and Edwin S. Fussell, *Edwin Arlington Robinson: The Literary Background of a Traditional Poet* (Berkeley, Calif., 1954).

The most useful bibliography is Lillian Lippincott, *A Bibliography of the Writings and Criticisms of Edwin Arlington Robinson* (Boston, 1937). Important listings of secondary material, including explications, are in Allen Tate, *Sixty American Poets, 1896-1944* (Washington, 1954), and Joseph M. Kuntz, *Poetry Explication* (Rev. ed.; Denver, 1962).

From Letter to Harry de Forest Smith

(dated GARDINER, *March 15, 1897)*

How long do you think a man can live in hell? I think he can live there a good many years—a hundred, perhaps, if his bowels keep in decent order—but he isn't going to have a very good time. No man can have a very good time—of the right sort, at any rate—until he understands things; and how the devil is a man to understand things in an age like this, when the whole trend of popular thought is in the wrong direction—not only that, but proud of the way it is taking? The age is all right, material progress is all right, Herbert Spencer is all right, hell is all right. These things are temporal necessities, but they are damned uninteresting to one who can get a glimpse of the real light through the clouds of time. It is that glimpse that makes me wish to live and see it out. If it were not for that glimpse, I should be tempted, as Tennyson used to be, to stick my nose into a rag soaked with chloroform and be done with it—that is, if I could screw up the courage. But now, thank God, that is not the kind of courage I am praying for; what I am after is the courage to see and to believe that my present life is the best thing for me, and that every man has it in his power to overcome whatever obstacles may be in his way—even that seeming obstacle we call by the name of Death. I have not said much about my life for the past three years—I mean the past ten—because with all its lack of anything like material hope and pleasure—it was tolerable. For all my long lean face, I never gave up; and I never shall give up. I can't do it; but I can suffer like damnation, which shows there is something wrong with me somewhere. The past three months of my life, however, are quite another thing. If they had come two years ago, or even one, I think they would have finished me. The book has helped me out a little—in fact, I was rather bewildered by its reception—but that counts (the praise, I mean) for very little. There are things here at home that are pulling me back, and I've got to look out for them. I can't get away, just now—I don't see how I can for a year—and the result is that all my best strength is required in keeping my thoughts in some sort of rational order. The one great pleasure of my life is the knowledge that my poor mother is out of it. I can't quite understand—yet—the laws of compensation that make a woman suffer what she did and from so many causes. We say she died of diphtheria. What does that mean? It means just this: she had endured all [she] could and was ready to die. I had been watching it for a year. If she had not had diphtheria, or membranous croup, or whatever it was that took her off so hellishly, she would have gone crazy. I am not going crazy, for I see some things she did not see—some things she could not see; but I am going to lose all those pleasures which are said to make up the happiness of this life and I'm glad of it. I'm glad to say that I am strong enough to do without them. There is a pleasure—a job—this is greater than all these little selfish notions and I have found the way to it through idealism. Once I thought I was in a way to be a Christian Scientist, but that will be impossible. The system is too dependent on unsubstantial inferences. As it is taught and managed it is not Christianity, though the claim is that the two terms are synonymous. It is rapidly developing into a sect, and one that will have a tremendous power in the world; but it is only a stepping stone to the truth. It has proved the power, however, of even a partial recognition, and thereby proved the utter fallacy of all existing notions of religion—popular notions, I mean.

The great scholars of the world are for the most part spiritual imbeciles, and there is where the trouble lies. The willingness "to be a child again" comes hard—so hard that it will never come to many who are in the world today. That is not what they are here for. "The world was made in order, and the atoms march in time." It is a damned queer time to us who are here now; but it is all right and we are all going to hear it as it is—when the mortal wax gets out of our ears. . . .

From Letter to L. N. Chase
(from PETERBOROUGH, *July 11, 1917)*

I find it rather difficult to answer your letter, much as I appreciate it and your motive in writing it. I am handicapped at the start in having no biography and no theories. You will find as much in Who's Who as I have to say about myself personally; and as for my work, I have hoped that it might speak—not very loudly, perhaps—for itself. Ten years ago I was called a radical, and most readers looked sideways at my work on account of its unconventional use of so-called simple language. I suppose that I have always depended rather more on context than on vocabulary for my poetical effects, and this offense has laid me open to the charge of over-subtlety on the part of the initiated and of dullness on the part of the dull. Whatever merit my work may or may not possess, I fancy that it will always be a waste of time for any reader who has not a fairly well developed sense of humor—which, as someone has said before, is a very serious thing—to bother with it. When I tell you that my poem called "The Gift of God" (in *The Man Against the Sky*) has been interpreted as a touching tribute to our Saviour, you will require no further comment upon this point.

When I was younger, I was very much under the influence of Wordsworth and Kipling, but never at all, so far as I am aware, under that of Browning, as many seem to believe. As a matter of fact, I have never been able to understand the alleged resemblance unless it can be attributed to my use of rather more colloquial language than "poetic diction" has usually sanctioned. I began the writing of verse long before I was old enough to know better, and I fancy that I am safe in saying that my style, such as it is, was pretty well formed by the time my first book was published, in 1896.

As for my methods of work, there does not seem to be much for me to say. As a rule I see the end of a thing before I begin it (if I don't see it then, I am likely never to see it) and the rest of the process is simply a matter of how the thing goes. Sometimes it goes rapidly, sometimes slowly; and so far as I can see, one method produces about the same result as the other, provided I know what I am trying to say. When occasionally I have become disgusted and thrown an unfinished poem away, it has always been because I had really nothing to write about. I have written a sonnet in twenty minutes as a joke ("Another Dark Lady") and I have tinkered others ("The Clerks," for example) for a month. Generally speaking, I should be inclined to say that if some sort of first draft doesn't form itself rather quickly, the final product is likely to be unsatisfactory; but with something definite and worth while to work on, any amount of labor may justify itself. Again, it may not. I imagine, however, that the worst poetry in the world has been written in the finest frenzy of inspiration; and so, probably, has the best.

When you ask me to annotate individual poems, I find myself in another difficulty. While nearly everything that I have written has a certain amount of personal coloring, I do not recall anything of mine that is a direct transcription of experience. For example, I have never liked the sound of church-bells; and the sound of their ringing one evening for the wedding of two people in whom I had not the remotest interest brought about a mood in me that made me write "On the Night of a Friend's Wedding"—a sonnet, by the way, that was begun suddenly, and later worked over for an immoderate length of time. But I was younger then than I am now, and time didn't count.

I thought nothing when I was writing my first book of working for a week over a single line; and while I don't do it any more, I am sure that my technique is better for those early grilling exercises. In fact, I am now more than inclined to believe that the technical flabbiness of many writers is due to the lack in earlier years of just such grilling—in the years when one is not conscious of how hard he is working and of how much time he is wasting—unless he is ready to gamble his life away for the sake of winning the possible conjunction of a few inevitable words. It seems an odd stake to play for so heavily, and perhaps it is fortunate for the race that so few are playing for it. Of course almost everyone is writing verse nowadays, but not many are taking it seriously enough to let it interfere with their meal tickets. . . .

Credo

I cannot find my way: there is no star
In all the shrouded heavens anywhere;
And there is not a whisper in the air
Of any living voice but one so far
That I can hear it only as a bar
Of lost, imperial music, played when fair
And angel fingers wove, and unaware,
Dead leaves to garlands where no roses are.

No, there is not a glimmer, nor a call,
For one that welcomes, welcomes when he fears,
The black and awful chaos of the night;
For through it all—above, beyond it all—
I know the far-sent message of the years,
I feel the coming glory of the Light.

1896

Luke Havergal

Go to the western gate, Luke Havergal,
There where the vines cling crimson on the wall,
And in the twilight wait for what will come.
The leaves will whisper there of her, and some,
Like flying words, will strike you as they fall;
But go, and if you listen she will call.
Go to the western gate, Luke Havergal—
Luke Havergal.

No, there is not a dawn in eastern skies
To rift the fiery night that's in your eyes;
But there, where western glooms are gathering,
The dark will end the dark, if anything:
God slays Himself with every leaf that flies,
And hell is more than half of paradise.
No, there is not a dawn in eastern skies—
In eastern skies.

Out of a grave I come to tell you this,
Out of a grave I come to quench the kiss
That flames upon your forehead with a glow
That blinds you to the way that you must go.
Yes, there is yet one way to where she is,
Bitter, but one that faith may never miss.
Out of a grave I come to tell you this—
To tell you this.

There is the western gate, Luke Havergal,
There are the crimson leaves upon the wall.
Go, for the winds are tearing them away,—
Nor think to riddle the dead words they say,
Nor any more to feel them as they fall;
But go, and if you trust her she will call.
There is the western gate, Luke Havergal—
Luke Havergal. 1896

Zola

Because he puts the compromising chart
Of hell before your eyes, you are afraid;
Because he counts the price that you have paid
For innocence, and counts it from the start,
You loathe him. But he sees the human heart
Of God meanwhile, and in His hand was weighed
Your squeamish and emasculate crusade
Against the grim dominion of his art.

Never until we conquer the uncouth
Connivings of our shamed indifference
(We call it Christian faith) are we to scan
The racked and shrieking hideousness of Truth
To find, in hate's polluted self-defence
Throbbing, the pulse, the divine heart of man.
1896

Boston

My northern pines are good enough for me,
But there's a town my memory uprears—
A town that always like a friend appears,
And always in the sunrise by the sea.
And over it, somehow, there seems to be
A downward flash of something new and fierce,
That ever strives to clear, but never clears
The dimness of a charmed antiquity. 1896

Aaron Stark

Withal a meagre man was Aaron Stark,
Cursed and unkempt, shrewd, shrivelled, and morose.
A miser was he, with a miser's nose,
And eyes like little dollars in the dark.
His thin, pinched mouth was nothing but a mark;
And when he spoke there came like sullen blows
Through scattered fangs a few snarled words and close,
As if a cur were chary of its bark.

Glad for the murmur of his hard renown,
Year after year he shambled through the town,
A loveless exile moving with a staff;
And oftentimes there crept into his ears
A sound of alien pity, touched with tears,—
And then (and only then) did Aaron laugh. 1896

Richard Cory

Whenever Richard Cory went down town,
We people on the pavement looked at him:
He was a gentleman from sole to crown,
Clean favored, and imperially slim.

And he was always quietly arrayed,
And he was always human when he talked;
But still he fluttered pulses when he said,
"Good-morning," and he glittered when he walked.

And he was rich—yes, richer than a king—
And admirably schooled in every grace:
In fine, we thought that he was everything
To make us wish that we were in his place.

So on we worked, and waited for the light,
And went without the meat, and cursed the bread;
And Richard Cory, one calm summer night,
Went home and put a bullet through his head.
1897

Miniver Cheevy

Miniver Cheevy, child of scorn,
  Grew lean while he assailed the seasons;
He wept that he was ever born,
  And he had reasons.

Miniver loved the days of old
  When swords were bright and steeds were prancing;
The vision of a warrior bold
  Would set him dancing.

Miniver sighed for what was not,
And dreamed, and rested from his labors;
He dreamed of Thebes and Camelot,
And Priam's neighbors.

Miniver mourned the ripe renown
That made so many a name so fragrant;
He mourned Romance, now on the town,
And Art, a vagrant.

Miniver loved the Medici,
Albeit he had never seen one;
He would have sinned incessantly
Could he have been one.

Miniver cursed the commonplace
And eyed a khaki suit with loathing;
He missed the mediaeval grace
Of iron clothing.

Miniver scorned the gold he sought,
But sore annoyed was he without it;
Miniver thought, and thought, and thought,
And thought about it.

Miniver Cheevy, born too late,
Scratched his head and kept on thinking;
Miniver coughed, and called it fate,
And kept on drinking. 1907

Cassandra

I heard one who said: "Verily,
What word have I for children here?
Your Dollar is your only Word,
The wrath of it your only fear.

"You build it altars tall enough
To make you see, but you are blind;
You cannot leave it long enough
To look before you or behind.

"When Reason beckons you to pause,
You laugh and say that you know best;
But what it is you know, you keep
As dark as ingots in a chest.

"You laugh and answer, 'We are young;
O leave us now, and let us grow.'—
Not asking how much more of this
Will Time endure or Fate bestow.

"Because a few complacent years
Have made your peril of your pride,
Think you that you are to go on
Forever pampered and untried?

"What lost eclipse of history,
What bivouac of the marching stars,
Has given the sign for you to see
Millenniums and last great wars?

"What unrecorded overthrow
Of all the world has ever known,
Or ever been, has made itself
So plain to you, and you alone?

"Your dollar, Dove and Eagle make
A Trinity that even you
Rate higher than you rate yourselves;
It pays, it flatters, and it's new.

"And though your very flesh and blood
Be what your Eagle eats and drinks,
You'll praise him for the best of birds,
Not knowing what the Eagle thinks.

"The power is yours, but not the sight;
You see not upon what you tread;
You have the ages for your guide,
But not the wisdom to be led.

"Think you to tread forever down
The merciless old verities?
And are you never to have eyes
To see the world for what it is?

"Are you to pay for what you have
With all you are?"—No other word
We caught, but with a laughing crowd
Moved on. None heeded, and few heard.

1914

Eros Turannos

She fears him, and will always ask
What fated her to choose him;
She meets in his engaging mask
All reasons to refuse him;
But what she meets and what she fears
Are less than are the downward years,
Drawn slowly to the foamless weirs
Of age, were she to lose him.

Between a blurred sagacity
That once had power to sound him,
And Love, that will not let him be
The Judas that she found him,
Her pride assuages her almost,
As if it were alone the cost,—
He sees that he will not be lost,
And waits and looks around him.

A sense of ocean and old trees
Envelops and allures him;
Tradition, touching all he sees,
Beguiles and reassures him;
And all her doubts of what he says
Are dimmed with what she knows of days—
Till even prejudice delays
And fades, and she secures him.

The falling leaf inaugurates
The reign of her confusion;
The pounding wave reverberates
The dirge of her illusion;
And home, where passion lived and died,
Becomes a place where she can hide,
While all the town and harbor side
Vibrate with her seclusion.

We tell you, tapping on our brows,
  The story as it should be,—
As if the story of a house
  Were told, or ever could be;
We'll have no kindly veil between
Her visions and those we have seen,—
As if we guessed what hers have been,
  Or what they are or would be.

Meanwhile we do no harm; for they
  That with a god have striven,
Not hearing much of what we say,
  Take what the god has given;
Though like waves breaking it may be,
Or like a changed familiar tree,
Or like a stairway to the sea
  Where down the blind are driven.

1914

Flammonde

The man Flammonde, from God knows where,
With firm address and foreign air,
With news of nations in his talk
And something royal in his walk,
With glint of iron in his eyes,
But never doubt, nor yet surprise,
Appeared, and stayed, and held his head
As one by kings accredited.

Erect, with his alert repose
About him, and about his clothes,
He pictured all tradition hears
Of what we owe to fifty years.
His cleansing heritage of taste
Paraded neither want nor waste;
And what he needed for his fee
To live, he borrowed graciously.

He never told us what he was,
Or what mischance, or other cause,
Had banished him from better days
To play the Prince of Castaways.

Meanwhile he played surpassing well
A part, for most, unplayable;
In fine, one pauses, half afraid
To say for certain that he played.

For that, one may as well forego
Conviction as to yes or no;
Nor can I say just how intense
Would then have been the difference
To several, who, having striven
In vain to get what he was given,
Would see the stranger taken on
By friends not easy to be won.

Moreover, many a malcontent
He soothed and found munificent;
His courtesy beguiled and foiled
Suspicion that his years were soiled;
His mien distinguished any crowd,
His credit strengthened when he bowed;
And women, young and old, were fond
Of looking at the man Flammonde.

There was a woman in our town
On whom the fashion was to frown;
But while our talk renewed the tinge
Of a long-faded scarlet fringe,
The man Flammonde saw none of that,
And what he saw we wondered at—
That none of us, in her distress,
Could hide or find our littleness.

There was a boy that all agreed
Had shut within him the rare seed
Of learning. We could understand,
But none of us could lift a hand.
The man Flammonde appraised the youth,
And told a few of us the truth;
And thereby, for a little gold,
A flowered future was unrolled.

There were two citizens who fought
For years and years, and over nought;
They made life awkward for their friends,
And shortened their own dividends.

The man Flammonde said what was wrong
Should be made right; nor was it long
Before they were again in line,
And had each other in to dine.

And these I mention are but four
Of many out of many more.
So much for them. But what of him—
So firm in every look and limb?
What small satanic sort of kink
Was in his brain? What broken link
Withheld him from the destinies
That came so near to being his?

What was he, when we came to sift
His meaning, and to note the drift
Of incommunicable ways
That make us ponder while we praise?
Why was it that his charm revealed
Somehow the surface of a shield?
What was it that we never caught?
What was he, and what was he not?

How much it was of him we met
We cannot ever know; nor yet
Shall all he gave us quite atone
For what was his, and his alone;
Nor need we now, since he knew best,
Nourish an ethical unrest:
Rarely at once will nature give
The power to be Flammonde and live.

We cannot know how much we learn
From those who never will return,
Until a flash of unforeseen
Remembrance falls on what has been.
We've each a darkening hill to climb;
And this is why, from time to time
In Tilbury Town, we look beyond
Horizons for the man Flammonde. 1915

The Man Against the Sky

Between me and the sunset, like a dome
Against the glory of a world on fire,
Now burned a sudden hill,
Bleak, round, and high, by flame-lit height made higher,
With nothing on it for the flame to kill
Save one who moved and was alone up there
To loom before the chaos and the glare
As if he were the last god going home
Unto his last desire.

Dark, marvelous, and inscrutable he moved on
Till down the fiery distance he was gone,
Like one of those eternal, remote things
That range across a man's imaginings
When a sure music fills him and he knows
What he may say thereafter to few men,—
The touch of ages having wrought
An echo and a glimpse of what he thought
A phantom or a legend until then;
For whether lighted over ways that save,
Or lured from all repose,
If he go on too far to find a grave,
Mostly alone he goes.

Even he, who stood where I had found him,
On high with fire all round him,
Who moved along the molten west,
And over the round hill's crest
That seemed half ready with him to go down,
Flame-bitten and flame-cleft,
As if there were to be no last thing left
Of a nameless unimaginable town,—
Even he who climbed and vanished may have taken
Down to the perils of a depth not known,
From death defended though by men forsaken,
The bread that every man must eat alone;
He may have walked while others hardly dared
Look on to see him stand where many fell;
And upward out of that, as out of hell,
He may have sung and striven

To mount where more of him shall yet be given,
Bereft of all retreat,
To sevenfold heat,—
As on a day when three in Dura shared
The furnace, and were spared
For glory by that king of Babylon
Who made himself so great that God, who heard,
Covered him with long feathers, like a bird.

Again, he may have gone down easily,
By comfortable altitudes, and found,
As always, underneath him solid ground
Whereon to be sufficient and to stand
Possessed already of the promised land,
Far stretched, and fair to see:
A good sight, verily,
And one to make the eyes of her who bore him
Shine glad with hidden tears.
Why question of his ease of who before him,
In one place or another where they left
Their names as far behind them as their bones,
And yet by dint of slaughter, toil and theft,
And shrewdly sharpened stones,
Carved hard the way for his ascendency
Through deserts of lost years?
Why trouble him now who sees and hears
No more than what his innocence requires,
And therefore to no other height aspires
Than one at which he neither quails nor tires?
He may do more by seeing what he sees
Than others eager for iniquities;
He may, by seeing all things for the best,
Incite futurity to do the rest.

Or with an even likelihood,
He may have met with atrabilious eyes
The fires of time on equal terms and passed
Indifferently down, until at last
His only kind of grandeur would have been,
Apparently, in being seen.
He may have had for evil or for good
No argument; he may have had no care
For what without himself went anywhere
To failure or to glory, and least of all

For such a stale, flamboyant miracle;
He may have been the prophet of an art
Immovable to old idolatries;
He may have been a player without a part,
Annoyed that even the sun should have the skies
For such a flaming way to advertise;
He may have been a painter sick at heart
With Nature's toiling for a new surprise;
He may have been a cynic, who now, for all
Of anything divine that his effete
Negation may have tasted,
Saw truth in his own image, rather small,
Forbore to fever the ephemeral,
Found any barren height a good retreat
From any swarming street,
And in the sun saw power superbly wasted:
And when the primitive old-fashioned stars
Came out again to shine on joys and wars
More primitive, and all arrayed for doom,
He may have proved a world a sorry thing
In his imagining,
And life a lighted highway to the tomb.

Or, mounting with infirm unsearching tread,
His hopes to chaos led,
He may have stumbled up there from the past,
And with an aching strangeness viewed the last
Absymal conflagration of his dreams,—
A flame where nothing seems
To burn but flame itself, by nothing fed;
And while it all went out,
Not even the faint anodyne of doubt
May then have eased a painful going down
From pictured heights of power and lost renown,
Revealed at length to his outlived endeavor
Remote and unapproachable forever;
And at his heart there may have gnawed
Sick memories of a dead faith foiled and flawed
And long dishonored by the living death
Assigned alike by chance
To brutes and hierophants;
And anguish fallen on those he loved around him
May once have dealt the last blow to confound him,
And so have left him as death leaves a child,

Who sees it all too near;
And he who knows no young way to forget
May struggle to the tomb unreconciled.
Whatever suns may rise or set
There may be nothing kinder for him here
Than shafts and agonies;
And under these
He may cry out and stay on horribly;
Or, seeing in death too small a thing to fear,
He may go forward like a stoic Roman
Where pangs and terrors in his pathway lie,—
Or, seizing the swift logic of a woman,
Curse God and die.

Or maybe there, like many another one
Who might have stood aloft and looked ahead,
Black-drawn against wild red,
He may have built, unawed by fiery gules
That in him no commotion stirred,
A living reason out of molecules
Why molecules occurred,
And one for smiling when he might have sighed
Had he seen far enough,
And in the same inevitable stuff
Discovered an odd reason too for pride
In being what he must have been by laws
Infrangible and for no kind of cause.
Deterred by no confusion or surprise
He may have seen with his mechanic eyes
A world without a meaning, and had room,
Alone amid magnificence and doom,
To build himself an airy monument
That should, or fail him in his vague intent,
Outlast an accidental universe—
To call it nothing worse—
Or, by the burrowing guile
Of Time disintegrated and effaced,
Like once-remembered mighty trees go down
To ruin, of which by man may now be traced
No part sufficient even to be rotten,
And in the book of things that are forgotten
Is entered as a thing not quite worth while.
He may have been so great
That satraps would have shivered at his frown,

And all he prized alive may rule a state
No larger than a grave that holds a clown;
He may have been a master of his fate,
And of his atoms,—ready as another
In his emergence to exonerate
His father and his mother;
He may have been a captain of a host,
Self-eloquent and ripe for prodigies,
Doomed here to swell by dangerous degrees,
And then give up the ghost.
Nahum's great grasshoppers were such as these,
Sun-scattered and soon lost.

Whatever the dark road he may have taken,
This man who stood on high
And faced alone the sky,
Whatever drove or lured or guided him,—
A vision answering a faith unshaken,
An easy trust assumed of easy trials,
A sick negation born of weak denials,
A crazed abhorrence of an old condition,
A blind attendance on a brief ambition,—
Whatever stayed him or derided him,
His way was even as ours;
And we, with all our wounds and all our powers,
Must each await alone at his own height
Another darkness or another light;
And there, of our poor self-dominion reft,
If inference and reason shun
Hell, Heaven, and Oblivion,
May thwarted will (perforce precarious,
But for our conservation better thus)
Have no misgiving left
Of doing yet what here we leave undone?
Or if unto the last of these we cleave,
Believing or protesting we believe
In such an idle and ephemeral
Florescence of the diabolical,—
If, robbed of two fond old enormities,
Our being had no onward auguries,
What then were this great love of ours to say
For launching other lives to voyage again
A little farther into time and pain,
A little faster in a futile chase

For a kingdom and a power and a Race
That would have still in sight
A manifest end of ashes and eternal night?
Is this the music of the toys we shake
So loud,—as if there might be no mistake
Somewhere in our indomitable will?
Are we no greater than the noise we make
Along one blind atomic pilgrimage
Whereon by crass chance billeted we go
Because our brains and bones and cartilage
Will have it so?
If this we say, then let us all be still
About our share in it, and live and die
More quietly thereby.

Where was he going, this man against the sky?
You know not, nor do I.
But this we know, if we know anything:
That we may laugh and fight and sing
And of our transience here make offering
To an orient World that will not be erased,
Or, save in incommunicable gleams
Too permanent for dreams,
Be found or known.
No tonic and ambitious irritant
Of increase or of want
Has made an otherwise insensate waste
Of ages overthrown
A ruthless, veiled, implacable foretaste
Of other ages that are still to be
Depleted and rewarded variously
Because a few, by fate's economy,
Shall seem to move the world the way it goes;
No soft evangel of equality,
Safe-cradled in a communal repose
That huddles into death and may at last
Be covered well with equatorial snows—
And all for what, the devil only knows—
Will aggregate an inkling to confirm
The credit of a sage or of a worm,
Or tell us why one man in five
Should have a care to stay alive
While in his heart he feels no violence
Laid on his humor and intelligence

When infant Science makes a pleasant face
And waves again that hollow toy, the Race;
No planetary trap where souls are wrought
For nothing but the sake of being caught
And sent again to nothing will attune
Itself to any key of any reason
Why man should hunger through another season
To find out why 'twere better late than soon
To go away and let the sun and moon
And all the silly stars illuminate
A place for creeping things,
And those that root and trumpet and have wings,
And herd and ruminate,
Or dive and flash and poise in rivers and seas,
Or by their loyal tails in lofty trees
Hang screeching lewd victorious derision
Of man's immortal vision.

Shall we, because Eternity records
Too vast an answer for the time-born words
We spell, whereof so many are dead that once
In our capricious lexicons
Were so alive and final, hear no more
The Word itself, the living word
That none alive has ever heard
Or ever spelt,
And few have ever felt
Without the fears and old surrenderings
And terrors that began
When Death let fall a feather from his wings
And humbled the first man?
Because the weight of our humility,
Wherefrom we gain
A little wisdom and much pain,
Falls here too sore and there too tedious,
Are we in anguish or complacency,
Not looking far enough ahead
To see by what mad couriers we are led
Along the roads of the ridiculous,
To pity ourselves and laugh at faith
And while we curse life bear it?
And if we see the soul's dead end in death,
Are we to fear it?
What folly is here that has not yet a name

Unless we say outright that we are liars?
What have we seen beyond our sunset fires
That lights again the way by which we came?
Why pay we such a price, and one we give
So clamoringly, for each racked empty day
That leads one more last human hope away,
As quiet fiends would lead past our crazed eyes
Our children to an unseen sacrifice?
If after all that we have lived and thought,
All comes to Nought,—
If there be nothing after Now,
And we be nothing anyhow,
And we know that,—why live?
'Twere sure but weaklings' vain distress
To suffer dungeons where so many doors
Will open on the cold eternal shores
That look sheer down
To the dark tideless floods of Nothingness
Where all who know may drown.   1916

Bewick Finzer

Time was when his half millon drew
  The breath of six per cent;
But soon the worm of what-was-not
  Fed hard on his content;
And something crumbled in his brain
  When his half million went.

Time passed, and filled along with his
  The place of many more;
Time came, and hardly one of us
  Had credence to restore,
From what appeared one day, the man
  Whom we had known before.

The broken voice, the withered neck,
  The coat worn out with care,
The cleanliness of indigence,
  The brillance of despair,
The fond imponderable dreams
  Of affluence,—all were there.

Poor Finzer, with his dreams and schemes,
Fares hard now in the race,
With heart and eye that have a task
When he looks in the face
Of one who might so easily
Have been in Finzer's place.

He comes unfailing for the loan
We give and then forget;
He comes, and probably for years
Will he be coming yet,—
Familiar as an old mistake,
And futile as regret. 1916

The Rat

As often as he let himself be seen
We pitied him, or scorned him, or deplored
The inscrutable profusion of the Lord
Who shaped as one of us a thing so mean—
Who made him human when he might have been
A rat, and so been wholly in accord
With any other creature we abhorred
As always useless and not always clean.

Now he is hiding all alone somewhere,
And in a final hole not ready then;
For now he is among those over there
Who are not coming back to us again.
And we who do the fiction of our share
Say less of rats and more of men. 1920

New England

Here where the wind is always north-north-east
And children learn to walk on frozen toes,
Wonder begets an envy of all those
Who boil elsewhere with such a lyric yeast
Of love that you will hear them at a feast
Where demons would appeal for some repose,
Still clamoring where the chalice overflows
And crying wildest who have drunk the least.

Passion is here a soilure of the wits,
We're told, and Love a cross for them to bear;
Joy shivers in the corner where she knits
And Conscience always has the rocking-chair,
Cheerful as when she tortured into fits
The first cat that was ever killed by Care. 1923

From *Tristram*

I

Isolt of the white hands, in Brittany,
Could see no longer northward anywhere
A picture more alive or less familiar
Than a blank ocean and the same white birds
Flying, and always flying, and still flying,
Yet never bringing any news of him
That she remembered, who had sailed away
The spring before—saying he would come back,
Although not saying when. Not one of them,
For all their flying, she thought, had heard the name
Of Tristram, or of him beside her there
That was the King, her father. The last ship
Was out of sight, and there was nothing now
For her to see before the night came down
Except her father's face. She looked at him
And found him smiling in the way she feared,
And loved the while she feared it. The King took
One of her small still hands in one of his
That was so large and hard to be so kind,
And weighed a question, not for the first time:

"Why should it be that I must have a child
Whose eyes are wandering always to the north?
The north is a bad region full of wolves
And bears and hairy men that have no manners.
Why should her eyes be always on the north,
I wonder, when all's here that one requires
Of comfort, love, and of expediency?
You are not cheered, I see, or satisfied
Entirely by the sound of what I say.
You are too young, may be, to make yourself
A nest of comfort and expediency."

"I may be that," she said, and a quick flush
Made a pink forage of her laughing face.
At which he smiled again. "But not so young
As to be told for ever how young I am.
I have been growing for these eighteen years,
And waiting here, for one thing and another.
Besides, his manners are as good as yours,
And he's not half so hairy as you are,
Even though you be the King of Brittany,
Or the great Jove himself, and then my father."
With that she threw her arms around his neck,
Throbbing as if she were a child indeed.

"You are no heavier than a cat," said he,
"But otherwise you are somewhat like a tiger.
Relinquish your commendable affection
A little, and tell me why it is you dream
Of someone coming always from the north.
Are there no proper knights or princes else
Than one whose eyes, wherever they may be fixed,
Are surely not fixed hard on Brittany?
You are a sort of child, or many sorts,
Yet also are too high and too essential
To be much longer the quaint sport and food
Of shadowy fancies. For a time I've laughed
And let you dream, but I may not laugh always.
Because he praised you as a child one day,
And may have liked you as a child one day,
Why do you stare for ever into the north,
Over that water, where the good God placed
A land known only to your small white ears?"

"Only because the good God, I suppose,
Placed England somewhere north of Brittany—
Though not so far but one may come and go
As many a time as twice before he dies.
I know that's true, having been told about it.
I have been told so much about this world
That I have wondered why men stay in it.
I have been told of devils that are in it,
And some right here in Brittany. Griffon
Is one of them; and if he ever gets me
I'll pray for the best way to kill myself."

King Howel held his daughter closer to him,
As if a buried and forgotten fear
Had come to life and was confronting him
With a new face. "Never you mind the devils,"
He said, "be they in Brittany or elsewhere.
They are for my attention, if need be.
You will affright me and amuse me less
By saying, if you are ready, how much longer
You are to starve yourself with your delusion
Of Tristram coming back. He may come back,
Or Mark, his uncle, who tonight is making
Another Isolt his queen—the dark Isolt,
Isolt of Ireland—may be coming back,
Though I'd as lief he would remain at home
In Cornwall, with his new queen—if he keeps her."

"And who is this far-off Isolt of Ireland?"
She said, like a thing waiting to be hurt:
"A creature that one hears of constantly,
And one that no man sees, or none to say so,
Must be unusual—if she be at all."

"The few men who have told of her to me
Have told of silence and of Irish pride,
Inhabiting too much beauty for one woman.
My eyes have never seen her; and as for beauty,
My eyes would rather look on yours, my child.
And as for Tristram coming back, what then—
One of these days? Any one may come back.
King Arthur may come back; and as for that,
Our Lord and Saviour may come back some time,
Though hardly all for you. Have you kept hid
Some promise or protestation heretofore,
That you may shape a thought into a reason
For making always of a distant wish
A dim belief? You are too old for that—
If it will make you happy to be told so.
You have been told so much." King Howel smiled,
And waited, holding her white hands in his.

"I have been told that Tristram will come back,"
She said; "and it was he who told me so.
Also I have this agate that he gave me;
And I believe his eyes."

"Believe his agate,"
The king said, "for as long as you may save it.
An agate's a fair plaything for a child,
Though not so boundless and immovable
In magnitude but that a child may lose it.
Since you esteem it such an acquisition,
Treasure it more securely, and believe it
As a bright piece of earth, and nothing more.
Believe his agate, and forget his eyes;
And go to bed. You are not young enough,
I see, to stay awake and entertain
Much longer your exaggerated fancies.
And if he should come back? Would you prepare
Upon the ruinous day of his departure
To drown yourself, and with yourself his agate?"

Isolt, now on a cushion at his feet,
Finding the King's hard knees a meagre pillow,
Sat upright, thinking. "No, I should not do that;
Though I should never trust another man
So far that I should go away with him.
King's daughters, I suppose, are bought and sold,
But you would not sell me."

"You seize a question
As if it were an agate—or a fact,"
The King said, laughing at the calm gray eyes
That were so large in the small face before him.
"I might sell you, perhaps, at a fair bargain.
To play with an illustrious example,
If Modred were to overthrow King Arthur—
And there are prophets who see Arthur's end
In Modred, who's an able sort of reptile—
And come for you to go away with him,
And to be Queen of Britain, I might sell you,
Perhaps. You might say prayers that you be sold."

"I may say prayers that you be reasonable
And serious, and that you believe me so."
There was a light now in his daughter's eyes
Like none that he remembered having seen
In eyes before, whereat he paused and heard,
Not all amused. "He will come back," she said,
"And I shall wait. If he should not come back,

I shall have been but one poor woman more
Whose punishment for being born a woman
Was to believe and wait. You are my King,
My father, and of all men anywhere,
Save one, you are the world of men to me.
When I say this of him you must believe me,
As I believe his eyes. He will come back:
And what comes then I leave to him, and God."

Slowly the King arose, and with his hands
He lifted up Isolt, so frail, so light,
And yet, with all, mysteriously so strong.
He raised her patient face between his hands,
Observing it as if it were some white
And foreign flower, not certain in his garden
To thrive, nor like to die. Then with a vague
And wavering effect of shaking her
Affectionately back to his own world,
Which never would be hers, he smiled once more
And set her free. "You should have gone to bed
When first I told you. You had best go now,
And while you are still dreaming. In the morning
Your dreams, if you remember them, will all
Be less than one bird singing in a tree."

Isolt of the white hands, unchangeable,
Half childlike and half womanly, looked up
Into her father's eyes and shook her head,
Smiling, but less for joy than certainty:
"There's a bird then that I have never seen
In Brittany; and I have never heard him.
Good night, my father." She went slowly out,
Leaving him in the gloom.

"Good night, my child,
Good night," he said, scarce hearing his own voice
For crowded thoughts that were unseizable
And unforeseen within him. Like Isolt,
He stood now in the window looking north
Over the misty sea. A seven days' moon
Was in the sky, and there were a few stars
That had no fire. "I have no more a child,"
He thought, "and what she is I do not know.
It may be fancy and fantastic youth

That ails her now; it may be the sick touch
Of prophecy concealing disillusion.
If there were not inwoven so much power
And poise of sense with all her seeming folly,
I might assume a concord with her faith
As that of one elected soon to die.
But surely no infringement of the grave
In her conceits and her appearances
Encourages a fear that still is fear;
And what she is to know, I cannot say.
A changeling down from one of those white stars
Were more like her than like a child of mine."

Nothing in the cold glimmer of a moon
Over a still, cold ocean there before him
Would answer for him in the silent voice
Of time an idle question. So the King,
With only time for company, stood waiting
Alone there in the window, looking off
At the still sea between his eyes and England. 1927

Robert [Lee] Frost

(1874-1963)

CHRONOLOGY:

1874 Born March 26, San Francisco, California.

1885 Moved to Lawrence, Massachusetts, with mother and sister after death of father.

1894 "My Butterfly" published in *Independent*.

1895 Married Elinor Miriam White.

1897-99 Attended Harvard.

1900-10 Farmed at Derry, New Hampshire; wrote poetry; taught school.

1911-12 Taught psychology at Plymouth, New Hampshire.

1912 Moved to England with wife and four children.

1913 *A Boy's Will.*

1914 *North of Boston.*

1915 Returned to America; settled on farm at Franconia, New Hampshire.

1916 *Mountain Interval;* elected to National Institute of Arts and Letters.

1917 Began twenty-year intermittent association with Amherst College, as Professor of English.

1919 Moved to new farm, South Shaftsbury, Vermont.

1921-23 Poet in residence, University of Michigan; *Selected Poems; New Hampshire* (won Pulitzer Prize, 1924).

1928 *West-Running Brook.*

1930 *Collected Poems* (won Pulitzer Prize, 1931).

1936 *A Further Range* (won Pulitzer Prize, 1937); Professor of Poetry, Harvard University; *Selected Poetry.*

1938 Wife died.

1939 *Collected Poems.*

1942 *A Witness Tree* (won Pulitzer Prize, 1943).
1945 *A Masque of Reason.*
1947 *Steeple Bush; A Masque of Mercy.*
1949 *Complete Poems.*
1957 Awarded honorary degrees by Oxford and Cambridge and National University of Ireland.
1958 Appointed Consultant in Poetry to Library of Congress.
1959 Nation celebrated his 85th birthday.
1961 Read "The Gift Outright" at Inauguration of John F. Kennedy, January 20.
1962 *In the Clearing.*
1963 Died January 29, in Boston.

BIBLIOGRAPHY:

The full texts, through *A Masque of Mercy* (1947), are in the *Complete Poems of Robert Frost* (New York, 1949); his remaining poetry is in *In the Clearing* (New York, 1962). Two useful selections are *The Poems of Robert Frost* (New York: Modern Library, 1946) and *Selected Poems of Robert Frost*, with an Introduction by Robert Graves (New York: Rinehart, 1963). This last volume also contains a valuable list of books on Frost, a list of articles and critical comment, and a list of Frost's prose writings. An important collection of letters is Louis Untermeyer, ed., *The Letters of Robert Frost to Louis Untermeyer* (New York, 1963).

Two important collections of essays on Frost include Richard H. Thornton, *Recognition of Robert Frost* (New York, 1937), and James M. Cox, ed., *Robert Frost: A Collection of Critical Essays* (Englewood Cliffs, 1962).

For explications of individual poems, see Joseph M. Kuntz, *Poetry Explication* (Rev. ed.; Denver, 1962).

An Introduction to [Edwin Arlington Robinson's] *King Jasper*

It may come to the notice of posterity (and then again it may not) that this, our age, ran wild in the quest of new ways to be new. The one old way to be new no longer served. Science put it into our heads that there must be new ways to be new. Those tried were largely by subtraction—elimination. Poetry, for example, was tried without punctuation. It was tried without capital letters. It was tried without metric frame on which to measure the rhythm. It was tried without any images but those to the eye; and a loud general intoning had to be kept up to cover the total loss of specific images to the ear, those dramatic tones of voice which had hitherto constituted the better half of poetry. It was tried without content under the trade name of poesie pure. It was tried without phrase, epigram, coherence, logic and consistency. It was tried without ability. I took the confession of one who had had deliberately to unlearn what he knew. He made a back-pedalling movement of his hands to illustrate the process. It was tried premature like the delicacy of unborn calf in Asia. It was tried without feeling or sentiment like murder for small pay in the underworld. These many things was it tried without, and what had we left? Still something. The limits of poetry had been sorely strained, but the hope was that the idea had been somewhat brought out.

Robinson stayed content with the old-fashioned way to be new. I remember bringing the subject up with him. How does a man come on his difference, and how does he feel about it when he first finds it out? At first it may well frighten him, as his difference with the Church frightened Martin Luther. There is such a thing as being too willing to be different. And what shall we say to people who are not only willing but anxious? What assurance have they that their difference is not insane, eccentric, abortive, unintelligible? Two fears should follow us through life. There is the fear that we shan't prove worthy in the eyes of someone who knows us at least as well as we know ourselves. That is the fear of God. And there is the fear of Man—the fear that men won't understand us and we shall be cut off from them.

We began in infancy by establishing correspondence of eyes with eyes. We recognized that they were the same feature and we could do the same things with them. We went on to the visible motion of the lips—smile answered smile; then cautiously, by trial and error, to compare the invisible muscles of the mouth and throat. They were the same and could make the same sounds. We were still together. So far, so good. From here on the wonder grows. It has been said that recognition in art is all. Better say correspondence is all. Mind must convince mind that it can uncurl and wave the same filaments of subtlety, soul convince soul that it can give off the same shimmers of eternity. At no point would anyone but a brute fool want to break off this correspondence. It is all there is to satisfaction; and it is salutary to live in the fear of its being broken off.

The latest proposed experiment of the experimentalists is to use poetry as a vehicle of grievances against the un-Utopian state. As I say, most of their experiments have been by subtraction. This would be by addition of an ingredient that latter-day poetry has lacked. A distinction must be made between griefs and grievances. Grievances are probably more useful than griefs. I read in a sort of Sunday-school leaflet from Moscow, that the grievances of Chekhov against the sordidness and dullness of his home-town society have done away with the sordidness and dullness of home-town society all over Russia. They were celebrating the event. The grievances of the great Russians of the last century have given Russia a revolution. The grievances of their great followers in America may well give us, if not a revolution, at least some palliative pensions. We must suffer them to put life at its ugliest and forbid them not, as we value our reputation for liberality.

I had it from one of the youngest lately: "Whereas we once thought literature should be without content, we now know it should be charged full of propaganda." Wrong twice, I told him. Wrong twice and of theory prepense. But he returned to his position after a moment out for reassembly: "Surely art can be considered good only as it prompts to action." How soon, I asked him. But there is danger of undue levity in teasing the young. The experiment is evidently started. Grievances are certainly a power and are going to be turned on. We must be very tender of our dreamers. They may seem like picketers or members of the committee on rules for the moment. We shan't mind what they seem, if only they produce real poems.

But for me, I don't like grievances. I find I gently let them alone wherever published. What I like is griefs and I like them Robinsonianly profound. I suppose there is no use in asking, but I should think we might be indulged to the extent of having grievances restricted to prose if prose will accept the imposition, and leaving poetry free to go its way in tears.

Robinson was a prince of heartachers amid countless achers of another part. The sincerity he wrought in was all sad. He asserted the sacred right of poetry to lean its breast to a thorn and sing its dolefullest. Let weasels suck eggs. I know better where to look for melancholy. A few superficial irritable grievances, perhaps, as was only human, but these are forgotten in the depth of griefs to which he plunged us.

Grievances are a form of impatience. Griefs are a form of patience. We may be required by law to throw away patience as we have been required to surrender gold; since by throwing away patience and joining the impatient in one last rush on the citadel of evil, the hope is we may end the need of patience. There will be nothing left to be patient about. The day of perfection waits on unanimous social action. Two or three more good national elections should do the business. It has been similarly urged on us to give up courage, make cowardice a virtue, and see if that won't end war, and the need of courage. Desert religion for science, clean out the holes and corners of the residual unknown, and there will be no more need of religion. (Religion is merely consolation for what we don't know.) But suppose there was some mistake, and the evil stood siege, the war didn't end, and something remained unknowable. Our having disarmed would make our case worse than it had ever been before. Nothing in the latest advices from Wall Street, the League of Nations, or the Vatican incline me to give up my holdings in patient grief.

There were Robinson and I, it was years ago, and the place (near Boston Common) was the Place, as we liked afterwards to call it, of Bitters, because it was with bitters, though without bitterness, we could sit there and look out on the welter of dissatisfaction and experiment in the world around us. It was too long ago to remember who said what, but the sense of the meeting was, we didn't care how arrant a reformer or experimentalist a man was if he gave us real poems. For ourselves, we should hate to be read for any theory upon which we might be supposed to write. We doubted any poem could persist for any theory upon which it might have been written. Take the theory that poetry in our language could be treated as quantitative, for example. Poems had been written in spite of it. And poems are all that matter. The utmost of ambition is to lodge a few poems where they will be hard to get rid of, to lodge a few irreducible bits where Robinson lodged more than his share.

For forty years it was phrase on phrase on phrase with Robinson, and every one the closest delineation of something that *is* something. Any poet, to resemble him in the least, would have to resemble him in that grazing closeness to the spiritual realities. If books of verse were to be indexed by lines first in importance instead of lines first in position, many of Robinson's poems would be represented several times over. This should be seen to. The only possible objection is that it could not be done by any mere hireling of the moment, but would have to be the work of someone who had taken his impressions freely before he had any notion of their use. A particular poem's being represented several times would only increase the chance of its being located.

The first poet I ever sat down with to talk about poetry was Ezra Pound. It was in London in 1913. The first poet we talked about, to the best of my recollection, was Edwin Arlington Robinson. I was fresh from America and from having read *The Town Down the River*. Beginning at that book, I have slowly spread my reading of Robinson twenty years backward and forward, about equally in both directions.

I remember the pleasure with which Pound and I laughed over the fourth "thought" in

> Miniver thought, and thought, and thought,
> And thought about it.

Three "thoughts" would have been "adequate" as the critical praiseword then was. There would have been nothing to complain of, if it had been left at three. The fourth made the intolerable touch of poetry. With the fourth, the fun began. I was taken out on the strength of our community of opinion here, to be rewarded with an introduction to Miss May Sinclair, who had qualified as the patron authority on young and new poets by the sympathy she had shown them in *The Divine Fire*.

There is more to it than the number of "thoughts." There is the way the last one turns up by surprise round the corner, the way the shape of the stanza is played with, the easy way the obstacle of verse is turned to advantage. The mischief is in it.

> One pauses half afraid
> To say for certain that he played—

a man as sorrowful as Robinson. His death was sad to those who knew him, but nowhere near as sad as the lifetime of poetry to which he attuned our ears. Nevertheless, I say his much-admired restraint lies wholly in his never having let grief go further than it could in play. So far shall grief go, so far shall philosophy go, so far shall confidences go, and no further. Taste may set the limit. Humor is a surer dependence.

And once a man was there all night,
Expecting something every minute.

I know what the man wanted of Old King Cole. He wanted the heart out of his mystery. He was the friend who stands at the end of a poem ready in waiting to catch you by both hands with enthusiasm and drag you off your balance over the last punctuation mark into more than you meant to say. "I understand the poem all right, but please tell me what is behind it?" Such presumption needs to be twinkled at and baffled. The answer must be, "If I had wanted you to know, I should have told you in the poem."

We early have Robinson's word for it:

The games we play
To fill the frittered minutes of a day
Good glasses are to read the spirit through.

He speaks somewhere of Crabbe's stubborn skill. His own was a happy skill. His theme was unhappiness itself, but his skill was as happy as it was playful. There is that comforting thought for those who suffered to see him suffer. Let it be said at the risk of offending the humorless in poetry's train (for there are a few such): his art was more than playful; it was humorous.

The style is the man. Rather say the style is the way the man takes himself; and to be at all charming or even bearable, the way is almost rigidly prescribed. If it is with outer seriousness, it must be with inner humor. If it is with outer humor, it must be with inner seriousness. Neither one alone without the other under it will do. Robinson was thinking as much in his sonnet on Tom Hood. One ordeal of Mark Twain was the constant fear that his occluded seriousness would be overlooked. That betrayed him into his two or three books of out-and-out seriousness.

Miniver Cheevy was long ago. The glint I mean has kept coming to the surface of the fabric all down the years. Yesterday in conversation, I was using "The Mill." Robinson could make lyric talk like drama. What imagination for speech in "John Gorham"! He is at his height between quotation marks.

The miller's wife had waited long,
  The tea was cold, the fire was dead;
And there might yet be nothing wrong
  In how he went and what he said:
"There are no millers any more,"
  Was all that she had heard him say.

"There are no millers any more." It might be an edict of some power against industrialism. But no, it is of wider application. It is a sinister jest at the expense of all investors of life or capital. The market shifts and leaves them with a car-barn full of dead trolley cars. At twenty I commit myself to a life of religion. Now, if religion should go out of fashion in twenty-five years, there would I be, forty-five years old, unfitted for anything else and too old to learn anything else. It seems immoral to have to bet on such high things as lives of art, business, or the church. But in effect, we have no alternative. None but an all-wise and all-powerful government could take the responsibility of keeping us out of the gamble or of insuring us against loss once we were in.

The guarded pathos of "Mr. Flood's Party" is what makes it merciless. We are to bear in mind the number of moons listening. Two, as on the planet Mars. No less. No more ("No more, sir; that will do"). One moon (albeit a moon, no sun) would have laid grief too bare. More than two would have dissipated grief entirely and would have amounted to dissipation. The emotion had to be held at a point.

> He set the jug down slowly at his feet
> With trembling care, knowing that most things break;
> And only when assured that on firm earth
> It stood, as the uncertain lives of men
> Assuredly did not . . .

There twice it gleams. Nor is it lost even where it is perhaps lost sight of in the dazzle of all those golden girls at the ends of "The Sheaves." Granted a few fair days in a world where not all days are fair.

> "Well, Mr. Flood, we have the harvest moon
> Again, and we may not have many more;
> The bird is on the wing, the poet says,
> And you and I have said it here before.
> Drink to the bird."

Poetry transcends itself in the playfulness of the toast.

Robinson has gone to his place in American literature and left his human place among us vacant. We mourn, but with the qualification that, after all, his life was a revel in the felicites of language. And not just to no purpose. None has deplored

> The inscrutable profusion of the Lord
> Who shaped as one of us a thing

so sad and at the same time so happy in achievement. Not for me to search his sadness to its source. He knew how to forbid encroachment. And there is solid satisfaction in a sadness that is not just a fishing for ministration and consolation. Give us immedicable woes—woes that nothing can be done for—woes flat and final. And then to play. The play's the thing. Play's the thing. All virtue in "as if."

> As if the last of days
> Were fading and all wars were done.

As if they were. As if, as if!

1935

Mowing

There was never a sound beside the wood but one,
And that was my long scythe whispering to the ground.
What was it it whispered? I knew not well myself;
Perhaps it was something about the heat of the sun,
Something, perhaps, about the lack of sound—
And that was why it whispered and did not speak.
It was no dream of the gift of idle hours,
Or easy gold at the hand of fay or elf:
Anything more than the truth would have seemed too weak
To the earnest love that laid the swale in rows,
Not without feeble-pointed spikes of flowers
(Pale orchises), and scared a bright green snake.
The fact is the sweetest dream that labor knows.
My long scythe whispered and left the hay to make. 1913

The Tuft of Flowers

I went to turn the grass once after one
Who mowed it in the dew before the sun.

The dew was gone that made his blade so keen
Before I came to view the levelled scene.

I looked for him behind an isle of trees;
I listened for his whetstone on the breeze.

But he had gone his way, the grass all mown,
And I must be, as he had been,—alone.

"As all must be," I said within my heart,
"Whether they work together or apart."

But as I said it, swift there passed me by
On noiseless wing a bewildered butterfly,

Seeking with memories grown dim o'er night
Some resting flower of yesterday's delight.

And once I marked his flight go round and round,
As where some flower lay withering on the ground.

And then he flew as far as eye could see,
And then on tremulous wing came back to me.

I thought of questions that have no reply,
And would have turned to toss the grass to dry;

But he turned first, and led my eye to look
At a tall tuft of flowers beside a brook,

A leaping tongue of bloom the scythe had spared
Beside a reedy brook the scythe had bared.

I left my place to know them by their name,
Finding them butterfly weed when I came.

The mower in the dew had loved them thus,
By leaving them to flourish, not for us,

Nor yet to draw one thought of ours to him,
But from sheer morning gladness at the brim.

The butterfly and I had lit upon,
Nevertheless, a message from the dawn,

That made me hear the wakening birds around,
And hear his long scythe whispering to the ground,

And feel a spirit kindred to my own;
So that henceforth I worked no more alone;

But glad with him, I worked as with his aid,
And weary, sought at noon with him the shade;

And dreaming, as it were, held brotherly speech
With one whose thought I had not hoped to reach.

"Men work together," I told him from the heart,
"Whether they work together or apart."

1913

Mending Wall

Something there is that doesn't love a wall,
That sends the frozen-ground-swell under it,

And spills the upper bowlders in the sun;
And makes gaps even two can pass abreast.
The work of hunters is another thing:
I have come after them and made repair
Where they have left not one stone on a stone,
But they would have the rabbit out of hiding,
To please the yelping dogs. The gaps I mean,
No one has seen them made or heard them made,
But at spring mending-time we find them there.
I let my neighbor know beyond the hill;
And on a day we meet to walk the line
And set the wall between us once again.
We keep the wall between us as we go.
To each the boulders that have fallen to each.
And some are loaves and some so nearly balls
We have to use a spell to make them balance:
"Stay where you are until our backs are turned!"
We wear our fingers rough with handling them.
Oh, just another kind of out-door game,
One on a side. It comes to little more:
There where it is we do not need the wall:
He is all pine and I am apple orchard.
My apple trees will never get across
And eat the cones under his pines, I tell him.
He only says, "Good fences make good neighbors."
Spring is the mischief in me, and I wonder
If I could put a notion in his head:
"*Why* do they make good neighbors? Isn't it
Where there are cows? But here there are no cows.
Before I built a wall I'd ask to know
What I was walling in or walling out,
And to whom I was like to give offense.
Something there is that doesn't love a wall,
That wants it down." I could say "Elves" to him,
But it's not elves exactly, and I'd rather
He said it for himself. I see him there
Bringing a stone grasped firmly by the top
In each hand, like an old-stone savage armed.
He moves in darkness as it seems to me,
Not of woods only and the shade of trees.
He will not go behind his father's saying,
And he likes having thought of it so well
He says again, "Good fences make good neighbors."

1914

The Mountain

The mountain held the town as in a shadow.
I saw so much before I slept there once:
I noticed that I missed stars in the west,
Where its black body cut into the sky.
Near me it seemed: I felt it like a wall
Behind which I was sheltered from a wind.
And yet between the town and it I found,
When I walked forth at dawn to see new things,
Were fields, a river, and beyond, more fields.
The river at the time was fallen away,
And made a widespread brawl on cobble-stones;
But the signs showed what it had done in spring:
Good grass-land gullied out, and in the grass
Ridges of sand, and driftwood stripped of bark.
I crossed the river and swung round the mountain.
And there I met a man who moved so slow
With white-faced oxen in a heavy cart,
It seemed no harm to stop him altogether.

'What town is this?' I asked.

'This? Lunenburg.'

Then I was wrong: the town of my sojourn,
Beyond the bridge, was not that of the mountain,
But only felt at night its shadowy presence.
'Where is your village? Very far from here?'

'There is no village—only scattered farms,
We were but sixty voters last election.
We can't in nature grow to many more:
That thing takes all the room!' He moved his goad.
The mountain stood there to be pointed at.
Pasture ran up the side a little way,
And then there was a wall of trees with trunks;
After that only tops of trees, and cliffs
Imperfectly concealed among the leaves.
A dry ravine emerged from under boughs
Into the pasture.

'That looks like a path.
Is that the way to reach the top from here?—
Not for this morning, but some other time:
I must be getting back to breakfast now.'

'I don't advise your trying from this side.
There is no proper path, but those that *have*
Been up, I understand, have climbed from Ladd's.
That's five miles back. You can't mistake the place:
They logged it there last winter some way up.
I'd take you, but I'm bound the other way.'

'You've never climbed it?'

'I've been on the sides,
Deer-hunting and trout-fishing. There's a brook
That starts up on it somewhere—I've heard say
Right on the top, tip-top—a curious thing.
But what would interest you about the brook,
It's always cold in summer, warm in winter.
One of the great sights going is to see
It steam in winter like an ox's breath,
Until the bushes all along its banks
Are inch-deep with the frosty spines and bristles—
You know the kind. Then let the sun shine on it!'
'There ought to be a view around the world
From such a mountain—if it isn't wooded
Clear to the top.' I saw through leafy screens
Great granite terraces in sun and shadow,
Shelves one could rest a knee on getting up—
With depths behind him sheer a hundred feet.
Or turn and sit on and look out and down,
With little ferns in crevices at his elbow.

'As to that I can't say. But there's the spring,
Right on the summit, almost like a fountain.
That ought to be worth seeing.'

'If it's there.
You never saw it?'

'I guess there's no doubt
About its being there. I never saw it.

It may not be right on the very top:
It wouldn't have to be a long way down
To have some head of water from above,
And a *good distance* down might not be noticed
By anyone who'd come a long way up.
One time I asked a fellow climbing it
To look and tell me later how it was.'

'What did he say?'

'He said there was a lake
Somewhere in Ireland on a mountain top.'

'But a lake's different. What about the spring?'

'He never got up high enough to see.
That's why I don't advise your trying this side.
He tried this side. I've always meant to go
And look myself, but you know how it is:
It doesn't seem so much to climb a mountain
You've worked around the foot of all your life.
What would I do? Go in my overalls,
With a big stick, the same as when the cows
Haven't come down to the bars at milking time?
Or with a shotgun for a stray black bear?
'Twouldn't seem real to climb for climbing it.'
'I shouldn't climb it if I didn't want to—
Not for the sake of climbing. What's its name?'

'We call it Hor: I don't know if that's right.'

'Can one walk around it? Would it be too far?'

'You can drive round and keep in Lunenburg,
But it's as much as ever you can do,
The boundary lines keep in so close to it.
Hor is the township, and the township's Hor—
And a few houses sprinkled round the foot,
Like boulders broken off the upper cliff,
Rolled out a little farther than the rest.'

'Warm in December, cold in June you say?'

'I don't suppose the water's changed at all.
You and I know enough to know it's warm

Compared with cold, and cold compared with warm
But all the fun's in how you say a thing.'

'You've lived here all your life?'

'Ever since Hor
Was no bigger than a—' What, I did not hear.
He drew the oxen toward him with light touches
Of his slim goad on nose and offside flank,
Gave them their marching orders and was moving.

1914

Home Burial

He saw her from the bottom of the stairs
Before she saw him. She was starting down,
Looking back over her shoulder at some fear.
She took a doubtful step and then undid it
To raise herself and look again. He spoke
Advancing toward her: 'What is it you see
From up there always—for I want to know.'
She turned and sank upon her skirts at that,
And her face changed from terrified to dull.
He said to gain time: 'What is it you see,'
Mounting until she cowered under him.
'I will find out now—you must tell me, dear.'
She, in her place, refused him any help
With the least stiffening of her neck and silence.
She let him look, sure that he wouldn't see.
Blind creature; and awhile he didn't see.
But at last he murmured, 'Oh,' and again, 'Oh.'

'What is it—what?' she said.

'Just that I see.'

'You don't,' she challenged. 'Tell me what it is.'

'The wonder is I didn't see at once.
I never noticed it from here before.
I must be wonted to it—that's the reason.
The little graveyard where my people are!
So small the window frames the whole of it.
Not so much larger than a bedroom, is it?

There are three stones of slate and one of marble,
Broad-shouldered little slabs there in the sunlight
On the sidehill. We haven't to mind *those*.
But I understand: it is not the stones,
But the child's mound–'

'Don't, don't, don't, don't,' she cried.

She withdrew shrinking from beneath his arm
That rested on the bannister, and slid downstairs;
And turned on him with such a daunting look,
He said twice over before he knew himself:
'Can't a man speak of his own child he's lost?'

'Not you! Oh, where's my hat? Oh, I don't need it!
I must get out of here. I must get air.
I don't know rightly whether any man can.'

'Amy! Don't go to someone else this time.
Listen to me. I won't come down the stairs.'
He sat and fixed his chin between his fists.
'There's something I should like to ask you, dear.'

'You don't know how to ask it.'

'Help me, then.'

Her fingers moved the latch for all reply.

'My words are nearly always an offense.
I don't know how to speak of anything
So as to please you. But I might be taught
I should suppose. I can't say I see how.
A man must partly give up being a man
With women-folk. We could have some arrangement
By which I'd bind myself to keep hands off
Anything special you're a-mind to name.
Though I don't like such things 'twixt those that love.
Two that don't love can't live together without them.
But two that do can't live together with them.'
She moved the latch a little. 'Don't–don't go.
Don't carry it to someone else this time.
Tell me about it if it's something human.
Let me into your grief. I'm not so much
Unlike other folks as your standing there

Apart would make me out. Give me my chance.
I do think, though, you overdo it a little.
What was it brought you up to think it the thing
To take your mother-loss of a first child
So inconsolably—in the face of love.
You'd think his memory might be satisfied—'

'There you go sneering now!'

'I'm not, I'm not!
You make me angry. I'll come down to you.
God, what a woman! And it's come to this,
A man can't speak of his own child that's dead.'

'You can't because you don't know how to speak.
If you had any feelings, you that dug
With your own hand—how could you?—his little grave;
I saw you from that very window there,
Making the gravel leap and leap in air,
Leap up, like that, like that, and land so lightly
And roll back down the mound beside the hole.
I thought, Who is that man? I didn't know you.
And I crept down the stairs and up the stairs
To look again, and still your spade kept lifting.
Then you came in. I heard your rumbling voice
Out in the kitchen, and I don't know why,
But I went near to see with my own eyes.
You could sit there with the stains on your shoes
Of the fresh earth from your own baby's grave
And talk about your everyday concerns.
You had stood the spade up against the wall
Outside there in the entry, for I saw it.'

'I shall laugh the worst laugh I ever laughed.
I'm cursed. God, if I don't believe I'm cursed.'

'I can repeat the very words you were saying.
"Three foggy mornings and one rainy day
Will rot the best birch fence a man can build."
Think of it, talk like that at such a time!
What had how long it takes a birch to rot
To do with what was in the darkened parlor.
You *couldn't* care! The nearest friends can go
With anyone to death, comes so far short

They might as well not try to go at all.
No, from the time when one is sick to death,
One is alone, and he dies more alone.
Friends make pretense of following to the grave,
But before one is in it, their minds are turned
And making the best of their way back to life
And living people, and things they understand.
But the world's evil. I won't have grief so
If I can change it. Oh, I won't, I won't!'

'There, you have said it all and you feel better.
You won't go now. You're crying. Close the door.
The heart's gone out of it: why keep it up.
Amy! There's someone coming down the road!'

'*You*—oh, you think the talk is all. I must go—
Somewhere out of this house. How can I make you—'

'If—you—do!' She was opening the door wider.
'Where do you mean to go? First tell me that.
I'll follow and bring you back by force. I *will!*—'

1914

After Apple-Picking

My long two-pointed ladder's sticking through a tree
Toward heaven still,
And there's a barrel that I didn't fill
Beside it, and there may be two or three
Apples I didn't pick upon some bough.
But I am done with apple-picking now.
Essence of winter sleep is on the night,
The scent of apples: I am drowsing off.
I cannot rub the strangeness from my sight
I got from looking through a pane of glass
I skimmed this morning from the drinking trough
And held against the world of hoary grass.
It melted, and I let it fall and break.
But I was well
Upon my way to sleep before it fell,
And I could tell
What form my dreaming was about to take.
Magnified apples appear and disappear,

Stem end and blossom end,
And every fleck of russet showing clear.
My instep arch not only keeps the ache,
It keeps the pressure of a ladder-round.
I feel the ladder sway as the boughs bend.
And I keep hearing from the cellar bin
The rumbling sound
Of load on load of apples coming in.

For I have had too much
Of apple-picking: I am overtired
Of the great harvest I myself desired.
There were ten thousand thousand fruit to touch,
Cherish in hand, lift down, and not let fall.
For all
That struck the earth,
No matter if not bruised or spiked with stubble,
Went surely to the cider-apple heap
As of no worth.
One can see what will trouble
This sleep of mine, whatever sleep it is.
Were he not gone,
The woodchuck could say whether it's like his
Long sleep, as I describe its coming on,
Or just some human sleep. 1914

The Wood-Pile

Out walking in the frozen swamp one gray day,
I paused and said, 'I will turn back from here.
No, I will go on farther—and we shall see.'
The hard snow held me, save where now and then
One foot went through. The view was all in lines
Straight up and down of tall slim trees
Too much alike to mark or name a place by
So as to say for certain I was here
Or somewhere else: I was just far from home.
A small bird flew before me. He was careful
To put a tree between us when he lighted,
And say no word to tell me who he was
Who was so foolish as to think what *he* thought.
He thought that I was after him for a feather—
The white one in his tail; like one who takes

Everything said as personal to himself.
One flight out sideways would have undeceived him.
And then there was a pile of wood for which
I forgot him and let his little fear
Carry him off the way I might have gone,
Without so much as wishing him goodnight.
He went behind it to make his last stand.
It was a cord of maple, cut and split
And piled—and measured, four by four by eight.
And not another like it could I see.
No runner tracks in this year's snow looped near it.
And it was older sure than this year's cutting,
Or even last year's or the year's before.
The wood was grey and the bark warping off it
And the pile somewhat sunken. Clematis
Had wound strings round and round it like a bundle.
What held it though on one side was a tree
Still growing, and on one a stake and prop,
These latter about to fall. I thought that only
Someone who lived in turning to fresh tasks
Could so forget his handiwork on which
He spent himself, the labour of his ax,
And leave it there far from a useful fireplace
To warm the frozen swamp as best it could
With the slow smokeless burning of decay.

1914

Birches

When I see birches bend to left and right
Across the lines of straighter darker trees,
I like to think some boy's been swinging them.
But swinging doesn't bend them down to stay.
Ice-storms do that. Often you must have seen them
Loaded with ice a sunny winter morning
After a rain. They click upon themselves
As the breeze rises, and turn many colored
As the stir cracks and crazes their enamel.
Soon the sun's warmth makes them shed crystal shells
Shattering and avalanching on the snow-crust—
Such heaps of broken glass to sweep away
You'd think the inner dome of heaven had fallen.
They are dragged to the withered bracken by the load,

And they seem not to break; though once they are bowed
So low for long, they never right themselves:
You may see their trunks arching in the woods
Years afterwards, trailing their leaves on the ground
Like girls on hands and knees that throw their hair
Before them over their heads to dry in the sun.
But I was going to say when Truth broke in
With all her matter-of-fact about the ice-storm
I should prefer to have some boy bend them
As he went out and in to fetch the cows—
Some boy too far from town to learn baseball,
Whose only play was what he found himself,
Summer or winter, and could play alone.
One by one he subdued his father's trees
By riding them down over and over again
Until he took the stiffness out of them,
And not one but hung limp, not one was left
For him to conquer. He learned all there was
To learn about not launching out too soon
And so not carrying the tree away
Clear to the ground. He always kept his poise
To the top branches, climbing carefully
With the same pains you use to fill a cup
Up to the brim, and even above the brim.
Then he flung outward, feet first, with a swish,
Kicking his way down through the air to the ground.
So was I once myself a swinger of birches.
And so I dream of going back to be.
It's when I'm weary of considerations,
And life is too much like a pathless wood
Where your face burns and tickles with the cobwebs
Broken across it, and one eye is weeping
From a twig's having lashed across it open.
I'd like to get away from earth awhile
And then come back to it and begin over.
May no fate willfully misunderstand me
And half grant what I wish and snatch me away
Not to return. Earth's the right place for love:
I don't know where it's likely to go better.
I'd like to go by climbing a birch tree,
And climb black branches up a snow-white trunk
Toward heaven, till the tree could bear no more,
But dipped its top and set me down again.
That would be good both going and coming back.
One could do worse than be a swinger of birches.

1915

"Out, Out–"

The buzz-saw snarled and rattled in the yard
And made dust and dropped stove-length sticks of wood,
Sweet-scented stuff when the breeze drew across it.
And from there those that lifted eyes could count
Five mountain ranges one behind the other
Under the sunset far into Vermont.
And the saw snarled and rattled, snarled and rattled,
As it ran light, or had to bear a load.
And nothing happened: day was all but done.
Call it a day, I wish they might have said
To please the boy by giving him the half hour
That a boy counts so much when saved from work.
His sister stood beside them in her apron
To tell them "Supper." At the word, the saw,
As if to prove saws knew what supper meant,
Leaped out at the boy's hand, or seemed to leap–
He must have given the hand. However it was,
Neither refused the meeting. But the hand!
The boy's first outcry was a rueful laugh,
As he swung toward them holding up the hand
Half in appeal, but half as if to keep
The life from spilling. Then the boy saw all–
Since he was old enough to know, big boy
Doing a man's work, though a child at heart–
He saw all spoiled. "Don't let him cut my hand off–
The doctor, when he comes. Don't let him, sister!"
The doctor put him in the dark of ether.
So. But the hand was gone already.
He lay and puffed his lips out with his breath.
And then–the watcher at his pulse took fright.
No one believed. They listened at his heart.
Little–less–nothing!–and that ended it.
No more to build on there. And they, since they
Were not the one dead, turned to their affairs. 1916

Fire and Ice

Some say the world will end in fire,
Some say in ice.
From what I've tasted of desire

I hold with those who favor fire.
But if it had to perish twice,
I think I know enough of hate
To say that for destruction ice
Is also great
And would suffice. 1920

Stopping by Woods on a Snowy Evening

Whose woods these are I think I know.
His house is in the village though;
He will not see me stopping here
To watch his woods fill up with snow.

My little horse must think it queer
To stop without a farmhouse near
Between the woods and frozen lake
The darkest evening of the year.

He gives his harness bells a shake
To ask if there is some mistake.
The only other sound's the sweep
Of easy wind and downy flake.

The woods are lovely, dark and deep.
But I have promises to keep,
And miles to go before I sleep,
And miles to go before I sleep. 1923

West-Running Brook

'Fred, where is north?'

'North? North is there, my love.
The brook runs west.'

'West-running Brook then call it.'
(West-running Brook men call it to this day.)
'What does it think it's doing running west
When all the other country brooks flow east,
To reach the ocean? It must be the brook
Can trust itself to go by contraries

The way I can with you—and you with me—
Because we're—we're—I don't know what we are.
What are we?'

'Young or new?'

'We must be something.
We've said we two. Let's change that to we three.
As you and I are married to each other,
We'll both be married to the brook. We'll build
Our bridge across it, and the bridge shall be
Our arm thrown over it asleep beside it.
Look, look, it's waving to us with a wave
To let us know it hears me.'

'Why, my dear,
That wave's been standing off this jut of shore—'
(The black stream, catching on a sunken rock,
Flung backward on itself in one white wave,
And the white water rode the black forever,
Not gaining but not losing, like a bird
White feathers from the struggle of whose breast
Flecked the dark stream and flecked the darker pool
Below the point, and were at last driven wrinkled
In a white scarf against the far shore alders.)
'That wave's been standing off this jut of shore
Ever since rivers, I was going to say,
Were made in heaven. It wasn't waved to us.'

'It wasn't, yet it was. If not to you.
It was to me—in an annunciation.'

'Oh, if you take it off to lady-land,
As't were the country of the Amazons
We men must see you to the confines of
And leave you there, ourselves forbid to enter,—
It is your brook! I have no more to say.'

'Yes, you have, too. Go on. You thought of something.'

'Speaking of contraries, see how the brook
In that white wave runs counter to itself.
It is from that in water we were from
Long, long before we were from any creature.

Here we, in our impatience of the steps,
Get back to the beginning of beginnings,
The stream of everything that runs away.
Some say existence like a Pirouot
And Pirouette, forever in one place,
Stands still and dances, but it runs away,
It seriously, sadly, runs away
To fill the abyss' void with emptiness.
It flows beside us in this water brook,
But it flows over us. It flows between us
To separate us for a panic moment.
It flows between us, over us, and *with* us.
And it is time, strength, tone, light, life, and love—
And even substance lapsing unsubstantial;
The universal cataract of death
That spends to nothingness—and unresisted,
Save by some strange resistance in itself,
Not just a swerving, but a throwing back,
As if regret were in it and were sacred.
It has this throwing backward on itself
So that the fall of most of it is always
Raising a little, sending up a little.
Our life runs down in sending up the clock.
The brook runs down in sending up our life.
The sun runs down in sending up the brook.
And there is something sending up the sun.
It is this backward motion toward the source,
Against the stream, that most we see ourselves in,
The tribute of the current to the source.
It is from this in nature we are from.
It is most us.'

'Today will be the day
You said so.'

'No, today will be the day
You said the brook was called West-running Brook.'

'Today will be the day of what we both said.'

1928

A Soldier

He is that fallen lance that lies as hurled,
That lies unlifted now, come dew, come rust,
But still lies pointed as it plowed the dust.
If we who sight along it round the world,
See nothing worthy to have been its mark,
It is because like men we look too near,
Forgetting that as fitted to the sphere,
Our missiles always make too short an arc.
They fall, they rip the grass, they intersect
The curve of earth, and striking, break their own;
They make us cringe for metal-point on stone.
But this we know, the obstacle that checked
And tripped the body, shot the spirit on
Further than target ever showed or shone. 1928

What Fifty Said

When I was young my teachers were the old.
I gave up fire for form till I was cold.
I suffered like a metal being cast.
I went to school to age to learn the past.

Now I am old my teachers are the young.
What can't be moulded must be cracked and sprung.
I strain at lessons fit to start a suture.
I go to school to youth to learn the future. 1928

The Bear

The bear puts both arms around the tree above her
And draws it down as if it were a lover
And its choke cherries lips to kiss goodby,
Then lets it snap back upright in the sky.
Her next step rocks a boulder on the wall
(She's making her cross-country in the fall).
Her great weight creaks the barbed-wire in its staples
As she flings over and off down through the maples,
Leaving on one wire tooth a lock of hair.

Such is the uncaged progress of the bear.
The world has room to make a bear feel free;
The universe seems cramped to you and me.
Man acts more like the poor bear in a cage
That all day fights a nervous inward rage,
His mood rejecting all his mind suggests.
He paces back and forth and never rests
The toe-nail click and shuffle of his feet,
The telescope at one end of his beat,
And at the other end the microscope,
Two instruments of nearly equal hope,
And in conjunction giving quite a spread.
Or if he rests from scientific tread,
'Tis only to sit back and sway his head
Through ninety odd degrees of arc, it seems,
Between two metaphysical extremes.
He sits back on his fundamental butt
With lifted snout and eyes (if any) shut,
(He almost looks religious but he's not),
And back and forth he sways from cheek to cheek,
At one extreme agreeing with one Greek,
At the other agreeing with another Greek
Which may be thought, but only so to speak.
A baggy figure, equally pathetic
When sedentary and when peripatetic. 1928

Design

I found a dimpled spider, fat and white,
On a white heal-all, holding up a moth
Like a white piece of rigid satin cloth—
Assorted characters of death and blight
Mixed ready to begin the morning right,
Like the ingredients of a witches' broth—
A snow-drop spider, a flower like a froth,
And dead wings carried like a paper kite.

What had that flower to do with being white,
The wayside blue and innocent heal-all?
What brought the kindred spider to that height,
Then steered the white moth thither in the night?
What but design of darkness to appall?—
If design govern in a thing so small. 1936

The Silken Tent

She is as in a field a silken tent
At midday when a sunny summer breeze
Has dried the dew and all its ropes relent,
So that in guys it gently sways at ease,
And its supporting central cedar pole,
That is its pinnacle to heavenward
And signifies the sureness of the soul,
Seems to owe naught to any single cord,
But strictly held by none, is loosely bound
By countless silken ties of love and thought
To everything on earth the compass round,
And only by one's going slightly taut
In the capriciousness of summer air
Is of the slightest bondage made aware. 1942

The Subverted Flower

She drew back; he was calm:
'It is this that had the power.'
And he lashed his open palm
With the tender-headed flower.
He smiled for her to smile,
But she was either blind
Or willfully unkind.
He eyed her for a while
For a woman and a puzzle.
He flicked and flung the flower,
And another sort of smile
Caught up like finger tips
The corners of his lips
And cracked his ragged muzzle.
She was standing to the waist
In goldenrod and brake,
Her shining hair displaced.
He stretched her either arm
As if she made it ache
To clasp her—not to harm;
As if he could not spare

To touch her neck and hair.
'If this has come to us
And not to me alone–'
So she thought she heard him say;
Though with every word he spoke
His lips were sucked and blown
And the effort made him choke
Like a tiger at a bone.
She had to lean away.
She dared not stir a foot,
Lest movement should provoke
The demon of pursuit
That slumbers in a brute.
It was then her mother's call
From inside the garden wall
Made her steal a look of fear
To see if he could hear
And would pounce to end it all
Before her mother came.
She looked and saw the shame:
A hand hung like a paw,
An arm worked like a saw
As if to be persuasive,
An ingratiating laugh
That cut the snout in half,
An eye became evasive.
A girl could only see
That a flower had marred a man,
But what she could not see
Was that the flower might be
Other than base and fetid:
That the flower had done but part,
And what the flower began
Her own too meager heart
Had terribly completed.
She looked and saw the worst.
And the dog or what it was,
Obeying bestial laws,
A coward save at night,
Turned from the place and ran.
She heard him stumble first
And use his hands in flight.
She heard him bark outright.
And oh, for one so young

The bitter words she spit
Like some tenacious bit
That will not leave the tongue.
She plucked her lips for it,
And still the horror clung.
Her mother wiped the foam
From her chin, picked up her comb
And drew her backward home. 1942

Our Hold on the Planet

We asked for rain. It didn't flash and roar.
It didn't lose its temper at our demand
And blow a gale. It didn't misunderstand
And give us more than our spokesman bargained for;
And just because we owned to a wish for rain,
Send us a flood and bid us be damned and drown.
It gently threw us a glittering shower down.
And when we had taken that into the roots of grain,
It threw us another and then another still
Till the spongy soil again was natal wet.
We may doubt the just proportion of good to ill.
There is much in nature against us. But we forget:
Take nature altogether since time began,
Including human nature, in peace and war,
And it must be a little more in favor of man,
Say a fraction of one per cent at the very least,
Or our number living wouldn't be steadily more,
Our hold on the planet wouldn't have so increased.
1942

The Secret Sits

We dance round in a ring and suppose,
But the Secret sits in the middle and knows. 1942

Forgive, O Lord

Forgive, O Lord, my little jokes on Thee
And I'll forgive Thy great big one on me. 1962

Lines Written in Dejection on the Eve of Great Success

I once had a cow that jumped over the moon,
Not on to the moon but over.
I don't know what made her so lunar a loon;
All she'd been having was clover.

That was back in the days of my godmother Goose.
But though we are goosier now,
And all tanked up with mineral juice,
We haven't caught up with my cow.

POSTSCRIPT

But if over the moon I had wanted to go
And had caught my cow by the tail,
I'll bet she'd have made a melodious low
And put her foot in the pail;

Than which there is no indignity worse.
A cow did that once to a fellow
Who rose from the milking stool with a curse
And cried, "I'll larn you to bellow."

He couldn't lay hands on a pitchfork to hit her
Or give her a stab of the tine,
So he leapt on her hairy back and bit her
Clear into her marrow spine.

No doubt she would have preferred the fork.
She let out a howl of rage
That was heard as far away as New York
And made the papers' front page.

He answered her back, "Well, who begun it?"
That's what at the end of a war
We always say—not who won it,
Or what it was foughten for.   1962

The Figure a Poem Makes

Abstraction is an old story with the philosophers, but it has been like a new toy in the hands of the artists of our day. Why can't we have any one quality of poetry we choose by itself? We can have in thought. Then it will go hard if we can't in practice. Our lives for it.

Granted no one but a humanist much cares how sound a poem is if it is only *a* sound. The sound is the gold in the ore. Then we will have the sound out alone and dispense with the inessential. We do till we make the discovery that the object in writing poetry is to make all poems sound as different as possible from each other, and the resources for that of vowels, consonants, punctuation, syntax, words, sentences, meter are not enough. We need the help of context—meaning—subject matter. That is the greatest help towards variety. All that can be done with words is soon told. So also with meters—particularly in our language where there are virtually but two, strict iambic and loose iambic. The ancients with many were still poor if they depended on meters for all tune. It is painful to watch our sprung-rhythmists straining at the point of omitting one short from a foot for relief from monotony. The possibilities for tune from the dramatic tones of meaning struck across the rigidity of a limited meter are endless. And we are back in poetry as merely one more art of having something to say, sound or unsound. Probably better if sound, because deeper and from wider experience.

Then there is this wildness whereof it is spoken. Granted again that it has an equal claim with sound to being a poem's better half. If it is a wild tune, it is a poem. Our problem then is, as modern abstractionists, to have the wildness pure; to be wild with nothing to be wild about. We bring up as aberrationists, giving way to undirected associations and kicking ourselves from one chance suggestion to another in all directions as of a hot afternoon in the life of a grasshopper. Theme alone can steady us down. Just as the first mystery was how a poem could have a tune in such a straightness as meter, so the second mystery is how a poem can have wildness and at the same time a subject that shall be fulfilled.

It should be of the pleasure of a poem itself to tell how it can. The figure a poem makes. It begins in delight and ends in wisdom. The figure is the same as for love. No one can really hold that the ecstasy should be static and stand still in one place. It begins in delight, it inclines to the impulse, it assumes direction with the first line laid down, it runs a course of lucky events, and ends in a clarification of life—not necessarily a great clarification, such as sects and cults are founded on, but in a momentary

Written as a Preface to the 1939 *Collected Poems,* this celebrated statement was retained in the *Complete Poems* published ten years later.

stay against confusion. It has denouement. It has an outcome that though unforeseen was predestined from the first image of the original mood—and indeed from the very mood. It is but a trick poem and no poem at all if the best of it was thought of first and saved for the last. It finds its own name as it goes and discovers the best waiting for it in some final phrase at once wise and sad—the happy-sad blend of the drinking song.

No tears in the writer, no tears in the reader. No surprise for the writer, no surprise for the reader. For me the initial delight is in the surprise of remembering something I didn't know I knew. I am in a place, in a situation, as if I had materialized from cloud or risen out of the ground. There is a glad recognition of the long lost and the rest follows. Step by step the wonder of unexpected supply keeps growing. The impressions most useful to my purpose seem always those I was unaware of and so made no note of at the time when taken, and the conclusion is come to that like giants we are always hurling experience ahead of us to pave the future with against the day when we may want to strike a line of purpose across it for somewhere. The line will have the more charm for not being mechanically straight. We enjoy the straight crookedness of a good walking stick. Modern instruments of precision are being used to make things crooked as if by eye and hand in the old days.

I tell how there may be a better wildness of logic than of inconsequence. But the logic is backward, in retrospect, after the act. It must be more felt than seen ahead like prophecy. It must be a revelation, or a series of revelations, as much for the poet as for the reader. For it to be that there must have been the greatest freedom of the material to move about in it and to establish relations in it regardless of time and space, previous relation, and everything but affinity. We prate of freedom. We call our schools free because we are not free to stay away from them till we are sixteen years of age. I have given up my democratic prejudices and now willingly set the lower classes free to be completely taken care of by the upper classes. Political freedom is nothing to me. I bestow it right and left. All I would keep for myself is the freedom of my material—the condition of body and mind now and then to summons aptly from the vast chaos of all I have lived through.

Scholars and artists thrown together are often annoyed at the puzzle of where they differ. Both work from knowledge; but I suspect they differ most importantly in the way their knowledge is come by. Scholars get theirs with conscientious thoroughness along projected lines of logic; poets theirs cavalierly and as it happens in and out of books. They stick to nothing deliberately, but let what will stick to them like burrs where they walk in the fields. No acquirement is on assignment, or even self-assignment. Knowledge of the second kind is much more available in the wild free ways of wit and art. A schoolboy may be defined as one who can tell you what he knows in the order in which he learned it. The artist must value himself as he snatches a thing from some previous order in time and space into a new order with not so much as a ligature clinging to it of the old place where it was once organic.

More than once I should have lost my soul to radicalism if it had been the originality it was mistaken for by its young converts. Originality and initiative are what I ask for my country. For myself the originality need be no more than the freshness of a poem run in the way I have described: from delight to wisdom. The figure is the same as for love. Like a piece of ice on a hot stove the poem must ride on its own melting. A poem may be worked over once it is in being, but may not be worried into being. Its most precious quality will remain its having run itself and carried away the poet with it. Read it a hundred times: it will forever keep its freshness as a metal keeps its fragrance. It can never lose its sense of a meaning that once unfolded by surprise as it went.

1939

C H A P T E R
T W O

THE NEW FICTION

As late as 1930, on the occasion of receiving the Nobel Prize for Literature, Sinclair Lewis, the first American writer to be thus honored, characterized the American literary scene in these terms:

> . . . In America most of us—not readers alone but even writers—are still afraid of any literature which is not a glorification of our faults as well as our virtues. To be not only a best seller in America but to be really beloved, a novelist must assert that all American men are tall, handsome, rich, honest, and powerful at golf; that all country towns are filled with neighbors who do nothing from day to day save go about being kind to one another; that although American girls may be wild, they change always into perfect wives and mothers; and that, geographically, America is composed solely of New York, which is inhabited entirely by millionaires; of the West, which keeps unchanged all the boisterous heroism of 1870; and of the South, where every one lives on a plantation perpetually glossy with moonlight and scented with magnolia.

While this may have been true at the more popular literary levels, it was not true of the leading writers in 1930 and had not been true of them for at least three decades. It was not true of Lewis, whose best work was already behind him, nor of Dreiser, whose last good novel, *An American Tragedy,* came in 1925, and it had never been true for Willa Cather.

Lewis's biting attack is nonetheless a good introduction to modern American fiction, for it catches vividly the forces against which the new American novelists considered themselves to be in reaction. Later in the speech he was to say of Dreiser that, "more than any other man," he "cleared the trail from Victorian and Howellsian timidity and gentility in American fiction"; and of Willa Cather, that she had "been so untrue to America's patent . . . virtuousness as to picture [in *The Lost Lady*] an abandoned woman. . . ."

There had been, to be sure, lost ladies in American fiction before, most notably, perhaps, in Crane's *Maggie: a Girl of the Streets* (1896); and in Frank Norris's *McTeague: A Story of San Francisco* (1899), Victorian timidity is effectively dispelled. Although both these nineteenth-century novels were widely attacked, the taboos they challenged, taboos of subject matter no less than of treatment, were taboos the new writers also saw as their challenges. Jack London, Robert Herrick, and Upton Sinclair, among others, had fought the battle along with Crane and Norris. So too in different ways had Howells, James, and Edith Wharton. Even so, the consistent best sellers up to and after World War I were novelists such as Gene Stratton Porter, Harold Bell Wright, Zane Grey, or Eleanor H. Porter.

It is significant that Dreiser's first novel, *Sister Carrie,* was virtually suppressed from 1900 to 1911, whereas his *American Tragedy,* which is equally iconoclastic and certainly more explicitly critical of the American ideal, won wide and popular acclaim immediately upon publication in 1925. It is customary, although perhaps not totally accurate, to call Dreiser America's foremost "naturalistic" novelist. Certainly his major novels between *Sister Carrie* and *An American Tragedy*—*Jennie Gerhardt* (1911), *The Financier* (1912), *The Titan* (1914), and *The "Genius"* (1915) —are all constructed on the naturalistic principle which holds nature, heredity, and environment as the controlling forces in human behavior. Indeed, his background is an almost "classic" case for a naturalistic writer: ninth child of immigrant, highly religious, German parents; an impoverished and rootless boyhood in various parts of Indiana; difficult early years in Chicago as dish-washer, hardware clerk, scene painter; and newspaper work in midwestern and eastern cities. This background—and the encouragement of his famous song-writing brother, Paul Dresser—surely made its contribution to his celebrated talent for convincing detail, his sensitivity to the plight of the down-trodden, and his scarcely concealed admiration for men of power and fame. His early readings in Balzac, in Huxley, Tyndall, and Spencer, seem only to have confirmed what he already knew to be true: that human activity is controlled by exterior forces of environment or interior drives of fear, hunger, and sex; that strong personalities survive by crushing weaker ones; that social forces are what create these personalities; but that there exists a vast, impersonal force, a "chemism," which ultimately determines what one can and cannot do, what one can and cannot be.

In the sympathetically seen "sinful" women of both *Sister Carrie* and *Jennie Gerhardt,* which Dreiser based to some extent on his own sisters, there is a flaunting of conventional morality that shows first and in some ways best his acute awareness of the disparity between the American image and the American ideal. In his Cowperwood trilogy (*The Financier, The Titan,* and the posthumously published *The Stoic* [1947]) the idea seemingly most pervasively suggested by the industrial magnate Charles T. Yerkes (on whose life the trilogy was based) is that ingrained ruthlessness, even dishonest ambition, can be as intransigently compelling on the behavior of the powerful as ingrained ineptness, say, can be on the behavior of the weak. *The "Genius,"* a thinly disguised fictional account of Dreiser's own attempt to gain a literary foothold in New York, might better be read with his autobiographical works. But in *An American Tragedy* we see better than anywhere else in Dreiser the essence of the American dilemma: the fatal plight of young Clyde Griffiths' attempt to make for himself a place in a world whose demands he was incapable of meeting. Basing his novel on an actual murder and trial in upper New York state, Dreiser did careful research on his subject; and in the voluminous detail that makes up the tragedy (it was originally published in two volumes), he catches as nowhere else in his works a complex of forces that explains (yet somehow meaningfully does *not* account for) both his hero's aspirations and his inevitable, fatal failure. It is one of the "classic" American novels.

The controversial problems of Dreiser's sometimes awkward and cumbersome style are perhaps best left to the tastes of individual readers, but it can be said that he was too verbose and too little the craftsman to be a masterful short-story writer. He nonetheless published four volumes of short fiction during his career, and with an occasional scene, incident, or character he can be very moving. His formative and guiding ideas perhaps best come through in his autobiographical writings, such as *A Traveller at Forty* (1913) or *A Book About Myself* (1922), or in his essays, such as those collected in *Hey Rub-a-Dub-Dub* (1920), the volume from which the essay in this collection is taken. His plays and poetry are inconsequential, but his late political and social books, for example, *Dreiser Looks at Russia* (1928) or *Tragic America* (1931), are important, as his late fiction is not, in their description of the contradictory appeal that socialism and state planning had for a mind otherwise committed to a belief in an impersonal, seemingly chaotic cosmos.

Willa Cather's contribution to the new fiction is about as far removed from Dreiser's as one novelist's can be from that of another. It is equally important, however. Unlike Dreiser, she emerges from the American literary tradition best represented by Hawthorne, Henry James, and Sarah Orne Jewett, whom she specifically names as influences. Her approach to fiction is a quiet one, highly cerebral, controlled, selective—even though her most successful subjects are the magnificently expansive Nebraskan prairies, the old Southwest, and, somewhat less surprisingly, the Quebec of the early 1700's.

Her birth in Virginia and her first professional work as teacher, newspaper woman, and editor, in Pennsylvania and New York, appear to have been far less crucial to her artistic development than her early residence and education in Nebraska. After some early poetry, some significant short stories, and one unimportant novel, she turned (apparently at the suggestion of Sarah Orne Jewett) to the West of her youth for her subject matter. The three novels that first resulted are generally considered among her best work. *O Pioneers!* (1913) is set in Nebraska and beautifully portrays Alexandra Bergson's devotion to and success with the land in contrast to her Swedish immigrant family's unsuccessful struggle with American ways. *The Song of the Lark* (1915) portrays the transformation of Thea Kronborg from a passionate, troubled, eager daughter of immigrants to Moonstone, Colorado, into a famous opera singer. And *My Ántonia* (1918), the best of the three and still one of America's most realistic yet sensitive portraits of the Middle West, is the chronicle of an immigrant Bohemian farm family in Nebraska, especially as it relates to Antonia Shimerda, the daughter. The beauty of the land and its brutalizing demands on those who would master it are rendered with equal skill; and Ántonia's flight from and return to the land constitute perhaps one of the most memorable American records of a new people and a new frontier in primal conflict.

A retreat from and rejection of present "commercial" values begin to be indicated in both *A Lost Lady* (1923), her last Nebraska novel, and *The Professor's House* (1925), a despairing portrait of a sensitive professor's defeat by the forces of modernity. The rejection is complete in *Death Comes for the Archbishop* (1927), which turns to the historical past of the old Southwest for its setting and to the ageless values of the pioneering priesthood for its subject. Some consider it her most enduring book. Only slightly less highly regarded is her *Shadows on the Rock* (1931), set in seventeenth-century, Roman Catholic Quebec.

Miss Cather's later novels are minor, but in her short stories, especially those in the early *The Troll Garden* (1905)—which included "The Sculptor's Funeral," "A Wagner Matinée," and the frequently anthologized "Paul's Case"—she often caught beautifully the dilemma of the sensitive artist in an alien environment and thereby brought subject matter and theme into a stream of American fiction that Henry James's influence was so powerfully to dominate later in the century. Indeed, to retreat to the past as she did in her middle novels, when done as protest against the shabby and insensitive commercialism of the present, is to reveal affinities with naturalists such as Dreiser. They both deplored what they considered the inhumane brutalities of modern America. And if, in contrast, say, to Dreiser's voluminous detail and sprawling formlessness, Miss Cather valued a careful selectivity and an astringent control, it does not follow that their moral ends were necessarily opposed. Willa Cather's literary techniques were close to those to be followed by Fitzgerald, Hemingway, and Faulkner; Dreiser's were closer to those of Dos Passos, Thomas Wolfe, and James T. Farrell. That the new fiction contained both streams is of major significance. It would have been radically poorer otherwise.

It would also have been poorer without Sinclair Lewis, who somehow belongs to both traditions—and yet to neither. Much more the symbol of rebelliousness in American fiction than either Dreiser or Cather, he is much more difficult to "locate" historically. With the exception of Twain, there had been before Lewis no strong tradition of satire and parody in American fiction; and Lewis's tone is so far removed from Twain's, his method and his interests so unlike those of the author of *Huckleberry Finn,* that it is somewhat meretricious to suggest a link. Lewis took all America as his province. Middle-class complacency, small-town smugness, citified Rotarianism, institutionalized science, commercialized medicine; business, education, religion; salesmen, clubwomen, schoolteachers; boosters, racial bigots, industrialists—all are found in his long shelf of novels; and all are curiously the butt of his incredible talent for mimicry and parody and satire at the same time that some at least are equally the objects of love and affection. Drawn for the most part from Lewis's boyhood in the Midwest and early manhood in the East, what he caught seemed authentic to all America; for his George Babbitt, Carol Kennicott, Lowell Schmaltz, and Elmer Gantry were as "real," as familiar, to the Americans of the Deep South and Far West as they were to the natives of Minnesota. And to the world at large, at least for a time, Lewis's Americans were the only Americans.

Lewis's fiction before 1920 is inconsequential, and that which followed 1930 is for the most part inferior. But with *Main Street* (1920), *Babbitt* (1922), and *Arrowsmith* (1925), with *Elmer Gantry* (1927), *The Man Who Knew Coolidge* (1928), and *Dodsworth* (1929), his achievement is immense. The Gopher Prairie of *Main Street* became the symbol of the provincialism and rigidity of small towns everywhere. George Folansbee Babbitt not only added a word to our language; in his boosterism, in his gregariousness, and in his unquestioned acceptance of all of his own values, he has come to be seen in recent years to be as much a victim as a butt for scorn and ridicule. Dr. Martin Arrowsmith and his first wife Leora are probably the most rounded and sympathetic characters Lewis created, for in spite of the meanness, the corruption, and the outright willful obstruction they encounter, a modicum of nobility and idealism remain. Lewis himself considered this his best novel. However, his satiric powers had not yet diminished, for the religious opportunism of his Elmer Gantry and the pathetic smugness of his Lowell Schmaltz are faithfully caught. In the picture of contrasting civilizations that contributes much to the value of *Dodsworth,* Lewis was still able, as Philip Rahv has pointed out, to "make full use of his gift for reproducing national patterns of behavior with wonderful accuracy and efficiency."

If, after 1930, both his influence and his powers began to decline, his output did not. He continued to write critical novels, but mostly on specific social problems. His *It Can't Happen Here* (1935) explores the probabilities of native fascism in America; his *Gideon Planish* (1943), fakery in the academic world; and his *Kingsblood Royal* (1947), racial hatred. Although these and other later works were widely read, his reputation still stands primarily on the novels he wrote during the 1920's.

When those works are joined to the novels of Dreiser and Willa Cather, we see the new fiction firmly established in America. That fiction was not, of course, established only by these three, who themselves owed much to the American writing which preceded theirs. The new fiction also owed much to their late contemporaries, to Ellen Glasgow, to Sherwood Anderson and Scott Fitzgerald, to Dos Passos, Hemingway, and Faulkner, but the works of Dreiser, Cather, and Lewis constitute an ideal introduction to modern American fiction; their novels are still vibrant reading.

Theodore [Herman Albert] Dreiser

(1871-1945)

CHRONOLOGY:

1871 Born August 27, Terre Haute, Indiana.

1889-90 Attended Indiana University.

1892-95 Worked for newspapers and other periodicals in Chicago, St. Louis, Toledo, Pittsburgh, and New York.

1900 *Sister Carrie* published but not distributed for general sale.

1907 Made editor-in-chief of the *Delineator* and other Butterick publications; *Sister Carrie* released to the American public.

1910 Turned to full-time writing.

1911 *Jennie Gerhardt.*

1912 *The Financier.*

1913 *A Traveler at Forty,* autobiography.

1914 *The Titan.*

1915 *The "Genius."*

1916 *Plays of the Natural and Supernatural; A Hoosier Holiday,* autobiography.

1918 *The Hand of the Potter,* play; *Free and Other Stories.*

1919 *Twelve Men,* studies of actual persons, including one on his famous brother, Paul Dresser.

1920 *Hey, Rub-a-Dub-Dub: A Book of the Mystery and Terror and Wonder of Life,* essays.

1921-24 Lived in Hollywood.

1922 *A Book About Myself,* autobiography.

1923 *The Color of a Great City,* essays.

1925 *An American Tragedy.*

1926 *Moods, Cadenced and Declaimed,* poems.

1927 *Chains,* stories; visited Russia.

1928 *Dreiser Looks at Russia.*

1929 *My City,* sketches; *A Gallery of Women,* stories.

1931 *Dawn; Tragic America,* essays.
1941 *America Is Worth Saving,* essays.
1945 Died December 28, in Hollywood.
1946 *The Bulwark.*
1947 *The Stoic.*

BIBLIOGRAPHY:

There is no collected edition of Dreiser's works, although most of the fiction and some of the other writings have been collected in inexpensive reprints. Howard Fast edited *The Best Short Stories of Theodore Dreiser* (Cleveland, 1947).

The standard critical biography is Robert H. Elias, *Theodore Dreiser: Apostle of Nature* (New York, 1949), although one should also see F. O. Matthiessen, *Theodore Dreiser* (New York, 1951). An invaluable collection of critical essays is in Alfred Kazin and Charles Shapiro, eds., *The Stature of Theodore Dreiser: A Critical Survey of the Man and His Work* (Bloomington, 1955); it also contains a useful "Selected Bibliography of Dreiser's Biography and Criticism." Robert H. Elias edited *The Letters of Theodore Dreiser,* 3 vols. (Philadelphia, 1959).

For studies of individual novels, see Donna Gerstenberger and George Hendrick, *The American Novel, 1789-1959: A Checklist of Twentieth-Century Criticism* (Denver, 1961); for individual stories, Warren S. Walker, *Twentieth-Century Short Story Explication: Interpretations, 1900-1960 Inclusive, of Short Fiction Since 1800* (Hamden, Conn., 1961), Supplement, 1963.

From Hey, Rub-a-Dub-Dub!

(Taken from the notes of the late John Paradiso)

I have lived now to my fortieth year, and have seen a good deal of life. Just now, because of a stretch of poverty, I am living across the river from New York, in New Jersey, in sight of a splendid tower, the Woolworth Building on the lower end of Manhattan, which lifts its defiant spear of clay into the very maw of heaven. And although I am by no means as far from it as is Fifth Avenue, still I am a dweller in one of the shabbiest, most forlorn neighborhoods which the great metropolis affords. About me dwell principally Poles and Hungarians, who palaver in a lingo of which I know nothing and who live as I would despise to live, poor as I am. For, after all, in my hall-bedroom, which commands the river over the lumberyard, there is some attempt at intellectual adornment, whereas outside and around me there is little more than dull and to a certain extent aggrieved drudgery.

Not so very far from me is a church, a great yellow structure which lifts its walls out of a ruck of cheap frame houses, and those muddy, unpaved streets which are the pride of Jersey City and Hoboken. Here, if I will, I can hear splendid masses intoned, see bright altars and stained glass windows and people going to confession and burning votive candles before images. And if I go of a Sunday, which I rarely do, I can hear regularly that there is a Christ who died for men, and that He was the son of the living God who liveth and reigneth world without end.

I have no quarrel with this doctrine. I can hear it in a hundred thousand churches throughout the world. But I am one of those curious persons who cannot make up their minds about anything. I read and read, almost everything that I can lay hands on—history, politics, philosophy, art. But I find that one history contradicts another, one philosopher drives out another. Essayists, in the main, point out flaws and paradoxes in the current conception of things; novelists, dramatists and biographers spread tales of endless disasters, or silly illusions concerning life, duty, love, opportunity and the like. And I sit here and read and read, when I have time, wondering.

For, friends, I am a scrivener by trade—or try to be. Betimes, trying to make up my mind what to say about life, I am a motorman on a street-car at three dollars and twenty cents a day. I have been a handy man in a junk shop, and wagon driver, anything you will, so long as thereby I could keep body and soul together. I am not handsome, and therefore not attractive to women probably—at any rate I appear not to be—and in consequence am very much alone. Indeed, I am a great coward when it comes to women. Their least frown or mood of indifference frightens me and makes me turn inward to myself, where dwell innumerable beautiful women who smile and nod and hang on my arm and tell me they love me. Indeed, they whisper of scenes so beautiful and so comforting that I know they are not, and never could be, true. And so, in my best moments, I sit at my table and try to write stories which no doubt equally necessitous editors find wholly unavailable.

The things which keep me thinking and thinking are, first, my social and financial state; second, the difference between my point of view and that of thousands of other respectable citizens, who, being able to make up their minds, seem to find me queer, dull, recessive, or at any rate unsuited to their tastes and pleasures. I look at them, and while I say, "Well, thank heaven I am not like that," still I immediately ask myself, "Am I not all wrong? Should I not be happier if I, too, were like John Spitovesky, or Jacob Feilchenfeld, or Vaclav Melka?"—some of my present neighbors. For Spitovesky, to grow a little personal, is a small dusty man who has a tobacco store around the corner, and who would, I earnestly believe, run if he were threatened with a bath. He smokes his own three-for-fives (Flor de Sissel Grass), and deposits much of the ashes between his waistcoat and his gray striped cotton shirt. His hair, sticking bushily out over his ears, looks as though it were heavily peppered with golden snuff.

"Mr. Spitovesky," I said to him one day not long since, "have you been reading anything about the Colorado mining troubles?"

"I never read de papers," he said with a shrug of his shoulder.

"No? Not at all?" I pursued.

"Dere is nodding in dem—lies mosdly. Somedimes I look ad de baseball news in sommer."

"Oh, I see," I said hopelessly. Then, apropos of nothing, or because I was curious as to my neighbors, "Are you a Catholic?"

"I doaned belong to no church. I doaned mix in no politics, neider. Some hof de men aboud here get excided about politics; I got no time. I 'tend to mine store."

Seeing him stand for hours against his doorpost, or sitting out front smoking while his darksome little wife peels potatoes or sews or fusses with the children, I could never understand his "I got no time."

In a related sense there are my friends Jacob Feilchenfeld and Vaclav Melka, whom I sometimes envy because they are so different. The former, the butcher to whom I run for chops and pigs' feet for my landlady, Mrs. Wscrinkuus; the latter the keeper of a spirituous emporium whose windows read "Vynas, Scnapas." Jacob, like every other honest butcher worthy the name, is broad and beefy. He turns on me a friendly eye as he inquires, "About so thick?" or suggests that he has some nice fresh liver or beef tongue, things which he knows Mrs. Wscrinkuus likes. I can sum up Mr. Feilchenfeld's philosophy of life when I report that to every intellectual advance I make he exclaims in a friendly enough way, "I dunno," or "I ain't never heard about dot."

My pride in a sturdy, passive acceptance of things, however, is nearly realized in Vaclav Melka, the happy dispenser of "Vynas, Scnapsas." He also is frequently to be found leaning in his doorway in summer, business being not too brisk during the daytime, surveying the world with a reflective eye. He is dark, stocky, black-haired, black-eyed, a good Pole with a head like a wooden peg, almost flat at the top, and driven firmly albeit not ungracefully into his shoulders. He has a wife who is a slattern and nearly a slave, and three children who seem to take no noticeable harm from this saloon life. Leaning in coatless ease against his sticky bar of an evening, he has laid down the law concerning morals and ethics, thus: no lying or stealing—among friends; no brawling or assaults or murdering for any save tremendous reasons of passion; no truckling to priests or sisters who should mind their own business.

"Did you ever read a book, Melka?" I once asked him. It was apropos of a discussion as to a local brawl.

"Once. It was about a feller wot killed a woman. Mostly I ain't got no time to read. Once I was a bath-rubber, and I had time them, but that was long ago. Books ain't nutting for me."

Melka states, however, that he was a fool to come here. "A feller wanted me to take dis saloon, and here I am. I make a living. If my wife died I would go back to my old job, I think." He does not want his wife to die, I am sure. It does not make that much difference.

But over the river from all this is another picture which disturbs me even more than my present surroundings, because, as seen from here, it is seemingly beautiful and inviting. Its tall walls are those of a fabled city.

I can almost hear the tinkle of endless wealth in banks, the honks of auto mobiles, the fanfare of a great constructive trade life. At night all its myriad lights seem to wink at me and exclaim, "Why so incompetent? Why so idle, so poor? Why live in such a wretched neighborhood? Why not cross over and join the great gay throng, make a successful way for yourself? Why sit aside from this great game of materiality and pretend to ignore it or to feel superior?"

And as I sit and think, so it seems to me. But, alas, I haven't the least faculty for making money, not the least. Plainly beyond are all these wonderful things which are being done and made by men with that kind of ability which I appear to lack. I have no material, constructive sense. I can only think and write, in a way. I see these vast institutions (there are great warehouses on this side, too) filled to overflowing apparently with the financially interested and capable, but I—I have not the least idea how to do anything likewise. Yet I am not lazy. I toil over my stories or bounce out of bed and hurry to my work of a morning. But I have never earned more than thirty-five dollars a week in my whole life. No, I am not brilliant financially.

But the thing that troubles me most is the constant palaver going on in the papers and everywhere concerning right, truth, duty, justice, mercy and the like, things which I do not find expressed very clearly in my own motives nor in the motives of those immediately about me; and also the apparently earnest belief on the part of ever so many editors, authors, social reformers, et cetera, that every person, however weak or dull-appearing externally, contains within himself the seed or the mechanism for producing endless energy and ability, providing he can only be made to realize that he has it. In other words we are all Napoleons, only we don't know it. We are lazy Napoleons, idle Hannibals, wasteful and indifferent John D. Rockefellers. Turn the pages of any magazine—are there not advertisements of and treatises on How To Be Successful, with the authors thereof offering to impart their knowledge of how so to be for a comparative song?

Well, I am not one who can believe that. In my very humble estimation people are not so. They are, in the main, as I see it, weak and limited, exceedingly so, like Vaclav Melka or Mrs. Wscrinkuus, and to fill their humble brains with notions of an impossible supremacy, if it could be done, would be to send them forth to breast the ocean in a cockleshell. And, yet, here on my table, borrowed from the local library for purposes of idle or critical examination, is a silly book entitled "Take It!"—"It" meaning *"the world!"*; and another "It's Yours!"—the "It" in this case meaning that same great world! All you have to do is to decide so to do—and to try! Am I a fool to smile at this very stout doctrine, to doubt whether you can get more than four quarts out of any four-quart measure, if so much?

But to return to this same matter of right, truth, justice, mercy, so freely advertised in these days and so clearly defined, apparently, in every one's mind as open paths by which they may proceed. In the main, it seems to me that people are not concerned about right, or truth, or justice, or mercy, or duty, as abstract principles or working rules, nor do I believe that the average man knows clearly or even semi-clearly what is meant by the words. His only relation to them, so far as I can see, is that he finds them used in a certain reckless, thoughtless way to represent some method of adjustment by which he would like to think he is protected from assault or saved from misery, and so uses them himself. His concern for them as related to the other individual is that the other individual should not infringe on him, and I am now speaking of the common unsuccessful mass as well as of the successful.

Mrs. Wscrinkuus, poor woman, is stingy and slightly suspicious, although she goes to church Sundays and believes that Christ's Sermon on the Mount is the living truth. She does not want any one to be mean to her; she does not do anything mean to other people, largely because she has no particular taste or capacity in that direction. Supposing I should advise her to "Take It!" assure her that "It" was hers by right of capability! What would become of *right, truth, justice, mercy* in that case?

Or, once more, let us take Jacob Feilchenfeld and John Spitovesky, who care for no man beyond their trade and whose attitude toward right, truth, mercy, justice is as above. Suppose I should tell them to take "It," or assure them that "It" was theirs? Of what import would the message be? Vaclav Melka does favors only in return for favors. He does not like priests because they are always taking up collections. If you told him to take "It" he would proceed to take something away from the very good priests first of all. Everywhere I find the common man imbued with this feeling for self-protection and self-advancement. *Truth* is something that must be told to *him; justice* is what *he* deserves—although if it costs him nothing he will gladly see it extended to the other fellow.

But do not think for one moment because I say this that I think myself better or more deserving or wiser than any of these. As I said before, I do not understand life, although I like it; I may even say that I like this sharp, grasping scheme of things, and find that it works well. Plainly it produces all the fine spectacles I see. If it had not been for a certain hard, seeking ambition in Mr. Woolworth to get up and be superior to his fellows, where would his splendid tower have come from? It is only because I cannot understand why people cling so fatuitously to the idea that there is some fixed idyllic scheme or moral order handed down from on high, which is tender and charitable, punishes so-called evil and always rewards so-called good, that I write this. If it punishes evil, it is not all of the evil that I see. If it rewards good, then much of the good that I admire goes wholly unrewarded, on this earth at least.

But to return. The Catholics believe that Christ died on the Cross for them, and that unless the Buddhists, Shintoists, Mohammedans, et cetera, reform or find Christ they will be lost. Three hundred million Mohammedans believe quite otherwise. Two hundred and fifty million Buddhists believe something else. The Christians Scientists and Hicksites believe still differently. Then there are historians who doubt the authenticity of Christ (Gibbon; Vol. I, Chapters 15, 16). Where is a moral order which puts a false interpretation on history as in the case of sectarian literature (lists furnished on application), or allows fetiches to flourish like the grass of the new year?

I will admit that in cases such as lying, stealing and the like there is always a so-called moral thing to do or say when these so-called moral principles or beatitudes are inveighed against. You have ridden on a street-car; pay your fare. You have received five dollars from a given man; return it. You have had endless favors from a given individual; do not malign him. Such are the obvious and commonplace things with which these great words are concerned; and in these prima facie cases these so-called principles work well enough.

But take a case where temperament or body-needs or appetites fly in the face of man-made order, where a great spirit-thirst stands out against a life-made conviction. Here is a man-made law, and here is dire necessity. On which side is Right? On which side God?

(1) A girl falls in love with a boy to whom the father takes an instant dislike. The father is not better than the lover, just different. The girl and boy are aflame (no chemical law of their invention, mind you), and when the father opposes them they wed secretly. Result, rage. A weak temperament on the part of the father (no invention of his own) causes him to drink. On sight, in liquor, he kills the youth. The law says he must be hung unless justified. A lie on the part of the girl defaming the lover-husband will save the father. On which side now do right, truth, justice, mercy stand?

(2) A man has a great trade idea. He sees where by combining fourteen companies he can reduce cost of manufacture and sell a very necessary product to the public at a reduced rate, the while he makes himself rich. In the matter of principle and procedure (right, truth, justice, etc.), since his competitors will not sell out, he is confronted by the following propositions: (a) forming a joint stock company and permitting them all to share in the profits; (b) giving them the idea, asking nothing, and allowing them to form a company of their own, so helping humanity; (c) making a secret combination with four or five and underselling the others and so compel them to sell or quit; (d) doing nothing, letting time and chance work and the public wait. Now it so happens that the second and fourth are the only things that can be done without opposition. He

is a man of brains and ideals. What are his rights, duties, privileges? Where do justice, mercy, truth, fit in here, and how?

(3) A man's son has committed a crime. The man realizes that owing to deficiencies of his own he has never been able to give the boy a right training or a fair chance. The law demands that he give up his son, even though he loves him dearly and feels himself responsible. Where do right, justice, mercy work here, and can they be made harmonious and consonant?

These are but three of fifty instances out of the current papers which I daily read. I have cited them to show how topsy-turvy the world seems to me, how impossible of a fixed explanation or rule. Scarcely any two individuals but will be at variance on these propositions. Yet the religionists, the moralists, the editorial writers preach a faith and an obvious line of duty which they label grandiosely "right" or "true," "just" or "merciful." My observation and experience lead me to believe that there is scarcely a so-called "sane," right, merciful, true, just, solution to anything. I know that many will cry in answer "Look at all this great world! Look at all the interesting things made, the beautiful things, the pleasures provided. Are not these the intelligent directive product of a superior governing being, who is kind and merciful into the bargain and who has our interests at heart? Can you doubt, when you observe the exact laws that govern in mathematics, chemistry, physics, that there is an intelligent, kindly ruling power, truthful, merciful, etc?" My answer is: I can and do, for these things can be used as readily against right, truth, justice, mercy, as we understand those things, as they can for or with them. If you don't believe this, and are anti-German or anti-Japanese, or anti-anything else, see how those or any other so-called inimical powers can use all these magnificent forces or arts in its behalf and against the powers of light and worth such as you understand and approve of. And when justice and mercy are tacked on as attributes of this intelligence there is no possible appeal to *human* reason.

"But only look," some one is sure to cry, "at some of the beautiful, wonderful, helpful things which Divine Providence, or Life, or Force, or Energy has provided now and here for man! Railroads; telegraphy; the telephone; theaters; gas; electricity; clothing of all sorts; newspapers; books; hotels; stores; fire departments; hospitals; plumbing; the pleasures of love and sex; music." An admirable list, truly, and all provided by one struggling genius or another or by the slow, cataclysmic processes of nature: fires, deaths and painful births. Aside from the fact that all of these things can be and are used for *evil* as well as *good* purposes (trust oppression, enemy wars and the like), still it might as well be supplemented by such things as jails, detectives, penitentiaries, courts of law—good or evil things, as you choose to look at them. All of these things are good in the hands of good people, evil in the hands of the evil, and nature seems not to care which group uses them. A hospital will aid a scoundrel as readily as a good man, and vice versa.

Common dust swept into our atmosphere makes our beautiful sunsets and blue sky. Sidereal space, as we know it, is said to be one welter of strangely flowing streams of rock and dust, a wretched mass made attractive only by some vast compulsory coalition into a star. Stars clash and blaze, and the whole great complicated system seems one erosive, chaffering, bickering effort, with here and there a tendency to stillness and petrifaction. This world as we know it, the human race and the accompanying welter of animals and insects, do they not, aside from momentary phases of delight and beauty, often strike you as dull, aimless, cruel, useless? Are not the processes by which they are produced or those by which they live (the Chicago slaughter-houses, for instance), stark, relentless, brutal, shameful even?—life living on life, the preying of one on another, the compulsory aging of all, the hungers, thirsts, destroying losses and pains. . . .

But I was talking of Jersey City and my difficulty in adjusting myself to the life about me, thinking as I do. Yet such facts as I can gather only confound me the more. Take the daily papers which I have been reading to beguile my loneliness, and note that:

(1) Two old people who lived near me, after working hard for years to supply themselves with a competence, were ruined by the failure of a bank and were therefore forced to seek work. Not finding it, they were compelled to make a choice between subsisting on charity and dying. Desiring to be as agreeable to the world as possible and not to be a burden to it, they chose death by gas, locking the doors of their bare little home, stuffing paper and clothing into chinks and under doors and windows, and turning on the gas, seated side-by-side and hand-in-hand. Naturally the end came quickly enough, for Divine Mind has no objection to ordinary illuminating gas killing any one. It did not inform any one of their predicament. Impartial gas choked them as quickly as it would have lighted the room, and yet at the same time, according to the same papers, in this very same world—

(2) The sixteen-year-old son of a multi-millionaire real estate holder was left over fifty million dollars by his fond father, who did not know what else to do with it, the same son having not as yet exhibited any capacity for handling the money wisely or having done anything to deserve it save be the son of the aforesaid father.

(3) A somewhat bored group of Newport millionairesses give a dinner for the pet dogs of their equally wealthy friends, one particular dog or doggess being host or hostess.

(4) A Staten Island brewer worth twenty millions died of heart failure, induced by undue joy over the fact that he had been elected snare

drummer of a shriners' lodge, after spending thousands upon thousands in organizing a band of his own and developing sufficient influence to cause a shriners' organization to tolerate him.

(5) A millionaire politician and horse-racer erected a fifteen-thousand-dollar monument to a horse.

(6) An uneducated darkey, trying to make his way North, climbed upon the carriage trucks of a Pullman attached to a fast express and was swept North into a blizzard, where he was finally found dying of exhaustion, and did die—arms and legs frozen—a victim of an effort to better his condition.

Puzzle: locate Divine Mind, Light, Wisdom, Truth, Justice, Mercy in these items.

By these same papers, covering several months or more, I saw where:

(1) Several people died waiting in line on bundle day for bundles of cast-off clothing given by those who could not use the clothes any longer—not such people as you and I, perhaps, but those who were sick, or old, or weak.

(2) Mr. Ford, manufacturer of automobiles, was convinced that he could reform any criminal or bad character by giving him or her plenty of work to do at good wages and with the prospect of advancement; also that he was earning too much and wished to divide with his fellow man.

(3) August Belmont and J. P. Morgan, Jr., noting this item, concluded that they could not do anything for any one, intellectually, financially or otherwise.

(4) An attendant in an Odd Fellows Home, having tired of some old patients, chloroformed them all—a purely pagan event and not possible in an enlightened age and a Christian country.

(5) A priest, having murdered a girl and confessed to it, no way was found to electrocute him because of his cloth. Men whose services and aid he contemned insisted that he must be proved insane and not be electrocuted, though he did not agree with them.

(6) A young soldier and his bride, but one day married, walk out to buy furniture for their new home; a street fight in which three toughs assail each other with pistols breaks out and before they can take to cover a stray bullet instantly kills the soldier-husband. Subsequently the bride becomes morbid and goes insane.

(7) In nearly all the countries of the late great war a day of prayer for Divine intervention was indulged in, but prayer having been made and not answered the combatants proceeded to make more and worse war—Divine prohibition of combat, according to the Christian dogma, being no bar nor of any avail.

(8) A well-known Western financier and promoter of strong religious and moralistic leanings, having projected and built a well-known railroad and made it immensely prosperous by reducing the rates to the people of

his region was thereupon set upon by other financiers who wished to secure his property for little or nothing, and being attacked by false charges brought by a suborned stockholder and his road thrown into the hands of a receiver by a compliant judge, was so injured financially thereby as never to be able to recover his property. And those who attacked him justified themselves on the ground that he was a "rate-cutter" and so a disturbing element—a disturber of the peace and profits of other railroads adjacent and elsewhere. His dying statement (years later) was that American history would yet justify him and that God governed for good, if one could wait long enough!

(9) One man was given one year for a cold, brutal manslaughter in New York, whereas a whole family of colored people in the South was strung up and riddled with bullets for so little as that one of them fought with a deputy sheriff; while a woman who had shot another woman through a window because of jealousy (aroused by her husband's assumed attentions to said woman) was acquitted and then went on the stage, the general sentiment being that "one could not electrocute a woman."

(10) The principal charities aid society of New York had spent and was spending one hundred and fifty thousand dollars per year on running expenses, and something over ninety thousand dollars in actual relief work, though it was explained that the hundred and fifty thousand brought about much reference of worthy cases to other agencies and private charities, a thing which could not otherwise have been done.

(11) It is immoral, un-Christian and illegitimate to have a child without a husband, yet when six hundred thousand men are withdrawn from England to fight the Germans and twenty thousand virgins become war-brides it is proposed to legalize the children on the ground that it is nevertheless moral to preserve the nation from extinction.

(12) A doctor may advise against child-birth when that experience would endanger a woman or threaten her permanent disability, but if he gives information or furnishes contraceptal means which would prevent the trying situation he is guilty of a misdemeanor, subject to fine and the ruin of his career.

(13) The president of one of the largest street railway corporations in the world finds it wrong to fail to rise and give your seat to a woman, but right to run so few cars as to make available seats for only one-third of the traffic; wrong not to take extreme precaution in stepping off or on a car or crossing the tracks, but right to leave the cars without heat, the windows and floors dirty and the doors broken, making anger, delay and haste contribute to inattention and unfairness; wrong to read a newspaper wide open, to cross your legs or protrude your feet too far, thereby inconveniencing your fellow-passenger, but right to mulct the city, composed of these same passengers, of millions via stolen franchises, watered stock, avoided taxes, the refusal of transfers at principal intersections, to

say nothing of the prevention of fair competition via the jitney bus and other means which would relieve traffic pressure, and all with no excuse save that the corporation desires the money; and a tame public endures it with a little ineffectual murmuring.

(14) A man has been found in a Western penitentiary who had been there for twenty years and who had been sent there because of erroneous circumstantial evidence, the real offender having confessed on his death-bed.

(15) A certain landlord in New York compelled a certain family to move, because, not they, but some of their visitors, wore shabby, hence undesirable, clothes, thus lowering the social and material tone of the apartment house in question and causing their distant but still watchful fellow-tenants much distress of mind in being compelled to live in such an atmosphere. This was a Riverside Drive apartment.

But need I cite more, really?

It is because of these things that I sit in my hall-bedroom, a great panorama of beauty spread out before me, and in attempting to write of this thing, life, find myself confused. I do not know how to work right, truth, justice, mercy, etc., into these things, nor am I sure that life would be as fascinating without them, as driving or forceful. The scenes that I look upon here and everywhere are beautiful enough, sun, moon and stars swinging in their courses, seemingly mathematically and with great art or charm. I am willing to assume that their courses are calculated and intelligent, but no more and no further. And the river at this moment is begemmed with thousands of lights—a truly artistic and poetic spectacle and one not to be gainsaid. By day it is gray, or blue, or green, wondrous shades by turns; by night a jewel world. Gulls wheel over it; tugs strain cheerily to and fro, emitting gorgeous plumes of smoke. Snows, rains, warmths, colds come in endless variety, the endless fillip which gives force and color to our days.

Still I am confused. For, on the one hand, here is Vaclav Melka, who does not care much for this alleged charm; nor John Spitovesky; nor Jacob Feilchenfeld; nor many, many others like them. On the other hand, myself and many others like me, sitting and meditating on it, are so spellbound that we have scarcely any thought wherewith to earn a living. Life seems to prove but one thing to me, and that is that the various statements concerning right, truth, justice, mercy are palaver merely, an earnest and necessitous attempt, perhaps, at balance and equation where all things are so very much unbalanced, paradoxical and contradictory—the small-change names for a thing or things of which we have not yet caught the meaning. History teaches me little save that nothing is really dependable or assured, but all inexplicable and all shot through with a great desire on the part of many to do or say something by which they may escape the unutterable confusion of time and the feebleness of earthly memory. Current action, it appears, demonstrates much the same thing. Kings and emperors have risen and gone. Generals and captains have warred and departed. Philosophers have dreamed, poets have written; and I, mussing around among religions, philosophies, fictions and facts can find nothing wherewith to solve my vaulting egoism, no light, and no way to be anything more than the humblest servitor.

Among so much that is tempestuous and glittering I merely occasionally scrub and make bright my room. I look out at the river flowing by now, after hundreds of millions of years of loneliness where there was nothing but silence and waste (past so much now that is vivid, colorful, human), and say to myself: Well, where there is so much order and love of order in every one and everywhere there must be some great elemental spirit holding for order of sorts, at any rate. Stars do not swing in given obits for nothing surely, or at least I might have faith to that extent. But when I step out and encounter, as I daily do, lust and greed, plotting and trapping, and envy and all uncharitableness, including murder—all severely condemned by the social code, the Bible and a thousand wise saws and laws—and also see, as I daily do, vast schemes of chicane grinding the faces of the poor, and wars brutally involving the death of millions whose lives are precious to them because of the love of power on the part of some one or many, I am not so sure. Illusions hold too many; lust and greed, vast and bleary-eyed, dominate too many more. Ignorance, vast and almost unconquerable, hugs and licks its chains in reverence. Brute strength sits empurpled and laughs a throaty laugh.

Yet here is the great river—that is beautiful; and Mr. Woolworth's tower, a strange attempt on the part of man to seem more than he is; and a thousand other evidences of hopes and dreams, all too frail perhaps against the endless drag toward nothingness, but still lovely and comforting. And yet here also is Vaclav Melka, who wants to be a bath-rubber again! John Spitovesky, who doesn't care; Jacob Feilchenfeld, who never heard; and millions of others like them, and I—I think and grow confused, and earn nineteen-twenty a week or less—never more, apparently.

Come to think of it, is it not a wonder, holding such impossible views as I do, that I earn anything at all? 1920

Willa [Sibert] Cather

(1873-1947)

CHRONOLOGY:

1873 Born December 7, near Winchester, Virginia.

1883 Moved to Nebraska, near Red Cloud.

1891-95 University of Nebraska.

1895-1901 Worked on the Pittsburgh *Daily Leader*.

1901-06 Taught in Pennsylvania schools.

1903 *April Twilights*, poems.

1905 *The Troll Garden,* stories.
1906-11 Was on the staff of *McClure's Magazine.*
1912 *Alexander's Bridge.*
1913 *O, Pioneers!*
1914 *My Autobiography.*
1915 *The Song of the Lark.*
1918 *My Ántonia*
1920 *Youth and the Bright Medusa,* stories.
1922 *One of Ours;* won Pulitzer Prize.
1923 *A Lost Lady.*
1925 *The Professor's House.*
1926 *My Mortal Enemy.*
1927 *Death Comes for the Archbishop.*
1930 Awarded the Howells Medal by the American Academy of Arts and Letters.
1931 *Shadows on the Rock.*
1932 *Obscure Destinies,* stories.
1933 *December Night,* stories; was the first recipient of the *Prix Femina Américaine.*
1935 *Lucy Gayheart.*
1936 *Not Under Forty,* essays.
1940 *Sapphira and the Slave Girl.*
1944 Awarded a gold medal by the National Institute of Arts and Letters.
1947 Died April 24, in New York City.
1948 *The Old Beauty and Others.*
1949 *On Writing: Critical Studies on Writing as an Art.*
1950 *Writings from Willa Cather's Campus Years,* ed. by James R. Shively.
1956 *Willa Cather in Europe: Her Own Story of the First Journey,* ed. by George N. Kates.
1957 *Early Stories of Willa Cather,* ed. by Mildred R. Bennett.

BIBLIOGRAPHY:

The "Library Edition" of her fiction was collected as *The Novels and Stories of Willa Cather,* 13 vols. (Boston, 1941). Many of her novels have also been reprinted individually.

Biographical studies are numerous. Of major importance are E. K. Brown (completed by Leon Edel), *Willa Cather: A Critical Biography* (New York, 1953); Edith Lewis, *Willa Cather Living: A Personal Record* (New York, 1953); and Elizabeth Shepley Sergeant, *Willa Cather: A Memoir* (Philadelphia, 1953). Essential critical studies are David Daiches, *Willa Cather: A Critical Introduction* (Ithaca, 1951), and John H. Randall, III, *The Landscape and the Looking Glass* (New York, 1960), which includes a complete bibliography.

For studies of individual novels, see Donna Gerstenberger and George Hendrick, *The American Novel, 1789-1959: A Checklist* . . . (Denver, 1961); for individual stories, Warren S. Walker, *Twentieth-Century Short Story Explication* . . . (Hamden, Conn., 1961), Supplement, 1963.

From a "Preface" to *The Best Stories of Sarah Orne Jewett*

. . . . .

Pater said that every truly great drama must, in the end, linger in the reader's mind as a sort of ballad. Probably the same thing might be said of every great story. It must leave in the mind of the sensitive reader an intangible residuum of pleasure; a cadence, a quality of voice that is exclusively the writer's own, individual, unique. A quality that one can remember without the volume at hand, can experience over and over again in the mind but can never absolutely define, as one can experience in memory a melody, or the summer perfume of a garden. The magnitude of the subject-matter is not of primary importance, seemingly. An idyll of Theocritus, concerned with sheep and goats and shade and pastures, is today as much alive as the most dramatic passages of the *Iliad*—stirs the reader's feeling quite as much, perhaps, if the reader is a poet.

It is a common fallacy that a writer, if he is talented enough, can achieve this poignant quality by improving upon his subject-matter, using his "imagination" upon it and twisting it to suit his purpose. The truth is that by such a process (which is not imaginative at all!) he can at best produce only a brilliant sham, which, like a badly built and pretentious house, looks poor and shabby in a few years. If he achieves anything noble, anything enduring, it must be by giving himself absolutely to his material. And this gift of sympathy is his great gift; it is the fine thing in him that alone can make his work fine. He fades away into the land and people of his heart, he dies of love only to be born again. The artist spends a lifetime in loving the things that haunt him, in having his mind "teased" by them, in trying to get these conceptions down on paper exactly as they are to him and not in conventional poses supposed to reveal their character; trying this method and that, as a painter tries different lightings and different attitudes with his subject to catch the one that presents it more suggestively than any other. And at the end of a lifetime he emerges with much that is more or less happy experimenting, and comparatively little that is the very flower of himself and his genius. . . .

1925

The Sculptor's Funeral

A group of the townspeople stood on the station siding of a little Kansas town, awaiting the coming of the night train, which was already twenty minutes overdue. The snow had fallen thick over everything; in the pale starlight the line of bluffs across the wide, white meadows south of the town made soft, smoke-coloured curves against the clear sky. The men on the siding stood first on one foot and then on the other, their hands thrust deep into their trousers pockets, their overcoats open, their shoulders screwed up with the cold; and they glanced from time to time toward the southeast, where the railroad track wound along the river shore. They conversed in low tones and moved about restlessly, seeming uncertain as to what was expected of them. There was but one of the company who looked as though he knew exactly why he was there; and he kept conspicuously apart; walking to the far end of the platform, returning to the station door, then pacing up the track again, his chin sunk in the high collar of his overcoat, his burly shoulders drooping forward, his gait heavy and dogged. Presently he was approached by a tall, spare, grizzled man clad in a faded Grand Army suit, who shuffled out from the group and advanced with a certain deference, craning his neck forward until his back made the angle of a jack-knife three-quarters open:

"I reckon she's a-goin' to be pretty late agin tonight, Jim," he remarked in a squeaky falsetto. "S'pose it's the snow?"

"I don't know," responded the other man with a shade of annoyance, speaking from out an astonishing cataract of red beard that grew fiercely and thickly in all directions.

The spare man shifted the quill toothpick he was chewing to the other side of his mouth. "It ain't likely that anybody from the East will come with the corpse, I s'pose," he went on reflectively.

"I don't know," responded the other, more curtly than before.

"It's too bad he didn't belong to some lodge or other. I like an order funeral myself. They seem more appropriate for people of some repytation," the spare man continued, with an ingratiating concession in his shrill voice, as he carefully placed his toothpick in his vest pocket. He always carried the flag at the G.A.R. funerals in the town.

The heavy man turned on his heel, without replying, and walked up the siding. The spare man shuffled back to the uneasy group. "Jim's ez full ez a tick, ez ushel," he commented commiseratingly.

Just then a distant whistle sounded, and there was a shuffling of feet on the platform. A number of lanky boys of all ages appeared as suddenly and slimily as eels wakened by the crack of thunder; some came from the waiting-room, where they had been warming themselves by the red stove, or half asleep on the slat benches; others uncoiled themselves from baggage trucks or slid out of express wagons. Two clambered down from the driver's seat of a hearse that stood backed up against the siding. They straightened their stooping shoulders and lifted their heads, and a flash of momentary animation kindled their dull eyes at that cold, vibrant scream, the world-wide call for men. It stirred them like the note of a trumpet; just as it had often stirred the man who was coming home tonight, in his boyhood.

The night express shot, red as a rocket, from out the eastward marsh lands and wound along the river shore under the long lines of shivering poplars that sentinelled the meadows, the escaping steam hanging in grey masses against the pale sky and blotting out the Milky Way. In a moment the red glare from the headlight streamed up the snow-covered track before the siding and glittered on the wet, black rails. The burly man with the dishevelled red beard walked swiftly up the platform toward the approaching train, uncovering his head as he went. The group of men behind him hesitated, glanced questioningly at one another, and awkwardly followed his example. The train stopped, and the crowd shuffled up to the express car just as the door was thrown open, the spare man in the G.A.R. suit thrusting his head forward with curiosity. The express messenger appeared in the doorway, accompanied by a young man in a long ulster and travelling cap.

"Are Mr. Merrick's friends here?" inquired the young man.

The group on the platform swayed and shuffled uneasily. Philip Phelps, the banker, responded with dignity: "We have come to take charge of the body. Mr. Merrick's father is very feeble and can't be about."

"Send the agent out here," growled the express messenger, "and tell the operator to lend a hand."

The coffin was got out of its rough box and down on the snowy platform. The townspeople drew back enough to make room for it and then formed a close semicircle about it, looking curiously at the palm leaf which lay across the black cover. No one said anything. The baggage man stood by his truck, waiting to get at the trunks. The engine panted heavily, and the fireman dodged in and out among the wheels with his yellow torch and long oil-can, snapping the spindle boxes. The young Bostonian, one of the dead sculptor's pupils who had come with the body, looked about him helplessly. He turned to the banker, the only one of that black, uneasy, stoop-shouldered group who seemed enough of an individual to be addressed.

"None of Mr. Merrick's brothers are here?" he asked uncertainly.

The man with the red beard for the first time stepped up and joined the group. "No, they have not come yet; the family is scattered. The body will be taken directly to the house." He stooped and took hold of one of the handles of the coffin.

"Take the long hill road up, Thompson, it will be easier on the horses," called the liveryman as the undertaker snapped the door of the hearse and prepared to mount to the driver's seat.

Laird, the red-bearded lawyer, turned again to the stranger: "We didn't know whether there would be any one with him or not," he explained. "It's a long walk, so you'd better go up in the hack." He pointed to a single battered conveyance, but the young man replied stiffly: "Thank you, but I think I will go up with the hearse. If you don't object," turning to the undertaker, "I'll ride with you."

They clambered up over the wheels and drove off in the starlight up the long, white hill toward the town. The lamps in the still village were shining from under the low, snow-burdened roofs; and beyond, on every side, the plains reached out into emptiness, peaceful and wide as the soft sky itself, and wrapped in a tangible, white silence.

When the hearse backed up to a wooden sidewalk before a naked, weather-beaten frame house, the same composite, ill-defined group that had stood upon the station siding was huddled about the gate. The front yard was an icy swamp, and a couple of warped planks, extending from the sidewalk to the door, made a sort of rickety foot-bridge. The gate hung on one hinge, and was opened wide with difficulty. Steavens, the young stranger, noticed that something black was tied to the knob of the front door.

The grating sound made by the casket, as it was drawn from the hearse, was answered by a scream from the house; the front door was wrenched open, and a tall, corpulent woman rushed out bareheaded into the snow and flung herself upon the coffin, shrieking: "My boy, my boy! And this is how you've come home to me!"

As Steavens turned away and closed his eyes with a shudder of unutterable repulsion, another woman, also tall, but flat and angular, dressed entirely in black, darted out of the house and caught Mrs. Merrick by the shoulders, crying sharply: "Come, come, mother; you musn't go on like this!" Her tone changed to one of obsequious solemnity as she turned to the banker: "The parlour is ready, Mr. Phelps."

The bearers carried the coffin along the narrow boards, while the undertaker ran ahead with the coffin-rests. They bore it into a large, unheated room that smelled of dampness and disuse and furniture polish, and set it down under a hanging lamp ornamented with jingling glass prisms and before a "Rogers group" of John Alden and Priscilla, wreathed with smilax. Henry Steavens stared about him with the sickening conviction that there had been some horrible mistake, and that he had somehow arrived at the wrong destination. He looked painfully about over the clover-green Brussels, the fat plush upholstery; among the hand-painted china placques and panels, and vases, for some mark of identification, for something that might once conceivably have belonged to Harvey Merrick. It was not until he recognized his friend in the crayon portrait of a little boy in kilts and curls hanging above the piano, that he felt willing to let any of these people approach the coffin.

"Take the lid off, Mr. Thompson; let me see my boy's face," wailed the elder woman between her sobs. This time Steavens looked fearfully, almost beseechingly into her face, red and swollen under its masses of strong, black, shiny hair. He flushed, dropped his eyes, and then, almost incredulously, looked again. There was a kind of power about her face—a kind of brutal handsomeness, even, but it was scarred and furrowed by violence, and so coloured and coarsened by fiercer passions that grief seemed never to have laid a gentle finger there. The long nose was distended and knobbed at the end, and there were deep lines on either side of it; her heavy, black brows almost met across her forehead, her teeth were large and square, and set far apart—teeth that could tear. She filled the room; the men were obliterated, seemed tossed about like twigs in an angry water, and even Steavens felt himself being drawn into the whirlpool.

The daughter—the tall, raw-boned woman in crêpe, with a mourning comb in her hair which curiously lengthened her long face—sat stiffly upon the sofa, her hands, conspicuous for their large knuckles, folded in her lap, her mouth and eyes drawn down, solemnly awaiting the opening of the coffin. Near the door stood a mulatto woman, evidently a servant in the house, with a timid bearing and an emaciated face pitifully sad and gentle. She was weeping silently, the corner of her calico apron lifted to her eyes, occasionally suppressing a long, quivering sob. Steavens walked over and stood beside her.

Feeble steps were heard on the stairs, and an old man, tall and frail, odorous of pipe smoke, with shaggy, unkept grey hair and a dingy beard, tobacco stained about the mouth, entered uncertainly. He went slowly up to the coffin and stood rolling a blue cotton handkerchief between his hands, seeming so pained and embarrassed by his wife's orgy of grief that he had no consciousness of anything else.

"There, there, Annie, dear, don't take on so," he quavered timidly, putting out a shaking hand and awkwardly patting her elbow. She turned with a cry, and sank upon his shoulder with such violence that he tottered a little. He did not even glance toward the coffin, but continued to look at her with a dull, frightened, appealing expression, as a spaniel looks at the whip. His sunken cheeks slowly reddened and burned with miserable shame. When his wife rushed from the room, her daughter strode after her with set lips. The servant stole up to the coffin, bent over it for a moment, and then slipped away to the kitchen, leaving Steavens, the lawyer and the father to themselves. The old man stood trembling and looking down at his dead son's face. The sculptor's splendid head seemed even more noble in its rigid stillness than in life. The dark hair had crept low upon the wide forehead; the face seemed strangely long, but in it there was not that beautiful and chaste repose which we expect to find in the faces of the dead. The brows were so drawn that there were two deep lines above the beaked nose, and the chin was thrust forward defiantly. It was as though the strain of life had been so sharp and bitter that death could not at once wholly relax the tension and smooth the countenance into perfect peace—as though he were still guarding something precious and holy, which might even yet be wrested from him.

The old man's lips were working under his stained beard. He turned to the lawyer with timid deference: "Phelps and the rest are comin' back to set up with Harve, ain't they?" he asked. "Thank 'ee, Jim, thank 'ee." He brushed the hair back gently from his son's forehead. "He was a good boy, Jim; always a good boy. He was ez gentle ez a child and the kindest of 'em all—only we didn't none of us ever onderstand him." The tears trickled slowly down his beard and dropped upon the sculptor's coat.

"Martin, Martin. Oh, Martin! come here," his wife wailed from the top of the stairs. The old man started timorously: "Yes, Annie, I'm coming." He turned away, hesitated, stood for a moment in miserable indecision;

then reached back and patted the dead man's hair softly, and stumbled from the room.

"Poor old man, I didn't think he had any tears left. Seems as if his eyes would have gone dry long ago. At his age nothing cuts very deep," remarked the lawyer.

Something in his tone made Steavens glance up. While the mother had been in the room, the young man had scarcely seen any one else; but now, from the moment he first glanced into Jim Laird's florid face and blood-shot eyes, he knew that he had found what he had been heartsick at not finding before—the feeling, the understanding, that must exist in some one, even here.

The man was red as his beard, with features swollen and blurred by dissipation, and a hot, blazing blue eye. His face was strained—that of a man who is controlling himself with difficulty—and he kept plucking at his beard with a sort of fierce resentment. Steavens, sitting by the window, watched him turn down the glaring lamp, still its jangling pendants with an angry gesture, and then stand with his hands locked behind him, staring down into the master's face. He could not help wondering what link there could have been between the porcelain vessel and so sooty a lump of potter's clay.

From the kitchen an uproar was sounding; when the dining-room door opened, the import of it was clear. The mother was abusing the maid for having forgotten to make the dressing for the chicken salad which had been prepared for the watchers. Steavens had never heard anything in the least like it; it was injured, emotional, dramatic abuse, unique and masterly in its excruciating cruelty, as violent and unrestrained as had been her grief of twenty minutes before. With a shudder of disgust the lawyer went into the dining-room and closed the door into the kitchen.

"Poor Roxy's getting it now," he remarked when he came back. "The Merricks took her out of the poor-house years ago; and if her loyalty would let her, I guess the poor old thing could tell tales that would curdle your blood. She's the mulatto woman who was standing in here a while ago, with her apron to her eyes. The old woman is a fury; there never was anybody like her for demonstrative piety and ingenious cruelty. She made Harvey's life a hell for him when he lived at home; he was so sick ashamed of it. I never could see how he kept himself so sweet."

"He was wonderful," said Steavens slowly, "wonderful; but until to-night I have never known how wonderful."

"That is the true and eternal wonder of it, anyway; that it can come even from such a dung heap as this," the lawyer cried, with a sweeping gesture which seemed to indicate much more than the four walls within which they stood.

"I think I'll see whether I can get a little air. The room is so close I am beginning to feel rather faint," murmured Steavens, struggling with one of the windows. The sash was stuck, however, and would not yield, so he sat down dejectedly and began pulling at his collar. The lawyer came over, loosened the sash with one blow of his red fist and sent the window up a few inches. Steavens thanked him, but the nausea which had been gradually climbing into his throat for the last half hour left him with but one desire—a desperate feeling that he must get away from this place with what was left of Harvey Merrick. Oh, he comprehended well enough now the quiet bitterness of the smile that he had seen so often on his master's lips!

He remembered that once, when Merrick returned from a visit home, he brought with him a singularly feeling and suggestive bas-relief of a thin, faded old woman, sitting and sewing something pinned to her knee; while a full-lipped, full-blooded little urchin, his trousers held up by a single gallows, stood beside her, impatiently twitching her gown to call her attention to a butterfly he had caught. Steavens, impressed by the tender and delicate modelling of the thin, tired face, had asked him if it were his mother. He remembered the dull flush that had burned up in the sculptor's face.

The lawyer was sitting in a rocking-chair beside the coffin, his head thrown back and his eyes closed. Steavens looked at him earnestly, puzzled at the line of the chin, and wondering why a man should conceal a feature of such distinction under that disfiguring shock of beard. Suddenly, as though he felt the young sculptor's keen glance, he opened his eyes.

"Was he always a good deal of an oyster?" he asked abruptly. "He was terribly shy as a boy."

"Yes, he was an oyster, since you put it so," rejoined Steavens. "Although he could be very fond of people, he always gave one the impression of being detached. He disliked violent emotion; he was reflective, and rather distrustful of himself—except, of course, as regarded his work. He was sure-footed enough there. He distrusted men pretty thoroughly and women even more, yet somehow without believing ill of them. He was determined, indeed, to believe the best, but he seemed afraid to investigate."

"A burnt dog dreads the fire," said the lawyer grimly, and closed his eyes.

Steavens went on and on, reconstructing that whole miserable boyhood. All this raw, biting ugliness had been the portion of the man whose tastes were refined beyond the limits of the reasonable—whose mind was an exhaustless gallery of beautiful impressions, and so sensitive that the mere shadow of a poplar leaf flickering against a sunny wall would be etched and held there forever. Surely, if ever a man had the magic word in his finger tips, it was Merrick. Whatever he touched, he revealed its holiest secret; liberated it from enchantment and restored it to its pristine loveliness, like the Arabian prince who fought the enchantress spell for spell. Upon whatever he had come in contact with, he had left a beautiful record of the experience—a sort of ethereal signature; a scent, a sound, a colour that was his own.

Steavens understood now the real tragedy of his master's life; neither love nor wine, as many had conjectured; but a blow which had fallen earlier and cut deeper than these could have done—a shame not his, and yet so unescapably his, to hide in his heart from his very boyhood. And without—the frontier warfare; the yearning of a boy, cast ashore upon a desert of newness and ugliness and sordidness, for all that is chastened and old, and noble with traditions.

At eleven o'clock the tall, flat woman in black crêpe entered and announced that the watchers were arriving, and asked them "to step into the dining-room." As Steavens rose, the lawyer said dryly: "You go on —it'll be a good experience for you, doubtless; as for me, I'm not equal to that crowd to-night; I've had twenty years of them."

As Steavens closed the door after him he glanced back at the lawyer, sitting by the coffin in the dim light, with his chin resting on his hand.

The same misty group that had stood before the door of the express car shuffled into the dining-room. In the light of the kerosene lamp they separated and became individuals. The minister, a pale, feeble-looking man with white hair and blond chin-whiskers, took his seat beside a small side table and placed his Bible upon it. The Grand Army man sat down behind the stove and tilted his chair back comfortably against the wall, fishing his quill toothpick from his waistcoat pocket. The two bankers, Phelps and Elder, sat off in a corner behind the dinner-table, where they could finish their discussion of the new usury law and its effect on chattel security loans. The real estate agent, an old man with a smiling, hypocritical face, soon joined them. The coal and lumber dealer and the cattle shipper sat on opposite sides of the hard coal-burner, their feet on the nickel-work. Steavens took a book from his pocket and began to read. The talk around him ranged through various topics of local interest while the house was quieting down. When it was clear that the members of the family were in bed, the Grand Army man hitched his shoulders and, untangling his long legs, caught his heels on the rounds of his chair.

"S'pose there'll be a will, Phelps?" he queried in his weak falsetto.

The banker laughed disagreeably, and began trimming his nails with a pearl-handled pocket-knife.

"There'll scarcely be any need for one, will there?" he queried in his turn.

The restless Grand Army man shifted his position again, getting his knees still nearer his chin. "Why, the ole man says Harve's done right well lately," he chirped.

The other banker spoke up. "I reckon he means by that Harve ain't asked him to mortgage any more farms lately, so as he could go on with his education."

"Seems like my mind don't reach back to a time when Harve wasn't bein' edycated," tittered the Grand Army man.

There was a general chuckle. The minister took out his handkerchief and blew his nose sonorously. Banker Phelps closed his knife with a snap. "It's too bad the old man's sons didn't turn out better," he remarked with reflective authority. "They never hung together. He spent money enough on Harve to stock a dozen cattle-farms and he might as well have poured it into Sand Creek. If Harve had stayed at home and helped nurse what little they had, and gone into stock on the old man's bottom farm, they might all have been well fixed. But the old man had to trust everything to tenants and was cheated right and left."

"Harve never could have handled stock none," interposed the cattleman. "He hadn't it in him to be sharp. Do you remember when he bought Sander's mules for eight-year olds, when everybody in town knew that Sander's father-in-law give 'em to his wife for a wedding present eighteen years before, an' they was full-grown mules then."

Every one chuckled, and the Grand Army man rubbed his knees with a spasm of childish delight.

"Harve never was much account for anything practical, and he shore was never fond of work," began the coal and lumber dealer. "I mind the last time he was home; the day he left, when the old man was out to the barn helpin' his hand hitch up to take Harve to the train, and Cal Moots was patchin' up the fence, Harve, he come out on the step and sings out, in his ladylike voice: "Cal Moots, Cal Moots! please come cord my trunk."

"That's Harve for you," approved the Grand Army man gleefully. "I kin hear him howlin' yet when he was a big feller in long pants and his mother used to whale him with a rawhide in the barn for lettin' the cows git foundered in the cornfield when he was drivin' 'em home from pasture. He killed a cow of mine that-a-way onct—a pure Jersey and the best milker I had, an' the ole man had to put up for her. Harve, he was watchin' the sun set acrost the marshes when the anamile got away; he argued that sunset was oncommon fine."

"Where the old man made his mistake was in sending the boy East to school," said Phelps, stroking his goatee and speaking in a deliberate, judicial tone. "There was where he got his head full of trapseing to Paris and all such folly. What Harve needed, of all people, was a course in some first-class Kansas City business college."

The letters were swimming before Steavens's eyes. Was it possible that these men did not understand, that the palm on the coffin meant nothing to them? The very name of their town would have remained forever buried in the postal guide had it not been now and again mentioned in the world in connection with Harvey Merrick's. He remembered what his master had said to him on the day of his death, after the congestion of both lungs had shut off any probability of recovery, and the sculptor had asked his pupil to send his body home. "It's not a pleasant place to be lying while the world is moving and doing and bettering," he had said with a feeble smile, "but it rather seems as though we ought to go back to the place we came from in the end. The townspeople will come in for a look at me; and after they have had their say I shan't have much to fear from the judgment of God. The wings of the Victory, in there"—with a weak gesture toward his studio—"will not shelter me."

The cattleman took up the comment. "Forty's young for a Merrick to cash in; they usually hang on pretty well. Probably he helped it along with whisky."

"His mother's people were not long lived, and Harvey never had a robust constitution," said the minister mildly. He would have liked to say more. He had been the boy's Sunday-school teacher, and had been fond of him; but he felt that he was not in a position to speak. His own sons had turned out badly, and it was not a year since one of them had made his last trip home in the express car, shot in a gambling-house in the Black Hills.

"Nevertheless, there is no disputin' that Harve frequently looked upon the wine when it was red, also variegated, and it shore made an oncommon fool of him," moralized the cattleman.

Just then the door leading into the parlour rattled loudly and every one started involuntarily, looking relieved when only Jim Laird came out. His red face was convulsed with anger, and the Grand Army man ducked his head when he saw the spark in his blue, blood-shot eye. They were all afraid of Jim; he was a drunkard, but he could twist the law to suit his client's needs as no other man in all western Kansas could do; and there were many who tried. The lawyer closed the door gently behind him, leaned back against it and folded his arms, cocking his head a little to one side. When he assumed this attitude in the court-room, ears were always pricked up, as it usually foretold a flood of withering sarcasm.

"I've been with you gentlemen before," he began in a dry, even tone, "when you've sat by the coffins of boys born and raised in this town; and, if I remember rightly, you were never any too well satisfied when you checked them up. What's the matter, anyhow? Why is it that reputable young men are as scarce as millionaires in Sand City? It might almost seem to a stranger that there was some way something the matter with your progressive town. Why did Ruben Sayer, the brightest young lawyer you ever turned out, after he had come home from the university as straight as a die, take to drinking and forge a check and shoot himself? Why did Bill Merrit's son die of the shakes in a saloon in Omaha? Why was Mr. Thomas's son, here, shot in a gambling-house? Why did young Adams burn his mill to beat the insurance companies and go to the pen?"

The lawyer paused and unfolded his arms, laying one clenched fist quietly on the table. "I'll tell you why. Because you drummed nothing but money and knavery into their ears from the time they wore knickerbockers; because you carped away at them as you've been carping here to-night, holding our friends Phelps and Elder up to them for their models, as our grandfathers held up George Washington and John Adams. But the boys, worse luck, were young, and raw at the business you put them to; and how could they match coppers with such artists as Phelps and Elder? You wanted them to be successful rascals; they were only unsuccessful ones—that's all the difference. There was only one boy ever raised in this borderland between ruffianism and civilization, who didn't come to grief, and you hated Harvey Merrick more for winning out than you hated all the other boys who got under the wheels. Lord, Lord, how you did hate him! Phelps, here, is fond of saying that he could buy and sell us all out any time he's a mind to; but he knew Harve wouldn't have given a tinker's damn for his bank and all his cattle-farms put together; and a lack of appreciation, that way, goes hard with Phelps.

"Old Nimrod, here, thinks Harve drank too much; and this from such as Nimrod and me!

"Brother Elder says Harve was too free with the old man's money—fell short in filial consideration, maybe. Well, we can all remember the very tone in which brother Elder swore his own father was a liar, in the county court; and we all know that the old man came out of that partnership with his son as bare as a sheared lamb. But maybe I'm getting personal, and I'd better be driving ahead at what I want to say."

The lawyer paused a moment, squared his heavy shoulders, and went on: "Harvey Merrick and I went to school together, back East. We were dead in earnest, and we wanted you all to be proud of us some day. We meant to be great men. Even I, and I haven't lost my sense of humor, gentlemen, I meant to be a great man. I came back here to practise, and I found you didn't in the least want me to be a great man. You wanted me to be a shrewd lawyer—oh, yes! Our veteran here wanted me to get him an increase of pension, because he had dyspepsia; Phelps wanted a new county survey that would put the widow Wilson's little bottom farm inside his south line; Elder wanted to lend money at 5 per cent a month, and get it collected; old Stark here wanted to wheedle old women up in Vermont into investing their annuities in real-estate mortgages that are not worth the paper they are written on. Oh, you needed me hard enough, and you'll go on needing me; and that's why I'm not afraid to plug the truth home to you this once.

"Well, I came back here and became the damned shyster you wanted me to be. You pretend to have some sort of respect for me; and yet you'll stand up and throw mud at Harvey Merrick, whose soul you couldn't dirty and whose hands you couldn't tie. Oh, you're a discriminating lot of Christians! There have been times when the sight of Harvey's name in some Eastern paper has made me hang my head like a whipped dog; and, again, times when I liked to think of him off there in the world, away from all this hog-wallow, doing his great work and climbing the big, clean up-grade he'd set for himself.

"And we? Now that we've fought and lied and sweated and stolen, and hated as only the disappointed strugglers in a bitter, dead little Western town know how to do, what have we got to show for it? Harve Merrick wouldn't have given one sunset over your marshes for all you've got put together, and you know it. It's not for me to say why, in the inscrutable wisdom of God, a genius should ever have been called from this place of hatred and bitter waters; but I want this Boston man to know that the drivel he's been hearing here to-night is the only tribute any truly great man could ever have from such a lot of sick, side-tracked, burnt-dog, land-poor sharks as the here-present financiers of Sand City—upon which town may God have mercy!"

The lawyer thrust out his hand to Steavens as he passed him, caught up his overcoat in the hall, and had left the house before the Grand Army man had had time to lift his ducked head and crane his long neck about at his fellows.

Next day Jim Laird was drunk and unable to attend the funeral services. Steavens called twice at his office, but was compelled to start East without seeing him. He had a presentiment that he would hear from him again, and left his address on the lawyer's table; but if Laird found it, he never acknowledged it. The thing in him that Harvey Merrick had loved must have gone under ground with Harvey Merrick's coffin; for it never spoke again, and Jim got the cold he died of driving across the Colorado mountains to defend one of Phelps's sons who had got into trouble out there by cutting government timber.

1905

[Harry] Sinclair Lewis

(1885-1951)

CHRONOLOGY:

1885 Born February 7, at Sauk Centre, Minnesota.

1903-08 Attended Oberlin College in Ohio briefly and Yale University.

1906-07 Served a brief stint as janitor in Upton Sinclair's Helicon Hall, Englewood, New Jersey, and as writer and editor in New York City.

1908 Graduated from Yale.

1908-15 Was a reporter, editor, publisher's reader, and copy writer for advertising firms at various locations.

1912 *Hike and the Aeroplane,* juvenile (published under the pseudonym of Tom Graham).
1914 *Our Mr. Wren.*
1915 *The Trail of the Hawk.*
1917 *The Job; The Innocents.*
1920 *Main Street.*
1922 *Babbitt.*
1925 *Arrowsmith.*
1926 *Mantrap;* refused Pulitzer Prize for *Arrowsmith.*
1927 *Elmer Gantry.*
1928 *The Man Who Knew Coolidge.*
1929 *Dodsworth.*
1930 Awarded the Nobel Prize for Literature (first American to be thus honored).
1933 *Ann Vickers.*
1934 *Work of Art.*
1935 *Jayhawker: A Play in Three Acts* (with Lloyd Lewis); *Selected Short Stories; It Can't Happen Here.*
1938 *The Prodigal Parents.*
1940 *Bethel Merriday.*
1943 *Gideon Planish.*
1945 *Cass Timberlane.*
1947 *Kingsblood Royal.*
1949 *The God-Seeker.*
1951 Died January 10 in Rome. *World So Wide.*

BIBLIOGRAPHY:

There is no collected edition of Lewis's fiction, although inexpensive reprints of individual novels are numerous. Harry Maule and Melville Caine edited *The Man From Main Street: A Sinclair Lewis Reader, 1904-1950 (New York,* 1953).

The definitive critical biography is Mark Shorer, *Sinclair Lewis: An American Life* (New York, 1961), which also contains full bibliographies. Also important are Grace Hegger Lewis's (the novelist's first wife) *With Love from Gracie: Sinclair Lewis: 1912-1925* (New York, 1955), Harrison Smith, *From Main Street to Stockholm: Letters of Sinclair Lewis, 1919-1930* (New York, 1952), and Sheldon Grebstein, *Sinclair Lewis* (New York, 1962).

For studies of individual novels, see Donna Gerstenberger and George Hendrick, *The American Novel, 1789-1959: A Checklist . . .* (Denver, 1961).

Nobel Prize Address

MEMBERS OF THE SWEDISH ACADEMY,
LADIES AND GENTLEMEN:

Were I to express my feeling of honor and pleasure in having been awarded the Nobel Prize in Literature, I should be fulsome and perhaps tedious, and I present my gratitude with a plain "Thank you."

I wish, in this address, to consider certain trends, certain dangers, and certain high and exciting promises in present-day American literature. To discuss this with complete and unguarded frankness—and I should not insult you by being otherwise than completely honest, however indiscreet—it will be necessary for me to be a little impolite regarding certain institutions and persons of my own greatly beloved land.

But I beg of you to believe that I am in no case gratifying a grudge. Fortune has dealt with me rather too well. I have known little struggle, not much poverty, many generosities. Now and then I have, for my books or myself, been somewhat warmly denounced—there was one good pastor in California who upon reading my "Elmer Gantry" desired to lead a mob and lynch me, while another holy man in the State of Maine wondered if there was no respectable and righteous way of putting me in jail. And, much harder to endure than any raging condemnation, a certain number of old acquaintances among journalists, what in the galloping American slang we call the "I Knew Him When Club," have scribbled that since they know me personally, therefore I must be a rather low sort of fellow and certainly no writer. But if I have now and then received such cheering brickbats, still I, who have heaved a good many bricks myself, would be fatuous not to expect a fair number in return.

No, I have for myself no conceivable complaint to make, and yet for American literature in general, and its standing in a country where industrialism and finance and science flourish and the only arts that are vital and respected are architecture and the film, I have a considerable complaint.

I can illustrate by an incident which chances to concern the Swedish Academy and myself and which happened a few days ago, just before I took ship at New York for Sweden. There is in America a learned and most amiable old gentleman who has been a pastor, a university professor, and a diplomat. He is a member of the American Academy of Arts and Letters and no few universities have honored him with degrees. As a writer he is chiefly known for his pleasant little essays on the joy of fishing. I do not suppose that professional fishermen, whose lives depend on the run of cod or herring, find it altogether an amusing occupation, but from these essays I learned, as a boy, that there is something very important and spiritual about catching fish, if you have no need of doing so.

This scholar stated, and publicly, that in awarding the Nobel Prize to a person who has scoffed at American institutions as much as I have, the Nobel Committee and the Swedish Academy had insulted America. I don't know whether, as an ex-diplomat, he intends to have an international incident made of it, and perhaps demand of the American Government that they land Marines in Stockholm to protect American literary rights, but I hope not.

I should have supposed that to a man so learned as to have been made a Doctor of Divinity, a Doctor of Letters, and I do not know how many other imposing magnificences, the matter would have seemed different; I should have supposed that he would have reasoned, "Although personally I dislike this man's books, nevertheless the Swedish Academy has in choosing him honored America by assuming that the Americans are no longer a puerile backwoods clan, so inferior that they are afraid of criticism, but instead a nation come of age and able to consider calmly and maturely any dissection of their land, however scoffing."

I should even have supposed that so international a scholar would have believed that Scandinavia, accustomed to the works of Strindberg, Ibsen, and Pontoppidan, would not have been peculiarly shocked by a writer whose most anarchistic assertion has been that America, with all her wealth and power, has not yet produced a civilization good enough to satisfy the deepest wants of human creatures.

I believe that Strindberg rarely sang the "Star-Spangled Banner" or addressed Rotary Clubs, yet Sweden seems to have survived him.

I have at such length discussed this criticism of the learned fisherman not because it has any conceivable importance in itself, but because it does illustrate the fact that in America most of us—not readers alone but even writers—are still afraid of any literature which is not a glorification of everything American, a glorification of our faults as well as our virtues. To be not only a best-seller in America but to be really beloved, a novelist must assert that all American men are tall, handsome, rich, honest, and powerful at golf; that all country towns are filled with neighbors who do nothing from day to day save go about being kind to one another; that although American girls may be wild, they change always into perfect wives and mothers; and that, geographically, America is composed solely of New York, which is inhabited entirely by millionaires; of the West, which keeps unchanged all the boisterous heroism of 1870; and of the South, where every one lives on a plantation perpetually glossy with moonlight and scented with magnolias.

It is not today vastly more true than it was twenty years ago that such novelists of ours as you have read in Sweden, novelists like Dreiser and Willa Cather, are authentically popular and influential in America. As it was revealed by the venerable fishing Academician whom I have quoted, we still most revere the writers for the popular magazines who in a hearty and edifying chorus chant that the America of a hundred and twenty million population is still as simple, as pastoral, as it was when it had but forty million; that in an industrial plant with ten thousand employees, the relationship between the worker and the manager is still as neighborly and uncomplex as in a factory of 1840, with five employees; that the relationships between father and son, between husband and wife, are precisely the same in an apartment in a thirty-story palace today, with three motor cars awaiting the family below and five books on the library shelves and a divorce imminent in the family next week, as were those relationships in a rose-veiled five-room cottage in 1880; that, in fine, America has gone through the revolutionary change from rustic colony to world-empire without having in the least altered the bucolic and Puritanic simplicity of Uncle Sam.

I am, actually, extremely grateful to the fishing Academician for having somewhat condemned me. For since he is a leading member of the American Academy of Arts and Letters, he has released me, has given me the right to speak as frankly of that Academy as he has spoken of me.

And in any honest study of American intellectualism today, that curious institution must be considered.

Before I consider the Academy, however, let me sketch a fantasy which has pleased me the last few days in the unavoidable idleness of a rough trip on the Atlantic. I am sure that you know, by now, that the award to me of the Nobel Prize has by no means been altogether popular in America. Doubtless the experience is not new to you. I fancy that when you gave the award even to Thomas Mann, whose "Zauberberg" seems to me to contain the whole of intellectual Europe, even when you gave it to Kipling, whose social significance is so profound that it has been rather authoritatively said that he created the British Empire, even when you gave it to Bernard Shaw, there were countrymen of those authors who complained because you did not choose another.

And I imagined what would have been said had you chosen some American other than myself. Suppose you had taken Theodore Dreiser.

Now to me, as to many other American writers, Dreiser more than any other man, marching alone, usually unappreciated, often hated, has cleared the trail from Victorian and Howellsian timidity and gentility in American fiction to honesty and boldness and passion of life. Without his pioneering, I doubt if any of us could, unless we liked to be sent to jail, seek to express life and beauty and terror.

My great colleague Sherwood Anderson has proclaimed this leadership of Dreiser. I am delighted to join him. Dreiser's great first novel, "Sister Carrie," which he dared to publish thirty long years ago and which I read twenty-five years ago, came to housebound and airless America like a great free Western wind, and to our stuffy domesticity gave us the first fresh air since Mark Twain and Whitman.

Yet had you given the Prize to Mr. Dreiser, you would have heard groans from America; you would have heard that his style—I am not exactly sure what this mystic quality "style" may be, but I find the word so often in the writings of minor critics that I suppose it must exist—you would have heard that his style is cumbersome, that his choice of words is insensitive, that his books are interminable. And certainly respectable scholars would complain that in Mr. Dreiser's world, men and women are often sinful and tragic and despairing, instead of being forever sunny and full of song and virtue, as befits authentic Americans.

And had you chosen Mr. Eugene O'Neill, who has done nothing much in American drama save to transform it utterly, in ten or twelve years, from a false world of neat and competent trickery to a world of splendor and fear and greatness, you would have been reminded that he has done something far worse than scoffing—he has seen life as not to be neatly arranged in the study of a scholar but as a terrifying, magnificent and often quite horrible thing akin to the tornado, the earthquake, the devastating fire.

And had you given Mr. James Branch Cabell the Prize, you would have been told that he is too fantastically malicious. So would you have been told that Miss Willa Cather, for all the homely virtue of her novels concerning the peasants of Nebraska, has in her novel, "The Lost Lady," been so untrue to America's patent and perpetual and possibly tedious virtuousness as to picture an abandoned woman who remains, nevertheless, uncannily charming even to the virtuous, in a story without any moral; that Mr. Henry Mencken is the worst of all scoffers; that Mr. Sherwood Anderson viciously errs in considering sex as important a force in life as fishing; that Mr. Upton Sinclair, being a Socialist, sins against the perfectness of American capitalistic mass-production; that Mr. Joseph Hergesheimer is un-American in regarding graciousness of manner and beauty of surface as of some importance in the endurance of daily life; and that Mr. Ernest Hemingway is not only too young but, far worse, uses language which should be unknown to gentlemen; that he acknowledges drunkenness as one of men's eternal ways to happiness, and asserts that a soldier may find love more significant than the hearty slaughter of men in battle.

Yes, they are wicked, these colleagues of mine; you would have done almost as evilly to have chosen them as to have chosen me; and as a Chauvinistic American—only, mind you, as an American of 1930 and not of 1880—I rejoice that they are my countrymen and countrywomen, and that I may speak of them with pride even in the Europe of Thomas Mann, H. G. Wells, Galsworthy, Knut Hamsun, Arnold Bennett, Feuchtwanger, Selma Lagerlöf, Sigrid Undset, Verner von Heidenstam, D'Annunzio, Romain Rolland.

It is my fate in this paper to swing constantly from optimism to pessimism and back, but so is it the fate of any one who writes or speaks of anything in America—the most contradictory, the most depressing, the most stirring, of any land in the world today.

Thus, having with no muted pride called the roll of what seem to me to be great men and women in American literary life today, and having indeed omitted a dozen other names of which I should like to boast were there time, I must turn again and assert that in our contemporary American literature, indeed in all American arts save architecture and the film, we—yes, we who have such pregnant and vigorous standards in commerce and science—have no standards, no healing communication, no heroes to be followed nor villains to be condemned, no certain ways to be pursued and no dangerous paths to be avoided.

The American novelist or poet or dramatist or sculptor or painter must work alone, in confusion, unassisted save by his own integrity.

That, of course, has always been the lot of the artist. The vagabond and criminal François Villon had certainly no smug and comfortable refuge in which elegant ladies would hold his hand and comfort his starveling soul and more starved body. He, veritably a great man, destined to outlive in history all the dukes and puissant cardinals whose robes he was esteemed unworthy to touch, had for his lot the gutter and the hardened crust.

Such poverty is not for the artist in America. They pay us, indeed, only too well; that writer is a failure who cannot have his butler and motor and his villa at Palm Beach, where he is permitted to mingle almost in equality with the barons of banking. But he is oppressed ever by something worse than poverty—by the feeling that what he creates does not matter, that he is expected by his readers to be only a decorator or a clown, or that he is good-naturedly accepted as a scoffer whose bark probably is worse than his bite and who probably is a good fellow at heart, who in any case certainly does not count in a land that produces eighty-story buildings, motors by the million, and wheat by the billions of bushels. And he has no institution, no group, to which he can turn for inspiration, whose criticism he can accept and whose praise will be precious to him.

What institutions have we?

The American Academy of Arts and Letters does contain, along with several excellent painters and architects and statesmen, such a really distinguished university-president as Nicholas Murray Butler, so admirable and courageous a scholar as Wilbur Cross, and several first-rate writers: the poets Edwin Arlington Robinson and Robert Frost, the free-minded publicist James Truslow Adams, and the novelists Edith Wharton, Hamlin Garland, Owen Wister, Brand Whitlock and Booth Tarkington.

But it does not include Theodore Dreiser, Henry Mencken, our most vivid critic, George Jean Nathan who, though still young, is certainly the dean of our dramatic critics, Eugene O'Neill, incomparably our best dramatist, the really original and vital poets, Edna St. Vincent Millay and Carl Sandburg, Robinson Jeffers and Vachel Lindsay and Edgar Lee Masters, whose "Spoon River Anthology" was so utterly different from any other poetry ever published, so fresh, so authoritative, so free from any gropings and timidities that it came like a revelation, and created a new school of native American poetry. It does not include the novelists and short-story writers, Willa Cather, Joseph Hergesheimer, Sherwood Anderson, Ring Lardner, Ernest Hemingway, Louis Bromfield, Wilbur Daniel Steele, Fannie Hurst, Mary Austin, James Branch Cabell, Edna Ferber, nor Upton Sinclair, of whom you must say, whether you admire or detest his aggressive socialism, that he is internationally better known than any other American artist whosoever, be he novelist, poet, painter, sculptor, musician, architect.

I should not expect any Academy to be so fortunate as to contain all these writers, but one which fails to contain any of them, which thus cuts itself off from so much of what is living and vigorous and original in American letters, can have no relationship whatever to our life and aspirations. It does not represent literary America of today—it represents only Henry Wadsworth Longfellow.

It might be answered that, after all, the Academy is limited to fifty members; that, naturally, it cannot include everyone of merit. But the fact is that while most of our few giants are excluded, the Academy does have room to include three extraordinarily bad poets, two very melodramatic and insignificant playwrights, two gentlemen who are known only because they are university presidents, a man who was thirty years ago known as a rather clever humorous draughtsman, and several gentlemen of whom—I sadly confess my ignorance—I have never heard.

Let me again emphasize the fact—for it is a fact—that I am not attacking the American Academy. It is a hospitable and generous and decidedly dignified institution. And it is not altogether the Academy's fault that it does not contain many of the men who have significance in our letters. Sometimes it is the fault of those writers themselves. I cannot imagine that grizzly-bear Theodore Dreiser being comfortable at the serenely Athenian dinners of the Academy, and were they to invite Mencken, he would infuriate them with his boisterous jeering. No, I am not attacking—I am reluctantly considering the Academy because it is so perfect an example of the divorce in America of intellectual life from all authentic standards of importance and reality.

Our universities and colleges, or gymnasia, most of them, exhibit the same unfortunate divorce. I can think of four of them, Rollins College in Florida, Middlebury College in Vermont, the University of Michigan, and the University of Chicago—which has had on its roll so excellent a novelist as Robert Herrick, so courageous a critic as Robert Morss Lovett—which have shown an authentic interest in contemporary creative literature. Four of them. But universities and colleges and musical emporiums and schools for the teaching of theology and plumbing and sign-painting are as thick in America as the motor traffic. Whenever you see a public building with Gothic fenestration on a sturdy backing of Indiana concrete, you may be certain that it is another university, with anywhere from two hundred to twenty thousand students equally ardent about avoiding the disadvantage of becoming learned and about gaining the social prestige contained in the possession of a B.A. degree.

Oh, socially our universities are close to the mass of our citizens, and so are they in the matter of athletics. A great college football game is passionately witnessed by eighty thousand people, who have paid five dollars apiece and motored anywhere from ten to a thousand miles for the ecstasy of watching twenty-two men chase one another up and down a curiously marked field. During the football season, a capable player ranks very nearly with our greatest and most admired heroes—even with Henry Ford, President Hoover, and Colonel Lindbergh.

And in one branch of learning, the sciences, the lords of business who rule us are willing to do homage to the devotees of learning. However bleakly one of our trader aristocrats may frown upon poetry or the visions of a painter, he is graciously pleased to endure a Millikan, a Michelson, a Banting, a Theobald Smith.

But the paradox is that in the arts our universities are as cloistered, as far from reality and living creation, as socially and athletically and scientifically they are close to us. To a true-blue professor of literature in an American university, literature is not something that a plain human being, living today, painfully sits down to produce. No; it is something dead; it is something magically produced by superhuman beings who must, if they are to be regarded as artists at all, have died at least one hundred years before the diabolical invention of the typewriter. To any authentic don, there is something slightly repulsive in the thought that literature could be created by any ordinary human being, still to be seen walking the streets, wearing quite commonplace trousers and coat and looking not so unlike a chauffeur or a farmer. Our American professors like their literature clear and cold and pure and very dead.

I do not suppose that American universities are alone in this. I am aware that to the dons of Oxford and Cambridge, it would seem rather indecent to suggest that Wells and Bennett and Galsworthy and George Moore may, while they commit the impropriety of continuing to live, be compared to any one so beautifully and safely dead as Samuel Johnson. I suppose that in the Universities of Sweden and France and Germany there exist plenty of professors who prefer dissection to understanding. But in the new and vital and experimental land of America, one would expect the teachers of literature to be less monastic, more human, than in the traditional shadows of old Europe.

They are not.

There has recently appeared in America, out of the universities, an astonishing circus called "the New Humanism." Now of course "humanism" means so many things that it means nothing. It may infer anything from a belief that Greek and Latin are more inspiring than the dialect of contemporary peasants to a belief that any living peasant is more interesting than a dead Greek. But it is a delicate bit of justice that this nebulous word should have been chosen to label this nebulous cult.

Insofar as I have been able to comprehend them—for naturally in a world so exciting and promising as this today, a life brilliant with Zeppelins and Chinese revolutions and the Bolshevik industrialization of farming and ships and the Grand Canyon and young children and terrifying hunger and the lonely quest of scientists after God, no creative writer would have the time to follow all the chilly enthusiasms of the New Humanists—this newest of sects reasserts the dualism of man's nature. It would confine literature to the fight between man's soul and God, or man's soul and evil.

But, curiously, neither God nor the devil may wear modern dress, but must retain Grecian vestments. Oedipus is a tragic figure for the New Humanists; man, trying to maintain himself as the image of God under the menace of dynamos, in a world of high-pressure salesmanship, is not. And the poor comfort which they offer is that the object of life is to develop self-discipline—whether or not one ever accomplishes anything with this self-discipline. So this the whole movement results in the not particularly novel doctrine that both art and life must be resigned and negative. It is a doctrine of the blackest reaction introduced into a stirringly revolutionary world.

Strangely enough, this doctrine of death, this escape from the complexities and danger of living into the secure blankness of the monastery, has become widely popular among professors in a land where one would have expected only boldness and intellectual adventure, and it has more than ever shut creative writers off from any benign influence which might conceivably have come from the universities.

But it has always been so. America has never had a Brandes, a Taine, a Goethe, a Croce.

With a wealth of creative talent in America, our criticism has most of it been a chill and insignificant activity pursued by jealous spinsters, ex-baseball-reporters, and acid professors. Our Erasmuses have been village schoolmistresses. How should there be any standards when there has been no one capable of setting them up?

The great Cambridge-Concord circle of the middle of the Nineteenth Century—Emerson, Longfellow, Lowell, Holmes, the Alcotts—were sentimental reflections of Europe, and they left no school, no influence. Whitman and Thoreau and Poe and, in some degree, Hawthorne, were outcasts, men alone and despised, berated by the New Humanists of their generation. It was with the emergence of William Dean Howells that we first began to have something like a standard, and a very bad standard it was.

Mr. Howells was one of the gentlest, sweetest, and most honest of men, but he had the code of a pious old maid whose greatest delight was to have tea at the vicarage. He abhorred not only profanity and obscenity but all of what H. G. Wells has called "the jolly coarsenesses of life." In his fantastic vision of life, which he innocently conceived to be realistic, farmers and seamen and factory-hands might exist, but the farmer must never be covered with muck, the seaman must never roll out bawdy chanteys, the factory-hand must be thankful to his good kind employer, and all of them must long for the opportunity to visit Florence and smile gently at the quaintness of the beggars.

So strongly did Howells feel this genteel, this New Humanistic philosophy that he was able vastly to influence his contemporaries, down even to 1914 and the turmoil of the Great War.

He was actually able to tame Mark Twain, perhaps the greatest of our writers, and to put that fiery old savage into an intellectual frock coat and top hat. His influence is not altogether gone today. He is still worshipped by Hamlin Garland, an author who should in every way have been greater than Howells but who under Howells' influence was changed from a harsh and magnificent realist into a genial and insignificant lecturer. Mr. Garland is, so far as we have one, the dean of American letters today, and as our dean, he is alarmed by all of the younger writers who are so lacking in taste as to suggest that men and women do not always love in accordance with the prayer-book, and that common people sometimes use language which would be inappropriate at a women's literary club on Main Street. Yet this same Hamlin Garland, as a young man, before he had gone to Boston and become cultured and Howellsised, wrote two most valiant and revelatory works of realism, "Main-Travelled Roads" and "Rose of Dutcher's Coolly."

I read them as a boy in a prairie village in Minnesota—just such an environment as was described in Mr. Garland's tales. They were vastly exciting to me. I had realized in reading Balzac and Dickens that it was possible to describe French and English common people as one actually saw them. But it had never occurred to me that one might without indecency write of the people of Sauk Centre, Minnesota, as one felt about them. Our fictional tradition, you see, was that all of us in Midwestern villages were altogether noble and happy; that not one of us would exchange the neighborly bliss of living on Main Street for the heathen gaudiness of New York or Paris or Stockholm. But in Mr. Garland's "Main-Travelled Roads" I discovered that there was one man who believed that Midwestern peasants were sometimes bewildered and hungry and vile—and heroic. And, given this vision, I was released; I could write of life as living life.

I am afraid that Mr. Garland would be not pleased but acutely annoyed to know that he made it possible for me to write of America as I see it, and not as Mr. William Dean Howells so sunnily saw it. And it is his tragedy, it is a completely revelatory American tragedy, that in our land of freedom, men like Garland, who first blast the roads to freedom, become themselves the most bound.

But, all this time, while men like Howells were so effusively seeking to guide America into becoming a pale edition of an English cathedral town, there were surly and authentic fellows—Whitman and Melville, then Dreiser and James Huneker and Mencken—who insisted that our land had something more than tea-table gentility.

And so, without standards, we have survived. And for the strong young men, it has perhaps been well that we should have no standards. For, after seeming to be pessimistic about my own and much beloved land, I want to close this dirge with a very lively sound of optimism.

I have, for the future of American literature, every hope and every eager belief. We are coming out, I believe, of the stuffiness of safe, sane, and incredibly dull provincialism. There are young Americans today who are doing such passionate and authentic work that it makes me sick to see that I am a little too old to be one of them.

There is Ernest Hemingway, a bitter youth, educated by the most intense experience, disciplined by his own high standards, an authentic artist whose home is in the whole of life; there is Thomas Wolfe, a child of, I believe, thirty or younger, whose one and only novel, "Look Homeward, Angel," is worthy to be compared with the best in our literary production, a Gargantuan creature with great gusto of life; there is Thornton Wilder, who in an age of realism dreams the old and lovely dreams of the eternal romantics; there is John Dos Passos, with his hatred of the safe and sane standards of Babbitt and his splendor of revolution; there is Stephen Benét who, to American drabness, has restored the epic poem with his glorious memory of old John Brown; there are Michael Gold, who reveals the new frontier of the Jewish East Side, and William Faulkner, who has freed the South from hoop-skirts; and there are a dozen other young poets and fictioneers, most of them living now in Paris, most of them a little insane in the tradition of James Joyce, who, however insane they may be, have refused to be genteel and traditional and dull.

I salute them, with a joy in being not yet too far removed from their determination to give to the America that has mountains and endless prairies, enormous cities and lost far cabins, billions of money and tons of faith, to an America that is, as strange as Russia and as complex as China, a literature worthy of her vastness. 1930

From *The Man Who Knew Coolidge*

You Know How Women Are

—And I tell you, Walt, now we have a chance to sit down here by ourselves in your den and have a real chat—and say, from what I've seen, I don't believe there's a more elegant house for its size in Troy, and then of course you always were my favorite cousin, and one of the few people whose business judgment I'd trust and—

If you can see your way clear to making this loan, you'll never regret it. Business hasn't gone quite so good the last six months, as I admitted, but now I've got the exclusive Zenith agency for Zenith for these new cash registers—and say, what the cash register means, what it *means* to the modern and efficient conduct of business; it's almost, you might say, the symbol of modern industry, like the sword is of war—now I've got that, I can guarantee a big increase in turnover, taking one thing with another, and I want you to examine the analysis of my business with the greatest care.

And I certainly do admit all your criticisms, and I'm going to ponder on 'em and try to profit by 'em.

I'm afraid I do get too kind of talkee-talkee during business hours, and maybe waste time and money. And I admit what you said about my college course. It's perfectly true: I didn't quit Amherst because my Dad died—fact, he didn't die till nine months after I was fired, and it's true I was dropped for flunking all my college courses, as you said—though I thought you threw that up to me a little unnecessarily; almost hurt my feelings, in fact; don't know that I'd 've stood it from anybody but you, but of course you always were my favorite cousin—

You see, I don't go around telling everybody that version of the story, because what I figure is, what they don't know won't hurt 'em none, and it's none of their business.

But it's not true, as you kind of hinted and suggested, that I didn't know President Coolidge in college. It's a fact that for some years I did have him mixed up with another fellow in our class that looked something like him, but here some time ago I happened to run into this other fellow, and now I've got the two of 'em perfectly straight.

Why, I can remember just as if it was yesterday, Cal—as we used to call him—Cal and I were going into class together, and I says to him, "Cal, old boy," I said, "what's the Latin for 'battle'?" And he said—he said—well, he gave the word right out, without any hemming and hawing and beating around the bush.

But you're right, I do kind of get to talking too much. Henceforth I'm going to cut it short, and you'll never regret it if you put in that loan.

And I don't think that even you, with all the insight that you show into human nature, quite understand how and why it is that in certain moods I do run on a good deal. There's reasons for it. In the first place, I'm called on so constantly for speeches and oratory in Zenith—you've never been there and you couldn't understand, but—

Well, you take like this, for instance. I was attending a meeting of the Americanization Committee of the Zenith Chamber of Commerce, and we were discussing birth control. Well, the chairman insisted I make 'em a long speech on the subject.

"Shucks, boys," I said, "you know just as much about it as I do," but they talked and they insisted, and they wouldn't let me go until I'd made a long spiel for 'em, summing up the arguments on both sides and, you might say, kind of clarifying it for 'em. See how I mean? But you, Walt, you just think of business night and day, and prob'ly that's a more practical way to think of it. But I get dragged into all these public and influential occasions and get kind of into a habit of oratory and philosophy, see how I mean?

And then—

I hate to say it, and there isn't another human being living, Walt, that I'd tell this to, and I want you to treat it as strictly confidential, but—

The fact is, what really cramps my style is my wife.

That girl—

And in many ways I've got nothing but praise for Mamie. She means well, and as far as her lights lead her, she does everything she can for me, but the fact is she don't quite understand me, and say, the way she drives me and makes demands on me and everything, why say, it just about drives me crazy.

And Delmerine same way. Thinking the Old Man's *made* of money!

And what I've done for Mamie—yes, and what modern American science has done! Think of the advantage of canned goods, of delicatessen shops with every delicacy from salads to cold turkey, all ready to serve without any preparation; of baker's bread without having to bake bread at home. Think of the electric dish-washing machine, reducing the work of dish-washing to, you might say, practically a minimum, and the vacuum cleaner, and what an invention *that* is!—no more sweeping, no more beating rugs—why say, the preachers can talk about these mysteries and all like that, but I guess in the vacuum cleaner America has added to the world *its* own mystery, that'll last when the columns of the Acropolis have crumbled to mere dust!

And then think of the modern laundries with their marvelous machinery.

It's true that they don't wash the clothes quite as good as my old mother used to—fact, they simply tear hell out of my handkerchiefs, and I always was a man to appreciate a high grade of fine linen handkerchief. But still, think of the labor-saving.

And so I've provided Mame with every device to save her labor, so whether it's a question of her telling the maid what to do, or during those comparatively rare intervals when we haven't got a hired girl and she has to do some of the work herself, she can get it all done in a jiffy, you might say, and be free for all the pleasures and self-improvement of leisure. She's free to play bridge nearly every afternoon, and also to give a lot of attention to her literary club, the William Lyon Phelps Ladies' Book and Literary Society, and get a lot of culture.

Now myself, I've always given a lot of attention to intellectual matters. Of course I'm right up on history—I've read clear through both Wells' "Outline of History," or practically clear through it, and also Van Lear's

"Story of Mankind," especially studying the illustrations. And of course—maybe I'm a little rusty on it now, but as a boy I used to be able to chatter German like a native, you might say, as my father often talked it to us at home. And now I'm kind of specializing on philosophy. I've read a lot of this "Story of Philosophy" by—I can't at the moment exactly remember the professor's name, but it gives you the whole contents of all philosophy in one book; and while these business cares have for the moment interrupted my reading the book, I expect to go right on and finish it.

But Mame, she has the opportunity to go ahead and knock all *my* culture into a cocked hat. Here recently her club had a very fine lecture about the excavation of King Tut's tomb, from a gentleman that had been right there on the ground—of course he couldn't go *into* the tomb, because nobody's allowed inside it except the excavating staff, but he saw the place at first hand, and my wife learned a lot about Egyptology from him.

And they've had a whole course in dietetics. She learned, for example, that the ordinary housewife uses more butter in cooking than is at all necessary—that while maybe butter may make grub *taste* a little better, it doesn't add proportionately to the calories or whatever they are, and so she learned one way in which to economize. And my God, these days, what with the cost of gasoline and golf balls, a fellow has to economize on something.

So as I say, she has a chance to lead a free life and have a lot of dandy times, because I've provided her with all the household conveniences. But who paid for 'em? Where did the money to pay for 'em come from? From my toil and efforts, that's where it came from, and do you think I can get her to appreciate that? Not for one moment!

All day long I slave and work to keep her in luxury, and then when I come home at night all tired out, do I find her ready to comfort me? I do not!

I might as well not have a wife at all. And then when I try to make her understand what I've been doing—like telling her how hard I've worked to sell a new adding-machine to some fellow that didn't want it and maybe didn't need it, do you think she appreciates it? She does not!

Why, she always makes out like she wishes I was a doctor, or one of these he-lecturers that goes around spieling to women's clubs, or some darn' arty thing like that, and sometimes she practically up and says she wishes I could make love like one of these Wop counts, or a movie actor!

She says I just think of business and not of her. But I notice she's good and plenty glad to grab all the money I bring home from that business, all right!

It was—

Now I wouldn't say this to anybody else on God's green earth, and for heaven's sake don't you ever breathe a syllable of it, even to your wife, but I've been beginning to think here lately that it was all wrong with Mame and me right from the beginning!

Not that I'd ever do anything about it, you understand—even though I *have* got a lady friend in New York, simply a little darling and at least twelve years younger than Mame, too—but I don't believe in divorce, and then there's the children to think of. But it was all wrong—

I've learned a lot here lately. I've been studying and delving into psychoanalysis. Know anything about psychoanalysis?

Well, I do, and say, it certainly is a revelation. I've read almost clear through a manual on it—a very authoritive book written by a lady, Miss Alexandrine Applebaugh, that's a great authority on the subject, because she studied with a man that was a pupil of one of the biggest pupils of old Freud, and it was Freud that invented psychoanalysis.

Well, now I'll explain what psychoanalysis is. It's like this:

Everybody ought to have a rich, full sex-life, and all human activities are directed toward that. Whenever a guy is doing something, it's directed toward making himself attractive sexually, especially if it's something big and important—no matter whether it's painting a picture or putting over a big deal in Florida town-lots or discovering a new eclipse or pitching in a World Series game or preaching a funeral sermon or writing a big advertisement or any of them things. On the other hand, when fellows like us *do* put over something, we want to be appreciated, and we got a right to expect it, and if we don't get appreciated at home, we ought to find new mates, see how I mean?

Only you get into so doggone many complications and trouble and all that maybe it ain't practical, even with a cute girl like this one in New York I was speaking about—Ain't really worth it.

And then there's a lot in psychoanalysis about dreams. All dreams mean you ought to have a different kind of a wife—oh, they're *mighty* important!

And so now you'll understand psychoanalysis—as well as anybody does, anyway.

Well, as I say, now that I've mastered psychoanalysis, I can see things was all wrong with Mame and me from the beginning.

I was a young fellow, just come to Zenith, then, working in a wholesale paper house and living in a boarding-house out in the Benner Park district, and in those days that district was just like a small town. I met a dandy crowd of young people at the church and so on, and we used to have dances and picnics and sleigh-rides and everything—rube stuff, but lots of fun.

Well, Mame—her father was in the roofing business, did a pretty good business, too, for them days—she was one of the jolliest girls in the bunch, but she was awful on the level. There was some of the girls in our crowd that you could get pretty fresh with—nothing wrong, you understand, or not hardly ever, but still when you was all cuddled down together in the hay on a sleigh-ride, you could hold their hands and maybe even pat their knees a little.

But Mame—never! No sir! Why say, she was so pure and religious that one time at a dance when I tried to kiss her, she slapped hell out of me!

So of course that just led me on. Made me think she was the living wonder.

Maybe if I'd known then as much as I know now, I'd 've known that it isn't so bad for a girl that you're going to spend your life with, intimate, you might say, to have a little of the Old Nick in her and not be so dog-gone adverse to a little scientific cuddling—within reason I mean, of course, you see how I mean?

Well, so we got married and she never did get so she liked—

I mean, she hints around sometimes and kind of hints that it's because I'm just a poor plain plug American business man that she's never warmed up. But my God, I've never had any encouragement! I don't expect I'd ever be any Valentino, anyway, but how can I even begin to learn to show her a good time when she's always acted like she was afraid I *would* try to kiss her?

I tell you, Walt, I'm kind of puzzled. Sometimes I almost kind of wonder (though I wouldn't want to be quoted) whether with all the great things we got in this greatest nation in the world, with more autos and radios and furnaces and suits of clothes and miles of cement pavements and skyscrapers than the rest of the world put together, and with more deep learning—hundreds of thousands of students studying Latin and bookkeeping and doctoring and domestic science and literature and banking and window-dressing—even with all of this, I wonder if we don't lack something in American life when you consider that you almost never see an American married couple that really like each other and like to be with each other?

I wonder. But I guess it's too much for me. I just don't understand—

But I'm getting away from my subject. To return to Mame:

Aside from her apparently not wanting me to be anything whatsomever around the house except the guy that pays the bills and carves the duck and fixes the furnace and drives her car out of the garage so she can go off to a hen bridge-party, here lately we've got into kind of a bad way of quarreling.

Well, here's an example:

We used to have dogs for quite a while after we were married, and I always did like to have a good dog around the house. Kind of gives you somebody to talk to when you come home and there ain't anybody around—just sits and listens while you explain things to him, and looks like he *understood!* But here about six years ago, just at a moment when we didn't happen to have a dog, somebody gave Mrs. Schmaltz—gave Mamie, I mean—a very fine expensive cat by the name Minnie—not exactly a full-bred Persian, I guess, but pretty full-bred at that.

But at the same time, even appreciating how much money she was worth, I never did *like* that damn' cat!

You see, we also had a canary, a very valuable little canary named Dicky, a real genuwine Hertz Mountains canary, and intelligent—say, there's those that say a canary isn't intelligent, but I want to tell you that that canary *knew* me, and when I'd stand near the cage he'd chirp just like he was talking to me.

He was a lot of comfort to me, not having a dog at that time—I was looking for a high-class English setter, and hadn't been able to find one at the price I felt justified in paying.

Well sir, here was a surprising thing. We fed that cat and fed her—I'd hate to tot up all the money we've paid out for milk and meat for that cat—but even so, she was bound and determined she was going to get at that poor little canary. She'd hang around underneath the cage and look up at Dicky, absolutely bloodthirsty, and one time when somebody (and I always thought it was Mame did it herself, too, and not the hired girl) —when somebody left a chair right practically under the cage, Minnie lep' up on the chair and absolutely did her best to leap up and get at the cage.

Of course Mame and I had words about that—

And then that damn' cat never *would* be friendly, at least not to me.

I used to say to Mame, "Well, what does the fool cat *do* for its living, anyway? Think we're sent into the world just to loaf around and enjoy ourselves and sponge on other people?" I says.

Wouldn't sit in my lap—no sir, not for a minute. I used to get so sore at that cat that I'd kick it good and plenty hard, when nobody was looking—I showed it its place, by God—and *still* I couldn't get it to be friendly.

And we talked a lot about it, about the cat and the canary, and one thing often led to another—

You know how it is.

And when I talked about getting another dog, no *sir*, Mame wouldn't hear to it—said a dog would frighten her ittly, bittly, sweetsy, bitsy, high-hatting, canary-murdering damn' *cat*, by God!

Well, I made up my mind that I was going to be master in my own household, but—Oh well, things just kind of floated along for several months, and I didn't do anything special about buying a dog, and then one day—

I remember just like it was yesterday. I'd been out to the country club for a few holes of golf—I remember I was playing with Joe Minchin, the machinery king, Willis Ijams, our leading—or certainly one of the leading hardware dealers, and fellow named George Babbitt, the great real-estate dealer. But I was driving home alone, and I remember there was something wrong—car kept kind of bucking—couldn't exactly figure out what it was, so I stops the car right by the side of the road—it was late autumn—and I lifts the hood and I'm trying to figure out what's wrong when I hears a kind of a whining and a whimpering, and I looks down, and by golly there's a nice water spaniel—not very old, not more'n say two or maybe nearer two and a half years old, sitting there and looking up at me so pathetic—say, it was absolutely pathetic. And he held up his paw like it'd been hurt.

"Well, what's the trouble, old man?" I says to him.

And he looks up, so intelligent—By golly, I just loved that damn' tyke. Well, make a long story short, I looks at his paw, and way I figured it out, he'd cut it on some broken glass—but not bad. Fortunately I had some old but clean rags there in the door-pocket of the car, and so I sat down on the running-board and kind of bound up his paw, and meantime I noticed—and a good, high-grade dog he was, too—I noticed he didn't have any collar or license or anything. And when I'd finished, doggoned if he didn't jump up into my sedan like he belonged there.

"Well, who d'you think you are?" I says to him. "What are you trying to do, you old hijacker," I says to him. "Steal my car? Poor old Pop Schmaltz with his car stolen," I says.

And he just curls up on the back seat and wags his tail, much as to say, "You're a great little kidder, but I know which side my meat is buttered on."

Well, I looks up and down the road and there wasn't anybody in sight that looked like they were looking for a dog, and there was only a couple of houses in sight, and when I got the car to acting Christian again—seems the carburetor needed a little adjusting—I drives to both these houses, and *they* didn't know nothing about no lost dog, so I says, "Well, don't like to leave old Jackie here—"

That's what I named the pup, and that's what I call him to this very day.

"I'd better not leave him here to get run over," thinks I, "and when we get back home, I'll advertise and see if I can find his owner."

Well, when I got home, Robby—you remember my boy, Walt—Robby was just as crazy about having a dog as I was, but Mame gets sniffy about how the dog'd scare that damn' cat Minnie of hers. But she let me keep Jackie, that's the dog, out in the garage till I'd advertised.

Well, I advertised and I advertised—

No, come to think of it, I guess it was just one ad I put in, because I thinks to myself, "Jackie looks to me like a regular man's dog, and if his owner ain't keeping a look-out, can't expect *me* to do all the work!"

Anyway, never got an answer, and in 'long about a week, Mame wakes up and begins to realize, here I am with a dog that ain't going to be buddies with her cat—and say, was she right? Say, the first time Minnie comes pee-rading out on the lawn to see if she can't murder a few sparrows, Jackie, his paw was well enough for that, he takes one look at her, and say, honest, you'd 've laughed fit to bust; he chases her 'way clean up our elm tree, and keeps her there, too, by golly.

Well, after that, there was a hell of a powwow with Big Chief Wife, and no peace-pipe in sight. She gets me in the house, away from Robby, who'd 've backed me up, and she rides the wild mustango up and down the living-room, and throws her tomahawk into the tortured victims, meaning me, and she says:

"Lowell Schmaltz, I've told you, and if I've told you once, I've told you a hundred times, that Minnie is a *very* sensitive and high-bred cat, and I will not have her nerves all shattered by being annoyed by a lot of horrid dogs. I want you to find the rightful owner of this horrid dog and give him back."

"Give who back? The owner?" I says, just sitting down and lighting a cigar and trying to look like I was amused and there was nothing she could do or say that would get my goat. And of course I had her there: "Give who back? The owner?" I says.

"You know perfectly well and good what I mean," she says. "And I want you to find the horrid thing's owner at once!"

"Fine!" I says. "Sure! Of course all I've done is to advertise extensively in the *Advocate-Times*, which only has more circulation than any other two papers in this territory put together—or so they claim, and I've looked into it and I'm disposed to accept their figures," I says. "But of course that isn't enough. All right, I'll just tuck Jackie under my arm, and start right out—Let's see," I says, "there's only about six hundred thousand people in Zenith and the neighboring towns, within perhaps a twenty-eight or thirty mile radius of City Hall, and all I'll have to do will be to run around to *each* of 'em and say, 'Hey, mister, lost a dog?' That's all I'll have to do."

"Well, then, you can take the horrid beast out where you found him and leave him there," she says.

"I can, and I ain't going to," I says—flat. "I'm not going to have him run over by some damn' fool careless motorist," I says. "He's a valuable dog," I says.

"He's horrid—and he's terribly dirty. I never did see such a terribly dirty dog," she says.

"Oh, sure," I says. "Of course aside from the notorious fact that he's a water spaniel—and water spaniels' being, even if they ain't at present as fashionable as cocker spaniels or wire-haired terriers or Airdales, merely notoriously the cleanest dogs that exist," I says, "aside from that, you're dead right."

"But we don't need a dog anyway," she says.

Well say, that kind of got my goat.

"No," I says, "sure we don't. I don't, anyway. Think what I've got here to be chummy with in the evening. Elegant! This nice, fluffy, expensive feline cat, that hates me like hell, that won't sit in my lap, that cottons to you because you got nothing to do all day but stay home and pet it, while I have to be in my store, working my head off—to support a damn' cat! Fine!" I says.

But then I got serious, and after some remarks back and forth about how she *did* have things to do, like running the house and looking after my clothes and Robby and Delmerine—*you* know how any woman can make out like she works like a slave—after that I got serious, and I says:

"But seriously," I says, "when you come to look at it in a serious manner, what is a dog? What is a dog? What is he but man's greatest friend! Who so unselfish as a dog? Who so welcomes the weary man—yes, or woman, for that matter, if she treats 'em right!—when they come home weary from the day's labor? To say nothing of their being in many lands also useful in a practical way in helping to haul carts, also as watchmen.

"You forget," I told her, "all the wonderful things we've seen Rin Tin Tin do in the movies. Why say, I'll bet that dog's salary is higher than that of any film-author or even camera-man. But aside from that, think of some of the dogs of history. Think of those brave Saint Bernard dogs, going out with little barrels of brandy under their chins to rescue belated travelers in that pass in Germany, or wherever it was—though I never could understand," I admits, "why there were so many travelers that kept taking a chance and getting belated in the snow that they had to keep a whole corps of dogs running to rescue them all the time. But still, that was in old historic times, and maybe things were different from now, and of course no railroads—

"But in modern times," I told her, "I've heard an anecdote, and I got it mighty straight, from a fellow who knew the fellow who was in the story, and it seems this fellow was a trapper or a miner or a prospector or something like that, anyway he had a cabin 'way off in the Sierras or some place like that—high mountains, anyway—and seems it was the depth of winter, and this fellow's cabin was all snowed in, also the tracks and trails and all were deep buried in the snow.

"Well, seems this fellow had an accident, slipped down a crevasse or something like that, and busted his leg, seriously, but he managed to make his way. with great difficulty back to his cabin where his faithful dog, I never did learn the name of the dog, was waiting for him, and then as a result of the accident, he fell into a kind of fever, I suppose it was, and he lay there simply shot to pieces, and in great suffering, and attended only by this faithful dog, who couldn't, of course, do much to help him, but he did his best, and he was a mighty smart, clever dog, and the trapper, or whatever this fellow was, he trained this dog so's he'd bring a match or a drink of water or whatever it was the poor devil needed.

"But there wasn't any way of cooking any food—it goes without saying that that was something the dog couldn't help him with—and the trapper got worse and worse, and he was in great pain, and you could see the dog was worried about what to do, and then all of a sudden, one day by golly the dog gives a kind of a short quick yelp, and he dives right through the cabin window, head on, and he's gone—not one sound from him.

"Well, of course, the poor devil of a trapper, he thought his only friend had deserted him, and he gave himself up to die, and it was almost as bitter as the pain itself to think that he'd been deserted by the only friend he had.

"But all this time, the dog was not idle. He goes lickety-split, following the snow-obliterated trails as if by instinct, 'way down and down and down to the far-distant nearest village, and comes up to the doctor's house, where he'd been once several years before with his master.

"Well, the door is slightly ajar, and the dog busts in and whines at the feet of the doc, who was at dinner.

" 'You get to hell out of here—how'd you ever get in here anyway?' the doctor says, naturally not understanding the situation, and he chases the dog out and closes the door, but the dog stands there on the door-step, whining and otherwise trying to draw the attention of the doctor, till the doctor's wife begins to think something is wrong, and they cautiously let the dog in again and try to feed it, but it keeps tugging at the doc's pants-legs and refuses to eat a single morsel, till at last the doc says, 'Maybe I'm needed somewhere, and come to think of it, this dog looks like the dog that that trapper had back in the mountains when he came here one time.'

"So anyway, he takes a chance on it—of course he hasn't got any more idea than the man in the moon where this fellow lives, but he hitches up his cutter, and the dog runs along in front of them, picking out the best road, and they come to this cabin, hours and hours from anywhere, and the doc goes in, and here's this fellow with the fever and busted leg in dire need. Well, he tends to him and gets him some chow and is all ready to move him to civilization when he thinks of this poor dog that's saved him, and he turns to find him, and the poor little tyke has crawled into a corner and fallen dead, exhausted by his terrible race for life!

"That's what dogs can do," I tell her, and then I tells her some other absolutely authentic anecdotes about dogs and we pass a lot of remarks back and forth, and final result is, she says all right; she'll stand my keeping the dog, but he's got to stay out of the house, and I can build him a dog-kennel out beside the garage.

But you know how things go. One morning I gets up early and has breakfast by myself, and there's Jackie whining outside, and I takes a chance and lets him in and feeds him, and that cat comes marching into the room like a Episcopalopian rector leading a procession, and Jackie gets one squint at her and chases her up on the buffet, and just then Mamie comes in and–

Say, I didn't stop with no buffet; I didn't stop till I'd reached the top of the Second National Bank Tower. But seriously, though, she certainly give Jackie and me such an earful that–

Well, Joe Minchin had planned a poker party for that evening and I hadn't kind of intended to go, but Mame bawled hell out of me so at breakfast that later in the day I said I'd go, and I went, and I got lit to the eyebrows, if the truth be known–say, I was simply ossified.

So I comes home late, thinking I was both the King and Queen of Sheba, and then I got dizzy and just about the time Mame'd thought up her adjectives and was ready to describe me for the catalogue of domestic sons of guns, I couldn't tarry, oh, no longer–I had to be wending my way into the bathroom P.D.Q., and there, say, I lost everything but my tonsils. Wow!

Well, Mame was awful' nice to me. She helped me back into bed, and she bathed my forehead, and she got some black coffee for me–only what I wanted was a good cyanide of potassium cocktail–and when I woke up in the morning she just kind of laughed, and I thought I was going to get by without the matrimonial cat-o'-nine-tails–I actually thought that, and me married over twenty years to her!

So when my head gets itself reduced to not more'n six or seven normal times its ordinary or wearing size, and I gets up for breakfast, not more'n twenty or twenty-two hours late, and she's still bright and–oh God, what a blessing!–still keeping her trap shut and not telling me about salvation, why, I thinks I'm safe, and then just when I stagger up from breakfast and thinks I'll go down to my store, if I can remember where I left my garage last night, why, she smiles brighter'n ever, and says in a nice, sweet, cool, Frigidaire voice:

"Sit down a moment, will you please, Low. There's something I want to say to you."

Well–

Oh, I died with my face to the foemen. I tried to take the barricades in one gallant dash, like Douglas Fairbanks. I says briefly, "I know what you want to say," I says. "You want to say I was lit, last night. Say, that isn't any news. By this time it's so old and well known that you can find it among the problems in the sixth-grade arithmetic book," I says. "Look here," I says, "it wasn't entirely my fault. It was that God-awful bootleg hootch I got at Joe's. It'd been all right if it'd been honest liquor."

"You were *disgusting,*" she says. "If my poor father and mother hadn't passed away, and if my sister Edna wasn't such a crank about theosophy that nobody could live with her, I'd 've left you before dawn, let me tell you that."

Well, I got sore. I'm not a very bad-tempered cuss, as you know, but after along about twenty years, this threatening-to-leave-you business gets a little tiresome.

"Fine," I says. "You're always blowing about how much you know about clothes. I'll be glad to give you a knock-down to some of the big guys at Benson, Hanley and Koch's," I says, "and probably they'll make you buyer in the ladies' garments department," I says, "and you won't have to go on standing for a gorilla of a husband like me."

And she says all right, by God she'll do it!

And we seesaw back and forth, and I kind of apologizes, and she says she didn't mean it, and then we really gets down to business.

"But just the same," she says, "I'm not going to have that dog in the house again! You've not got the least consideration for my feelings. You talk so much about your dear old friends, like this horrible Joe Minchin, but you never give one moment's thought to what I need or like. You don't know what the word 'thoughtfulness' means."

"All right, I'll look it up in the dictionary," I says. "And speaking of *thoughtfulness,*" I says, "when I was going out last night, I found you'd been using my safety razor and hadn't cleaned it, and I was in a hurry and you'd neglected—By God," I says, "when I was a boy, a man had his sweaters to himself, without his wife or sister calmly up and using 'em, and he had his razor to himself, and he had his barber-shop to himself—"

"Yes, and he had his saloons to himself, and still has," she comes back at me. "And you talk about neglect! It isn't only me you neglect," she says, "when you go and get full of liquor, and it isn't simply the example you set the children, but it's the way you neglect the church and religion," she says.

"And of course I'm only a deacon in the church," I says. You know—sarcastic.

"Yes, and you know mighty good and well you only took the job because it'd give you a stand-in with the religious folks, and every Sunday you can, you sneak off and play golf instead of going to church. And that morning when Dr. Hickenlooper came in from Central Methodist and preached for us—that time when poor Dr. Edwards was sick and couldn't preach himself—"

"Sick? He was sick like a fox," I told her. "He just had a sore throat because he'd been off on a lecture trip, shooting his mouth off before a lot of women's clubs to rake in some extra dough, when he ought to stayed home here and tended to his job."

"That's entirely aside from the question," she says, "and anyway, instead of listening to Dr. Hickenlooper like you ought to, you and a couple other deacons stayed out in the lobby of the church."

"Yuh, there's something to what you say," I told her. "Hickenlooper is a fine man. He's all for charity—providing some rich man provides the money for the charity. I don't believe he's ever smoked a cigar or had a nip of liquor in his life. He's a credit to the Methodist clergy. It's true he does bawl out his wife and his kids all the time, and it's true he nags his secretary all day long, but you can't blame a man that's busy with the Lord's work for being maybe a little irritable. In fact there's only one trouble with the holy man—he's the worst and most consistent liar in seven counties!

"I've heard him tell as his own experience things I know he read in books, because I've seen the books. And here's a story that our own pastor, Edwards, told us. Seems Hickenlooper met him in front of our church one Monday morning, and Hickenlooper says, 'Well, Dr. Edwards, my brother-in-law heard you preach yesterday, and he said it was the best sermon he ever heard in his life.'

" 'Well, that's nice,' Dr. Edwards says, 'but it just happens that I didn't preach yesterday.'

"I guess I'm a kind of a blowhard," I says to Mamie, "and in general I'm just a plug business man, while Hickenlooper addresses Chautauquas and addresses colleges and addresses Methodist conferences and writes articles for the magazines and writes lovely books about how chummy he and God and the sunsets are, but say, if that holy liar knew what even poor, ordinary business men like me really thought about him and what they said privately, he'd sneak off to a desert and never open his mouth again!"

Well say, that had Mamie wild—and don't you think for one moment, Walt, that she let me get by without a few interruptions that I haven't put into the story. And what I've just told you about this Hickenlooper bird—he looks like a prize-fighter and talks like a glad-hand circus ballyhooer, and he lies like a politician—was all straight, and she knew it. I've done a little lying myself, but I've never made a three-ring circus of it like him. But Mamie had a sneaking kind of admiration for him, I guess because he's big and strong and a great baby-kisser and girl-jollier. And she let loose on me, and what she said—Whee!

She said I encouraged Robby to smoke. She said I never used an ashtray—always scattered my ashes around the house—and I'm afraid she had me there. And she said she was sick of having my friends around the house all the time, and I bawled her out for high-hattin' 'em, and she said something about my driving too fast, and I come back with a few short sweet words about back-seat driving—she's the best single-handed non-participating Major Seagrove of the entire inhabited world. And—

And so on.

And that's just typical of a few home Board of Directors conferences we been having, and I'm pretty sick of it.

Not but what I'm just as mean as she is, at that, I suppose.

But I did by God keep old Jackie!

But I'm getting sick of the whole business—

Not, you understand, but what Mame is just as nice a pal as you'd want to find, in between tantrums. That time we were here and saw you and then went on and had our long talk with Coolidge in Washington, she was jolly the whole time. But more and more—

Say, I don't know as I ought to tell you about this, hardly, but this girl I was speaking of in New York—well, she isn't exactly a girl any more, but she's only thirty-eight and that's seventeen years younger'n I am—Erica, her name is, and say, she's one of the most talented little women I ever met.

By rights, she ought to be a world-renowned portrait-painter, but she's always run into the damnedest hard luck, and just now for a few years she's been working for the Pillstein and Lipshutz Christmas and Easter Greeting Card Company, where I always get my greeting cards. Of course by rights I'm not a stationer but stick right to office supplies, but same time, along at these holiday times, I feel it does kind of brighten up the business to stock a few handsome cards, and pay—say, it brings me in hundreds a year.

Well, Erica designs a lot of cards—*darn'* smart intelligent girl—does the drawings and the poems and the whole thing. Say, you've probably seen some of her cards. It was her that wrote that famous one that had such a big sale—the one with the two kids shaking hands in front of an old schoolhouse, and then a lot of holly and so on, and the poem:

Dear friend, this season of ice and snow
Does not make love the colder grow,
But on contrary pries apart
Wider the cockles of the heart.

'Tis years since we were boys together
In jolly winter and summer weather,
'Tis years indeed since we have met,
But our old friendship I'll ne'er forget.

Say, it'd surprise you how many of those cards a lot of hard-boiled old business men buy .to send to fellows they haven't seen for years. I tell you, that fellow Manny Pillstein is a genius. Of course there've been greeting cards for years, but he was the first one to put the business on a scientific, nationally advertised basis, and really standardize and Ford-ize all this Holiday Good Will so it'd amount to something. They say he's increased the business 10,000 per cent—made it as practical as chain grocery stores or even Mother's Day.

Well, I met Erica there at his place, and I was alone in New York, and I invited her to dinner, and I blew her to a nice little feed with a bottle of real domestic Chianti. Well, we got to talking and telling our ideas and so on, and come to find out, poor kid, she was pretty near as lonely in New York as I was.

And then every time I blew into the Big Burg—alone—I'd see her, and—

Now say, her relations and mine was just as pure as the driven snow. Maybe I'd kiss her in a taxicab, or something like that, and tell the truth I don't know how far I'd 've gone if I'd got her off to Atlantic City or something like that, but my God, with my position and my responsibilities, both financial and social, I didn't want to get into no complications. To tell the truth (and I'd never tell another living soul but you), one evening I did go up to her flat—But only that once! And I got scared, and just used to see her at restaurants.

But be the cause what it may, our relations were entirely and absolutely friendly and intellectual, and know what she told me?

When I told her what I thought of her work—and to me, and I told her so, she's the best greeting-card artist in the country—she told me my appreciation was the greatest encouragement and the greatest incentive to go onward and upward to finer and better art that she'd ever received! And let me tell you, I've never had anything buck *me* up, in turn, like her appreciation of my appreciation. Whereas at home—

If I try to tell Mame that she plays a good mitt of bridge, or that I think she's got on an elegant new dress, or she sang some song at some church affair real pretty, or like that, she just looks like she was saying, "Who the hell ever told you *you* was a connooser?"

Oh God, I suppose we'll always go on, just about the same way, but if I was younger—

Well, I ain't!

Well, Walt, I guess it's getting late and about time for us to turn in—you'll have to be in your office tomorrow, and I think I'll take that 12:18 for home, if I can get a Pullman.

It's been a mighty great privilege to have this frank talk with you. I certainly will take your advice. I'll try to keep from talking and running on so much—you noticed this evening at supper I hardly said a word, but just listened to your good wife. You bet. I've learned my lesson. I'm going to concentrate on selling the goods, and not discuss subjects and topics all the time.

And I hope you'll give my schedule a mighty close once-over and see your way to advance me the loan.

You remember how I've always turned to you. Remember that month I spent with you boys on your granddad's farm when we were 'long about twelve?

God, what fun that was! Regular idyl, you might say, like a fellow can't touch again in these later care-ridden and less poetic years. Remember how we stole those mushmelons from that old farmer, and when he got sassy about it we went back and smashed all the rest of 'em? Remember how we hid the alarm-clock in the church so it went off during the sermon? Remember how we greased the springboard so's that Irish kid slipped on it and almost busted his back? Gosh, I had to laugh!

Oh, those were great days, and you and me always did understand each other, Walt, and don't forget that there's no firm in the world could give you better security for the loan.

1928

CHAPTER THREE

IMAGISTS AND REGIONAL POETS

It is significant that the three first practitioners of the new fiction just examined all came from the Midwest. Rebellion against the conventional standards and conservative policies of the established centers of culture in the East—especially Boston and New York—was one of the first signs of "modern" literature in America, in poetry and fiction. Flight to Europe, as Frost and many other poets and novelists considered themselves forced into, or a turn toward Chicago and Harriet Monroe's *Poetry,* where some of Robinson's early verses appeared, became for a while the established patterns. Later there was to be critical dissension between the expatriates and those who had turned toward Chicago and remained, but for a time they made a common cause of their rebellion against the standards of the East. The Midwestern group is well represented by the triumvirate of Vachel Lindsay, Edgar Lee Masters, and Carl Sandburg; the expatriated Imagists, by Amy Lowell; and a special form of Eastern rebellion, by Edna St. Vincent Millay.

Born within a decade of one another (Lindsay and Sandburg were born in Illinois; Masters moved there from Kansas when still a baby), the Midwestern group came to be known as "the Prairie poets." Sandburg towers over the group, but Lindsay and Masters made important contributions also, if in quite different ways.

Vachel Lindsay, a voracious reader of Poe but more significantly in the tradition of Whitman, had an evangelical passion for reform. His crusading spirit took many directions, including early lectures for the YMCA and the Anti-Saloon League. What he wanted most was to bring to the "folk" of America a sense of its Beauty, to see, as Whitman had seen, that America itself was the greatest poem, and that the "myth" of America could best be shaped out of the American experience.

It is not surprising therefore that he would find American historical and folk heroes as ideal subjects: Andy Jackson, Abe Lincoln, Johnny Appleseed, Daniel Boone. His celebrated walking tours—from the South into the North in 1906, and, more importantly, from Springfield toward California in 1912—suggest a passionate involvement with the problem of communicating directly with the people, a direct involvement that probably has no parallel in American literature. The "tone" of this involvement is well suggested by the preface to his *Handy Guide for Beggars*, reprinted in this volume, as well as the better known *Rhymes To Be Traded for Bread*, the slim, sixteen-page volume of poems he took with him on his second tour to be sold or bartered for sustenance.

His interest in the oral tradition of poetry, no less than his earnestness, certainly helps account for the popularity of his "General William Booth Enters into Heaven," when it appeared in Harriet Monroe's *Poetry* in 1913. Poetry was best when it was "performed," sometimes to musical accompaniment, sometimes not, but almost always to the rhythms of popular songs or hymns and with careful marginal notations as to the appropriate pace, volume, and inflection it should carry. There is also always a quiet, lyrical side to Lindsay's poetry—as there is to both Whitman's and Sandburg's—that suggests a melancholy brooding only seemingly at variance with his "louder" voices. Lindsay's "A Net to Snare the Moonlight" and "The Flower-Fed Buffaloes" are both good examples. That the passionate and enthusiastic evangelism of his early years was followed by a deepening morbidity culminating in his suicide in 1931 is perhaps another aspect of this same dichotomy.

Although often linked with Lindsay, whose biography he wrote, Edgar Lee Masters, the second of the prairie poets, has very little in common with the troubadour. Misanthropic and cynical where Lindsay was ebullient and optimistic—a hater of Lincoln, for example, in contrast to Lindsay's reverent admiration of him—Masters' reputation rests almost entirely on one book, his *Spoon River Anthology* (1915, 1916), although he penned many verses before this and many more afterwards, in addition to novels, essays, and biographies of Whitman, Lincoln, and Mark Twain. It is difficult, however, to overestimate the impact made by his Spoon River poems.

His successful career as a practicing Chicago lawyer and the prolix but inconsequential volumes of verse he had turned out as early as 1910 would not seemingly have justified a prediction of the achievement of his *Spoon River Anthology*. However, his boyhood experiences in Petersburg and Lewistown, the Illinois villages from which he compounded his fictional Spoon River; his legalistic training which led him to look beneath what people appear to be and to see what they really are; his admiration for Sandburg's success with free-verse forms; and, most importantly, his reading of *The Greek Anthology*, pressed on him by William Marion

Reedy, St. Louis editor of *Reedy's Mirror* and an early admirer of Masters' verse—all coalesced into those still shocking "lives" he recounted in *Spoon River.* The epitaph form was ideal for his purposes: it allowed each person to give the lie to the words or symbols carved on his gravestone at the same time that it allowed contrasting points of view about a given incident, episode, or character. More than the usual number of epitaphs are given in this collection to suggest the interrelatedness of the poems, although their scope is best seen only when all 246 poems are read together. Thirty-two important, new poems were added to the 1916 edition of the *Anthology*. The continuity of the *Anthology* was seen with fresh vitality late in 1963 when a dramatic review based on Spoon River opened to high critical praise in New York's Booth Theater.

Masters' thumbnail biographies of his Spoon River inhabitants—his dreamers and poets and saints, his drunkards and skinflints and atheists, for whom life was a fulfillment or a burden, an accomplishment or a frustration, a satisfaction or a meaningless torture—hit America with unprecedented force. The "revolt from the village" was thus underway in poetry sometime before the comparable revolts (in fiction) of Sherwood Anderson's *Winesburg, Ohio* and Lewis' *Main Street.*

Perhaps, however, the misnamed "Midwestern Renaissance" has its best poetical representative in Carl Sandburg, certainly the dean of the prairie poets. In both spirit and practice, he was much more closely allied with Lindsay than he was with Masters: Sandburg also was in the tradition of Whitman; he was a faithful recorder of the literature of the "folk," a collector of their songs and ballads; and his biography of Lincoln is among the most highly regarded in its field. Few American poets have recorded the prairie states more memorably, the occupations and panoramas of their rural aspects no less than their metropolitan ones, especially as represented by Chicago. If he saw that what was most enduring in America was in the beliefs, the proverbs, the stories, and the idioms of the people, he clearly saw also that the people's spirit was as much caught in the clean coldness of steel and the upward thrust of skyscrapers as in its fields of grain.

Sandburg has a strong social conscience. He has never been blind to the problems and injustices accorded the common man when confronted by the complexities of an industrialized civilization. If he truly is a laureate of industrial America, he is no less truly a lyricist. "Nocturne in a Deserted Brickyard" and "Flowers Tell Months" reveal affinities with the Imagists as clear-cut as his more famous "Chicago" poems do with Whitman. His deliberate disregard of conventional form, his use of slang and colloquialisms, his avoidance of rhyme, his occasional prosiness are as characteristic of his quiet moods as of his declamatory ones.

Sandburg's books for children, beginning with the memorable *Rootabaga Stories* (1922), are already accepted classics. At the age of seventy he wrote his first novel, *Remembrance Rock* (1948), and his autobiographical account of his Midwestern youth, *Always the Young Strangers,* appeared in 1952.

Since Sandburg's voice is still strong and vigorous, it is difficult to remember that his early Chicago poems, like Lindsay's early works, found their first wide audience through Harriet Monroe's *Poetry,* some fifty years ago. When they are joined with Masters', however, we see a contribution to the new poetry that is at once vital and varied. Their particularized poetic voices are the most authentic we have of the modern Midwestern rebellion in early twentieth-century American poetry.

Amy Lowell's militant advocacy of imagism represents a different stream of poetic rebelliousness, although the enemy—conventional moralizing and standardized verse patterns—was a common one. Unlike the prairie poets, she emerged from the East, from the distinguished Massachusetts family of Lowells, and from a traditional Brahmin education: tutors, private schools, travel abroad.

Close to thirty before she definitely selected a literary career, she was almost forty when her first book of poems appeared, *A Dome of Many-Coloured Glass* (1912), a conventional and for the most part undistinguished volume. The next year, in England, she met the Imagist group—Pound, Hilda Doolittle, Richard Aldington, and John Gould Fletcher, among others—who were in the vanguard of the expatriated new poetry movement. Their aggressive advocacy of imagism represented exactly the kind of cause she could support. Her second volume, *Sword Blades and Poppy Seed* (1914), clearly reveals her attraction to the new principles: precision, clarity, and accuracy of description; the language of common speech; new rhythms; absolute freedom in the choice of subject matter; concentration.

Pound soon found himself displaced as leader of the movement—it had degenerated into "amygism," he later charged—and for the next few years Amy Lowell became America's most militant supporter of the new poetry. She edited, after Pound, the annual anthologies of *Some Imagist Poets.* She travelled widely to lecture and read—and crusade. She wrote two critical volumes related to influences upon and principles of the Imagists, and she firmly established for herself a place among the poets of her day with her *Men, Women and Ghosts* (1916), perhaps the most important collection of her own verse. Without Amy Lowell the new poetry movement would have been far less turbulent, perhaps less influential, certainly far less exciting than it was.

Edna St. Vincent Millay's poetic rebellion was in quite another direction. Precocious enough as a child to publish verses in the *St. Nicholas* magazine, her first fame came in 1912 (she was only twenty) when her poem "Renascence" appeared in Mitchell Kennerley's anthology *The Lyric Year* but was not awarded its prize, a distinction many readers and

critics thought it should have had. It eventually won her a patr
however, and she was able to attend Barnard College and later Va
from which she graduated in 1917, the same year *Renascence,* her
and perhaps most influential volume of verses, was published. She then moved to Greenwich Village, became a leader of female bohemianism, supported herself with articles and stories (under various pseudonyms), became associated with some productions of the Provincetown Players, and capped her capacity for the notorious with a second volume of verses deliberately calculated to bait the bourgeoisie, *A Few Figs from Thistles* (1920).

The reputation she thereby gained as a female spokesman for "flaming youth," as a Jazz Age iconoclast among the Lost Generation of Fitzgerald and Hemingway, perhaps obscured for a time her talent for the delicate lyric and the classical sonnet. Even so, it was for the quieter vein of her *Harp Weaver and Other Poems* (1923) that she was awarded a Pulitzer Prize. The sonnets and lyrics of her later volumes, when coupled with the poems of the early *Renascence,* are now considered her most enduring work, in spite of her concern in the 1930's and '40's with the ugly realities of that world.

The new poetry in America was marked by exceptional variety and experimentation. All these poets were impatient with rigidity and propriety, with convention and precedent, as Robinson and Frost had been. Yet, with all the bombast, there was in each a quiet lyrical strain—sometimes brooding, sometimes ecstatic—that was all the more memorable because of individualized discoveries of effective ways to reveal the truth. In one way or another, a significant part of modern American poetry is what these five poets made it.

[Nicholas] Vachel Lindsay

(1879-1931)

CHRONOLOGY:

1879 Born November 10, in Springfield, Illinois.

1897-1900 Hiram College, Ohio.

1900-03 Studied at The Chicago Art Institute.

1904-05 Studied at the New York School of Art; began Anti-Saloon and YMCA lecturing.

1906 Made walking tour in the South.

1909 *The Tramp's Excuse and Other Poems.*

1912 Made walking tour through the Midwest and Southwest; *Rhymes To Be Traded for Bread.*

1913 *General William Booth Enters into Heaven and Other Poems.*

1914 *Adventures While Preaching the Gospel of Beauty; The Congo and Other Poems.*

1915 *The Art of the Moving Pictures.*
1916 *A Handy Guide for Beggars.*
1917 *The Chinese Nightingale and Other Poems.*
1920 *The Golden Whales of California, and Other Rhymes in the American Language; The Golden Book of Springfield.*
1923 *Going-to-the-Sun; Collected Poems.*
1926 *Going-to-the-Stars; The Candle in the Cabin: A Weaving Together of Script and Singing.*
1929 *The Litany of Washington Street; Every Soul Is a Circus.*
1931 Committed suicide on December 5, at Springfield.

BIBLIOGRAPHY:

Collected Poems by Vachel Lindsay (New York, 1923; revised and illustrated, 1925) is still the only collected edition of his poetry. Hazelton Spencer's edition, *Selected Poems of Vachel Lindsay* (New York, 1931), is, however, a good sampling.

Two biographies are significant: Edgar Lee Master's *Vachel Lindsay* (New York, 1935), and Mark Harris' *City of Discontent: An Interpretive Biography* (Indianapolis, 1952).

An important bibliography is in Allen Tate, *Sixty American Poets, 1896-1944* (Rev. ed.; Washington, 1954); for studies of individual poems, see Joseph M. Kuntz, *Poetry Explication* (Rev. ed.; Denver, 1962).

From A Handy Guide for Beggars, *Especially Those of the Poetic Fraternity, Being sundry explorations, made while afoot and penniless in Florida, Georgia, North Carolina, Tennessee, Kentucky, New Jersey, and Pennsylvania. These adventures convey and illustrate the rule of beggary for poets and some others.*

Dedication and Preface of *A Handy Guide for Beggars*

There are one hundred new poets in the villages of the land. This Handy Guide is dedicated first of all *to them.*

It is also dedicated to the younger sons of the wide earth, to the runaway boys and girls getting further from home every hour, to the prodigals who are still wasting their substance in riotous living, be they gamblers or blasphemers or plain drunks; to those heretics of whatever school to whom life is a rebellion with banners; to those who are willing to accept counsel if it be made counsel.

This book is also dedicated to those budding philosophers who realize that every creature is a beggar in the presence of the beneficient sun, to those righteous ones who know that all righteousness is as filthy rags.

Moreover, as an act of contrition, reënlistment and fellowship this book is dedicated to all the children of Don Quixote who see giants where most folks see windmills: those Galahads dear to Christ and those virgin sisters of Joan of Arc who serve the lepers on their knees and march in shabby armor against the proud, who look into the lightning with the eyes of the mountain cat. They do more soldierly things every day than this book records, yet they are mine own people, my nobler kin to whom I have been recreant, and so I finally dedicate this book *to them.*

These are the rules of the road:—
(1) Keep away from the Cities;
(2) Keep away from the railroads;
(3) Have nothing to do with money and carry no baggage;
(4) Ask for dinner about quarter after eleven;
(5) Ask for supper, lodging and breakfast about quarter of five;
(6) Travel alone;
(7) Be neat, deliberate, chaste and civil;
(8) Preach the Gospel of Beauty.

And without further parley, let us proceed to inculcate these, by illustration, precept and dogma.

Vachel Lindsay.

Springfield, Illinois,
November, 1916

A Net to Snare the Moonlight

(WHAT THE MAN OF FAITH SAID)

The dew, the rain and moonlight
All prove our Father's mind.
The dew, the rain and moonlight
Descend to bless mankind.

Come, let us see that all men
Have land to catch the rain,
Have grass to snare the spheres of dew,
And fields spread for the grain.

Yea, we would give to each poor man
Ripe wheat and poppies red,—
A peaceful place at evening
With the stars just overhead:

A net to snare the moonlight
A sod spread to the sun,
A place of toil by daytime,
Of dreams when toil is done. 1913

General William Booth Enters into Heaven

(To be sung to the tune of "The Blood of the Lamb" with indicated instruments.)

I

(Bass drum beaten loudly.)
Booth led boldly with his big bass drum,
(Are you washed in the blood of the Lamb?)
The saints smiled gravely, and they said,
"He's come."
(Are you washed in the blood of the Lamb?)
Walking lepers followed, rank on rank,
Lurching bravos from the ditches dank,
Drabs from the alleyways and drug-fiends pale–
Minds still passion-ridden, soul-powers frail!
Vermin-eaten saints with moldy breath
Unwashed legions with the ways of death–
(Are you washed in the blood of the Lamb?)

(Banjos.)
Every slum had sent its half-a-score
The round world over.–(Booth had groaned for more.)
Every banner that the wide world flies
Bloomed with glory and transcendent dyes.
Big-voiced lasses made their banjos bang!
Tranced, fanatical, they shrieked and sang;–
"Are you washed in the blood of the Lamb?"
Hallelujah! It was queer to see
Bull-necked convicts with that land make free!
Loons with trumpets blowed a blare, blare, blare–
On, on, upward thro' the golden air!
(Are you washed in the blood of the Lamb?)

II

(Bass drum slower and softer.)
Booth died blind, and still by faith he trod,
Eyes still dazzled by the ways of God.
Booth led boldly, and he looked the chief:
Eagle countenance in sharp relief,
Beard a-flying, air of high command
Unabated in that holy land.

(Sweet flute music.)
Jesus came from out the Courthouse door,
Stretched His hands above the passing poor.
Booth saw not, but led his queer ones there
'Round and 'round the mighty Courthouse square.
Yet in an instant all that blear review
Marched on spotless, clad in raiment new.
The lame were straightened, withered limbs uncurled,
And blind eyes opened on a new sweet world.

(Bass drum louder.)
Drabs and vixens in a flash made whole!
Gone was the weasel-head, the snout, the jowl!
Sages and sibyls now, and athletes clean,
Rulers of empires, and of forests green!

(Grand chorus of all instruments. Tambourines to the foreground.)
The hosts were sandaled and their wings were fire!
    (Are you washed in the blood of the Lamb?)
But their noise played havoc with the angel-choir.
    (Are you washed in the blood of the Lamb?)
Oh, shout Salvation! it was good to see
Kings and Princes by the Lamb set free.
The banjos rattled and the tambourines
Jing-jing-jingled in the hands of Queens!

(Reverently sung, no instruments.)
And when Booth halted by the curb for prayer
He saw his Master thro' the flag-filled air.
Christ came gently with a robe and crown
For Booth the soldier, while the throng knelt down.
He saw King Jesus. They were face to face,
And he knelt a-weeping in that holy place.
    Are you washed in the blood of the Lamb? 1913

Abraham Lincoln Walks at Midnight

(IN SPRINGFIELD, ILLINOIS)

It is portentous, and a thing of state
That here at midnight, in our little town
A mourning figure walks, and will not rest,
Near the old court-house pacing up and down,

Or by his homestead, or in shadowed yards
He lingers where his children used to play,
Or through the market, on the well-worn stones
He stalks until the dawn-stars burn away.

A bronzed, lank man! His suit of ancient black,
A famous high top-hat and plain worn shawl
Make him the quaint great figure that men love,
The prairie-lawyer, master of us all.

He cannot sleep upon his hillside now.
He is among us:—as in times before!
And we who toss and lie awake for long
Breathe deep, and start, to see him pass the door.

His head is bowed. He thinks on men and kings.
Yea, when the sick world cries, how can he sleep?
Too many peasants fight, they know not why,
Too many homesteads in black terror weep.

The sins of all the war-lords burn his heart.
He sees the dreadnaughts scouring every main.
He carries on his shawl-wrapped shoulders now
The bitterness, the folly and the pain.

He cannot rest until a spirit-dawn
Shall come;—the shining hope of Europe free:
The league of sober folk, the Workers' Earth,
Bringing long peace to Cornland, Alp and Sea.

It breaks his heart that kings must murder still,
That all his hours of travail here for men
Seem yet in vain. And who will bring white peace
That he may sleep upon his hill again? 1914

The Flower-Fed Buffaloes

The flower-fed buffaloes of the spring
In the days of long ago,
Ranged where the locomotives sing
And the prairie flowers lie low:—
The tossing, blooming, perfumed grass
Is swept away by the wheat,
Wheels and wheels and wheels spin by

In the spring that still is sweet.
But the flower-fed buffaloes of the spring
Left us, long ago.
They gore no more, they bellow no more,
They trundle around the hills no more:—
With the Blackfeet, lying low.
With the Pawnees, lying low,
Lying low. 1924

Edgar Lee Masters

(1868-1950)

CHRONOLOGY:

1868 Born on August 23, in Garnett, Kansas.

1869 Moved to New Salem, Illinois.

1880 Settled in Lewistown, Illinois (which, with neighboring Petersburg, became his fictional "Spoon River").

1889-90 Attended Knox College, Galesburg, Illinois.

1891 Admitted to the Bar.

1892 Moved to Chicago to write and practice law.

1893-1914 Published eleven volumes, among them: *A Book of Verse* (1898); *Maximilian: A Play* (1902); *The New Star Chamber and Other Essays* (1904); *The Blood of the Prophets*, verse (1905).

1905 Began association with William Marion Reedy, and *Reedy's Mirror*.

1915 *Spoon River Anthology*.

1916 *Spoon River Anthology* (2nd ed., with thirty-two new poems).

1916-23 Published ten more books, including *Songs and Satires* (1916); *Domesday Book* (1920); *Children of the Market Place* (1922).

1923 Moved to New York.

1924-30 Published many more volumes, including *The New Spoon River* (1924); *Selected Poems* (1925); *The Fate of the Jury: An Epilogue to Domesday Book* (1929).

1931 *Lincoln, the Man* (perhaps his most notorious book).

1933-42 Additional volumes of verse, plays, novels; his biographies: on Vachel Lindsay (1935), Whitman (1937), Mark Twain (1938); and his autobiography, *Across Spoon River* (1936).

1950 He died on May 5.

BIBLIOGRAPHY:

No collected edition of Masters' poems has been published since his *Selected Poems* (New York, 1925). One of the best critical and biographical accounts is in Bernard Duffey's *The Chicago Renaissance in American Letters* (East Lansing, 1954).

For a bibliographical listing, see Allen Tate, *Sixty American Poets, 1896-1944* (Rev. ed.; Washington, 1954); for studies of individual poems, Joseph M. Kuntz, *Poetry Explication* (Rev. ed.; Denver, 1962).

From *Spoon River Anthology*

The Hill

Where are Elmer, Herman, Bert, Tom and Charley,
The weak of will, the strong of arm, the clown, the boozer, the fighter?
All, all, are sleeping on the hill.

One passed in a fever,
One was burned in a mine,
One was killed in a brawl,
One died in a jail,
One fell from a bridge toiling for children and wife—
All, all are sleeping, sleeping, sleeping on the hill.

Where are Ella, Kate, Mag, Lizzie and Edith,
The tender heart, the simple soul, the loud, the proud, the happy one?—
All, all, are sleeping on the hill.

One died in shameful child-birth,
One of a thwarted love,
One at the hands of a brute in a brothel,
One of a broken pride, in the search for heart's desire,
One after life in far-away London and Paris
Was brought to her little space by Ella and Kate and Mag—
All, all are sleeping, sleeping, sleeping on the hill.

Where are Uncle Isaac and Aunt Emily,
And old Towny Kincaid and Sevigne Houghton,
And Major Walker who had talked
With venerable men of the revolution?—
All, all, are sleeping on the hill.

They brought them dead sons from the war,
And daughters whom life had crushed,
And their children fatherless, crying—
All, all are sleeping, sleeping, sleeping on the hill.

Where is Old Fiddler Jones
Who played with life all his ninety years,
Braving the sleet with bared breast,
Drinking, rioting, thinking neither of wife nor kin,
Nor gold, nor love, nor heaven?
Lo! he babbles of the fish-frys of long ago,
Of the horse-races of long ago at Clary's Grove,
Of what Abe Lincoln said
One time at Springfield.

1915

Cassius Hueffer

They have chiseled on my stone the words:
'His life was gentle, and the elements so mixed in him
That nature might stand up and say to all the world,
This was a man.'
Those who knew me smile
As they read this empty rhetoric.
My epitaph should have been:
'Life was not gentle to him,
And the elements so mixed in him
That he made warfare on life,
In the which he was slain.'
While I lived I could not cope with slanderous tongues,
Now that I am dead I must submit to an epitaph
Graven by a fool! 1915

Knowlt Hoheimer

I was the first fruits of the battle of Missionary Ridge.
When I felt the bullet enter my heart
I wished I had staid at home and gone to jail
For stealing the hogs of Curl Trenary,
Instead of running away and joining the army.
Rather a thousand times the county jail
Than to lie under this marble figure with wings,
And this granite pedestal
Bearing the words, "*Pro Patria.*"
What do they mean, anyway? 1915

Lydia Puckett

Knowlt Hoheimer ran away to the war
The day before Curl Trenary
Swore out a warrant through Justice Arnett
For stealing hogs.
But that's not the reason he turned a soldier.
He caught me running with Lucius Atherton.
We quarreled and I told him never again
To cross my path.
Then he stole the hogs and went to the war—
Back of every soldier is a woman. 1915

Margaret Fuller Slack

I would have been as great as George Eliot
But for an untoward fate.
For look at the photograph of me made by Penniwit,
Chin resting on hand, and deep-set eyes—
Gray, too, and far-searching.
But there was the old, old problem:
Should it be celibacy, matrimony or unchastity?
Then John Slack, the rich druggist, wooed me,
Luring me with the promise of leisure for my novel,
And I married him, giving birth to eight children,
And had no time to write.
It was all over with me, anyway,
When I ran the needle in my hand
While washing the baby's things,
And died from lock-jaw, an ironical death.
Hear me, ambitious souls,
Sex is the curse of life! 1915

Editor Whedon

To be able to see every side of every question;
To be on every side, to be everything, to be nothing long;
To pervert truth, to ride it for a purpose,
To use great feelings and passions of the human family
For base designs, for cunning ends,
To wear a mask like the Greek actors—
Your eight-page paper—behind which you huddle,
Bawling through the megaphone of big type:
'This is I, the giant.'
Thereby also living the life of a sneak-thief,
Poisoned with the anonymous words
Of your clandestine soul.
To scratch dirt over scandal for money,
And exhume it to the winds for revenge,
Or to sell papers,
Crushing reputations, or bodies, if need be,
To win at any cost, save your own life.
To glory in demoniac power, ditching civilization,
As a paranoiac boy puts a log on the track

And derails the express train.
To be an editor, as I was.
Then to lie here close by the river over the place
Where the sewage flows from the village,
And the empty cans and garbage are dumped,
And abortions are hidden. 1915

Daisy Fraser

Did you ever hear of Editor Whedon
Giving to the public treasury any of the money he received
For supporting candidates for office?
Or for writing up the canning factory
To get people to invest?
Or for suppressing the facts about the bank,
When it was rotten and ready to break?
Did you ever hear of the Circuit Judge
Helping anyone except the "Q" railroad,
Or the bankers? Or did Rev. Peet or Rev. Sibley
Give any part of their salary, earned by keeping still,
Or speaking out as the leaders wished them to do,
To the building of the water works?
But I—Daisy Fraser who always passed
Along the streets through rows of nods and smiles,
And coughs and words such as "there she goes,"
Never was taken before Justice Arnett
Without contributing ten dollars and costs
To the School fund of Spoon River! 1915

Mrs. Kessler

Mr. Kessler, you know, was in the army,
And he drew six dollars a month as a pension,
And stood on the corner talking politics,
Or sat at home reading Grant's Memoirs;
And I supported the family by washing,
Learning the secrets of all the people
From their curtains, counterpanes, shirts and skirts.
For things that are new grow old at length,
They're replaced with better or none at all:
People are prospering or falling back.
And rents and patches widen with time;

No thread or needle can pace decay,
And there are stains that baffle soap,
And there are colors that run in spite of you,
Blamed though you are for spoiling a dress.
Handkerchiefs, napery, have their secrets–
The laundress, Life, knows all about it.
And I, who went to all the funerals
Held in Spoon River, swear I never
Saw a dead face without thinking it looked
Like something washed and ironed. 1915

Harry Wilmans

I was just turned twenty-one,
And Henry Phipps, the Sunday-school superintendent,
Made a speech in Bindle's Opera House.
"The honor of the flag must be upheld," he said,
"Whether it be assailed by a barbarous tribe of Tagalogs
Or the greatest power in Europe."
And we cheered and cheered the speech and the flag he waved
As he spoke.
And I went to the war in spite of my father,
And followed the flag till I saw it raised
By our camp in a rice field near Manila,
And all of us cheered and cheered it.
But there were flies and poisonous things;
And there was the deadly water,
And the cruel heat,
And the sickening, putrid food;
And the smell of the trench just back of the tents
Where the soldiers went to empty themselves;
And there were the whores who followed us, full of syphilis;
And beastly acts between ourselves or alone,
With bullying, hatred, degradation among us,
And days of loathing and nights of fear
To the hour of the charge through the steaming swamp,
Following the flag,
Till I fell with a scream, shot through the guts.
Now there's a flag over me in Spoon River!
A flag! A flag! 1915

Godwin James

Harry Wilmans! You who fell in a swamp
Near Manila, following the flag,
You were not wounded by the greatness of a dream,
Or destroyed by ineffectual work,
Or driven to madness by Satanic snags;
You were not torn by aching nerves,
Nor did you carry great wounds to your old age.
You did not starve, for the government fed you.
You did not suffer yet cry "forward"
To an army which you led
Against a foe with mocking smiles,
Sharper than bayonets. You were not smitten down
By invisible bombs. You were not rejected
By those for whom you were defeated.
You did not eat the savorless bread
Which a poor alchemy had made from ideals.
You went to Manila, Harry Wilmans,
While I enlisted in the bedraggled army
Of fright-eyed, divine youths,
Who surged forward, who were driven back and fell,
Sick, broken, crying, shorn of faith,
Following the flag of the Kingdom of Heaven.
You and I, Harry Wilmans, have fallen
In our several ways, not knowing
Good from bad, defeat from victory,
Nor what face it is that smiles
Behind the demoniac mask. 1915

Lucinda Matlock

I went to the dances at Chandlerville,
And played snap-out at Winchester.
One time we changed partners,
Driving home in the moonlight of middle June,
And then I found Davis.
We were married and lived together for seventy years,
Enjoying, working, raising the twelve children,
Eight of whom we lost
Ere I had reached the age of sixty.

I spun, I wove, I kept the house, I nursed the sick,
I made the garden, and for holiday
Rambled over the fields where sang the larks,
And by Spoon River gathering many a shell,
And many a flower and medicinal weed—
Shouting to the wooded hills, singing to the green valleys.
At ninety-six I had lived enough, that is all,
And passed to a sweet repose.
What is this I hear of sorrow and weariness,
Anger, discontent and drooping hopes?
Degenerate sons and daughters,
Life is too strong for you—
It takes life to love Life.

1915

Carl [Charles August] Sandburg
(1878-)

CHRONOLOGY:

1878 Born on January 6, in Galesburg, Illinois.
1891-97 Occupied at various menial jobs during a wandering tour of the West.
1898 Served in Puerto Rico during Spanish-American War.
1898-1902 Attended Lombard College, Galesburg.
1904 *In Reckless Ecstasy*, privately printed.
1907-08 Was organizer for the Wisconsin Social-Democratic party and worked on Milwaukee newspapers.
1910-12 Was secretary to Emil Seidel, first socialist mayor of Milwaukee.
1914 "Chicago" and other early poems appeared in *Poetry*.
1916 *Chicago Poems.*
1918 *Cornhuskers.*
1919 *The Chicago Race Riots.*
1920 *Smoke and Steel.*
1922 *Slabs of the Sunburnt West; Rootabaga Stories.*
1923 *Rootabaga Pigeons.*
1926 *Abraham Lincoln: The Prairie Years*, biography.
1927 Edited *The American Songbag.*
1928 *Good Morning, America;* Phi Beta Kappa poet, Harvard University.
1929 *Steichen, the Photographer*, criticism.
1930 *Potato Face; Early Moon.*
1932 (with Paul M. Angle) *Mary Lincoln, Wife and Widow.*
1936 *The People, Yes.*
1938 Edited *A Lincoln and Whitman Miscellany.*
1939 *Abraham Lincoln: The War Years*, awarded a Pulitzer Prize the next year.
1943 *Home Front Memo*, sketches and miscellany.
1948 *Remembrance Rock*, novel.
1950 *Complete Poems* (awarded Pulitzer Prize the next year.)
1953 *Always the Young Strangers*, autobiography.
1960 *Wind Song.*

BIBLIOGRAPHY:

Sandburg's *Complete Poems* (New York, 1950) is the standard edition. His *Abraham Lincoln: The Prairie Years and the War Years* (New York, 1946) is a one-volume distillation of the six-volume biography. *The Sandburg Range* (New York, 1957) is a useful representative selection from his entire work, including some previously unpublished material.

Three book-length studies are Karl W. Detzer, *Carl Sandburg: A Study in Personality and Background* (New York, 1941), and those by Harry Golden (in 1961) and Richard Crowder (in 1964).

A bibliographical listing is in Allen Tate, *Sixty American Poets, 1896-1944* (Rev. ed.; Washington, 1954); for studies of individual poems, see Joseph M. Kuntz, *Poetry Explication* (Rev. ed.; Denver, 1962).

From Notes for a Preface

. . . . .

At the age of six, as my fingers first found how to shape the alphabet, I decided to become a person of letters. At the age of ten I had scrawled letters on slates, on paper, on boxes and walls and I formed an ambition to become a sign-painter. At twenty I was an American soldier in Puerto Rico writing letters printed in the home town paper. At twenty-one I went to West Point, being a classmate of Douglas MacArthur and Ulysses S. Grant III—for two weeks—returning home after passing in spelling, geography, history, failing in arithmetic and grammar. At twenty-three I edited a college paper and wrote many a paragraph that after a lapse of fifty years still seems funny, the same applying to the college yearbook I edited the following year. Across several years I wrote many odd pieces—two slim books—not worth later reprint. In a six-year period came four books of poetry having a variety of faults, no other person more keenly aware of their accomplishments and shortcomings than myself. In the two books for children, in this period, are a few cornland tales that go on traveling, one about "The Two Skyscrapers Who Decided to Have a Child." At fifty I had published a two-volume biography and *The American Songbag*, and there was puzzlement as to whether I was a poet, a biographer, a wandering troubadour with a guitar, a midwest Hans Christian Andersen, or a historian of current events whose newspaper reporting was gathered into a book *The Chicago Race Riots*. At fifty-one I wrote America's first biography of a photographer. At sixty-one came a four-volume biography, bringing doctoral degrees at Harvard, Yale, New York University, Wesleyan, Lafayette, Lincoln Memorial, Syracuse, Rollins, Dartmouth—Augustana and Uppsala at Stockholm. I am still studying verbs and the mystery of how they connect nouns. I am more suspicious of adjectives than at any other time in all my born days.

I have forgotten the meaning of twenty or thirty of my poems written thirty or forty years ago. I still favor several simple poems published long ago which continue to have an appeal for simple people. I have written by different methods and in a wide miscellany of moods and have seldom been afraid to travel in lands and seas where I met fresh scenes and new songs. All my life I have been trying to learn to read, to see and hear, and to write. At sixty-five I began my first novel, and the five years lacking a month I took to finish it, I was still traveling, still a seeker. I should like to think that as I go on writing there will be sentences truly alive, with verbs quivering, with nouns giving color and echoes. It could be, in the grace of God, I shall live to be eighty-nine, as did Hokusai, and speaking my farewell to earthly scenes, I might paraphrase: "If God had let me live five years longer I should have been a writer." 1950

Chicago

Hog Butcher for the World,
Tool Maker, Stacker of Wheat,
Player with Railroads and the Nation's Freight Handler;
Stormy, husky, brawling,
City of the Big Shoulders:

They tell me you are wicked and I believe them, for I have seen your painted women under the gas lamps luring the farm boys.
And they tell me you are crooked, and I answer: Yes, it is true I have seen the gunman kill and go free to kill again.
And they tell me you are brutal and my reply is: On the faces of women and children I have seen the marks of wanton hunger.
And having answered so I turn once more to those who sneer at this my city, and I give them back the sneer and say to them:
Come and show me another city with lifted head singing so proud to be alive and coarse and strong and cunning.
Flinging magnetic curses amid the toil of piling job on job, here is a tall bold slugger set vivid against the little soft cities;
Fierce as a dog with tongue lapping for action, cunning as a savage pitted against the wilderness,
        Bareheaded,
        Shoveling,
        Wrecking,
        Planning,
    Building, breaking, rebuilding,
Under the smoke, dust all over his mouth, laughing with white teeth,
Under the terrible burden of destiny laughing as a young man laughs,

Laughing even as an ignorant fighter laughs who has never lost a battle,
Bragging and laughing that under his wrist is the pulse, and under his ribs the heart of the people.
Laughing!
Laughing the stormy, husky, brawling laughter of youth; half-naked, sweating, proud to be Hog Butcher, Tool Maker, Stacker of Wheat, Player with Railroads, and Freight Handler to the Nation. 1914

Monotone

The monotone of the rain is beautiful,
And the sudden rise and slow relapse
Of the long multitudinous rain.

The sun on the hills is beautiful,
Or a captured sunset sea-flung,
Bannered with fire and gold.

A face I know is beautiful—
With fire and gold of sky and sea,
And the peace of long warm rain. 1916

Nocturne in a Deserted Brickyard

Stuff of the moon
Runs on the lapping sand
Out to the longest shadows.
Under the curving willows,
And round the creep of the wave line,
Fluxions of yellow and dusk on the waters
Make a wide dreaming pansy of an old pond in the night.
1916

I Am the People, the Mob

I am the people—the mob—the crowd—the mass.
Do you know that all the great work of the world is done through me?
I am the workingman, the inventor, the maker of the world's food and clothes.

I am the audience that witnesses history. The Napoleons come from me and the Lincolns. They die. And then I send forth more Napoleons and Lincolns.
I am the seed ground. I am a prairie that will stand for much plowing. Terrible storms pass over me. I forget. The best of me is sucked out and wasted. I forget. Everything but Death comes to me and makes me work and give up what I have. And I forget.
Sometimes I growl, shake myself and spatter a few red drops for history to remember. Then—I forget.
When I, the People, learn to remember, when I, the People, use the lessons of yesterday and no longer forget who robbed me last year, who played me for a fool,—then there will be no speaker in all the world say the name: "The People," with any fleck of a sneer in his voice or any far-off smile of derision.
The mob—the crowd—the mass—will arrive then. 1916

Under a Hat Rim

While the hum and the hurry
Of passing footfalls
Beat in my ear like the restless surf
Of a wind-blown sea,
A soul came to me
Out of the look on a face.

Eyes like a lake
Where a storm-wind roams
Caught me from under
The rim of a hat.
I thought of a midsea wreck
and bruised fingers clinging
to a broken state-room door. 1916

Flux

Sand of the sea runs red
Where the sunset reaches and quivers.
Sand of the sea runs yellow
Where the moon slants and wavers. 1916

Broken-face Gargoyles

All I can give you is broken-face gargoyles.
It is too early to sing and dance at funerals,
Though I can whisper to you I am looking for an undertaker humming a lullaby and throwing his feet in a swift and mystic buck-and-wing, now you see it and now you don't.

Fish to swim a pool in your garden flashing a speckled silver,
A basket of wine-saps filling your room with flame-dark for your eyes and the tang of valley orchards for your nose,
Such a beautiful pail of fish, such a beautiful peck of apples, I cannot bring you now.
It is too early and I am not footloose yet.

I shall come in the night when I come with a hammer and saw.
I shall come near your window, where you look out when your eyes open in the morning,
And there I shall slam together bird-houses and bird-baths for wing-loose wrens and hummers to live in, birds with yellow wing tips to blur and buzz soft all summer,
So I shall make little fool homes with doors, always open doors for all and each to run away when they want to.

I shall come just like that even though now it is early and I am not yet footloose,
Even though I am still looking for an undertaker with a raw, wind-bitten face and a dance in his feet.
I make a date with you (put it down) for six o'clock in the evening a thousand years from now.

All I can give you now is broken-face gargoyles.
All I can give you now is a double gorilla head with two fish mouths and four eagle eyes hooked on a street wall, spouting water and looking two ways to the ends of the street for the new people, the young strangers, coming, coming, always coming.

It is early.
I shall yet be footloose.   1920

Accomplished Facts

Every year Emily Dickinson sent one friend the first arbutus bud in her garden.

In a last will and testament Andrew Jackson remembered a friend with the gift of George Washington's pocket spy-glass.

Napoleon too, in a last testament, mentioned a silver watch taken from the bedroom of Frederick the Great, and passed along this trophy to a particular friend.

O. Henry took a blood carnation from his coat lapel and handed it to a country girl starting work in a bean bazaar, and scribbled: "Peach blossoms may or may not stay pink in city dust."

So it goes. Some things we buy, some not.
Tom Jefferson was proud of his radishes, and Abe
Lincoln blacked his own boots, and Bismarck called
Berlin a wilderness of brick and newspapers.

So it goes. There are accomplished facts.
Ride, ride, ride on in the great new blimps—
Cross unheard-of oceans, circle the planet.
When you come back we may sit by five hollyhocks.
We might listen to boys fighting for marbles.
The grasshopper will look good to us.

So it goes . . . 1920

Flowers Tell Months

Gold buttons in the garden today—
Among the brown-eyed susans the golden spiders are gambling
The blue sisters of the white asters speak to each other.

After the travel of the snows—
Buttercups come in a yellow rain,
Johnny-jump-ups in a blue mist—
Wild azaleas with a low spring cry. 1928

From *The People, Yes*

The people will live on.
The learning and blundering people will live on.
They will be tricked and sold and again sold
And go back to the nourishing earth for rootholds,
The people so peculiar in renewal and comeback
You can't laugh off their capacity to take it.
The mammoth rests between his cyclonic dramas.

The people so often sleepy, weary, enigmatic,
is a vast huddle with many units saying:
"I earn my living.
I make enough to get by
and it takes all my time.
If I had more time
I could do more for myself
and maybe for others.
I could read and study
and talk things over
and find out about things.
It takes time.
I wish I had the time."

The people is a tragic and comic two-face: hero and hoodlum: phantom and gorilla twisting to moan with a gargoyle mouth: "They buy me and sell me . . . it's a game . . . sometime I'll break loose . . ."

Once having marched
Over the margins of animal necessity,
Over the grim line of sheer subsistence
Then man came
To the deeper rituals of his bones,
To the lights lighter than any bones,
To the time for thinking things over,
To the dance, the song, the story,
Or the hours given over to dreaming,
Once having so marched.
Between the finite limitations of the five senses
and the endless yearnings of man for the beyond
the people hold to the humdrum bidding of work and food
while reaching out when it comes their way
for lights beyond the prison of the five senses,
for keepsakes lasting beyond any hunger or death.
This reaching is alive.
The panderers and liars have violated and smutted it.
Yet this reaching is alive yet
for lights and keepsakes.

The people know the salt of the sea
and the strength of the winds
lashing the corners of the earth.
The people to take the earth
as a tomb of rest and a cradle of hope.

Who else speaks for the Family of Man?
They are in tune and step
with constellations of universal law.
The people is a polychrome,
a spectrum and a prism
held in a moving monolith,
a console organ of changing themes,
a clavilux of color poems
wherein the sea offers fog
and the fog moves off in rain
and the labrador sunset shortens
to a nocturne of clear stars
serene over the shot spray
of northern lights.

The steel mill sky is alive.
The fire breaks white and zigzag
shot on a gun-metal gloaming.
Man is a long time coming.
Man will yet win.
Brother may yet line up with brother:

This old anvil laughs at many broken hammers.
There are men who can't be bought.
The fireborn are at home in fire.
The stars make no noise.
You can't hinder the wind from blowing.
Time is a great teacher.
Who can live without hope?

In the darkness with a great bundle of grief the people march.
In the night, and overhead a shovel of stars for keeps, the people march:
"Where to? what next?" 1936

Public Letter to Emily Dickinson

Five little roses spoke
for God to be near them,
for God to be witness.

Flame and thorn were there
in and around five roses,
winding flame, speaking thorn.

Pour from the sea
one hand of salt.
Take from a star
one finger of mist.
Pick from a heart
one cry of silver.

Let be, give over
to the moving blue
of the chosen shadow.

Let be, give over
to the ease of gongs,
to the might of gongs.

Share with the flamewon,
choose from your thorns,
for God to be near you,
for God to be witness. 1950

Amy [Lawrence] Lowell

(1874-1925)

CHRONOLOGY:

1874 Born February 9, in Brookline, Massachusetts.
1882 First of many trips to Europe.
1887 *Dream Drops; or, Stories from Fairy Land* (with Katherine Lowell Bowkley and Katherine Bigelow Lowell).
1902 Decided on a poetic career.
1910 First poem published in *Atlantic Monthly*.
1912 *A Dome of Many-Coloured Glass*.
1913 Met Ezra Pound in England.
1914 *Sword Blades and Poppy Seed*.
1915 Lectured in Boston, New York, and Chicago; *Six French Poets*.
1916 *Men, Women and Ghosts*.
1917 *Tendencies in Modern American Poetry*.
1918 Phi Beta Kappa poet at Tufts College; *Can Grande's Castle*.
1919 *Pictures of the Floating World*.
1920 Phi Beta Kappa poet at Columbia University.
1921 *Legends*.
1922 *A Critical Fable*.
1924 Awarded Helen Haire Levison Prize of *Poetry*.
1925 *John Keats*, biography; *What's O'clock*, awarded Pulitzer Prize next year; died May 12 in Massachusetts.
1926 *East Wind*.
1927 *Ballads for Sale; The Madonna of Carthagena; Fool o' the Moon*.
1930 *Poetry and Poets: Essays*.

BIBLIOGRAPHY:

Louis Untermeyer edited, with an introduction, *The Complete Poetical Works of Amy Lowell* (Boston, 1955). *Selected Poems* was edited by John Livingston Lowes (Boston, 1928); and *Florence Ayscough and Amy Lowell:*

Correspondence of a Friendship (Chicago, 1945) was edited by Harley F. MacNair.

The most recent critical biography is Horace Gregory, *Amy Lowell: Portrait of the Poet in Her Time* (New York, 1958); still useful is S. Foster Damon, *Amy Lowell: A Chronicle, with Extracts from Her Correspondence* (Boston, 1935).

For bibliography and explications, see Allen Tate, *Sixty American Poets, 1896-1944* (Rev. ed.; Washington, 1954) and Joseph M. Kuntz, *Poetry Explication* (Rev. ed.; Denver, 1962).

Patterns

I walk down the garden paths,
And all the daffodils
Are blowing, and the bright blue squills.
I walk down the patterned garden paths
In my stiff, brocaded gown.
With my powdered hair and jewelled fan,
I too am a rare
Pattern. As I wander down
The garden paths.

My dress is richly figured,
And the train
Makes a pink and silver stain
On the gravel, and the thrift
Of the borders.
Just a plate of current fashion,
Tripping by in high-heeled, ribboned shoes.
Not a softness anywhere about me,
Only whalebone and brocade.
And I sink on a seat in the shade
Of a lime tree. For my passion
Wars against the stiff brocade.
The daffodils and squills
Flutter in the breeze
As they please.
And I weep;
For the lime tree is in blossom
And one small flower has dropped upon my bosom.

And the plashing of waterdrops
In the marble fountain
Comes down the garden paths.
The dripping never stops.
Underneath my stiffened gown
Is the softness of a woman bathing in a marble basin,

A basin in the midst of hedges grown
So thick, she cannot see her lover hiding,
But she guesses he is near,
And the sliding of the water
Seems the stroking of a dear
Hand upon her.
What is summer in a fine brocaded gown!
I should like to see it lying in a heap upon the ground.
All the pink and silver crumpled up on the ground.

I would be the pink and silver as I ran along the paths,
And he would stumble after,
Bewildered by my laughter.
I should see the sun flashing from his sword-hilt and the buckles on
his shoes.
I would choose
To lead him in a maze along the patterned paths,
A bright and laughing maze for my heavy-booted lover.
Till he caught me in the shade,
And the buttons of his waistcoat bruised my body as he clasped me,
Aching, melting, unafraid.
With the shadows of the leaves and the sundrops,
And the plopping of the waterdrops,
All about us in the open afternoon—
I am very like to swoon
With the weight of this brocade,
For the sun sifts through the shade.

Underneath the fallen blossom
In my bosom,
Is a letter I have hid.
It was brought to me this morning by a rider from the Duke.
"Madam, we regret to inform you that Lord Hartwell
Died in action Thursday se'nnight."
As I read it in the white, morning sunlight,
The letters squirmed like snakes.
"Any answer, Madam," said my footman.
"No," I told him.
"See that the messenger takes some refreshment.
No, no answer."
And I walked into the garden,
Up and down the patterned paths,
In my stiff, correct brocade.
The blue and yellow flowers stood up proudly in the sun,
Each one.

I stood upright too,
Held rigid to the pattern
By the stiffness of my gown.
Up and down I walked,
Up and down.

In a month he would have been my husband.
In a month, here, underneath this lime,
We would have broke the pattern;
He for me, and I for him,
He as Colonel, I as Lady,
On this shady seat.
He had a whim
That sunlight carried blessing.
And I answered, "It shall be as you have said."
Now he is dead.

In summer and in winter I shall walk
Up and down
The patterned garden paths
In my stiff, brocaded gown.
The squills and daffodils
Will give place to pillared roses, and to asters, and to snow.
I shall go
Up and down,
In my gown.
Gorgeously arrayed,
Boned and stayed.
And the softness of my body will be guarded from embrace
By each button, hook, and lace.
For the man who should loose me is dead,
Fighting with the Duke in Flanders,
In a pattern called a war.
Christ! What are patterns for? 1916

Edna St. Vincent Millay

(1892-1950)

CHRONOLOGY:

1892 Born on February 22, in Rockland, Maine.

1908-10 Published youthful verse in *St. Nicholas magazine.*

1912 "Renascence" appeared in *The Lyric Year.*

1913-17 Entered Barnard but transferred to Vassar, from which she graduated.

1917 *Renascence;* moved to Greenwich Village, New York City.
1920 *A Few Figs from Thistles;* awarded prize by *Poetry.*
1921 *The Lamp and the Bell, Aria da Capo, Two Slatterns and a King* (plays); *Second April.*
1923 *The Harp Weaver and Other Poems* (awarded Pulitzer Prize).
1924 *Distressing Dialogues* (under pseudonym of Nancy Boyd).
1926-27 *The King's Henchmen,* used as libretto of opera by Deems Taylor, performed at Metropolitan Opera.
1928 *The Buck in the Snow and Other Poems.*
1931 *Fatal Interview;* awarded Helen Haire Levison Prize by *Poetry.*
1932 *The Princess Marries the Page* (play).
1934 *Wine from These Grapes.*
1937 *Conversation at Midnight.*
1939 *Huntsman, What Quarry?*
1940 *Make Bright the Arrows.*
1942 *The Murder of Lidice.*
1950 Died on October 19.
1954 *Mine the Harvest,* edited by Norma Millay.

BIBLIOGRAPHY:

The standard edition is *Collected Poems of Edna St. Vincent Millay,* ed. Norma Millay (New York, 1956). *Letters of Edna St. Vincent Millay* (New York, 1952) was edited by Allan Ross Macdougall.

The only book-length biographical study is Vincent Sheean, *The Indigo Bunting: A Memoir of Edna St. Vincent Millay* (New York, 1951); but one should also see Edmund Wilson's account in *The Shores of Light* (New York, 1952).

The most recent bibliographical listing is in Allen Tate, *Sixty American Poets 1896-1944* (Rev. ed.; Washington, 1954); for explications, see Joseph M. Kuntz, *Poetry Explication* (Rev. ed.; Denver, 1962).

Renascence

All I could see from where I stood
Was three long mountains and a wood;
I turned and looked another way
And saw three islands in a bay.
So with my eyes I traced the line
Of the horizon, thin and fine,
Straight around till I was come
Back to where I started from;
And all I saw from where I stood
Was three long mountains and a wood.
Over these things I could not see;
These were the things that bounded me;
And I could touch them with my hand,—
Almost, I thought, from where I stand.
And all at once things seemed so small
My breath came short, and scarce at all.
But, sure, the sky is big, I said;
Miles and miles above my head;
So here upon my back I'll lie
And look my fill into the sky.

And so I looked, and, after all,
The sky was not so very tall.
The sky, I said, must somewhere stop,
And—sure enough!—I see the top.
The sky, I thought, is not so grand;
I 'most could touch it with my hand!
And, reaching up my hand to try,
I screamed to feel it touch the sky.
I screamed, and—lo!—Infinity
Came down and settled over me;
And, pressing of the Undefined
The definition on my mind,
Held up before my eyes a glass
Through which my shrinking sight did pass
Until it seemed I must behold
Immensity made manifold;
Whispered to me a word whose sound
Deafened the air for worlds around,
And brought unmuffled to my ears
The gossiping of friendly spheres,
The creaking of the tented sky,
The ticking of Eternity.

I saw and heard, and knew at last
The How and Why of all things, past,
And present, and forevermore.
The universe, cleft to the core,
Lay open to my probing sense
That, sick'ning, I would fain pluck thence
But could not—nay! But needs must suck
At the great wound, and could not pluck
My lips away till I had drawn
All venom out—Ah, fearful pawn!
For my omniscience paid I toll
In infinite remorse of soul.
All sin was of my sinning, all
Atoning mine, and mine the gall
Of all regret. Mine was the weight
Of every brooded wrong, the hate
That stood behind each envious thrust,
Mine every greed, mine every lust.
And all the while for every grief,
Each suffering, I craved relief
With individual desire—

Craved all in vain! And felt fierce fire
About a thousand people crawl;
Perished with each—then mourned for all!
A man was starving in Capri;
He moved his eyes and looked at me;
I felt his gaze, I heard his moan,
And knew his hunger as my own.
I saw at sea a great fog-bank
Between two ships that struck and sank;
A thousand screams the heavens smote;
And every scream tore through my throat.
No hurt I did not feel, no death
That was not mine; mine each last breath
That, crying, met an answering cry
From the compassion that was I.
All suffering mine, and mine its rod;
Mine, pity like the pity of God.
Ah, awful weight! Infinity
Pressed down upon the finite me!
My anguished spirit, like a bird,
Beating against my lips I heard;
Yet lay the weight so close about
There was no room for it without.
And so beneath the weight lay I
And suffered death, but could not die.

Deep in the earth I rested now;
Cool is its hand upon the brow
And soft its breast beneath the head
Of one who is so gladly dead.
And all at once, and over all,
The pitying rain began to fall;
I lay and heard each pattering hoof
Upon my lowly, thatchèd roof,
And seemed to love the sound far more
Than ever I had done before.
For rain it hath a friendly sound
To one who's six feet underground;
And scarce the friendly voice or face:
A grave is such a quiet place.

The rain, I said, is kind to come
And speak to me in my new home.
I would I were alive again
To kiss the fingers of the rain,

To drink into my eyes the shine
Of every slanting silver line,
To catch the freshened, fragrant breeze
From drenched and dripping apple-trees.
For soon the shower will be done,
And then the broad face of the sun
Will laugh above the rain-soaked earth
Until the world with answering mirth
Shakes joyously, and each round drop
Rolls, twinkling, from its grass-blade top.
How can I bear it; buried here,
While overhead the sky grows clear
And blue again after the storm?
O, multi-coloured, multiform,
Belovèd beauty over me,
That I shall never, never see
Again! Spring-silver, autumn-gold
That I shall never more behold!
Sleeping your myriad magics through,
Close-sepulchred away from you!
O God, I cried, give me new birth,
And put me back upon the earth!
Upset each cloud's gigantic gourd
And let the heavy rain, down-poured
In one big torrent, set me free,
Washing my grave away from me!
I ceased; and, through the breathless hush
That answered me, the far-off rush
Of herald wings came whispering,
Like music down the vibrant string
Of my ascending prayer, and—crash!
Before the wild wind's whistling lash
The startled storm-clouds reared on high
And plunged in terror down the sky,
And the big rain in one black wave
Fell from the sky and struck my grave.

I know not how such things can be,
I only know there came to me
A fragrance such as never clings
To aught save happy living things;
A sound as of some joyous elf
Singing sweet songs to please himself,
And, through and over everything,

A sense of glad awakening.
The grass, a tip-toe at my ear,
Whispering to me I could hear;
I felt the rain's cool finger-tips
Brushed tenderly across my lips,
Laid gently on my sealèd sight,
And all at once the heavy night
Fell from my eyes and I could see—
A drenched and dripping apple-tree,
A last long line of silver rain,
A sky grown clear and blue again.
And as I looked a quickening gust
Of wind blew up to me and thrust
Into my face a miracle
Of orchard-breath, and with the smell—
I know not how such things can be!—
I breathed my soul back into me.
Ah! Up then from the ground sprang I
And hailed the earth with such a cry
As is not heard save from a man
Who has been dead, and lives again.
About the trees my arms I wound;
Like one gone mad I hugged the ground;
I raised my quivering arms on high;
I laughed and laughed into the sky,
Till at my throat a strangling sob
Caught fiercely, and a great heart-throb
Sent instant tears into my eyes;
O God, I cried, no dark disguise
Can e'er hereafter hide from me
Thy radiant identity!
Thou canst not move across the grass
But my quick eyes will see Thee pass,
Nor speak, however silently,
But my hushed voice will answer Thee.
I know the path that tells Thy way
Through the cool eve of every day;
God, I can push the grass apart
And lay my finger on Thy heart!
The world stands out on either side
No wider than the heart is wide;
Above the world is stretched the sky—
No higher than the soul is high.
The heart can push the sea and land

Farther away on either hand;
The soul can split the sky in two,
And let the face of God shine through.
But East and West will pinch the heart
That cannot keep them pushed apart;
And he whose soul is flat—the sky
Will cave in on him by and by. 1912

If I Should Learn, in Some Quite Casual Way

If I should learn, in some quite casual way,
That you were gone, not to return again—
Read from the back-page of a paper, say,
Held by a neighbor in a subway train,
How at the corner of this avenue
And such a street (so are the papers filled)
A hurrying man, who happened to be you,
At noon today had happened to be killed—
I should not cry aloud—I could not cry
Aloud, or wring my hands in such a place—
I should but watch the station sights rush by
With a more careful interest on my face;
Or raise my eyes and read with greater care
Where to store furs and how to treat the hair. 1917

Euclid Alone Has Looked on Beauty Bare

Euclid alone has looked on Beauty bare.
Let all who prate of Beauty hold their peace,
And lay them prone upon the earth and cease
To ponder on themselves, the while they stare
At nothing, intricately drawn nowhere
In shapes of shifting lineage; let geese
Gabble and hiss, but heroes seek release
From dusty bondage into luminous air.
O blinding hour, O holy, terrible day,
When first the shaft into his vision shone
Of light anatomized! Euclid alone
Has looked on Beauty bare. Fortunate they
Who, though once only and then but far away,
Have heard her massive sandal set on stone. 1923

NEW ACHIEVEMENTS

CHAPTER FOUR

THE TRIUMPH OF THE EXPATRIATES

Although they were all born in the Midwest, as the prairie poets had been, the fame that Sherwood Anderson, F. Scott Fitzgerald, and Ernest Hemingway achieved was not as regional writers. "You are all," said Gertrude Stein to Ernest Hemingway, in a phrase the whole world now knows, "a lost generation." Miss Stein's "all," of course, referred to a good deal more than these three writers. Although she was joking, Hemingway—and the world—took her seriously. Yet, with the possible exception of Pound's "Hugh Selwyn Mauberley" or of Eliot's "The Waste Land," it is Hemingway's first novel, *The Sun Also Rises* (1926), that seems most spectacularly to have personified the phrase, even as it quoted it. Hemingway himself had crucial relations with both Anderson and Fitzgerald, as all had with Gertrude Stein, in a way that makes of these three writers a significant and cohesive embodiment of one of the strains of modern American fiction that is generally considered to be among its finest.

These three writers of fiction cohere, of course, in many other ways also. They were all highly individualized stylists, for example, and brought to modern fiction a revolutionary concern for words that was paralleled in nineteenth-century American fiction only in the works of Mark Twain, Stephen Crane, and perhaps Henry James. It was a concern for *expression* in fiction comparable to that shown by the new poets in their renaissance. Moreover, unlike Lewis and Dreiser, they were all as accomplished with the short-story form as they were with the novel—some think more so. Certainly their best short fiction reflects those qualities that our modern age has come to value most highly: subtlety of conception; a carefully contrived style that is accurate, sensitive, and suggestive; a conscious use of symbols, Freudian and otherwise; a belief in the integrity of the short story as a respectable literary genre; and a talent for intricately constructing this short literary form. Although there are still other important ways these three writers could be viewed as constituting a collective, cohesive force in modern American fiction, an introduction to them by Gertrude Stein is a good way of approaching their works.

Miss Stein could only have been an American. Although she visited her homeland only once during the forty-odd years she resided in Europe, her "tone" was always an American tone—as "schoolmarm" to every American visitor to Europe with artistic aspirations; as *grande dame* of the post-World War I expatriates; as stylistic word-juggler *extraordinaire;* as patron and *confrère* to the painters Picasso, Matisse, and Bracque (not to mention sculptors and musicians); as a public and jealous antagonist to her art-critic brother, Leo; as pseudo-plagiarist of her nurse, secretary, chef, friend, and confidante, Alice B. Toklas; as a fervent lover of France; even as a creator of a home-away-from-home for Allied and American soldiers during and after both World Wars.

Yet, her place in modern American literature is difficult to determine. Clear enough is her influence on the prose of those American writers who flocked to her salon at 27 Rue de Fleurus for encouragement and direction, for more often than not it was acknowledged and specified by the writers themselves. Moreover, that influence had been paralleled to some extent by the influence of Pound and the Imagists in England on the poetry of a slightly earlier generation. The great bulk of her experimental work still needs proper assessment, in spite of the critical acceptance of her memoirs published as the supposed *Autobiography of Alice B. Toklas* (1933); the three novellas in *Three Lives* (1908); the critical pronouncements of her *Composition as Explanation* (1926); her play *Four Saints in Three Acts* (1934); and two or three other works.

Sherwood Anderson's ties with the Midwest were much stronger than those of Fitzgerald and Hemingway, his ties with the expatriates much looser. Yet, the achievement of his masterpiece, *Winesburg, Ohio* (1919), has behind it important germs from both directions. Essential, of course, was his own late adolescence in Clyde, Ohio; his close association with members of the Chicago group such as Floyd Dell, Ben Hecht, Sandburg, Dreiser, Margaret Anderson, and others; and, most importantly, Masters' *Spoon River Anthology,* with its structural scheme much like the scheme of Anderson's related stories. Sigmund Freud and D. H. Lawrence are also back of *Winesburg,* and so is Gertrude Stein. Although Anderson did not meet Miss Stein until after the publication of his masterpiece, it was her early *Three Lives* (according to Mark Schorer) that "helped him discover the language that he . . . wanted to use"—the colloquial, free, easy, sensitive, supple language of Mark Twain.

Although the best "whole" book he ever wrote, even *Winesburg, Ohio* is not as good as its parts—not as good as a totality as are several of its short stories taken separately—or perhaps even as some stories that were to come later, such as "I Want to Know Why" from *The Triumph of the Egg* (1921), "I'm a Fool" from *Horses and Men* (1923), or "Death in the Woods" from a volume by the same title (1933). Not in the line of the "pure" naturalism of Dreiser or even the "impressionistic" naturalism of Stephen Crane (though closer to the latter), Anderson's special gift was profound insight into the repressed, inarticulate yearnings of men and women whose longing for emotional or spiritual release had been thwarted by industrialization, respectability, or convention. Traditional plotting is abandoned for revelation of character, and the tenderness and pity he reveals for the warped or trapped "grotesques" who people his best short stories exemplify first and in some ways best (among American short-story writers) what has since come to be known as the Joycean epiphany. Anderson was especially good at depicting the young, as so many American writers had been and were to be, and the theme of initiation into manhood pervades many of his best stories.

Unlike Fitzgerald's and Hemingway's, Anderson's novels were never considered as good as his short stories. Only *Dark Laughter* (1925) was a popular success, although his influence was widespread during the 1920's, especially on younger writers, notably Hemingway and Faulkner. His autobiographical memoirs are unreliable as fact but reveal an engaging personality, and if his other late writings are essentially journalistic, his memoirs and letters nevertheless evoke one strain of the "tone" of his time in a compelling and memorable way.

It is F. Scott Fitzgerald, however, who most flamboyantly and indelibly represents "The Jazz Age," "The Roaring Twenties," the decade of boom and booze. It is also F. Scott Fitzgerald, it later came to be seen, who, of all his generation, saw most clearly that the beautiful are also the damned (even as one of his own titles specified); that bust must follow boom; that underneath glitter and tinsel inevitably reside corruption and disaster. Fitzgerald's deep awareness of this paradox is intrinsic to his talent and is the source of much of his power as a writer. Indeed, it is his unique "double vision" that often reveals the true moral center of his best fiction, whether long or short.

Like Crane's *The Red Badge of Courage,* Fitzgerald's *The Great Gatsby* (1925) is his single perfectly constructed novel. His first novel, *This Side of Paradise* (1920), was sensationally received and helped give the Jazz Age its definition. His second, *The Beautiful and the Damned* (1922), although less autobiographical and better structured than the first, had not that beautiful, precarious balance of which he was capable. Only *Tender Is the Night* (1934) approaches the achievement of *Gatsby* among Fitzgerald's novels; and although it is a more ambitious work (and even for some a more successful one), it has problems of structure that he perhaps never finally solved. His unfinished novel of Hollywood,

The Last Tycoon (posthumously edited by Edmund Wilson and published in 1941), shows great promise indeed, but *The Great Gatsby* is a truly "finished" work; it is an almost perfect conjunction of form and content, of the right subject treated in the right way. Jay Gatsby represents something generic in the American character, something elusive of easy definition but as undeniably "there" for its time and place as Hester Prynne, Captain Ahab, and Huckleberry Finn are for theirs.

A half-dozen or more of Fitzgerald's short stories are equally accomplished. "Babylon Revisited," "May Day," "The Diamond as Big as the Ritz," "Winter Dreams," "Crazy Sunday"—all brilliantly evoke worlds, be they of Paris, New York, or Hollywood, that inevitably judge even as they charm. For far too many years, Fitzgerald's life—in its flamboyant aspects no less than its tragic ones—got in the way of a proper appreciation of his fiction, much as Poe's did for an even longer period. In the 1940's and '50's, however, revaluations began which progressively defined a "place" for Fitzgerald in American letters as secure as that held by any modern writer of fiction.

Ernest Hemingway might well be approached by first looking backward in American literature—by looking back to Mark Twain and Stephen Crane. Hemingway's acknowledgement of the influence of *Huckleberry Finn* on his own celebrated style is well known. His links with Stephen Crane are also apparent, and have been acknowledged: Crane's puzzling pessimism, his nihilism, his resort to symbolism are all present in Hemingway's work, even if Crane's occasional tag-word preaching never is. Gertrude Stein, Ezra Pound, and Sherwood Anderson also importantly influenced the early Hemingway. One might also look to Henry James, who saw in art the world's saving grace, who saw artistic perfection as the one thing that gives order and meaning and intelligibility to the pervasive chaos of existence. Hemingway's work is everywhere marked by the same ideal—as if the distilled re-creation of the world around him, when *perfectly* distilled, when *precisely* evoked, when done, that is, according to the right laws, with integrity, somehow thereby makes of life something worthwhile and valuable, whatever the ups and downs, the pains and jealousies and fears and injustices and disasters that characterize life as we commonly know it.

From the early *In Our Time* (1925) up through *The Old Man and the Sea* (1952), in book after book and story after story, victory is seemingly defined in terms of how one plays the game. There are, of course, other values and worths, weaknesses and strengths of various kinds, stories and novels and essays about war and bullfighting and hunting big game, about fishing, about the lost generation, about prize fighters, gamblers, prostitutes, and perverts—but common to them all is an attitude both within and without the writing that sees some sort of victory in the courage, felicity, and fidelity with which life's odds are met. To the extent to which Hemingway himself maintained this courage and felicity and fidelity—by being what he called true and honest with his material, not sentimentalizing, not romanticizing, not falsifying what his material honestly appeared to him to be—to just that extent did he consider his work successful. Within his fiction, the heroes are ones who, in effect, do the same thing. In one important sense, then, a Hemingway hero is to be tested and judged by the extent to which he is an artist; the artist by the extent to which he is a hero.

At the end of *In Our Time* the young Nick Adams is wounded, alienated from society, alone; he will nevertheless endure, for if without hope, he is also without self-pity. Jake Barnes in *The Sun Also Rises* (1926) is a hero because he can meet with integrity the odds of being both emasculated and in love. Frederick Henry is tested in *A Farewell to Arms* (1929) when he runs away from the war with a nurse he has gotten pregnant and is forced to watch her die as she gives birth to his child. Robert Jordan faces death and defeat at the end of *For Whom the Bell Tolls* (1940). And in *The Old Man and the Sea* (1952) the old fisherman gets to shore only the skeleton of the giant marlin he has killed. In the famous short story, "The Snows of Kilimanjaro" (1936), it is the writer who is tested as he faces on his deathbed the reality of a wasted, thrown-away talent, of dissipated creative energies. In its companion piece, "The Short Happy Life of Francis Macomber" (1936), it is perhaps the code itself that has to be tested.

Hemingway's talent was a remarkably even one. Only three of his works met widespread critical disdain or public indifference, or both: his early declaration of independence from the influence of Sherwood Anderson, the cruel parody, *The Torrents of Spring* (1926); his bow to the impact of the depression and the need for social responsibility, *To Have and Have Not* (1937); and his novel of World War II, *Across the River and into the Trees* (1950). Two of his expository volumes—*Death in the Afternoon* (1932) and *Green Hills of Africa* (1935)—are as provocative as his fiction, compounds as they both are of the ostensible subject at hand (bullfighting and hunting big game in Africa), personal creeds and artistic principles, and a kind of memoir writing.*

His many short stories are as sharp and polished as any in the language and, for some critics, represent his talent at its highest pitch. The influence of his hard, sparse prose was the most pervasive of that of any twentieth-century novelist, on English no less than on other languages, on the sub-literary level of the hard-boiled detective school and *New Yorker* off-shoots such as John O'Hara, no less than on sophisticated Brit-

* Late in 1963 it was announced in New York by Hemingway's widow that a novel, a number of short stories, a travel book, and some poetry were among "50 pounds of manuscript and typescript" that the author left at his death in 1961. These are in addition to Hemingway's memoirs of Paris in the 1920's, *A Moveable Feast* (New York, 1964).

ish writers such as Graham Greene. Embellished prose was to return to American fiction through the gate of Hemingway's great contemporaries, Thomas Wolfe and William Faulkner, but even so, style was never again to be in America what it would have been without his example.

Hemingway's suicide in 1961 rounded out with shocking symmetry his more than symbolic ties with Anderson and Fitzgerald, both of whose deaths had their own ironic overtones: the former from a fatal infection acquired at a cocktail party, the latter from a tragically early heart attack which was certainly related to his drinking. Thus was their age given its final peal. But, it must be remembered, they (with Gertrude Stein) also revolutionized the style of prose fiction in modern America; they brought the short story to a level of perfection that has not yet been surpassed; they left a literary heritage of their age seemingly as enduring as that of any of their contemporaries.

Gertrude Stein

(1874-1946)

CHRONOLOGY:

1874 Born on February 3, in Allegheny, Pennsylvania.
1893-97 Studied at Radcliffe with William James.
1897-1901 Studied medicine at Johns Hopkins University.
1903 Moved to France.
1909 *Three Lives.*
1914 *Tender Buttons.*
1922 *Geography and Plays.*
1925 *The Making of Americans.*
1926 *Composition as Explanation.*
1928 *Useful Knowledge.*
1930 *Lucy Church Amiably.*
1931 *How to Write.*
1932 *Operas and Plays.*
1933 *The Autobiography of Alice B. Toklas; Matisse, Picasso and Gertrude Stein.*
1934 Visited America; *Four Saints in Three Acts* (set to music by Virgil Thompson, produced and published).
1935 *Narration: Four Lectures; Lectures in America.*
1936 *The Geographical History of America.*
1937 *Everybody's Autobiography.*
1938 *A Wedding Bouquet: Ballet; Anciens et Modernes: Picasso.*
1939 *The World Is Round.*
1940 *Paris France; What Are Masterpieces.*
1941 *Ida: A Novel.*
1945 *Wars I Have Seen.*
1946 Died in France on July 27; *In Savoy or "Yes" is for the Yes for a Very Young Man* (produced on Broadway, 1949); *Brewsie and Willie.*
1947 *Four in America; Kisses Can; Literally True; The Mother of Us All* (set to music by Virgil Thompson and produced as an opera).
1948 *Blood on the Dining Room Floor.*
1949 *Last Operas and Plays.*
1955 *Absolutely Bob Brown; or, Bobbed Brown.*
1957 *To Bobchen Hass.*

BIBLIOGRAPHY:

Although there is no collected edition, the Yale Edition of the Unpublished Writings of Gertrude Stein, under the general editorship of Carl

Van Vechten, had brought out eight volumes between 1951 and 1958. Carl Van Vechten's *Selected Writings* (New York, 1946) includes "Melanchtha," *The Autobiography of Alice B. Toklas*, and a liberal sampling of other works. There are paperback editions of *Three Lives* and *The Autobiography*.

Among the many memoirs and studies, perhaps of first importance as biography and criticism are Donald Sutherland's *Gertrude Stein, a Biography of Her Work* (New Haven, 1951); Elizabeth Sprigge, *Gertrude Stein: Her Life and Work* (New York, 1957); and John Malcolm Brinnin, *The Third Rose: Gertrude Stein and Her World* (New York, 1959).

From *The Autobiography of Alice B. Toklas*

. . . .

I remember very well the impression I had of Hemingway that first afternoon. He was an extraordinarily good-looking young man, twenty-three years old. It was not long after that that everybody was twenty-six. It became the period of being twenty-six. During the next two or three years all the young men were twenty-six years old. It was the right age apparently for that time and place. There were one or two under twenty, for example George Lynes but they did not count as Gertrude Stein carefully explained to them. If they were young men they were twenty-six. Later on, much later on they were twenty-one and twenty-two.

So Hemingway was twenty-three, rather foreign looking, with passionately interested, rather than interesting eyes. He sat in front of Gertrude Stein and listened and looked.

They talked then, and more and more, a great deal together. He asked her to come and spend an evening in their apartment and look at his work. Hemingway had then and has always a very good instinct for finding apartments in strange but pleasing localities and good femmes de ménage and good food. This his first apartment was just off the place du Tertre. We spent the evening there and he and Gertrude Stein went over all the writing he had done up to that time. He had begun the novel that it was inevitable he would begin and there were the little poems afterwards printed by McAlmon in the Contact Edition. Gertrude Stein rather liked the poems, they were direct, Kiplingesque, but the novel she found wanting. There is a great deal of description in this, she said, and not particularly good description. Begin over again and concentrate, she said.

Hemingway was at this time Paris correspondent for a canadian newspaper. He was obliged there to express what he called the canadian viewpoint.

He and Gertrude Stein used to walk together and talk together a great deal. One day she said to him, look here, you say you and your wife have a little money between you. Is it enough to live on if you live quietly. Yes, he said. Well, she said, then do it. If you keep on doing newspaper work you will never see things, you will only see words and that will not do, that is of course if you intend to be a writer. Hemingway said he undoubtedly intended to be a writer. He and his wife went away on a trip and shortly after Hemingway turned up alone. He came to the house about ten o'clock in the morning and he stayed, he stayed for lunch, he stayed all afternoon, he stayed for dinner and he stayed until about ten o'clock at night and then all of a sudden he announced that his wife was enceinte and then with great bitterness, and I, I am too young to be a father. We consoled him as best we could and sent him on his way.

When they came back Hemingway said that he had made up his mind. They would go back to America and he would work hard for a year and with what he would earn and what they had they would settle down and he would give up newspaper work and make himself a writer. They went away and well within the prescribed year they came back with a new born baby. Newspaper work was over.

The first thing to do when they came back was as they thought to get the baby baptised. They wanted Gertrude Stein and myself to be godmothers and an english war comrade of Hemingway was to be god-father. We were all born in different religions and most of us were not practising any, so it was rather difficult to know in what church the baby could be baptised. We spent a great deal of time that winter, all of us, discussing the matter. Finally it was decided that it should be baptised episcopalian and episcopalian it was. Just how it was managed with the assortment of god-parents I am sure I do not know, but it was baptised in the episcopalian chapel.

Writer or painter god-parents are notoriously unreliable. That is, there is certain before long to be a cooling of friendship. I know several cases of this, poor Paulot Picasso's god-parents have wandered out of sight and just as naturally it is a long time since any of us have seen or heard of our Hemingway god-child.

However in the beginning we were active god-parents, I particularly. I embroidered a little chair and I knitted a gay coloured garment for the god-child. In the meantime the god-child's father was very earnestly at work making himself a writer.

Gertrude Stein never corrects any detail of anybody's writing, she sticks strictly to general principles, the way of seeing what the writer chooses to see, and the relation between that vision and the way it gets down. When the vision is not complete the words are flat, it is very simple, there can be no mistake about it, so she insists. It was at this time that Hemingway began the short things that afterwards were printed in a volume called In Our Time.

One day Hemingway came in very excited about Ford Madox Ford and the Transatlantic. Ford Madox Ford had started the Transatlantic some months before. A good many years before, indeed before the war, we had met Ford Madox Ford who was at that time Ford Madox Hueffer. He was married to Violet Hunt and Violet Hunt and Gertrude Stein were next to each other at the tea table and talked a great deal together. I was next to Ford Madox Hueffer and I liked him very much and I liked his stories of Mistral and Tarascon and I liked his having been followed about in that land of the french royalist, on account of his resemblance to the Bourbon claimant. I had never seen the Bourbon claimant but Ford at that time undoubtedly might have been a Bourbon.

We had heard that Ford was in Paris, but we had not happened to meet. Gertrude Stein had however seen copies of the Transatlantic and found it interesting but had thought nothing further about it.

Hemingway came in then very excited and said that Ford wanted something of Gertrude Stein's for the next number and he, Hemingway, wanted The Making of Americans to be run in it as a serial and he had to have the first fifty pages at once. Gertrude Stein was of course quite overcome with her excitement at this idea, but there was no copy of the manuscript except the one that we had had bound. That makes no difference, said Hemingway, I will copy it. And he and I between us did copy it and it was printed in the next number of the Transatlantic. So for the first time a piece of the monumental work which was the beginning, really the beginning of modern writing, was printed, and we were very happy. Later on when things were difficult between Gertrude Stein and Hemingway, she always remembered with gratitude that after all it was Hemingway who first caused to be printed a piece of The Making of Americans. She always says, yes sure I have a weakness for Hemingway. After all he was the first of the young men to knock at my door and he did make Ford print the first piece of The Making of Americans.

I myself have not so much confidence that Hemingway did do this. I have never known what the story is but I have always been certain that there was some other story behind it all. That is the way I feel about it.

Gertrude Stein and Sherwood Anderson are very funny on the subject of Hemingway. The last time that Sherwood was in Paris they often talked about him. Hemingway had been formed by the two of them and they were both a little proud and a little ashamed of the work of their minds. Hemingway had at one moment, when he had repudiated Sherwood Anderson and all his works, written him a letter in the name of american literature which he, Hemingway, in company with his contemporaries was about to save, telling Sherwood just what he, Hemingway thought about Sherwood's work, and, that thinking, was in no sense complimentary. When Sherwood came to Paris Hemingway naturally was afraid. Sherwood as naturally was not.

As I say he and Gertrude Stein were endlessly amusing on the subject. They admitted that Hemingway was yellow, he is, Gertrude Stein insisted, just like the flat-boat men on the Mississippi river as described by Mark Twain. But what a book, they both agreed, would be the real story of Hemingway, not those he writes but the confessions of the real Ernest Hemingway. It would be for another audience than the audience Hemingway now has but it would be very wonderful. And then they both agreed that they have a weakness for Hemingway because he is such a good pupil. He is a rotten pupil, I protested. You don't understand, they both said, it is so flattering to have a pupil who does it without understanding it, in other words he takes training and anybody who takes training is a favourite pupil. They both admit it to be a weakness. Gertrude Stein added further, you see he is like Derain. You remember Monsieur de Tuille said, when I did not understand why Derain was having the success he was having that it was because he looks like a modern and he smells of the museums. And that is Hemingway, he looks like a modern and he smells of the museums. But what a story that of the real Hem, and one he should tell himself but alas he never will. After all, as he himself once murmured, there is the career, the career.

But to come back to the events that were happening.

Hemingway did it all. He copied the manuscript and corrected the proof. Correcting proofs is, as I said before, like dusting, you learn the values of the thing as no reading suffices to teach it to you. In correcting these proofs Hemingway learned a great deal and he admired all that he learned. It was at this time that he wrote to Gertrude Stein saying that it was she who had done the work in writing The Making of Americans and he and all his had but to devote their lives to seeing that it was published.

He had hopes of being able to accomplish this. Some one, I think by the name of Sterne, said that he could place it with a publisher. Gertrude Stein and Hemingway believed that he could, but soon Hemingway reported that Sterne had entered into his period of unreliability. That was the end of that.

In the meantime and sometime before this Mina Loy had brought McAlmon to the house and he came from time to time and he brought his wife and brought William Carlos Williams. And finally he wanted to print The Making of Americans in the Contact Edition and finally he did. I will come to that.

In the meantime McAlmon had printed the three poems and ten stories of Hemingway and William Bird had printed In Our Time and Hemingway was getting to be known. He was coming to know Dos Passos and Fitzgerald and Bromfield and George Antheil and everybody else and Harold Loeb was once more in Paris. Hemingway had become a writer. He was also a shadow-boxer, thanks to Sherwood, and he heard about bull-fighting from me. I have always loved spanish dancing and spanish bull-fighting and I loved to show the photographs of bull-fighters and bull-fighting. I also loved to show the photograph where Gertrude Stein and I were in the front row and had our picture taken there accidentally. In these days Hemingway was teaching some young chap how to box. The boy did not know how, but by accident he knocked Hemingway out. I believe this sometimes happens. At any rate in these days Hemingway although a sportsman was easily tired. He used to get quite worn out walking from his house to ours. But then he had been worn by the war. Even now he is, as Hélène says all men are, fragile. Recently a robust friend of his said to Gertrude Stein, Ernest is very fragile, whenever he does anything sporting something breaks, his arm, his leg, or his head.

In those early days Hemingway liked all his contemporaries except Cummings. He accused Cummings of having copied everything, not from anybody but from somebody. Gertrude Stein who had been much impressed by The Enormous Room said that Cummings did not copy, he was the natural heir of the New England tradition with its aridity and its sterility, but also with its individuality. They disagreed about this. They also disagreed about Sherwood Anderson. Gertrude Stein contended that Sherwood Anderson had a genius for using the sentence to convey a direct emotion, this was in the great american tradition, and that really except Sherwood there was no one in America who could write a clear and passionate sentence. Hemingway did not believe this, he did not like Sherwood's taste. Taste has nothing to do with sentences, contended Gertrude Stein. She also added that Fitzgerald was the only one of the younger writers who wrote naturally in sentences.

Gertrude Stein and Fitzgerald are very peculiar in their relation to each other. Gertrude Stein had been very much impressed by This Side of Paradise. She read it when it came out and before she knew any of the young american writers. She said of it that it was this book that really created for the public the new generation. She has never changed her opinion about this. She thinks this equally true of The Great Gatsby. She thinks Fitzgerald will be read when many of his well known contemporaries are forgotten. Fitzgerald always says that he thinks Gertrude Stein says these things just to annoy him by making him think that she means them, and he adds in his favourite way, and her doing it is the cruellest thing I ever heard. They always however have a very good time when they meet. And the last time they met they had a good time with themselves and Hemingway.

Then there was McAlmon. McAlmon had one quality that appealed to Gertrude Stein, abundance, he could go on writing, but she complained that it was dull.

There was also Glenway Wescott but Glenway Wescott at no time interested Gertrude Stein. He has a certain syrup but it does not pour.

So then Hemingway's career was begun. For a little while we saw less of him and then he began to come again. He used to recount to Gertrude Stein the conversations that he afterwards used in The Sun Also Rises and they talked endlessly about the character of Harold Loeb. At this time Hemingway was preparing his volume of short stories to submit to publishers in America. One evening after we had not seen him for a while he turned up with Shipman. Shipman was an amusing boy who was to inherit a few thousand dollars when he came of age. He was not of age. He was to buy the Transatlantic Review when he came of age, so Hemingway said. He was to support a surrealist review when he came of age, André Masson said. He was to buy a house in the country when he came of age, Josette Gris said. As a matter of fact when he came of age nobody who had known him then seemed to know what he did do with his inheritance. Hemingway brought him with him to the house to talk about buying the Transatlantic and incidentally he brought the manuscript he intended sending to America. He handed it to Gertrude Stein. He had added to his stories a little story of meditations and in these he said that The Enormous Room was the greatest book he had ever read. It was then that Gertrude Stein said, Hemingway, remarks are not literature.

After this we did not see Hemingway for quite a while and then we went to see some one, just after The Making of Americans was printed, and Hemingway who was there came up to Gertrude Stein and began to explain why he would not be able to write a review of the book. Just then a heavy hand fell on his shoulder and Ford Madox Ford said, young man it is I who wish to speak to Gertrude Stein. Ford then said to her, I wish to ask your permission to dedicate my new book to you. May I. Gertrude Stein and I were both awfully pleased and touched.

For some years after this Gertrude Stein and Hemingway did not meet. And then we heard that he was back in Paris and telling a number of people how much he wanted to see her. Don't you come home with Hemingway on your arm, I used to say when she went out for a walk. Sure enough one day she did come back bringing him with her.

They sat and talked a long time. Finally I heard her say, Hemingway, after all you are ninety percent Rotarian. Can't you, he said, make it eighty percent. No, said she regretfully, I can't. After all, as she always says, he did, and I may say, he does have moments of disinterestedness.

After that they met quite often. Gertrude Stein always says she likes to see him, he is so wonderful. And if he could only tell his own story. In their last conversation she accused him of having killed a great many of his rivals and put them under the sod. I never, said Hemingway, seriously killed anybody but one man and he was a bad man and, he deserved it, but if I killed anybody else I did it unknowingly, and so I am not responsible.

It was Ford who once said of Hemingway, he comes and sits at my feet and praises me. It makes me nervous. Hemingway also said once, I turn my flame which is a small one down and down and then suddenly there is a big explosion. If there were nothing but explosions my work would be so exciting nobody could bear it.

However, whatever I say, Gertrude Stein always says, yes I know but I have a weakness for Hemingway.

1933

Sherwood Anderson

(1879-1941)

CHRONOLOGY:

1876 Born September 13, in Camden, Ohio.
1896 Worked in Chicago.
1898 Served as a soldier in the Spanish American War.
1899 Attended the Wittenberg Academy, Springfield, Ohio.
1912 Deserted family and job in Elyria, Ohio, for advertising and writing in Chicago.
1916 *Windy McPherson's Son.*
1917 *Marching Men.*
1918 *Mid-American Chants,* verse.
1919 *Winesburg. Ohio.*
1920 *Poor White.*
1921 *The Triumph of the Egg;* given the *Dial* Award; met Gertrude Stein in Paris.
1923 *Many Marriages; Horses and Men.*
1924 *A Story-Teller's Story,* autobiography.
1925 *Dark Laughter; The Modern Writer,* criticism; bought two newspapers in Virginia and edited them with his son.
1926 *Sherwood Anderson's Notebook; Tar: A Midwest Childhood,* autobiography.
1927 *A New Testament,* verse.
1929 *Alice and the Lost Novel,* criticism; *Hello Towns!,* journalism.
1930 *The American County Fair,* journalism.
1931 *Perhaps Women,* journalism.
1932 *Beyond Desire.*
1933 *Death in the Woods,* stories.
1934 *No Swank,* criticism.
1935 *Puzzled America,* journalism.
1936 *Kit Brandon: A Portrait.*
1937 *Plays: Winesburg and Others.*
1940 *Home Town,* journalism.
1941 Died March 8, in Colon, Panama.
1942 *Sherwood Anderson's Memoirs.*

BIBLIOGRAPHY:

There is no collected edition of Anderson's works, but there are several inexpensive reprints of *Winesburg, Ohio.* Useful collections are *The Portable Sherwood Anderson* (New York, 1949), edited by Horace Gregory; and the *Sherwood Anderson Reader* (Boston, 1947), edited by Paul Rosenfield. Indispensable is Howard Mumford Jones and Walter B. Rideout, eds., *The Letters of Sherwood Anderson* (Boston, 1953).

The standard biography is James E. Scheville, *Sherwood Anderson, His Life and Work* (Denver, 1951); but one should also see Irving Howe, *Sherwood Anderson* (New York, 1951).

A useful bibliography is in Fred B. Millett, *Contemporary American Authors* (New York, 1940). For studies of individual stories, see Warren S. Walker, *Twentieth-Century Short Story Explication . . .* (Hamden, Conn., 1961), Supplement, 1963.

From *Winesburg, Ohio*

The Book of the Grotesque

The writer, an old man with a white mustache, had some difficulty in getting into bed. The windows of the house in which he lived were high and he wanted to look at the trees when he awoke in the morning. A carpenter came to fix the bed so that it would be on a level with the window.

Quite a fuss was made about the matter. The carpenter, who had been a soldier in the Civil War, came into the writer's room and sat down to talk of building a platform for the purpose of raising the bed. The writer had cigars lying about and the carpenter smoked.

For a time the two men talked of the raising of the bed and then they talked of other things. The soldier got on the subject of the war. The writer, in fact, led him to that subject. The carpenter had once been a prisoner in Andersonville prison and had lost a brother. The brother had died of starvation, and whenever the carpenter got upon that subject he cried. He, like the old writer, had a white mustache, and when he cried he puckered up his lips and the mustache bobbed up and down. The weeping old man with the cigar in his mouth was ludicrous. The plan the writer had for the raising of his bed was forgotten and later the carpenter did it in his own way and the writer, who was past sixty, had to help himself with a chair when he went to bed at night.

In his bed the writer rolled over on his side and lay quite still. For years he had been beset with notions concerning his heart. He was a hard smoker and his heart fluttered. The idea had got into his mind that he would some time die unexpectedly and always when he got into bed he thought of that. It did not alarm him. The effect in fact was quite a special thing and not easily explained. It made him more alive, there in bed, than at any other time. Perfectly still he lay and his body was old and not of much use any more, but something inside him was altogether young. He was like a pregnant woman, only that the thing inside him was not a baby but a youth. No, it wasn't a youth, it was a woman, young, and wearing a coat of mail like a knight. It is absurd, you see, to try to tell what was inside the old writer as he lay on his high bed and listened to the fluttering of his heart. The thing to get at is what the writer, or the young thing within the writer, was thinking about.

The old writer, like all of the people in the world, had got, during his long life, a great many notions in his head. He had once been quite handsome and a number of women had been in love with him. And then, of course, he had known people, many people, known them in a peculiarly intimate way that was different from the way in which you and I know people. At least that is what the writer thought and the thought pleased him. Why quarrel with an old man concerning his thoughts?

In the bed the writer had a dream that was not a dream. As he grew somewhat sleepy but was still conscious, figures began to appear before his eyes. He imagined the young indescribable thing within himself was driving a long procession of figures before his eyes.

You see the interest in all this lies in the figures that went before the eyes of the writer. They were all grotesques. All of the men and women the writer had ever known had become grotesques.

The grotesques were not all horrible. Some were amusing, some almost beautiful, and one, a woman all drawn out of shape, hurt the old man by her grotesqueness. When she passed he made a noise like a small dog whimpering. Had you come into the room you might have supposed the old man had unpleasant dreams or perhaps indigestion.

For an hour the procession of grotesques passed before the eyes of the old man, and then, although it was a painful thing to do, he crept out of bed and began to write. Some one of the grotesques had made a deep impression on his mind and he wanted to describe it.

At his desk the writer worked for an hour. In the end he wrote a book which he called "The Book of the Grotesque." It was never published, but I saw it once and it made an indelible impression on my mind. The book had one central thought that is very strange and has always remained with me. By remembering it I have been able to understand many people and things that I was never able to understand before. The thought was involved but a simple statement of it would be something like this:

That in the beginning when the world was young there were a great many thoughts but no such thing as a truth. Man made the truths himself and each truth was a composite of a great many vague thoughts. All about in the world were the truths and they were all beautiful.

The old man had listed hundreds of the truths in his book. I will not try to tell you of all of them. There was the truth of virginity and the truth of passion, the truth of wealth and of poverty, of thrift and of profligacy, of carelessness and abandon. Hundreds and hundreds were the truths and they were all beautiful.

And then the people came along. Each as he appeared snatched up one of the truths and some who were quite strong snatched up a dozen of them.

It was the truths that made the people grotesques. The old man had quite an elaborate theory concerning the matter. It was his notion that the moment one of the people took one of the truths to himself, called it his truth, and tried to live his life by it, he became a grotesque and the truth he embraced became a falsehood.

You can see for yourself how the old man, who had spent all of his life writing and was filled with words, would write hundreds of pages concerning this matter. The subject would become so big in his mind that he himself would be in danger of becoming a grotesque. He didn't, I suppose, for the same reason that he never published the book. It was the young thing inside him that saved the old man.

Concerning the old carpenter who fixed the bed for the writer, I only mentioned him because he, like many of what are called very common people, became the nearest thing to what is understandable and lovable of all the grotesques in the writer's book.

From *Winesburg, Ohio*

Sophistication

It was early evening of a day in the late fall and the Winesburg County Fair had brought crowds of country people into town. The day had been clear and the night came on warm and pleasant. On the Trunion Pike, where the road after it left town stretched away between berry fields now covered with dry brown leaves, the dust from passing wagons arose in clouds. Children, curled into little balls, slept on the straw scattered on wagon beds. Their hair was full of dust and their fingers black and sticky. The dust rolled away over the fields and the departing sun set it ablaze with colors.

In the main street of Winesburg crowds filled the stores and the sidewalks. Night came on, horses whinnied, the clerks in the stores ran madly about, children became lost and cried lustily, an American town worked terribly at the task of amusing itself.

Pushing his way through the crowds in Main Street, young George Willard concealed himself in the stairway leading to Doctor Reefy's office and looked at the people. With feverish eyes he watched the faces drifting past under the store lights. Thoughts kept coming into his head and he did not want to think. He stamped impatiently on the wooden steps and looked sharply about. "Well, is she going to stay with him all day? Have I done all this waiting for nothing?" he muttered.

George Willard, the Ohio village boy, was fast growing into manhood and new thoughts had been coming into his mind. All that day, amid the jam of people at the Fair, he had gone about feeling lonely. He was about to leave Winesburg to go away to some city where he hoped to get work on a city newspaper and he felt grown up. The mood that had taken possession of him was a thing known to men and unknown to boys. He felt old and a little tired. Memories awoke in him. To his mind his new sense of maturity set him apart, made of him a half-tragic figure. He wanted someone to understand the feeling that had taken possession of him after his mother's death.

There is a time in the life of every boy when he for the first time takes the backward view of life. Perhaps that is the moment when he crosses the line into manhood. The boy is walking through the street of his town. He is thinking of the future and of the figure he will cut in the world. Ambitions and regrets awake within him. Suddenly something happens; he stops under a tree and waits as for a voice calling his name. Ghosts of old things creep into his consciousness; the voices outside of himself whisper a message concerning the limitations of life. From being quite sure of himself and his future he becomes not at all sure. If he be an imaginative boy a door is torn open and for the first time he looks out upon the world, seeing, as though they marched in procession before him, the countless figures of men who before his time have come out of nothingness into the world, lived their lives and again disappeared into nothingness. The sadness of sophistication has come to the boy. With a little gasp he sees himself as merely a leaf blown by the wind through the streets of his village. He knows that in spite of all the stout talk of his fellows he must live and die in uncertainty, a thing blown by the winds, a thing destined like corn to wilt in the sun. He shivers and looks eagerly about. The eighteen years he has lived seem but a moment, a breathing space in the long march of humanity. Already he hears death calling. With all his heart he wants to come close to some other human, touch someone with his hands, be touched by the hand of another. If he prefers that the other be a woman, that is because he believes that a woman will be gentle, that she will understand. He wants, most of all, understanding.

When the moment of sophistication came to George Willard his mind turned to Helen White, the Winesburg banker's daughter. Always he had been conscious of the girl growing into womanhood as he grew into manhood. Once on a summer night when he was eighteen, he had walked with her on a country road and in her presence had given way to an impulse to boast, to make himself appear big and significant in her eyes. Now he wanted to see her for another purpose. He wanted to tell her of the new impulses that had come to him. He had tried to make her think of him as a man when he knew nothing of manhood and now he wanted to be with her and to try to make her feel the change he believed had taken place in his nature.

As for Helen White, she also had come to a period of change. What George felt, she in her young woman's way felt also. She was no longer a girl and hungered to reach into the grace and beauty of womanhood. She had come home from Cleveland, where she was attending college, to spend a day at the Fair. She also had begun to have memories. During the day she sat in the grandstand with a young man, one of the instructors from the college, who was a guest of her mother's. The young man was of a pedantic turn of mind and she felt at once he would not do for her purpose. At the Fair she was glad to be seen in his company as he was well dressed and a stranger. She knew that the fact of his presence would create an impression. During the day she was happy, but when night came on she began to grow restless. She wanted to drive the instructor away, to get out of his presence. While they sat together in the grandstand and while the eyes of former schoolmates were upon them, she paid so much attention to her escort that he grew interested. "A scholar needs money. I should marry a woman with money," he mused.

Helen White was thinking of George Willard even as he wandered gloomily through the crowds thinking of her. She remembered the summer evening when they had walked together and wanted to walk with him again. She thought that the months she had spent in the city, the going to theatres and the seeing of great crowds wandering in lighted thoroughfares, had changed her profoundly. She wanted him to feel and be conscious of the change in her nature.

The summer evening together that had left its mark on the memory of both the young man and woman had, when looked at quite sensibly, been rather stupidly spent. They had walked out of town along a country road. Then they had stopped by a fence near a field of young corn and George had taken off his coat and let it hang on his arm. "Well, I've stayed here in Winesburg—yes—I've not yet gone away but I'm growing up," he had said. "I've been reading books and I've been thinking. I'm going to try to amount to something in life.

"Well," he explained, "that isn't the point. Perhaps I'd better quit talking."

The confused boy put his hand on the girl's arm. His voice trembled. The two started to walk back along the road toward town. In his desperation George boasted, "I'm going to be a big man, the biggest that ever lived here in Winesburg," he declared. "I want you to do something, I don't know what. Perhaps it is none of my business. I want you to try to be different from other women. You see the point. It's none of my business I tell you. I want you to be a beautiful woman. You see what I want."

The boy's voice failed and in silence the two came back into town and went along the street to Helen White's house. At the gate he tried to say something impressive. Speeches he had thought out came into his head, but they seemed utterly pointless. "I thought—I used to think—I had it in my mind you would marry Seth Richmond. Now I know you won't," was all he could find to say as she went through the gate and toward the door of her house.

On the warm fall evening as he stood in the stairway and looked at the crowd drifting through Main Street, George thought of the talk beside the field of young corn and was ashamed of the figure he had made of himself. In the street the people surged up and down like cattle confined in a pen. Buggies and wagons almost filled the narrow thoroughfare. A band played and small boys raced along the sidewalk, diving between the legs of men. Young men with shining red faces walked awkwardly about with girls on their arms. In a room above one of the stores, where a dance was to be held, the fiddlers tuned their instruments. The broken sounds floated down through an open window and out across the murmur of voices and the loud blare of the horns of the band. The medley of sounds got on young Willard's nerves. Everywhere, on all sides, the sense of crowding, moving life closed in about him. He wanted to run away by himself and think. "If she wants to stay with that fellow she may. Why should I care? What difference does it make to me?" he growled and went along Main Street and through Hern's grocery into a side street.

George felt so utterly lonely and dejected that he wanted to weep but pride made him walk rapidly along, swinging his arms. He came to Westley Moyer's livery barn and stopped in the shadows to listen to a group of men who talked of a race Westley's stallion, Tony Tip, had won at the Fair during the afternoon. A crowd had gathered in front of the barn and before the crowd walked Westley, prancing up and down and boasting. He held a whip in his hand and kept tapping the ground. Little puffs of dust arose in the lamplight. "Hell, quit your talking," Westley exclaimed. "I wasn't afraid, I knew I had 'em beat all the time. I wasn't afraid."

Ordinarily George Willard would have been intensely interested in the boasting of Moyer, the horseman. Now it made him angry. He turned and hurried away along the street. "Old wind-bag," he sputtered. "Why does he want to be bragging? Why don't he shut up?"

George went into a vacant lot and as he hurried along, fell over a pile of rubbish. A nail protruding from an empty barrel tore his trousers. He sat down on the ground and swore. With a pin he mended the torn place and then arose and went on. "I'll go to Helen White's house, that's what I'll do. I'll walk right in. I'll say that I want to see her. I'll walk right in and sit down, that's what I'll do," he declared, climbing over a fence and beginning to run.

. . . . .

On the veranda of Banker White's house Helen was restless and distraught. The instructor sat between the mother and daughter. His talk wearied the girl. Although he had also been raised in an Ohio town, the instructor began to put on the airs of the city. He wanted to appear cosmopolitan. "I like the chance you have given me to study the background out of which most of our girls come," he declared. "It was good of you, Mrs. White, to have me down for the day." He turned to Helen and laughed. "Your life is still bound up with the life of this town?" he asked. "There are people here in whom you are interested?" To the girl his voice sounded pompous and heavy.

Helen arose and went into the house. At the door leading to a garden at the back she stopped and stood listening. Her mother began to talk. "There is no one here fit to associate with a girl of Helen's breeding," she said.

Helen ran down a flight of stairs at the back of the house and into the garden. In the darkness she stopped and stood trembling. It seemed to her that the world was full of meaningless people saying words. Afire with eagerness she ran through a garden gate and turning a corner by the banker's barn, went into a little side street. "George! Where are you, George?" she cried, filled with nervous excitement. She stopped running, and leaned against a tree to laugh hysterically. Along the dark little street came George Willard, still saying words. "I'm going to walk right into her house. I'll go right in and sit down," he declared as he came up to her. He stopped and stared stupidly. "Come on," he said and took hold of her hand. With hanging heads they walked away along the street under the trees. Dry leaves rustled under foot. Now that he had found her George wondered what he had better do and say.

. . . . .

At the upper end of the fair ground, in Winesburg, there is a half decayed old grand-stand. It has never been painted and the boards are all warped out of shape. The fair ground stands on top of a low hill rising out of the valley of Wine Creek and from the grand-stand one can see at night, over a cornfield, the lights of the town reflected against the sky.

George and Helen climbed the hill to the fair ground, coming by the path past Waterworks Pond. The feeling of loneliness and isolation that had come to the young man in the crowded streets of his town was both broken and intensified by the presence of Helen. What he felt was reflected in her.

In youth there are always two forces fighting in people. The warm unthinking little animal struggles against the thing that reflects and remembers, and the older, the more sophisticated thing had possession of George Willard. Sensing his mood, Helen walked beside him filled with respect. When they got to the grand-stand they climbed up under the roof and sat down on one of the long bench-like seats.

There is something memorable in the experience to be had by going into a fair ground that stands at the edge of a Middle Western town on a night after the annual fair has been held. The sensation is one never to be forgotten. On all sides are ghosts, not of the dead, but of living people. Here, during the day just passed, have come the people pouring in from the town and the country around. Farmers with their wives and children and all the people from the hundreds of little frame houses have gathered within these board walls. Young girls have laughed and men with beards have talked of the affairs of their lives. The place has been filled to overflowing with life. It has itched and squirmed with life and now it is night and the life has all gone away. The silence is almost terrifying. One conceals oneself standing silently beside the trunk of a tree and what there is of a reflective tendency in his nature is intensified. One shudders at the thought of the meaninglessness of life while at the same instant, and if the people of the town are his people, one loves life so intensely that tears come into the eyes.

In the darkness under the roof of the grandstand, George Willard sat beside Helen White and felt very keenly his own insignificance in the scheme of existence. Now that he had come out of town where the presence of the people stirring about, busy with a multitude of affairs, had been so irritating the irritation was all gone. The presence of Helen renewed and refreshed him. It was as though her woman's hand was assisting him to make some minute readjustment of the machinery of his life. He began to think of the people in the town where he had always lived with something like reverence. He had reverence for Helen. He wanted to love and to be loved by her, but he did not want at the moment to be confused by her womanhood. In the darkness he took hold of her hand and when she crept close put a hand on her shoulder. A wind began to blow and he shivered. With all his strength he tried to hold and to understand the mood that had come upon him. In that high place in the darkness the two oddly sensitive human atoms held each other tightly and waited. In the mind of each was the same thought. "I have come to this lonely place and here is this other," was the substance of the thing felt.

In Winesburg the crowded day had run itself out into the long night of the late fall. Farm horses jogged away along lonely country roads pulling their portion of weary people. Clerks began to bring samples of goods in off the sidewalks and lock the doors of stores. In the Opera House a crowd had gathered to see a show and further down Main Street the fiddlers, their instruments tuned, sweated and worked to keep the feet of youth flying over a dance floor.

In the darkness in the grand-stand Helen White and George Willard remained silent. Now and then the spell that held them was broken and they turned and tried in the dim light to see into each other's eyes. They kissed but that impulse did not last. At the upper end of the fair ground a half dozen men worked over horses that had raced during the afternoon. The men had built a fire and were heating kettles of water. Only their legs could be seen as they passed back and forth in the light. When the wind blew the little flames of the fire danced crazily about.

George and Helen arose and walked away into the darkness. They went along a path past a field of corn that had not yet been cut. The wind whispered among the dry corn blades. For a moment during the walk back into town the spell that held them was broken. When they had come to the crest of Waterworks Hill they stopped by a tree and George again put his hands on the girl's shoulders. She embraced him eagerly and then again they drew quickly back from that impulse. They stopped kissing and stood a little apart. Mutual respect grew big in them. They were both embarrassed and to relieve their embarrassment dropped into the animalism of youth. They laughed and began to pull and haul at each other. In some way chastened and purified by the mood they had been in they became, not man and woman, not boy and girl, but excited little animals.

It was so they went down the hill. In the darkness they played like two splendid young things in a young world. Once, running swiftly forward, Helen tripped George and he fell. He squirmed and shouted. Shaking with laughter, he rolled down the hill. Helen ran after him. For just a moment she stopped in the darkness. There is no way of knowing what woman's thoughts went through her mind but, when the bottom of the hill was reached and she came up to the boy, she took his arm and walked beside him in dignified silence. For some reason they could not have explained they had both got from their silent evening together the thing needed. Man or boy, woman or girl, they had for a moment taken hold of the thing that makes the mature life of men and women in the modern world possible.

1919

F[rancis] Scott [Key] Fitzgerald

(1896-1940)

CHRONOLOGY:

1896 Born on September 24, in St. Paul, Minnesota.

1911 Attended the Newman School, Hackensack, New Jersey.

1913-17 Attended Princeton University, where he met and became friends with Edmund Wilson and John Peale Bishop, among others.

1917-19 Served in the army but did not go overseas.

1920 *This Side of Paradise; Flappers and Philosophers,* stories; married Zelda Sayre of Montgomery, Alabama.

1922 *The Beautiful and the Damned; Tales of the Jazz Age.*

1925 *The Great Gatsby.*

1926 *All the Sad Young Men,* stories.

1934 *Tender Is the Night.*

1935 *Taps at Reveille,* stories.

1940 Died December 20, in Hollywood.

1941 *The Last Tycoon,* unfinished novel edited by Edmund Wilson.

1957 *Afternoon of an Author,* uncollected stories and essays, edited by Arthur Mizener.

1962 *The Pat Hobby Stories,* late, uncollected stories introduced here by Arnold Gingrich.

BIBLIOGRAPHY:

There is no collected edition of Fitzgerald's works, but a major reprinting is *Three Novels: The Great Gatsby, Tender Is the Night* (both edited by Malcolm Cowley) *and The Last Tycoon: An Unfinished Novel,* ed. by Edmund Wilson (New York, 1953). Malcolm Cowley also selected the *Stories of F. Scott Fitzgerald* (New York, 1951). There are inexpensive paperbacks of the major works.

Three indispensable biographical studies are Arthur Mizener, *The Far Side of Paradise, A Biography of F. Scott Fitzgerald* (Boston, 1951); Sheilah Graham, *Beloved Infidel* (New York, 1958); and Andrew Turnbull, *F. Scott Fitzgerald* (New York, 1962). Turnbull also edited the *Letters of F. Scott Fitzgerald* (New York, 1963). James E. Miller's *The Fictional Technique of Scott Fitzgerald* (The Hague, 1957) and Alfred Kazin's collection of critical essays, *F. Scott Fitzgerald: The Man and His Work* (Cleveland, 1951) provide valuable critical tools and bibliographies.

Both the *Princeton University Library Chronicle,* XII (Summer, 1951) and *Modern Fiction Studies,* VII (Spring, 1961) are special Fitzgerald issues. The check list of studies of Fitzgerald's fiction in the latter journal can be supplemented by Warren S. Walker's *Twentieth-Century Short Story Explication . . .* (Hamden, Conn., 1961), Supplement, 1963.

From The Crack-Up

February, 1936

Of course all life is a process of breaking down, but the blows that do the dramatic side of the work—the big sudden blows that come, or seem to come, from outside—the ones you remember and blame things on and, in moments of weakness, tell your friends about, don't show their effect all at once. There is another sort of blow that comes from within—that you don't feel until it's too late to do anything about it, until you realize with finality that in some regard you will never be as good a man again. The first sort of breakage seems to happen quick—the second kind happens almost without your knowing it but is realized suddenly indeed.

Before I go on with this short history, let me make a general observation—the test of a first-rate intelligence is the ability to hold two opposed ideas in the mind at the same time, and still retain the ability to function. One should, for example, be able to see that things are hopeless and yet be determined to make them otherwise. This philosophy fitted on to my early adult life, when I saw the improbable, the implausible, often the "impossible," come true. Life was something you dominated if you were any good. Life yielded easily to intelligence and effort, or to what proportion could be mustered of both. It seemed a romantic business to be a successful literary man—you were not ever going to be as famous as a movie star but what note you had was probably longer-lived—you were never going to have the power of a man of strong political or religious convictions but you were certainly more independent. Of course within the practice of your trade you were forever unsatisfied—but I, for one, would not have chosen any other.

As the twenties passed, with my own twenties marching a little ahead of them, my two juvenile regrets—at not being big enough (or good enough) to play football in college, and at not getting overseas during the war—resolved themselves into childish waking dreams of imaginary heroism that were good enough to go to sleep on in restless nights. The big problems of life seemed to solve themselves, and if the business of fixing them was difficult, it made one too tired to think of more general problems.

Life, ten years ago, was largely a personal matter. I must hold in balance the sense of the futility of effort and the sense of the necessity to struggle; the conviction of the inevitability of failure and still the determination to "succeed"—and, more than these, the contradiction between the dead hand of the past and the high intentions of the future. If I could do this through the common ills—domestic, professional and personal—then the ego would continue as an arrow shot from nothingness to nothingness with such force that only gravity would bring it to earth at last.

For seventeen years, with a year of deliberate loafing and resting out in the center—things went on like that, with a new chore only a nice prospect for the next day. I was living hard, too, but: "Up to forty-nine it'll be all right," I said. "I can count on that. For a man who's lived as I have, that's all you could ask."

—And then, ten years this side of forty-nine, I suddenly realized that I had prematurely cracked.

Crazy Sunday

I

It was Sunday—not a day, but rather a gap between two other days. Behind, for all of them, lay sets and sequences, the long waits under the crane that swung the microphone, the hundred miles a day by automobiles to and fro across a county, the struggles of rival ingenuities in the conference rooms, the ceaseless compromise, the clash and strain of many personalities fighting for their lives. And now Sunday, with individual life starting up again, with a glow kindling in eyes that had been glazed with monotony the afternoon before. Slowly as the hours waned they came awake like "Puppenfeen" in a toy shop: an intense colloquy in a corner, lovers disappearing to neck in a hall. And the feeling of "Hurry, it's not too late, but for God's sake hurry before the blessed forty hours of leisure are over."

Joel Coles was writing continuity. He was twenty-eight and not yet broken by Hollywood. He had had what were considered nice assignments since his arrival six months before and he submitted his scenes and sequences with enthusiasm. He referred to himself modestly as a hack but really did not think of it that way. His mother had been a successful actress; Joel had spent his childhood between London and New York trying to separate the real from the unreal, or at least to keep one guess ahead. He was a handsome man with the pleasant cow-brown eyes that in 1913 had gazed out at Broadway audiences from his mother's face.

When the invitation came it made him sure that he was getting somewhere. Ordinarily he did not go out on Sundays but stayed sober and took work home with him. Recently they had given him a Eugene O'Neill play destined for a very important lady indeed. Everything he had done so far had pleased Miles Calman, and Miles Calman was the only director on the lot who did not work under a supervisor and was responsible to the money men alone. Everything was clicking into place in Joel's career. ("This is Mr. Calman's secretary. Will you come to tea from four to six Sunday—he lives in Beverly Hills, number——.")

Joel was flattered. It would be a party out of the top-drawer. It was a tribute to himself as a young man of promise. The Marion Davies crowd, the high-hats, the big currency numbers, perhaps even Dietrich and Garbo and the Marquise, people who were not seen everywhere, would probably be at Calman's.

"I won't take anything to drink," he assured himself. Calman was audibly tired of rummies, and thought it was a pity the industry could not get along without them.

Joel agreed that writers drank too much—he did himself, but he wouldn't this afternoon. He wished Miles would be within hearing when the cocktails were passed to hear his succinct, unobtrusive, "No, thank you."

Miles Calman's house was built for great emotional moments—there was an air of listening as if the far silences of its vistas hid an audience, but this afternoon it was thronged, as though people had been bidden rather than asked. Joel noted with pride that only two other writers from the studio were in the crowd, an ennobled limey and, somewhat to his surprise, Nat Keogh, who had evoked Calman's impatient comment on drunks.

Stella Calman (Stella Walker, of course) did not move on to her other guests after she spoke to Joel. She lingered—she looked at him with the sort of beautiful look that demands some sort of acknowledgment and Joel drew quickly on the dramatic adequacy inherited from his mother:

"Well, you look about sixteen! Where's your kiddy car?"

She was visibly pleased; she lingered. He felt that he should say something more, something confident and easy—he had first met her when she was struggling for bits in New York. At the moment a tray slid up and Stella put a cocktail glass into his hand.

"Everybody's afraid, aren't they?" he said, looking at it absently. "Everybody watches for everybody else's blunders, or tries to make sure they're with people that'll do them credit. Of course that's not true in your house," he covered himself hastily. "I just meant generally in Hollywood."

Stella agreed. She presented several people to Joel as if he were very important. Reassuring himself that Miles was at the other side of the room, Joel drank the cocktail.

"So you have a baby?" he said. "That's the time to look out. After a pretty woman has had her first child, she's very vulnerable, because she wants to be reassured about her own charm. She's got to have some new man's unqualified devotion to prove to herself she hasn't lost anything."

"I never get anybody's unqualified devotion," Stella said rather resentfully.

"They're afraid of your husband."

"You think that's it?" She wrinkled her brow over the idea; then the conversation was interrupted at the exact moment Joel would have chosen.

Her attentions had given him confidence. Not for him to join safe groups, to slink to refuge under the wings of such acquaintances as he saw about the room. He walked to the window and looked out toward the Pacific, colorless under its sluggish sunset. It was good here—the American Riviera and all that, if there were ever time to enjoy it. The handsome, well-dressed people in the room, the lovely girls, and the—well, the lovely girls. You couldn't have everything.

He saw Stella's fresh boyish face, with the tired eyelid that always drooped a little over one eye, moving about among her guests and he wanted to sit with her and talk a long time as if she were a girl instead of a name; he followed her to see if she paid anyone as much attention as she had paid him. He took another cocktail—not because he needed confidence but because she had given him so much of it. Then he sat down beside the director's mother.

"Your son's gotten to be a legend, Mrs. Calman—Oracle and a Man of Destiny and all that. Personally, I'm against him but I'm in a minority. What do you think of him? Are you impressed? Are you surprised how far he's gone?"

"No, I'm not surprised," she said calmly. "We always expected a lot from Miles."

"Well now, that's unusual," remarked Joel. "I always think all mothers are like Napoleon's mother. My mother didn't want me to have anything to do with the entertainment business. She wanted me to go to West Point and be safe."

"We always had every confidence in Miles." . . .

He stood by the built-in bar of the dining room with the good-humored, heavy-drinking, highly paid Nat Keogh.

"—I made a hundred grand during the year and lost forty grand gambling, so now I've hired a manager."

"You mean an agent," suggested Joel.

"No, I've got that too. I mean a manager. I make over everything to my wife and then he and my wife get together and hand me out the money. I pay him five thousand a year to hand me out my money."

"You mean your agent."

"No, I mean my manager, and I'm not the only one—a lot of other irresponsible people have him."

"Well, if you're irresponsible why are you responsible enough to hire a manager?"

"I'm just irresponsible about gambling. Look here——"

A singer performed; Joel and Nat went forward with the others to listen.

II

The singing reached Joel vaguely; he felt happy and friendly toward all the people gathered there, people of bravery and industry, superior to a bourgeois that outdid them in ignorance and loose living, risen to a position of the highest prominence in a nation that for a decade had wanted only to be entertained. He liked them—he loved them. Great waves of good feeling flowed through him.

As the singer finished his number and there was a drift toward the hostess to say good-by, Joel had an idea. He would give them "Building It Up," his own composition. It was his only parlor trick, it had amused several parties and it might please Stella Walker. Possessed by the hunch, his blood throbbing with the scarlet corpuscles of exhibitionism, he sought her.

"Of course," she cried. "Please! Do you need anything?"

"Someone has to be the secretary that I'm supposed to be dictating to."

"I'll be her."

As the word spread, the guests in the hall, already putting on their coats to leave, drifted back and Joel faced the eyes of many strangers. He had a dim foreboding, realizing that the man who had just performed was a famous radio entertainer. Then someone said "Sh!" and he was alone with Stella, the center of a sinister Indian-like half-circle. Stella smiled up at him expectantly—he began.

His burlesque was based upon the cultural limitations of Mr. Dave Silverstein, an independent producer; Silverstein was presumed to be dictating a letter outlining a treatment of a story he had bought.

"—a story of divorce, the younger generation and the Foreign Legion," he heard his voice saying, with the intonations of Mr. Silverstein. "But we got to build it up, see?"

A sharp pang of doubt struck through him. The faces surrounding him in the gently molded light were intent and curious, but there was no ghost of a smile anywhere; directly in front the Great Lover of the screen glared at him with an eye as keen as the eye of a potato. Only Stella Walker looked up at him with a radiant, never faltering smile.

"If we make him a Menjou type, then we get a sort of Michael Arlen only with a Honolulu atmosphere."

Still not a ripple in front, but in the rear a rustling, a perceptible shift toward the left, toward the front door.

"—then she says she feels this sex appil for him and he burns out and says 'Oh, go on destroy yourself——' "

At some point he heard Nat Keogh snicker and here and there were a few encouraging faces, but as he finished he had the sickening realization that he had made a fool of himself in view of an important section of the picture world, upon whose favor depended his career.

For a moment he existed in the midst of a confused silence, broken by a general trek for the door. He felt the undercurrent of derision that rolled through the gossip; then—all this was in the space of ten seconds—the Great Lover, his eye hard and empty as the eye of a needle, shouted "Boo! Boo!" voicing in an overtone what he felt was the mood of the crowd. It was the resentment of the professional toward the amateur, of the community toward the stranger, the thumbs-down of the clan.

Only Stella Walker was still standing near and thanking him as if he had been an unparalleled success, as if it hadn't occurred to her that anyone hadn't liked it. As Nat Keogh helped him into his overcoat, a great wave of self-disgust swept over him and he clung desperately to his rule of never betraying an inferior emotion until he no longer felt it.

"I was a flop," he said lightly, to Stella. "Never mind, it's a good number when appreciated. Thanks for your coöperation."

The smile did not leave her face—he bowed rather drunkenly and Nat drew him toward the door. . . .

The arrival of his breakfast awakened him into a broken and ruined world. Yesterday he was himself, a point of fire against an industry, today he felt that he was pitted under an enormous disadvantage, against those faces, against individual contempt and collective sneer. Worse than that, to Miles Calman he was become one of those rummies, stripped of dignity, whom Calman regretted he was compelled to use. To Stella Walker on whom he had forced a martyrdom to preserve the courtesy of her house—her opinion he did not dare to guess. His gastric juices ceased to flow and he set his poached eggs back on the telephone table. He wrote:

"Dear Miles: You can imagine my profound self-disgust. I confess to a taint of exhibitionism, but at six o'clock in the afternoon, in broad daylight! Good God! My apologies to your wife.

"Yours ever,

"Joel Coles."

Joel emerged from his office on the lot only to slink like a malefactor to the tobacco store. So suspicious was his manner that one of the studio police asked to see his admission card. He had decided to eat lunch outside when Nat Keogh, confident and cheerful, overtook him.

"What do you mean you're in permanent retirement? What if that Three-Piece Suit did boo you?

"Why, listen," he continued, drawing Joel into the studio restaurant. "The night of one of his premières at Grauman's, Joe Squires kicked his tail while he was bowing to the crowd. The ham said Joe'd hear from him later but when Joe called him up at eight o'clock next day and said, 'I thought I was going to hear from you,' he hung up the phone."

The preposterous story cheered Joel, and he found a gloomy consolation in staring at the group at the next table, the sad, lovely Siamese twins, the mean dwarfs, the proud giant from the circus picture. But looking beyond at the yellow-stained faces of pretty women, their eyes all melancholy and startling with mascara, their ball gowns garish in full day, he saw a group who had been at Calman's and winced.

"Never again," he exclaimed aloud, "absolutely my last social appearance in Hollywood!"

The following morning a telegram was waiting for him at his office:

"You were one of the most agreeable people at our party. Expect you at my sister June's buffet supper next Sunday.

"Stella Walker Calman."

The blood rushed fast through his veins for a feverish minute. Incredulously he read the telegram over.

"Well, that's the sweetest thing I ever heard of in my life!"

III

Crazy Sunday again. Joel slept until eleven, then he read a newspaper to catch up with the past week. He lunched in his room on trout, avocado salad and a pint of California wine. Dressing for the tea, he selected a pin-check suit, a blue shirt, a burnt orange tie. There were dark circles of fatigue under his eyes. In his second-hand car he drove to the Riviera apartments. As he was introducing himself to Stella's sister, Miles and Stella arrived in riding clothes—they had been quarreling fiercely most of the afternoon on all the dirt roads back of Beverly Hills.

Miles Calman, tall, nervous, with a desperate humor and the unhappiest eyes Joel ever saw, was an artist from the top of his curiously shaped head to his niggerish feet. Upon these last he stood firmly—he had never made a cheap picture though he had sometimes paid heavily for the luxury of making experimental flops. In spite of his excellent company, one could not be with him long without realizing that he was not a well man.

From the moment of their entrance Joel's day bound itself up inextricably with theirs. As he joined the group around them Stella turned away from it with an impatient little tongue click—and Miles Calman said to the man who happened to be next to him:

"Go easy on Eva Goebel. There's hell to pay about her at home." Miles turned to Joel, "I'm sorry I missed you at the office yesterday. I spent the afternoon at the analyst's."

"You being psychoanalyzed?"

"I have been for months. First I went for claustrophobia, now I'm trying to get my whole life cleared up. They say it'll take over a year."

"There's nothing the matter with your life," Joel assured him.

"Oh, no? Well, Stella seems to think so. Ask anybody—they can all tell you about it," he said bitterly.

A girl perched herself on the arm of Miles' chair; Joel crossed to Stella, who stood disconsolately by the fire.

"Thank you for your telegram," he said. "It was darn sweet. I can't imagine anybody as good-looking as you are being so good-humored."

She was a little lovelier than he had ever seen her and perhaps the unstinted admiration in his eyes prompted her to unload on him—it did not take long, for she was obviously at the emotional bursting point.

"—and Miles has been carrying on this thing for two years, and I never knew. Why, she was one of my best friends, always in the house. Finally when people began to come to me, Miles had to admit it."

She sat down vehemently on the arm of Joel's chair. Her riding breeches were the color of the chair and Joel saw that the mass of her hair was made up of some strands of red gold and some of pale gold, so that it could not be dyed, and that she had on no make-up. She was that good-looking——

Still quivering with the shock of her discovery, Stella found unbearable the spectacle of a new girl hovering over Miles; she led Joel into a bedroom, and seated at either end of a big bed they went on talking. People on their way to the washroom glanced in and made wisecracks, but Stella, emptying out her story, paid no attention. After a while Miles stuck his head in the door and said, "There's no use trying to explain something to Joel in half an hour that I don't understand myself and the psychoanalyst says will take a whole year to understand."

She talked on as if Miles were not there. She loved Miles, she said—under considerable difficulties she had always been faithful to him.

"The psychoanalyst told Miles that he had a mother complex. In his first marriage he transferred his mother complex to his wife, you see—and then his sex turned to me. But when we married the thing repeated itself—he transferred his mother complex to me and all his libido turned toward this other woman."

Joel knew that this probably wasn't gibberish—yet it sounded like gibberish. He knew Eva Goebel; she was a motherly person, older and probably wiser than Stella, who was a golden child.

Miles now suggested impatiently that Joel come back with them since Stella had so much to say, so they drove out to the mansion in Beverly Hills. Under the high ceilings the situation seemed more dignified and tragic. It was an eerie bright night with the dark very clear outside of all the windows and Stella all rose-gold raging and crying around the room. Joel did not quite believe in picture actresses' grief. They have other preoccupations—they are beautiful rose-gold figures blown full of life by writers and directors, and after hours they sit around and talk in whispers and giggle innuendoes, and the ends of many adventures flow through them.

Sometimes he pretended to listen and instead thought how well she was got up—sleek breeches with a matched set of legs in them, an Italian-colored sweater with a little high neck, and a short brown chamois coat. He couldn't decide whether she was an imitation of an English lady or an English lady was an imitation of her. She hovered somewhere between the realest of realities and the most blatant of impersonations.

"Miles is so jealous of me that he questions everything I do," she cried scornfully. "When I was in New York I wrote him that I'd been to the theater with Eddie Baker. Miles was so jealous he phoned me ten times in one day."

"I was wild," Miles snuffled sharply, a habit he had in times of stress. "The analyst couldn't get any results for a week."

Stella shook her head despairingly. "Did you expect me just to sit in the hotel for three weeks?"

"I don't expect anything. I admit that I'm jealous. I try not to be. I worked on that with Dr. Bridgebane, but it didn't do any good. I was jealous of Joel this afternoon when you sat on the arm of his chair."

"You were?" She started up. "You were! Wasn't there somebody on the arm of your chair? And did you speak to me for two hours?"

"You were telling your troubles to Joel in the bedroom."

"When I think that that woman"—she seemed to believe that to omit Eva Goebel's name would be to lessen her reality—"used to come here——"

"All right—all right," said Miles wearily. "I've admitted everything and I feel as bad about it as you do." Turning to Joel he began talking about pictures, while Stella moved restlessly along the far walls, her hands in her breeches pockets.

"They've treated Miles terribly," she said, coming suddenly back into the conversation as if they'd never discussed her personal affairs. "Dear, tell him about old Beltzer trying to change your picture."

As she stood hovering protectively over Miles, her eyes flashing with indignation in his behalf, Joel realized that he was in love with her. Stifled with excitement he got up to say good night.

With Monday the week resumed its workaday rhythm, in sharp contrast to the theoretical discussions, the gossip and scandal of Sunday; there was the endless detail of script revision—"Instead of a lousy dissolve, we can leave her voice on the sound track and cut to a medium shot of the taxi from Bell's angle or we can simply pull the camera back to include the station, hold it a minute and then pan to the row of taxis"—by Monday afternoon Joel had again forgotten that people whose business was to provide entertainment were ever privileged to be entertained. In the evening he phoned Miles' house. He asked for Miles but Stella came to the phone.

"Do things seem better?"

"Not particularly. What are you doing next Saturday evening?"

"Nothing."

"The Perrys are giving a dinner and theater party and Miles won't be here—he's flying to South Bend to see the Notre Dame-California game. I thought you might go with me in his place."

After a long moment Joel said, "Why—surely. If there's a conference I can't make dinner but I can get to the theater."

"Then I'll say we can come."

Joel walked his office. In view of the strained relations of the Calmans, would Miles be pleased, or did she intend that Miles shouldn't know of it? That would be out of the question—if Miles didn't mention it Joel would. But it was an hour or more before he could get down to work again.

Wednesday there was a four-hour wrangle in a conference room crowded with planets and nebulae of cigarette smoke. Three men and a woman paced the carpet in turn, suggesting or condemning, speaking sharply or persuasively, confidently or despairingly. At the end Joel lingered to talk to Miles.

The man was tired—not with the exaltation of fatigue but life-tired, with his lids sagging and his beard prominent over the blue shadows near his mouth.

"I hear you're flying to the Notre Dame game."

Miles looked beyond him and shook his head.

"I've given up the idea."

"Why?"

"On account of you." Still he did not look at Joel.

"What the hell, Miles?"

"That's why I've given it up." He broke into a perfunctory laugh at himself. "I can't tell what Stella might do just out of spite—she's invited you to take her to the Perrys', hasn't she? I wouldn't enjoy the game."

The fine instinct that moved swiftly and confidently on the set, muddled so weakly and helplessly through his personal life.

"Look, Miles," Joel said frowning. "I've never made any passes whatsoever at Stella. If you're really seriously canceling your trip on account of me, I won't go to the Perrys' with her. I won't see her. You can trust me absolutely."

Miles looked at him, carefully now.

"Maybe." He shrugged his shoulders. "Anyhow there'd just be somebody else. I wouldn't have any fun."

"You don't seem to have much confidence in Stella. She told me she'd always been true to you."

"Maybe she has." In the last few minutes several more muscles had sagged around Miles' mouth. "But how can I ask anything of her after what's happened? How can I expect her—" He broke off and his face grew harder as he said, "I'll tell you one thing, right or wrong and no matter what I've done, if I ever had anything on her I'd divorce her. I can't have my pride hurt—that would be the last straw."

His tone annoyed Joel, but he said:

"Hasn't she calmed down about the Eva Goebel thing?"

"No." Miles snuffled pessimistically. "I can't get over it either."

"I thought it was finished."

"I'm trying not to see Eva again, but you know it isn't easy just to drop something like that—it isn't some girl I kissed last night in a taxi. The psychoanalyst says——"

"I know," Joel interrupted. "Stella told me." This was depressing. "Well, as far as I'm concerned if you go to the game I won't see Stella. And I'm sure Stella has nothing on her conscience about anybody."

"Maybe not," Miles repeated listlessly. "Anyhow I'll stay and take her to the party. Say," he said suddenly, "I wish you'd come too. I've got to have somebody sympathetic to talk to. That's the trouble—I've influenced Stella in everything. Especially I've influenced her so that she likes all the men I like—it's very difficult."

"It must be," Joel agreed.

IV

Joel could not get to the dinner. Self-conscious in his silk hat against the unemployment, he waited for the others in front of the Hollywood Theater and watched the evening parade: obscure replicas of bright, particular picture stars, spavined men in polo coats, a stomping dervish with the beard and staff of an apostle, a pair of chic Filipinos in collegiate clothes, reminder that this corner of the Republic opened to the seven seas, a long fantastic carnival of young shouts which proved to be a fraternity initiation. The line split to pass two smart limousines that stopped at the curb.

There she was, in a dress like ice-water, made in a thousand pale-blue pieces, with icicles trickling at the throat. He started forward.

"So you like my dress?"

"Where's Miles?"

"He flew to the game after all. He left yesterday morning—at least I think—" She broke off. "I just got a telegram from South Bend saying that he's starting back. I forgot—you know all these people?"

The party of eight moved into the theater.

Miles had gone after all and Joel wondered if he should have come. But during the performance, with Stella a profile under the pure grain of light hair, he thought no more about Miles. Once he turned and looked at her and she looked back at him, smiling and meeting his eyes for as long as he wanted. Between the acts they smoked in the lobby and she whispered:

"They're all going to the opening of Jack Johnson's night club—I don't want to go, do you?"

"Do we have to?"

"I suppose not." She hesitated. "I'd like to talk to you. I suppose we could go to our house—if I were only sure——"

Again she hesitated and Joel asked:

"Sure of what?"

"Sure that—oh, I'm haywire I know, but how can I be sure Miles went to the game?"

"You mean you think he's with Eva Goebel?"

"No, not so much that—but supposing he was here watching everything I do. You know Miles does odd things sometimes. Once he wanted a man with a long beard to drink tea with him and he sent down to the casting agency for one, and drank tea with him all afternoon."

"That's different. He sent you a wire from South Bend—that proves he's at the game."

After the play they said good night to the others at the curb and were answered by looks of amusement. They slid off along the golden garish thoroughfare through the crowd that had gathered around Stella.

"You see he could arrange the telegrams," Stella said, "very easily."

That was true. And with the idea that perhaps her uneasiness was justified, Joel grew angry: if Miles had trained a camera on them he felt no obligations toward Miles. Aloud he said:

"That's nonsense."

There were Christmas trees already in the shop windows and the full moon over the boulevard was only a prop, as scenic as the giant boudoir lamps of the corners. On into the dark foliage of Beverly Hills that flamed as eucalyptus by day, Joel saw only the flash of a white face under his own, the arc of her shoulder. She pulled away suddenly and looked up at him.

"Your eyes are like your mother's," she said. "I used to have a scrap book full of pictures of her."

"Your eyes are like your own and not a bit like any other eyes," he answered.

Something made Joel look out into the grounds as they went into the house, as if Miles were lurking in the shrubbery. A telegram waited on the hall table. She read aloud:

"CHICAGO.

"Home tomorrow night. Thinking of you. Love.

"MILES."

"You see," she said, throwing the slip back on the table, "he could easily have faked that." She asked the butler for drinks and sandwiches and ran upstairs, while Joel walked into the empty reception rooms. Strolling about he wandered to the piano where he had stood in disgrace two Sundays before.

"Then we could put over," he said aloud, "a story of divorce, the younger generation and the Foreign Legion."

His thoughts jumped to another telegram.

"You were one of the most agreeable people at our party——"

An idea occurred to him. If Stella's telegram had been purely a gesture of courtesy then it was likely that Miles had inspired it, for it was Miles who had invited him. Probably Miles had said:

"Send him a wire—he's miserable—he thinks he's queered himself."

It fitted in with "I've influenced Stella in everything. Especially I've influenced her so that she likes all the men I like." A woman would do a thing like that because she felt sympathetic—only a man would do it because he felt responsible.

When Stella came back into the room he took both her hands.

"I have a strange feeling that I'm a sort of pawn in a spite game you're playing against Miles," he said.

"Help yourself to a drink."

"And the odd thing is that I'm in love with you anyhow."

The telephone rang and she freed herself to answer it.

"Another wire from Miles," she announced. "He dropped it, or it says he dropped it, from the airplane at Kansas City."

"I suppose he asked to be remembered to me."

"No, he just said he loved me. I believe he does. He's so very weak."

"Come sit beside me," Joel urged her.

It was early. And it was still a few minutes short of midnight a half-hour later, when Joel walked to the cold hearth, and said tersely:

"Meaning that you haven't any curiosity about me?"

"Not at all. You attract me a lot and you know it. The point is that I suppose I really do love Miles."

"Obviously."

"And tonight I feel uneasy about everything."

He wasn't angry—he was even faintly relieved that a possible entanglement was avoided. Still as he looked at her, the warmth and softness of her body thawing her cold blue costume, he knew she was one of the things he would always regret.

"I've got to go," he said. "I'll phone a taxi."

"Nonsense—there's a chauffeur on duty."

He winced at her readiness to have him go, and seeing this she kissed him lightly and said, "You're sweet, Joel." Then suddenly three things happened: he took down his drink at a gulp, the phone rang loud through the house and a clock in the hall struck in trumpet notes.

Nine—ten—eleven—twelve——

V

It was Sunday again. Joel realized that he had come to the theater this evening with the work of the week still hanging about him like cerements. He had made love to Stella as he might attack some matter to be cleaned up hurriedly before the day's end. But this was Sunday—the lovely, lazy perspective of the next twenty-four hours unrolled before him—every minute was something to be approached with lulling indirection, every moment held the germ of innumerable possibilities. Nothing was impossible—everything was just beginning. He poured himself another drink.

With a sharp moan, Stella slipped forward inertly by the telephone. Joel picked her up and laid her on the sofa. He squirted soda-water on a handkerchief and slapped it over her face. The telephone mouthpiece was still grinding and he put it to his ear.

"—the plane fell just this side of Kansas City. The body of Miles Calman has been identified and——"

He hung up the receiver.

"Lie still," he said, stalling, as Stella opened her eyes.

"Oh, what's happened?" she whispered. "Call them back. Oh, what's happened?"

"I'll call them right away. What's your doctor's name?"

"Did they say Miles was dead?"

"Lie quiet—is there a servant still up?"

"Hold me—I'm frightened."

He put his arm around her.

"I want the name of your doctor," he said sternly. "It may be a mistake but I want someone here."

"It's Doctor—Oh, God, is Miles dead?"

Joel ran upstairs and searched through strange medicine cabinets for spirits of ammonia. When he came down Stella cried:

"He isn't dead—I know he isn't. This is part of his scheme. He's torturing me. I know he's alive. I can feel he's alive."

"I want to get hold of some close friend of yours, Stella. You can't stay here alone tonight."

"Oh, no," she cried. "I can't see anybody. You stay. I haven't got any friend." She got up, tears streaming down her face. "Oh, Miles is my only friend. He's not dead—he can't be dead. I'm going there right away and see. Get a train. You'll have to come with me."

"You can't. There's nothing to do tonight. I want you to tell me the name of some woman I can call: Lois? Joan? Carmel? Isn't there somebody?"

Stella stared at him blindly.

"Eva Goebel was my best friend," she said.

Joel thought of Miles, his sad and desperate face in the office two days before. In the awful silence of his death all was clear about him. He was the only American-born director with both an interesting temperament and an artistic conscience. Meshed in an industry, he had paid with his ruined nerves for having no resilience, no healthy cynicism, no refuge—only a pitiful and precarious escape.

There was a sound at the outer door—it opened suddenly, and there were footsteps in the hall.

"Miles!" Stella screamed. "Is it you, Miles? Oh, it's Miles."

A telegraph boy appeared in the doorway.

"I couldn't find the bell. I heard you talking inside."

The telegram was a duplicate of the one that had been phoned. While Stella read it over and over, as though it were a black lie, Joel telephoned. It was still early and he had difficulty getting anyone; when finally he succeeded in finding some friends he made Stella take a stiff drink.

"You'll stay here, Joel," she whispered, as though she were half-asleep. "You won't go away. Miles liked you—he said you—" She shivered violently, "Oh, my God, you don't know how alone I feel." Her eyes closed, "Put your arms around me. Miles had a suit like that." She started bolt upright. "Think of what he must have felt. He was afraid of almost everything, anyhow."

She shook her head dazedly. Suddenly she seized Joel's face and held it close to hers.

"You won't go. You like me—you love me, don't you? Don't call up anybody. Tomorrow's time enough. You stay here with me tonight."

He stared at her, at first incredulously, and then with shocked understanding. In her dark groping Stella was trying to keep Miles alive by sustaining a situation in which he had figured—as if Miles' mind could not die so long as the possibilities that had worried him still existed. It was a distraught and tortured effort to stave off the realization that he was dead.

Resolutely Joel went to the phone and called a doctor.

"Don't, oh, don't call anybody!" Stella cried. "Come back here and put your arms around me."

"Is Doctor Bales in?"

"Joel," Stella cried. "I thought I could count on you. Miles liked you. He was jealous of you—Joel, come here."

Ah then—if he betrayed Miles she would be keeping him alive—for if he were really dead how could he be betrayed?

"—has just had a very severe shock. Can you come at once, and get hold of a nurse?"

"Joel!"

Now the door-bell and the telephone began to ring intermittently, and automobiles were stopping in front of the door.

"But you're not going," Stella begged him. "You're going to stay, aren't you?"

"No," he answered. "But I'll be back, if you need me."

Standing on the steps of the house which now hummed and palpitated with the life that flutters around death like protective leaves, he began to sob a little in his throat.

"Everything he touched he did something magical to," he thought. "He even brought that little gamin alive and made her a sort of masterpiece."

And then:

"What a hell of a hole he leaves in this damn wilderness—already!"

And then with a certain bitterness. "Oh, yes, I'll be back—I'll be back!"

1932

Ernest [Miller] Hemingway

(1899-1961)

CHRONOLOGY:

1899 Born on July 21, in Oak Park, Illinois.

1917 Was a reporter on the Kansas City *Star*.

1918 Served with the ambulance corp in Italy; wounded on the Italian front on July 8.

1921 Returned to Europe as a reporter for the Toronto *Star*.

1922 Settled in Paris and met Gertrude Stein, Ezra Pound, and others.

1923 *Three Stories & Ten Poems.*

1924-25 *In Our Time* (both Paris and American editions).

1926 *The Torrents of Spring; Today Is Friday,* story; *The Sun Also Rises.*

1927 *Men Without Women,* stories.

1929 *A Farewell to Arms;* Hemingway's father committed suicide.

1932 *Death in the Afternoon.*
1933 *God Rest You Merry Gentlemen*, story; *Winner Take Nothing*, stories.
1935 *Green Hills of Africa.*
1936 Went to Spain to support the Loyalists in the Spanish Civil War.
1937 *To Have and Have Not.*
1938 *The Spanish Earth*, film script; *The Fifth Column and the First Forty-Nine Stories*, play and collected stories.
1940 *For Whom the Bell Tolls.*
1942-45 Reported on and participated in World War II.
1950 *Across the River and into the Trees.*
1950-60 Settled in Cuba.
1952 *The Old Man and the Sea.*
1954 Awarded the Nobel Prize for Literature.
1961 Committed suicide on July 2, in Idaho.
1964 *A Moveable Feast.*

BIBLIOGRAPHY:

In 1953 Charles Scribner's Sons began issuing a uniform edition of Hemingway's works; the same publisher has also issued paperback editions of most of the major novels and short stories. Useful selections are in Malcolm Cowley, ed., *The Portable Hemingway* (New York, 1944) and Charles Poore, ed., *The Hemingway Reader* (New York, 1953).

Hemingway has attracted much critical attention. Of first importance is Carlos Baker, *Hemingway: The Writer as Artist* (3rd ed.; Princeton, 1963), with an extensive bibliography. Also useful are Philip Young, *Ernest Hemingway* (New York, 1952) and Charles Fenton, *The Apprenticeship of Ernest Hemingway: The Early Years* (New York, 1954). Important collections of critical essays are in John K. M. McCaffery, ed., *Ernest Hemingway: The Man and His Work* (Cleveland, 1950) and Carlos Baker, *Hemingway and His Critics: An International Anthology* (New York, 1961), with an extensive check list of additional critical studies.

For current studies of the stories, see Warren S. Walker's *Twentieth-Century Short Story Explication . . .* (Hamden, Conn., 1961), Supplement, 1963.

From *Green Hills of Africa*

. . . . .

"And tell me, who is the greatest writer in America?"

"My husband," said my wife.

"No. I do not mean for you to speak from family pride. I mean who really? Certainly not Upton Sinclair. Certainly not Sinclair Lewis. Who is your Thomas Mann? Who is your Valery?"

"We do not have great writers," I said. "Something happens to our good writers at a certain age. I can explain but it is quite long and may bore you."

"Please explain," he said. "This is what I enjoy. This is the best part of life. The life of the mind. This is not killing kudu."

"You haven't heard it yet," I said.

"Ah, but I can see it coming. You must take more beer to loosen your tongue."

"It's loose," I told him. "It's always too bloody loose. But *you* don't drink anything."

"No, I never drink. It is not good for the mind. It is unnecessary. But tell me. Please tell me."

"Well," I said, "we have had, in America, skillful writers. Poe is a skillful writer. It is skillful, marvellously constructed, and it is dead. We have had writers of rhetoric who had the good fortune to find a little, in a chronicle of another man and from voyaging, of how things, actual things, can be, whales for instance, and this knowledge is wrapped in the rhetoric like plums in a pudding. Occasionally it is there, alone, unwrapped in pudding, and it is good. This is Melville. But the people who praise it, praise it for the rhetoric which is not important. They put a mystery in which is not there."

"Yes," he said. "I see. But it is the mind working, its ability to work, which makes the rhetoric. Rhetoric is the blue sparks from the dynamo."

"Sometimes. And sometimes it is only blue sparks and what is the dynamo driving?"

"So. Go on."

"I've forgotten."

"No. Go on. Do not pretend to be stupid."

"Did you ever get up before daylight—"

"Every morning," he said. "Go on."

"All right. There were others who wrote like exiled English colonials from an England of which they were never a part to a newer England that they were making. Very good men with the small, dried, and excellent wisdom of Unitarians; men of letters; Quakers with a sense of humor."

"Who were these?"

"Emerson, Hawthorne, Whittier, and Company. All our early classics who did not know that a new classic does not bear any resemblance to the classics that have preceded it. It can steal from anything that it is better than, anything that is not a classic, all classics do that. Some writers are only born to help another writer to write one sentence. But it cannot derive from or resemble a previous classic. Also all these men were gentlemen, or wished to be. They were all very respectable. They did not use the words that people always have used in speech, the words that survive in language. Nor would you gather that they had bodies. They had minds, yes. Nice, dry, clean minds. This is all very dull, I would not state it except that you ask for it."

"Go on."

"There is one at that time that is supposed to be really good, Thoreau. I cannot tell you about it because I have not yet been able to read it. But that means nothing because I cannot read other naturalists unless they are being extremely accurate and not literary. Naturalists should all work alone and some one else should correlate their findings for them. Writers should work alone. They should see each other only after their work is done, and not too often then. Otherwise they become like writers in New York. All angleworms in a bottle, trying to derive knowledge and nourishment from their own contact and from the bottle. Sometimes the bottle is shaped art, sometimes economics, sometimes economic-religion. But once they are in the bottle they stay there. They are lonesome outside of the bottle. They do not want to be lonesome. They are afraid to be alone in their beliefs and no woman would love any of them enough so that they could kill their lonesomeness in that woman, or pool it with hers, or make something with her that makes the rest unimportant."

"But what about Thoreau?"

"You'll have to read him. Maybe I'll be able to later. I can do nearly everything later."

"Better have some more beer, Papa."

"All right."

"What about the good writers?"

"The good writers are Henry James, Stephen Crane, and Mark Twain. That's not the order they're good in. There is no order for good writers."

"Mark Twain is a humorist. The others I do not know."

"All modern American literature comes from one book by Mark Twain called *Huckleberry Finn*. If you read it you must stop where the Nigger Jim is stolen from the boys. That is the real end. The rest is just cheating. But it's the best book we've had. All American writing comes from that. There was nothing before. There has been nothing as good since."

"What about the others?"

"Crane wrote two fine stories. *The Open Boat* and *The Blue Hotel*. The last one is the best."

"And what happened to him?"

"He died. That's simple. He was dying from the start."

"But the other two?"

"They both lived to be old men but they did not get any wiser as they got older. I don't know what they really wanted. You see we make our writers into something very strange."

"I do not understand."

"We destroy them in many ways. First, economically. They make money. It is only by hazard that a writer makes money although good books always make money eventually. Then our writers when they have made some money increase their standard of living and they are caught. They have to write to keep up their establishments, their wives, and so on, and they write slop. It is slop not on purpose but because it is hurried. Because they write when there is nothing to say or no water in the well. Because they are ambitious. Then, once they have betrayed themselves, they justify it and you get more slop. Or else they read the critics.

If they believe the critics when they say they are great then they must believe them when they say they are rotten and they lose confidence. At present we have two good writers who cannot write because they have lost confidence through reading critics. If they wrote, sometimes it would be good and sometimes not so good and sometimes it would be quite bad, but the good would get out. But they have read the critics and they must write masterpieces. The masterpieces the critics said they wrote. They weren't masterpieces, of course. They were just quite good books. So now they cannot write at all. The critics have made them impotent."

"Who are these writers?"

"Their names would mean nothing to you and by now they may have written, become frightened, and be impotent again."

"But what is it that happens to American writers? Be definite."

"I was not here in the old days so I cannot tell you about them, but now there are various things. At a certain age the men writers change into Old Mother Hubbard. The women writers became Joan of Arc without the fighting. They become leaders. It doesn't matter who they lead. If they do not have followers they invent them. It is useless for those selected as followers to protest. They are accused of disloyalty. Oh, hell. There are too many things happen to them. That is one thing. The others try to save their souls with what they write. That is an easy way out. Others are ruined by the first money, the first praise, the first attack, the first time they find they cannot write, or the first time they cannot do anything else, or else they get frightened and join organizations that do their thinking for them. Or they do not know what they want. Henry James wanted to make money. He never did, of course."

"And you?"

"I am interested in other things. I have a good life but I must write because if I do not write a certain amount I do not enjoy the rest of my life."

"And what do you want?"

"To write as well as I can and learn as I go along. At the same time I have my life which I enjoy and which is a damned good life."

"Hunting kudu?"

"Yes. Hunting kudu and many other things."

"What other things?"

"Plenty of other things."

"And you know what you want?"

"Yes."

"You really like to do this, what you do now, this silliness of kudu?"

"Just as much as I like to be in the Prado."

"One is not better than the other?"

"One is as necessary as the other. There are other things, too."

"Naturally. There must be. But this sort of thing means something to you, really?"

"Truly."

"And you know what you want?"

"Absolutely, and I get it all the time."

"But it takes money."

"I could always make money and besides I have been very lucky."

"Then you are happy?"

"Except when I think of other people."

"Then you think of other people?"

"Oh, yes."

"But you do nothing for them?"

"No."

"Nothing?"

"Maybe a little."

"Do you think your writing is worth doing—as an end in itself?"

"Oh, yes."

"You are sure?"

"Very sure."

"That must be very pleasant."

"It is," I said. "It is the one altogether pleasant thing about it."

"This is getting awfully serious," my wife said.

"It's a damned serious subject."

"You see, he is really serious about something," Kandisky said. "I knew he must be serious on something besides kudu."

"The reason every one now tries to avoid it, to deny that it is important, to make it seem vain to try to do it, is because it is so difficult. Too many factors must combine to make it possible."

"What is this now?"

"The kind of writing that can be done. How far prose can be carried if any one is serious enough and has luck. There is a fourth and fifth dimension that can be gotten."

"You believe it?"

"I know it."

"And if a writer can get this?"

"Then nothing else matters. It is more important than anything he can do. The chances are, of course, that he will fail. But there is a chance that he succeeds."

"But that is poetry you are talking about."

"No. It is much more difficult than poetry. It is a prose that has never been written. But it can be written, without tricks and without cheating. With nothing that will go bad afterwards."

"And why has it not been written?"

"Because there are too many factors. First, there must be talent, much talent. Talent such as Kipling had. Then there must be discipline. The discipline of Flaubert. Then there must be the conception of what it can be and an absolute conscience as unchanging as the standard meter in Paris, to prevent faking. Then the writer must be intelligent and disinterested and above all he must survive. Try to get all these in one person and have him come through all the influences that press on a writer. The hardest thing, because time is so short, is for him to survive and get his work done. But I would like us to have such a writer and to read what he would write. What do you say? Should we talk about something else?"

"It is interesting what you say. Naturally I do not agree with everything."

"Naturally."

"What about a gimlet?" Pop asked. "Don't you think a gimlet might help?"

"Tell me first what are the things, the actual, concrete things that harm a writer?"

I was tired of the conversation which was becoming an interview. So I would make it an interview and finish it. The necessity to put a thousand intangibles into a sentence, now, before lunch, was too bloody.

"Politics, women, drink, money, ambition. And the lack of politics, women, drink, money and ambition," I said profoundly.

"He's getting much too easy now," Pop said.

* * * * *

. . . It was very hot climbing back up the sandy ravine and I was glad to lean my back against the tree trunk and read in Tolstoi's *Sevastopol*. It was a very young book and had one fine description of fighting in it, where the French take the redoubt and I thought about Tolstoi and about what a great advantage an experience of war was to a writer. It was one of the major subjects and certainly one of the hardest to write truly of and those writers who had not seen it were always very jealous and tried to make it seem unimportant, or abnormal, or a disease as a subject, while, really, it was just something quite irreplaceable that they had missed. Then Sevastopol made me think of the Boulevard Sevastopol in Paris, about riding a bicycle down it in the rain on the way home from Strassburg and the slipperiness of the rails of the tram cars and the feeling of riding on greasy, slippery asphalt and cobble stones in traffic in the rain, and how we had nearly lived on the Boulevard du Temple that time, and I remembered the look of that apartment, how it was arranged, and the wall paper, and instead we had taken the upstairs of the pavilion in Notre Dame des Champs in the courtyard with the sawmill (*and the sudden whine of the saw, the smell of sawdust and the chestnut tree over the roof with a mad woman downstairs*) and the year worrying about money (*all of the stories back in the mail that came in through a slit in the saw-mill door, with notes of rejection that would never call them stories, but always anecdotes, sketches, contes, etc. They did not want them, and we lived on poireaux and drank cahors and water*) and how fine the fountains were at the Place de L'Observatoire (*water sheen rippling on the bronze of horses' manes, bronze breasts and shoulders, green under thin-flowing water*) and when they put up the bust of Flaubert in the Luxembourg on the short cut through the gardens on the way to the rue Soufflot (*one that we believed in, loved without criticism, heavy now in stone as an idol should be*). He had not seen war but he had seen a revolution and the Commune and a revolution is much the best if you do not become bigoted because every one speaks the same language. Just as civil war is the best war for a writer, the most complete. Stendhal had seen a war and Napoleon taught him to write. He was teaching everybody then; but no one else learned. Dostoevsky was made by being sent to Siberia. Writers are forged in injustice as a sword is forged. I wondered if it would make a writer of him, give him the necessary shock to cut the overflow of words and give him a sense of proportion, if they sent Tom Wolfe to Siberia or to the Dry Tortugas. Maybe it would and maybe it wouldn't. He seemed sad, really, like Carnera. Tolstoi was a small man. Joyce was of medium height and he wore his eyes out. And that last night, drunk, with Joyce and the thing he kept quoting from Edgar Quinet, "Fraîche et rose comme au jour de la bataille." I didn't have it right I knew. And when you saw him he would take up a conversation interrupted three years before. It was nice to see a great writer in our time.

What I had to do was work. I did not care, particularly, how it all came out. I did not take my own life seriously any more, any one else's life, yes, but not mine. They all wanted something that I did not want and I would get it without wanting it, if I worked. To work was the only thing, it was the one thing that always made you feel good, and in the meantime it was my own damned life and I would lead it where and how I pleased. And where I had led it now pleased me very much. This was a better sky than Italy. The hell it was. The best sky was in Italy and Spain and Northern Michigan in the fall and in the fall in the Gulf off Cuba. You could beat this sky; but not the country.

All I wanted to do now was get back to Africa. We had not left it, yet, but when I would wake in the night I would lie, listening, homesick for it already.

Now, looking out the tunnel of trees over the ravine at the sky with white clouds moving across in the wind, I loved the country so that I was happy as you are after you have been with a woman that you really love, when, empty, you feel it welling up again and there it is and you can never have it all and yet what there is, now, you can have, and you want more and more, to have, and be, and live in, to possess now again for always, for that long, sudden-ended always; making time stand still, sometimes so very still that afterwards you wait to hear it move, and it is slow in starting. But you are not alone, because if you have ever really loved her happy and untragic, she loves you always; no matter whom she loves nor where she goes she loves you more. So if you have loved some woman and some country you are very fortunate and, if you die afterwards it makes no difference. Now, being in Africa, I was hungry for more of it, the changes of the seasons, the rains with no need to travel, the discomforts that you paid to make it real, the names of the trees, of the small animals, and all the birds, to know the language and have time to be in it and to move slowly. I had loved country all my life; the country was always better than the people. I could only care about people a very few at a time. . . .

1935

Big Two-Hearted River

PART I

The train went on up the track out of sight, around one of the hills of burnt timber. Nick sat down on the bundle of canvas and bedding the baggage man had pitched out of the door of the baggage car. There was no town, nothing but the rails and the burned-over country. The thirteen saloons that had lined the one street of Seney had not left a trace. The foundations of the Mansion House hotel stuck up above the ground. The stone was chipped and split by the fire. It was all that was left of the town of Seney. Even the surface had been burned off the ground.

Nick looked at the burned-over stretch of hillside, where he had expected to find the scattered houses of the town and then walked down the railroad track to the bridge over the river. The river was there. It swirled against the log spiles of the bridge. Nick looked down into the clear, brown water, colored from the pebbly bottom, and watched the trout keeping themselves steady in the current with wavering fins. As he watched them they changed their positions by quick angles, only to hold steady in the fast water again. Nick watched them a long time.

He watched them holding themselves with their noses into the current, many trout in deep, fast moving water, slightly distorted as he watched far down through the glassy convex surface of the pool, its surface pushing and swelling smooth against the resistance of the log-driven piles of the bridge. At the bottom of the pool were the big trout. Nick did not see them at first. Then he saw them at the bottom of the pool, big trout looking to hold themselves on the gravel bottom in a varying mist of gravel and sand, raised in spurts by the current.

Nick looked down into the pool from the bridge. It was a hot day. A kingfisher flew up the stream. It was a long time since Nick had looked into a stream and seen trout. They were very satisfactory. As the shadow of the kingfisher moved up the stream, a big trout shot upstream in a long angle, only his shadow marking the angle, then lost his shadow as he came through the surface of the water, caught the sun, and then, as he went back into the stream under the surface, his shadow seemed to float down the stream with the current, unresisting, to his post under the bridge where he tightened facing up into the current.

Nick's heart tightened as the trout moved. He felt all the old feeling.

He turned and looked down the stream. It stretched away, pebbly-bottomed with shallows and big boulders and a deep pool as it curved away around the foot of a bluff.

Nick walked back up the ties to where his pack lay in the cinders beside the railway track. He was happy. He adjusted the pack harness around the bundle, pulling straps tight, slung the pack on his back, got his arms through the shoulder straps and took some of the pull off his shoulders by leaning his forehead against the wide band of the tumpline. Still, it was too heavy. It was much too heavy. He had his leather rod-case in his hand and leaning forward to keep the weight of the pack high on his shoulders he walked along the road that paralleled the railway track, leaving the burned town behind in the heat, and then turned off around a hill with a high, fire-scarred hill on either side onto a road that went back into the country. He walked along the road feeling the ache from the pull of the heavy pack. The road climbed steadily. It was hard work walking up-hill. His muscles ached and the day was hot, but Nick felt happy. He felt he had left everything behind, the need for thinking, the need to write, other needs. It was all back of him.

From the time he had gotten down off the train and the baggage man had thrown his pack out of the open car door things had been different. Seney was burned, the country was burned over and changed, but it did not matter. It could not all be burned. He knew that. He hiked along the road, sweating in the sun, climbing to cross the range of hills that separated the railway from the pine plains.

The road ran on, dipping occasionally, but always climbing. Nick went on up. Finally the road after going parallel to the burnt hillside reached the top. Nick leaned back against a stump and slipped out of the pack harness. Ahead of him, as far as he could see, was the pine plain. The burned country stopped off at the left with the range of hills. On ahead islands of dark pine trees rose out of the plain. Far off to the left was the line of the river. Nick followed it with his eye and caught glints of the water in the sun.

There was nothing but the pine plain ahead of him, until the far blue hills that marked the Lake Superior height of land. He could hardly see them, faint and far away in the heat-light over the plain. If he looked too steadily they were gone. But if he only half-looked they were there, the far-off hills of the height of land.

Nick sat down against the charred stump and smoked a cigarette. His pack balanced on the top of the stump, harness holding ready, a hollow molded in it from his back. Nick sat smoking, looking out over the country. He did not need to get his map out. He knew where he was from the position of the river.

As he smoked, his legs stretched out in front of him, he noticed a grasshopper walk along the ground and up onto his woolen sock. The grasshopper was black. As he had walked long the road, climbing, he had started many grasshoppers from the dust. They were all black. They were not the big grasshoppers with yellow and black or red and black wings whirring out from their black wing sheathing as they fly up. These were just ordinary hoppers, but all a sooty black in color. Nick had wondered about them as he walked, without really thinking about them. Now, as he watched the black hopper that was nibbling at the wool of his sock with its four-way lip, he realized that they had all turned black from living in the burned-over land. He realized that the fire must have come the year before, but the grasshoppers were all black now. He wondered how long they would stay that way.

Carefully he reached his hand down and took hold of the hopper by the wings. He turned him up, all his legs walking in the air, and looked at his jointed belly. Yes, it was black too, irridescent where the back and head were dusty.

"Go on, hopper," Nick said, speaking out loud for the first time. "Fly away somewhere."

He tossed the grasshopper up into the air and watched him sail away to a charcoal stump across the road.

Nick stood up. He leaned his back against the weight of his pack where it rested upright on the stump and got his arms through the shoulder straps. He stood with the pack on his back on the brow of the hill looking out across the country, toward the distant river and then struck down the hillside away from the road. Underfoot the ground was good walking. Two hundred yards down the hillside the fire line stopped. Then it was sweet fern, growing ankle high, to walk through, and clumps of jack pines; a long undulating country with frequent rises and descents, sandy underfoot and the country alive again.

Nick kept his direction by the sun. He knew where he wanted to strike the river and he kept on through the pine plain, mounting small rises to see other rises ahead of him and sometimes from the top of a rise a great solid island of pines off to his right or his left. He broke off some sprigs of the heathery sweet fern, and put them under his pack straps. The chafing crushed it and he smelled it as he walked.

He was tired and very hot, walking across the uneven, shadeless pine plain. At any time he knew he could strike the river by turning off to his left. It could not be more than a mile away. But he kept on toward the north to hit the river as far upstream as he could go in one day's walking.

For some time as he walked Nick had been in sight of one of the big islands of pine standing out above the rolling high ground he was crossing. He dipped down and then as he came slowly up to the crest of the bridge he turned and made toward the pine trees.

There was no underbrush in the island of pine trees. The trunks of the trees went straight up or slanted toward each other. The trunks were straight and brown without branches. The branches were high above. Some interlocked to make a solid shadow on the brown forest floor. Around the grove of trees was a bare space. It was brown and soft underfoot as Nick walked on it. This was the over-lapping of the pine needle floor, extending out beyond the width of the high branches. The trees had grown tall and the branches moved high, leaving in the sun this bare space they had once covered with shadow. Sharp at the edge of this extension of the forest floor commenced the sweet fern.

Nick slipped off his pack and lay down in the shade. He lay on his back and looked up into the pine trees. His neck and back and the small of his back rested as he stretched. The earth felt good against his back. He looked up at the sky, through the branches, and then shut his eyes. He opened them and looked up again. There was a wind high up in the branches. He shut his eyes again and went to sleep.

Nick woke stiff and cramped. The sun was nearly down. His pack was heavy and the straps painful as he lifted it on. He leaned over with the pack on and picked up the leather rod-case and started out from the pine trees across the sweet fern swale, toward the river. He knew it could not be more than a mile.

He came down a hillside covered with stumps into a meadow. At the edge of the meadow flowed the river. Nick was glad to get to the river. He walked upstream through the meadow. His trousers were soaked with the dew as he walked. After the hot day, the dew had come quickly and heavily. The river made no sound. It was too fast and smooth. At the edge of the meadow, before he mounted to a piece of high ground to make camp, Nick looked down the river at the trout rising. They were rising to insects come from the swamp on the other side of the stream when the sun went down. The trout jumped out of water to take them. While Nick walked through the little stretch of meadow alongside the stream, trout had jumped high out of water. Now as he looked down the river, the insects must be settling on the surface, for the trout were feeding steadily all down the stream. As far down the long stretch as he could see, the trout were rising, making circles all down the surface of the water, as though it were starting to rain.

The ground rose, wooded and sandy, to overlook the meadow, the stretch of river and the swamp. Nick dropped his pack and rod-case and looked for a level piece of ground. He was very hungry and he wanted to make his camp before he cooked. Between two jack pines, the ground was quite level. He took the ax out of the pack and chopped out two projecting roots. That leveled a piece of ground large enough to sleep on. He smoothed out the sandy soil with his hand and pulled all the sweet fern bushes by their roots. His hands smelled good from the sweet fern. He smoothed the uprooted earth. He did not want anything making lumps under the blankets. When he had the ground smooth, he spread his three blankets. One he folded double, next to the ground. The other two he spread on top.

With the ax he slit off a bright slab of pine from one of the stumps and split it into pegs for the tent. He wanted them long and solid to hold in the ground. With the tent unpacked and spread on the ground, the pack, leaning against a jack pine, looked much smaller. Nick tied the rope that served the tent for a ridge-pole to the trunk of one of the pine trees and pulled the tent up off the ground with the other end of the rope and tied it to the other pine. The tent hung on the rope like a canvas blanket on a clothesline. Nick poked a pole he had cut up under the back peak of the canvas and then made it a tent by pegging out the sides. He pegged the sides out taut and drove the pegs deep, hitting them down into the ground with the flat of the ax until the rope loops were buried and the canvas was drum tight.

Across the open mouth of the tent Nick fixed cheesecloth to keep out mosquitoes. He crawled inside under the mosquito bar with various things from the pack to put at the head of the bed under the slant of the canvas. Inside the tent the light came through the brown canvas. It smelled pleasantly of canvas. Already there was something mysterious and homelike. Nick was happy as he crawled inside the tent. He had not been unhappy all day. This was different though. Now things were done. There had been this to do. Now it was done. It had been a hard trip. He was very tired. That was done. He had made his camp. He was settled. Nothing could touch him. It was a good place to camp. He was there, in the good place. He was in his home where he had made it. Now he was hungry.

He came out, crawling under the cheesecloth. It was quite dark outside. It was lighter in the tent.

Nick went over to the pack and found, with his fingers, a long nail in a paper sack of nails, in the bottom of the pack. He drove it into the pine tree, holding it close and hitting it gently with the flat of the ax. He hung the pack up on the nail. All his supplies were in the pack. They were off the ground and sheltered now.

Nick was hungry. He did not believe he had ever been hungrier. He opened and emptied a can of pork and beans and a can of spaghetti into the frying pan.

"I've got a right to eat this kind of stuff, if I'm willing to carry it," Nick said. His voice sounded strange in the darkening woods. He did not speak again.

He started a fire with some chunks of pine he got with the ax from a stump. Over the fire he stuck a wire grill, pushing the four legs down into the ground with his boot. Nick put the frying pan on the grill over the flames. He was hungrier. The beans and spaghetti warmed. Nick stirred them and mixed them together. They began to bubble, making little bubbles that rose with difficulty to the surface. There was a good smell. Nick got out a bottle of tomato catchup and cut four slices of bread. The little bubbles were coming faster now. Nick sat down beside the fire and lifted the frying pan off. He poured about half the contents out into the tin plate. It spread slowly on the plate. Nick knew it was too hot. He poured on some tomato catchup. He knew the beans and spaghetti were still too hot. He looked at the fire, then at the tent, he was not going to spoil it all by burning his tongue. For years he had never enjoyed fried bananas because he had never been able to wait for them to cool. His tongue was very sensitive. He was very hungry. Across the river in the swamp, in the almost dark, he saw a mist rising. He looked at the tent once more. All right. He took a full spoonful from the plate.

"Chrise," Nick said, "Geezus Chrise," he said happily.

He ate the whole plateful before he remembered the bread. Nick finished the second plateful with the bread, mopping the plate shiny. He had not eaten since a cup of coffee and a ham sandwich in the station restaurant at St. Ignace. It had been a very fine experience. He had been that hungry before, but had not been able to satisfy it. He could have made camp hours before if he had wanted to. There were plenty of good places to camp on the river. But this was good.

Nick tucked two big chips of pine under the grill. The fire flared up. He had forgotten to get water for the coffee. Out of the pack he got a folding canvas bucket and walked down the hill, across the edge of the meadow, to the stream. The other bank was in the white mist. The grass was wet and cold as he knelt on the bank and dipped the canvas bucket into the stream. It bellied and pulled hard in the current. The water was ice cold. Nick rinsed the bucket and carried it full up to the camp. Up away from the stream it was not so cold.

Nick drove another big nail and hung up the bucket full of water. He dipped the coffee pot half full, put some more chips under the grill onto the fire and put the pot on. He could not remember which way he made coffee. He could remember an argument about it with Hopkins, but not which side he had taken. He decided to bring it to a boil. He remembered now that was Hopkins's way. He had once argued about everything with Hopkins. While he waited for the coffee to boil, he opened a small can of apricots. He liked to open cans. He emptied the can of apricots out into a tin cup. While he watched the coffee on the fire, he drank the juice syrup of the apricots, carefully at first to keep from spilling, then meditatively, sucking the apricots down. They were better than fresh apricots.

The coffee boiled as he watched. The lid came up and coffee and grounds ran down the side of the pot. Nick took it off the grill. It was a triumph for Hopkins. He put sugar in the empty apricot cup and poured some of the coffee out to cool. It was too hot to pour and he used his hat to hold the handle of the coffee pot. He would not let it steep in the pot at all. Not the first cup. It should be straight Hopkins all the way. Hop deserved that. He was a very serious coffee drinker. He was the most serious man Nick had ever known. Not heavy, serious. That was a long time ago. Hopkins spoke without moving his lips. He had played polo. He made millions of dollars in Texas. He had borrowed carfare to go to Chicago, when the wire came that his first big well had come in. He could have wired for money. That would have been too slow. They called Hop's girl the Blonde Venus. Hop did not mind because she was not his real girl. Hopkins said very confidently that none of them would make fun of his real girl. He was right. Hopkins went away when the telegram came. That was on the Black River. It took eight days for the telegram to reach him. Hopkins gave away his .22 caliber Colt automatic pistol to Nick. He gave his camera to Bill. It was to remember him always by. They were all going fishing again next summer. The Hop Head was rich. He would get a yacht and they would all cruise along the north shore of Lake Superior. He was excited but serious. They said good-bye and all felt bad. It broke up the trip. They never saw Hopkins again. That was a long time ago on the Black River.

Nick drank the coffee, the coffee according to Hopkins. The coffee was bitter. Nick laughed. It made a good ending to the story. His mind was starting to work. He knew he could choke it because he was tired enough. He spilled the coffee out of the pot and shook the grounds loose into the fire. He lit a cigarette and went inside the tent. He took off his shoes and trousers, sitting on the blankets, rolled the shoes up inside the trousers for a pillow and got in between the blankets.

Out through the front of the tent he watched the glow of the fire, when the night wind blew on it. It was a quiet night. The swamp was perfectly quiet. Nick stretched under the blanket comfortably. A mosquito hummed close to his ear. Nick sat up and lit a match. The mosquito was on the canvas, over his head. Nick moved the match quickly up to it. The mosquito made a satisfactory hiss in the flame. The match went out. Nick lay down again under the blanket. He turned on his side and shut his eyes. He was sleepy. He felt sleep coming. He curled up under the blanket and went to sleep.

PART II

In the morning the sun was up and the tent was starting to get hot. Nick crawled out under the mosquito netting stretched across the mouth of the tent, to look at the morning. The grass was wet on his hands as he came out. He held his trousers and his shoes in his hands. The sun was just up over the hill. There was the meadow, the river and the swamp. There were birch trees in the green of the swamp on the other side of the river.

The river was clear and smoothly fast in the early morning. Down about two hundred yards were three logs all the way across the stream. They made the water smooth and deep above them. As Nick watched, a mink crossed the river on the logs and went into the swamp. Nick was excited. He was excited by the early morning and the river. He was really too hurried to eat breakfast, but he knew he must. He built a little fire and put on the coffee pot.

While the water was heating in the pot he took an empty bottle and went down over the edge of the high ground to the meadow. The meadow was wet with dew and Nick wanted to catch grasshoppers for bait before the sun dried the grass. He found plenty of good grasshoppers. They were at the base of the grass stems. Sometimes they clung to a grass stem. They were cold and wet with the dew, and could not jump until the sun warmed them. Nick picked them up, taking only the medium-sized brown ones, and put them into the bottle. He turned over a log and just under the shelter of the edge were several hundred hoppers. It was a grasshopper lodging house. Nick put about fifty of the medium browns into the bottle. While he was picking up the hoppers the others warmed in the sun and commenced to hop away. They flew when they hopped. At first they made one flight and stayed stiff when they landed, as though they were dead.

Nick knew that by the time he was through with breakfast they would be as lively as ever. Without dew in the grass it would take him all day to catch a bottle full of good grasshoppers and he would have to crush many of them, slamming at them with his hat. He washed his hands at the stream. He was excited to be near it. Then he walked up to the tent. The hoppers were already jumping stiffly in the grass. In the bottle, warmed by the sun, they were jumping in a mass. Nick put in a pine stick as a cork. It plugged the mouth of the bottle enough, so the hoppers could not get out and left plenty of air passage.

He had rolled the log back and knew he could get grasshoppers there every morning.

Nick laid the bottle full of jumping grasshoppers against a pine trunk.

Rapidly he mixed some buckwheat flour with water and stirred it smooth, one cup of flour, one cup of water. He put a handful of coffee in the pot and dipped a lump of grease out of a can and slid it sputtering across the hot skillet. On the smoking skillet he poured smoothly the buckwheat batter. It spread like lava, the grease spitting sharply. Around the edges the buckwheat cake began to firm, then brown, then crisp. The surface was bubbling slowly to porousness. Nick pushed under the browned under surface with a fresh pine chip. He shook the skillet sideways and the cake was loose on the surface. I won't try and flop it, he thought. He slid the chip of clean wood all the way under the cake, and flopped it over onto its face. It sputtered in the pan.

When it was cooked Nick regreased the skillet. He used all the batter. It made another big flapjack and one smaller one.

Nick ate a big flapjack and a smaller one, covered with apple butter. He put apple butter on the third cake, folded it over twice, wrapped it in oiled paper and put it in his shirt pocket. He put the apple butter jar back in the pack and cut bread for two sandwiches.

In the pack he found a big onion. He sliced it in two and peeled the silky outer skin. Then he cut one half into slices and made onion sandwiches. He wrapped them in oiled paper and buttoned them in the other pocket of his khaki shirt. He turned the skillet upside down on the grill, drank the coffee, sweetened and yellow brown with the condensed milk in it, and tidied up the camp. It was a good camp.

Nick took his fly rod out of the leather rod-case, jointed it, and shoved the rod-case back into the tent. He put on the reel and threaded the line through the guides. He had to hold it from hand to hand, as he threaded it, or it would slip back through its own weight. It was a heavy, double tapered fly line. Nick had paid eight dollars for it a long time ago. It was made heavy to lift back in the air and come forward flat and heavy and straight to make it possible to cast a fly which has no weight. Nick opened the aluminum leader box. The leaders were coiled between the damp flannel pads. Nick had wet the pads at the water cooler on the train up to St. Ignace. In the damp pads the gut leaders had softened and Nick unrolled one and tied it by a loop at the end to the heavy fly line. He fastened a hook on the end of the leader. It was a small hook; very thin and springy.

Nick took it from his hook book, sitting with the rod across his lap. He tested the knot and the spring of the rod by pulling the line taut. It was a good feeling. He was careful not to let the hook bite into his finger.

He started down to the stream, holding his rod, the bottle of grasshoppers hung from his neck by a thong tied in half hitches around the neck of the bottle. His landing net hung by a hook from his belt. Over his shoulder was a long flour sack tied at each corner into an ear. The cord went over his shoulder. The sack flapped against his legs.

Nick felt awkward and professionally happy with all his equipment hanging from him. The grasshopper bottle swung against his chest. In his shirt the breast pockets bulged against him with the lunch and his fly book.

He stepped into the stream. It was a shock. His trousers clung tight to his legs. His shoes felt the gravel. The water was a rising cold shock.

Rushing, the current sucked against his legs. Where he stepped in, the water was over his knees. He waded with the current. The gravel slid under his shoes. He looked down at the swirl of water below each leg and tipped up the bottle to get a grasshopper.

The first grasshopper gave a jump in the neck of the bottle and went out into the water. He was sucked under in the whirl by Nick's right leg and came to the surface a little way down stream. He floated rapidly, kicking. In a quick circle, breaking the smooth surface of the water, he disappeared. A trout had taken him.

Another hopper poked his face out of the bottle. His antennæ wavered. He was getting his front legs out of the bottle to jump. Nick took him by the head and held him while he threaded the slim hook under his chin, down through his thorax and into the last segments of his abdomen. The grasshopper took hold of the hook with his front feet, spitting tobacco juice on it. Nick dropped him into the water.

Holding the rod in his right hand he let out line against the pull of the grasshopper in the current. He stripped off line from the reel with his left hand and let it run free. He could see the hopper in the little waves of the current. It went out of sight.

There was a tug on the line. Nick pulled against the taut line. It was his first strike. Holding the now living rod across the current, he brought in the line with his left hand. The rod bent in jerks, the trout pumping against the current. Nick knew it was a small one. He lifted the rod straight up in the air. It bowed with the pull.

He saw the trout in the water jerking with his head and body against the shifting tangent of the line in the stream.

Nick took the line in his left hand and pulled the trout, thumping tiredly against the current, to the surface. His back was mottled the clear, water-over-gravel color, his side flashing in the sun. The rod under his right arm, Nick stooped, dipping his right hand into the current. He held the trout, never still, with his moist right hand, while he unhooked the barb from his mouth, then dropped him back into the stream.

He hung unsteadily in the current, then settled to the bottom beside a stone. Nick reached down his hand to touch him, his arm to the elbow under water. The trout was steady in the moving stream, resting on the gravel, beside a stone. As Nick's fingers touched him, touched his smooth, cool, underwater feeling he was gone, gone in a shadow across the bottom of the stream.

He's all right, Nick thought. He was only tired.

He had wet his hand before he touched the trout, so he would not disturb the delicate mucus that covered him. If a trout was touched with a dry hand, a white fungus attacked the unprotected spot. Years before when he had fished crowded streams, with fly fishermen ahead of him and behind him, Nick had again and again come on dead trout, furry with white fungus, drifted against a rock, or floating belly up in some pool. Nick did not like to fish with other men on the river. Unless they were of your party, they spoiled it.

He wallowed down the stream, above his knees in the current, through the fifty yards of shallow water above the pile of logs that crossed the stream. He did not rebait his hook and held it in his hand as he waded. He was certain he could catch small trout in the shallows, but he did not want them. There would be no big trout in the shallows this time of day.

Now the water deepened up his thighs sharply and coldly. Ahead was the smooth dammed-back flood of water above the logs. The water was smooth and dark; on the left, the lower edge of the meadow; on the right the swamp.

Nick leaned back against the current and took a hopper from the bottle. He threaded the hopper on the hook and spat on him for good luck. Then he pulled several yards of line from the reel and tossed the hopper out ahead onto the fast, dark water. It floated down towards the logs, then the weight of the line pulled the bait under the surface. Nick held the rod in his right hand, letting the line run out through his fingers.

There was a long tug. Nick struck and the rod came alive and dangerous, bent double, the line tightening, coming out of water, tightening, all in a heavy, dangerous, steady pull. Nick felt the moment when the leader would break if the strain increased and let the line go.

The reel ratcheted into a mechanical shriek as the line went out in a rush. Too fast. Nick could not check it, the line rushing out, the reel note rising as the line ran out.

With the core of the reel showing, his heart feeling stopped with the excitement, leaning back against the current that mounted icily his thighs, Nick thumbed the reel hard with his left hand. It was awkward getting his thumb inside the fly reel frame.

As he put on pressure the line tightened into sudden hardness and beyond the logs a huge trout went high out of water. As he jumped, Nick lowered the tip of the rod. But he felt, as he dropped the tip to ease the strain, the moment when the strain was too great; the hardness too tight. Of course, the leader had broken. There was no mistaking the feeling when all spring left the line and it became dry and hard. Then it went slack.

His mouth dry, his heart down, Nick reeled in. He had never seen so big a trout. There was a heaviness, a power not to be held, and then the bulk of him, as he jumped. He looked as broad as a salmon.

Nick's hand was shaky. He reeled in slowly. The thrill had been too much. He felt, vaguely, a little sick, as though it would be better to sit down.

The leader had broken where the hook was tied to it. Nick took it in his hand. He thought of the trout somewhere on the bottom, holding himself steady over the gravel, far down below the light, under the logs, with the hook in his jaw. Nick knew the trout's teeth would cut through the snell of the hook. The hook would imbed itself in his jaw. He'd bet the trout was angry. Anything that size would be angry. That was a trout. He had been solidly hooked. Solid as a rock. He felt like a rock, too, before he started off. By God, he was a big one. By God, he was the biggest one I ever heard of.

Nick climbed out onto the meadow and stood, water running down his trousers and out of his shoes, his shoes squelchy. He went over and sat on the logs. He did not want to rush his sensations any.

He wriggled his toes in the water, in his shoes, and got out a cigarette from his breast pocket. He lit it and tossed the match into the fast water below the logs. A tiny trout rose at the match, as it swung around in the fast current. Nick laughed. He would finish the cigarette.

He sat on the logs, smoking, drying in the sun, the sun warm on his back, the river shallow ahead entering the woods, curving into the woods, shallows, light glittering, big water-smooth rocks, cedars along the bank and white birches, the logs warm in the sun, smooth to sit on, without bark, gray to the touch; slowly the feeling of disappointment left him. It went away slowly, the feeling of disappointment that came sharply after the thrill that made his shoulders ache. It was all right now. His rod lying out on the logs, Nick tied a new hook on the leader, pulling the gut tight until it grimped into itself in a hard knot.

He baited up, then picked up the rod and walked to the far end of the logs to get into the water, where it was not too deep. Under and beyond the logs was a deep pool. Nick walked around the shallow shelf near the swamp shore until he came out on the shallow bed of the stream.

On the left, where the meadow ended and the woods began, a great elm tree was uprooted. Gone over in a storm, it lay back into the woods, its roots clotted with dirt, grass growing in them, rising a solid bank beside the stream. The river cut to the edge of the uprooted tree. From where Nick stood he could see deep channels, like ruts, cut in the shallow bed of the stream by the flow of the current. Pebbly where he stood and pebbly and full of boulders beyond; where it curved near the tree roots, the bed of the stream was marly and between the ruts of deep water green weed fronds swung in the current.

Nick swung the rod back over his shoulder and forward, and the line, curving forward, laid the grasshopper down on one of the deep channels in the weeds. A trout struck and Nick hooked him.

Holding the rod far out toward the uprooted tree and sloshing backward in the current, Nick worked the trout, plunging, the rod bending alive, out of the danger of the weeds into the open river. Holding the rod, pumping alive against the current, Nick brought the trout in. He rushed, but always came, the spring of the rod yielding to the rushes, sometimes jerking under water, but always bringing him in. Nick eased downstream with the rushes. The rod above his head he led the trout over the net, then lifted.

The trout hung heavy in the net, mottled trout back and silver sides in the meshes. Nick unhooked him; heavy sides, good to hold, big undershot jaw, and slipped him, heaving and big sliding, into the long sack that hung from his shoulders in the water.

Nick spread the mouth of the sack against the current and it filled, heavy with water. He held it up, the bottom in the stream, and the water poured out through the sides. Inside at the bottom was the big trout, alive in the water.

Nick moved downstream. The sack out ahead of him sunk heavy in the water, pulling from his shoulders.

It was getting hot, the sun hot on the back of his neck.

Nick had one good trout. He did not care about getting many trout. Now the stream was shallow and wide. There were trees along both banks. The trees of the left bank made short shadows on the current in the forenoon sun. Nick knew there were trout in each shadow. In the afternoon, after the sun had crossed toward the hills, the trout would be in the cool shadows on the other side of the stream.

The very biggest ones would lie up close to the bank. You could always pick them up there on the Black. When the sun was down they all moved out into the current. Just when the sun made the water blinding in the glare before it went down, you were liable to strike a big trout anywhere in the current. It was almost impossible to fish then, the surface of the water was blinding as a mirror in the sun. Of course, you could fish upstream, but in a stream like the Black, or this, you had to wallow against the current and in a deep place, the water piled up on you. It was no fun to fish upstream with this much current.

Nick moved along through the shallow stretch watching the banks for deep holes. A beech tree grew close beside the river, so that the branches hung down into the water. The stream went back in under the leaves. There were always trout in a place like that.

Nick did not care about fishing that hole. He was sure he would get hooked in the branches.

It looked deep though. He dropped the grasshopper so the current took it under water, back in under the overhanging branch. The line pulled hard and Nick struck. The trout threshed heavily, half out of water in the leaves and branches. The line was caught. Nick pulled hard and the trout was off. He reeled in and holding the hook in his hand, walked down the stream.

Ahead, close to the left bank, was a big log. Nick saw it was hollow; pointing up river the current entered it smoothly, only a little ripple spread each side of the log. The water was deepening. The top of the hollow log was gray and dry. It was partly in the shadow.

Nick took the cork out of the grasshopper bottle and a hopper clung to it. He picked him off, hooked him and tossed him out. He held the rod far out so that the hopper on the water moved into the current flowing into the hollow log. Nick lowered the rod and the hopper floated in. There was a heavy strike. Nick swung the rod against the pull. It felt as though he were hooked into the log itself, except for the live feeling.

He tried to force the fish out into the current. It came, heavily.

The line went slack and Nick thought the trout was gone. Then he saw him, very near, in the current, shaking his head, trying to get the hook out. His mouth was clamped shut. He was fighting the hook in the clear flowing current.

Looping in the line with his left hand, Nick swung the rod to make the line taut and tried to lead the trout toward the net, but he was gone, out of sight, the line pumping. Nick fought him against the current, letting him thump in the water against the spring of the rod. He shifted the rod to his left hand, worked the trout upstream, holding his weight, fighting on the rod, and then let him down into the net. He lifted him clear of the water, a heavy half circle in the net, the net dripping, unhooked him and slid him into the sack.

He spread the mouth of the sack and looked down in at the two big trout alive in the water.

Through the deepening water, Nick waded over to the hollow log. He took the sack off, over his head, the trout flopping as it came out of water, and hung it so the trout were deep in the water. Then he pulled himself up on the log and sat, the water from his trouser and boots running down into the stream. He laid his rod down, moved along to the shady end of the log and took the sandwiches out of his pocket. He dipped the sandwiches in the cold water. The current carried away the crumbs. He ate the sandwiches and dipped his hat full of water to drink, the water running out through his hat just ahead of his drinking.

It was cool in the shade, sitting on the log. He took a cigarette out and struck a match to light it. The match sunk into the gray wood, making a tiny furrow. Nick leaned over the side of the log, found a hard place and lit the match. He sat smoking and watching the river.

Ahead the river narrowed and went into a swamp. The river became smooth and deep and the swamp looked solid with cedar trees, their trunks close together, their branches solid. It would not be possible to walk through a swamp like that. The branches grew so low. You would have to keep almost level with the ground to move at all. You could not crash through the branches. That must be why the animals that lived in swamps were built the way they were, Nick thought.

He wished he had brought something to read. He felt like reading. He did not feel like going on into the swamp. He looked down the river. A big cedar slanted all the way across the stream. Beyond that the river went into the swamp.

Nick did not want to go in there now. He felt a reaction against deep wading with the water deepening up under his armpits, to hook big trout in places impossible to land them. In the swamp the banks were bare, the big cedars came together overhead, the sun did not come through, except in patches; in the fast deep water, in the half light, the fishing would be tragic. In the swamp fishing was a tragic adventure. Nick did not want it. He did not want to go down the stream any further today.

He took out his knife, opened it and stuck it in the log. Then he pulled up the sack, reached into it and brought out one of the trout. Holding him near the tail, hard to hold, alive, in his hand, he whacked him against the log. The trout quivered, rigid. Nick laid him on the log in the shade and broke the neck of the other fish the same way. He laid them side by side on the log. They were fine trout.

Nick cleaned them, slitting them from the vent to the tip of the jaw. All the insides and the gills and tongue came out in one piece. They were both males; long gray-white strips of milt, smooth and clean. All the insides clean and compact, coming out all together. Nick tossed the offal ashore for the minks to find.

He washed the trout in the stream. When he held them back up in the water they looked like live fish. Their color was not gone yet. He washed his hands and dried them on the log. Then he laid the trout on the sack spread out on the log, rolled them up in it, tied the bundle and put it in the landing net. His knife was still standing, blade stuck in the log. He cleaned it on the wood and put it in his pocket.

Nick stood up on the log, holding his rod, the landing net hanging heavy, then stepped into the water and splashed ashore. He climbed the bank and cut up into the woods, toward the high ground. He was going back to camp. He looked back. The river just showed through the trees. There were plenty of days coming when he could fish the swamp.

1925

CHAPTER FIVE

THE TRIUMPH OF 'MODERN POETRY'

The variety of ways in which achievement marks the complex, critical, and creative activities of Ezra Pound, T. S. Eliot, and Wallace Stevens makes it difficult to generalize about their collective talents. Pound, for example, touches in one way or another—and on both sides of the Atlantic—the most eclectic group of poets and literary movements now considered of consequence during the early decades of this century. Among them are some of the most important little magazines (*Poetry*, *Little Review*, *Blast*, *Exile*); various new poetry movements (the Imagists and the Vorticists, among others); American poets as varied as Frost and Sandburg, William Carlos Williams and Hart Crane, E. E. Cummings and Archibald MacLeish; and distinguished non-Americans such as Tagore, Lawrence, Joyce, and Yeats. Pound helped the young Hemingway in Paris; and the effect of his collaborative association with Eliot, at least up through the period of *The Waste Land,* is probably difficult to overemphasize. Eliot himself is commonly characterized as the most influential literary figure of his age. His influence as a critic was, if anything, even more pervasive than his influence as a poet. He also wrote distinguished drama in verse and saw it successfully produced. His magisterial role as arbiter of literary taste, at least for a time, had not had a comparable parallel in English literature since the age and example of Dr. Johnson. Wallace Stevens, in the meantime, in a comparatively quiet and unobtrusive manner, methodically went about the business of perfecting verse which some consider among the most distinguished any modern American has produced. As Hayden Carruth has phrased it, his was the most "determinedly individualistic course" of all.

Although born in Idaho, educated, in part, in Pennsylvania, and for a very short time an instructor at Wabash College in Indiana, Ezra Pound's long stay in Europe was a removal from mid-continental America and its characteristic activities in a good many more ways than geographical distance. American democracy and the so-called common man were both anathemas to Pound. Yet, Carl Sandburg could describe him as "the greatest single influence in American poetry." A good many English poets might have said the same, for the twelve or so years he spent in England (after about 1908) were among the most influential of a long career. His widespread collaborations and encouragements, his various editings, his broadsides, manifestoes, and criticisms were never more vigorous than during his London years.

Equally influential was his own hard, precise verse, effectively a mixture of both the unadorned and the recondite. His enormous erudition led him, in his own poetry, to make few concessions to the cultural or linguistic limitations of his readers. Like the early T. S. Eliot, who followed him, Pound thus restored to poetry literary allusion as an effective technique. They both demanded of their readers some knowledge of the classics, of the major productions of the Renaissance in both England and Italy, and of specialized areas of continental and eastern literatures. Pound was also a gifted translator, and his renditions of ancient Chinese, Japanese, Italian, Provençal, and Anglo-Saxon poetry into modern English constitute, for some, his major achievements.

His two major poetic undertakings are his *Personae* and his still unfinished *Cantos*. *Personae* became the title under which he collected his poetry in 1926, suggesting as it does both the masks or "faces" worn by Greek actors and the need for a poet to objectify his expression through an imagined point of view. We see the technique at its best in the selection from *Hugh Selwyn Mauberley* (1920) collected here. His *Cantos* are an even more ambitious project. Originally to have been, like Dante's *The Divine Comedy*, 100 in number, they presently number 109, and their subject embraces nothing less than the whole of human civilization. They are difficult and obscure with violent juxtapositions of ancient languages and modern witticisms, free, personal associations, and socio-economic philosophizings. In spite of voluminous critical attention and widespread acknowledgement from poets of their influence, there is still no established consensus of their worth.

Pound had fled from England in 1920 as he had from America in 1908, and after four years in France, he moved to Italy. There his conversion to Mussolini's state socialism (and, especially, his anti-American broadcasts to Allied troops on the Italian state radio) eventually led, near the end of World War II, to his arrest for treason, his return to the United States, and his internment for insanity in St. Elizabeth's hospital in Washington. While thus interned, Pound was selected (in 1948) by a committee of the Fellows in American Literature of the Library of Congress for the first annual Bollingen Award for Poetry. The resulting furor over the social responsibility of the artist was among the most dynamic "literary" debates ever witnessed in America. For some it is still a sensitive issue. Yet, even his bitterest critics would freely admit his importance as an influence and an innovator. In 1958 he was released from St. Elizabeth's and allowed to return to Italy.

In T. S. Eliot's literary reputation are few of the vagaries one finds in Pound's. Eliot has been disliked, to be sure; his influence has been deplored by some; but there is a splendid originality in the best of his poetry and of his criticism that no serious historian of modern literature would deny. It had become a widespread critical commonplace, long before his death in early 1965, to designate the modern period as "The Age of Eliot"—a rare tribute to a writer during his own lifetime.

Interestingly enough, Eliot, like his early mentor, Pound, was born in the American Midwest (St. Louis), began his formal education in the East (Harvard), and at a relatively young age dissociated himself from America, moving permanently to England in 1914. A student of philosophy at Harvard, Eliot was strongly influenced by both Babbitt and Santayana, was an editor of the *Harvard Advocate* (where some of his earliest poetry appeared), and finished three years of Ph.D. study there (in Indic philology, Sanskrit, and philosophy) between a year at the Sorbonne (1910-11) and a year at Oxford (1914-15). His subsequent infrequent returns to America (like Henry James's, after about 1880) were in effect no more than visits.

He inevitably met Pound in England, and it was the discerning Ezra who sent Eliot's first major poem, "The Love Song of J. Alfred Prufrock," to Harriet Monroe's *Poetry*, where it appeared in 1915. It was collected in his first volume of verse, *Prufrock and Other Observations* (1917). Although one of his earliest poems and probably begun while still a student at Harvard, "Prufrock" was a remarkably effective and prophetic work: in its characteristic use of a Browning-like dramatic monologue (not unlike Pound's "*personae*" or "masks"); in its reflections of the influence of the French Symbolists and major figures of the English and Italian Renaissances; in its "metaphysical" juxtaposition of seemingly incongruous images; and in its devices of associative transitions, precisely controlled free verse, concise yet ironic diction, and multiple if indirect allusions.

It was also prophetic in its ideology. Its portrait of a personified neurotic impotency is also a portrait of the cultural and spiritual decay of Eliot's time. The poet's dismay, later articulated, at the decay of religious values in the Western world is already implicit in the scheme of "Prufrock." It was, generally speaking, these same devices and meanings (now more intricately refined and more dexterously perfected) that, two volumes of verse and seven years later, gave to his masterpiece, *The Waste Land* (edited by and significantly dedicated to Pound), its unprecedented impact. *The Waste Land* was *the* poem of Western culture between the two wars. It literally spawned a whole generation of poets in

England (Auden, Spender, C. Day Lewis) and America (Tate, Hart Crane, Archibald MacLeish). Its impact can scarcely be measured. *The Hollow Men* (1925) is another effective if somewhat different projection of the spiritual plight of Western man.

The first major work to follow Eliot's controversial self-definition (in 1928, a year after he became a British citizen) as "a classicist in literature, a royalist in politics, and an Anglo-Catholic in religion" was the magnificently controlled *Ash Wednesday* (1930). Although in a way a direct descendent of all of the major poetry since "Prufrock," it first heralds in explicit terms the religious affirmation that more intricately follows in the verse drama, *Murder in the Cathedral* (1935), and the highly accomplished *Four Quartets* (1943), which some critics consider Eliot's most successful poem. His later verse plays, *The Cocktail Party* (1950), *The Confidential Clerk* (1953), and *The Elder Statesman* (1958), continue the explicit spiritual probings first seen clearly in *Ash Wednesday*, but they, along with his later light verse, have evoked critical reservations strongly at variance with the reputation of his other poetry and criticism.

Eliot's critical essays parallel the practice and development of his poetry; he consistently practiced (in his poetry) what he preached (in his criticism). The two perhaps should not be separated. Following his early tribute to Pound (*His Metric and Poetry*, 1917), his various collections of essays—among them *The Sacred Wood* (1920), *Homage to John Dryden* (1924), *For Lancelot Andrewes* (1928), *Selected Essays* (1932, 1950)—created as much excitement, critical comment, and homage as his poetry. In them Eliot literally revised literary tradition for the modern world, finding that "tradition" not in the romantic poets of the late eighteenth and nineteenth centuries but in the metaphysical ones of the seventeenth century—notably Ben Jonson, Milton (after some early reservations), Marvell, and, especially, John Donne. It was not for a time remembered that earlier American poets had made similar turns to similar sources, that Edward Taylor, Emerson, and Emily Dickinson had in a sense already practiced what Eliot himself later so persuasively preached and practiced. Eliot's criticism undoubtedly deepened the modern appreciation of these earlier American poets—as it did, strangely, enough, that of the fiction of Hemingway. He was surely the so-called "New Criticism's" most effective voice, the creator of much of its vocabulary and the ideal model of its procedures. Moreover, neither the extreme classicism of his tastes, as spelled out, for example, in *What Is a Classic?* (1945) nor the traditionalism of his theology, as in *The Idea of a Christian Society* (1940), ever dispelled the effectiveness of his method. When, in 1948, he was awarded the Nobel Prize for Literature, there was probably less critical dissent about the appropriateness of the choice than has been the case with any other American writer thus honored.

Wallace Stevens is a heady contrast to both Pound and Eliot. His conventional education (in the study of law at Harvard and New York University), his well-ordered professional life (as an eminently successful executive with a Hartford insurance firm for over thirty years), and his late, relatively quiet and meager output of verse are all radically at variance with the critical flamboyance that accompanied so much of the poetic activity of these other two writers. Yet, Stevens too never compromised with the limitations of his readers; he absorbed, at least in his early work, some of the techniques of both the French Symbolists and the Imagists; and he maintained uniformly high standards for all the verse he allowed to appear in print.

His reputation, although it grew slowly, grew steadily almost from the beginning. His verse first appeared, as so much of the new poetry had done, in the flourishing little magazines, including Harriet Monroe's *Poetry.* Stevens was forty-three years old when his first collection, *Harmonium,* came out in 1923. His second book, an expanded version of *Harmonium,* did not appear until eight years later. Then, in comparatively rapid order, appeared *Ideas of Order* (1935), *Owl's Clover* (1936), and *The Man with the Blue Guitar and Other Poems* (1937). With these five slim volumes his reputation was secure.

Stevens' poetry is not so much difficult or obscure, as some have thought, as it is simply uncompromising. Its imperviousness to paraphrase is ultimately a mark of its esthetic integrity. Its ideology is everywhere permeated with "imagined" order as the most meaningful "reality" mankind can apprehend. Imagined order, to be sure, is a subtle order, a toned order, a conjunctive order of both thing and idea. The reality the imagination thus orders is consequently the ultimate reality—a position, strangely enough, equally the position and the practice of other American writers as varied as Thoreau, Henry James, and Ernest Hemingway. They, like Stevens, saw in artistic creation the ultimate reality, "the supreme fiction," and they also had equally high respect for the ordering imagination, "the necessary angel," as the ultimate means whereby the ultimate truth could reveal itself.

In Stevens' later volumes—*Notes Toward a Supreme Fiction* (1942), *Esthétique du Mal* (1945), *Transport to Summer* (1947), *A Primitive Like an Orb* (1948), and *Auroras of Autumn* (1950)—he became increasingly concerned with the epistemology of esthetics. His later poetry thus became more and more a definition of poetry, as all supreme poetry ultimately does, but always in a way that intensified (rather than loosened) the conjunction between imagined "reality" and the other "realities" we conventionally know. The essays and addresses in both *The Necessary Angel* (1951) and in the posthumously published *Opus Posthumous* (1957) reaffirm with startling clarity the esthetic integrity his poetry had been affirming all along.

Pound, Eliot, and Wallace Stevens thus represent a pole of poetic achievement in modern American verse different from the pole of Robinson and Frost. More varied, more intellectualized, and, in a way, more flamboyant (at least in the responses they evoked), the three poets here grouped together are testimony enough, when added to Robinson and Frost, of the variety of ways in which poetic achievement had come of age in modern America.

Ezra [Loomis] Pound

(1885-)

CHRONOLOGY:

1885 Born on October 30, in Hailey, Idaho.

1905 Graduated from Hamilton College.

1905-06 Did graduate work at the University of Pennsylvania.

1906 Travelled in Europe (Spain, Italy, France).

1907-08 Was an instructor, Wabash College, Indiana (four months).

1908-20 Lived in London.

1908 *A Lume Spento,* first poems, published in Italy.

1909 *Personae; Exaltations.*

1910 *Provença; The Spirit of Romance,* criticism.

1911 *Canzoni.*

1912 *Ripostes; The Sonnets and Ballate of Guido Cavalcanti,* trans.

1914 Edited *Des Imagistes.*

1915 *Cathay,* trans.

1916 *Lustra; Gaudier-Brzeska,* biography; *Noh—or, Accomplishment,* trans; *Certain Noble Plays of Japan,* trans.

1918 *Pavannes and Divisions,* criticism.

1919 *Quia Pauper Amavi.*

1920 *Hugh Selwyn Mauberley; Umbra; Instigations,* criticism.

1920-24 Lived in Paris.

1921 *Poems, 1918-21.*

1923 *Indiscretions,* autobiography.

1924 *Antheil and the Treatise on Harmony,* criticism.

1924-45 Lived in Rapallo, Italy.

1925 *A Draft of XVI Cantos.*

1926 *Personae: The Collected Poems of Ezra Pound.*

1928 *A Draft of the Cantos 17-27.*

1930 *A Draft of XXX Cantos; Imaginary Letters,* criticism.

1931 *How to Read,* criticism.

1933 *ABC of Economics.*

1934 *Eleven New Cantos: XXXI-XLI; Homage to Sexus Propertius; ABC of Reading,* criticism; *Make It New,* criticism.

1935 *Jefferson and/or Mussolini,* prose.

1937 *The Fifth Decad of Cantos; Polite Essays.*

1938 *Culture,* criticism.

1940 *Cantos LII-LXXI.*

1945-58 Interned in Washington, D.C.

1947 *Confucius: The Unwobbling Pivot and the Great Digest,* trans.

1948 *The Pisan Cantos [74-84]* (awarded the Bollinger Prize for Poetry and precipitated controversy); *The Cantos of Ezra Pound [1-84]; If This Be Treason . . .*

1950-52 *Money Pamphlets by Pound* (reprinted from essays previously published between 1934-1944).

1950 *Patria Mia* (written before 1913); *The Letters of Ezra*

Pound (ed. by D. D. Paige).

1953 *Secondo Biglietto da Visita; The Translations of Ezra Pound.*

1954 *The Literary Essays of Ezra Pound,* (ed. by T. S. Eliot); *The Classic Anthology Defined by Confucius,* trans.

1956 *Section: Rock-Drill, 85-95 De Los Cantares.*

1957 *Sophocles: Women of Trachis,* trans.

1958 *Pavannes and Divagations;* returned to Italy.

1959 *Thrones: 96-109 De Los Cantares.*

1960 *Impact: Essays on Ignorance and the Decline of American Civilization* (ed. by Noel Stock).

BIBLIOGRAPHY:

Personae: The Collected Poems (New York, 1950) is a re-issue of the 1926 Liveright edition with two new appendices. The *Cantos of Ezra Pound* (New York, 1948) does not contain the recent additions. *Selected Poems* (Norfolk, Conn., 1949) is a good sampling. T. S. Eliot's edition of *The Literary Essays of Ezra Pound* (Norfolk, Conn., 1954) is the most useful single volume of essays. And D. E. Paige's *The Letters of Ezra Pound, 1907-1941* (New York, 1950) is possibly the most important collection of correspondence in modern criticism.

Indispensable book-length studies of Pound are T. S. Eliot's early *Ezra Pound: His Metric and His Poetry* (New York, 1917); Hugh Kenner's *The Poetry of Ezra Pound* (Norfolk, Conn., 1951); H. H. Watts' *Ezra Pound and the Cantos* (Chicago, 1952); and John J. Espy's *Ezra Pound's Mauberley: A Study in Composition* (Berkeley, 1955). Three important collections of essays are Peter Russell, ed., *An Examination of Ezra Pound* (Norfolk, Conn., 1950); Lewis Leary, ed., *Motive and Method in the Cantos of Ezra Pound* (New York, 1954); and Walter Sutton, ed., *Ezra Pound: A Collection of Critical Essays* (Englewood Cliffs, 1963). The first full-length biography is Charles Norman, *Ezra Pound* (New York, 1960). The Bollingen Prize Award controversy is well covered in W. V. O'Connor and Edward Stone, eds., *A Casebook on Ezra Pound* (New York, 1959).

A bibliographical listing is in Allen Tate, *Sixty American Poets, 1896-1944* (Rev. ed.; Washington, 1954); for studies of individual poems, see Joseph M. Kuntz, *Poetry Explications* (Rev. ed.; Denver, 1962).

A Retrospect

There has been so much scribbling about a new fashion in poetry, that I may perhaps be pardoned this brief recapitulation and retrospect.

In the spring or early summer of 1912, "H. D.," Richard Aldington and myself decided that we were agreed upon the three principles following:

1. Direct treatment of the "thing" whether subjective or objective.

2. To use absolutely no word that does not contribute to the presentation.

3. As regarding rhythm: to compose in the sequence of the musical phrase, not in sequence of a metronome.

Upon many points of taste and of predilection we differed, but agreeing upon these three positions we thought we had as much right to a group name, at least as much right, as a number of French "schools" proclaimed by Mr. Flint in the August number of Harold Monro's magazine for 1911.

This school has since been "joined" or "followed" by numerous people who, whatever their merits, do not show any signs of agreeing with the second specification. Indeed *vers libre* has become as prolix and as verbose as any of the flaccid varieties that preceded it. It has brought faults of its own. The actual language and phrasing is often as bad as that of our elders without even the excuse that the words are shovelled in to fill a metric pattern or to complete the noise of a rhyme-sound. Whether or no the phrases followed by the followers are musical must be left to the reader's decision. At times I can find a marked metre in "vers libres," as stale and hackneyed as any pseudo-Swinburnian, at times the writers seem to follow no musical structure whatever. But it is, on the whole, good that the field should be ploughed. Perhaps a few good poems have come from the new method, and if so it is justified.

Criticism is not a circumscription or a set of prohibitions. It provides fixed points of departure. It may startle a dull reader into alertness. That little of it which is good is mostly in stray phrases; or if it be an older artist helping a younger it is in great measure but rules of thumb, cautions gained by experience.

I set together a few phrases on practical working about the time the first remarks on imagisme were published. The first use of the word "Imagiste" was in my note to T. E. Hulme's five poems, printed at the end of my "Ripostes" in the autumn of 1912. I reprint my cautions from *Poetry* for March, 1913.

A FEW DON'TS

An "Image" is that which presents an intellectual and emotional complex in an instant of time. I use the term "complex" rather in the technical sense employed by the newer psychologists, such as Hart, though we might not agree absolutely in our application.

It is the presentation of such a "complex" instantaneously which gives that sense of sudden liberation; that sense of freedom from time limits and space limits; that sense of sudden growth, which we experience in the presence of the greatest works of art.

It is better to present one Image in a lifetime than to produce voluminous works.

All this, however, some may consider open to debate. The immediate necessity is to tabulate A LIST OF DON'TS for those beginning to write verses. I can not put all of them into Mosaic negative.

To begin with, consider the three propositions (demanding direct treatment, economy of words, and the sequence of the musical phrase), not as dogma—never consider anything as dogma—but as the result of long contemplation, which, even if it is some one else's contemplation, may be worth consideration.

Pay no attention to the criticism of men who have never themselves written a notable work. Consider the discrepancies between the actual writing of the Greek poets and dramatists, and the theories of the Graeco-Roman grammarians, concocted to explain their metres.

LANGUAGE

Use no superfluous word, no adjective which does not reveal something.

Don't use such an expression as "dim lands *of peace.*" It dulls the image. It mixes an abstraction with the concrete. It comes from the writer's not realizing that the natural object is always the *adequate* symbol.

Go in fear of abstractions. Do not retell in mediocre verse what has already been done in good prose. Don't think any intelligent person is going to be deceived when you try to shirk all the difficulties of the unspeakably difficult art of good prose by chopping your composition into line lengths.

What the expert is tired of today the public will be tired of tomorrow.

Don't imagine that the art of poetry is any simpler than the art of music, or that you can please the expert before you have spent at least as much effort on the art of verse as the average piano teacher spends on the art of music.

Be influenced by as many great artists as you can, but have the decency either to acknowledge the debt outright, or to try to conceal it.

Don't allow "influence" to mean merely that you mop up the particular decorative vocabulary of some one or two poets whom you happen to admire. A Turkish war correspondent was recently caught red-handed babbling in his despatches of "dove-grey" hills, or else it was "pearl-pale," I can not remember.

Use either no ornament or good ornament.

RHYTHM AND RHYME

Let the candidate fill his mind with the finest cadences he can discover, preferably in a foreign language,[1] so that the meaning of the words may be less likely to divert his attention from the movement; e.g. Saxon charms, Hebridean Folk Songs, the verse of Dante, and the lyrics of Shakespeare—if he can dissociate the vocabulary from the cadence. Let him dissect the lyrics of Goethe coldly into their component sound values, syllables long and short, stressed and unstressed, into vowels and consonants.

It is not necessary that a poem should rely on its music, but if it does rely on its music that music must be such as will delight the expert.

[1] This is for rhythm; his vocabulary must of course be found in his native tongue.

Let the neophyte know assonance and alliteration, rhyme immediate and delayed, simple and polyphonic, as a musician would expect to know harmony and counterpoint and all the minutiae of his craft. No time is too great to give to these matters or to any one of them, even if the artist seldom have need of them.

Don't imagine that a thing will "go" in verse just because it's too dull to go in prose.

Don't be "viewy"—leave that to the writers of pretty little philosophic essays. Don't be descriptive; remember that the painter can describe a landscape much better than you can, and that he has to know a deal more about it.

When Shakespeare talks of the "Dawn in russet mantle clad" he presents something which the painter does not present. There is in this line of his nothing that one can call description; he presents.

Consider the way of the scientists rather than the way of an advertising agent for a new soap.

The scientist does not expect to be acclaimed as a great scientist until he has *discovered* something. He begins by learning what has been discovered already. He goes from that point onward. He does not bank on being a charming fellow personally. He does not expect his friends to applaud the results of his freshman class work. Freshmen in poetry are unfortunately not confined to a definite and recognizable class room. They are "all over the shop." Is it any wonder "the public is indifferent to poetry?"

Don't chop your stuff into separate *iambs*. Don't make each line stop dead at the end, and then begin every next line with a heave. Let the beginning of the next line catch the rise of the rhythm wave, unless you want a definite longish pause.

In short, behave as a musician, a good musician, when dealing with that phase of your art which has exact parallels in music. The same laws govern, and you are bound by no others.

Naturally, your rhythmic structure should not destroy the shape of your words, or their natural sound, or their meaning. It is improbable that, at the start, you will be able to get a rhythm-structure strong enough to affect them very much, though you may fall a victim to all sorts of false stopping due to line ends and cæsurae.

The Musician can rely on pitch and the volume of the orchestra. You can not. The term harmony is misapplied in poetry; it refers to simultaneous sounds of different pitch. There is, however, in the best verse a sort of residue of sound which remains in the ear of the hearer and acts more or less as an organ-base.

A rhyme must have in it some slight element of surprise if it is to give pleasure; it need not be bizarre or curious, but it must be well used if used at all.

Vide further Vildrac and Duhamel's notes on rhyme in "*Technique Poétique.*"

That part of your poetry which strikes upon the imaginative *eye* of the reader will lose nothing by translation into a foreign tongue; that which appeals to the ear can reach only those who take it in the original.

Consider the definiteness of Dante's presentation, as compared with Milton's rhetoric. Read as much of Wordsworth as does not seem too unutterably dull.

If you want the gist of the matter go to Sappho, Catullus, Villon, Heine when he is in the vein, Gautier when he is not too frigid; or, if you have not the tongues, seek out the leisurely Chaucer. Good prose will do you no harm, and there is good discipline to be had by trying to write it.

Translation is likewise good training, if you find that your original matter "wobbles" when you try to rewrite it. The meaning of the poem to be translated can not "wobble."

If you are using a symmetrical form, don't put in what you want to say and then fill up the remaining vacuums with slush.

Don't mess up the perception of one sense by trying to define it in terms of another. This is usually only the result of being too lazy to find the exact word. To this clause there are possibly exceptions.

The first three simple prescriptions will throw out nine-tenths of all the bad poetry now accepted as standard and classic; and will prevent you from many a crime of production.

". . . *Mais d'abord il faut être un poète,*" as MM. Duhamel and Vildrac have said at the end of their little book, "*Notes sur la Technique Poétique.*"

Since March 1913, Ford Madox Hueffer has pointed out that Wordsworth was so intent on the ordinary or plain word that he never thought of hunting for *le mot juste.*

John Butler Yeats has handled or man-handled Wordsworth and the Victorians, and his criticism, contained in letters to his son, is now printed and available.

I do not like writing *about* art, my first, at least I think it was my first essay on the subject, was a protest against it. 1918

A Virginal

No, no! Go from me. I have left her lately.
I will not spoil my sheath with lesser brightness,
For my surrounding air has a new lightness;
Slight are her arms, yet they have bound me straitly
And left me cloaked as with a gauze of æther;
As with sweet leaves; as with a subtle clearness.
Oh, I have picked up magic in her nearness
To sheathe me half in half the things that sheathe her.

No, no! Go from me. I have still the flavor,
Soft as spring wind that's come from birchen bowers.
Green come the shoots, aye April in the branches,
As winter's wound with her sleight hand she staunches,
Hath of the trees a likeness of the savor:
As white their bark, so white this lady's hours. 1909

The Jewel Stairs' Grievance

The jewelled steps are already quite white with dew,
It is so late that the dew soaks my gauze stockings,
And I let down the crystal curtain
And watch the moon through the clear autumn.

—By Rihaku 1909

The Beautiful Toilet

Blue, blue is the grass about the river
And the willows have overfilled the close garden.
And within, the mistress, in the midmost of her youth,
White, white of face, hesitates, passing the door.
Slender, she puts forth a slender hand;

And she was a courtezan in the old days,
And she has married a sot,
Who now goes drunkenly out
And leaves her too much alone.

—By Mei Sheng, 140 B.C.
1909

The Rest

O helpless few in my country,
O remnant enslaved!

Artists broken against her,
Astray, lost in the villages,
Mistrusted, spoken against,

Lovers of beauty, starved,
Thwarted with systems,
Helpless against the control;

You who cannot wear yourselves out
By persisting to successes,
You who can only speak,
Who cannot steel yourselves into reiteration;

You of the finer sense,
Broken against false knowledge,
You who can know at first hand,
Hated, shut in, mistrusted:

Take thought:
I have weatherd the storm,
I have beaten out my exile. 1913

A Pact

I make a pact with you, Walt Whitman—
I have detested you long enough.
I come to you as a grown child
Who has had a pig-headed father;
I am old enough now to make friends.
It was you that broke the new wood,
Now is a time for carving.
We have one sap and one root—
Let there be commerce between us. 1913

From *Hugh Selwyn Mauberley*

E. P. Ode pour l'Election de Son Sepulchre

[ODE ON THE CHOICE OF HIS TOMB]

Life and Contacts
Vocat Æstus in Umbram
—NEMESIANUS EC. IV.

For three years, out of key with his time,
He strove to resuscitate the dead art
Of poetry; to maintain "the sublime"
In the old sense. Wrong from the start—

No, hardly, but seeing he had been born
In a half-savage country, out of date;
Bent resolutely on wringing lilies from the acorn;
Capaneus; trout for factitious bait;

Ἴδμεν γάρ τοι πάνθ', ὅσ' ἐνὶ Τροίῃ
Caught in the unstopped ear;
Giving the rocks small lee-way
The chopped seas held him, therefore, that year.

His true Penelope was Flaubert,
He fished by obstinate isles;
Observed the elegance of Circe's hair
Rather than the mottoes on sun-dials.

Unaffected by "the march of events,"
He passed from men's memory in *l'an trentiesme*
De son eage; the case presents
No adjunct to the Muses' diadem.

II

The age demanded an image
Of its accelerated grimace,
Something for the modern stage,
Not, at any rate, an Attic grace;

Not, not certainly, the obscure reveries
Of the inward gaze;
Better mendacities
Than the classics in paraphrase!

The "age demanded" chiefly a mould in plaster,
Made with no loss of time,
A prose kinema, not, not assuredly, alabaster
Or the "sculpture" of rhyme.

III

The tea-rose tea-gown, etc.
Supplants the mousseline of Cos,
The pianola "replaces"
Sappho's barbitos.

Christ follows Dionysus,
Phallic and ambrosial
Made way for macerations;
Caliban casts out Ariel

All things are a flowing,
Sage Heracleitus says;
But a tawdry cheapness
Shall outlast our days.

Even the Christian beauty
Defects—after Samothrace;
We see τὸ καλὸν
Decreed in the market place.

Faun's flesh is not to us,
Nor the saint's vision.
We have the Press for wafer;
Franchise for circumcision.

All men, in law, are equals.
Free of Pisistratus,
We choose a knave or an eunuch
To rule over us.

O bright Apollo,
τίν' ἄνδρα, τίν' ἥρωα, τίνα θεόν
What god, man, or hero
Shall I place a tin wreath upon!

IV

These fought in any case,
and some believing,
        pro domo, in any case . . .

Some quick to arm,
some for adventure,

some from fear of weakness,
some from fear of censure,
some for love of slaughter, in imagination,
learning later . . .
some in fear, learning love of slaughter;

Died some, pro patria,
        non "dulce" non "et decor" . . .
walked eye-deep in hell
believing in old men's lies, then unbelieving
came home, home to a lie,
home to many deceits,
home to old lies and new infamy;
usury age-old and age-thick
and liars in public places.
Daring as never before, wastage as never before.
Young blood and high blood,
fair cheeks, and fine bodies;

fortitude as never before,

frankness as never before,
disillusions as never told in the old days,
hysterias, trench confessions,
laughter out of dead bellies.

v

There died a myriad,
And of the best, among them,
For an old bitch gone in the teeth,
For a botched civilization,

Charm, smiling at the good mouth,
Quick eyes gone under earth's lid,

For two gross of broken statues,
For a few thousand battered books.   1919

Envoi (1919)

Go, dumb-born book,
Tell her that sang me once that song of Lawes:
Hadst thou but song
As thou hast subjects known,
Then were there cause in thee that should condone

Even my faults that heavy upon me lie,
And build her glories their longevity.

Tell her that sheds
Such treasure in the air,
Recking naught else but that her graces give
Life to the moment,
I would bid them live
As roses might, in magic amber laid,
Red overwrought with orange and all made
One substance and one colour
Braving time.

Tell her that goes
With song upon her lips
But sings not out the song, nor knows
The maker of it, some other mouth,
May be as fair as hers,
Might, in new ages, gain her worshippers,
When our two dusts with Waller's shall be laid,
Siftings on siftings in oblivion,
Till change hath broken down
All things save Beauty alone. 1920

Letter to T. S. Eliot—1921

Paris, 24 Saturnus, An 1, [24 December]

Caro mio: MUCH improved. I think your instinct had led you to put the remaining superfluities at the end. I think you had better leave 'em, abolish 'em altogether or for the present.

IF you MUST keep 'em, put 'em at the beginning before the "April cruelest month." The POEM ends with the "Shantih, shantih, shantih."

One test is whether anything would be lacking if the last three were omitted. I don't think it would.

The song has only two lines which you can use in the body of the poem. The other two, at least the first, does not advance on earlier stuff. And even the sovegna doesn't hold with the rest; which does hold.

(It also, to your horror probably, reads aloud very well. Mouthing out his OOOOOOze.)

I doubt if Conrad is weighty enough to stand the citation.

The thing now runs from "April . . ." to "shantih" without a break. That is 19 pages, and let us say the longest poem in the English langwidge. Don't try to bust all records by prolonging it three pages further.

The bad nerves is O.K. as now led up to.

My squibs are now a bloody impertinence. I send 'em as requested; but don't use 'em with *Waste Land*.

You can tack 'em onto a collected edtn, or use 'em somewhere where they would be decently hidden and swamped by the bulk of accompanying matter. They'd merely be an extra and wrong note with the 19-page version.

Complimenti, you bitch. I am wracked by the seven jealousies, and cogitating an excuse for always exuding my deformative secretions in my own stuff, and never getting an outline. I go into nacre and objets d'art. Some day I shall lose my temper, blaspheme Flaubert, lie like a — and say "Art should embellish the umbelicus."

SAGE HOMME

These are the poems of Eliot
By the Uranian Muse begot;
A Man their Mother was,
A Muse their Sire.
How did the printed Infancies result
From Nuptials thus doubly difficult?

If you must needs enquire
Know diligent Reader
That on each Occasion
Ezra performed the Caesarean Operation.
Cauls and grave clothes he brings,
Fortune's outrageous stings,
About which odour clings,
Of putrefaction,
Bleichstein's dank rotting clothes
Affect the dainty nose,
He speaks of common woes
Deploring action.

He writes of A.B.C.s
And flaxseed poultices,
Observing fate's hard decrees
Sans satisfaction;
Breeding of animals,
Humans and cannibals,
But above all else of smells
Without attraction.

Vates cum fistula

It is after all a grrrreat litttttttary period. Thanks for the Aggymemnon.

T[homas] S[tearns] Eliot

(1888-1965)

CHRONOLOGY:

1888 Born September 26, in St. Louis, Missouri.

1906-10 Attended Harvard University.

1910-11 Attended the Sorbonne, Paris.

1911-14 Studied Indic philology, Sanskrit, philosophy at Harvard University.

1914-15 Attended Merton College, Oxford; remained in England.

1915 "The Love Song of J. Alfred Prufrock" appeared in *Poetry*.

1917-19 Helped edit the *Egoist*.

1917 *Prufrock and Other Observations; Ezra Pound: His Metric and Poetry.*

1919 *Poems.*

1920 *Poems; The Sacred Wood*, criticism.

1922 *The Waste Land.*

1923-39 Founded and edited *The Criterion.*

1924 *Homage to John Dryden*, criticism.

1925 *Poems, 1909-1925;* joined the British publishing firm of Faber and Faber, then called Faber and Gwyer.

1927 Became a British citizen; *The Journey of the Magi; Shakespeare and the Stoicism of Seneca.*

1928 *For Lancelot Andrewes*, criticism; *A Song for Simeon.*

1929 *Dante; Animula.*

1930 *Ash-Wednesday; Marina*

1931 *Charles Whibley: A Memoir; Triumphal March; Thoughts After Lambeth.*

1932 *John Dryden the Poet, the Dramatist, the Critic; Sweeney Agonistes.*

1933 *The Use of Poetry and the Use of Criticism.*

1934 *After Strange Gods*, criticism; *The Rock: A Pageant Play; Elizabethan Essays.*

1935 *Murder in the Cathedral*, verse drama.

1936 *Essays, Ancient and Modern.*

1939 *The Idea of a Christian Society; The Family Reunion: A Play; Old Possum's Book of Practical Cats*, juvenile verse.

1942 *The Music of Poetry; The Classics and the Man of Letters.*

1943 *Four Quartets.*

1945 *What Is a Classic?*

1947 *On Poetry; A Practical Possum*, juvenile verse; *Milton.*

1948 Awarded the Nobel Prize for Literature; *Notes Toward the Definition of Culture; From Poe to Valéry.*

1949 *The Aims of Poetic Drama.*

1950 *The Cocktail Party*, verse drama; *Talk on Dante.*

1951 *Poetry and Drama.*

1952 Appointed president of the London Library.

1953 *The Three Voices of Poetry; American Literature and the American Language.*

1954 *The Confidential Clerk*, verse drama; *Religious Drama: Mediaeval and Modern.*

1955 *The Literature of Politics.*

1956 *The Frontiers of Criticism.*

1957 *On Poetry and Poets.*

1958 *The Elder Statesman*, verse drama.

1963 *Collected Poems, 1909-1962.*

1965 Died January 4, in London.

BIBLIOGRAPHY:

The Complete Poems and Plays, 1909-1950 (New York, 1950) is only partly superseded by *Collected Poems,*

1909-1962 (New York, 1963). Although not complete, *Selected Essays* (Rev. ed.; New York, 1950) and *On Poets and Poetry* (New York, 1957) together constitute a wide and representative sampling of the criticism. John Hayward compiled *Poems Written in Early Youth* (Stockholm, 1950). Donald Gallup's *T. S. Eliot: A Bibliography* (Rev. ed.; New York, 1953) is thus far the most complete listing. Editions of *Selected Poems* and *Selected Essays* are available in paperback editions.

No biography of Eliot has yet appeared, although there is biographical information in a number of the many critical studies published. One of the most important of those is F. O. Matthiessen, *The Achievement of T. S. Eliot* (3rd ed. with an additional chapter by C. L. Barber, New York, 1958). Other important book-length studies include Elizabeth Drew, *T. S. Eliot: The Design of His Poetry* (New York, 1949); Helen Louise Gardner, *The Art of T. S. Eliot* (London, 1949); D. E. S. Maxwell, *The Poetry of T. S. Eliot* (London, 1952); George Williamson, *A Reader's Guide to T. S. Eliot: A Poem-by-Poem Analysis* (New York, 1953); Hugh Kenner, *The Invisible Poet: T. S. Eliot* (New York, 1959); and Grover Smith, Jr., *T. S. Eliot's Poetry and Plays: A Study in Sources and Meanings* (Rev. ed.; Chicago, 1960).

The most comprehensive collection of essays about Eliot is Leonard Unger, ed., *T. S. Eliot: A Selected Critique* (New York, 1948); but also useful are Balachandra Rajan, ed., *T. S. Eliot: A Study of His Writings by Several Hands* (London, 1947), and Richard March and Tambimuttu, eds., *T. S. Eliot: A Symposium* (London, 1948).

For useful explications see Allen Tate, *Sixty American Poets, 1896-1944* (Rev. ed.; Washington, 1954) and Joseph M. Kuntz, *Poetry Explication* (Rev. ed.; Denver, 1962).

The Function of Criticism

I

Writing several years ago on the subject of the relation of the new to the old in art, I formulated a view to which I still adhere, in sentences which I take the liberty of quoting, because the present paper is an application of the principle they express:

'The existing monuments form an ideal order among themselves, which is modified by the introduction of the new (the really new) work of art among them. The existing order is complete before the new work arrives; for order to persist after the supervention of novelty, the *whole* existing order must be, if ever so slightly, altered; and so the relations, proportions, values of each work of art toward the whole are readjusted; and this is conformity between the old and the new. Whoever has approved this idea of order, of the form of European, of English literature, will not find it preposterous that the past should be altered by the present as much as the present is directed by the past.'

I was dealing then with the artist, and the sense of tradition which, it seemed to me, the artist should have; but it was generally a problem of order; and the function of criticism seems to be essentially a problem of order too. I thought of literature then, as I think of it now, of the literature of the world, of the literature of Europe, of the literature of a single country, not as a collection of the writings of individuals, but as 'organic wholes,' as systems in relation to which, and only in relation to which, individual works of literary art, and the works of individual artists, have their significance. There is accordingly something outside of the artist to which he owes allegiance, a devotion to which he must surrender and sacrifice himself in order to earn and to obtain his unique position. A common inheritance and a common cause unite artists consciously or unconsciously: it must be admitted that the union is mostly unconscious. Between the true artists of any time there is, I believe, an unconscious community. And, as our instincts of tidiness imperatively command us not to leave to the haphazard of unconsciousness what we can attempt to do consciously, we are forced to conclude that what happens unconsciously we could bring about, and form into a purpose, if we made a conscious attempt. The second-rate artist, of course, cannot afford to surrender himself to any common action; for his chief task is the assertion of all the trifling differences which are his distinction: only the man who has so much to give that he can forget himself in his work can afford to collaborate, to exchange, to contribute.

If such views are held about art, it follows that *a fortiori* whoever holds them must hold similar views about criticism. When I say criticism, I mean of course in this place the commentation and exposition of works of art by means of written words; for of the general use of the word 'criticism' to mean such writings, as Matthew Arnold uses it in his essay, I shall presently make several qualifications. No exponent of criticism (in this limited sense) has, I presume, ever made the preposterous assumption that criticism is an autotelic activity. I do not deny that art may be affirmed to serve ends beyond itself; but art is not required to be aware of these ends, and indeed performs its function, whatever that may be, according to various theories of value, much better by indifference to them. Criticism, on the other hand, must always profess an end in view, which, roughly speaking, appears to be the elucidation of works of art and the correction of taste. The critic's task, therefore, appears to be quite clearly cut out for him; and it ought to be comparatively easy to decide whether he performs it satisfactorily, and in general, what kinds of criticism are useful and what are otiose. But on giving the matter a little attention, we perceive that criticism, far from being a simple and orderly field of beneficent activity, from which impostors can be readily ejected, is no better than a Sunday park of contending and contentious orators, who have not even arrived at the articulation of their differences. Here, one would suppose, was a place for quiet co-operative labour. The critic, one would suppose, if he is to justify his existence, should endeavour to discipline his personal prejudices and cranks—tares to which we are all subject—and compose his differences with as many of his fellows as possible, in the common pursuit of true judgment. When we find that quite the contrary prevails, we begin to suspect that the critic owes his livelihood to the violence and extremity of his opposition to other critics, or else to some trifling oddities of his own with which he contrives to season the opinions which men already hold, and which out of vanity or sloth they prefer to maintain. We are tempted to expel the lot.

Immediately after such an eviction, or as soon as relief has abated our rage, we are compelled to admit that there remain certain books, certain essays, certain sentences, certain men, who have been 'useful' to us. And our next step is to attempt to classify these, and find out whether we establish any principles for deciding what kinds of book should be preserved, and what aims and methods of criticism should be followed.

II

The view of the relation of the work of art to art, of the work of literature to literature, of 'criticism' to criticism, which I have outlined above, seemed to me natural and self-evident. I owe to Mr. Middleton Murry my perception of the contentious character of the problem; or rather, my perception that there is a definite and final choice involved. To Mr. Murry I feel an increasing debt of gratitude. Most of our critics are occupied in labour of obnubilation; in reconciling, in hushing up, in patting down, in squeezing in, in glozing over, in concocting pleasant sedatives, in pretending that the only difference between themselves and others is that they are nice men and the others of very doubtful repute. Mr. Murry is not one of these. He is aware that there are definite positions to be taken, and that now and then one must actually reject something and select something else. He is not the anonymous writer who in a literary paper several years ago asserted that Romanticism and Classicism are much the same thing, and that the true Classical Age in France was the Age which produced the Gothic cathedrals and—Jeanne d'Arc. With Mr. Murry's formulation of Classicism and Romanticism I cannot agree; the difference seems to me rather the difference between the complete and the fragmentary, the adult and the immature, the orderly and the chaotic. But what Mr. Murry does show is that there are at least two attitudes toward literature and toward everything, and that you cannot hold both. And the attitude which he professes appears to imply that the other has no standing in England whatever. For it is made a national, a racial issue.

Mr. Murry makes his issue perfectly clear. 'Catholicism', he says, 'stands for the principle of unquestioned spiritual authority outside the individual; that is also the principle of Classicism in literature.' Within the orbit within which Mr. Murry's discussion moves, this seems to me an unimpeachable definition, though it is of course not all that there is to be said about either Catholicism or Classicism. Those of us who find ourselves supporting what Mr. Murry calls Classicism believe that men cannot get on without giving allegiance to something outside themselves. I am aware that 'outside' and 'inside' are terms which provide unlimited opportunity for quibbling, and that no psychologist would tolerate a discussion which shuffled such base coinage; but I will presume that Mr. Murry and myself can agree that for our purpose these counters are adequate, and concur in disregarding the admonitions of our psychological friends. If you find that you have to imagine it as outside, then it is outside. If, then, a man's interest is political, he must, I presume, profess an allegiance to principles, or to a form of government, or to a monarch; and if he is interested in religion, and has one, to a Church; and if he happens to be interested in literature, he must acknowledge, it seems to me, just that sort of allegiance which I endeavoured to put forth in the preceding section. There is, nevertheless, an alternative, which Mr. Murry has expressed. 'The English writer, the English divine, the English statesman, inherit no rules from their forebears; they inherit only this: a sense that in the last resort they must depend upon the inner voice.' This statement does, I admit, appear to cover certain cases; it throws a flood of light upon Mr. Lloyd George. But why *'in the last resort'*? Do they, then, avoid the dictates of the inner voice up to the last extremity? My belief is that those who possess this inner voice are ready enough to hearken to it, and will hear no other. The inner voice, in fact, sounds remarkably like an old principle which has been formulated by an elder critic in the now familiar phrase of 'doing as one likes'. The possessors of the inner voice ride ten in a compartment to a football match at Swansea, listening to the inner voice, which breathes the eternal message of vanity, fear, and lust.

Mr. Murry will say, with some show of justice, that this is a wilful misrepresentation. He says: 'If they (the English writer, divine, statesman) dig *deep enough* in their pursuit of self-knowledge—a piece of mining done not with the intellect alone, but with the whole man—they will come upon a self that is universal'—an exercise far beyond the strength of our football enthusiasts. It is an exercise, however, which I believe was of enough interest to Catholicism for several handbooks to be written on its practice. But the Catholic practitioners were, I believe, with the possible exception of certain heretics, not palpitating Narcissi; the Catholic did not believe that God and himself were identical. 'The man who truly interrogates himself will ultimately hear the voice of God', Mr. Murry says. In theory, this leads to a form of pantheism which I maintain is not European—just as Mr. Murry maintains that 'Classicism' is not English. For its practical results, one may refer to the verses of *Hudibras*.

I did not realise that Mr. Murry was the spokesman for a considerable sect, until I read in the editorial columns of a dignified daily that 'magnificent as the representatives of the classical genius have been in England, they are not the sole expressions of the English character, which remains at bottom obstinately "humorous" and nonconformist'. This writer is moderate in using the qualification *sole,* and brutally frank in attributing this 'humorousness' to 'the unreclaimed Teutonic element in us'. But it strikes me that Mr. Murry, and this other voice, are either too obstinate or too tolerant. The question is, the first question, *not* what comes natural or what comes *easy* to us, but what is right? Either one attitude is better than the other, or else it is indifferent. But how can such a choice be indifferent? Surely the reference to racial origins, or the mere statement that the French are thus, and the English otherwise, is not expected to settle the question: which, of two antithetical views, is *right?* And I cannot understand why the opposition between Classicism and Romanticism should be profound enough in Latin countries (Mr. Murry says it is) and yet of no significance among ourselves. For if the French are *naturally* classical, why should there be any 'opposition' in France, any more than there is here? And if Classicism is not natural to them, but something acquired, why not acquire it here? Were the French in the year 1600 classical, and the English in the same year romantic? A more important difference, to my mind, is that the French in the year 1600 *had already a more mature prose.*

III

This discussion may seem to have led us a long way from the subject of this paper. But it was worth my while to follow Mr. Murry's comparison of Outside Authority with the Inner Voice. For to those who obey the inner voice (perhaps 'obey' is not the word) nothing that I can say about criticism will have the slightest value. For they will not be interested in the attempt to find any common principles for the pursuit of criticism. Why have principles, when one has the inner voice? If I like a thing, that is all I want; and if enough of us, shouting all together, like it, that should be all that *you* (who don't like it) ought to want. The law of art, said Mr. Clutton Brock, is all case law. And we can not only like whatever we like to like but we can like it for any reason we choose. We are not, in fact, concerned with literary *perfection* at all—the search for perfection is a sign of pettiness, for it shows that the writer has admitted the existence of an unquestioned spiritual authority outside himself, to which he has attempted to *conform.* We are not in fact interested in art. We will not worship Baal. 'The principle of classical leadership is that obeisance is made to the office or to the tradition, never to the man.' And we want, not principles, but men.

Thus speaks the Inner Voice. It is a voice to which, for convenience, we may give a name: and the name I suggest is Whiggery.

IV

Leaving, then, those whose calling and election are sure and returning to those who shamefully depend upon tradition and the accumulated wisdom of time, and restricting the discussion to those who sympathise with each other in this frailty, we may comment for a moment upon the use of the terms 'critical' and 'creative' by one whose place, on the whole, is with the weaker brethren. Matthew Arnold distinguishes far too bluntly, it seems to me, between the two activities: he overlooks the capital importance of criticism in the work of creation itself. Probably, indeed, the larger part of the labour of an author in composing his work is critical labour; the labour of sifting, combining, constructing, expunging, correcting, testing: this frightful toil is as much critical as creative. I maintain even that the criticism employed by a trained and skilled writer on his own work is the most vital, the highest kind of criticism; and (as I think I have said before) that some creative writers are superior to others solely because their critical faculty is superior. There is a tendency, and I think it is a whiggery tendency, to decry this critical toil of the artist; to propound the thesis that the great artist is an unconscious artist, unconsciously inscribing on his banner the words Muddle Through. Those of us who are Inner Deaf Mutes are, however, sometimes compensated by a humble conscience, which, though without oracular expertness, counsels us to do the best we can, reminds us that our compositions ought to be as free from defects as possible (to atone for their lack of inspiration), and, in short, makes us waste a good deal of time. We are aware, too, that the critical discrimination which comes so hardly to us has in more fortunate men flashed in the very heat of creation; and we do not assume that because works have been composed without apparent critical labour, no critical labour has been done. We do not know what previous labours have prepared, or what goes on, in the way of criticism, all the time in the minds of the creators.

But this affirmation recoils upon us. If so large a part of creation is really criticism, is not a large part of what is called 'critical writing' really creative? If so, is there not creative criticism in the ordinary sense? The answer seems to be, that there is no equation. I have assumed as axiomatic that a creation, a work of art, is autotelic; and that criticism, by definition, is *about* something other than itself. Hence you cannot fuse creation with criticism as you can fuse criticism with creation. The critical activity finds its highest, its true fulfilment in a kind of union with creation in the labour of the artist.

But no writer is completely self-sufficient, and many creative writers have a critical activity which is not all discharged into their work. Some seem to require to keep their critical powers in condition for the real work by exercising them miscellaneously; others, on completing a work, need to continue the critical activity by commenting on it. There is no general rule. And as men can learn from each other, so some of these treatises have been useful to other writers. And some of them have been useful to those who were not writers.

At one time I was inclined to take the extreme position that the *only* critics worth reading were the critics who practised, and practised well, the art of which they wrote. But I had to stretch this frame to make some important inclusions; and I have since been in search of a formula which should cover everything I wished to include, even if it included more than I wanted. And the most important qualification which I have been able to find, which accounts for the peculiar importance of the criticism of practitioners, is that a critic must have a very highly developed sense of fact. This is by no means a trifling or frequent gift. And it is not one which easily wins popular commendations. The sense of fact is something very slow to develop, and its complete development means perhaps the very pinnacle of civilisation. For there are so many spheres of fact to be mastered, and our outermost sphere of fact, of knowledge, of control, will be ringed with narcotic fancies in the sphere beyond. To the member of the Browning Study Circle, the discussion of poets about poetry may seem arid, technical, and limited. It is merely that the practitioners have clarified and reduced to a state of fact all the feelings that the member can only enjoy in the most nebulous form; the dry technique implies, for those who have mastered it, all that the member thrills to; only that has been made into something precise, tractable, under control. That, at all events, is one reason for the value of the practitioner's criticism—he is dealing with his facts, and he can help us to do the same.

And at every level of criticism I find the same necessity regnant. There is a large part of critical writing which consists in 'interpreting' an author, a work. This is not on the level of the Study Circle either; it occasionally happens that one person obtains an understanding of another, or a creative writer, which he can partially communicate, and which we feel to be true and illuminating. It is difficult to confirm the 'interpretation' by external evidence. To anyone who is skilled in fact on this level there will be evidence enough. But who is to prove his own skill? And for every success in this type of writing there are thousands of impostures. Instead of insight, you get a fiction. Your test is to apply it again and again to the original, with your view of the original to guide you. But there is no one to guarantee your competence, and once again we find ourselves in a dilemma.

We must ourselves decide what is useful to us and what is not; and it is quite likely that we are not competent to decide. But it is fairly certain that 'interpretation' (I am not touching upon the acrostic element in literature) is only legitimate when it is not interpretation at all, but merely putting the reader in possession of facts which he would otherwise have missed. I have had some experience of Extension lecturing, and I have found only two ways of leading any pupils to like anything with the right liking: to present them with a selection of the simpler kind of facts about a work—its conditions, its setting, its genesis—or else to spring the work on them in such a way that they were not prepared to be prejudiced against it. There were many facts to help them with Elizabethan drama: the poems of T. E. Hulme only needed to be read aloud to have immediate effect.

Comparison and analysis, I have said before, and Remy de Gourmont has said before me (a real master of fact—sometimes, I am afraid, when he moved outside of literature, a master illusionist of fact), are the chief tools of the critic. It is obvious indeed that they *are* tools, to be handled with care, and not employed in an inquiry into the number of times giraffes are mentioned in the English novel. They are not used with conspicuous success by many contemporary writers. You must know what to compare and what to analyse. The late Professor Ker had skill in the use of these tools. Comparison and analysis need only the cadavers on the table; but interpretation is always producing parts of the body from its pockets, and fixing them in place. And any book, any essay, any note in *Notes and Queries,* which produces a fact even of the lowest order about a work of art is a better piece of work than nine-tenths of the most pretentious critical journalism, in journals or in books. We assume, of course, that we are masters and not servants of facts, and that we know that the discovery of Shakespeare's laundry bills would not be of much use to us; but we must always reserve final judgment as to the futility of the research which has discovered them, in the possibility that some genius will appear who will know of a use to which to put them. Scholarship, even in its humblest forms, has its rights; we assume that we know how to use it, and how to neglect it. Of course the multiplication of critical books and essays may create, and I have seen it create, a vicious taste for reading about works of art instead of reading the works themselves, it may supply opinion instead of educating taste. But *fact* cannot corrupt taste; it can at worst gratify one taste—a taste for history, let us say, or antiquities, or biography—under the illusion that it is assisting another. The real corrupters are those who supply opinion or fancy; and Goethe and Coleridge are not guiltless—for what is Coleridge's *Hamlet:* is it an honest inquiry as far as the data permit, or is it an attempt to present Coleridge in an attractive costume?

We have not succeeded in finding such a test as anyone can apply; we have been forced to allow ingress to innumerable dull and tedious books; but we have, I think, found a test which, for those who are able to apply it, will dispose of the really vicious ones. And with this test we may return to the preliminary statement of the polity of literature and of criticism. For the kinds of critical work which we have admitted, there is the possibility of cooperative activity, with the further possibility of arriving at something outside of ourselves, which may provisionally be called truth. But if anyone complains that I have not defined truth, or fact, or reality, I can only say apologetically that it was no part of my purpose to do so, but only to find a scheme into which, whatever they are, they will fit, if they exist.

1923

The Love Song of J. Alfred Prufrock

S'io credesse che mia risposta fosse
A persona che mai tornasse al mondo,
Questa fiamma staria senza piu scosse.
Ma perciocche giammai di questo fondo
Non torno vivo alcun, s'i'odo il vero,
Senza tema d'infamia ti rispondo.

Let us go then, you and I,
When the evening is spread out against the sky
Like a patient etherized upon a table;
Let us go, through certain half-deserted streets,
The muttering retreats
Of restless nights in one-night cheap hotels
And sawdust restaurants with oyster-shells:
Streets that follow like a tedious argument
Of insidious intent
To lead you to an overwhelming question . . .
Oh, do not ask, 'What is it?'
Let us go and make our visit.

In the room the women come and go
Talking of Michelangelo.

The yellow fog that rubs its back upon the window-panes,
The yellow smoke that rubs its muzzle on the window-panes
Licked its tongue into the corners of the evening,
Lingered upon the pools that stand in drains,
Let fall upon its back the soot that falls from chimneys,
Slipped by the terrace, made a sudden leap,
And seeing that it was a soft October night,
Curled once about the house, and fell asleep.

And indeed there will be time
For the yellow smoke that slides along the street,
Rubbing its back upon the window-panes;

There will be time, there will be time
To prepare a face to meet the faces that you meet;
There will be time to murder and create,
And time for all the works and days of hands
That lift and drop a question on your plate;
Time for you and time for me,
And time yet for a hundred indecisions,
And for a hundred visions and revisions,
Before the taking of a toast and tea.

In the room the women come and go
Talking of Michelangelo.

And indeed there will be time
To wonder, 'Do I dare?' and, 'Do I dare?'
Time to turn back and descend the stair,
With a bald spot in the middle of my hair—
(They will say: 'How his hair is growing thin!')
My morning coat, my collar mounting firmly to the chin,
My necktie rich and modest, but asserted by a simple pin—
(They will say: 'But how his arms and legs are thin!')
Do I dare
Disturb the universe?
In a minute there is time
For decisions and revisions which a minute will reverse.

For I have known them all already, known them all:—
Have known the evenings, mornings, afternoons,
I have measured out my life with coffee spoons;
I know the voices dying with a dying fall
Beneath the music from a farther room.
  So how should I presume?

And I have known the eyes already, known them all—
The eyes that fix you in a formulated phrase,
And when I am formulated, sprawling on a pin,
When I am pinned and wriggling on the wall,
Then how should I begin
To spit out all the butt-ends of my days and ways?
  And how should I presume?

And I have known the arms already, known them all—
Arms that are braceleted and white and bare
(But in the lamplight, downed with light brown hair!)
Is it perfume from a dress
That makes me so digress?

Arms that lie along a table, or wrap about a shawl.
  And should I then presume?
  And how should I begin?

. . . . . .

Shall I say, I have gone at dusk through narrow streets
And watched the smoke that rises from the pipes
Of lonely men in shirt-sleeves, leaning out of windows? . . .

I should have been a pair of ragged claws
Scuttling across the floors of silent seas.

. . . . . .

And the afternoon, the evening, sleeps so peacefully!
Smoothed by long fingers,
Asleep . . . tired . . . or it malingers,
Stretched on the floor, here beside you and me.
Should I, after tea and cakes and ices,
Have the strength to force the moment to its crisis?
But though I have wept and fasted, wept and prayed,
Though I have seen my head (grown slightly bald) brought in upon
    a platter,
I am no prophet—and here's no great matter;
I have seen the moment of my greatness flicker,
And I have seen the eternal Footman hold my coat, and snicker,
And in short, I was afraid.

And would it have been worth it, after all,
After the cups, the marmalade, the tea,
Among the porcelain, among some talk of you and me,
Would it have been worth while,
To have bitten off the matter with a smile,
To have squeezed the universe into a ball
To roll it toward some overwhelming question,
To say: 'I am Lazarus, come from the dead,
Come back to tell you all, I shall tell you all'—
If one, settling a pillow by her head,
  Should say: 'That is not what I meant at all,
  That is not it, at all.'

. . . . . .

And would it have been worth it, after all,
Would it have been worth while,
After the sunsets and the dooryards and the sprinkled streets,

After the novels, after the teacups, after the skirts that trail along
the floor—
And this, and so much more?—
It is impossible to say just what I mean!
But as if a magic lantern threw the nerves in patterns on a screen:
Would it have been worth while
If one, settling a pillow or throwing off a shawl,
And turning toward the window, should say:
'That is not it at all,
That is not what I meant, at all.'

. . . . . .

No! I am not Prince Hamlet, nor was meant to be;
Am an attendant lord, one that will do
To swell a progress, start a scene or two,
Advise the prince; no doubt, an easy tool,
Deferential, glad to be of use,
Politic, cautious, and meticulous;
Full of high sentence, but a bit obtuse;
At times, indeed, almost ridiculous—
Almost, at times, the Fool.

I grow old . . . I grow old . . .
I shall wear the bottoms of my trousers rolled.

Shall I part my hair behind? Do I dare to eat a peach?
I shall wear white flannel trousers, and walk upon the beach.
I have heard the mermaids singing, each to each.

I do not think that they will sing to me.

I have seen them riding seaward on the waves
Combing the white hair of the waves blown back
When the wind blows the water white and black.

We have lingered in the chambers of the sea
By sea-girls wreathed with seaweed red and brown
Till human voices wake us, and we drown. 1915

The Hippopotamus

Similiter et omnes revereantur Diaconos, ut mandatum Jesu Christi; et Episcopum, ut Jesum Christum, existentem filium Patris; Presbyteros autem, ut concilium Dei et conjunctionem Apostolorum. Sine his Ecclesia non vocatur; de quibus suadeo vos sic habeo.

S. IGNATII AD TRALLIANOS

And when this epistle is read among you, cause that it be read also in the church of the Laodiceans.

The broad-backed hippopotamus
Rests on his belly in the mud;
Although he seems so firm to us
He is merely flesh and blood.

Flesh and blood is weak and frail,
Susceptible to nervous shock;
While the True Church can never fail
For it is based upon a rock.

The hippo's feeble steps may err
In compassing material ends,
While the True Church need never stir
To gather in its dividends.

The 'potamus can never reach
The mango on the mango-tree;
But fruits of pomegranate and peach
Refresh the Church from over sea.

At mating time the hippo's voice
Betrays inflexions hoarse and odd;
But every week we hear rejoice
The Church at being one with God.

The hippopotamus's day
Is passed in sleep; at night he hunts;
God works in a mysterious way—
The Church can sleep and feed at once.

I saw the 'potamus take wing
Ascending from the damp savannas,
And quiring angels round him sing
The praise of God, in loud hosannas.

Blood of the Lamb shall wash him clean
And him shall heavenly arms enfold,
Among the saints he shall be seen
Performing on a harp of gold.

He shall be washed as white as snow,
By all the martyr'd virgins kist,
While the True Church remains below
Wrapt in the old miasmal mist. 1920

The Waste Land*

"NAM Sibyllam quidem Cumis ego ipse oculis meis vidi in ampulla pendere, et cum illi pueri dicerent: Σίβυλλα τί θέλεις; *respondebat illa:* ἀποθανεῖν θέλω."

For EZRA POUND
il miglior fabbro.

I. THE BURIAL OF THE DEAD

April is the cruellest month, breeding
Lilacs out of the dead land, mixing
Memory and desire, stirring
Dull roots with spring rain.
Winter kept us warm, covering
Earth in forgetful snow, feeding
A little life with dried tubers.
Summer surprised us, coming over the Starnbergersee
With a shower of rain; we stopped in the colonnade,
And went on in sunlight, into the Hofgarten,
And drank coffee, and talked for an hour.
Bin gar keine Russin, stamm' aus Litauen, echt deutsch.
And when we were children, staying at the archduke's,
My cousin's, he took me out on a sled,
And I was frightened. He said, Marie,

* [All the notes are by T. S. Eliot.] Not only the title, but the plan and a good deal of the incidental symbolism of the poem were suggested by Miss Jessie L. Weston's book on the Grail legend: *From Ritual to Romance* (Cambridge). Indeed, so deeply am I indebted, Miss Weston's book will elucidate the difficulties of the poem much better than my notes can do; and I recommend it (apart from the great interest of the book itself) to any who think such elucidation of the poem worth the trouble. To another work of anthropology I am indebted in general, one which has influenced our generation profoundly; I mean *The Golden Bough;* I have used especially the two volumes *Adonis, Attis, Osiris.* Anyone who is acquainted with these works will immediately recognise in the poem certain references to vegetation ceremonies.

Marie, hold on tight. And down we went.
In the mountains, there you feel free.
I read, much of the night, and go south in the winter.

What are the roots that clutch, what branches grow
Out of this stony rubbish? Son of man,[1]
You cannot say, or guess, for you know only
A heap of broken images, where the sun beats,
And the dead tree gives no shelter, the cricket no relief,[2]
And the dry stone no sound of water. Only
There is shadow under this red rock,
(Come in under the shadow of this red rock),
And I will show you something different from either
Your shadow at morning striding behind you
Or your shadow at evening rising to meet you;
I will show you fear in a handful of dust.
Frisch weht der Wind
Der Heimat zu
Mein Irisch Kind,
Wo weilest du?[3]
"You gave me hyacinths first a year ago;
"They called me the hyacinth girl."
—Yet when we came back, late, from the Hyacinth garden,
Your arms full, and your hair wet, I could not
Speak, and my eyes failed, I was neither
Living nor dead, and I knew nothing,
Looking into the heart of light, the silence.
Oed' und leer das Meer.[4]

Madame Sosostris, famous clairvoyante,
Had a bad cold, nevertheless
Is known to be the wisest woman in Europe,
With a wicked pack of cards.[5] Here, said she,
Is your card, the drowned Phoenician Sailor,
(Those are pearls that were his eyes. Look!)
Here is Belladonna, the Lady of the Rocks,

[1] Cf. Ezekiel II, i.

[2] Cf. Ecclesiastes XII, v.

[3] V. Tristan und Isolde, I, verses 5-8.

[4] Id. III, verse 24.

[5] I am not familiar with the exact constitution of the Tarot pack of cards, from which I have obviously departed to suit my own convenience. The Hanged Man, a member of the traditional pack, fits my purpose in two ways: because he is associated in my mind with the Hanged God of Frazer, and because I associate him with the hooded figure in the passage of the disciples to Emmaus in Part V. The Phoenician Sailor and the Merchant appear later; also the "crowds of people," and Death by Water is executed in Part IV. The Man with Three Staves (an authentic member of the Tarot pack) I associate, quite arbitrarily, with the Fisher King himself.

The lady of situations.
Here is the man with three staves, and here the Wheel,
And here is the one-eyed merchant, and this card,
Which is blank, is something he carries on his back,
Which I am forbidden to see. I do not find
The Hanged Man. Fear death by water.
I see crowds of people, walking round in a ring.
Thank you. If you see dear Mrs. Equitone,
Tell her I bring the horoscope myself:
One must be so careful these days.

Unreal City,[6]
Under the brown fog of a winter dawn,
A crowd flowed over London Bridge, so many,
I had not thought death had undone so many.[7]
Sighs, short and infrequent, were exhaled,[8]
And each man fixed his eyes before his feet.
Flowed up the hill and down King William Street,
To where Saint Mary Woolnoth kept the hours
With a dead sound on the final stroke of nine.[9]
There I saw one I knew, and stopped him, crying: "Stetson!
"You who were with me in the ships at Mylae!
"That corpse you planted last year in your garden,
"Has it begun to sprout? Will it bloom this year?
"Or has the sudden frost disturbed its bed?
"Oh keep the Dog far hence, that's friend to men,[10]
"Or with his nails he'll dig it up again!
"You! hypocrite lecteur!—mon semblable,—mon frère!"[11]

II. A GAME OF CHESS

The Chair she sat in, like a burnished throne,[12]
Glowed on the marble, where the glass
Held up by standards wrought with fruited vines
From which a golden Cupidon peeped out
(Another hid his eyes behind his wing)
Doubled the flames of sevenbranched candelabra
Reflecting light upon the table as

[6] Cf. Baudelaire:
"Fourmillante cité, cité pleine de rêves,
"Où le spectre en plein jour raccroche le passant."

[7] Cf. Inferno III, 55-57:
"si lunga tratta
di gente, ch'io non avrei mai creduto
che morte tanta n'avesse disfatta."

[8] Cf. Inferno IV, 25-27:
"Quivi, secondo che per ascoltare,
"non avea pianto, ma' che di sospiri,
"che l'aura eterna facevan tremare."

[9] A phenomenon which I have often noticed.

[10] Cf. the Dirge in Webster's *White Devil.*

[11] V. Baudelaire, Preface to *Fleurs du Mal.*

[12] Cf. *Antony and Cleopatra,* II, ii, l. 190.

The glitter of her jewels rose to meet it,
From satin cases poured in rich profusion;
In vials of ivory and coloured glass
Unstoppered, lurked her strange synthetic perfumes,
Unguent, powdered, or liquid—troubled, confused
And drowned the sense in odours; stirred by the air
That freshened from the window, these ascended
In fattening the prolonged candle-flames,
Flung their smoke into the laquearia,[13]
Stirring the pattern on the coffered ceiling.
Huge sea-wood fed with copper
Burned green and orange, framed by the coloured stone,
In which sad light a carvèd dolphin swam.
Above the antique mantel was displayed
As though a window gave upon the sylvan scene[14]
The change of Philomel, by the barbarous king[15]
So rudely forced; yet there the nightingale[16]
Filled all the desert with inviolable voice
And still she cried, and still the world pursues,
"Jug Jug" to dirty ears.
And other withered stumps of time
Were told upon the walls; staring forms
Leaned out, leaning, hushing the room enclosed.
Footsteps shuffled on the stair.
Under the firelight, under the brush, her hair
Spread out in fiery points
Glowed into words, then would be savagely still.

"My nerves are bad to-night. Yes, bad. Stay with me.
"Speak to me. Why do you never speak. Speak.
"What are you thinking of? What thinking? What?
"I never know what you are thinking. Think."

I think we are in rats' alley[17]
Where the dead men lost their bones.

"What is that noise?"
The wind under the door.[18]
"What is that noise now? What is the wind doing?"
Nothing again nothing.

[13] Laquearia. V. *Aeneid,* I, 726: dependent lychni laquearibus aureis incensi, et noctem flammis funalia vincunt.

[14] Sylvan scene. V. Milton, *Paradise Lost,* IV, 140.

[15] V. Ovid, *Metamorphoses,* VI, Philomela.

[16] Cf. Part III, l. 204.

[17] Cf. Part III, l. 195.

[18] Cf. Webster: "Is the wind in that door still?"

"Do
"You know nothing? Do you see nothing? Do you remember
"Nothing?"

I remember
Those are pearls that were his eyes.
"Are you alive, or not? Is there nothing in your head?"[19]
But
O O O O that Shakespeherian Rag—
It's so elegant
So intelligent
"What shall I do now? What shall I do?"
"I shall rush out as I am, and walk the street
"With my hair down, so. What shall we do tomorrow?
"What shall we ever do?"
The hot water at ten.
And if it rains, a closed car at four.
And we shall play a game of chess,
Pressing lidless eyes and waiting for a knock upon the door.[20]
When Lil's husband got demobbed, I said—
I didn't mince my words, I said to her myself,
HURRY UP PLEASE ITS TIME
Now Albert's coming back, make yourself a bit smart.
He'll want to know what you done with that money he gave you
To get yourself some teeth. He did, I was there.
You have them all out, Lil, and get a nice set,
He said, I swear, I can't bear to look at you.
And no more can't I, I said, and think of poor Albert,
He's been in the army four years, he wants a good time,
And if you don't give it him, there's others will, I said.
Oh is there, she said. Something o' that, I said.
Then I'll know who to thank, she said, and give me a straight look.
HURRY UP PLEASE ITS TIME
If you don't like it you can get on with it, I said.
Others can pick and choose if you can't.
But if Albert makes off, it won't be for lack of telling.
You ought to be ashamed, I said, to look so antique.
(And her only thirty-one.)
I can't help it, she said, pulling a long face,
It's them pills I took, to bring it off, she said.
(She's had five already, and nearly died of young George.)
The chemist said it would be all right, but I've never been the same.

[19] Cf. Part I, l. 37, 48.
[20] Cf. the game of chess in Middleton's *Women beware Women*.

You *are* a proper fool, I said.
Well, if Albert won't leave you alone, there it is, I said,
What you get married for if you don't want children?
HURRY UP PLEASE ITS TIME
Well, that Sunday Albert was home, they had a hot gammon,
And they asked me in to dinner, to get the beauty of it hot–
HURRY UP PLEASE ITS TIME
HURRY UP PLEASE ITS TIME
Goonight Bill. Goonight Lou. Goonight May. Goonight.
Ta ta. Goonight. Goonight.
Good night, ladies, good night, sweet ladies, good night, good night.

III. THE FIRE SERMON

The river's tent is broken: the last fingers of leaf
Clutch and sink into the wet bank. The wind
Crosses the brown land, unheard. The nymphs are departed.
Sweet Thames, run softly, till I end my song.[21]
The river bears no empty bottles, sandwich papers,
Silk handkerchiefs, cardboard boxes, cigarette ends
Or other testimony of summer nights. The nymphs are departed.
And their friends, the loitering heirs of city directors;
Departed, have left no addresses.
By the waters of Leman I sat down and wept . . .
Sweet Thames, run softly till I end my song,
Sweet Thames, run softly, for I speak not loud or long.
But at my back in a cold blast I hear
The rattle of the bones, and chuckle spread from ear to ear.
A rat crept softly through the vegetation
Dragging its slimy belly on the bank
While I was fishing in the dull canal
On a winter evening round behind the gashouse
Musing upon the king my brother's wreck
And on the king my father's death before him.[22]
White bodies naked on the low damp ground
And bones cast in a little low dry garret,
Rattled by the rat's foot only, year to year.
But at my back from time to time I hear[23]
The sound of horns and motors, which shall bring[24]
Sweeney to Mrs. Porter in the spring.

[21] V. Spenser, *Prothalamion*.
[22] Cf. *The Tempest*, I, ii.
[23] Cf. Marvell, *To His Coy Mistress*.
[24] Cf. Day, *Parliament of Bees*:
"When of the sudden, listening, you shall hear,
"A noise of horns and hunting, which shall bring
"Actaeon to Diana in the spring,
"Where all shall see her naked skin . . ."

O the moon shone bright on Mrs. Porter[25]
And on her daughter
They wash their feet in soda water
Et O ces voix d'enfants, chantant dans la coupole![26]

Twit twit twit
Jug jug jug jug jug jug
So rudely forc'd.
Tereu

Unreal City
Under the brown fog of a winter noon
Mr. Eugenides, the Smyrna merchant
Unshaven, with a pocket full of currants[27]
C.i.f. London: documents at sight,
Asked me in demotic French
To luncheon at the Cannon Street Hotel
Followed by a weekend at the Metropole.
At the violet hour, when the eyes and back
Turn upward from the desk, when the human engine waits
Like a taxi throbbing waiting,
I Tiresias, though blind, throbbing between two lives,[28]
Old man with wrinkled female breasts, can see
At the violet hour, the evening hour that strives

[25] I do not know the origin of the ballad from which these lines are taken: it was reported to me from Sydney, Australia.

[26] V. Verlaine, *Parsifal*.

[27] The currants were quoted at a price "carriage and insurance free to London"; and the Bill of Lading etc. were to be handed to the buyer upon payment of the sight draft.

[28] Tiresias, although a mere spectator and not indeed a "character," is yet the most important personage in the poem, uniting all the rest. Just as the one eyed merchant, seller of currants, melts into the Phoenician Sailor, and the latter is not wholly distinct from Ferdinand Prince of Naples, so all the women are one woman, and the two sexes meet in Tiresias. What Tiresias *sees*, in fact, is the substance of the poem. The whole passage from Ovid is of great anthropological interest:

'. . . Cum Iunone iocos et maior vestra profecto est
Quam, quae contingit maribus,' dixisse, 'voluptas.'
Illa negat; placuit quae sit sententia docti
Quaerere Tiresiae: venus huic erat utraque nota.
Nam duo magnorum viridi coeuntia silva
Corpora serpentum baculi violaverat ictu
Deque viro factus, mirabile, femina septem
Egerat autumnos; octavo rursus eosdem
Vidit et 'est vestrae si tanta potentia plagae,'
Dixit 'ut auctoris sortem in contraria mutet,
Nunc quoque vos feriam!' percussis anguibus isdem
Forma prior rediit genetivaque venit imago.
Arbiter hic igitur sumptus de lite iocosa
Dicta Iovis firmat; gravius Saturnia iusto
Nec pro materia fertur doluisse suique
Iudicis aeterna damnavit lumina nocte,
At pater omnipotens (neque enim licet inrita cuiquam
Facta dei fecisse deo) pro lumine adempto
Scire futura dedit poenamque levavit honore.

Homeward, and brings the sailor home from sea,[29]
The typist home at teatime, clears her breakfast, lights
Her stove, and lays out food in tins.
Out of the window perilously spread
Her drying combinations touched by the sun's last rays,
On the divan are piled (at night her bed)
Stockings, slippers, camisoles, and stays.
I Tiresias, old man with wrinkled dugs
Perceived the scene, and foretold the rest—
I too awaited the expected guest.
He, the young man carbuncular, arrives,
A small house agent's clerk, with one bold stare,
One of the low on whom assurance sits
As a silk hat on a Bradford millionaire.
The time is now propitious, as he guesses,
The meal is ended, she is bored and tired,
Endeavours to engage her in caresses
Which still are unreproved, if undesired.
Flushed and decided, he assaults at once;
Exploring hands encounter no defence;
His vanity requires no response,
And makes a welcome of indifference.
(And I Tiresias have foresuffered all
Enacted on this same divan or bed;
I who have sat by Thebes below the wall
And walked among the lowest of the dead.)
Bestows one final patronising kiss,
And gropes his way, finding the stairs unlit . . .

She turns and looks a moment in the glass,
Hardly aware of her departed lover;
Her brain allows one half-formed thought to pass:
"Well now that's done: and I'm glad it's over."
When lovely woman stoops to folly and[30]
Paces about her room again, alone,
She smoothes her hair with automatic hand,
And puts a record on the gramophone.

"This music crept by me upon the waters"[31]
And along the Strand, up Queen Victoria Street.

[29] This may not appear as exact as Sappho's lines, but I had in mind the "longshore" or "dory" fisherman, who returns at nightfall.

[30] V. Goldsmith, the song in *The Vicar of Wakefield*.

[31] V. *The Tempest*, as above.

O City city, I can sometimes hear
Beside a public bar in Lower Thames Street,
The pleasant whining of a mandoline
And a clatter and a chatter from within
Where fishmen lounge at noon: where the walls
Of Magnus Martyr hold[32]
Inexplicable splendour of Ionian white and gold.

The river sweats[33]
Oil and tar
The barges drift
With the turning tide
Red sails
Wide
To leeward, swing on the heavy spar.
The barges wash
Drifting logs
Down Greenwich reach
Past the Isle of Dogs.
Weialala leia
Wallala leialala

Elizabeth and Leicester[34]
Beating oars
The stern was formed
A gilded shell
Red and gold
The brisk swell
Rippled both shores
Southwest wind
Carried down stream
The peal of bells
White towers
Weialala leia
Wallala leialala

[32] The interior of St. Magnus Martyr is to my mind one of the finest among Wren's interiors. See *The Proposed Demolition of Nineteen City Churches:* (P. S. King & Son, Ltd.).

[33] The Song of the (three) Thames-daughters begins here. From line 292 to 306 inclusive they speak in turn. V. *Götterdämmerung,* III, i: the Rhine-daughters.

[34] V. Froude, *Elizabeth,* Vol. I, ch. iv, letter of De Quadra to Philip of Spain: "In the afternoon we were in a barge, watching the games on the river. (The queen) was alone with Lord Robert and myself on the poop, when they began to talk nonsense, and went so far that Lord Robert at last said, as I was on the spot there was no reason why they should not be married if the queen pleased."

"Trams and dusty trees.
Highbury bore me. Richmond and Kew[35]
Undid me. By Richmond I raised my knees
Supine on the floor of a narrow canoe."

"My feet are at Moorgate, and my heart
Under my feet. After the event
He wept. He promised 'a new start.'
I made no comment. What should I resent?"

"On Margate Sands.
I can connect
Nothing with nothing.
The broken fingernails of dirty hands.
My people humble people who expect
Nothing."
la la

To Carthage then I came[36]
Burning burning burning burning[37]
O Lord Thou pluckest me out[38]
O Lord Thou pluckest

burning

IV. DEATH BY WATER

Phlebas the Phoenician, a fortnight dead,
Forgot the cry of gulls, and the deep sea swell
And the profit and loss.
A current under sea
Picked his bones in whispers. As he rose and fell
He passed the stages of his age and youth
Entering the whirlpool.
Gentile or Jew
O you who turn the wheel and look to windward,
Consider Phlebas, who was once handsome and tall as you.

[35] Cf. *Purgatorio,* V, 133:
"Ricorditi di me, che son la Pia;
"Siena mi fe', disfecemi Maremma."

[36] V. St. Augustine's *Confessions:* "to Carthage then I came, where a cauldron of unholy loves sang all about mine ears."

[37] The complete text of the Buddha's Fire Sermon (which corresponds in importance to the Sermon on the Mount) from which these words are taken, will be found translated in the late Henry Clarke Warren's *Buddhism in Translation* (Harvard Oriental Series). Mr. Warren was one of the great pioneers of Buddhist studies in the Occident.

[38] From St. Augustine's *Confessions* again. The collocation of these two representatives of eastern and western asceticism, as the culmination of this part of the poem, is not an accident.

V. WHAT THE THUNDER SAID[39]

After the torchlight red on sweaty faces
After the frosty silence in the gardens
After the agony in stony places
The shouting and the crying
Prison and palace and reverberation
Of thunder of spring over distant mountains
He who was living is now dead
We who were living are now dying
With a little patience

Here is no water but only rock
Rock and no water and the sandy road
The road winding above among the mountains
Which are mountains of rock without water
If there were water we should stop and drink
Amongst the rock one cannot stop or think
Sweat is dry and feet are in the sand
If there were only water amongst the rock
Dead mountain mouth of carious teeth that cannot spit
Here one can neither stand nor lie nor sit
There is not even silence in the mountains
But dry sterile thunder without rain
There is not even solitude in the mountains
But red sullen faces sneer and snarl
From doors of mudcracked houses
If there were water
And no rock
If there were rock
And also water
And water
A spring
A pool among the rock
If there were the sound of water only
Not the cicada
And dry grass singing
But sound of water over a rock
Where the hermit-thrush sings in the pine trees[40]

[39] In the first part of Part V three themes are employed: the journey to Emmaus, the approach to the Chapel Perilous (see Miss Weston's book) and the present decay of eastern Europe.

[40] This is *Turdus aonalaschkae pallasii*, the hermit-thrush which I have heard in Quebec County. Chapman says (*Handbook of Birds of Eastern North America*) "it is most at home in secluded woodland and thickety retreats. . . . Its notes are not remarkable for variety or volume, but in purity and sweetness of tone and exquisite modulation they are unequalled." Its "water-dripping song" is justly celebrated.

Drip drop drip drop drop drop drop
But there is no water

Who is the third who walks always beside you?
When I count, there are only you and I together[41]
But when I look ahead up the white road
There is always another one walking beside you
Gliding wrapt in a brown mantle, hooded
I do not know whether a man or a woman
—But who is that on the other side of you?

What is that sound high in the air
Murmur of maternal lamentation
Who are those hooded hordes swarming
Over endless plains, stumbling in cracked earth
Ringed by the flat horizon only
What is the city over the mountains
Cracks and reforms and bursts in the violet air
Falling towers
Jerusalem Athens Alexandria
Vienna London
Unreal[42]

A woman drew her long black hair out tight
And fiddled whisper music on those strings
And bats with baby faces in the violet light
Whistled, and beat their wings
And crawled head downward down a blackened wall
And upside down in air were towers
Tolling reminiscent bells, that kept the hours
And voices singing out of empty cisterns and exhausted wells.

In this decayed hole among the mountains
In the faint moonlight, the grass is singing
Over the tumbled graves, about the chapel
There is the empty chapel, only the wind's home.

[41] The following lines were stimulated by the account of one of the Antarctic expeditions (I forget which, but I think one of Shackleton's): it was related that the party of explorers, at the extremity of their strength, had the constant delusion that there was *one more member* than could actually be counted.

[42] Cf. Hermann Hesse, *Blick ins Chaos:* "Schon ist halb Europa, schon ist zumindest der halbe Osten Europas auf dem Wege zum Chaos, fährt betrunken im heiligem Wahn am Abgrund entlang und singt dazu, singt betrunken und hymnisch wie Dmitri Karamasoff sang. Ueber diese Lieder lacht der Bürger beleidigt, der Heilige und Seher hört sie mit Tränen."

It has no windows, and the door swings,
Dry bones can harm no one.
Only a cock stood on the rooftree
Co co rico co co rico
In a flash of lightning. Then a damp gust
Bringing rain

Ganga was sunken, and the limp leaves
Waited for rain, while the black clouds
Gathered far distant, over Himavant.
The jungle crouched, humped in silence.
Then spoke the thunder
DA
Datta: what have we given?[43]
My friend, blood shaking my heart
The awful daring of a moment's surrender
Which an age of prudence can never retract
By this, and this only, we have existed
Which is not to be found in our obituaries
Or in memories draped by the beneficent spider[44]
Or under seals broken by the lean solicitor
In our empty rooms
DA
Dayadhvam: I have heard the key[45]
Turn in the door once and turn once only
We think of the key, each in his prison
Thinking of the key, each confirms a prison
Only at nightfall, aethereal rumours
Revive for a moment a broken Coriolanus

[43] "Datta, dayadhvam, damyata" (Give, sympathise, control). The fable of the meaning of the Thunder is found in the *Brihadaranyaka—Upanishad,* 5, 1. A translation is found in Deussen's *Sechzig Upanishads des Veda,* p. 489.

[44] Cf. Webster, *The White Devil,* V, vi:

"... they'll remarry
Ere the worm pierce your winding-sheet, ere the spider
Make a thin curtain for your epitaphs."

[45] Cf. *Inferno,* XXXIII, 46:
"ed io sentii chiavar l'uscio di sotto all'orribile torre."

Also F. H. Bradley, *Appearance and Reality*, p. 346.
"My external sensations are no less private to myself than are my thoughts or my feelings. In either case my experience falls within my own circle, a circle closed on the outside; and, with all its elements alike, every sphere is opaque to the others which surround it. . . . In brief, regarded as an existence which appears in a soul, the whole world for each is peculiar and private to that soul."

DA
Damyata: The boat responded
Gaily, to the hand expert with sail and oar
The sea was calm, your heart would have responded
Gaily, when invited, beating obedient
To controlling hands

I sat upon the shore
Fishing, with the arid plain behind me[46]
Shall I at least set my lands in order?
London Bridge is falling down falling down falling down
Poi s'ascose nel foco che gli affina[47]
Quando fiam uti chelidon—O swallow swallow[48]
Le Prince d'Aquitaine à la tour abolie[49]
These fragments I have shored against my ruins
Why then Ile fit you. Hieronymo's mad againe.[50]
Datta. Dayadhvam. Damyata.
Shantih shantih shantih[51] 1922

The Hollow Men

A penny for the Old Guy

I

We are the hollow men
We are the stuffed men
Leaning together
Headpiece filled with straw. Alas!
Our dried voices, when
We whisper together
Are quite meaningless
As wind in dry grass
Or rats' feet over broken glass
In our dry cellar

[46] V. Weston: *From Ritual to Romance;* chapter on the Fisher King.

[47] V. *Purgatorio,* XXVI, 148.
"'Ara vos prec per aquella valor
'que vos guida al som de l'escalina,
'sovegna vos a temps de ma dolor.'
Poi s'ascose nel foco che gli affina."

[48] V. *Pervigilium Veneris.* Cf. Philomela in Parts II and III.

[49] V. Gerard de Nerval, Sonnet *El Desdichado.*

[50] V. Kyd's *Spanish Tragedy.*

[51] Shantih. Repeated as here, a formal ending to an Upanishad. "The Peace which passeth understanding" is our equivalent to this word.

Shape without form, shade without colour,
Paralysed force, gesture without motion;

Those who have crossed
With direct eyes, to death's other Kingdom
Remember us—if at all—not as lost
Violent souls, but only
As the hollow men
The stuffed men.

II

Eyes I dare not meet in dreams
In death's dream kingdom
These do not appear:
There, the eyes are
Sunlight on a broken column
There, is a tree swinging
And voices are
In the wind's singing
More distant and more solemn
Than a fading star.

Let me be no nearer
In death's dream kingdom
Let me also wear
Such deliberate disguises
Rat's skin, crowskin, crossed staves
In a field
Behaving as the wind behaves
No nearer—

Not that final meeting
In the twilight kingdom

III

This is the dead land
This is cactus land
Here the stone images
Are raised, here they receive
The supplication of a dead man's hand
Under the twinkle of a fading star.

Is it like this
In death's other kingdom
Waking alone
At the hour when we are
Trembling with tenderness

Lips that would kiss
Form prayers to broken stone.

IV

The eyes are not here
There are no eyes here
In this valley of dying stars
In this hollow valley
This broken jaw of our lost kingdoms

In this last of meeting places
We grope together
And avoid speech
Gathered on this beach of the tumid river

Sightless, unless
The eyes reappear
As the perpetual star
Multifoliate rose
Of death's twilight kingdom
The hope only
Of empty men.

V

Here we go round the prickly pear
Prickly pear prickly pear
Here we go round the prickly pear
At five o'clock in the morning.

Between the idea
And the reality
Between the motion
And the act
Falls the Shadow
For Thine is the Kingdom

Between the conception
And the creation
Between the emotion
And the response
Falls the Shadow
Life is very long

Between the desire
And the spasm
Between the potency
And the existence
Between the essence

And the descent
Falls the Shadow
For Thine is the Kingdom

For Thine is
Life is
For Thine is the

This is the way the world ends
This is the way the world ends
This is the way the world ends
Not with a bang but a whimper. 1925

Ash-Wednesday

I

Because I do not hope to turn again
Because I do not hope
Because I do not hope to turn
Desiring this man's gift and that man's scope
I no longer strive to strive towards such things
(Why should the agèd eagle stretch its wings?)
Why should I mourn
The vanished power of the usual reign?

Because I do not hope to know again
The infirm glory of the positive hour
Because I do not think
Because I know I shall not know
The one veritable transitory power
Because I cannot drink
There, where trees flower, and springs flow, for there is nothing again

Because I know that time is always time
And place is always and only place
And what is actual is actual only for one time
And only for one place
I rejoice that things are as they are and
I renounce the blessèd face
And renounce the voice

Because I cannot hope to turn again
Consequently I rejoice, having to construct something
Upon which to rejoice

And pray to God to have mercy upon us
And I pray that I may forget
These matters that with myself I too much discuss
Too much explain
Because I do not hope to turn again
Let these words answer
For what is done, not to be done again
May the judgement not be too heavy upon us

Because these wings are no longer wings to fly
But merely vans to beat the air
The air which is now thoroughly small and dry
Smaller and dryer than the will
Teach us to care and not to care
Teach us to sit still.

Pray for us sinners now and at the hour of our death
Pray for us now and at the hour of our death.

II

Lady, three white leopards sat under a juniper-tree
In the cool of the day, having fed to satiety
On my legs my heart my liver and that which had been contained
In the hollow round of my skull. And God said
Shall these bones live? shall these
Bones live? And that which had been contained
In the bones (which were already dry) said chirping:
Because of the goodness of this Lady
And because of her loveliness, and because
She honours the Virgin in meditation,
We shine with brightness. And I who am here dissembled
Proffer my deeds to oblivion, and my love
To the posterity of the desert and the fruit of the gourd.
It is this which recovers
My guts the strings of my eyes and the indigestible portions
Which the leopards reject. The Lady is withdrawn
In a white gown, to contemplation, in a white gown.
Let the whiteness of bones atone to forgetfulness.
There is no life in them. As I am forgotten
And would be forgotten, so I would forget
Thus devoted, concentrated in purpose. And God said
Prophesy to the wind, to the wind only for only
The wind will listen. And the bones sang chirping
With the burden of the grasshopper, saying

Lady of silences
Calm and distressed
Torn and most whole
Rose of memory
Rose of forgetfulness
Exhausted and life-giving
Worried reposeful
The single Rose
Is now the Garden
Where all loves end
Terminate torment
Of love unsatisfied
The greater torment
Of love satisfied
End of the endless
Journey to no end
Conclusion of all that
Is inconclusible
Speech without word and
Word of no speech
Grace to the Mother
For the Garden
Where all love ends.

Under a juniper-tree the bones sang, scattered and shining
We are glad to be scattered, we did little good to each other,
Under a tree in the cool of the day, with the blessing of sand,
Forgetting themselves and each other, united
In the quiet of the desert. This is the land which ye
Shall divide by lot. And neither division nor unity
Matters. This is the land. We have our inheritance.

III

At the first turning of the second stair
I turned and saw below
The same shape twisted on the banister
Under the vapour in the fetid air
Struggling with the devil of the stairs who wears
The deceitful face of hope and of despair.

At the second turning of the second stair
I left them twisting, turning below;
There were no more faces and the stair was dark,
Damp, jaggèd, like an old man's mouth drivelling, beyond repair,
Or the toothed gullet of an agèd shark.

At the first turning of the third stair
Was a slotted window bellied like the fig's fruit
And beyond the hawthorn blossom and a pasture scene
The broadbacked figure drest in blue and green
Enchanted the maytime with an antique flute.
Blown hair is sweet, brown hair over the mouth blown,
Lilac and brown hair;
Distraction, music of the flute, stops and steps of the mind over
    the third stair,
Fading, fading; strength beyond hope and despair
Climbing the third stair.

Lord, I am not worthy
Lord, I am not worthy

        but speak the word only.

IV

Who walked between the violet and the violet
Who walked between
The various ranks of varied green
Going in white and blue, in Mary's colour,
Talking of trivial things
In ignorance and in knowledge of eternal dolour
Who moved among the others as they walked,
Who then made strong the fountains and made fresh the springs

Made cool the dry rock and made firm the sand
In blue of larkspur, blue of Mary's colour,
Sovegna vos

Here are the years that walk between, bearing
Away the fiddles and the flutes, restoring
One who moves in the time between sleep and waking, wearing

White light folded, sheathed about her, folded.
The new years walk, restoring
Through a bright cloud of tears, the years, restoring
With a new verse the ancient rhyme. Redeem
The time, Redeem
The unread vision in the higher dream
While jewelled unicorns draw by the gilded hearse.

The silent sister veiled in white and blue
Between the yews, behind the garden god,
Whose flute is breathless, bent her head and signed but spoke
    no word

But the fountain sprang up and the bird sang down
Redeem the time, redeem the dream
The token of the word unheard, unspoken

Till the wind shake a thousand whispers from the yew

And after this our exile

V

If the lost word is lost, if the spent word is spent
If the unheard, unspoken
Word is unspoken, unheard;
Still is the unspoken word, the Word unheard,
The Word without a word, the Word within
The world and for the world;
And the light shone in darkness and
Against the Word the unstilled world still whirled
About the centre of the silent Word.

O my people, what have I done unto thee.

Where shall the word be found, where will the word
Resound? Not here, there is not enough silence
Not on the sea or on the islands, not
On the mainland, in the desert or the rain land,
For those who walk in darkness
Both in the day time and in the night time
The right time and the right place are not here
No place of grace for those who avoid the face
No time to rejoice for those who walk among noise and deny the voice

Will the veiled sister pray for
Those who walk in darkness, who chose thee and oppose thee,
Those who are torn on the horn between season and season, time and time, between
Hour and hour, word and word, power and power, those who wait
In darkness? Will the veiled sister pray
For children at the gate
Who will not go away and cannot pray:
Pray for those who chose and oppose

O my people, what have I done unto thee.

Will the veiled sister between the slender
Yew trees pray for those who offend her
And are terrified and cannot surrender
And affirm before the world and deny between the rocks

In the last desert between the last blue rocks
The desert in the garden the garden in the desert
Of drouth, spitting from the mouth the withered apple-seed.

O my people.

VI

Although I do not hope to turn again
Although I do not hope
Although I do not hope to turn

Wavering between the profit and the loss
In this brief transit where the dreams cross
The dreamcrossed twilight between birth and dying
(Bless me father) though I do not wish to wish these things
From the wide window towards the granite shore
The white sails still fly seaward, seaward flying
Unbroken wings

And the lost heart stiffens and rejoices
In the lost lilac and the lost sea voices
And the weak spirit quickens to rebel
For the bent golden-rod and the lost sea smell
Quickens to recover
The cry of quail and the whirling plover
And the blind eye creates
The empty forms between the ivory gates
And smell renews the salt savour of the sandy earth

This is the time of tension between dying and birth
The place of solitude where three dreams cross
Between blue rocks
But when the voices shaken from the yew-tree drift away
Let the other yew be shaken and reply.

Blessèd sister, holy mother, spirit of the fountain, spirit of the garden,
Suffer us not to mock ourselves with falsehood
Teach us to care and not to care
Teach us to sit still
Even among these rocks,
Our peace in His will
And even among these rocks
Sister, mother
And spirit of the river, spirit of the sea,
Suffer me not to be separated

And let my cry come unto Thee. 1930

Wallace Stevens

(1879-1955)

CHRONOLOGY:

1879 Born October 2, in Reading, Pennsylvania.
1897-1903 Attended Harvard University and New York Law School.
1904 Admitted to the Bar.
1904-16 Practiced law in New York City.
1914 Published four early poems in *Poetry.*
1916 Moved to Hartford, Connecticut, and joined the Hartford Accident and Indemnity Company.
1923 *Harmonium.*
1931 *Harmonium,* expanded and enlarged.
1935 *Ideas of Order.*
1936 *Owl's Clover.*
1937 *The Man with the Blue Guitar and Other Poems.*
1942 *Parts of a World; Notes Toward a Supreme Fiction.*
1945 *Esthétique du Mal.*
1947 *Transport to Summer; Three Academic Pieces.*
1948 *A Primitive Like an Orb.*
1949 Awarded the Bollingen Prize for Poetry.
1950 *The Auroras of Autumn.*
1951 Awarded the National Book Award for Poetry; *The Necessary Angel: Essays on Reality and the Imagination.*
1953 *Raoul Dufy, a Note.*
1954 *Collected Poems.*
1955 Died August 2, in Hartford, Connecticut; awarded the National Book Award for Poetry and the Pulitzer Prize for Poetry.
1957 *Opus Posthumous* (ed. by S. F. Morse).

BIBLIOGRAPHY:

The standard edition is *Collected Poems* (New York, 1954). Samuel French Morse's edition of *Opus Posthumous* (New York, 1957) collects some poems and essays that had not been published before. Morse also compiled the standard bibliography, *Wallace Stevens: A Checklist of His Published Writings, 1894-1954* (New Haven, 1954).

Two important book-length analyses are William Van O'Connor, *The Shaping Spirit: A Study of Wallace Stevens* (Chicago, 1950) and Robert Pack, *Wallace Stevens: An Approach to His Poetry* (New Brunswick, N.J., 1958). Two special issues devoted exclusively to Stevens include the *Trinity Review,* VII (May, 1954), and *Perspective,* VII (Autumn, 1954). *The Achievement of Wallace Stevens,* ed. Ashley Brown and R. S. Haller (Philadelphia, 1962), is a useful collection of critical studies.

For useful check lists and explications, see Allen Tate, *Sixty American Poets, 1896-1944* (Rev. ed.; Washington, 1954) and Joseph M. Kuntz, *Poetry Explication* (Rev. ed.; Denver, 1962).

On Poetic Truth

Poetry has to do with reality in its most individual aspect. An isolated fact, cut loose from the universe, has no significance for the poet. It derives its significance from the reality to which it belongs. To see things in their true perspective, for example, we require to draw very extensively upon experiences that are past. All that we see and hear is given a meaning in this way. It is the function of science to complete this interpretation. The scientist can tell me much which I cannot know from ordinary observation. But however exhaustive information of this kind may be there is something which it does not cover and that is particularity here and now. There is in reality, whether we think of it as animate or inanimate, human or subhuman, an aspect of individuality at which many forms of rational explanation stop short.

For Plato the only reality that mattered is exemplified best for us in the principles of mathematics. The aim of our lives should be to draw ourselves away as much as possible from the unsubstantial fluctuating facts of the world about us and establish some communion with the objects which are apprehended by thought and not sense. This was the source of Plato's asceticism. It must suffice here to note the dismissal of the individual and particular facts of experience as of no importance in themselves. Plato would describe himself as a realist in the sense that it is by breaking away from the world of facts that we make contact with reality.

What do we learn? Just this; that poetry has to do with reality in that concrete and individual aspect of it which the mind can never tackle altogether on its own terms, with matter that is foreign and alien in a way in which abstract systems, ideas in which we detect an inherent pattern, a structure that belongs to the ideas themselves, can never be. It is never familiar to us in the way in which Plato wished the conquests of the mind to be familiar. On the contrary its function, the need which it meets and which has to be met in some way in every age that is not to become decadent or barbarous is precisely this contact with reality as it impinges on us from the outside, the sense that we can touch and feel a solid reality which does not wholly dissolve itself into the conceptions of our own minds. It is the individual and particular that does this. And the wonder and mystery of art, as indeed of religion in the last resort, is the revelation of something "wholly other" by which the inexpressible loneliness of thinking is broken and enriched. To know facts as facts in the ordinary way has, indeed, no particular power or worth. But a quickening of our awareness of the irrevocability by which a thing is what it is, has such power, and it is, I believe, the very soul of art. But no fact is a bare fact, no individual is a universe in itself. The artist exhibits affinities in the *actual* structure of objects by which their significance is deepened and enhanced. What I desire to stress is that there is a unity rooted in the individuality of objects and discovered in a different way from the apprehension of rational connections.

The extraction of a meaning from a poem and appraisement of it by rational standards of truth has mainly been due to enthusiasm for moral or religious truth. But that is not usual today. Politics is our culprit. It would be fantastic to suggest that the overt meaning, what the poem seems to say, contributes little to the artistic significance and merit of a poem. We merely protest against the abstraction of this content from the whole and appraisement of it by other than aesthetic standards. The "something said" is important, but it is important for the poem only in so far as the saying of that particular something in a special way is a revelation of reality. The form derives its significance from the whole. Form has no significance except in relation to the reality that is being revealed.

The genuine artist is never "true to life." He sees what is real, but not as we are normally aware of it. We do not go storming through life like actors in a play. Art is never real life. The poet sees with a poignancy and penetration that is altogether unique. What matters is that the poet must be true to his art and not "true to life," whether his art is simple or complex, violent or subdued. Emotion is thought to lie at the center of aesthetic experience. That, however, is not how the matter appears to me. If I am right, the essence of art is insight of a special kind into reality. But such insight is bound to be accompanied by remarkable emotions. A poem would be nothing without some meaning. The truth is that meaning is an awareness and a communication. But it is no ordinary awareness, no ordinary communication.

Novelty must be inspired. But there must be novelty. This crisis is most evident in religion. The theologians whose thought is most astir today do make articulate a supreme need, and one that has now become also imperative, as their urgency shows, the need to infuse into the ages of enlightenment an awareness of reality adequate to their achievements and such as will not be attenuated by them. There is one most welcome and authentic note; it is the insistence on a reality that forces itself upon our consciousness and refuses to be managed and mastered. It is here that the affinity of art and religion is most evident today. Both have to mediate for us a reality not ourselves. This is what the poet does. The supreme virtue here is humility, for the humble are they that move about the world with the love of the real in their hearts.

1957

Disillusionment of Ten O'Clock

The houses are haunted
By white night-gowns.
None are green,
Or purple with green rings,
Or green with yellow rings,
Or yellow with blue rings.
None of them are strange,

With socks of lace
And beaded ceintures.
People are not going
To dream of baboons and periwinkles.
Only, here and there, an old sailor,
Drunk and asleep in his boots,
Catches tigers
In red weather. 1915

Anecdote of the Jar

I placed a jar in Tennessee,
And round it was, upon a hill.
It made the slovenly wilderness
Surround that hill.

The wilderness rose up to it,
And sprawled around, no longer wild.
The jar was round upon the ground
And tall and of a port in air.

It took dominion everywhere.
The jar was gray and bare.
It did not give of bird or bush,
Like nothing else in Tennessee. 1919

A High-Toned Old Christian Woman

Poetry is the supreme fiction, madame.
Take the moral law and make a nave of it
And from the nave build haunted heaven. Thus,
The conscience is converted into palms,
Like windy citherns hankering for hymns.
We agree in principle. That's clear. But take
The opposing law and make a peristyle,
And from the peristyle project a masque
Beyond the planets. Thus, our bawdiness,
Unpurged by epitaph, indulged at last,
Is equally converted into palms,
Squiggling like saxophones. And palm for palm,
Madame, we are where we began. Allow,
Therefore, that in the planetary scene

Your disaffected flagellants, well-stuffed,
Smacking their muzzy bellies in parade,
Proud of such novelties of the sublime,
Such tink and tank and tunk-a-tunk-tunk,
May, merely may, madame, whip from themselves
A jovial hullabaloo among the spheres.
This will make widows wince. But fictive things
Wink as they will. Wink most when widows wince.

1922

The Emperor of Ice-Cream

Call the roller of big cigars,
The muscular one, and bid him whip
In kitchen cups concupiscent curds.
Let the wenches dawdle in such dress
As they are used to wear, and let the boys
Bring flowers in last month's newspapers.
Let be be finale of seem.
The only emperor is the emperor of ice-cream.

Take from the dresser of deal,
Lacking the three glass knobs, that sheet
On which she embroidered fantails once
And spread it so as to cover her face.
If her horny feet protrude, they come
To show how cold she is, and dumb.
Let the lamp affix its beam.
The only emperor is the emperor of ice-cream.

1922

The Plot Against the Giant

FIRST GIRL

When this yokel comes maundering,
Whetting his hacker,
I shall run before him,
Diffusing the civilest odors
Out of geraniums and unsmelled flowers.
It will check him.

SECOND GIRL

I shall run before him,
Arching cloths besprinkled with colors

As small as fish-eggs.
The threads
Will abash him.

THIRD GIRL

Oh, la . . . le pauvre!
I shall run before him,
With a curious puffing.
He will bend his ear then.
I shall whisper
Heavenly labials in a world of gutturals.
It will undo him. 1923

Floral Decorations for Bananas

Well, Nuncle, this plainly won't do.
These insolent, linear peels
And sullen, hurricane shapes
Won't do with your eglantine.
They require something serpentine.
Blunt yellow in such a room!

You should have had plums tonight,
In an eighteenth-century dish,
And pettifogging buds,
For the women of primrose and purl,
Each one in her decent curl.
Good God! What a precious light!

But bananas hacked and hunched . . .
The table was set by an ogre,
His eye on an outdoor gloom
And a stiff and noxious place.
Pile the bananas on planks.
The women will be all shanks
And bangles and slatted eyes.

And deck the bananas in leaves
Plucked from the Carib trees,
Fibrous and dangling down,
Oozing cantankerous gum
Out of their purple maws,
Darting out of their purple craws
Their musky and tingling tongues. 1923

The Idea of Order at Key West

She sang beyond the genius of the sea.
The water never formed to mind or voice,
Like a body wholly body, fluttering
Its empty sleeves; and yet its mimic motion
Made constant cry, caused constantly a cry,
That was not ours although we understood,
Inhuman, of the veritable ocean.

The sea was not a mask. No more was she.
The song and water were not medleyed sound
Even if what she sang was what she heard,
Since what she sang was uttered word by word.
It may be that in all her phrases stirred
The grinding water and the gasping wind;
But it was she and not the sea we heard.

For she was the maker of the song she sang.
The ever-hooded, tragic-gestured sea
Was merely a place by which she walked to sing.
Whose spirit is this? we said, because we knew
It was the spirit that we sought and knew
That we should ask this often as she sang.

If it was only the dark voice of the sea
That rose, or even colored by many waves;
If it was only the outer voice of sky
And cloud, of the sunken coral water-walled,
However clear, it would have been deep air,
The heaving speech of air, a summer sound
Repeated in a summer without end
And sound alone. But it was more than that,
More even than her voice, and ours, among
The meaningless plungings of water and the wind,
Theatrical distances, bronze shadows heaped
On high horizons, mountainous atmospheres
Of sky and sea.
It was her voice that made
The sky acutest at its vanishing.
She measured to the hour its solitude.
She was the single artificer of the world
In which she sang. And when she sang, the sea,
Whatever self it had, became the self

That was her song, for she was the maker. Then we,
As we beheld her striding there alone,
Knew that there never was a world for her
Except the one she sang and, singing, made.

Ramon Fernandez, tell me, if you know,
Why, when the singing ended and we turned
Toward the town, tell why the glassy lights,
The lights in the fishing boats at anchor there,
As the night descended, tilting in the air,
Mastered the night and portioned out the sea,
Fixing emblazoned zones and fiery poles,
Arranging, deepening, enchanting night.

Oh! Blessed rage for order, pale Ramon,
The maker's rage to order words of the sea,
Words of the fragrant portals, dimly-starred,
And of ourselves and of our origins,
In ghostlier demarcations, keener sounds. 1934

Of Modern Poetry

The poem of the mind in the act of finding
What will suffice. It has not always had
To find: the scene was set; it repeated what
Was in the script.
Then the theatre was changed
To something else. Its past was a souvenir.

It has to be living, to learn the speech of the place.
It has to face the men of the time and to meet
The women of the time. It has to think about war
And it has to find what will suffice. It has
To construct a new stage. It has to be on that stage
And, like an insatiable actor, slowly and
With meditation, speak words that in the ear,
In the delicatest ear of the mind, repeat,
Exactly, that which it wants to hear, at the sound
Of which, an invisible audience listens,
Not to the play, but to itself, expressed
In an emotion as of two people, as of two
Emotions becoming one. The actor is
A metaphysician in the dark, twanging
An instrument, twanging a wiry string that gives

Sounds passing through sudden rightnesses, wholly
Containing the mind, below which it cannot descend,
Beyond which it has no will to rise.
It must
Be the finding of a satisfaction, and may
Be of a man skating, a woman dancing, a woman
Combing. The poem of the act of the mind. 1940

Study of Two Pears

I

Opusculum paedagogum.
The pears are not viols,
Nudes or bottles.
They resemble nothing else.

II

They are yellow forms
Composed of curves
Bulging toward the base.
They are touched red.

III

They are not flat surfaces
Having curved outlines.
They are round
Tapering toward the top.

IV

In the way they are modelled
There are bits of blue.
A hard dry leaf hangs
From the stem.

V

The yellow glistens.
It glistens with various yellows,
Citrons, oranges and greens
Flowering over the skin.

VI

The shadows of the pears
Are blobs on the green cloth.
The pears are not seen
As the observer wills. 1942

The Ultimate Poem Is Abstract

This day writhes with what? The lecturer
On This Beautiful World Of Ours composes himself
And hems the planet rose and haws it ripe,

And red, and right. The particular question—here
The particular answer to the particular question
Is not in point—the question is in point.

If the day writhes, it is not with revelations.
One goes on asking questions. That, then, is one
Of the categories. So said, this placid space

Is changed. It is not so blue as we thought. To be blue,
There must be no questions. It is an intellect
Of windings round and dodges to and fro,

Writhings in wrong obliques and distances,
Not an intellect in which we are fleet: present
Everywhere in space at once, cloud-pole

Of communication. It would be enough
If we were ever, just once, at the middle, fixed
In This Beautiful World Of Ours and not as now,

Helplessly at the edge, enough to be
Complete, because at the middle, if only in sense,
And in that enormous sense, merely enjoy. 1950

CHAPTER SIX

THE TRIUMPH OF MODERN AMERICAN DRAMA

Although Eugene O'Neill is clearly the giant of modern American drama, he did not develop in a theatrical vacuum. The late rise of significant American drama (the latter half of the second decade of the present century) is a curious literary phenomenon, but when drama did come into its own, its intrinsic achievements and its influence on the world were to be among the most dynamic that modern American literature was to exert in any of the literary genres. That one of the oldest of the arts should have become one of the newest of any consequence in America is an involved and complex story, the major threads of which have already been recounted in the Introduction (see pp. 2 and 4). Obviously, the three plays here collected and the three playwrights represented (Elmer Rice, Eugene O'Neill, and Tennessee Williams) are by no means the only playwrights (with the exception of O'Neill) or the only plays that could demonstrate, within so small a compass, the scope and depth of the dramatic achievement in modern America. These three plays, however, are radically different, one from the other. The playwrights themselves form a sequence which spans the period of the founding and the flourishing of a successful dramatic movement in America from about World War I to the present. They provide, in short, without any claim to exclusiveness or uniqueness, a valid sampling of three ways modern American drama has achieved a literary success.

Although Elmer Rice's first play, *On Trial,* dates from 1914, his most influential years were during the 1920's, the most flourishing decade of the new drama, as it had been for both poetry and fiction. Always a knowledgeable and careful theatrical craftsman (he had used the "flashback" successfully in his first play), Rice ideally exemplifies the American playwright's concern for the social problems of contemporary life.

His keen, passionate social conscience is evident in all his plays, his various ventures into production, and his signal service to the Federal Theater movement during the depression-ridden 1930's. His early training as a lawyer reveals a similar bent, in his interest in questions of censorship, arbitration, and legal rights, no less than in his many plays involving court-room scenes and decisions.

His plays, however, show a wide variety of accomplished theatrical techniques. After the early and commercially successful *On Trial,* three plays and nine years intervened before the Theater Guild produced his *The Adding Machine* (1923), according to Barrett Clark, "one of the first really original American plays" accepted by that famous group. It is, moreover, one of the American theater's earliest and most successful adaptations of the so-called German expressionistic techniques that mark some of the best work of O'Neill and Williams. The theme and tone of *The Adding Machine* are characteristically American—in social implications; in racy, colloquial language; and in ruthless exhibition of the nonhero, Mr. Zero, as an unsentimentalized, unpitied victim of a particular kind of American social and economic regimentation. The play's use of mordant and extravagant fantasy to dramatize inner states usually hidden by appearances results in still-exciting theatrical productions.

His next widely applauded play was *Street Scene* (1929), which was ruthlessly realistic in detail and technique yet also successful in its poetic evocation of the sounds and rhythms of its metropolitan scenes. Reproduced in an operatic version in 1947, with music supplied by Kurt Weil, it was called by one New York critic "a musical play of magnificence and glory." Rice's competent craftsmanship and range are adequately shown in the many other plays between the two versions of *Street Scene*—*Counselor-at-Law* (1931), an effective satire on the legal profession; *The Left Bank* (1931), a portrait of ineffective expatriates; *Judgment Day* (1934), *Between Two Worlds* and *American Landscapes* (both 1938), pictures of the threat abroad and at home of various forms of totalitarianism; and *Dream Girl* (1945), the best received of his plays since *Street Scene.* His relatively few plays of the '50's—*The Grand Tour* (1951), *The Winner* (1954)—have not been so well received, but his affecting *Autobiography* appeared in 1962 and was warmly reviewed. Both *The Adding Machine* and *Street Scene* are still frequently produced and anthologized, as examples of theatrical achievement in two directions by one American dramatist who contributed no small part to whatever the accomplishment is of the modern theater in America.

Perhaps the most decisive period in the life of Eugene O'Neill was the winter of 1912-13, when he was hospitalized in a New England sanatorium for tuberculosis. Wide reading, during that winter, in the world's dramatic literature, especially that of Ibsen and Strindberg, apparently determined him to become a playwright. In spite of a theatrical family (his father, James O'Neill, was the celebrated romantic actor), little else in his early years seems to have pointed toward the career that developed. He had toured with his father's company, to be sure, but his early education in various Catholic and private schools, his expulsion from Princeton after a year of indifferent study, and his amazing wanderings over the world in a wide variety of jobs (seaman, gold prospector, reporter) hardly would have suggested what followed. After the period of convalescence, however, his development was in a fairly straight line: enrollment in Professor Baker's famous "47 Workshop" at Harvard, a bit of Bohemian life in Greenwich Village, association with the Provincetown Players, who produced his one-act plays (first in the Wharf Theater and later in their MacDougal Street theater in New York), publication of other one-act plays in Mencken and Nathan's magazine, *The Smart Set,* and two collections of those early plays. He "arrived" on Broadway in 1920, when his first full-length play, *Beyond the Horizon,* opened to widespread critical and popular approval, winning the Pulitzer Prize.

During the next fourteen years new O'Neill plays were to be running on Broadway almost continuously. Each of the plays was unmistakably O'Neill's own, an indelible embodiment of his individualized vision of man's tragically maladjusted relation to the universe; nevertheless, they were to embody the widest and most varied theatrical "experiments" of any American playwright, before or since. *Beyond the Horizon,* with a realism of dialogue and treatment new to the American stage, contrasts the dual fate of two brothers who deny their natural inclinations, the "farmer" who goes to sea, and the "sailor" who stays home on the farm. *The Emperor Jones* (1920) and *The Hairy Ape* (1922) are both expressionistic in technique, realistic in theme and attitude: the first depicting the disintegration of an American Negro as he succumbs to inner forces his apparent "rise" had only superficially freed him from; the latter, the disintegration of a stoker from a merchant ship who comes to see that there is nothing to which he belongs. *Anna Christie* (1921) reveals the tragic bond the sea exerts on those who serve her. In *Desire Under the Elms* (1924), a domestic tragedy set in New England, we see, back of an apparently "naturalistic" conception, everywhere the impact of Freudian psychology.

Two of O'Neill's most baffling plays are of this same decade. *The Great God Brown* (1926) and *Lazarus Laughed* (1927) both employ the classic device of masks. They both show the influence of Jung and Nietzsche, especially in the former's stress on the Dionysian, and both make few concessions to the exigencies of production. Critics and public were kinder to two equally ambitious plays that followed, although these too made unconventional demands. *Strange Interlude* (1928), a psychological study of a neurotic woman deprived of her lover, bravely uses the stream-of-consciousness techniques through the Elizabethan device of asides. Although its nine acts made necessary an intermission for dinner, it was popular on Broadway for a year and a half. In *Mourning Becomes Electra* (1931) O'Neill adapts the classic story of Clytemnestra and Agamemnon, Orestes and Electra, into a New England tragedy of the period following the Civil War. A trilogy of three complete plays in thirteen acts, it too had a remarkably long run, in spite of the fact that each performance ran from mid-afternoon until late at night. Then, as if to show his versatility, O'Neill released *Ah, Wilderness!* (1933), a delightfully rich contrast, warm in its humor and nostalgic in its comic depiction of first love in an adolescent boy.

Perhaps because of failing health, O'Neill was not to have a new play on Broadway from 1934 until 1946. *The Iceman Cometh* of that year received a mixed reaction. Reconsideration began, however, after his death in 1953, with posthumous productions of *A Long Day's Journey Into Night* (1956), *A Moon for the Misbegotten* (1957), *A Touch of the Poet* (1958), and *Hughie* (1959). Intrinsic evaluation of these perhaps still needs to be made.

Yet, some of O'Neill's remarkable achievements are unmistakable and clear-cut. No other American playwright so widely reflects so many of the intellectual currents of modern American life: Darwin, Marx, Freud, Jung, and Nietzsche are all discernible in his works, as are most of their esthetic ramifications in the literary techniques of realism, naturalism, expressionism, and primitivism. The revolutions of the new poetry and the new fiction in modern America are nowhere so dependent on one writer's achievement as the new drama is dependent upon O'Neill's, though his work undoubtedly does parallel those developments. He first liberated the American theater by showing with undeniable authority that American drama could also be literature. The devices of continental literature that he brought into his plays opened to the drama of the whole English-speaking world, not simply of America, dramatic techniques that still dominate its theaters.

Tennessee Williams, for example, could not have enjoyed the successes he has enjoyed during the last two decades without the liberating influences and examples of O'Neill and his contemporaries during the two or more decades preceding him. His subject matter, his technique, and his theatrical expression would have been neither permitted nor understood without the revolutionary innovations successfully practiced by American playwrights during the 1920's and '30's. The contemporary playwrights who seem, with Williams, most fruitfully to be keeping the American theater alive, contemporaries such as Arthur Miller and the young Edward Albee, are as indebted to O'Neill's generation as Williams is.

Williams has been, on the whole, the most continuously productive of the post-World War II American playwrights. His first successful Broadway production, the play here reproduced, *The Glass Menagerie* (1945), is the tenderest of his plays, even as its theme, the contradictory appeals of illusion and reality to a lovely young girl, is perhaps his most pervasive one. The play is quietly symbolical without rejecting the realistic demands of its conception, unconventional in structure (its seven-scene length is effectively "framed" by narration), and strangely affecting in its uncomplicated but evocative language. Williams' subject matter, however, now and again was to become much more sensational: *A Streetcar Named Desire* (1947), another sensitive picture of an illusion-ridden woman, also depicts a brutalizing hero, brazenly exploits violence, and introduces candid suggestions of sexual aberrations. *Summer and Smoke* (1948), still another portrait of a lost heroine, joins the wistfulness of *A Glass Menagerie* to some of the sexual emphasis of *Streetcar*. Completely different in tone is *The Rose Tatoo* (1951), a picture of Gulf Coast Sicilians in all their boisterous ribaldry. *Cat on a Hot Tin Roof* (1955) won Williams his second Pulitzer Prize; it catches tensions in a wealthy Southern family in a way that lead some to consider it his most successful play. Perhaps the most sensational Williams play is *Suddenly, Last Summer* (1958), produced with *Something Unspoken* under the title *Garden District*. A possessive mother, a homosexual son, and the devouring of the latter by a group of starving children surely represent an extreme in choice of subject matter unmatched by any other major American playwright who has been successfully produced on Broadway.

Williams' most recent plays—*Sweet Bird of Youth* (1959), *Period of Adjustment* (1960), the highly successful *The Night of the Iguana* (1961), and *The Milk Train Doesn't Stop Here Anymore* (1963)—continue to testify to his skill as a craftsman, his mastery of the language, his general theatrical versatility. Frequent charges of sensationalism, of an excessive devotion to violence and sex, have not deterred Williams from dramatic experimentation or his conviction of the universal primitivism close to the veneer that so often is the face society, culture, convention, and even history present to the world.

As a consequence, Williams will have to be a major consideration in whatever judgments are ultimately made about American drama during the last two decades. And when his plays are joined to those of Elmer Rice and O'Neill, the result is certainly no radical distortion of some of the major faults and achievements of whatever American drama has been from about 1920 to the present.

Elmer Rice

(1892-)

CHRONOLOGY:

1892 Born September 28, in New York City, under the name of Elmer Reizenstein.
1912 Received LL.B. *cum laude* from New York Law School.
1914 *On Trial.*
1917 *The Home of the Free.*
1919 *For the Defense.*
1921 *Wake Up, Jonathan!* (in collaboration with Hatcher Hughes).
1923 *The Adding Machine.*
1924 *Close Harmony; or, The Lady Next Door* (in collaboration with Dorothy Parker).
1928 *Cock Robin* (in collaboration with Philip Barry).
1929 *Street Scene* (awarded Pulitzer Prize); *The Subway; See Naples and Die.*
1930 *A Voyage to Purilia,* novel.
1931 *Counselor-at-Law; The Left Bank.*
1932 *The House in Blind Alley; Black Sheep.*
1933 *We, the People.*
1934 *Judgment Day; The Passing of Chow-Chow; Three Plays Without Words; Between Two Worlds.*
1935 Appointed regional director of Federal Theater Project; *Not for Children.*
1937 *Imperial City: A Novel.*
1938 *American Landscape.*
1940 *Two on an Island.*
1941 *Flight to the West.*
1944 *A New Life.*
1945 *Dream Girl.*
1947 Operatic version of *Street Scene,* with music by Kurt Weil.
1949 *The Show Must Go On,* a novel.
1951 *The Grand Tour: A Play in Two Acts.*
1954 *The Winner: A Play in Four Scenes.*
1962 *Autobiography.*

BIBLIOGRAPHY:

The only collection of Rice's plays is his *Seven Plays* (New York, 1950) from among the more than two score he has written. There is at present no biography, although his *Autobiography* (New York, 1962) contains important primary material. Significant criticism is in Joseph W. Krutch, *The American Drama Since 1918* (Rev. ed.; New York, 1957) and Alan S. Downer, *Fifty Years of American Drama, 1900-1950* (Chicago, 1951). For later studies, see the annual bibliographies in *PMLA.*

The Adding Machine

CHARACTERS

(IN ORDER OF APPEARANCE)

MR. ZERO
MRS. ZERO
DAISY DIANA DOROTHEA DEVORE
THE BOSS
MR. ONE
MRS. ONE
MR. TWO
MRS. TWO
MR. THREE
MRS. THREE
MR. FOUR
MRS. FOUR
MR. FIVE
MRS. FIVE
MR. SIX
MRS. SIX
POLICEMAN
THE GUIDE
A TALL LADY
A STOUT LADY
CHARLEY
LITTLE LORD FAUNTLEROY
HIS MOTHER
THE NOTE-TAKING YOUTH
A BOY OF FOURTEEN
HIS FATHER
SEVERAL
A MAN
THE FIXER
GUARD
MAN
JUDY O'GRADY
YOUNG MAN
SHRDLU
A HEAD
LIEUTENANT CHARLES
JOE

SYNOPSIS OF SCENES

SCENE ONE—A bedroom
SCENE TWO—An office
SCENE THREE—A living room
SCENE FOUR—A place of justice
SCENE FIVE—A cage
SCENE SIX—A graveyard
SCENE SEVEN—A pleasant place
SCENE EIGHT—Another office

SCENE ONE

SCENE: *A small bedroom containing an "installment plan" bed, dresser, and chairs. An ugly electric-light fixture over the bed with a single glaring, naked lamp. One small window with the shade drawn. The walls are papered with sheets of foolscap covered with columns of figures.*

MR. ZERO *is lying on the bed, facing the audience, his head and shoulders visible. He is thin, sallow, undersized, and partially bald.* MRS. ZERO *is standing before the dresser arranging her hair for night. She is forty-five, sharp-featured, gray streaks in her hair. She is shapeless in her long-sleeved cotton nightgown. She is wearing her shoes, over which sag her ungartered stockings.*

MRS. ZERO (*as she takes down her hair*): I'm gettin' sick o' them Westerns. All of them cowboys ridin' around an' foolin' with them ropes. I don't care nothin' about that. I'm sick of 'em. I don't see why they don't have more of them stories like *For Love's Sweet Sake*. I like them sweet little love stories. They're nice an' wholesome. Mrs. Twelve was sayin' to me only yesterday, "Mrs. Zero," says she, "what I like is one of them wholesome stories, with just a sweet, simple little love story." "You're right, Mrs. Twelve," I says. "That's what I like too." They're showin' too many Westerns at the Rosebud. I'm gettin' sick of them. I think we'll start goin' to the Peter Stuyvesant. They got a good bill there Wednesday night. There's a Chubby Delano comedy called *Sea-Sick*. Mrs. Twelve was tellin' me about it. She says it's a scream. They're havin' a picnic in the country and they sit Chubby next to an old maid with a great big mouth. So he gets sore an' when she ain't lookin' he goes and catches a frog and drops it in her clam chowder. An' when she goes to eat the chowder the frog jumps out of it an' right into her mouth. Talk about laugh! Mrs. Twelve was tellin' me she laughed so she nearly passed out. He sure can pull some funny ones. An' they got that big Grace Darling feature, *A Mother's Tears*. She's sweet. But I don't like her clothes. There's no style to them. Mrs. Nine was tellin' me she read in *Pictureland* that she ain't livin' with her husband. He's her second too. I don't know whether they're divorced or just separated. You wouldn't think it to see her on the screen. She looks so sweet and innocent. Maybe it ain't true. You can't believe all you read. They say some Pittsburgh millionaire is crazy about her and that's why she ain't livin' with her husband. Mrs. Seven was tellin' me her brother-in-law has a friend that used to go to school with Grace Darling. He says her name ain't Grace Darling at all. Her right name is Elizabeth Dugan, he says, an' all them stories about her gettin' five thousand a week is the bunk, he says. She's sweet though. Mrs. Eight was tellin' me that *A Mother's Tears* is the best picture she ever made. "Don't miss it, Mrs. Zero," she says. "It's sweet," she says. "Just sweet and wholesome. Cry!" she says, "I nearly cried my eyes out." There's one part in it where this big bum of an Englishman—he's a married man too—an' she's this little simple country girl. An' she nearly falls for him too. But she's sittin' out in the garden, one day, and she looks up and there's her mother lookin' at her, right out of the clouds. So that night she locks the door of her room. An' sure enough, when everybody's in bed, along comes this big bum of an Englishman an' when she won't let him in what does he do but go an' kick open the door. "Don't miss it, Mrs. Zero," Mrs. Eight was tellin' me. It's at the Peter Stuyvesant Wednesday night, so don't be tellin' me you want to go to the Rosebud. The Eights seen it downtown at the Strand. They go downtown all the time. Just like us—nit! I guess by the time it gets to the Peter Stuyvesant all that part about kickin' in the door will be cut out. Just like they cut out that big cabaret scene in *The Price of Virtue*. They sure are pullin' some rough stuff in the pictures nowadays. "It's no place for a young girl," I was tellin' Mrs. Eleven, only the other day. An' by the time they get uptown half of it is cut out. But you wouldn't go downtown—not if wild horses was to drag you. You can wait till they come uptown! Well, I don't want to wait, see? I want to see 'em when everybody else is seein' 'em an' not a month later. Now don't go tellin' me you ain't got the price. You could dig up the price all right, all right, if you wanted to. I notice you always got the price to go to the ball game. But when it comes to me havin' a good time, then it's always: "I ain't got the price, I gotta start savin'." A fat lot you'll ever save! I got all I can do now makin' both ends meet, an' you talkin' about savin'. (*She seats herself on a chair and begins removing her shoes and stockings.*) An' don't go pullin' that stuff about bein' tired. "I been workin' hard all day. Twice a day in the subway's enough for me." Tired! Where do you get that tired stuff, anyhow? What about me? Where do I come in? Scrubbin' floors an' cookin' your meals an' washin' your dirty clothes. An' you sittin' on a chair all day, just addin' figgers an' waitin' for five-thirty. There's no five-thirty for me. I don't wait for no whistle. I don't get no vacations neither. And what's more I don't get no pay envelope every Saturday night neither. I'd like to know where you'd be without me. An' what have I got to show for it? —slavin' my life away to give you a home. What's in it for me, I'd like to know? But it's my own fault, I guess. I was a fool for marryin' you. If I'd 'a' had any sense, I'd 'a' known what you were from the start. I wish I had it to do over again, I hope to tell you. You was goin' to do wonders, you was! You wasn't goin' to be a bookkeeper long—oh, no, not you. Wait till you got started—you was goin' to show 'em. There wasn't no job in the store that was too big for you. Well, I've been waitin'—waitin' for you to get started—see? It's been a good long wait too. Twenty-five years! An' I ain't seen nothin' happen. Twenty-five years in the same job. Twenty-five years tomorrow! You're proud of it, ain't you? Twenty-five years in the same job an' never missed a day! That's somethin' to be proud of, ain't it? Sittin' for twenty-five years on the same chair, addin' up figgers. What about bein' store manager? I guess you forgot about that, didn't you? An' me at home here lookin' at the same four walls an' workin' my fingers to the bone to make both ends meet. Seven years since you got a raise! An' if you don't get one tomorrow, I'll bet a nickel you won't have the guts to go an' ask for one. I didn't pick much when I picked you, I'll tell the world. You ain't much to be proud of. (*She rises, goes to the window, and raises the shade. A few lighted windows are visible on the other side of the closed court. Looking out for a moment*) She ain't walkin' around tonight, you can bet your sweet life on that. An' she won't be walkin' around any more nights neither. Not in this house, anyhow. (*She turns away from the window.*) The dirty bum!

The idea of her comin' to live in a house with respectable people. They should 'a' gave her six years, not six months. If I was the judge I'd of gave her life. A bum like that. (*She approaches the bed and stands there a moment.*) I guess you're sorry she's gone. I guess you'd like to sit home every night an' watch her goin's-on. You're somethin' to be proud of, you are! (*She stands on the bed and turns out the light. . . . A thin stream of moonlight filters in from the court. The two figures are dimly visible.* MRS. ZERO *gets into bed.*) You'd better not start nothin' with women, if you know what's good for you. I've put up with a lot, but I won't put up with that. I've been slavin' away for twenty-five years, makin' a home for you an' nothin' to show for it. If you was any kind of a man you'd have a decent job by now an' I'd be gettin' some comfort out of life—instead of bein' just a slave, washin' pots an' standin' over the hot stove. I've stood it for twenty-five years an' I guess I'll have to stand it twenty-five more. But don't you go startin' nothin' with women—(*She goes on talking as the curtain falls.*)

(*Curtain*)

SCENE TWO

SCENE: *An office in a department store. Wood and glass partitions. In the middle of the room two tall desks back to back. At one desk on a high stool is* ZERO. *Opposite him at the other desk, also on a high stool, is* DAISY DIANA DOROTHEA DEVORE, *a plain, middle-aged woman. Both wear green eyeshades and paper sleeve-protectors. A pendent electric lamp throws light upon both desks.* DAISY *reads aloud figures from a pile of slips which lie before her. As she reads the figures* ZERO *enters them upon a large square sheet of ruled paper which lies before him.*

DAISY (*reading aloud*): Three ninety-eight. Forty-two cents. A dollar fifty. A dollar fifty. A dollar twenty-five. Two dollars. Thirty-nine cents. Twenty-seven fifty.

ZERO (*petulantly*): Speed it up a little, cancha?

DAISY: What's the rush? Tomorrer's another day.

ZERO: Aw, you make me sick.

DAISY: An' you make me sicker.

ZERO: Go on. Go on. We're losin' time.

DAISY: Then quit bein' so bossy. (*She reads.*) Three dollars. Two sixty-nine. Eighty-one fifty. Forty dollars. Eight seventy-five. Who do you think you are, anyhow?

ZERO: Never mind who I think I am. You tend to your work.

DAISY: Aw, don't be givin' me so many orders. Sixty cents. Twenty-four cents. Seventy-five cents. A dollar fifty. Two fifty. One fifty. One fifty. Two fifty. I don't have to take it from you and what's more I won't.

ZERO: Aw, quit talkin'.

DAISY: I'll talk all I want. Three dollars. Fifty cents. Fifty cents. Seven dollars. Fifty cents. Two fifty. Three fifty. Fifty cents. One fifty. Fifty cents.

(*She goes on, bending over the slips and transferring them from one pile to another.* ZERO *bends over his desk, busily entering the figures.*)

ZERO (*without looking up*): You make me sick. Always shootin' off your face about somethin'. Talk, talk, talk. Just like all the other women. Women make me sick.

DAISY (*busily fingering the slips*): Who do you think you are, anyhow? Bossin' me around. I don't have to take it from you, and what's more I won't.

(*They both attend closely to their work, neither looking up. Throughout, each intones figures during the other's speeches.*)

ZERO: Women make me sick. They're all alike. The judge gave her six months. I wonder what they do in the workhouse. Peel potatoes. I'll bet she's sore at me. Maybe she'll try to kill me when she gets out. I better be careful. Hello—Girl Slays Betrayer. Jealous Wife Slays Rival. You can't tell what a woman's liable to do. I better be careful.

DAISY: I'm gettin' sick of it. Always pickin' on me about somethin'. Never a decent word out of you. Not even the time o' day.

ZERO: I guess she wouldn't have the nerve at that. Maybe she don't even know it's me. They didn't even put my name in the paper, the big bums. Maybe she's been in the workhouse before. A bum like that. She didn't have nothin' on that one time—nothin' but a shirt. (*He glances up quickly, then bends over again.*) You make me sick. I'm sick of lookin' at your face.

DAISY: Gee, ain't that whistle ever goin' to blow? You didn't used to be like that. Not even good mornin' or good evenin'. I ain't done nothin' to you. It's the young girls. Goin' around without corsets.

ZERO: Your face is gettin' all yeller. Why don't you put some paint on it? She was puttin' on paint that time. On her cheeks and on her lips. And that blue stuff on her eyes. Just sittin' there in a shimmy puttin' on the paint. An' walkin' around the room with her legs all bare.

DAISY: I wish I was dead.

ZERO: I was a goddam fool to let the wife get on to me. She oughta get six months at that. The dirty bum. Livin' in a house with respectable people. She'd be livin' there yet if the wife hadn't o' got on to me. Damn her!

DAISY: I wish I was dead.

ZERO: Maybe another one'll move in. Gee, that would be great. But the wife's got her eye on me now.

DAISY: I'm scared to do it though.

ZERO: You oughta move into that room. It's cheaper than where you're livin' now. I better tell you about it. I don't mean to be always pickin' on you.

DAISY: Gas. The smell of it makes me sick.

(ZERO *looks up and clears his throat.*)

DAISY: (*looking up, startled*): Whadja say?

ZERO: I didn't say nothin'.

DAISY: I thought you did.

ZERO: You thought wrong.

(*They bend over their work again.*)

DAISY: A dollar sixty. A dollar fifty. Two ninety. One sixty-two.

ZERO: Why the hell should I tell you? Fat chance of you forgettin' to pull down the shade!

DAISY: If I asked for carbolic they might get on to me.

ZERO: Your hair's gettin' gray. You don't wear them shirtwaists any more with the low collars. When you'd bend down to pick somethin' up—

DAISY: I wish I knew what to ask for. Girl Takes Mercury After All-Night Party. Woman In Ten-Story Death Leap.

ZERO: I wonder where'll she go when she gets out. Gee, I'd like to make a date with her. Why didn't I go over there the night my wife went to Brooklyn? She never woulda found out.

DAISY: I seen Pauline Frederick do it once. Where could I get a pistol though?

ZERO: I guess I didn't have the nerve.

DAISY: I'll bet you'd be sorry then that you been so mean to me. How do I know though? Maybe you wouldn't.

ZERO: Nerve! I got as much nerve as anybody. I'm on the level, that's all. I'm a married man and I'm on the level.

DAISY: Anyhow, why ain't I got a right to live? I'm as good as anybody else. I'm too refined, I guess. That's the whole trouble.

ZERO: The time the wife had pneumonia I thought she was goin' to pass out. But she didn't. The doctor's bill was eighty-seven dollars. (*Looking up*) Hey, wait a minute! Didn't you say eighty-seven dollars?

DAISY (*looking up*): What?

ZERO: Was the last you said eighty-seven dollars?

DAISY (*consulting the slip*): Forty-two fifty.

ZERO: Well, I made a mistake. Wait a minute. (*He busies himself with an eraser.*) All right. Shoot.

DAISY: Six dollars. Three fifteen. Two twenty-five. Sixty-five cents. A dollar twenty. You talk to me as if I was dirt.

ZERO: I wonder if I could kill the wife without anybody findin' out. In bed some night. With a pillow.

DAISY: I used to think you was stuck on me.

ZERO: I'd get found out though. They always have ways.

DAISY: We used to be so nice and friendly together when I first came here. You used to talk to me then.

ZERO: Maybe she'll die soon. I noticed she was coughin' this mornin'.

DAISY: You used to tell me all kinds o' things. You were goin' to show them all. Just the same, you're still sittin' here.

ZERO: Then I could do what I damn please. Oh, boy!

DAISY: Maybe it ain't all your fault neither. Maybe if you'd had the right kind o' wife—somebody with a lot of common sense, somebody refined—me!

ZERO: At that, I guess I'd get tired of bummin' around. A feller wants some place to hang his hat.

DAISY: I wish she would die.

ZERO: And when you start goin' with women you're liable to get into trouble. And lose your job maybe.

DAISY: Maybe you'd marry me.

ZERO: Gee, I wish I'd gone over there that night.

DAISY: Then I could quit workin'.

ZERO: Lots o' women would be glad to get me.

DAISY: You could look a long time before you'd find a sensible, refined girl like me.

ZERO: Yes, sir, they could look a long time before they'd find a steady meal-ticket like me.

DAISY: I guess I'd be too old to have any kids. They say it ain't safe after thirty-five.

ZERO: Maybe I'd marry you. You might be all right, at that.

DAISY: I wonder—if you don't want kids—whether—if there's any way—

ZERO (*looking up*): Hey! Hey! Can't you slow up? What do you think I am—a machine?

DAISY (*looking up*): Say, what do you want, anyhow? First it's too slow an' then it's too fast. I guess you don't know what you want.

ZERO: Well, never mind about that. Just you slow up.

DAISY: I'm gettin' sick o' this. I'm goin' to ask to be transferred.

ZERO: Go ahead. You can't make me mad.

DAISY: Aw, keep quiet. (*She reads.*) Two forty-five. A dollar twenty. A dollar fifty. Ninety cents. Sixty-three cents.

ZERO: Marry you! I guess not! You'd be as bad as the one I got.

DAISY: You wouldn't care if I did ask. I got a good mind to ask.

ZERO: I was a fool to get married.

DAISY: Then I'd never see you at all.

ZERO: What chance has a guy got with a woman tied around his neck?

DAISY: That time at the store picnic—the year your wife couldn't come—you were nice to me then.

ZERO: Twenty-five years holdin' down the same job!

DAISY: We were together all day—just sittin' around under the trees.

ZERO: I wonder if the boss remembers about it bein' twenty-five years.

DAISY: And comin' home that night—you sat next to me in the big delivery wagon.

ZERO: I got a hunch there's a big raise comin' to me.

DAISY: I wonder what it feels like to be really kissed. Men—dirty pigs! They want the bold ones.

ZERO: If he don't come across I'm goin' right up to the front office and tell him where he gets off.

DAISY: I wish I was dead.

ZERO: "Boss," I'll say, "I want to have a talk with you." "Sure," he'll say, "sit down. Have a Corona Corona." "No," I'll say, "I don't smoke." "How's that?" he'll say. "Well, boss," I'll say, "it's this way. Every time I feel like smokin' I just take a nickel and put it in the old sock. A penny saved is a penny earned, that's the way I look at it." "Damn sensible," he'll say. "You got a wise head on you, Zero."

DAISY: I can't stand the smell of gas. It makes me sick. You coulda kissed me if you wanted to.

ZERO: "Boss," I'll say, "I ain't quite satisfied. I been on the job twenty-five years now and if I'm gonna stay I gotta see a future ahead of me." "Zero," he'll say, "I'm glad you came in. I've had my eye on you, Zero. Nothin' gets by me." "Oh, I know that, boss," I'll say. That'll hand him a good laugh, that will. "You're a valuable man, Zero," he'll say, "and I want you right up here with me in the front office. You're done addin' figgers. Monday mornin' you move up here."

DAISY: Them kisses in the movies—them long ones—right on the mouth—

ZERO: I'll keep a-goin' right on up after that. I'll show some of them birds where they get off.

DAISY: That one the other night—*The Devil's Alibi*—he put his arms around her—and her head fell back and her eyes closed—like she was in a daze.

ZERO: Just give me about two years and I'll show them birds where they get off.

DAISY: I guess that's what it's like—a kinda daze—when I see them like that, I just seem to forget everything.

ZERO: Then me for a place in Jersey. And maybe a little Buick. No tin Lizzie for mine. Wait till I get started—I'll show 'em.

DAISY: I can see it now when I kinda half close my eyes. The way her head fell back. And his mouth pressed right up against hers. Oh, Gawd! it must be grand!

(*There is a sudden shrill blast from a steam whistle.*)

DAISY AND ZERO (*together*): The whistle!

(*With great agility they get off their stools, remove their eyeshades and sleeve-protectors and put them on the desks. Then each produces* *from behind the desk a hat—*ZERO, *a dusty derby,* DAISY, *a frowsy straw.* DAISY *puts on her hat and turns toward* ZERO *as though she were about to speak to him. But he is busy cleaning his pen and pays no attention to her. She sighs and goes toward the door at the left.*)

ZERO (*looking up*): G'night, Miss Devore.

(*But she does not hear him and exits.* ZERO *takes up his hat and goes left. The door at the right opens and the* BOSS *enters—middle-aged, stoutish, bald, well dressed.*)

THE BOSS (*calling*): Oh—er—Mister—er—

(ZERO *turns in surprise, sees who it is, and trembles nervously.*)

ZERO (*obsequiously*) : Yes, sir. Do you want me, sir?

BOSS: Yes. Just come here a moment, will you?

ZERO: Yes, sir. Right away, sir. (*He fumbles his hat, picks it up, stumbles, recovers himself, and approaches the* BOSS, *every fiber quivering.*)

BOSS: Mister—er—er—

ZERO: Zero.

BOSS: Yes, Mr. Zero. I wanted to have a little talk with you.

ZERO (*with a nervous grin*): Yes, sir, I been kinda expectin' it.

BOSS (*staring at him*): Oh, have you?

ZERO: Yes, sir.

BOSS: How long have you been with us, Mister—er—Mister—

ZERO: Zero.

BOSS: Yes, Mr. Zero.

ZERO: Twenty-five years today.

BOSS: Twenty-five years! That's a long time.

ZERO: Never missed a day.

BOSS: And you've been doing the same work all the time?

ZERO: Yes, sir. Right here at this desk.

BOSS: Then, in that case, a change probably won't be unwelcome to you.

ZERO: No, sir, it won't. And that's the truth.

BOSS: We've been planning a change in this department for some time.

ZERO: I kinda thought you had your eye on me.

BOSS: You were right. The fact is that my efficiency experts have recommended the installation of adding machines.

ZERO (*staring at him*): Addin' machines?

BOSS: Yes, you've probably seen them. A mechanical device that adds automatically.

ZERO: Sure. I've seen them. Keys—and a handle that you pull. (*He goes through the motions in the air.*)

BOSS: That's it. They do the work in half the time and a high-school girl can operate them. Now, of course, I'm sorry to lose an old and faithful employee—

ZERO: Excuse me, but would you mind sayin' that again?

BOSS: I say I'm sorry to lose an employee who's been with me for so many years—

(*Soft music is heard—the sound of the mechanical player of a distant merry-go-round. The part of the floor upon which the desk and stools are standing begins to revolve very slowly.*)

BOSS: But, of course, in an organization like this, efficiency must be the first consideration—

(*The music becomes gradually louder and the revolutions more rapid.*)

BOSS: You will draw your salary for the full month. And I'll direct my secretary to give you a letter of recommendation—

ZERO: Wait a minute, boss. Let me get this right. You mean I'm canned?

BOSS (*barely making himself heard above the increasing volume of sound*): I'm sorry—no other alternative—greatly regret—old employee—efficiency—economy—business—*business*—BUSINESS—

(*His voice is drowned by the music. The platform is revolving rapidly now.* ZERO *and the* BOSS *face each other. They are entirely motionless save for the* BOSS*'s jaws, which open and close incessantly. But the words are inaudible. The music swells and swells. To it is added every offstage effect of the theater: the wind, the waves, the galloping horses, the locomotive whistle, the sleigh bells, the automobile siren, the glass-crash. New Year's Eve, Election Night, Armistice Day, and Mardi Gras. The noise is deafening, maddening, unendurable. Suddenly it culminates in a terrific peal of thunder. For an instant there is a flash of red and then everything is plunged into blackness.*)

(*Curtain*)

SCENE THREE

SCENE: *The* ZERO *dining room. Entrance door at right. Doors to kitchen and bedroom at left. The walls, as in the first scene, are papered with foolscap sheets covered with columns of figures. In the middle of the room, upstage, a table set for two. Along each side wall seven chairs are ranged in symmetrical rows.*

At the rise of the curtain MRS. ZERO *is seen seated at the table looking alternately at the entrance door and a clock on the wall. She wears a bungalow apron over her best dress.*

After a few moments the entrance door opens and ZERO *enters. He hangs his hat on a rack behind the door and, coming over to the table, seats himself at the vacant place. His movements throughout are quiet and abstracted.*

MRS. ZERO (*breaking the silence*): Well, it was nice of you to come home. You're only an hour late and that ain't very much. The supper don't get very cold in an hour. An' of course the part about our havin' a lot of company tonight don't matter. (*They begin to eat.*)

Ain't you even got sense enough to come home on time? Didn't I tell you we're goin' to have a lot o' company tonight? Didn't you know the Ones are comin'? An' the Twos? An' the Threes? An' the Fours? An' the Fives? And the Sixes? Didn't I tell you to be home on time? I might as well talk to a stone wall. (*They eat for a few moments in silence.*)

I guess you musta had some important business to attend to. Like watchin' the scoreboard. Or was two kids havin' a fight an' you was the referee? You sure do have a lot of business to attend to. It's a wonder you have time to come home at all. You gotta tough life, you have. Walk in, hang up your hat, an' put on the nosebag. An' me in the hot kitchen all day, cookin' your supper an' waitin' for you to get good an' ready to come home! (*Again they eat in silence.*)

Maybe the boss kept you late tonight. Tellin' you what a big noise you are and how the store couldn't 'a' got along if you hadn't been pushin' a pen for twenty-five years. Where's the gold medal he pinned on you? Did some blind old lady take it away from you or did you leave it on the seat of the boss's limousine when he brought you home? (*Again a few moments of silence*)

I'll bet he gave you a big raise, didn't he? Promoted you from the third floor to the fourth, maybe. Raise? A fat chance you got o' gettin' a raise. All they gotta do is put an ad in the paper. There's ten thousand like you layin' around the streets. You'll be holdin' down the same job at the end of another twenty-five years—if you ain't forgot how to add by that time.

(*A noise is heard offstage, a sharp clicking such as is made by the operation of the keys and levers of an adding machine.* ZERO *raises his head for a moment but lowers it almost instantly.*)

MRS. ZERO: There's the doorbell. The company's here already. And we ain't hardly finished supper. (*She rises.*) But I'm goin' to clear off the table whether you're finished or not. If you want your supper, you got a right to be home on time. Not standin' around lookin' at scoreboards. (*As she piles up the dishes* ZERO *rises and goes toward the entrance door.*) Wait a minute! Don't open the door yet. Do you want the company to see all the mess? An' go an' put on a clean collar. You got red ink all over it. (ZERO *goes toward bedroom door.*) I should think after pushin' a pen for twenty-five years, you'd learn how to do it without gettin' ink on your collar. (ZERO *exits to bedroom.* MRS. ZERO *takes dishes to kitchen, talking as she goes.*)

I guess I can stay up all night now washin' dishes. You should worry! That's what a man's got a wife for, ain't it? Don't he buy her her clothes an' let her eat with him at the same table? An' all she's gotta do is cook the meals an' do the washin' an' scrub the floor, an' wash the dishes when the company goes. But, believe me, you're goin' to sling a mean dish towel when the company goes tonight!

(*While she is talking* ZERO *enters from bedroom. He wears a clean collar and is cramming the soiled one furtively into his pocket.* MRS. ZERO *enters from kitchen. She has removed her apron and carries a table cover which she spreads hastily over the table. The clicking noise is heard again.)*

MRS. ZERO: There's the bell again. Open the door, cancha?

(ZERO *goes to the entrance door and opens it. Six men and six women file into the room in a double column. The men are all shapes and sizes, but their dress is identical with that of* ZERO *in every detail. Each, however, wears a wig of a different color. The women are all dressed alike too, except that the dress of each is of a different color.)*

MRS. ZERO (*taking the first woman's hand*): How de do, Mrs. One.

MRS. ONE: How de do, Mrs. Zero.

(MRS. ZERO *repeats this formula with each woman in turn.* ZERO *does the same with the men except that he is silent throughout. The files now separate, each man taking a chair from the right wall and each woman one from the left wall. Each sex forms a circle with the chairs very close together. The men—all except* ZERO*—smoke cigars. The women munch chocolates.)*

SIX: Some rain we're havin'.

FIVE: Never saw the like of it.

FOUR: Worst in fourteen years, paper says.

THREE: Y' can't always go by the papers.

TWO: No, that's right too.

ONE: We're liable to forget from year to year.

SIX: Yeh, come t' think, last year was pretty bad too.

FIVE: An' how about two years ago?

FOUR: Still, this year's pretty bad.

THREE: Yeh, no gettin' away from that.

TWO: Might be a whole lot worse.

ONE: Yeh, it's all the way you look at it. Some rain though.

MRS. SIX: I like them little organdie dresses.

MRS. FIVE: Yeh, with a little lace trimmin' on the sleeves.

MRS. FOUR: Well, I like 'em plain myself.

MRS. THREE: Yeh, what I always say is the plainer the more refined.

MRS. TWO: Well, I don't think a little lace does any harm.

MRS. ONE: No, it kinda dresses it up.

MRS. ZERO: Well, I always say it's all a matter of taste.

MRS. SIX: I saw you at the Rosebud Movie Thursday night, Mr. One.

ONE: Pretty punk show, I'll say.

TWO: They're gettin' worse all the time.

MRS. SIX: But who was the charming lady, Mr. One?

ONE: Now don't you go makin' trouble for me. That was my sister.

MRS. FIVE: Oho! That's what they all say.

MRS. FOUR: Never mind! I'll bet Mrs. One knows what's what, all right.

MRS. ONE: Oh, well, he can do what he likes—'slong as he behaves himself.

THREE: You're in luck at that, One. Fat chance I got of gettin' away from the frau even with my sister.

MRS. THREE: You oughta be glad you got a good wife to look after you.

THE OTHER WOMEN (*in unison*): That's right, Mrs. Three.

FIVE: I guess I know who wears the pants in your house, Three.

MRS. ZERO: Never mind. I saw them holdin' hands at the movie the other night.

THREE: She musta been tryin' to get some money away from me.

MRS. THREE: Swell chance anybody'd have of gettin' any money away from you.

(*General laughter*)

FOUR: They sure are a loving couple.

MRS. TWO: Well, I think we oughta change the subject.

MRS. ONE: Yes, let's change the subject.

SIX (*sotto voce*): Did you hear the one about the travelin' salesman?

FIVE: It seems this guy was in a sleeper.

FOUR: Goin' from Albany to San Diego.

THREE: And in the next berth was an old maid.

TWO: With a wooden leg.

ONE: Well, along about midnight—

(*They all put their heads together and whisper.*)

MRS. SIX (*sotto voce*): Did you hear about the Sevens?

MRS. FIVE: They're gettin' a divorce.

MRS. FOUR: It's the second time for him.

MRS. THREE: They're two of a kind, if you ask me.

MRS. TWO: One's as bad as the other.

MRS. ONE: Worse.

MRS. ZERO: They say that she—

(*They all put their heads together and whisper.*)

SIX: I think this woman suffrage is the bunk.

FIVE: It sure is! Politics is a man's business.

FOUR: Woman's place is in the home.

THREE: That's it! Lookin' after the kids, 'stead of hangin' around the streets.

TWO: You hit the nail on the head that time.

ONE: The trouble is they don't know what they want.

MRS. SIX: Men sure get me tired.

MRS. FIVE: They sure are a lazy lot.

MRS. FOUR: And dirty.

MRS. THREE: Always grumblin' about somethin'.

MRS. TWO: When they're not lyin'!

MRS. ONE: Or messin' up the house.

MRS. ZERO: Well, believe me, I tell mine where he gets off.

SIX: Business conditions are sure bad.

FIVE: Never been worse.

FOUR: I don't know what we're comin' to.

THREE: I look for a big smash-up in about three months.

TWO: Wouldn't surprise me a bit.

ONE: We're sure headin' for trouble.

MRS. SIX: My aunt has gallstones.

MRS. FIVE: My husband has bunions.

MRS. FOUR: My sister expects next month.

MRS. THREE: My cousin's husband has erysipelas.

MRS. TWO: My niece has St. Vitus's dance.

MRS. ONE: My boy has fits.

MRS. ZERO: I never felt better in my life. Knock wood!

SIX: Too damn much agitation, that's at the bottom of it.

FIVE: That's it! Too damn many strikes.

FOUR: Foreign agitators, that's what it is.

THREE: They ought be run outa the country.

TWO: What the hell do they want anyhow?

ONE: They don't know what they want, if you ask me.

SIX: America for the Americans is what I say!

ALL (*in unison*): That's it! Damn foreigners! Damn dagoes! Damn Catholics! Damn sheenies! Damn niggers! Jail 'em! Shoot 'em! Hang 'em! Lynch 'em! Burn 'em! (*They all rise.*)

ALL (*sing in unison*): "My country 'tis of thee,
Sweet land of liberty!"

MRS. FOUR: Why so pensive, Mr. Zero?

ZERO (*speaking for the first time*): I'm thinkin'.

MRS. FOUR: Well, be careful not to sprain your mind.

(*Laughter*)

MRS. ZERO: Look at the poor men all by themselves. We ain't very sociable.

ONE: Looks like we're neglectin' the ladies.

(*The women cross the room and join the men, all chattering loudly. The doorbell rings.*)

MRS. ZERO: Sh! The doorbell!

(*The volume of sound slowly diminishes. Again the doorbell.*)

ZERO (*quietly*): I'll go. It's for me.

(*They watch curiously as* ZERO *goes to the door and opens it, admitting a* POLICEMAN. *There is a murmur of surprise and excitement.*)

POLICEMAN: I'm lookin' for Mr. Zero.

(*They all point to* ZERO)

ZERO: I've been expectin' you.

POLICEMAN: Come along!

ZERO: Just a minute. (*He puts his hand in his pocket.*)

POLICEMAN: What's he tryin' to pull? (*He draws a revolver.*) I got you covered.

ZERO: Sure, that's all right. I just want to give you somethin'. (*He takes the collar from his pocket and gives it to the* POLICEMAN.)

POLICEMAN (*suspiciously*): What's that?

ZERO: The collar I wore.

POLICEMAN: What do I want it for?

ZERO: It's got bloodstains on it.

POLICEMAN (*pocketing it*): All right, come along!

ZERO (*turning to* MRS. ZERO): I gotta go with him. You'll have to dry the dishes yourself.

MRS. ZERO (*rushing forward*): What are they takin' you for?

ZERO (*calmly*): I killed the boss this afternoon.

(*The* POLICEMAN *takes him off.*)

(*Quick Curtain*)

SCENE FOUR

SCENE: *A court of justice. Three bare white walls without door or windows except for a single door in the right wall. At the right is a jury box in which are seated* MESSRS. ONE, TWO, THREE, FOUR, FIVE, *and* SIX *and their respective wives. On either side of the jury box stands a uniformed officer. Opposite the jury box is a long, bare oak table piled high with law books. Behind the books* ZERO *is seated, his face buried in his hands. There is no other furniture in the room. A moment after the rise of the curtain one of the officers rises and, going around the table, taps* ZERO *on the shoulder.* ZERO *rises and accompanies the officer. The officer escorts him to the great empty space in the middle of the courtroom, facing the jury. He motions to* ZERO *to stop, then points to the jury and resumes his place beside the jury box.* ZERO *stands there looking at the jury, bewildered and half afraid. The jurors give no sign of having seen him. Throughout they sit with folded arms, staring stolidly before them.*

ZERO (*beginning to speak, haltingly*): Sure I killed him. I ain't sayin' I didn't, am I? Sure I killed him. Them lawyers! They give me a good stiff pain, that's what they give me. Half the time I don't know what the hell they're talkin' about. Objection sustained. Objection overruled. What's the big idea anyhow? You ain't heard me do any objectin', have you? Sure not! What's the idea of objectin'? You got a right to know. What I say is, if one bird kills another bird, why you got a right to call him for it. That's what I say. I know all about that. I been on the jury too. Them lawyers! Don't let 'em fill you full of bunk. All that bull about it bein' red ink on the bill file. Red ink nothin'! It was blood, see? I want you to get that right. I killed him, see? Right through the heart with the bill file, see? I want you to get that right—all of you. One, two, three, four, five, six, seven, eight, nine, ten, eleven, twelve. Twelve of you. Six and six. That makes twelve. I figgered it up often enough. Six and six makes twelve. And five is seventeen. And eight is twenty-five. And three is twenty-eight. Eight and carry two. Aw, cut it out! Them damn figgers! I can't forget 'em. Twenty-five years, see? Eight hours a day, exceptin' Sundays. And July and August half-day Saturday. One week's vacation with pay. And another week without pay if you want it. Who the hell wants it? Layin' around the house listenin' to the wife tellin' you where you get off. Nix! An' legal holidays. I nearly forgot them. New Year's, Washington's Birthday, Decoration Day, Fourth o' July, Labor Day, Election Day, Thanksgivin', Christmas. Good Friday if you want it. An' if you're a Jew, Young Kipper an' the other one—I forget what they call it. The dirty sheenies—always gettin' two to the other bird's one. An' when a holiday comes on Sunday, you get Monday off. So that's fair enough. But when the Fourth o' July comes on Saturday, why you're out o' luck on account of Saturday bein' a half-day anyhow. Get me? Twenty-five years—I'll tell you somethin' funny. Decoration Day an' the Fourth o' July are always on the same day o' the week. Twenty-five years. Never missed a day, and never more'n five minutes late. Look at my time card if you don't believe me. Eight twenty-seven, eight thirty, eight twenty-nine, eight twenty-seven, eight thirty-two. Eight an' thirty-two's forty an'—Goddam them figgers! I can't forget 'em. They're funny things, them figgers. They look like people sometimes. The eights, see? Two dots for the eyes and a dot for the nose. An' a line. That's the mouth, see? An' there's others remind you of other things—but I can't talk about them, on account of there bein' ladies here. Sure I killed him. Why didn't he shut up? If he'd only shut up! Instead o' talkin' an' talkin' about how sorry he was an' what a good guy I was an' this an' that. I felt like sayin' to him: "For Christ's sake, shut up!" But I didn't have the nerve, see? I didn't have the nerve to say that to the boss. An' he went on talkin', sayin' how sorry he was, see? He was standin' right close to me. An' his coat only had two buttons on it. Two an' two makes four an'—aw, can it! An' there was the bill file on the desk. Right where I could touch it. It ain't right to kill a guy. I know that. When I read all about him in the paper an' about his three kids I felt like a cheapskate, I tell you. They had the kids' pictures in the paper, right next to mine. An' his wife too. Gee, it must be swell to have a wife like that. Some guys sure is lucky. An' he left fifty thousand dollars just for a rest room for the girls in the store. He was a good guy at that. Fifty thousand. That's more'n twice as much as I'd have if I saved every nickel I ever made. Let's see. Twenty-five an' twenty-five an' twenty-five an'—aw, cut it out! An' the ads had a big, black border around 'em; an' all it said was that the store would be closed for three days on account of the boss bein' dead. That nearly handed me a laugh, that did. All them floorwalkers an' buyers an' high-muck-a-mucks havin' me to thank for gettin' three days off. I hadn't oughta killed him. I ain't sayin' nothin' about that. But I thought he was goin' to give me a raise, see? On account of bein' there twenty-five years. He never talked to me before, see? Except one mornin' we happened to come in the store together and I held the door open for him and he said "Thanks." Just like that, see? "Thanks!" That was the only time he ever talked to me. An' when I seen him comin' up to my desk, I didn't know where I got off. A big guy like that comin' up to my desk. I felt like I was chokin' like and all of a sudden I got a kind o' bad taste in my mouth like when you get up in the mornin'. I didn't have no right to kill him. The district attorney is right about that. He read the law to you, right out o' the book. Killin' a bird—that's wrong. But there was that girl, see? Six months they gave her. It was a dirty trick tellin' the cops on her like that. I shouldn't 'a' done that. But what was I gonna do? The wife woudn't let up on me. I hadda do it. She used to walk around the room, just in her undershirt, see? Nothin' else on. Just her undershirt. An' they gave her six months. That's the last I'll ever see of her. Them birds—how do they get away with it? Just grabbin' women, the way you see 'em do in the pictures. I've seen lots I'd like to grab like that, but I ain't got the nerve—in the subway an' on the street an' in the store buyin' things. Pretty soft for them shoe salesmen, I'll say, lookin' at women's legs all day. Them lawyers! They give me a pain, I tell you—a pain! Sayin' the same thing over an' over again. I never said I didn't kill him. But that ain't the same as bein' a regular murderer. What good did it do me to kill him? I didn't make nothin' out of it. Answer yes or no! Yes or no, me elbow! There's some things you can't answer yes or no. Give me the once-over, you guys. Do I look like a murderer? Do I? I never did no harm to nobody. Ask the wife. She'll tell you. Ask anybody. I never got into trouble. You wouldn't count that one time at the Polo Grounds. That was just fun like. Everybody was yellin', "Kill the empire! Kill the empire!" An' before I knew what I was doin' I fired the pop bottle. It was on account of everybody yellin' like that. Just in fun like, see? The yeller dog! Callin' that one a strike—a mile away from the plate. Anyhow, the bottle didn't hit him. An' when I seen the cop comin' up the aisle, I beat it. That didn't hurt nobody. It was just in fun like, see? An' that time in the subway. I was readin' about a lynchin', see? Down in Georgia. They took the nigger an' they tied him to a tree. An' they poured kerosene on him and lit a big fire under him. The dirty nigger! Boy, I'd of liked to been there, with a gat in each hand, pumpin' him full of lead. I was readin' about it in the subway, see? Right at Times Square where the big crowd gets on. An' all of a sudden this big nigger steps right on my foot. It was lucky for him I didn't have a gun on me. I'd of killed him sure, I guess. I guess he couldn't help it all right on account of the crowd, but a nigger's got no right to step on a white man's foot. I told him where he got off all right. The dirty nigger. But that didn't hurt nobody either. I'm a pretty steady guy, you gotta admit that. Twenty-five years in one job an' I never missed a day. Fifty-two weeks in a year. Fifty-two an' fifty-two an' fifty-two an'— They didn't have t' look for me, did they? I didn't try to run away, did I? Where was I goin' to run to! I wasn't thinkin' about it at all, see? I'll tell you what I was thinkin' about—how I was goin' to break it to the wife about bein' canned. He canned me after twenty-five years, see? Did the lawyers tell you about that? I forget. All that talk gives me a headache. Objection sustained. Objection overruled. Answer yes or no. It gives me a headache. And I can't get the figgers outta my head neither. But that's what I was thinkin' about—how I was goin' t' break it to the wife about bein' canned. An' what Miss Devore would think when she heard about me killin' him. I bet she never thought I had the nerve to do it. I'd of married her if the wife had passed out. I'd be holdin' down my job yet if he hadn't o' canned me. But he kept talkin' an' talkin'. An' there was the bill file right where I could reach it. Do you get me? I'm just a regular guy like anybody else. Like you birds, now. (*For the first time the jurors relax, looking indignantly at each other and whispering.*)

Suppose you was me, now. Maybe you'd 'a' done the same thing. That's the way you oughta look at it, see? Suppose you was me—

JURORS (*rising as one and shouting in unison*): *GUILTY!*

(ZERO *falls back, stunned for a moment by their vociferousness. The* JURORS *right-face in their places and file quickly out of the jury box and toward the door in a double column.*)

ZERO (*recovering speech as the* JURORS *pass out at the door*): Wait a minute. Jest a minute. You don't get me right. Jest give me a chance an' I'll tell you how it was. I'm all mixed up, see? On account of them lawyers. And the figgers in my head. But I'm goin' to tell you how it was. I was there twenty-five years, see? An' they gave her six months, see?

(*He goes on haranguing the empty jury box as the curtain falls.*)

(*Curtain*)

SCENE FIVE*

SCENE: *In the middle of the stage is a large cage with bars on all four sides. The bars are very far apart and the interior of the cage is clearly visible. The floor of the cage is about six feet above the level of the stage. A flight of wooded steps lead up to it on the side facing the audience.* ZERO *is discovered in the middle of the cage seated at a table above which is suspended a single naked electric light. Before him is an enor-*

* This scene, which follows the courtroom scene, was part of the original script. It was omitted, however, when the play was produced, and was performed for the first time (in its present revised form) when the play was revived at the Phoenix Theatre in New York in February, 1956.

mous platter of ham and eggs which he eats voraciously with a large wooden spoon. He wears a uniform of very broad black and white horizontal stripes. A few moments after the rise of the curtain a man enters at left, wearing the blue uniform and peaked cap of a GUIDE. *He is followed by a miscellaneous crowd of* MEN, WOMEN *and* CHILDREN—*about a dozen in all.*

THE GUIDE (*stopping in front of the cage*): Now ladies and gentlemen, if you'll kindly step right this way! (THE CROWD *straggles up and forms a loose semi-circle around him.*) Step right up, please. A little closer so's everybody can hear. (THEY *move up closer.* ZERO *pays no attention whatever to them.*) This, ladies and gentlemen, is a very in-ter-est-in' specimen; the North American murderer, Genus homo sapiens, Habitat North America (*A titter of excitement.* THEY *all crowd up around the cage.*) Don't push. There's room enough for everybody.

A TALL LADY: Oh, how interesting!

A STOUT LADY (*excitedly*): Look, Charley, he's eating!

CHARLEY (*bored*): Yeh, I see him.

THE GUIDE (*repeating by rote*): This specimen, ladies and gentlemen, exhibits the characteristics which are typical of his kind—

A SMALL BOY (*in a little Lord Fauntleroy suit, whiningly*): Mama!

HIS MOTHER: Be quiet, Eustace, or I'll take you right home.

THE GUIDE: He has the opposable thumbs, the large cranial capacity and the highly developed pre-frontal areas which distinguish him from all other species.

A YOUTH (*who has been taking notes*): What areas did you say?

THE GUIDE (*grumpily*): Pre-front-al areas. He learns by imitation and has a language which is said by some eminent philologists to bear many striking resemblances to English.

A BOY OF FOURTEEN: Pop, what's a philologist?

HIS FATHER: Keep quiet, can't you, and listen to what he's sayin'.

THE GUIDE: He thrives and breeds freely in captivity. This specimen was taken alive in his native haunts shortly after murdering his boss. (*Murmurs of great interest*)

THE TALL LADY: Oh, how charming.

THE NOTE-TAKING YOUTH: What was that last? I didn't get it.

SEVERAL (*helpfully*): Murdering his boss.

THE YOUTH: Oh—thanks.

THE GUIDE: He was tried, convicted and sentenced in one hour, thirteen minutes and twenty-four seconds, which sets a new record for this territory east of the Rockies and north of the Mason and Dixon line.

LITTLE LORD FAUNTLEROY (*whiningly*): Ma-ma!

HIS MOTHER: Be quiet, Eustace, or Mama won't let you ride in the choo-choo.

THE GUIDE: Now take a good look at him, ladies and gents. It's his last day here. He's goin' to be executed at noon. (*Murmurs of interest*)

THE TALL LADY: Oh, how lovely!

A MAN: What's he eating?

THE GUIDE: Ham and eggs.

THE STOUT LADY: He's quite a big eater, ain't he?

THE GUIDE: Oh, he don't always eat that much. You see we always try to make 'em feel good on their last day. So about a week in advance we let them order what they want to eat on their last day. They can have eight courses and they can order anything they want—don't make no difference what it costs or how hard it is to get. Well, he couldn't make up his mind till last night and then he ordered eight courses of ham and eggs. (THEY *all push and stare*)

THE BOY OF FOURTEEN: Look pop! He's eatin' with a spoon. Don't he know how to use a knife and fork?

THE GUIDE: (*overhearing him*): We don't dare trust him with a knife and fork, sonny. He might try to kill himself.

THE TALL LADY: Oh, how fascinating!

THE GUIDE (*resuming his official tone*): And now friends if you'll kindly give me your kind attention for just a moment. (*He takes a bundle of folders from his pocket.*) I have a little souvenir folder, which I'm sure you'll all want to have. It contains twelve beautiful colored views, relating to the North American Murderer you have just been looking at. These include a picture of the murderer, a picture of the murderer's wife, the blood-stained weapon, the murderer at the age of six, the spot where the body was found, the little red school house where he went to school, and his vine-covered boyhood home in southern Illinois, with his sweet-faced white-haired old mother plainly visible in the foreground. And many other interesting views. I'm now going to distribute these little folders for your examination. (*Sotto voice*) Just pass them back, will you. (*In louder tones*) Don't be afraid to look at them. You don't have to buy them if you don't want to. It don't cost anything to look at them. (*To the* NOTE-TAKING YOUTH *who is fumbling with a camera*) Hey, there, young feller, no snapshots allowed. All right now friends, if you'll just step this way. Keep close together and follow me. A lady lost her little boy here one time and by the time we found him, he was smoking cigarettes and hollering for a razor.

(*Much laughter as* THEY *all follow him off left.* ZERO *finishes eating and pushes away his plate. As the* CROWD *goes at left,* MRS. ZERO *enters at right. She is dressed in mourning garments. She carries a large parcel. She goes up the steps to the cage, opens the door and enters.* ZERO *looks up and sees her*)

MRS. ZERO: Hello.

ZERO: Hello, I didn't think you were comin' again.

MRS. ZERO: Well, I thought I'd come again. Are you glad to see me?

ZERO: Sure. Sit down. (*She complies.*) You're all dolled up, ain't you?

MRS. ZERO: Yeh, don't you like it? (*She gets up and turns about like a mannequin*)

ZERO: Gee. Some class.

MRS. ZERO: I always look good in black. There's some weight to this veil though I'll tell the world. I got a fierce headache.

ZERO: How much did all that set you back?

MRS. ZERO: Sixty-four dollars and twenty cents. And I gotta get a pin yet and some writin' paper—you know, with black around the edges.

ZERO: You'll be scrubbin' floors in about a year, if you go blowin' your coin like that.

MRS. ZERO: Well, I gotta do it right. It don't happen every day. (*She rises and takes up the parcel*) I brought you somethin'.

ZERO (*interested*): Yeh, what?

MRS. ZERO (*opening the parcel*): You gotta guess.

ZERO: Er—er—gee, search me.

MRS. ZERO: Somethin' you like. (*She takes out a covered plate*)

ZERO (*with increasing interest*): Looks like somethin' to eat.

MRS. ZERO (*nodding*): Yeh. (*She takes off the top plate*) Ham an' eggs!

ZERO (*joyfully*): Oh, boy! Just what I feel like eatin! (*He takes up the wooden spoon and begins to eat avidly*)

MRS. ZERO (*pleased*): Are they good?

ZERO (*his mouth full*): Swell.

MRS. ZERO (*a little sadly*): They're the last ones I'll ever make for you.

ZERO (*busily eating*): Uh-huh.

MRS. ZERO: I'll tell you somethin'—shall I?

ZERO: Sure.

MRS. ZERO (*hesitantly*): Well, all the while they were cookin' I was cryin!

ZERO: Yeh? (*He leans over and pats her hand*)

MRS. ZERO: I just couldn't help it. The thought of it just made me cry.

ZERO: Well—no use cryin' about it.

MRS. ZERO: I just couldn't help it.

ZERO: Maybe this time next year you'll be fryin' eggs for some other bird.

MRS. ZERO: Not on your life.

ZERO: You never can tell.

MRS. ZERO: Not me. Once is enough for me.

ZERO: I guess you're right at that. Still, I dunno. You might just happen to meet some guy—

MRS. ZERO: Well, if I do, there'll be time enough to think about it. No use borrowin' trouble.

ZERO: How do you like bein' alone in the house?

MRS. ZERO: Oh, it's all right.

ZERO: You got plenty room in the bed now, ain't you?

MRS. ZERO: Oh yeh. (*A brief pause*) It's kinda lonesome though—you know, wakin' up in the mornin' and nobody around to talk to.

ZERO: Yeh, I know. It's the same with me.

MRS. ZERO: Not that we ever did much talkin'.

ZERO: Well, that ain't it. It's just the idea of havin' somebody there in case you want to talk.

MRS. ZERO: Yeh, that's it. (*Another brief pause*) I guess maybe I use t'bawl you out quite a lot, didn't I?

ZERO: Oh well—no use talkin' about it now.

MRS. ZERO: We were always at it, weren't we?

ZERO: No more than any other married folks, I guess.

MRS. ZERO (*dubiously*): I dunno—

ZERO: I guess I gave you cause, all right.

MRS. ZERO: Well,—I got my faults too.

ZERO: None of us are perfect.

MRS. ZERO: We got along all right, at that, didn't we?

ZERO: Sure! Better'n most.

MRS. ZERO: Remember them Sundays at the beach, in the old days?

ZERO: You bet. (*With a laugh*) Remember that time I ducked you. Gee you was mad!

MRS. ZERO (*with a laugh*): I didn't talk to you for a whole week.

ZERO (*chuckling*): Yeh, I remember.

MRS. ZERO: And the time I had pneumonia and you brought me them roses. Remember?

ZERO: Yeh, I remember. And when the doctor told me maybe you'd pass out, I nearly sat down and cried.

MRS. ZERO: Did you?

ZERO: I sure did.

MRS. ZERO: We had some pretty good times at that, didn't we?

ZERO: I'll say we did!

MRS. ZERO (*with a sudden soberness*): It's all over now.

ZERO: All over is right. I ain't got much longer.

MRS. ZERO (*rising and going over to him*): Maybe—Maybe—if we had to do it over again, it would be different.

ZERO (*taking her hand*): Yeh. We live and learn.

MRS. ZERO (*crying*): If we only had another chance.

ZERO: It's too late now.

MRS. ZERO: It don't seem right, does it?

ZERO: It ain't right. But what can you do about it?

MRS. ZERO: Ain't there somethin'—somethin' I can do for you—before—

ZERO: No. Nothin'. Not a thing.

MRS. ZERO: Nothin' at all?

ZERO: No. I can't think of anything. (*Suddenly*) You're takin' good care of that scrap-book, ain't you, with all the clippings in it?

MRS. ZERO: Oh, sure. I got it right on the parlor table. Right where everybody can see it.

ZERO (*pleased*): It must be pretty near full, ain't it?

MRS. ZERO: All but three pages.

ZERO: Well, there'll be more tomorrow. Enough to fill it, maybe. Be sure to get them all, will you?

MRS. ZERO: I will. I ordered the papers already.

ZERO: Gee, I never thought I'd have a whole book full of clippings all about myself. (*Suddenly*) Say, that's somethin' I'd like to ask you.

MRS. ZERO: What?

ZERO: Suppose you should get sick or be run over or somethin', what would happen to the book?

MRS. ZERO: Well, I kinda thought I'd leave it to little Beatrice Elizabeth.

ZERO: Who? Your sister's kid?

MRS. ZERO: Yeh.

ZERO: What would she want with it?

MRS. ZERO: Well, it's nice to have, ain't it? And I wouldn't know who else to give it to.

ZERO: Well, I don't want her to have it. That fresh little kid puttin' her dirty fingers all over it.

MRS. ZERO: She ain't fresh and she ain't dirty. She's a sweet little thing.

ZERO: I don't want her to have it.

MRS. ZERO: Who do you want to have it then?

ZERO: Well, I kinda thought I'd like Miss Devore to have it.

MRS. ZERO: Miss Devore?

ZERO: Yeh. You know. Down at the store.

MRS. ZERO: Why should she have it?

ZERO: She'd take good care of it. And anyhow, I'd like her to have it.

MRS. ZERO: Oh you would, would you?

ZERO: Yes.

MRS. ZERO: Well, she ain't goin' to have it. Miss Devore! Where does she come in, I'd like to know, when I got two sisters and a niece.

ZERO: I don't care nothin' about your sisters and your niece.

MRS. ZERO: Well, I do! And Miss Devore ain't goin' to get it. Now put that in your pipe and smoke it.

ZERO: What have you got to say about it? It's my book, ain't it?

MRS. ZERO: No, it ain't. It's mine now—or it will be tomorrow. And I'm goin' to do what I like with it.

ZERO: I should have given it to her in the first place—that's what I should have done.

MRS. ZERO: Oh, should you? And what about me? Am I your wife or ain't I?

ZERO: Why remind me of my troubles?

MRS. ZERO: So it's Miss Devore all of a sudden, is it. What's been goin' on, I'd like to know, between you and Miss Devore?

ZERO: Aw, tie a can to that!

MRS. ZERO: Why didn't you marry Miss Devore, if you think so much of her?

ZERO: I would if I'd of met her first.

MRS. ZERO (*shrieking*): Ooh! A fine way to talk to me. After all I've done for you. You bum! You dirty bum! I won't stand for it! I won't stand for it!

(*In a great rage she takes up the dishes and smashes them on the floor. Then crying hysterically she opens the cage door, bangs it behind her, comes down the steps and goes off towards left.* ZERO *stands gazing ruefully after her for a moment, and then with a shrug and a sigh begins picking up the pieces of broken crockery. As* MRS. ZERO *exits at left a door in the back of the cage opens and* A MAN *enters. He is dressed in a sky-blue padded silk dressing-gown which is fitted with innumerable pockets. Under this he wears a pink silk union-suit. His bare feet are in sandals. He wears a jaunty Panama hat with a red feather stuck in the brim. Wings are fastened to his sandals and to the shoulders of his dressing-gown.* ZERO *who is busy picking up the broken crockery does not notice him at first.* THE MAN *takes a gold toothpick and begins carefully picking his teeth, waiting for* ZERO *to notice him.* ZERO *happens to look up and suddenly sees the man. He utters a cry of terror and shrinks into a corner of the cage, trembling with fear.*)

ZERO (*hoarsely*): Who are you?

THE MAN (*calmly, as he pockets his toothpick*): I'm the Fixer—from the Claim Department.

ZERO: Whaddya want?

THE FIXER: It's no use, Zero. There are no miracles.

ZERO: I don't know what you're talking about.

THE FIXER: Don't lie, Zero. (*Holding up his hand*) And now that your course is run—now that the end is already in sight, you still believe that some thunderbolt, some fiery bush, some celestial apparition will intervene between you and extinction. But it's no use, Zero. You're done for.

ZERO (*vehemently*): It ain't right! It ain't fair! I ain't gettin' a square deal!

THE FIXER (*wearily*): They all say that, Zero. (*Mildly*) Now just tell me why you're not getting a square deal.

ZERO: Well, that addin' machine. Was that a square deal—after twenty-five years?

THE FIXER: Certainly—from any point of view, except a sentimental one. (*Looking at his wrist watch*) The machine is quicker, it never makes a mistake, it's always on time. It presents no problems of housing, traffic congestion, water supply, sanitation.

ZERO: It costs somethin' to buy them machines, I'll tell you that!

THE FIXER: Yes, you're right there. In one respect you have the advantage over the machine—the cost of manufacture. But we've learned from many years' experience, Zero, that the original cost is an inconsequential item compared to upkeep. Take the dinosaurs, for example. They literally ate themselves out of existence. I held out for them to the last. They were damned picturesque—but when it came to a question of the nitrate supply, I simply had to yield. (*He begins to empty and clean his pipe*) And so with you, Zero. It costs a lot to keep up all that delicate mechanism of eye and ear and hand and brain which you've never put to any use. We can't afford to maintain it in idleness—and so you've got to go. (*He puts the pipe in one of his pockets*)

ZERO (*falling to his knees, supplicatingly*): Gimme a chance, gimme another chance!

THE FIXER: What would you do if I gave you another chance?

ZERO: Well—first thing I'd go out and look for a job.

THE FIXER: Adding figures?

ZERO: Well—I ain't young enough to take up somethin' new. (*The* FIXER *takes out a police whistle and blows shrilly. Instantly two guards enter*)

THE FIXER: Put the skids under him boys, and make it snappy. (*He strolls away to the other side of the cage, and taking a nail clipper from a pocket, begins to clip his nails as the* GUARDS *seize* ZERO)

ZERO (*struggling and shrieking*): No! No! Don't take me away! Don't kill me! Gimme a chance! Gimme another chance!

GUARD (*soothingly*): Ah come on! Be a good fellow! It'll all be over in a minute!

ZERO: I don't want to die! I don't want to die! I want to live! (*The* GUARDS *look at each other dubiously. Then one of them walks rather timidly over to the* FIXER *who is busy with his nails*)

GUARD (*clearing his throat*): H'm!

THE FIXER (*looking up*): Well?

GUARD (*timidly*): He says he wants to live.

THE FIXER: No. He's no good.

GUARD (*touching his cap, deferentially*): Yes sir! (*He goes back to his companion and the* TWO OF THEM *drag* ZERO *out at the back of the cage, still struggling and screaming.* THE FIXER *puts away his nail clippers, yawns, then goes to the table and sits on the edge of it. From a pocket he takes an enormous pair of horn-rimmed spectacles. Then from another pocket he takes a folded newspaper, which he unfolds carefully. It is a colored comic supplement. He holds it up in front of him and becomes absorbed in it. A moment later the door at the back of the cage opens and a tall, brawny, bearded* MAN *enters. He wears a red flannel undershirt and carries a huge blood-stained axe.* THE FIXER, *absorbed in the comic supplement, does not look up.)*

MAN (*hoarsely*): O.K.

THE FIXER (*looking up*): What?

MAN: O.K.

THE FIXER (*nodding*): Oh, all right. (*The* MAN *bows deferentially and goes out at the back.* THE FIXER *puts away his spectacles and folds the comic supplement carefully. As he folds the paper*:) That makes a total of 2137 black eyes for Jeff. (*He puts away the paper, turns out the electric light over his head, and leaves the cage by the front door. Then he takes a padlock from a pocket, attaches it to the door, and saunters off as the curtain falls.)*

(Curtain)

SCENE SIX

SCENE: *A graveyard in full moonlight. It is a second-rate graveyard—no elaborate tombstones or monuments, just simple headstones and here and there a cross. At the back is an iron fence with a gate in the middle. At first no one is visible, but there are occasional sounds throughout: the hooting of an owl, the whistle of a distant whippoorwill, the croaking of a bullfrog, and the yowling of a serenading cat. After a few moments two figures appear outside the gate—a man and a woman. She pushes the gate and it opens with a rusty creak. The couple enter. They are now fully visible in the moonlight—*JUDY O'GRADY *and a* YOUNG MAN.

JUDY (*advancing*): Come on, this is the place.

YOUNG MAN (*hanging back*): This! Why this here is a cemetery.

JUDY: Aw, quit yer kiddin'!

YOUNG MAN: You don't mean to say—

JUDY: What's the matter with this place?

YOUNG MAN: A cemetery!

JUDY: Sure. What of it?

YOUNG MAN: You must be crazy.

JUDY: This place is all right, I tell you. I been here lots o' times.

YOUNG MAN: Nix on this place for me!

JUDY: Ain't this place as good as another? Whaddya afraid of? They're all dead ones here! They don't bother you. (*With sudden interest*) Oh, look, here's a new one.

YOUNG MAN: Come on out of here.

JUDY: Wait a minute. Let's see what it says. (*She kneels on a grave in the foreground and putting her face close to headstone spells out the inscription*) Z-E-R-O. Z-e-r-o. Zero! Say, that's the guy—

YOUNG MAN: Zero? He's the guy killed his boss, ain't he?

JUDY: Yeh, that's him, all right. But what I'm thinkin' of is that I went to the hoosegow on account of him.

YOUNG MAN: What for?

JUDY: You know, same old stuff. Tenement House Law. (*Mincingly*) Section blaa-blaa of the Penal Code. Third offense. Six months.

YOUNG MAN: And this bird—

JUDY (*contemptuously*): Him? He was mama's white-haired boy. We lived in the same house. Across the airshaft, see? I used to see him lookin' in my window. I guess his wife musta seen him too. Anyhow, they went and turned the bulls on me. And now I'm out and he's in. (*Suddenly*) Say—say—(*She bursts into a peal of laughter.*)

YOUNG MAN (*nervously*): What's so funny?

JUDY (*rocking with laughter*): Say, wouldn't it be funny—if—if—(*She explodes again.*) That would be a good joke on him, all right. He can't do nothin' about it now, can he?

YOUNG MAN: Come on out of here. I don't like this place.

JUDY: Aw, you're a bum sport. What do you want to spoil my joke for? (*A cat yammers mellifluously.*)

YOUNG MAN (*half hysterically*): What's that?

JUDY: It's only the cats. They seem to like it here all right. But come on if you're afraid. (*They go toward the gate. As they go out*) You nervous men sure are the limit.

(*They go out through the gate. As they disappear* ZERO'*s grave opens suddenly and his head appears.*)

ZERO (*looking about*): That's funny! I thought I heard her talkin' and laughin'. But I don't see nobody. Anyhow, what would she be doin' here? I guess I must 'a' been dreamin'. But how could I be dreamin' when I ain't been asleep? (*He looks about again.*) Well, no use goin' back. I can't sleep anyhow. I might as well walk around a little. (*He rises out of the ground, very rigidly. He wears a full-dress suit of very antiquated cut and his hands are folded stiffly across his breast.*)

ZERO (*walking woodenly*): Gee! I'm stiff! (*He slowly walks a few steps, then stops.*) Gee, it's lonesome here! (*He shivers and walks on aimlessly*). I should 'a' stayed where I was. But I thought I heard her laughin'.

(*A loud sneeze is heard.* ZERO *stands motionless, quaking with terror. The sneeze is repeated.*)

ZERO (*hoarsely*): What's that?

A MILD VOICE: It's all right. Nothing to be afraid of.

(*From behind a headstone* SHRDLU *appears. He is dressed in a shabby and ill-fitting cutaway. He wears silver-rimmed spectacles and is smoking a cigarette.*)

SHRDLU: I hope I didn't frighten you.

ZERO (*still badly shaken*): No-o. It's all right. You see, I wasn't expectin' to see anybody.

SHRDLU: You're a newcomer, aren't you?

ZERO: Yeh, this is my first night. I couldn't seem to get to sleep.

SHRDLU: I can't sleep either. Suppose we keep each other company, shall we?

ZERO (*eagerly*): Yeh, that would be great. I been feelin' awful lonesome.

SHRDLU (*nodding*): I know. Let's make ourselves comfortable.

(*He seats himself easily on a grave.* ZERO *tries to follow his example but he is stiff in every joint and groans with pain.*)

ZERO: I'm kinda stiff.

SHRDLU: You mustn't mind the stiffness. It wears off in a few days. (*He produces a package of cigarettes.*) Will you have a Camel?

ZERO: No, I don't smoke.

SHRDLU: I find it helps keep the mosquitoes away. (*He lights a cigarette. Suddenly taking the cigarette out of his mouth*) Do you mind if I smoke, Mr.—Mr.—?

ZERO: No, go right ahead.

SHRDLU (*replacing the cigarette*): Thank you, I didn't catch your name. (ZERO *does not reply. Mildly*) I say I didn't catch your name.

ZERO: I heard you the first time. (*Hesitantly*) I'm scared if I tell you who I am and what I done, you'll be off me.

SHRDLU (*sadly*): No matter what your sins may be, they are as snow compared to mine.

ZERO: You got another guess comin'. (*He pauses dramatically.*) My name's Zero. I'm a murderer.

SHRDLU (*nodding calmly*): Oh, yes, I remember reading about you, Mr. Zero.

ZERO (*a little piqued*): And you still think you're worse than me?

SHRDLU (*throwing away his cigarette*): Oh, a thousand times worse, Mr. Zero—a million times worse.

ZERO: What did you do?

SHRDLU: I, too, am a murderer.

ZERO (*looking at him in amazement*): Go on! You're kiddin' me!

SHRDLU: Every word I speak is the truth, Mr. Zero. I am the foulest, the most sinful of murderers! You only murdered your employer, Mr. Zero. But I—I murdered my mother. (*He covers his face with his hands and sobs.*)

ZERO (*horrified*): The hell yer say!

SHRDLU (*sobbing*): Yes, my mother! My beloved mother!

ZERO (*suddenly*): Say, you don't mean to say you're Mr.—

SHRDLU (*nodding*): Yes. (*He wipes his eyes, still quivering with emotion.*)

ZERO: I remember readin' about you in the papers.

SHRDLU: Yes, my guilt has been proclaimed to all the world. But that would be a trifle if only I could wash the stain of sin from my soul.

ZERO: I never heard of a guy killin' his mother before. What did you do it for?

SHRDLU: Because I have a sinful heart—there is no other reason.

ZERO: Did she always treat you square and all like that?

SHRDLU: She was a saint—a saint, I tell you. She cared for me and watched over me as only a mother can.

ZERO: You mean to say you didn't have a scrap or nothin'?

SHRDLU: Never a harsh or an unkind word. Nothing except loving care and good advice. From my infancy she devoted herself to guiding me on the right path. She taught me to be thrifty, to be devout, to be unselfish, to shun evil companions, and to shut my ears to all the temptations of the flesh—in short, to become a virtuous, respectable, and God-fearing man. (*He groans.*) But it was a hopeless task. At fourteen I began to show evidence of my sinful nature.

ZERO (*breathlessly*): You didn't kill anybody else, did you?

SHRDLU: No, thank God, there is only one murder on my soul. But I ran away from home.

ZERO: You did!

SHRDLU: Yes. A companion lent me a profane book—the only profane book I have ever read, I'm thankful to say. It was called *Treasure Island.* Have you ever read it?

ZERO: No, I never was much on readin' books.

SHRDLU: It is a wicked book—a lurid tale of adventure. But it kindled in my sinful heart a desire to go to sea. And so I ran away from home.

ZERO: What did you do—get a job as a sailor?

SHRDLU: I never saw the sea—not to the day of my death. Luckily my mother's loving intuition warned her of my intention and I was sent back home. She welcomed me with open arms. Not an angry word, not a look of reproach. But I could read the mute suffering in her eyes as we prayed together all through the night.

ZERO (*sympathetically*): Gee, that must 'a' been tough. Gee, the mosquitoes are bad, ain't they? (*He tries awkwardly to slap at them with his stiff hands.*)

SHRDLU (*absorbed in his narrative*): I thought that experience had cured me of evil and I began to think about a career. I wanted to go in foreign missions at first, but we couldn't bear the thought of the separation. So we finally decided that I should become a proofreader.

ZERO: Say, slip me one o' them Camels, will you? I'm gettin' all bit up.

SHRDLU: Certainly. (*He hands* ZERO *cigarettes and matches.*)

ZERO (*lighting up*): Go ahead. I'm listenin'.

SHRDLU: By the time I was twenty I had a good job reading proof for a firm that printed catalogues. After a year they promoted me and let me specialize in shoe catalogues.

ZERO: Yeh? That must 'a' been a good job.

SHRDLU: It was a very good job. I was on the shoe catalogues for thirteen years. I'd been on them yet, if I hadn't—(*He chocks back a sob.*)

ZERO: They oughta put a shot o' citronella in that embalmin' fluid.

SHRDLU (*sighs*): We were so happy together. I had my steady job. And Sundays we would go to morning, afternoon, and evening service. It was an honest and moral mode of life.

ZERO: It sure was.

SHRDLU: Then came that fatal Sunday. Dr. Amaranth, our minister, was having dinner with us—one of the few pure spirits on earth. When he had finished saying grace, we had our soup. Everything was going along as usual—we were eating our soup and discussing the sermon, just like every other Sunday I could remember. Then came the leg of lamb—(*He breaks off, then resumes in a choking voice.*) I see the whole scene before me so plainly—it never leaves me—Dr. Amaranth at my right, my mother at my left, the leg of lamb on the table in front of me and the cuckoo clock on the little shelf between the windows. (*He stops and wipes his eyes.*)

ZERO: Yeh, but what happened?

SHRDLU: Well, as I started to carve the lamb—Did you ever carve a leg of lamb?

ZERO: No, corned beef was our speed.

SHRDLU: It's very difficult on account of the bone. And when there's gravy in the dish there's danger of spilling it. So Mother always used to hold the dish for me. She leaned forward, just as she always did, and I could see the gold locket around her neck. It had my picture in it and one of my baby curls. Well, I raised my knife to carve the leg of lamb—and instead I cut my mother's throat! (*He sobs.*)

ZERO: You must 'a' been crazy!

SHRDLU (*raising his head, vehemently*): No! Don't try to justify me. I wasn't crazy. They tried to prove at the trial that I was crazy. But Dr. Amaranth saw the truth! He saw it from the first! He knew that it was my sinful nature—and he told me what was in store for me.

ZERO (*trying to be comforting*): Well, your troubles are over now.

SHRDLU (*his voice rising*): Over! Do you think this is the end?

ZERO: Sure. What more can they do to us?

SHRDLU (*his tones growing shriller and shriller*): Do you think there can ever be any peace for such as we are—murderers, sinners? Don't you know what awaits us—flames, eternal flames!

ZERO (*nervously*): Keep your shirt on, buddy—they wouldn't do that to us.

SHRDLU: There's no escape—no escape for us, I tell you. We're doomed!

We're doomed to suffer unspeakable torments through all eternity. (*His voice rises higher and higher.*)

(*A grave opens suddenly and a head appears.*)

THE HEAD: Hey, you birds! Can't you shut up and let a guy sleep?

(ZERO *scrambles painfully to his feet.*)

ZERO (*to* SHRDLU): Hey, put on the soft pedal.

SHRDLU (*too wrought up to attend*): It won't be long now! We'll receive our summons soon.

THE HEAD: Are you goin' to beat it or not? (*He calls into the grave*) Hey, Bill, lend me your head a minute. (*A moment later his arm appears holding a skull.*)

ZERO (*warningly*): Look out! (*He seizes* SHRDLU *and drags him away just as* THE HEAD *throws the skull.*)

THE HEAD (*disgustedly*): Missed 'em. Damn old tabby cats! I'll get 'em next time. (*A prodigious yawn*) Ho-hum! Me for the worms!

(THE HEAD *disappears as the curtain falls.*)

(*Curtain*)

SCENE SEVEN

SCENE: *A pleasant place. A scene of pastoral loveliness. A meadow dotted with fine old trees and carpeted with rich grass and field flowers. In the background are seen a number of tents fashioned of gay-striped silks, and beyond gleams a meandering river. Clear air and a fleckless sky. Sweet distant music throughout.*

At the rise of the curtain SHRDLU *is seen seated under a tree in the foreground in an attitude of deep dejection. His knees are drawn up and his head is buried in his arms. He is dressed as in the preceding scene.*

A few minutes later ZERO *enters at right. He walks slowly and looks about him with an air of half-suspicious curiosity. He too is dressed as in the preceding scene. Suddenly he sees* SHRDLU *seated under the tree. He stands still and looks at him half fearfully. Then, seeing something familiar in him, goes closer.* SHRDLU *is unaware of his presence. At last* ZERO *recognizes him and grins in pleased surprise.*

ZERO: Well, if it ain't—! (*He claps* SHRDLU *on the shoulder.*) Hello, buddy!

(SHRDLU *looks up slowly, then, recognizing* ZERO, *he rises gravely and extends his hand courteously.*)

SHRDLU: How do you do, Mr. Zero? I'm very glad to see you again.

ZERO: Same here. I wasn't expectin' to see you either. (*Looking about*) This is a kinda nice place. I wouldn't mind restin' here a while.

SHRDLU: You may if you wish.

ZERO: I'm kinda tired. I ain't used to bein' outdoors. I ain't walked so much in years.

SHRDLU: Sit down here, under the tree.

ZERO: Do they let you sit on the grass?

SHRDLU: Oh, yes.

ZERO (*seating himself*): Boy, this feels good. I'll tell the world my feet are sore. I ain't used to so much walkin'. Say, I wonder would it be all right if I took my shoes off; my feet are tired.

SHRDLU: Yes. Some of the people here go barefoot.

ZERO: Yeh? They sure must be nuts. But I'm goin' t' leave 'em off for a while. So long as it's all right. The grass feels nice and cool. (*He stretches out comfortably.*) Say, this is the life of Riley all right, all right. This sure is a nice place. What do they call this place, anyhow?

SHRDLU: The Elysian Fields.

ZERO: The which?

SHRDLU: The Elysian Fields.

ZERO (*dubiously*): Oh! Well, it's a nice place, all right.

SHRDLU: They say that this is the most desirable of all places. Only the most favored remain here.

ZERO: Yeh? Well, that lets me out, I guess. (*Suddenly*) But what are you doin' here? I thought you'd be burned by now.

SHRDLU (*sadly*): Mr. Zero, I am the most unhappy of men.

ZERO (*in mild astonishment*): Why, because you ain't bein' roasted alive?

SHRDLU (*nodding*): Nothing is turning out as I expected. I saw everything so clearly—the flames, the tortures, an eternity of suffering as the just punishment for my unspeakable crime. And it has all turned out so differently.

ZERO: Well, that's pretty soft for you, ain't it?

SHRDLU (*wailingly*): No, no, no! It's right and just that I should be punished. I could have endured it stoically. All through those endless ages of indescribable torment I should have exulted in the magnificence of divine justice. But this—this is maddening! What becomes of justice? What becomes of morality? What becomes of right and wrong? It's maddening—simply maddening! Oh, if Dr. Amaranth were only here to advise me! (*He buries his face and groans.*)

ZERO (*trying to puzzle it out*): You mean to say they ain't called you for cuttin' your mother's throat?

SHRDLU: No! It's terrible—terrible! I was prepared for anything—anything but this.

ZERO: Well, what did they say to you?

SHRDLU (*looking up*): Only that I was to come here and remain until I understood.

ZERO: I don't get it. What do they want you to understand?

SHRDLU (*despairingly*): I don't know—I don't know! If I only had an inkling of what they meant—(*Interrupting himself*) Just listen quietly for a moment; do you hear anything?

(*They are both silent, straining their ears.*)

ZERO (*at last*): Nope.

SHRDLU: You don't hear any music? Do you?

ZERO: Music? No, I don't hear nothin'.

SHRDLU: The people here say that the music never stops.

ZERO: They're kiddin' you.

SHRDLU: Do you think so?

ZERO: Sure thing. There ain't a sound.

SHRDLU: Perhaps. They're capable of anything. But I haven't told you of the bitterest of my disappointments.

ZERO: Well, spill it. I'm gettin' used to hearin' bad news.

SHRDLU: When I came to this place my first thought was to find my dear mother. I wanted to ask her forgiveness. And I wanted her to help me to understand.

ZERO: An' she couldn't do it?

SHRDLU (*with a deep groan*): She's not here! Mr. Zero! Here where only the most favored dwell, that wisest and purest of spirits is nowhere to be found. I don't understand it.

A WOMAN'S VOICE (*in the distance*): Mr. Zero! Oh, Mr. Zero!

(ZERO *raises his head and listens attentively.*)

SHRDLU: (*going on, unheedingly*): If you were to see some of the people here—the things they do—

ZERO (*interrupting*): Wait a minute, will you? I think somebody's callin' me.

THE VOICE (*somewhat nearer*): Mr. Ze-ro! Oh! Mr. Ze-ro!

ZERO: Who the hell's that now? I wonder if the wife's on my trail already. That would be swell, wouldn't it? An' I figgered on her bein' good for another twenty years anyhow.

THE VOICE (*nearer*): Mr. Ze-ro! Yoo-hoo!

ZERO: No. That ain't her voice. (*Calling savagely*) Yoo-hoo. (*To* SHRDLU) Ain't that always the way? Just when a guy is takin' life easy an' havin' a good time! (*He rises and looks off left.*) Here she comes, whoever she is. (*In sudden amazement*) Well, I'll be—! Well, what do you know about that!

(*He stands looking in wonderment as* DAISY DIANA DOROTHEA DEVORE *enters. She wears a much-beruffled white muslin dress which is a size too small and fifteen years too youthful for her. She is red-faced and breathless.*)

DAISY (*panting*): Oh! I thought I'd never catch up to you. I've been followin' you for days—callin' an' callin'. Didn't you hear me?

ZERO: Not till just now. You look kinda winded.

DAISY: I sure am. I can't hardly catch my breath.

ZERO: Well, sit down an' take a load off your feet. (*He leads her to the tree.*)

(DAISY *sees* SHRDLU *for the first time and shrinks back a little.*)

ZERO: It's all right, he's a friend of mine. (*To* SHRDLU) Buddy, I want you to meet my friend, Miss Devore.

SHRDLU (*rising and extending his hand couteously*): How do you do, Miss Devore?

DAISY (*self-consciously*): How do!

ZERO (*to* DAISY): He's a friend of mine. (*To* SHRDLU) I guess you don't mind if she sits here a while an' cools off, do you?

SHRDLU: No, no, certainly not.

(*They all seat themselves under the tree.* ZERO *and* DAISY *are a little self-conscious.* SHRDLU *gradually becomes absorbed in his own thoughts.*)

ZERO: I was just takin' a rest myself. I took my shoes off on account of my feet bein' so sore.

DAISY: Yeh, I'm kinda tired too. (*Looking about*) Say, ain't it pretty here though?

ZERO: Yeh, it is at that.

DAISY: What do they call this place?

ZERO: Why—er—let's see. He was tellin' me just a minute ago. The—er—I don't know. Some kind o' fields. I forget now. (*To* SHRDLU) Say, buddy, what do they call this place again? (SHRDLU, *absorbed in his thoughts, does not hear him. To* DAISY) He don't hear me. He's thinkin' again.

DAISY (*sotto voce*): What's the matter with him?

ZERO: Why, he's the guy that murdered his mother—remember?

DAISY (*interested*): Oh, yeh! Is that him?

ZERO: Yeh. An' he had it all figgered out how they was goin' t' roast him or somethin'. And now they ain't goin' to do nothin' to him an' it's kinda got his goat.

DAISY (*sympathetically*): Poor feller!

ZERO: Yeh. He takes it kinda hard.

DAISY: He looks like a nice young feller.

ZERO: Well, you sure are good for sore eyes. I never expected to see you here.

DAISY: I thought maybe you'd be kinda surprised.

ZERO: Surprised is right. I thought you was alive an' kickin'. When did you pass out?

DAISY: Oh, right after you did—a coupla days.

ZERO (*interested*): Yeh? What happened? Get hit by a truck or somethin'?

DAISY: No. (*Hesitantly*) You see—it's this way. I blew out the gas.

ZERO (*astonished*): Go on! What was the big idea?

DAISY (*falteringly*): Oh, I don't know. You see, I lost my job.

ZERO: I'll bet you're sorry you did it now, ain't you?

DAISY (*with conviction*): No, I ain't sorry. Not a bit. (*Then hesitantly*) Say, Mr. Zero, I been thinkin'—(*She stops.*)

ZERO: What?

DAISY (*plucking up courage*): I been thinkin' it would be kinda nice—if you an' me—if we could kinda talk things over.

ZERO: Yeh. Sure. What do you want to talk about?

DAISY: Well—I don't know—but you and me—we ain't really ever talked things over, have we?

ZERO: No, that's right, we ain't. Well, let's go to it.

DAISY: I was thinkin' if we could be alone—just the two of us, see?

ZERO: Oh, yeh! Yeh, I get you. (*He turns to* SHRDLU *and coughs loudly.* SHRDLU *does not stir.*)

ZERO (*to* DAISY): He's dead to the world. (*He turns to* SHRDLU.) Say, buddy! (*No answer*) Say, buddy!

SHRDLU (*looking up with a start*): Were you speaking to me?

ZERO: Yeh. How'd you guess it? I was thinkin' that maybe you'd like to walk around a little and look for your mother.

SHRDLU (*shaking his head*): It's no use. I've looked everywhere. (*He relapses into thought again.*)

ZERO: Maybe over there they might know.

SHRDLU: No, no! I've searched everywhere. She's not here.

(ZERO *and* DAISY *look at each other in despair.*)

ZERO: Listen, old shirt, my friend here and me—see?—we used to work in the same store. An' we got some things to talk over—business, see?—kinda confidential. So if it ain't askin' too much—

SHRDLU (*springing to his feet*): Why, certainly! Excuse me!

(*He bows politely to* DAISY *and walks off.* DAISY *and* ZERO *watch him until he has disappeared.*)

ZERO (*with a forced laugh*): He's a good guy at that.

(*Now that they are alone, both are very self-conscious, and for a time they sit in silence.*)

DAISY (*breaking the silence*): It sure is pretty here, ain't it?

ZERO: Sure is.

DAISY: Look at the flowers! Ain't they just perfect! Why, you'd think they was artificial, wouldn't you?

ZERO: Yeh, you would.

DAISY: And the smell of them. Like perfume.

ZERO: Yeh.

DAISY: I'm crazy about the country, ain't you?

ZERO: Yeh. It's nice for a change.

DAISY: Them store picnics—remember?

ZERO: You bet. They sure was fun.

DAISY: One time—I guess you don't remember—the two of us—me and you—we sat down on the grass together under a tree—just like we're doin' now.

ZERO: Sure I remember.

DAISY: Go on! I'll bet you don't.

ZERO: I'll bet I do. It was the year the wife didn't go.

DAISY (*her face brightening*): That's right! I didn't think you'd remember.

ZERO: An' comin' home we sat together in the truck.

DAISY (*eagerly, rather shamefacedly*): Yeh! There's somethin' I've always wanted to ask you.

ZERO: Well, why didn't you?

DAISY: I don't know. It didn't seem refined. But I'm goin' to ask you now anyhow.

ZERO: Go ahead. Shoot.

DAISY: (*falteringly*): Well—while we was comin' home—you put your arm up on the bench behind me—and I could feel your knee kinda pressin' against mine. (*She stops.*)

ZERO (*becoming more and more interested*): Yeh—well, what about it?

DAISY: What I wanted to ask you was—was it just kinda accidental?

ZERO (*with a laugh*): Sure it was accidental. Accidental on purpose.

DAISY (*eagerly*): Do you mean it?

ZERO: Sure I mean it. You mean to say you didn't know it?

DAISY: No. I've been wantin' to ask you—

ZERO: Then why did you get sore at me?

DAISY: Sore? I wasn't sore! When was I sore?

ZERO: That night. Sure you was sore. If you wasn't sore why did you move away?

DAISY: Just to see if you meant it. I thought if you meant it you'd move up closer. An' then when you took your arm away I was sure you didn't mean it.

ZERO: An' I thought all the time you was sore. That's why I took my arm away. I thought if I moved up you'd holler and then I'd be in a jam, like you read in the paper all the time about guys gettin' pulled in for annoyin' women.

DAISY: An' I was wishin' you'd put your arm around me—just sittin' there wishin' all the way home.

ZERO: What do you know about that? That sure is hard luck, that is. If I'd 'a' only knew! You know what I felt like doin'—only I didn't have the nerve?

DAISY: What?

ZERO: I felt like kissin' you.

DAISY (*fervently*): I wanted you to.

ZERO (*astonished*): You would 'a' let me?

DAISY: I wanted you to! I wanted you to! Oh, why didn't you—why didn't you?

ZERO: I didn't have the nerve. I sure was a dumbbell.

DAISY: I would 'a' let you all you wanted to. I wouldn't 'a' cared. I know it would 'a' been wrong but I wouldn't 'a' cared. I wasn't thinkin' about right an' wrong at all. I didn't care—see? I just wanted you to kiss me.

ZERO (*feelingly*): If I'd only knew. I wanted to do it, I swear I did. But I didn't think you cared nothin' about me.

DAISY (*passionately*): I never cared nothin' about nobody else.

ZERO: Do you mean it—on the level? You ain't kiddin' me, are you?

DAISY: No, I ain't kiddin'. I mean it. I'm tellin' you the truth. I ain't never had the nerve to tell you before—but now I don't care. It don't make no difference now. I mean it—every word of it.

ZERO (*dejectedly*): If I'd only knew it.

DAISY: Listen to me. There's somethin' else I want to tell you. I may as well tell you everything now. It don't make no difference now. About my blowin' out the gas—see? Do you know why I done it?

ZERO: Yeh, you told me—on account o' bein' canned.

DAISY: I just told you that. That ain't the real reason. The real reason is on account o' you.

ZERO: You mean to say on account o' me passin' out—?

DAISY: Yeh. That's it. I didn't want to go on livin'. What for? What did I want to go on livin' for? I didn't have nothin' to live for with you gone. I often thought of doin' it before. But I never had the nerve. An' anyhow I didn't want to leave you.

ZERO: An' me bawlin' you out, about readin' too fast an' readin' too slow.

DAISY (*reproachfully*): Why did you do it?

ZERO: I don't know, I swear I don't. I was always stuck on you. An' while I'd be addin' them figgers, I'd be thinkin' how if the wife died, you an' me could get married.

DAISY: I used to think o' that too.

ZERO: An' then before I knew it I was bawlin' you out.

DAISY: Them was the times I'd think o' blowin' out the gas. But I never did till you was gone. There wasn't nothin' to live for then. But it wasn't so easy to do anyhow. I never could stand the smell o'gas. An' all the while I was gettin' ready, you know, stuffin' up all the cracks, the way you read about in the paper—I was thinkin' of you and hopin' that maybe I'd meet you again. An' I made up my mind if I ever did see you, I'd tell you.

ZERO (*taking her hand*): I'm sure glad you did. I'm sure glad. (*Ruefully*) But it don't do much good now, does it?

DAISY: No, I guess it don't. (*Summoning courage*) But there's one thing I'm goin' to ask you.

ZERO: What's that?

DAISY (*in a low voice*): I want you to kiss me.

ZERO: You bet I will! (*He leans over and kisses her cheek.*)

DAISY: Not like that. I don't mean like that. I mean really kiss me. On the mouth. I ain't never been kissed like that.

(ZERO *puts his arms about her and presses his lips to hers. A long embrace. At last they separate and sit side by side in silence.*)

DAISY (*putting her hands to her cheeks*): So that's what it's like. I didn't know it could be like that. I didn't know anythin' could be like that.

ZERO (*fondling her hand*): Your cheeks are red. They're all red. And your eyes are shinin'. I never seen your eyes shinin' like that before.

DAISY (*holding up her hand*): Listen—do you hear it? Do you hear the music?

ZERO: No, I don't hear nothin'!

DAISY: Yeh—music. Listen an' you'll hear it.

(*They are both silent for a moment.*)

ZERO (*excitedly*): Yeh! I hear it! He said there was music, but I didn't hear it till just now.

DAISY: Ain't it grand?

ZERO: Swell! Say, do you know what?

DAISY: What?

ZERO: It makes me feel like dancin'.

DAISY: Yeh? Me too.

ZERO (*springing to his feet*): Come on! Let's dance! (*He seizes her hands and tries to pull her up.*)

DAISY (*resisting laughingly*): I can't dance. I ain't danced in twenty years.

ZERO: That's nothin'. I ain't neither. Come on! I feel just like a kid! (*He pulls her to her feet and seizes her about the waist.*)

DAISY: Wait a minute! Wait till I fix my skirt. (*She turns back her skirts and pins them above the ankles.*)

(ZERO *seizes her about the waist. They dance clumsily but with gay abandon.* DAISY'*s hair becomes loosened and tumbles over her shoulders. She lends herself more and more to the spirit of the dance. But* ZERO *soon begins to tire and dances with less and less zest.*)

ZERO (*stopping at last, panting for breath*): Wait a minute! I'm all winded.

(*He releases* DAISY, *but before he can turn away, she throws her arms about him and presses her lips to his.*)

ZERO (*freeing himself*): Wait a minute! Let me get my wind!

(*He limps to the tree and seats himself under it, gasping for breath.* DAISY *looks after him, her spirits rather dampened.*)

ZERO: Whew! I sure am winded! I ain't used to dancin'.

(*He takes off his collar and tie and opens the neckband of his shirt.* DAISY *sits under the tree near him, looking at him longingly. But he is busy catching his breath.*)

ZERO: Gee, my heart's goin' a mile a minute.

DAISY: Why don't you lay down an' rest? You could put your head on my lap.

ZERO: That ain't a bad idea. (*He stretches out, his head in* DAISY'*s lap.*)

DAISY (*fondling his hair*): It was swell, wasn't it?

ZERO: Yeh. But you gotta be used to it.

DAISY: Just imagine if we could stay here all the time—you an' me together—wouldn't it be swell?

ZERO: Yeh. But there ain't a chance.

DAISY: Won't they let us stay?

ZERO: No. This place is only for the good ones.

DAISY: Well, we ain't so bad, are we?

ZERO: Go on! Me a murderer an' you committin' suicide. Anyway, they wouldn't stand for this—the way we been goin' on.

DAISY: I don't see why.

ZERO: You don't! You know it ain't right. Ain't I got a wife?

DAISY: Not any more you ain't. When you're dead that ends it. Don't they always say "until death do us part"?

ZERO: Well, maybe you're right about that but they wouldn't stand for us here.

DAISY: It would be swell—the two of us together—we could make up for all them years.

ZERO: Yeh, I wish we could.

DAISY: We sure were fools. But I don't care. I've got you now. (*She kisses his forehead and cheeks and mouth.*)

ZERO: I'm sure crazy about you. I never saw you lookin' so pretty before, with your cheeks all red. An' your hair hangin' down. You got swell hair. (*He fondles and kisses her hair.*)

DAISY (*ecstatically*): We got each other now, ain't we?

ZERO: Yeh. I'm crazy about you. Daisy! That's a pretty name. It's a flower, ain't it? Well—that's what you are—just a flower.

DAISY (*happily*): We can always be together now, can't we?

ZERO: As long as they'll let us. I sure am crazy about you. (*Suddenly he sits upright.*) Watch your step!

DAISY (*alarmed*): What's the matter?

ZERO (*nervously*): He's comin' back.

DAISY: Oh, is that all? Well, what about it?

ZERO: You don't want him to see us layin' around like this, do you?

DAISY: I don't care if he does.

ZERO: Well, you oughta care. You don't want him to think you ain't a refined girl, do you? He's an awful moral bird, he is.

DAISY: I don't care nothin' about him. I don't care nothin' about anybody but you.

ZERO: Sure, I know. But we don't want people talkin' about us. You better fix your hair an' pull down your skirts.

(DAISY *complies rather sadly. They are both silent as* SHRDLU *enters.)*

ZERO (*with feigned nonchalance*): Well, you got back all right, didn't you?

SHRDLU: I hope I haven't returned too soon.

ZERO: No, that's all right. We were just havin' a little talk. You know—about business an' things.

DAISY (*boldly*): We were wishin' we could stay here all the time.

SHRDLU: You may if you like.

ZERO AND DAISY (*in astonishment*): What!

SHRDLU: Yes. Anyone who likes may remain—

ZERO: But I thought you were tellin' me—

SHRDLU: Just as I told you, only the most favored do remain. But anyone may.

ZERO: I don't get it. There's a catch in it somewheres.

DAISY: It don't matter as long as we can stay.

ZERO (*to* SHRDLU): We were thinkin' about gettin' married, see?

SHRDLU: You may or not, just as you like.

ZERO: You don't mean to say we could stay if we didn't, do you?

SHRDLU: Yes. They don't care.

ZERO: An' there's some here that ain't married?

SHRDLU: Yes.

ZERO (*to* DAISY): I don't know about this place, at that. They must be kind of a mixed crowd.

DAISY: It don't matter, so long as we got each other.

ZERO: Yeh, I know, but you don't want to mix with people that ain't respectable.

DAISY (*to* SHRDLU): Can we get married right away? I guess there must be a lot of ministers here, ain't there?

SHRDLU: Not as many as I had hoped to find. The two who seem most beloved are Dean Swift and the Abbé Rabelais. They are both much admired for some indecent tales which they have written.

ZERO (*shocked*): What! Ministers writin' smutty stories! Say, what kind of a dump is this anyway?

SHRDLU (*despairingly*): I don't know, Mr. Zero. All these people here are so strange, so unlike the good people I've known. They seem to think of nothing but enjoyment or of wasting their time in profitless occupations. Some paint pictures from morning until night, or carve blocks of stone. Others write songs or put words together, day in and day out. Still others do nothing but lie under the trees and look at the sky. There are men who spend all their time reading books and women who think only of adorning themselves. And forever they are telling stories and laughing and singing and drinking and dancing. There are drunkards, thieves, vagabonds, blasphemers, adulterers. There is one—

ZERO: That's enough. I heard enough. (*He seats himself and begins putting on his shoes.*)

DAISY (*anxiously*): What are you goin' to do?

ZERO: I'm goin' to beat it, that's what I'm goin' to do.

DAISY: You said you liked it here.

ZERO (*looking at her in amazement*): Liked it! Say, you don't mean to say you want to stay here, do you, with a lot of rummies an' loafers an' bums?

DAISY: We don't have to bother with them. We can just sit here together an' look at the flowers an' listen to the music.

SHRDLU (*eagerly*): Music! Did you hear music?

DAISY: Sure. Don't you hear it?

SHRDLU: No, they say it never stops. But I've never heard it.

ZERO (*listening*): I thought I heard it before but I don't hear nothin' now. I guess I must 'a' been dreamin'. (*Looking about*) What's the quickest way out of this place?

DAISY (*pleadingly*): Won't you stay just a little longer?

ZERO: Didn't yer hear me say I'm goin'? Good-by, Miss Devore. I'm goin' to beat it.

(*He limps off at the right.* DAISY *follows him slowly.*)

DAISY (*to* SHRDLU): I won't ever see him again.

SHRDLU: Are you goin' to stay here?

DAISY: It don't make no difference now. Without him I might as well be alive.

(*She goes off right.* SHRDLU *watches her a moment, then sighs and seating himself under the tree, buries his head on his arm.*)

(*Curtain*)

SCENE EIGHT

SCENE: *Before the curtain rises the clicking of an adding machine is heard. The curtain rises upon an office similar in appearance to that in Scene Two except that there is a door in the back wall through which can be seen a glimpse of the corridor outside. In the middle of the room* ZERO *is seated completely absorbed in the operation of an adding machine. He presses the keys and pulls the lever with mechanical precision. He still wears his full-dress suit but he has added to it sleeve-protectors and a green eyeshade. A strip of white paper-tape flows steadily from the machine as* ZERO *operates. The room is filled with this tape—streamers, festoons, billows of it everywhere. It covers the floor and the furniture, it climbs the walls and chokes the doorways. A few moments later* LIEUTENANT CHARLES *and* JOE *enter at the left.* LIEUTENANT CHARLES *is middle-aged and inclined to corpulence. He has an air of world-weariness. He is barefooted, wears a Panama hat, and is dressed in bright red tights which are a very bad fit—too tight in some places, badly wrinkled in others.* JOE *is a youth with a smutty face dressed in dirty blue overalls.*

CHARLES (*after contemplating* ZERO *for a few moments*): All right, Zero, cease firing.

ZERO (*looking up, surprised*): Whaddja say?

CHARLES: I said stop punching that machine.

ZERO (*bewildered*): Stop? (*He goes on working mechanically.*)

CHARLES (*impatiently*): Yes. Can't you stop? Here, Joe, give me a hand. He can't stop.

(JOE *and* CHARLES *each take one of* ZERO's *arms and with enormous effort detach him from the machine. He resists passively—mere inertia. Finally they succeed and swing him around on his stool.* CHARLES *and* JOE *mop their foreheads.*)

ZERO (*querulously*): What's the idea? Can't you lemme alone?

CHARLES (*ignoring the question*): How long have you been here?

ZERO: Jes' twenty-five years. Three hundred months, ninety-one hundred and thirty-one days, one hundred thirty-six thousand—

CHARLES (*impatiently*): That'll do! That'll do!

ZERO (*proudly*): I ain't missed a day, not an hour, not a minute. Look at all I got done. (*He points to the maze of paper.*)

CHARLES: It's time to quit.

ZERO: Quit? Whaddye mean quit? I ain't goin' to quit!

CHARLES: You've got to.

ZERO: What for? What do I have to quit for?

CHARLES: It's time for you to go back.

ZERO: Go back where? Whaddya talkin' about?

CHARLES: Back to earth, you dub. Where do you think?

ZERO: Aw, go on, Cap, who are you kiddin'?

CHARLES: I'm not kidding anybody. And don't call me Cap. I'm a lieutenant.

ZERO: All right, Lieutenant, all right. But what's this you're tryin' to tell me about goin' back?

CHARLES: Your time's up, I'm telling you. You must be pretty thick. How many times do you want to be told a thing?

ZERO: This is the first time I heard about goin' back. Nobody ever said nothin' to me about it before.

CHARLES: You didn't think you were going to stay here forever, did you?

ZERO: Sure. Why not? I did my bit, didn't I? Forty-five years of it. Twenty-five years in the store. Then the boss canned me and I knocked him cold. I guess you ain't heard about that—

CHARLES (*interrupting*): I know all about that. But what's that got to do with it?

ZERO: Well, I done my bit, didn't I? That oughta let me out.

CHARLES (*jeeringly*): So you think you're all through, do you?

ZERO: Sure, I do. I did the best I could while I was there and then I passed out. And now I'm sittin' pretty here.

CHARLES: You've got a fine idea of the way they run things, you have. Do you think they're going to all of the trouble of making a soul just to use it once?

ZERO: Once is often enough, it seems to me.

CHARLES: It seems to you, does it? Well, who are you? And what do you know about it? Why, man, they use a soul over and over again—over and over until it's worn out.

ZERO: Nobody ever told me.

CHARLES: So you thought you were all through, did you? Well, that's a hot one, that is.

ZERO (*sullenly*): How was I to know?

CHARLES: Use your brains! Where would we put them all! We're crowded enough as it is. Why, this place is nothing but a kind of repair and service station—a sort of cosmic laundry, you might say. We get the souls in here by the bushelful. Then we get busy and clean them up. And you ought to see some of them. The muck and the slime. Phoo! And as full of holes as a flour sifter. But we fix them up. We disinfect them and give them a kerosene rub and mend the holes and back they go—practically as good as new.

ZERO: You mean to say I've been here before—before the last time, I mean!

CHARLES: Been here before? Why, you poor boob—you've been here thousands of times—fifty thousand at least.

ZERO (*suspiciously*): How is it I don't remember nothin' about it?

CHARLES: Well—that's partly because you're stupid. But it's mostly because that's the way they fix it. (*Musingly*) They're funny that way—every now and then they'll do something white like that—when you'd least expect it. I guess economy's at the bottom of it though. They figure that the souls would get worn out quicker if they remembered.

ZERO: And don't any of 'em remember?

CHARLES: Oh, some do. You see there's different types: there's the type that gets a little better each time it goes back—we just give them a wash and send them right through. Then there's another type—the type that gets a little worse each time. That's where you belong!

ZERO (*offended*): Me? You mean to say I'm gettin' worse all the time?

CHARLES (*nodding*): Yes. A little worse each time.

ZERO: Well—what was I when I started? Somethin' big? A king or somethin'?

CHARLES (*laughing derisively*): A king! That's a good one! I'll tell you what you were the first time—if you want to know so much—a monkey.

ZERO (*shocked and offended*): A monkey!

CHARLES (*nodding*): Yes, sir—just a hairy, chattering, long-tailed monkey.

ZERO: That musta been a long time ago.

CHARLES: Oh, not so long. A million years or so. Seems like yesterday to me.

ZERO: Then look here, whaddya mean by sayin' I'm gettin' worse all the time?

CHARLES: Just what I said. You weren't so bad as a monkey. Of course, you did just what all the other monkeys did, but still it kept you out in the open air. And you weren't woman-shy—there was one little red-headed monkey—Well, never mind. Yes, sir, you weren't so bad then. But even in those days there must have been some bigger and brainier monkey that you kowtowed to. The mark of the slave was on you from the start.

ZERO (*sullenly*): You ain't very particular about what you call people, are you?

CHARLES: You wanted the truth, didn't you? If there ever was a soul in the world that was labeled slave it's yours. Why, all the bosses and kings that there ever were have left their trademarks on your backside.

ZERO: It ain't fair, if you ask me.

CHARLES (*shrugging his shoulders*): Don't tell me about it. I don't make the rules. All I know is, you've been getting worse—worse each time. Why, even six thousand years ago you weren't so bad. That was the time you were hauling stones for one of those big pyramids in a place they call Africa. Ever hear of the pyramids?

ZERO: Them big pointy things?

CHARLES (*nodding*): That's it.

ZERO: I seen a picture of them in the movies.

CHARLES: Well, you helped build them. It was a long step down from the happy days in the jungle, but it was a good job—even though you didn't know what you were doing and your back was striped by the foreman's whip. But you've been going down, down. Two thousand years ago you were a Roman galley slave. You were on one of the triremes that knocked the Carthaginian fleet for a goal. Again the whip. But you had muscles then—chest muscles, back muscles, biceps. (*He feels* ZERO'*s arm gingerly and turns away in disgust.*) Phoo! A bunch of mush! (*He notices that* JOE *has fallen asleep. Walking over, he kicks him in the shin.*)

Wake up, you mutt! Where do you think you are! (*He turns to* ZERO *again.*) And then another thousand years and you were a serf—a lump of clay digging up other lumps of clay. You wore an iron collar then—white ones hadn't been invented yet. Another long step down. But where you dug, potatoes grew, and that helped fatten the pigs. Which was something. And now—well, I don't want to rub it in—

ZERO: Rub it in is right! Seems to me I got a pretty healthy kick comin'. I ain't had a square deal! Hard work! That's all I've ever had!

CHARLES (*callously*): What else were you ever good for?

ZERO: Well, that ain't the point. The point is I'm through! I had enough! Let 'em find somebody else to do the dirty work. I'm sick of bein' the goat! I quit right here and now! (*He glares about defiantly. There is a thunderclap and a bright flash of lightning. Screaming*) Ooh! What's that? (*He clings to* CHARLES.)

CHARLES: It's all right. Nobody's going to hurt you. It's just their way of telling you that they don't like you to talk that way. Pull yourself together and calm down. You can't change the rules—nobody can—they've got it all fixed. It's a rotten system—but what are you going to do about it?

ZERO: Why can't they stop pickin' on me? I'm satisfied here—doin' my day's work. I don't want to go back.

CHARLES: You've got to, I tell you. There's no way out of it.

ZERO: What chance have I got—at my age? Who'll give me a job?

CHARLES: You big boob, you don't think you're going back the way you are, do you?

ZERO: Sure, how then?

CHARLES: Why, you've got to start all over.

ZERO: All over?

CHARLES (*nodding*): You'll be a baby again—a bald, red-faced little animal, and then you'll go through it all again. There'll be millions of others like you—all with their mouths open, squalling for food. And then when you get a little older you'll begin to learn things—and you'll learn all the wrong things and learn them all in the wrong way. You'll eat the wrong food and wear the wrong clothes, and you'll live in swarming dens where there's no light and no air! You'll learn to be a liar and a bully and a braggart and a coward and a sneak. You'll learn to fear the sunlight and to hate beauty. By that time you'll be ready for school. There they'll tell you the truth about a great many things that you don't give a damn about, and they'll tell you lies about all the things you ought to know—and about all the things you want to know they'll tell you nothing at all. When you get through you'll be equipped for your life work. You'll be ready to take a job.

ZERO (*eagerly*): What'll my job be? Another adding machine?

CHARLES: Yes. But not one of these antiquated adding machines. It will be a superb, super-hyper-adding machine, as far from this old piece of junk as you are from God. It will be something to make you sit up and take notice, that adding machine. It will be an adding machine which will be installed in a coal mine and which will record the individual output of each miner. As each miner down in the lower galleries takes up a shovelful of coal, the impact of his shovel will automatically set in motion a graphite pencil in your gallery. The pencil will make a mark in white upon a blackened, sensitized drum. Then your work comes in. With the great toe of your right foot you release a lever which focuses a violet ray on the drum. The ray, playing upon and through the white mark, falls upon a selenium cell which in turn sets the keys of the adding apparatus in motion. In this way the individual output of each miner is recorded without any human effort except the slight pressure of the great toe of your right foot.

ZERO (*in breathless, round-eyed wonder*): Say, that'll be some machine, won't it?

CHARLES: Some machine is right. It will be the culmination of human effort—the final triumph of the evolutionary process. For millions of years the nebulous gases swirled in space. For more millions of years the gases cooled and then through inconceivable ages they hardened into rocks. And then came life. Floating green things on the waters that covered the earth. More millions of years and a step upward—an animate organism in the ancient slime. And so on—step by step, down through the ages—a gain here, a gain there—the mollusk, the fish, the reptile, then mammal, man! And all so that you might sit in the gallery of a coal mine and operate the super-hyper-adding machine with the great toe of your right foot!

ZERO: Well, then—I ain't so bad after all.

CHARLES: You're a failure, Zero, a failure. A waste product. A slave to a contraption of steel and iron. The animal's instincts, but not his strength and skill. The animal's appetites, but not his unashamed indulgence of them. True, you move and eat and digest and excrete and reproduce. But any microscopic organism can do as much. Well—time's up! Back you go—back to your sunless groove—the raw material of slums and wars—the ready prey of the first jingo or demagogue or political adventurer who takes the trouble to play upon your ignorance and credulity and provincialism. You poor, spineless, brainless boob—I'm sorry for you!

ZERO (*falling to his knees*): Then keep me here! Don't send me back! Let me stay!

CHARLES: Get up. Didn't I tell you I can't do anything for you? Come on, time's up!

ZERO: I can't! I can't! I'm afraid to go through it all again.

CHARLES: You've got to, I tell you. Come on, now!

ZERO: What did you tell me so much for? Couldn't you just let me go, thinkin' everythin' was goin' to be all right?

CHARLES: You wanted to know, didn't you?

ZERO: How did I know what you were goin' to tell me? Now I can't stop thinkin' about it! I can't stop thinkin'! I'll be thinkin' about it all the time.

CHARLES: All right! I'll do the best I can for you. I'll send a girl with you to keep you company.

ZERO: A girl? What for? What good will a girl do me?

CHARLES: She'll help make you forget.

ZERO (*eagerly*): She will? Where is she?

CHARLES: Wait a minute, I'll call her. (*He calls in a loud voice.*) Oh! Hope! Yoo-hoo! (*He turns his head aside and speaks in the manner of a ventriloquist imitating a distant feminine voice.*) Ye-es. (*Then in his own voice*) Come here, will you? There's a fellow who wants you to take him back. (*Ventriloquously again*) All right. I'll be right over, Charlie dear. (*He turns to* ZERO.) Kind of familiar, isn't she? Charlie dear!

ZERO: What did you say her name is?

CHARLES: Hope. H-o-p-e.

ZERO: Is she good-lookin'?

CHARLES: Is she good-looking! Oh, boy, wait until you see her! She's a blonde with big blue eyes and red lips and little white teeth and—

ZERO: Say, that listens good to me. Will she be long?

CHARLES: She'll be here right away. There she is now! Do you see her?

ZERO: No. Where?

CHARLES: Out in the corridor. No, not there. Over farther. To the right. Don't you see her blue dress? And the sunlight on her hair?

ZERO: Oh, sure! Now I see her! What's the matter with me anyhow? Say, she's some jane! Oh, you baby vamp!

CHARLES: She'll make you forget your troubles.

ZERO: What troubles are you talkin' about?

CHARLES: Nothing. Go on. Don't keep her waiting.

ZERO: You bet I won't! Oh, Hope! Wait for me! I'll be right with you! I'm on my way!

(*He stumbles out eagerly.* JOE *bursts into uproarious laughter.*)

CHARLES (*eying him in surprise and anger*): What in hell's the matter with you?

JOE (*shaking with laughter*): Did you get that? He thinks he saw somebody and he's following her! (*He rocks with laughter.*)

CHARLES (*punching him in the jaw*): Shut your face!

JOE (*nursing his jaw*): What's the idea? Can't I even laugh when I see something funny?

CHARLES: Funny! You keep your mouth shut or I'll show you something funny. Go on, hustle out of here and get something to clean up this mess with. There's another fellow moving in. Hurry now. (*He makes a threatening gesture.* JOE *exits hastily.* CHARLES *goes to chair and seats himself. He looks weary and dispirited. Shaking his head*) Hell, I'll tell the world this is a lousy job! (*He takes a flask from his pocket, uncorks it, and slowly drains it.*)

(*Curtain*)

1923

Eugene [Gladstone] O' Neill

(1888-1953)

CHRONOLOGY:

1888 Born October 16, in New York City.

1906-07 Attended Princeton University before being expelled.

1912-13 Wandered among the waterfront slums of the world's chief cities.

1914 *Thirst and Other One-Act Plays;* enrolled in Professor G. P. Baker's "47 Workshop," at Harvard.

1916 Joined the Provincetown Players; *Bound East for Cardiff; Before Breakfast.*

1919 *The Moon of the Caribbees, and Six Other Plays of the Sea.*

1920 *Beyond the Horizon* (awarded Pulitzer Prize); *Gold.*

1921 *The Emperor Jones; Diff'rent; The Straw.*

1922 *The Hairy Ape; Anna Christie* (awarded Pulitzer Prize); *The First Man; The Dreamy Kid.*

1924 *All God's Chillun Got Wings; Welded.*

1925 *Desire Under the Elms.*

1926 *The Great God Brown; The Fountain; The Moon of the Caribbees, and Other Plays.*

1927 *Marco Millions; Lazarus Laughed.*

1928 *Strange Interlude* (awarded Pulitzer Prize).

1929 *Dynamo.*

1931 *Mourning Becomes Electra.*

1933 *Ah, Wilderness!*

1934 *Days Without End.*

1936 Awarded the Nobel Prize for Literature.

1946 *The Iceman Cometh.*

1950 *Lost Plays* (collected by Lawrence Gellert).

1952 *A Moon for the Misbegotten.*

1953 Died November 27, in Boston.

1956 *Long Day's Journey into Night.*

1958 *A Touch of the Poet.*

1959 *Hughie.*

BIBLIOGRAPHY:

All of the plays except the earliest and the posthumous ones are collected in *The Plays of Eugene O'Neill,* 3 Vols. (Rev. ed.; New York, 1951). The posthumous plays have been published one by one by the Yale University Press (see Chronology). A still useful reprint is *Nine Plays . . . Selected by the Author,* with an Introduction by Joseph Wood Krutch (New York: Modern Library, 1941).

Critical and biographical attention to O'Neill has been extensive. Among the important book-length studies are Barrett H. Clark, *Eugene O'Neill: The Man and His Plays* (Rev. ed.; New York, 1947); Edwin Engel, *The Haunted Heroes of Eugene O'Neill* (Cambridge, 1953); Doris Falk, *Eugene O'Neill and the Tragic Tension* (New Brunswick, 1958); and Crosswell Bowen, *The Curse of the Misbegotten* (New York, 1959). Agnes Boulton's *Part of a Long Story* (New York, 1958) is the memoirs of O'Neill's second wife. The standard biography is Arthur and Barbara Gelb, *O'Neill* (New York, 1962).

The most important collection of criticism is *O'Neill and His Plays* (New York, 1961), ed. by Oscar Cargill, N. Bryllion Fagin, and William J. Fisher; this volume also contains extensive bibliographical material.

Desire Under the Elms

CHARACTERS

EPHRAIM CABOT

SIMEON
PETER } *His sons*
EBEN

ABBIE PUTNAM

Young Girl, Two Farmers, The Fiddler, A Sheriff, and other folk from the neighboring farms.

The action of the entire play takes place in, and immediately outside of, the Cabot farmhouse in New England, in the year 1850. The south end of the house faces front to a stone wall with a wooden gate at center opening on a country road. The house is in good condition but in need of paint. Its walls are a sickly grayish, the green of the shutters faded. Two enormous elms are on each side of the house. They bend their trailing branches down over the roof. They appear to protect and at the same time subdue. There is a sinister maternity in their aspect, a crushing, jealous absorption. They have developed from their intimate contact with the life of man in the house an appalling humaneness. They brood oppressively over the house. They are like exhausted women resting their sagging breasts and hands and hair on its roof, and when it rains their tears trickle down monotonously and rot on the shingles.

There is a path running from the gate around the right corner of the house to the front door. A narrow porch is on this side. The end wall facing us has two windows in its upper story, two larger ones on the floor below. The two upper are those of the father's bedroom and that of the brothers. On the left, ground floor, is the kitchen—on the right, the parlor, the shades of which are always drawn down.

PART ONE—SCENE ONE

Exterior of the Farmhouse. It is sunset of a day at the beginning of summer in the year 1850. There is no wind and everything is still. The sky above the roof is suffused with deep colors, the green of the elms glows, but the house is in shadow, seeming pale and washed out by contrast.

A door opens and EBEN CABOT *comes to the end of the porch and stands looking down the road to the right. He has a large bell in his hand and this he swings mechanically, awakening a deafening clangor. Then he puts his hands on his hips and stares up at the sky. He sighs with a puzzled awe and blurts out with halting appreciation.*

EBEN. God! Purty! (*His eyes fall and he stares about him frowningly.*

He is twenty-five, tall and sinewy. His face is well-formed, good-looking, but its expression is resentful and defensive. His defiant, dark eyes remind one of a wild animal's in captivity. Each day is a cage in which he finds himself trapped but inwardly unsubdued. There is a fierce repressed vitality about him. He has black hair, mustache, a thin curly trace of beard. He is dressed in rough farm clothes.

He spits on the ground with intense disgust, turns and goes back into the house.

SIMEON *and* PETER *come in from their work in the fields. They are tall men, much older than their half-brother* [SIMEON *is thirty-nine and* PETER *thirty-seven*], *built on a squarer, simpler model, fleshier in body, more bovine and homelier in face, shrewder and more practical. Their shoulders stoop a bit from years of farm work. They clump heavily along in their clumsy thick-soled boots caked with earth. Their clothes, their faces, hands, bare arms and throats are earth-stained. They smell of earth. They stand together for a moment in front of the house and, as if with the one impulse, stare dumbly up at the sky, leaning on their hoes. Their faces have a compressed, unresigned expression. As they look upward, this softens*).

SIMEON. (*grudgingly*) Purty.

PETER. Ay-eh.

SIMEON. (*suddenly*) Eighteen year ago.

PETER. What?

SIMEON. Jenn. My woman. She died.

PETER. I'd fergot.

SIMEON. I rec'lect—now an' agin. Makes it lonesome. She'd hair long's a hoss' tail—an' yaller like gold!

PETER. Waal—she's gone. (*This with indifferent finality—then after a pause*) They's gold in the West, Sim.

SIMEON. (*still under the influence of sunset—vaguely*) In the sky?

PETER. Waal—in a manner o' speakin'—thar's the promise. (*Growing excited*) Gold in the sky—in the West—Golden Gate—Californi-a!—Goldest West!—fields o' gold!

SIMEON. (*excited in his turn*) Fortunes layin' just atop o' the ground waitin' t' be picked! Solomon's mines, they says! (*For a moment they continue looking up at the sky—then their eyes drop*).

PETER. (*with sardonic bitterness*) Here—it's stones atop o' the ground—stones atop o' stones—makin' stone walls—year atop o' year—him 'n' yew 'n' me 'n' then Eben—makin' stone walls fur him to fence us in!

SIMEON. We've wuked. Give our strength. Give our years. Plowed 'em under in the ground,—(*he stamps rebelliously*)—rottin'—makin' soil for his crops! (*A pause*) Waal—the farm pays good for hereabouts.

PETER. If we plowed in Californi-a, they'd be lumps o' gold in the furrow!

SIMEON. Californi-a's t'other side o' earth, a'most. We got t' calc'late—

PETER. (*after a pause*) 'Twould be hard fur me, too, to give up what we've 'arned here by our sweat. (*A pause.* EBEN *sticks his head out of the dining-room window, listening*).

SIMEON. Ay-eh. (*A pause*) Mebbe—he'll die soon.

PETER. (*doubtfully*) Mebbe.

SIMEON. Mebbe—fur all we knows—he's dead now.

PETER. Ye'd need proof.

SIMEON. He's been gone two months—with no word.

PETER. Left us in the fields an evenin' like this. Hitched up an' druv off into the West. That's plum onnateral. He hain't never been off this farm 'ceptin' t' the village in thirty year or more, not since he married Eben's maw. (*A pause. Shrewdly*) I calc'late we might git him declared crazy by the court.

SIMEON. He skinned 'em too slick. He got the best o' all on 'em. They'd never b'lieve him crazy. (*A pause*) We got t' wait—till he's under ground.

EBEN. (*with a sardonic chuckle*) Honor thy father! (*They turn, startled, and stare at him. He grins, then scowls*) I pray he's died. (*They stare at him. He continues matter-of-factly*) Supper's ready.

SIMEON *and* PETER. (*together*) Ay-eh.

EBEN. (*gazing up at the sky*) Sun's downin' purty.

SIMEON *and* PETER. (*together*) Ay-eh. They's gold in the West.

EBEN. Ay-eh. (*Pointing*) Yonder atop o' the hill pasture, ye mean?

SIMEON *and* PETER. (*together*) In Californi-a!

EBEN. Hunh? (*Stares at them indifferently for a second, then drawls*) Waal—supper's gittin' cold. (*He turns back into kitchen*).

SIMEON. (*startled—smacks his lips*) I air hungry!

PETER. (*sniffing*) I smells bacon!

SIMEON. (*with hungry appreciation*) Bacon's good!

PETER. (*in same tone*) Bacon's bacon! (*They turn, shouldering each other, their bodies bumping and rubbing together as they hurry clumsily to their food, like two friendly oxen toward their evening meal. They disappear around the right corner of house and can be heard entering the door*).

CURTAIN

SCENE TWO

The color fades from the sky. Twilight begins. The interior of the kitchen is now visible. A pine table is at center, a cookstove in the right rear corner, four rough wooden chairs, a tallow candle on the table. In the middle of the rear wall is fastened a big advertising poster with a ship in full sail and the word "California" in big letters. Kitchen utensils hang from nails. Everything is neat and in order but the atmosphere is of a men's camp kitchen rather than that of a home.

Places for three are laid. EBEN *takes boiled potatoes and bacon from the stove and puts them on the table, also a loaf of bread and a crock of water.* SIMEON *and* PETER *shoulder in, slump down in their chairs without a word.* EBEN *joins them. The three eat in silence for a moment, the two elder as naturally unrestrained as beasts of the field,* EBEN *picking at his food without appetite, glancing at them with a tolerant dislike.*

SIMEON. (*suddenly turns to* EBEN) Looky here! Ye'd oughtn't t' said that, Eben.

PETER. 'Twa'n't righteous.

EBEN. What?

SIMEON. Ye prayed he'd died.

EBEN. Waal—don't yew pray it? (*A pause.*)

PETER. He's our Paw.

EBEN. (*violently*) Not mine!

SIMEON. (*dryly*) Ye'd not let no one else say that about yer Maw! Ha! (*He gives one abrupt sardonic guffaw.* PETER *grins*).

EBEN. (*very pale*) I meant—I hain't his'n—I hain't like him—he hain't me!

PETER. (*dryly*) Wait till ye've growed his age!

EBEN. (*intensely*) I'm Maw—every drop o' blood! (*A pause. They stare at him with indifferent curiosity*).

PETER. (*reminiscently*) She was good t' Sim 'n' me. A good Stepmaw's scurse.

SIMEON. She was good t' everyone.

EBEN. (*greatly moved, gets to his feet and makes an awkward bow to each of them—stammering*) I be thankful t' ye. I'm her—her heir. (*He sits down in confusion*).

PETER. (*after a pause—judicially*) She was good even t' him.

EBEN. (*fiercely*) An' fur thanks he killed her!

SIMEON. (*after a pause*) No one never kills nobody. It's allus somethin'. That's the murderer.

EBEN. Didn't he slave Maw t' death?

PETER. He's slaved himself t' death. He's slaved Sim 'n' me 'n' yew t' death—on'y none o' us hain't died—yit.

SIMEON. It's somethin'—drivin' him—t' drive us!

EBEN. (*vengefully*) Waal—I hold him t' jedgment! (*Then scornfully*) Somethin'! What's somethin'?

SIMEON. Dunno.

EBEN. (*sardonically*) What's drivin' yew to Californi-a, mebbe? (*They look at him in surprise*) Oh, I've heerd ye! (*Then, after a pause*) But ye'll never go t' the gold fields!

PETER. (*assertively*) Mebbe!

EBEN. Whar'll ye git the money?

PETER. We kin walk. It's an a'mighty ways—Californi-a—but if yew was t' put all the steps we've walked on this farm end t' end we'd be in the moon!

EBEN. The Injuns'll skulp ye on the plains.

SIMEON. (*with grim humor*) We'll mebbe make 'em pay a hair fur a hair!

EBEN. (*decisively*) But t'aint that. Ye won't never go because ye'll wait here fur yer share o' the farm, thinkin' allus he'll die soon.

SIMEON. (*after a pause*) We've a right.

PETER. Two-thirds belongs t'us.

EBEN. (*jumping to his feet*) Ye've no right! She wa'n't yewr Maw! It was her farm! Didn't he steal it from her? She's dead. It's my farm.

SIMEON. (*sardonically*) Tell that t' Paw—when he comes! I'll bet ye a dollar he'll laugh—fur once in his life. Ha! (*He laughs himself in one single mirthless bark*).

PETER. (*amused in turn, echoes his brother*) Ha!

SIMEON. (*after a pause*) What've ye got held agin us, Eben? Year arter year it's skulked in yer eye—somethin'.

PETER. Ay-eh.

EBEN. Ay-eh. They's somethin'. (*Suddenly exploding*) Why didn't ye never stand between him 'n' my Maw when he was slavin' her to her grave—t' pay her back fur the kindness she done t' yew? (*There is a long pause. They stare at him in surprise*).

SIMEON. Waal—the stock'd got t' be watered.

PETER. 'R they was woodin' t' do.

SIMEON. 'R plowin'.

PETER. 'R hayin'.

SIMEON. 'R spreadin' manure.

PETER. 'R weedin'.

SIMEON. 'R prunin'.

PETER. 'R milkin'.

EBEN. (*breaking in harshly*) An' makin' walls—stone atop o' stone—makin' walls till yer heart's a stone ye heft up out o' the way o' growth onto a stone wall t' wall in yer heart!

SIMEON. (*matter-of-factly*) We never had no time t' meddle.

PETER. (*to* EBEN) Yew was fifteen afore yer Maw died—an' big fur yer age. Why didn't ye never do nothin'?

EBEN. (*harshly*) They was chores t' do, wa'n't they? (*A pause—then slowly*) It was on'y arter she died I come to think o' it. Me cookin'—doin' her work—that made me know her, suffer her sufferin'—she'd come back t' help—come back t' bile potatoes—come back t' fry bacon—come back t' bake biscuits—come back all cramped up t' shake the fire, an' carry ashes, her eyes weepin' an' bloody with smoke an' cinders same's they used t' be. She still comes back—stands by the stove thar in the evenin'—she can't find it nateral sleepin' an' restin' in peace. She can't git used t' bein' free—even in her grave.

SIMEON. She never complained none.

EBEN. She'd got too tired. She'd got too used t' bein' too tired. That was what he done. (*With vengeful passion*) An' sooner'r later, I'll meddle. I'll say the thin's I didn't say then t' him! I'll yell 'em at the top o' my lungs. I'll see t' it my Maw gits some rest an' sleep in her grave! (*He sits down again, relapsing into a brooding silence. They look at him with a queer indifferent curiosity*).

PETER. (*after a pause*) Whar in tarnation d'ye s'pose he went, Sim?

SIMEON. Dunno. He druv off in the buggy, all spick an' span, with the mare all breshed an' shiny, druv off clackin' his tongue an' wavin' his whip. I remember it right well. I was finishin' plowin', it was spring an' May an' sunset, an' gold in the West, an' he druv off into it. I yells "Whar ye goin', Paw?" an' he hauls up by the stone wall a jiffy. His old snake's eyes was glitterin' in the sun like he'd been drinkin' a jugful an' he says with a mule's grin: "Don't ye run away till I come back!"

PETER. Wonder if he knowed we was wantin' fur Californi-a?

SIMEON. Mebbe. I didn't say nothin' and he says, lookin' kinder queer an' sick: "I been hearin' the hens cluckin' an' the roosters crowin' all the durn day. I been listenin' t' the cows lowin' an' everythin' else kickin' up till I can't stand it no more. It's spring an' I'm feelin' damned," he says. "Damned like an old bare hickory tree fit on'y fur burnin'," he says. An' then I calc'late I must've looked a mite hopeful, fur he adds real spry and vicious: "But don't git no fool idee I'm dead. I've sworn t' live a hundred an' I'll do it, if on'y t' spite yer sinful greed! An' now I'm ridin' out t' learn God's message t' me in the spring, like the prophets done. An' yew git back t' yer plowin'," he says. An' he druv off singin' a hymn. I thought he was drunk—'r I'd stopped him goin'.

EBEN. (*scornfully*) No, ye wouldn't! Ye're scared o' him. He's stronger —inside—than both o' ye put together!

PETER. (*sardonically*) An' yew—be yew Samson?

EBEN. I'm gittin' stronger. I kin feel it growin' in me—growin' an' growin'—till it'll bust out—! (*He gets up and puts on his coat and a hat. They watch him, gradually breaking into grins.* EBEN *avoids their eyes sheepishly*) I'm goin' out fur a spell—up the road.

PETER. T' the village?

SIMEON. T' see Minnie?

EBEN. (*defiantly*) Ay-eh!

PETER. (*jeeringly*) The Scarlet Woman!

SIMEON. Lust—that's what's growin' in ye!

EBEN. Waal—she's purty!

PETER. She's been purty fur twenty year!

SIMEON. A new coat o' paint'll make a heifer out of forty.

EBEN. She hain't forty!

PETER. If she hain't, she's teeterin' on the edge.

EBEN. (*desperately*) What d'yew know—

PETER. All they is . . . Sim knew her—an' then me arter—

SIMEON. An' Paw kin tell yew somethin' too! He was fust!

EBEN. D'ye mean t' say he . . . ?

SIMEON. (*with a grin*) Ay-eh! We air his heirs in everythin'!

EBEN. (*intensely*) That's more to it! That grows on it! It'll bust soon! (*Then violently*) I'll go smash my fist in her face! (*He pulls open the door in rear violently*).

SIMEON. (*with a wink at* PETER—*drawlingly*) Mebbe—but the night's wa'm—purty—by the time ye git thar mebbe ye'll kiss her instead!

PETER. Sart'n he will! (*They both roar with coarse laughter.* EBEN *rushes out and slams the door—then the outside front door—comes around the corner of the house and stands still by the gate, staring up at the sky*).

SIMEON. (*looking after him*) Like his Paw.

PETER. Dead spit an' image!

SIMEON. Dog'll eat dog!

PETER. Ay-eh. (*Pause. With yearning*) Mebbe a year from now we'll be in Californi-a.

SIMEON. Ay-eh. (*A pause. Both yawn*) Let's git t'bed. (*He blows out the candle. They go out door in rear.* EBEN *stretches his arms up to the sky—rebelliously*).

EBEN. Waal—thar's a star, an' somewhar's they's him, an' here's me, an' thar's Min up the road—in the same night. What if I does kiss her? She's like t'night, she's soft 'n' wa'm, her eyes kin wink like a star, her mouth's wa'm, her arms're wa'm, she smells like a wa'm plowed field, she's purty . . . Ay-eh! By God A'mighty she's purty, an' I don't give a damn how many sins she's sinned afore mine or who she's sinned 'em with, my sin's as purty as any one on 'em (*He strides off down the road to the left*).

SCENE THREE

It is the pitch darkness just before dawn. EBEN *comes in from the left and goes around to the porch, feeling his way, chuckling bitterly and cursing half-aloud to himself.*

EBEN. The cussed old miser! (*He can be heard going in the front door. There is a pause as he goes upstairs, then a loud knock on the bedroom door of the brothers*) Wake up!

SIMEON. (*startedly*) Who's thar?

EBEN. (*pushing open the door and coming in, a lighted candle in his hand. The bedroom of the brothers is revealed. Its ceiling is the sloping roof. They can stand upright only close to the center dividing wall of the *upstairs.* SIMEON *and* PETER *are in a double bed front.* EBEN'S *cot is to the rear.* EBEN *has a mixture of silly grin and vicious scowl on his face)* I be!

PETER. (*angrily*) What in hell's fire . . . ?

EBEN. I got news fur ye! Ha! (*He gives one abrupt sardonic guffaw*).

SIMEON. (*angrily*) Couldn't ye hold it 'til we'd got our sleep?

EBEN. It's nigh sunup. (*Then explosively*) He's gone an' married agen!

SIMEON *and* PETER. (*explosively*) Paw?

EBEN. Got himself hitched to a female 'bout thirty-five—an' purty, they says . . .

SIMEON. (*aghast*) It's a durn lie!

PETER. Who says?

SIMEON. They been stringin' ye!

EBEN. Think I'm a dunce, do ye? The hull village says. The preacher from New Dover, he brung the news—told it t'our preacher—New Dover, that's whar the old loon got himself hitched—that's whar the woman lived—

PETER. (*no longer doubting—stunned*) Waal . . . !

SIMEON. (*the same*) Waal . . . !

EBEN. (*sitting down on a bed—with vicious hatred*) Ain't he a devil out o' hell? It's just t' spite us—the damned old mule!

PETER. (*after a pause*) Everythin'll go t' her now.

SIMEON. Ay-eh. (*A pause—dully*) Waal—if it's done—

PETER. It's done us. (*Pause—then persuasively*) They's gold in the fields o' Californi-a, Sim. No good a-stayin' here now.

SIMEON. Jest what I was a-thinkin'. (*Then with decision*) S'well fust's last! Let's light out and git this mornin'.

PETER. Suits me.

EBEN. Ye must like walkin'.

SIMEON. (*sardonically*) If ye'd grow wings on us we'd fly thar!

EBEN. Ye'd like ridin' better—on a boat, wouldn't ye? (*Fumbles in his pocket and takes out a crumpled sheet of foolscap*) Waal, if ye sign this ye kin ride on a boat. I've had it writ out an' ready in case ye'd ever go. It says fur three hundred dollars t' each ye agree yewr shares o' the farm is sold t' me. (*They look suspiciously at the paper. A pause*).

SIMEON. (*wonderingly*) But if he's hitched agen—

PETER. An' whar'd yew git that sum o' money, anyways?

EBEN. (*cunningly*) I know whar it's hid. I been waitin'—Maw told me. She knew whar it lay fur years, but she was waitin' . . . It's her'n—the money he hoarded from her farm an' hid from Maw. It's my money by rights now.

PETER. Whar's it hid?

EBEN. (*cunningly*) Whar yew won't never find it without me. Maw spied on him—'r she'd never knowed. (*A pause. They look at him suspiciously, and he at them*) Waal, is it fa'r trade?

SIMEON. Dunno.

PETER. Dunno.

SIMEON. (*looking at window*) Sky's grayin'.

PETER. Ye better start the fire, Eben.

SIMEON. An' fix some vittles.

EBEN. Ay-eh. (*Then with a forced jocular heartiness*) I'll git ye a good one. If ye're startin' t' hoof it t' Californi-a ye'll need somethin' that'll stick t' yer ribs. (*He turns to the door, adding meaningly*) But ye kin ride on a boat if ye'll swap. (*He stops at the door and pauses. They stare at him*).

SIMEON. (*suspiciously*) Whar was ye all night?

EBEN. (*defiantly*) Up t' Min's. (*Then slowly*) Walkin' thar, fust I felt 's if I'd kiss her; then I got a-thinkin' o' what ye'd said o' him an' her an' I says, I'll bust her nose fur that! Then I got t' the village an' heerd the news an' I got madder'n hell an' run all the way t' Min's not knowin' what I'd do—(*He pauses—then sheepishly but more defiantly*) Waal—when I seen her, I didn't hit her—nor I didn't kiss her nuther—I begun t' beller like a calf an' cuss at the same time, I was so durn mad—an' she got scared—an' I jest grabbed holt an' tuk her! (*Proudly*) Yes, sirree! I tuk her. She may've been his'n—an' your'n, too—but she's mine now!

SIMEON. (*dryly*) In love, air yew?

EBEN. (*with lofty scorn*) Love! I don't take no stock in sech slop!

PETER. (*winking at* SIMEON) Mebbe Eben's aimin' t' marry, too.

SIMEON. Min'd make a true faithful he'pmeet! (*They snicker*).

EBEN. What do I care fur her—'ceptin' she's round an' wa'm? The p'int is she was his'n—an' now she b'longs t' me! (*He goes to the door—then turns—rebelliously*) An' Min hain't sech a bad un. They's worse'n Min in the world, I'll bet ye! Wait'll we see this cow the Old Man's hitched t'! She'll beat Min, I got a notion! (*He starts to go out*).

SIMEON. (*suddenly*) Mebbe ye'll try t' make her your'n, too?

PETER. Ha! (*He gives a sardonic laugh of relish at this idea*).

EBEN. (*spitting with disgust*) Her—here—sleepin' with him—stealin' my Maw's farm! I'd as soon pet a skunk 'r kiss a snake! (*He goes out. The two stare after him suspiciously. A pause. They listen to his steps receding*).

PETER. He's startin' the fire.

SIMEON. I'd like t' ride t' Californi-a—but—

PETER. Min might o' put some scheme in his head.

SIMEON. Mebbe it's all a lie 'bout Paw marryin'. We'd best wait an' see the bride.

PETER. An' don't sign nothin' till we does!

SIMEON. Nor till we've tested it's good money! (*Then with a grin*) But if Paw's hitched we'd be sellin' Eben somethin' we'd never git nohow!

PETER. We'll wait an' see. (*Then with sudden vindictive anger*) An' till he comes, let's yew 'n' me not wuk a lick, let Eben tend to thin's if he's a mind t', let's us jest sleep an' eat an drink likker, an' let the hull damned farm go t' blazes!

SIMEON. (*excitedly*) By God, we've 'arned a rest! We'll play rich fur a change. I hain't a-going to stir outa bed till breakfast's ready.

PETER. An' on the table!

SIMEON. (*after a pause—thoughtfully*) What d'ye calc'late she'll be like—our new Maw? Like Eben thinks?

PETER. More'n' likely.

SIMEON. (*vindictively*) Waal—I hope she's a she-devil that'll make him wish he was dead an' livin' in the pit o' hell fur comfort!

PETER. (*fervently*) Amen!

SIMEON. (*imitating his father's voice*) "I'm ridin' out t' learn God's message t' me in the spring like the prophets done," he says. I'll bet right then an' thar he knew plumb well he was goin' whorin', the stinkin' old hypocrite!

SCENE FOUR

Same as Scene Two—shows the interior of the kitchen with a lighted candle on table. It is gray dawn outside. SIMEON *and* PETER *are just finishing their breakfast.* EBEN *sits before his plate of untouched food, brooding frowningly.*

PETER. (*glancing at him rather irritably*) Lookin' glum don't help none.

SIMEON. (*sarcastically*) Sorrowin' over his lust o' the flesh!

PETER. (*with a grin*) Was she yer fust?

EBEN. (*angrily*) None o' yer business. (*A pause*) I was thinkin' o' him. I got a notion he's gittin' near—I kin feel him comin' on like yew kin feel malaria chill afore it takes ye.

PETER. It's too early yet.

SIMEON. Dunno. He'd like t' catch us nappin'—jest t' have somethin' t' hoss us 'round over.

PETER. (*mechanically gets to his feet.* SIMEON *does the same*) Waal—let's git t' wuk. (*They both plod mechanically toward the door before they realize. Then they stop short*).

SIMEON. (*grinning*) Ye're a cussed fool, Pete—and I be wuss! Let him see we hain't wukin'! We don't give a durn!

PETER. (*as they go back to the table*) Not a damned durn! It'll serve t' show him we're done with him. (*They sit down again.* EBEN *stares from one to the other with surprise*).

SIMEON. (*grins at him*) We're aimin' t' start bein' lilies o' the field.

PETER. Nary a toil 'r spin 'r lick o' wuk do we put in!

SIMEON. Ye're sole owner—till he comes—that's what ye wanted. Waal, ye got t' be sole hand, too.

PETER. The cows air bellerin'. Ye better hustle at the milkin'.

EBEN. (*with excited joy*) Ye mean ye'll sign the paper?

SIMEON. (*dryly*) Mebbe.

PETER. Mebbe.

SIMEON. We're considerin'. (*Peremptorily*) Ye better git t' wuk.

EBEN. (*with queer excitement*) It's Maw's farm agen! It's my farm! Them's my cows! I'll milk my durn fingers off fur cows o' mine! (*He goes out door in rear, they stare after him indifferently*).

SIMEON. Like his Paw.

PETER. Dead spit 'n' image!

SIMEON. Waal—let dog eat dog! (EBEN *comes out of front door and around the corner of the house. The sky is beginning to grow flushed with sunrise.* EBEN *stops by the gate and stares around him with glowing, possessive eyes. He takes in the whole farm with his embracing glance of desire*).

EBEN. It's purty! It's damned purty! It's mine! (*He suddenly throws his head back boldly and glares with hard, defiant eyes at the sky*) Mine, d'ye hear? Mine! (*He turns and walks quickly off left, rear, toward the barn. The two brothers light their pipes*).

SIMEON. (*putting his muddy boots up on the table, tilting back his chair, and puffing defiantly*) Waal—this air solid comfort—fur once.

PETER. Ay-eh. (*He follows suit. A pause. Unconsciously they both sigh*).

SIMON. (*suddenly*) He never was much o' a hand at milkin', Eben wa'n't.

PETER. (*with a snort*) His hands air like hoofs! (*A pause*).

SIMEON. Reach down the jug thar! Let's take a swaller. I'm feelin' kind o' low.

PETER. Good idee! (*He does so—gets two glasses—they pour out drinks of whisky*) Here's t' the gold in Californi-a!

SIMEON. An' luck t' find it! (*They drink—puff resolutely—sigh—take their feet down from the table*).

PETER. Likker don't pear t' sot right.

SIMEON. We hain't used t' it this early. (*A pause. They become very restless*).

PETER. Gittin' close in this kitchen.

SIMEON. (*with immense relief*) Let's git a breath o' air. (*They arise briskly and go out rear—appear around house and stop by the gate. They stare up at the sky with a numbed appreciation*).

PETER. Purty!

SIMEON. Ay-eh. Gold's t' the East now.

PETER. Sun's startin' with us fur the Golden West.

SIMEON. (*staring around the farm, his compressed face tightened, unable to conceal his emotion*) Waal—it's our last mornin'—mebbe.

PETER. (*the same*) Ay-eh.

SIMEON. (*stamps his foot on the earth and addresses it desperately*) Waal—ye've thirty year o' me buried in ye—spread out over ye—blood an' bone an' sweat—rotted away—fertilizin' ye—richin' yer soul—prime manure, by God, that's what I been t' ye!

PETER. Ay-eh! An' me!

SIMEON. An' yew, Peter. (*He sighs—then spits*) Waal—no use'n cryin' over split milk.

PETER. They's gold in the West—an' freedom, mebbe. We been slaves t' stone walls here.

SIMEON. (*defiantly*) We hain't nobody's slaves from this out—nor no thin's slaves nuther. (*A pause—restlessly*) Speakin' o' milk, wonder how Eben's managin'?

PETER. I s'pose he's managin'.

SIMEON. Mebbe we'd ought t' help—this once.

PETER. Mebbe. The cows knows us.

SIMEON. An' likes us. They don't know him much.

PETER. An' the hosses, an' pigs, an' chickens. They don't know him much.

SIMEON. They knows us like brothers—an' likes us! (*Proudly*) Hain't we raised 'em t' be fust-rate, number one prize stock?

PETER. We hain't—not no more.

SIMEON. (*dully*) I was fergittin'. (*Then resignedly*) Waal, let's go help Eben a spell an' git waked up.

PETER. Suits me. (*They are starting off down left, rear, for the barn when* EBEN *appears from there hurrying toward them, his face excited*).

EBEN. (*breathlessly*) Waal—har they be! The old mule an' the bride! I seen 'em from the barn down below at the turnin'.

PETER. How could ye tell that far?

EBEN. Hain't I as far-sight as he's near-sight? Don't I know the mare 'n' buggy, an' two people settin' in it? Who else . . . ? An' I tell ye I kin feel 'em a-comin', too! (*He squirms as if he had the itch*).

PETER. (*beginning to be angry*) Waal—let him do his own unhitchin'!

SIMEON. (*angry in his turn*) Let's hustle in an' git our bundles an' be a-goin' as he's a-comin'. I don't want never t' step inside the door agen arter he's back. (*They both start back around the corner of the house.* EBEN *follows them*).

EBEN. (*anxiously*) Will ye sign it afore ye go?

PETER. Let's see the color o' the old skinflint's money an' we'll sign. (*They disappear left. The two brothers clump upstairs to get their bundles.* EBEN *appears in the kitchen, runs to window, peers out, comes back and pulls up a strip of flooring in under stove, takes out a canvas bag and puts it on table, then sets the floorboard back in place. The two brothers appear a moment after. They carry old carpet bags*).

EBEN. (*puts his hand on bag guardingly*) Have ye signed?

SIMEON. (*shows paper in his hand*) Ay-eh. (*Greedily*) Be that the money?

EBEN. (*opens bag and pours out pile of twenty-dollar gold pieces*) Twenty-dollar pieces—thirty on 'em. Count 'em. (PETER *does so, arranging them in stacks of five, biting one or two to test them*).

PETER. Six hundred. (*He puts them in bag and puts it inside his shirt carefully*).

SIMEON. (*handing paper to* EBEN) Har ye be.

EBEN. (*after a glance, folds it carefully and hides it under his shirt—gratefully*) Thank yew.

PETER. Thank yew fur the ride.

SIMEON. We'll send ye a lump o' gold fur Christmas. (*A pause.* EBEN *stares at them and they at him*).

PETER. (*awkwardly*) Waal—we're a-goin'.

SIMEON. Comin' out t' the yard?

EBEN. No. I'm waitin' in here a spell. (*Another silence. The brothers edge awkwardly to door in rear—then turn and stand*).

SIMEON. Waal—good-by.

PETER. Good-by.

EBEN. Good-by. (*They go out. He sits down at the table, faces the stove and pulls out the paper. He looks from it to the stove. His face, lighted up by the shaft of sunlight from the window, has an expression of trance. His lips move. The two brothers come out to the gate*).

PETER. (*looking off toward barn*) Thar he be—unhitchin'.

SIMEON. (*with a chuckle*) I'll bet ye he's riled!

PETER. An' thar she be.

SIMEON. Let's wait 'n' see what our new Maw looks like.

PETER. (*with a grin*) An' give him our partin' cuss!

SIMEON. (*grinning*) I feel like raisin' fun. I feel light in my head an' feet.

PETER. Me, too. I feel like laffin' till I'd split up the middle.

SIMEON. Reckon it's the likker?

PETER. No. My feet feel itchin' t' walk an' walk—an' jump high over thin's—an'. . . .

SIMEON. Dance? (*A pause*).

PETER. (*puzzled*) It's plumb onnateral.

SIMEON. (*a light coming over his face*) I calc'late it's 'cause school's out. It's holiday. Fur once we're free!

PETER. (*dazedly*) Free?

SIMEON. The halter's broke—the harness is busted—the fence bars is down—the stone walls air crumblin' an' tumblin'! We'll be kickin' up an' tearin' away down the road!

PETER. (*drawing a deep breath—oratorically*) Anybody that wants this stinkin' old rock-pile of a farm kin hev it. T'ain't our'n, no sirree!

SIMEON. (*takes the gate off its hinges and puts it under his arm*) We harby 'bolishes shet gates, an' open gates, an' all gates, by thunder!

PETER. We'll take it with us fur luck an' let 'er sail free down some river.

SIMEON. (*as a sound of voices comes from left, rear*) Har they comes! (*The two brothers congeal into two stiff, grim-visaged statues.* EPHRAIM CABOT *and* ABBIE PUTNAM *come in.* CABOT *is seventy-five, tall and gaunt, with great, wiry, concentrated power, but stoop-shouldered from toil. His face is as hard as if it were hewn out of a boulder, yet there is a weakness in it, a petty pride in its own narrow strength. His eyes are small, close together, and extremely near-sighted, blinking continually in the effort to focus on objects, their stare having a straining, ingrowing quality. He is dressed in his dismal black Sunday suit.* ABBIE *is thirty-five, buxom, full of vitality. Her round face is pretty but marred by its rather gross sensuality. There is strength and obstinacy in her jaw, a hard determination in her eyes, and about her whole personality the same unsettled, untamed, desperate quality which is so apparent in* EBEN).

CABOT. (*as they enter—a queer strangled emotion in his dry cracking voice*) Har we be t' hum, Abbie.

ABBIE. (*with lust for the word*) Hum! (*Her eyes gloating on the house without seeming to see the two stiff figures at the gate*) It's purty—purty! I can't b'lieve it's r'ally mine.

CABOT. (*sharply*) Yewr'n? Mine! (*He stares at her penetratingly. She stares back. He adds relentingly*) Our'n—mebbe! It was lonesome too long. I was growin' old in the spring. A hum's got t' hev a woman.

ABBIE. (*her voice taking possession*) A woman's got t' hev a hum!

CABOT. (*nodding uncertainly*) Ay-eh. (*Then irritably*) Whar be they? Ain't thar nobody about—'r wukin'—r' nothin'?

ABBIE. (*sees the brothers. She returns their stare of cold appraising contempt with interest—slowly*) Thar's two men loafin' at the gate an' starin' at me like a couple o' strayed hogs.

CABOT. (*straining his eyes*) I kin see 'em—but I can't make out. . . .

SIMEON. It's Simeon.

PETER. It's Peter.

CABOT. (*exploding*) Why hain't ye wukin'?

SIMEON. (*dryly*) We're waitin' t' welcome ye hum—yew an' the bride!

CABOT. (*confusedly*) Huh? Waal—this be yer new Maw, boys. (*She stares at them and they at her*).

SIMEON. (*turns away and spits contemptuously*) I see her!

PETER. (*spits also*) An' I see her!

ABBIE. (*with the conqueror's conscious superiority*) I'll go in an' look at *my* house. (*She goes slowly around to porch*).

SIMEON. (*with a snort*) *Her* house!

PETER. (*calls after her*) Ye'll find Eben inside. Ye better not tell him it's *yewr* house.

ABBIE. (*mouthing the name*) Eben. (*Then quietly*) I'll tell Eben.

CABOT. (*with a contemptuous sneer*) Ye needn't heed Eben. Eben's a dumb fool—like his Maw—soft an' simple!

SIMEON. (*with his sardonic burst of laughter*) Ha! Eben's a chip o' yew—spit 'n' image—hard 'n' bitter's a hickory tree! Dog'll eat dog. He'll eat ye yet, old man!

CABOT. (*commandingly*) Ye git t' wuk!

SIMEON. (*as* ABBIE *disappears in house—winks at* PETER *and says tauntingly*) So that thar's our new Maw, be it? Whar in hell did ye dig her up? (*He and* PETER *laugh*).

PETER. Ha! Ye'd better turn her in the pen with the other sows. (*They laugh uproariously, slapping their thighs*).

CABOT. (*so amazed at their effrontery that he stutters in confusion*) Simeon! Peter! What's come over ye? Air ye drunk?

SIMEON. We're free, old man—free o' yew an' the hull damned farm! (*They grow more and more hilarious and excited*).

PETER. An' we're startin' out fur the gold fields o' Californi-a!

SIMEON. Ye kin take this place an' burn it!

PETER. An' bury it—fur all we cares!

SIMEON. We're free, old man! (*He cuts a caper*).

PETER. Free! (*He gives a kick in the air*).

SIMEON. (*in a frenzy*) Whoop!

PETER. Whoop! (*They do an absurd Indian war dance about the old man who is petrified between rage and the fear that they are insane*).

SIMEON. We're free as Injuns! Lucky we don't skulp ye!

PETER. An' burn yer barn an' kill the stock!

SIMEON. An' rape yer new woman! Whoop! (*He and* PETER *stop their dance, holding their sides, rocking with wild laughter*).

CABOT. (*edging away*) Lust fur gold—fur the sinful, easy gold o' Californi-a! It's made ye mad!

SIMEON. (*tauntingly*) Wouldn't ye like us to send ye back some sinful gold, ye old sinner?

PETER. They's gold besides what's in Californi-a! (*He retreats back beyond the vision of the old man and takes the bag of money and flaunts it in the air above his head, laughing*).

SIMEON. And sinfuller, too!

PETER. We'll be voyagin' on the sea! Whoop! (*He leaps up and down*).

SIMEON. Livin' free! Whoop! (*He leaps in turn*).

CABOT. (*suddenly roaring with rage*) My cuss on ye!

SIMEON. Take our'n in trade fur it! Whoop!

CABOT. I'll hev ye both chained up in the asylum!

PETER. Ye old skinflint! Good-by!

SIMEON. Ye old blood sucker! Good-by!

CABOT. Go afore I. . . !

PETER. Whoop! (*He picks a stone from the road.* SIMEON *does the same*).

SIMEON. Maw'll be in the parlor.

PETER. Ay-eh! One! Two!

CABOT. (*frightened*) What air ye . . . ?

PETER. Three! (*They both throw, the stones hitting the parlor window with a crash of glass, tearing the shade*).

SIMEON. Whoop!

PETER. Whoop!

CABOT. (*in a fury now, rushing toward them*) If I kin lay hands on ye—I'll break yer bones fur ye! (*But they beat a capering retreat before him,* SIMEON *with the gate still under his arm.* CABOT *comes back, panting with impotent rage. Their voices as they go off take up the song of the gold-seekers to the old tune of "Oh, Susannah!"*

"I jumped aboard the Liza ship,
And traveled on the sea,
And every time I thought of home
I wished it wasn't me!
Oh! Californi-a,
That's the land fur me!
I'm off to Californi-a!
With my wash bowl on my knee."

(*In the meantime, the window of the upper bedroom on right is raised and* ABBIE *sticks her head out. She looks down at* CABOT—*with a sigh of relief*).

ABBIE. Waal—that's the last o' them two, hain't it? (*He doesn't answer. Then in possessive tones*) This here's a nice bedroom, Ephraim. It's a r'al nice bed. Is it my room, Ephraim?

CABOT. (*grimly—without looking up*) Our'n! (*She cannot control a grimace of aversion and pulls back her head slowly and shuts the window. A sudden horrible thought seems to enter* CABOT'S *head*) They been up to somethin'! Mebbe—mebbe they've pizened the stock—'r somethin'! (*He almost runs off down toward the barn. A moment later the kitchen door is slowly pushed open and* ABBIE *enters. For a moment she stands looking at* EBEN. *He does not notice her at first. Her eyes take him in penetratingly with a calculating appraisal of his strength as against hers. But under this her desire is dimly awakened by his youth and good looks. Suddenly he becomes conscious of her presence and looks up. Their eyes meet. He leaps to his feet, glowering at her speechlessly*).

ABBIE. (*in her most seductive tones which she uses all through this scene*) Be you—Eben? I'm Abbie—(*She laughs*) I mean, I'm yer new Maw.

EBEN. (*viciously*) No, damn ye!

ABBIE. (*as if she hadn't heard—with a queer smile*) Yer Paw's spoke a lot o' yew. . . .

EBEN. Ha!

ABBIE. Ye mustn't mind him. He's an old man. (*A long pause. They stare at each other*) I don't want t' pretend playin' Maw t' ye, Eben. (*Admiringly*) Ye're too big an' too strong fur that. I want t' be frens with ye. Mebbe with me fur a fren ye'd find ye'd like livin' here better. I kin make it easy fur ye with him, mebbe. (*With a scornful sense of power*) I calc'late I kin git him t' do most anythin' fur me.

EBEN. (*with bitter scorn*) Ha! (*They stare again,* EBEN *obscurely moved, physically attracted to her—in forced stilted tones)* Yew kin go t' the devil!

ABBIE. (*calmly*) If cussin' me does ye good, cuss all ye've a mind t'. I'm all prepared t' have ye agin me—at fust. I don't blame ye nuther. I'd feel the same at any stranger comin' t' take my Maw's place. (*He shudders. She is watching him carefully*) Yew must've cared a lot fur yewr Maw, didn't ye? My Maw died afore I'd growed. I don't remember her none. (*A pause*) But yew won't hate me long, Eben. I'm not the wust in the world—an' yew an' me've got a lot in common. I kin tell that by lookin' at ye. Waal—I've had a hard life, too—oceans o' trouble an' nuthin' but wuk fur reward. I was a orphan early an' had t' wuk fur others in other folks' hums. Then I married an' he turned out a drunken spreer an' so he had to wuk fur others an' me too agen in other folks' hums, an' the baby died, an' my husband got sick an' died too, an' I was glad sayin' now I'm free fur once, on'y I diskivered right away all I was free fur was t' wuk agen in other folks' hums, doin' other folks' wuk till I'd most give up hope o' ever doin' my own wuk in my own hum, an' then your Paw come. . . . (CABOT *appears returning from the barn. He comes to the gate and looks down the road the brothers have gone. A faint strain of their retreating voices is heard: "Oh, Californi-a! That's the place for me." He stands glowering, his fist clenched, his face grim with rage*).

EBEN. (*fighting against his growing attraction and sympathy—harshly)* An' bought yew—like a harlot! (*She is stung and flushes angrily. She has been sincerely moved by the recital of her troubles. He adds furiously*) An' the price he's payin' ye—this farm—was my Maw's, damn ye!—an' mine now!

ABBIE. (*with a cool laugh of confidence*) Yewr'n? We'll see 'bout that! (*Then strongly*) Waal—what if I did need a hum? What else'd I marry an old man like him fur?

EBEN. (*maliciously*) I'll tell him ye said that!

ABBIE. (*smiling*) I'll say ye're lyin' a-purpose—an' he'll drive ye off the place!

EBEN. Ye devil!

ABBIE. (*defying him*) This be my farm—this be my hum—this be my kitchen—!

EBEN. (*furiously, as if he were going to attack her*) Shut up, damn ye!

ABBIE. (*walks up to him—a queer coarse expression of desire in her face and body—slowly*) An' upstairs—that be my bedroom—an my bed! (*He stares into her eyes, terribly confused and torn. She adds softly*) I hain't bad nor mean—'ceptin' fur an enemy—but I got t' fight fur what's due me out o' life, if I ever 'spect t' git it. (*Then putting her hand on his arm—seductively*) Let's yew 'n' me be frens, Eben.

EBEN. (*stupidly—as if hypnotized*) Ay-eh. (*Then furiously flinging off her arm*) No, ye durned old witch! I hate ye! (*He rushes out the door*).

ABBIE. (*looks after him smiling satisfiedly—then half to herself, mouthing the word*) Eben's nice. (*She looks at the table, proudly*) I'll wash up *my* dishes now. (EBEN *appears outside, slamming the door behind him. He comes around corner, stops on seeing his father, and stands staring at him with hate*).

CABOT. (*raising his arms to heaven in the fury he can no longer control*) Lord God o' Hosts, smite the undutiful sons with Thy wust cuss!

EBEN. (*breaking in violently*) Yew 'n' yewr God! Allus cussin' folks—allus naggin' 'em!

CABOT. (*oblivious to him—summoningly*) God o' the old! God o' the lonesome!

EBEN. (*mockingly*) Naggin' His sheep t' sin! T' hell with yewr God! (CABOT *turns. He and* EBEN *glower at each other*).

CABOT. (*harshly*) So it's yew. I might've knowed it. (*Shaking his finger threateningly at him*) Blasphemin' fool! (*Then quickly*) Why hain't ye t' wuk?

EBEN. Why hain't yew? They've went. I can't wuk it all alone.

CABOT. (*contemptuously*) Nor noways! I'm wuth ten o' ye yit, old's I be! Ye'll never be more'n half a man! (*Then, matter-of-factly*) Waal—let's git t' the barn. (*They go. A last faint note of the "Californi-a" song is heard from the distance.* ABBIE *is washing her dishes*).

CURTAIN

PART TWO—SCENE ONE

The exterior of the farmhouse, as in Part One—a hot Sunday afternoon two months later. ABBIE, *dressed in her best, is discovered sitting in a rocker at the end of the porch. She rocks listlessly, enervated by the heat, staring in front of her with bored, half-closed eyes.*

EBEN *sticks his head out of his bedroom window. He looks around furtively and tries to see—or hear—if anyone is on the porch, but although he has been careful to make no noise,* ABBIE *has sensed his movement. She stops rocking, her face grows animated and eager, she waits attentively.* EBEN *seems to feel her presence, he scowls back his thoughts of her and spits with exaggerated disdain—then withdraws back into the room.* ABBIE *waits, holding her breath as she listens with passionate eagerness for every sound within the house.*

EBEN *comes out. Their eyes meet. His falter, he is confused, he turns away and slams the door resentfully. At this gesture,* ABBIE *laughs tantalizingly, amused but at the same time piqued and irritated. He scowls, strides off the porch to the path and starts to walk past her to the road with a grand swagger of ignoring her existence. He is dressed in his store suit, spruced up, his face shines from soap and water.* ABBIE *leans forward on her chair, her eyes hard and angry now, and, as he passes her, gives a sneering, taunting chuckle.*

EBEN. (*stung—turns on her furiously*) What air yew cacklin' 'bout?

ABBIE. (*triumphant*) Yew!

EBEN. What about me?

ABBIE. Ye look all slicked up like a prize bull.

EBEN. (*with a sneer*) Waal—ye hain't so durned purty yerself, be ye? (*They stare into each other's eyes, his held by hers in spite of himself, hers glowingly possessive. Their physical attraction becomes a palpable force quivering in the hot air*).

ABBIE. (*softly*) Ye don't mean that, Eben. Ye may think ye mean it, mebbe, but ye don't. Ye can't. It's agin nature, Eben. Ye been fightin' yer nature ever since the day I come—tryin' t' tell yerself I hain't purty t'ye. (*She laughs a low humid laugh without taking her eyes from his. A pause—her body squirms desirously—she murmurs languorously*) Hain't the sun strong an' hot? Ye kin feel it burnin' into the earth—Nature—makin' thin's grow—bigger 'n' bigger—burnin' inside ye—makin' ye want to grow—into somethin' else—till ye're jined with it—an' it's your'n—but it owns ye, too—an' makes ye grow bigger—like a tree—like them elums—(*She laughs again softly, holding his eyes. He takes a step toward her, compelled against his will*) Nature'll beat ye, Eben. Ye might's well own up t' it fust 's last.

EBEN. (*trying to break from her spell—confusedly*) If Paw'd hear ye goin' on. . . . (*Resentfully*) But ye've made such a damned idjit out o' the old devil . . . ! (ABBIE *laughs*).

ABBIE. Waal—hain't it easier fur yew with him changed softer?

EBEN. (*defiantly*) No. I'm fightin' him—fightin' yew—fightin' fur Maw's rights t' her hum! (*This breaks her spell for him. He glowers at her*) An' I'm onto ye. Ye hain't foolin' me a mite. Ye're aimin' t' swaller up everythin' an' make it your'n. Waal, you'll find I'm a heap sight bigger hunk nor yew kin chew! (*He turns from her with a sneer*).

ABBIE. (*trying to regain her ascendancy—seductively*) Eben!

EBEN. Leave me be! (*He starts to walk away*).

ABBIE. (*more commandingly*) Eben!

EBEN. (*stops—resentfully*) What d'ye want?

ABBIE. (*trying to conceal a growing excitement*) Whar air ye goin'?

EBEN. (*with malicious nonchalance*) Oh—up the road a spell.

ABBIE. T' the village?

EBEN. (*airily*) Mebbe.

ABBIE. (*excitedly*) T' see that Min, I s'pose?

EBEN. Mebbe.

ABBIE. (*weakly*) What d'ye want t' waste time on her fur?

EBEN. (*revenging himself now—grinning at her*) Ye can't beat Nature, didn't ye say? (*He laughs and again starts to walk away*).

ABBIE. (*bursting out*) An ugly old hake!

EBEN. (*with a tantalizing sneer*) She's purtier'n yew be!

ABBIE. That every wuthless drunk in the country has. . . .

EBEN. (*tauntingly*) Mebbe—but she's better'n yew. She owns up fa'r 'n' squar' t' her doin's.

ABBIE. (*furiously*) Don't ye dare compare. . . .

EBEN. She don't go sneakin' an' stealin'—what's mine.

ABBIE. (*savagely seizing on his weak point*) Your'n? Yew mean—my farm?

EBEN. I mean the farm yew sold yerself fur like any other old whore—my farm!

ABBIE. (*stung—fiercely*) Ye'll never live t' see the day when even a stinkin' weed on it 'll belong t' ye! (*Then in a scream*) Git out o' my sight! Go on t' yer slut—disgracin' yer Paw 'n' me! I'll git yer Paw t' horsewhip ye off the place if I want t'! Ye're only livin' here 'cause I tolerate ye! Git along! I hate the sight o' ye! (*She stops, panting and glaring at him*).

EBEN. (*returning her glance in kind*) An' I hate the sight o' yew! (*He turns and strides off up the road. She follows his retreating figure with concentrated hate. Old* CABOT *appears coming up from the barn. The hard, grim expression of his face has changed. He seems in some queer way softened, mellowed. His eyes have taken on a strange, incongruous dreamy quality. Yet there is no hint of physical weakness about him—rather he looks more robust and younger.* ABBIE *sees him and turns away quickly with unconcealed aversion. He comes slowly up to her*).

CABOT. (*mildly*) War yew an' Eben quarrelin' agen?

ABBIE. (*shortly*) No.

CABOT. Ye was talkin' a'mighty loud. (*He sits down on the edge of porch*).

ABBIE. (*snappishly*) If ye heerd us they hain't no need askin' questions.

CABOT. I didn't hear what ye said.

ABBIE. (*relieved*) Waal—it wa'n't nothin' t' speak on.

CABOT. (*after a pause*) Eben's queer.

ABBIE. (*bitterly*) He's the dead spit 'n' image o' yew!

CABOT. (*queerly interested*) D'ye think so, Abbie? (*After a pause, ruminatingly*) Me 'n' Eben's allus fit 'n' fit. I never could b'ar him noways. He's so thunderin' soft—like his Maw.

ABBIE. (*scornfully*) Ay-eh! 'Bout as soft as yew be!

CABOT. (*as if he hadn't heard*) Mebbe I been too hard on him.

ABBIE. (*jeeringly*) Waal—ye're gittin' soft now—soft as slop! That's what Eben was sayin'.

CABOT. (*his face instantly grim and ominous*) Eben was sayin'? Waal, he'd best not do nothin' t' try me 'r he'll soon diskiver. . . . (*A pause. She keeps her face turned away. His gradually softens. He stares up at the sky*) Purty, hain't it?

ABBIE. (*crossly*) I don't see nothin' purty.

CABOT. The sky. Feels like a wa'm field up thar.

ABBIE. (*sarcastically*) Air yew aimin' t' buy up over the farm too? (*She snickers contemptuously*).

CABOT. (*strangely*) I'd like t' own my place up thar. (*A pause*) I'm gittin' old, Abbie. I'm gittin' ripe on the bough. (*A pause. She stares at him mystified. He goes on*) It's allus lonesome cold in the house—even when it's bilin' hot outside. Hain't yew noticed?

ABBIE. No.

CABOT. It's wa'm down t' the barn—nice smellin' an' warm—with the cows. (*A pause*) Cows is queer.

ABBIE. Like yew?

CABOT. Like Eben. (*A pause*) I'm gittin' t' feel resigned t' Eben—jest as I got t' feel 'bout his Maw. I'm gittin' t' learn to b'ar his softness—jest like her'n. I calc'late I c'd a'most take t' him—if he wa'n't sech a dumb fool! (*A pause*) I s'pose it's old age a-creepin' in my bones.

ABBIE. (*indifferently*) Waal—ye hain't dead yet.

CABOT. (*roused*) No, I hain't, yew bet—not by a hell of a sight—I'm sound 'n' tough as hickory! (*Then moodily*) But arter three score and ten the Lord warns ye t' prepare. (*A pause*) That's why Eben's come in my head. Now that his cussed sinful brothers is gone their path t' hell, they's no one left but Eben.

ABBIE. (*resentfully*) They's me, hain't they? (*Agitatedly*) What's all this sudden likin' ye've tuk to Eben? Why don't ye say nothin' 'bout me? Hain't I yer lawful wife?

CABOT. (*simply*) Ay-eh. Ye be. (*A pause—he stares at her desirously—his eyes grow avid—then with a sudden movement he seizes her hands and squeezes them, declaiming in a queer camp meeting preacher's tempo*) Yew air my Rose o' Sharon! Behold, yew air fair; yer eyes air doves; yer lips air like scarlet; yer two breasts air like two fawns; yer navel be like a round goblet; yer belly be like a heap o' wheat. . . . (*He covers her hand with kisses. She does not seem to notice. She stares before her with hard angry eyes*).

ABBIE. (*jerking her hands away—harshly*) So ye're plannin' t' leave the farm t' Eben, air ye?

CABOT. (*dazedly*) Leave. . . ? (*Then with resentful obstinacy*) I hain't a-givin' it t' no one!

ABBIE. (*remorselessly*) Ye can't take it with ye.

CABOT. (*thinks a moment—then reluctantly*) No, I calc'late not. (*After a pause—with a strange passion*) But if I could, I would, by the Etarnal! 'R if I could, in my dyin' hour, I'd set it afire an' watch it burn—this house an' every ear o' corn an' every tree down t' the last blade o' hay! I'd sit and know it was all a-dying with me and no one else'd ever own what was mine, what I'd made out o' nothin' with my own sweat 'n' blood! (*A pause—then he adds with a queer affection*) 'Ceptin' the cows. Them I'd turn free.

ABBIE. (*harshly*) An' me?

CABOT. (*with a queer smile*) Ye'd be turned free, too.

ABBIE. (*furiously*) So that's the thanks I git fur marryin' ye—t' have ye change kind to Eben who hates ye, an' talk o' turnin' me out in the road.

CABOT. (*hastily*) Abbie! Ye know I wa'n't. . . .

ABBIE (*vengefully*) Just let me tell ye a thing or two 'bout Eben! Whar's he gone? T' see that harlot, Min! I tried fur t' stop him. Disgracin' yew an' me—on the Sabbath, too!

CABOT. (*rather guiltily*) He's a sinner—nateral-born. It's lust eatin' his heart.

ABBIE (*enraged beyond endurance—wildly vindictive*) An' his lust fur me! Kin ye find excuses fur that?

CABOT. (*stares at her—after a dead pause*) Lust—fur yew?

ABBIE. (*defiantly*) He was tryin' t' make love t' me—when ye heerd us quarrelin'.

CABOT. (*stares at her—then a terrible expression of rage comes over his face—he springs to his feet shaking all over*) By the A'mighty God—I'll end him!

ABBIE. (*frightened now for Eben*) No! Don't ye!

CABOT. (*violently*) I'll git the shotgun an' blow his soft brains t' the top o' them elums!

ABBIE. (*throwing her arms around him*) No, Ephraim!

CABOT. (*pushing her away violently*) I will, by God!

ABBIE. (*in a quieting tone*) Listen, Ephraim. 'Twa'n't nothin' bad—on'y a boy's foolin'—'twa'n't meant serious—jest jokin' an teasin'. . . .

CABOT. Then why did ye say—lust?

ABBIE. It must hev sounded wusser'n I meant. An' I was mad at thinkin' —ye'd leave him the farm.

CABOT. (*quieter but still grim and cruel*) Waal then, I'll horsewhip him off the place if that much'll content ye.

ABBIE. (*reaching out and taking his hand*) No. Don't think o' me! Ye mustn't drive him off. 'Tain't sensible. Who'll ye get to help ye on the farm? They's no one hereabouts.

CABOT. (*considers this—then nodding his appreciation*) Ye got a head on ye. (*Then irritably*) Waal, let him stay. (*He sits down on the edge of the porch. She sits beside him. He murmurs contemptuously*) I oughtn't t' git riled so—at that 'ere fool calf. (*A pause*) But har's the p'int. What son o' mine'll keep on here t' the farm—when the Lord does call me? Simeon an' Peter air gone t' hell—an' Eben's follerin' 'em.

ABBIE. They's me.

CABOT. Ye're on'y a woman.

ABBIE. I'm yewr wife.

CABOT. That hain't me. A son is me—my blood—mine. Mine ought t' git mine. An' then it's still mine—even though I be six foot under. D'ye see?

ABBIE. (*giving him a look of hatred*) Ay-eh. I see. (*She becomes very thoughtful, her face growing shrewd, her eyes studying* CABOT *craftily*).

CABOT. I'm gittin' old—ripe on the bough. (*Then with a sudden forced reassurance*) Not but what I hain't a hard nut t' crack even yet—an' fur many a year t' come! By the Etarnal, I kin break most o' the young feller's backs at any kind o' work any day o' the year!

ABBIE. (*suddenly*) Mebbe the Lord'll give *us* a son.

CABOT. (*turns and stares at her eagerly*) Ye mean—a son—t' me 'n' yew?

ABBIE. (*with a cajoling smile*) Ye're a strong man yet, hain't ye? 'Tain't noways impossible, be it? We know that. Why d'ye stare so? Hain't ye never thought o' that afore? I been thinkin' o' it all along. Ay-eh —an' I been prayin' it'd happen, too.

CABOT. (*his face growing full of joyous pride and a sort of religious ecstasy*) Ye been prayin', Abbie?—fur a son?—t' us?

ABBIE. Ay-eh. (*With a grim resolution*) I want a son now.

CABOT. (*excitedly clutching both of her hands in his*) It'd be the blessin' o' God, Abbie—the blessin' o' God A'mighty on me—in my old age—in my lonesomeness! They hain't nothin' I wouldn't do fur ye then, Abbie. Ye'd hev on'y t' ask it—anythin' ye'd a mind t'!

ABBIE. (*interrupting*) Would ye will the farm t' me then—t' me an' it. . . ?

CABOT. (*vehemently*) I'd do anythin' ye axed, I tell ye! I swar it! May I be everlastin' damned t' hell if I wouldn't! (*He sinks to his knees pulling her down with him. He trembles all over with the fervor of his hopes*) Pray t' the Lord agen, Abbie. It's the Sabbath! I'll jine ye! Two prayers air better nor one. "An' God hearkened unto Rachel"! An' God hearkened unto Abbie! Pray, Abbie! Pray fur him to hearken! (*He bows his head, mumbling. She pretends to do likewise but gives him a side glance of scorn and triumph*).

SCENE TWO

About eight in the evening. The interior of the two bedrooms on the top floor is shown. EBEN *is sitting on the side of his bed in the room on the left. On account of the heat he has taken off everything but his undershirt and pants. His feet are bare. He faces front, brooding moodily, his chin propped on his hands, a desperate expression on his face.*

In the other room CABOT *and* ABBIE *are sitting side by side on the edge of their bed, an old four-poster with feather mattress. He is in his night shirt, she in her nightdress. He is still in the queer, excited mood into which the notion of a son has thrown him. Both rooms are lighted dimly and flickeringly by tallow candles.*

CABOT. The farm needs a son.

ABBIE. I need a son.

CABOT. Ay-eh. Sometimes ye air the farm an' sometimes the farm be yew. That's why I clove t' ye in my lonesomeness. (*A pause. He pounds his knee with his fist*) Me an' the farm has got t' beget a son!

ABBIE. Ye'd best go t' sleep. Ye're gittin' thin's all mixed.

CABOT. (*with an impatient gesture*) No, I hain't. My mind's clear's a well. Ye don't know me, that's it. (*He stares hopelessly at the floor*).

ABBIE. (*indifferently*) Mebbe. (*In the next room* EBEN *gets up and paces up and down distractedly.* ABBIE *hears him. Her eyes fasten on the intervening wall with concentrated attention.* EBEN *stops and stares. Their hot glances seem to meet through the wall. Unconsciously he stretches out his arms for her and she half rises. Then aware, he mutters a curse at himself and flings himself face downward on the bed, his clenched fists above his head, his face buried in the pillow.* ABBIE *relaxes with a faint sigh but her eyes remain fixed on the wall; she listens with all her attention for some movement from* EBEN).

CABOT. (*suddenly raises his head and looks at her—scornfully*) Will ye ever know me—'r will any man 'r woman? (*Shaking his head*) No. I calc'late 't wa'n't t' be. (*He turns away.* ABBIE *looks at the wall. Then, evidently unable to keep silent about his thoughts, without looking at his wife, he puts out his hand and clutches her knee. She starts violently, looks at him, sees he is not watching her, concentrates again on the wall and pays no attention to what he says*) Listen, Abbie. When I come here fifty odd year ago—I was jest twenty an' the strongest an' hardest ye ever seen—ten times as strong an' fifty times as hard as Eben. Waal—this place was nothin' but fields o' stones. Folks laughed when I tuk it. They couldn't know what I knowed. When ye kin make corn sprout out o' stones, God's livin' in yew! They wa'n't strong enuf fur that! They reckoned God was easy. They laughed. They don't laugh no more. Some died hereabouts. Some went West an' died. They're all under ground—fur follerin' arter an easy God. God hain't easy. (*He shakes his head slowly*) An' I growed hard. Folks kept allus sayin' he's a hard man like 'twas sinful t' be hard, so's at last I said back at 'em: Waal then, by thunder, ye'll git me hard an' see how ye like it! (*Then suddenly*) But I give in t' weakness once. 'Twas arter I'd been here two year. I got weak—despairful—they was so many stones. They was a party leavin', givin' up, goin' West. I jined 'em. We tracked on 'n' on. We come t' broad medders, plains, whar the soil was black an' rich as gold. Nary a stone. Easy. Ye'd on'y to plow an' sow an' then set an' smoke yer pipe an' watch thin's grow. I could o' been a rich man—but somethin' in me fit me an' fit me—the voice o' God sayin': "This hain't wuth nothin' t' Me. Git ye back t' hum!" I got afeerd o' that voice an' I lit out back t' hum here, leavin' my claim an' crops t' whoever'd a mind t' take 'em. Ay-eh. I actoolly give up what was rightful mine! God's hard, not easy! God's in the stones! Build my church on a rock—out o' stones an' I'll be in them! That's what He meant t' Peter! (*He sighs heavily—a pause*) Stones. I picked 'em up an' piled 'em into walls. Ye kin read the years o' my life in them walls, every day a hefted stone, climbin' over the hills up and down, fencin' in the fields that was mine, whar I'd made thin's grow out o' nothin'—like the will o' God, like the servant o' His hand. It wa'n't easy. It was hard an' He made me hard fur it. (*He pauses*) All the time I kept gittin' lonesomer. I tuk a wife. She bore Simeon an' Peter. She was a good woman. She wuked hard. We was married twenty year. She never knowed me. She helped but she never knowed what she was helpin'. I was allus lonesome. She died. After that it wa'n't so lonesome fur a spell. (*A pause*) I lost count o' the years. I had no time t' fool away countin' 'em. Sim an' Peter helped. The farm growed. It was all mine! When I thought o' that I didn't feel lonesome. (*A pause*) But ye can't hitch yer mind t' one thin' day an' night. I tuk another wife—Eben's Maw. Her folks was contestin' me at law over my deeds t' the farm—my farm! That's why Eben keeps a-talkin' his fool talk o' this bein' his Maw's farm. She bore Eben. She was purty—but soft. She tried t' be hard. She couldn't. She never knowed me nor nothin'. It was lonesomer 'n hell with her. After a matter o' sixteen odd years, she died. (*A pause*) I lived with the boys. They hated me 'cause I was hard. I hated them 'cause they was soft. They coveted the farm without knowin' what it meant. It made me bitter 'n wormwood. It aged me—them coveting what I'd made fur mine. Then this spring the call come—the voice o' God cryin' in my wilderness, in my lonesomeness—t' go out an' seek an' find! (*Turning to her with strange passion*) I sought ye an' I found ye! Yew air my Rose o' Sharon! Yer eyes air like. . . . (*She has turned a blank face, resentful eyes to his. He stares at her for a moment—then harshly*) Air ye any the wiser fur all I've told ye?

ABBIE. (*confusedly*) Mebbe.

CABOT. (*pushing her away from him—angrily*) Ye don't know nothin'—

nor never will. If ye don't hev a son t' redeem ye. . . . (*This in a tone of cold threat*).

ABBIE. (*resentfully*) I've prayed, hain't I?

CABOT. (*bitterly*) Pray agen—fur understandin'!

ABBIE. (*a veiled threat in her tone*) Ye'll have a son out o' me, I promise ye.

CABOT. How kin ye promise?

ABBIE. I got second-sight mebbe. I kin foretell. (*She gives a queer smile*).

CABOT. I believe ye have. Ye give me the chills sometimes. (*He shivers*) It's cold in this house. It's oneasy. They's thin's pokin' about in the dark—in the corners. (*He pulls on his trousers, tucking in his night shirt, and pulls on his boots*).

ABBIE. (*surprised*) Whar air ye goin'?

CABOT (*queerly*) Down whar it's restful—whar it's warm—down t' the barn. (*Bitterly*) I kin talk t' the cows. They know. They know the farm an' me. They'll give me peace. (*He turns to go out the door*).

ABBIE. (*a bit frightenedly*) Air ye ailin' tonight, Ephraim?

CABOT. Growin'. Growin' ripe on the bough. (*He turns and goes, his boots clumping down the stairs.* EBEN *sits up with a start, listening.* ABBIE *is conscious of his movement and stares at the wall.* CABOT *comes out of the house around the corner and stands by the gate, blinking at the sky. He stretches up his hands in a tortured gesture*) God A'mighty, call from the dark! (*He listens as if expecting an answer. Then his arms drop, he shakes his head and plods off toward the barn.* EBEN *and* ABBIE *stare at each other through the wall.* EBEN *sighs heavily and* ABBIE *echoes it. Both become terribly nervous, uneasy. Finally* ABBIE *gets up and listens, her ear to the wall. He acts as if he saw every move she was making, he becomes resolutely still. She seems driven into a decision—goes out the door in rear determinedly. His eyes follow her. Then as the door of his room is opened softly, he turns away, waits in an attitude of strained fixity.* ABBIE *stands for a second staring at him, her eyes burning with desire. Then with a little cry she runs over and throws her arms about his neck, she pulls his head back and covers his mouth with kisses. At first, he submits dumbly; then he puts his arms about her neck and returns her kisses, but finally, suddenly aware of his hatred, he hurls her away from him, springing to his feet. They stand speechless and breathless, panting like two animals*).

ABBIE. (*at last—painfully*) Ye shouldn't, Eben—ye shouldn't—I'd make ye happy!

EBEN. (*harshly*) I don't want t' be happy—from yew!

ABBIE. (*helplessly*) Ye do, Eben! Ye do! Why d'ye lie?

EBEN. (*viciously*) I don't take t'ye. I tell ye! I hate the sight o' ye!

ABBIE. (*with an uncertain troubled laugh*) Waal, I kissed ye anyways—an' ye kissed back—yer lips was burnin'—ye can't lie 'bout that! (*Intensely*) If ye don't care, why did ye kiss me back—why was yer lips burnin'?

EBEN. (*wiping his mouth*) It was like pizen on 'em. (*Then tauntingly*) When I kissed ye back, mebbe I thought 'twas someone else.

ABBIE. (*wildly*) Min?

EBEN. Mebbe.

ABBIE. (*torturedly*) Did ye go t' see her? Did ye r'ally go? I thought ye mightn't. Is that why ye throwed me off jest now?

EBEN. (*sneeringly*) What if it be?

ABBIE. (*raging*) Then ye're a dog, Eben Cabot!

EBEN. (*threateningly*) Ye can't talk that way t' me!

ABBIE. (*with a shrill laugh*) Can't I? Did ye think I was in love with ye—a weak thin' like yew? Not much! I on'y wanted ye fur a purpose o' my own—an' I'll hev ye fur it yet 'cause I'm stronger'n yew be!

EBEN. (*resentfully*) I knowed well it was on'y part o' yer plan t' swaller everythin'!

ABBIE. (*tauntingly*) Mebbe!

EBEN. (*furious*) Git out o' my room!

ABBIE. This air my room an' ye're on'y hired help!

EBEN. (*threateningly*) Git out afore I murder ye!

ABBIE. (*quite confident now*) I hain't a mite afeerd. Ye want me, don't ye? Yes, ye do! An' yer Paw's son'll never kill what he wants! Look at yer eyes! They's lust fur me in 'em, burnin' 'em up! Look at yer lips now! They're tremblin' an' longin' t' kiss me, an' yer teeth t' bite! (*He is watching her now with a horrible fascination. She laughs a crazy triumphant laugh*) I'm a-goin' t' make all o' this hum my hum! They's one room hain't mine yet, but it's a-goin' t' be tonight. I'm a-goin' down now an' light up! (*She makes him a mocking bow*) Won't ye come courtin' me in the best parlor, Mister Cabot?

EBEN. (*staring at her—horribly confused—dully*) Don't ye dare! It hain't been opened since Maw died an' was laid out thar! Don't ye. . . ! (*But her eyes are fixed on his so burningly that his will seems to wither before hers. He stands swaying toward her helplessly*).

ABBIE. (*holding his eyes and putting all her will into her words as she backs out the door*) I'll expect ye afore long, Eben.

EBEN. (*stares after her for a while, walking toward the door. A light appears in the parlor window. He murmurs*) In the parlor? (*This seems to arouse connotations for he comes back and puts on his white shirt, collar, half ties the tie mechanically, puts on coat, takes his hat, stands barefooted looking about him in bewilderment, mutters wonderingly*) Maw! Whar air yew? (*Then goes slowly toward the door in rear*).

SCENE THREE

A few minutes later. The interior of the parlor is shown. A grim, repressed room like a tomb in which the family has been interred alive. ABBIE *sits on the edge of the horsehair sofa. She has lighted all the candles and the room is revealed in all its preserved ugliness. A change has come over the woman. She looks awed and frightened now, ready to run away.*

The door is opened and EBEN *appears. His face wears an expression of obsessed confusion. He stands staring at her, his arms hanging disjointedly from his shoulders, his feet bare, his hat in his hand.*

ABBIE. (*after a pause—with a nervous, formal politeness*) Won't ye set?

EBEN. (*dully*) Ay-eh. (*Mechanically he places his hat carefully on the floor near the door and sits stiffly beside her on the edge of the sofa. A pause. They both remain rigid, looking straight ahead with eyes full of fear*).

ABBIE. When I fust come in—in the dark—they seemed somethin' here.

EBEN. (*simply*) Maw.

ABBIE. I kin still feel—somethin'. . . .

EBEN. It's Maw.

ABBIE. At fust I was feered o' it. I wanted t' yell an' run. Now—since yew come—seems like it's growin' soft an' kind t' me. (*Addressing the air—queerly*) Thank yew.

EBEN. Maw allus loved me.

ABBIE. Mebbe it knows I love yew, too. Mebbe that makes it kind t' me.

EBEN. (*dully*) I dunno. I should think she'd hate ye.

ABBIE. (*with certainty*) No. I kin feel it don't—not no more.

EBEN. Hate ye fur stealin' her place—here in her hum—settin' in her parlor whar she was laid—(*He suddenly stops, staring stupidly before him*).

ABBIE. What is it, Eben?

EBEN. (*in a whisper*) Seems like Maw didn't want me t' remind ye.

ABBIE. (*excitedly*) I knowed, Eben! It's kind t' me! It don't b'ar me no grudges fur what I never knowed an' couldn't help!

EBEN. Maw b'ars him a grudge.

ABBIE. Waal, so does all o' us.

EBEN. Ay-eh. (*With passion*) I does, by God!

ABBIE. (*taking one of his hands in hers and patting it*) Thar! Don't git riled thinkin' o' him. Think o' yer Maw who's kind t' us. Tell me about yer Maw, Eben.

EBEN. They hain't nothin' much. She was kind. She was good.

ABBIE. (*putting one arm over his shoulder. He does not seem to notice—passionately*) I'll be kind an' good t' ye!

EBEN. Sometimes she used t' sing fur me.

ABBIE. I'll sing fur ye!

EBEN. This was her hum. This was her farm.

ABBIE. This is my hum! This is my farm!

EBEN. He married her t' steal 'em. She was soft an' easy. He couldn't 'preciate her.

ABBIE. He can't 'preciate me!

EBEN. He murdered her with his hardness.

ABBIE. He's murderin' me!

EBEN. She died. (*A pause*) Sometimes she used to sing fur me. (*He bursts into a fit of sobbing*).

ABBIE. (*both her arms around him—with wild passion*) I'll sing fur ye! I'll die fur ye! (*In spite of her overwhelming desire for him, there is a sincere maternal love in her manner and voice—a horribly frank mixture of lust and mother love*) Don't cry, Eben! I'll take yer Maw's place! I'll be everythin' she was t' ye! Let me kiss ye, Eben! (*She pulls his head around. He makes a bewildered pretense of resistance. She is tender*) Don't be afeered! I'll kiss ye pure, Eben—same 's if I was a Maw t' ye—an' ye kin kiss me back 's if yew was my son—my boy—sayin' good-night t' me! Kiss me, Eben. (*They kiss in restrained fashion. Then suddenly wild passion overcomes her. She kisses him lustfully again and again and he flings his arms about her and returns her kisses. Suddenly, as in the bedroom, he frees himself from her violently and springs to his feet. He is trembling all over, in a strange state of terror.* ABBIE *strains her arms toward him with fierce pleading*) Don't ye leave me, Eben! Can't ye see it hain't enuf—lovin' ye like a Maw—can't ye see it's got t' be that an' more—much more—a hundred times more—fur me t' be happy—fur yew t' be happy?

EBEN. (*to the presence he feels in the room*) Maw! Maw! What d'ye want? What air ye tellin' me?

ABBIE. She's tellin' ye t' love me. She knows I love ye an' I'll be good t' ye. Can't ye feel it? Don't ye know? She's tellin' ye t' love me, Eben!

EBEN. Ay-eh. I feel—mebbe she—but—I can't figger out—why—when ye've stole her place—here in her hum—in the parlor whar she was—

ABBIE. (*fiercely*) She knows I love ye!

EBEN. (*his face suddenly lighting up with a fierce, triumphant grin*) I see it! I sees why. It's her vengeance on him—so's she kin rest quiet in her grave!

ABBIE. (*wildly*) Vengeance o' God on the hull o' us! What d'we give a durn? I love ye, Eben! God knows I love ye! (*She stretches out her arms for him*).

EBEN. (*throws himself on his knees beside the sofa and grabs her in his arms—releasing all his pent-up passion*) An' I love yew, Abbie!—now I kin say it! I been dyin' fur want o' ye—every hour since ye come! I love ye! (*Their lips meet in a fierce, bruising kiss*).

SCENE FOUR

Exterior of the farmhouse. It is just dawn. The front door at right is opened and EBEN *comes out and walks around to the gate. He is dressed in his working clothes. He seems changed. His face wears a bold and confident expression, he is grinning to himself with evident satisfaction. As he gets near the gate, the window of the parlor is heard opening and the shutters are flung back and* ABBIE *sticks her head out. Her hair tumbles over her shoulders in disarray, her face is flushed, she looks at* EBEN *with tender, languorous eyes and calls softly*).

ABBIE. Eben. (*As he turns—playfully*) Jest one more kiss afore ye go. I'm goin' to miss ye fearful all day.

EBEN. An' me yew, ye kin bet! (*He goes to her. They kiss several times. He draws away, laughingly*) Thar. That's enuf, hain't it? Ye won't hev none left fur next time.

ABBIE. I got a million o' 'em left fur yew! (*Then a bit anxiously*) D'ye r'ally love me, Eben?

EBEN. (*emphatically*) I like ye better'n any gal I ever knowed! That's gospel!

ABBIE. Likin' hain't lovin'.

EBEN. Waal then—I love ye. Now air yew satisfied?

ABBIE. Ay-eh, I be. (*She smiles at him adoringly*).

EBEN. I better git t' the barn. The old critter's liable t' suspicion an' come sneakin' up.

ABBIE. (*with a confident laugh*) Let him! I kin allus pull the wool over his eyes. I'm goin' t' leave the shutters open and let in the sun 'n' air. This room's been dead long enuf. Now it's goin' t' be my room!

EBEN. (*frowning*) Ay-eh.

ABBIE. (*hastily*) I meant—our room.

EBEN. Ay-eh.

ABBIE. We made it our'n last night, didn't we? We give it life—our lovin' did. (*A pause*).

EBEN. (*with a strange look*) Maw's gone back t' her grave. She kin sleep now.

ABBIE. May she rest in peace! (*Then tenderly rebuking*) Ye oughtn't t' talk o' sad thin's—this mornin'.

EBEN. It jest come up in my mind o' itself.

ABBIE. Don't let it. (*He doesn't answer. She yawns*) Waal, I'm a-goin' t' steal a wink o' sleep. I'll tell the Old Man I hain't feelin' pert. Let him git his own vittles.

EBEN. I see him comin' from the barn. Ye better look smart an git upstairs.

ABBIE. Ay-eh. Good-by. Don't ferget me. (*She throws him a kiss. He grins—then squares his shoulders and awaits his father confidently.*

CABOT *walks slowly up from the left, staring up at the sky with a vague face*).

EBEN. (*jovially*) Mornin', Paw. Star-gazin' in daylight?

CABOT. Purty, hain't it?

EBEN. (*looking around him possessively*) It's a durned purty farm.

CABOT. I mean the sky.

EBEN. (*grinning*) How d'ye know? Them eyes o' your'n can't see that fur. (*This tickles his humor and he slaps his thigh and laughs*) Ho-ho! That's a good un!

CABOT. (*grimly sarcastic*) Ye're feelin' right chipper, hain't ye? Whar'd ye steal the likker?

EBEN. (*good-naturedly*) 'Tain't likker. Jest life. (*Suddenly holding out his hand—soberly*) Yew 'n' me is quits. Let's shake hands.

CABOT. (*suspiciously*) What's come over ye?

EBEN. Then don't. Mebbe it's jest as well. (*A moment's pause*) What's come over me? (*Queerly*) Didn't ye feel her passin'—goin' back t' her grave?

CABOT. (*dully*) Who?

EBEN. Maw. She kin rest now an' sleep content. She's quits with ye.

CABOT. (*confusedly*) I rested. I slept good—down with the cows. They know how t' sleep. They're teachin' me.

EBEN. (*suddenly jovial again*) Good fur the cows! Waal—ye better git t' work.

CABOT. (*grimly amused*) Air yew bossin' me, ye calf?

EBEN. (*beginning to laugh*) Ay-eh! I'm bossin' yew! Ha-ha-ha! See how ye like it! Ha-ha-ha! I'm the prize rooster o' this roost. Ha-ha-ha! (*He goes off toward the barn laughing*).

CABOT. (*looks after him with scornful pity*) Soft-headed. Like his Maw. Dead spit 'n' image. No hope in him! (*He spits with contemptuous disgust*) A born fool! (*Then matter-of-factly*) Waal—I'm gittin' peckish. (*He goes toward door*).

CURTAIN

PART THREE—SCENE ONE

A night in late spring the following year. The kitchen and the two bedrooms upstairs are shown. The two bedrooms are dimly lighted by a tallow candle in each. EBEN *is sitting on the side of the bed in his room, his chin propped on his fists, his face a study of the struggle he is making to understand his conflicting emotions. The noisy laughter and music from below where a kitchen dance is in progress annoy and distract him. He scowls at the floor.*

In the next room a cradle stands beside the double bed.

In the kitchen all is festivity. The stove has been taken down to give more room to the dancers. The chairs, with wooden benches added, have been pushed back against the walls. On these are seated, squeezed in tight against one another, farmers and their wives and their young folks of both sexes from the neighboring farms. They are all chattering and laughing loudly. They evidently have some secret joke in common. There is no end of winking, of nudging, of meaning nods of the head toward CABOT *who, in a state of extreme hilarious excitement increased by the amount he has drunk, is standing near the rear door where there is a small keg of whisky and serving drinks to all the men. In the left corner, front, dividing the attention with her husband,* ABBIE *is sitting in a rocking chair, a shawl wrapped about her shoulders. She is very pale, her face is thin and drawn, her eyes are fixed anxiously on the open door in rear as if waiting for someone.*

The musician is tuning up his fiddle, seated in the far right corner. He is a lanky young fellow with a long, weak face. His pale eyes blink incessantly and he grins about him slyly with a greedy malice.

ABBIE. (*suddenly turning to a young girl on her right*) Whar's Eben?

YOUNG GIRL. (*eying her scornfully*) I dunno, Mrs. Cabot. I hain't seen Eben in ages. (*Meaningly*) Seems like he's spent most o' his time t' hum since yew come.

ABBIE. (*vaguely*) I tuk his Maw's place.

YOUNG GIRL. Ay-eh. So I've heerd. (*She turns away to retail this bit of gossip to her mother sitting next to her.* ABBIE *turns to her left to a big stoutish middle-aged man whose flushed face and starting eyes show the amount of "likker" he has consumed*).

ABBIE. Ye hain't seen Eben, hev ye?

MAN. No, I hain't. (*Then he adds with a wink*) If yew hain't, who would?

ABBIE. He's the best dancer in the county. He'd ought t' come an' dance.

MAN. (*with a wink*) Mebbe he's doin' the dutiful an' walkin' the kid t' sleep. It's a boy, hain't it?

ABBIE. (*nodding vaguely*) Ay-eh—born two weeks back—purty's a picter.

MAN. They all is—t' their Maws. (*Then in a whisper, with a nudge and a leer*) Listen, Abbie—if ye ever git tired o' Eben, remember me! Don't fergit now! (*He looks at her uncomprehending face for a second—then grunts disgustedly*) Waal—guess I'll likker agin. (*He goes over and joins* CABOT *who is arguing noisily with an old farmer over cows. They all drink*).

ABBIE. (*this time appealing to nobody in particular*) Wonder what Eben's a-doin'? (*Her remark is repeated down the line with many a guffaw and titter until it reaches the fiddler. He fastens his blinking eyes on* ABBIE).

FIDDLER. (*raising his voice*) Bet I kin tell ye, Abbie, what Eben's doin'! He's down t' the church offerin' up prayers o' thanksgivin'. (*They all titter expectantly*).

A MAN. What fur? (*Another titter*).

FIDDLER. 'Cause unto him a—(*He hesitates just long enough*) brother is born! (*A roar of laughter. They all look from* ABBIE *to* CABOT. *She is oblivious, staring at the door.* CABOT, *although he hasn't heard the words, is irritated by the laughter and steps forward, glaring about him. There is an immediate silence*).

CABOT. What're ye all bleatin' about—like a flock o' goats? Why don't ye dance, damn ye? I axed ye here t' dance—t' eat, drink an' be merry—an' thar ye set cacklin' like a lot o' wet hens with the pip! Ye've swilled my likker an' guzzled my vittles like hogs, hain't ye? Then dance fur me, can't ye? That's fa'r an' squar', hain't it? (*A grumble of resentment goes around but they are all evidently in too much awe of him to express it openly*).

FIDDLER. (*slyly*) We're waitin' fur Eben. (*A suppressed laugh*).

CABOT. (*with a fierce exultation*) T'hell with Eben! Eben's done fur now! I got a new son! (*His mood switching with drunken suddenness*) But ye needn't t' laugh at Eben, none o' ye! He's my blood, if he be a dumb fool. He's better nor any o' yew! He kin do a day's work a'most up t' what I kin—an' that'd put any o' yew pore critters t' shame!

FIDDLER. An' he kin do a good night's work, too! (*A roar of laughter*).

CABOT. Laugh, ye damn fools! Ye're right jist the same, Fiddler. He kin work day an' night too, like I kin, if need be!

OLD FARMER. (*from behind the keg where he is weaving drunkenly back and forth—with great simplicity*) They hain't many t' touch ye, Ephraim—a son at seventy-six. That's a hard man fur ye! I be on'y sixty-eight an' I couldn't do it. (*A roar of laughter in which* CABOT *joins uproariously*).

CABOT. (*slapping him on the back*) I'm sorry fur ye, Hi. I'd never suspicion sech weakness from a boy like yew!

OLD FARMER. An' I never reckoned yew had it in ye nuther, Ephraim. (*There is another laugh*).

CABOT. (*suddenly grim*) I got a lot in me—a hell of a lot—folks don't know on. (*Turning to the fiddler*) Fiddle 'er up, durn ye! Give 'em somethin' t' dance t'! What air ye, an ornament? Hain't this a celebration? Then grease yer elbow an' go it!

FIDDLER. (*seizes a drink which the* OLD FARMER *holds out to him and downs it*) Here goes! (*He starts to fiddle "Lady of the Lake." Four young fellows and four girls form in two lines and dance a square dance. The* FIDDLER *shouts directions for the different movements, keeping his words in the rhythm of the music and interspersing them with jocular personal remarks to the dancers themselves. The people seated along the walls stamp their feet and clap their hands in unison.* CABOT *is especially active in this respect. Only* ABBIE *remains apathetic, staring at the door as if she were alone in a silent room*).

FIDDLER. Swing your partner t' the right! That's it, Jim! Give her a b'ar hug! Her Maw hain't lookin'. (*Laughter*) Change partners! That suits ye, don't it, Essie, now ye got Reub afore ye? Look at her redden up, will ye? Waal, life is short an' so's love, as the feller says. (*Laughter*).

CABOT. (*excitedly, stamping his foot*) Go it, boys! Go it, gals!

FIDDLER. (*with a wink at the others*) Ye're the spryest seventy-six ever I sees, Ephraim! Now if ye'd on'y good eye-sight . . . ! (*suppressed laughter. He gives* CABOT *no chance to retort but roars*) Promenade! Ye're walkin' like a bride down the aisle, Sarah! Waal, while they's life they's allus hope, I've heerd tell. Swing your partner to the left! Gosh A'mighty, look at Johnny Cook high-steppin'! They hain't goin' t'be much strength left fur howin' in the corn lot t'morrow. (*Laughter*).

CABOT. Go it! Go it! (*Then suddenly, unable to restrain himself any longer, he prances into the midst of the dancers, scattering them, waving his arms about wildly*) Ye're all hoofs! Git out o' my road! Give me room! I'll show ye dancin'. Ye're all too soft! (*He pushes them roughly away. They crowd back toward the walls, muttering, looking at him resentfully*).

FIDDLER. (*jeeringly*) Go it, Ephraim! Go it! (*He starts "Pop Goes the Weasel," increasing the tempo with every verse until at the end he is fiddling crazily as fast as he can go*).

CABOT. (*starts to dance, which he does very well and with tremendous vigor. Then he begins to improvise, cuts incredibly grotesque capers, leaping up and cracking his heels together, prancing around in a circle with body bent in an Indian war dance, then suddenly straightening up and kicking as high as he can with both legs. He is like a monkey on a string. And all the while he intersperses his antics with shouts and derisive comments*) Whoop! Here's dancin' fur ye! Whoop! See that! Seventy-six, if I'm a day! Hard as iron yet! Beatin' the young 'uns like I allus done! Look at me! I'd invite ye t' dance on my hundredth birthday on'y ye'll all be dead by then. Ye're a sickly generation! Yer hearts air pink, not red! Yer veins is full o' mud an' water! I be the on'y man in the county! Whoop! See that! I'm a Injun! I've killed Injuns in the West afore ye was born—an' skulped 'em too! They's a arrer wound on my backside I c'd show ye! The hull tribe chased me. I outrun 'em all—with the arrer stuck in me! An' I tuk vengeance on 'em. Ten eyes fur an eye, that was my motter! Whoop! Look at me! I kin kick the ceilin' off the room! Whoop!

FIDDLER. (*stops playing—exhaustedly*) God A'mighty, I got enuf. Ye got the devil's strength in ye.

CABOT. (*delightedly*) Did I beat yew, too? Wa'al, ye played smart.

Hev a swig. (*He pours whisky for himself and* FIDDLER. *They drink. The others watch* CABOT *silently with cold, hostile eyes. There is a dead pause. The* FIDDLER *rests.* CABOT *leans against the keg, panting, glaring around him confusedly. In the room above,* EBEN *gets to his feet and tiptoes out the door in rear, appearing a moment later in the other bedroom. He moves silently, even frightenedly, toward the cradle and stands there looking down at the baby. His face is as vague as his reactions are confused, but there is a trace of tenderness, of interested discovery. At the same moment that he reaches the cradle,* ABBIE *seems to sense something. She gets up weakly and goes to* CABOT).

ABBIE. I'm goin' up t' the baby.

CABOT. (*with real solicitation*) Air ye able fur the stairs? D'ye want me t' help ye, Abbie?

ABBIE. No. I'm able. I'll be down agen soon.

CABOT. Don't ye git wore out! He needs ye, remember—our son does! (*He grins affectionately, patting her on the back. She shrinks from his touch*).

ABBIE. (*dully*) Don't—tech me. I'm goin'—up. (*She goes.* CABOT *looks after her. A whisper goes around the room.* CABOT *turns. It ceases. He wipes his forehead streaming with sweat. He is breathing pantingly*).

CABOT. I'm a-goin' out t' git fresh air. I'm feelin' a mite dizzy. Fiddle up thar! Dance, all o' ye! Here's likker fur them as wants it. Enjoy yerselves. I'll be back. (*He goes, closing the door behind him*).

FIDDLER. (*sarcastically*) Don't hurry none on our account! (*A suppressed laugh. He imitates* ABBIE) Whar's Eben? (*More laughter*).

A WOMAN (*loudly*) What's happened in this house is plain as the nose on yer face! (ABBIE *appears in the doorway upstairs and stands looking in surprise and adoration at* EBEN *who does not see her*).

A MAN. Ssshh! He's li'ble t' be listenin' at the door. That'd be like him. (*Their voices die to an intensive whispering. Their faces are concentrated on this gossip. A noise as of dead leaves in the wind comes from the room.* CABOT *has come out from the porch and stands by the gate, leaning on it, staring at the sky blinkingly.* ABBIE *comes across the room silently.* EBEN *does not notice her until quite near*).

EBEN. (*starting*) Abbie!

ABBIE. Ssshh! (*She throws her arms around him. They kiss—then bend over the cradle together*) Ain't he purty?—dead spit 'n' image o' yew!

EBEN. (*pleased*) Air he? I can't tell none.

ABBIE. E-zactly like!

EBEN. (*frowningly*) I don't like this. I don't like lettin' on what's mine's his'n. I been doin' that all my life. I'm gittin' t' the end of b'arin' it!

ABBIE. (*putting her finger on his lips*) We're doin' the best we kin. We got t' wait. Somethin's bound t' happen. (*She puts her arms around him*) I got t' go back.

EBEN. I'm goin' out. I can't b'ar it with the fiddle playin' an' the laughin'.

ABBIE. Don't git feelin' low. I love ye, Eben. Kiss me. (*He kisses her. They remain in each other's arms*).

CABOT. (*at the gate, confusedly*) Even the music can't drive it out—somethin'. Ye kin feel it droppin' off the elums, climbin' up the roof, sneakin' down the chimney, pokin' in the corners! They's no peace in houses, they's no rest livin' with folks. Somethin's always livin' with ye. (*With a deep sigh*) I'll go t' the barn an' rest a spell. (*He goes wearily toward the barn*).

FIDDLER. (*tuning up*) Let's celebrate the old skunk gittin' fooled! We kin have some fun now he's went. (*He starts to fiddle "Turkey in the Straw." There is real merriment now. The young folks get up to dance*).

SCENE TWO

*A half hour later—Exterior—*EBEN *is standing by the gate looking up at the sky, an expression of dumb pain bewildered by itself on his face.* CABOT *appears, returning from the barn, walking wearily, his eyes on the ground. He sees* EBEN *and his whole mood immediately changes. He becomes excited, a cruel, triumphant grin comes to his lips, he strides up and slaps* EBEN *on the back. From within comes the whining of the fiddle and the noise of stamping feet and laughing voices.*

CABOT. So har ye be!

EBEN. (*startled, stares at him with hatred for a moment—then dully*) Ay-eh.

CABOT. (*surveying him jeeringly*) Why hain't ye been in t' dance? They was all axin' fur ye.

EBEN. Let 'em ax!

CABOT. They's a hull passel o' purty gals.

EBEN. T' hell with 'em!

CABOT. Ye'd ought t' be marryin' one o' 'em soon.

EBEN. I hain't marryin' no one.

CABOT. Ye might 'arn a share o' a farm that way.

EBEN. (*with a sneer*) Like yew did, ye mean? I hain't that kind.

CABOT. (*stung*) Ye lie! 'Twas yer Maw's folks aimed t' steal my farm from me.

EBEN. Other folks don't say so. (*After a pause—defiantly*) An' I got a farm, anyways!

CABOT. (*derisively*) Whar?

EBEN. (*stamps a foot on the ground*) Har!

CABOT. (*throws his head back and laughs coarsely*) Ho-ho! Ye hev, hev ye? Waal, that's a good un!

EBEN. (*controlling himself—grimly*) Ye'll see!

CABOT. (*stares at him suspiciously, trying to make him out—a pause—

then with scornful confidence) Ay-eh. I'll see. So'll ye. It's ye that's blind —blind as a mole underground. (EBEN *suddenly laughs, one short sardonic bark: "Ha." A pause.* CABOT *peers at him with renewed suspicion*) Whar air ye hawin' 'bout? (EBEN *turns away without answering.* CABOT *grows angry*) God A'mighty, yew air a dumb dunce! They's nothin' in that thick skull o' your'n but noise—like a empty keg it be! (EBEN *doesn't seem to hear.* CABOT'*s rage grows*) Yewr farm! God A'mighty! If ye wa'n't a born donkey ye'd know ye'll never own stick nor stone on it, specially now arter him bein' born. It's his'n, I tell ye—his'n arter I die—but I'll live a hundred jest t' fool ye all—an' he'll be growed then—yewr age a'most! (EBEN *laughs again his sardonic "Ha." This drives* CABOT *into a fury*) Ha? Ye think ye kin git 'round that someways, do ye? Waal, it'll be her'n, too—Abbie's—ye won't git 'round her—she knows yer tricks—she'll be too much fur ye—she wants the farm her'n—she was afeerd o' ye—she told me ye was sneakin' 'round tryin' t' make love t' her t' get her on yer side . . . ye . . . ye mad fool, ye! (*He raises his clenched fists threateningly*).

EBEN. (*is confronting him choking with rage*) Ye lie, ye old skunk! Abbie never said no sech thing!

CABOT. (*suddenly triumphant when he sees how shaken* EBEN *is*) She did. An' I says, I'll blow his brains t' the top o' them elums—an' she says no, that hain't sense, who'll ye git t'help ye on the farm in his place—an' then she says yew'n me ought t' have a son—I know we kin, she says—an' I says, if we do, ye kin have anythin' I've got ye've a mind t'. An' she says, I wants Eben cut off so's this farm'll be mine when ye die! (*With terrible gloating*) An' that's what's happened, hain't it? An the farms her'n! An' the dust o' the road—that's you'rn! Ha! Now who's hawin'?

EBEN. (*has been listening, petrified with grief and rage—suddenly laughs wildly and brokenly*) Ha-ha-ha! So that's her sneakin' game—all along!—like I suspicioned at fust—t' swaller it all—an' me, too . . . ! (*Madly*) I'll murder her! (*He springs toward the porch but* CABOT *is quicker and gets in between*).

CABOT. No, ye don't!

EBEN. Git out o' my road! (*He tries to throw* CABOT *aside. They grapple in what becomes immediately a murderous struggle. The old man's concentrated strength is too much for* EBEN. CABOT *gets one hand on his throat and presses him back across the stone wall. At the same moment,* ABBIE *comes out on the porch. With a stifled cry she runs toward them*).

ABBIE. Eben! Ephraim! (*She tugs at the hand on* EBEN'*s throat*) Let go, Ephraim! Ye're chokin' him!

CABOT. (*removes his hand and flings* EBEN *sideways full length on the grass, gasping and choking. With a cry,* ABBIE *kneels beside him, trying to take his head on her lap, but he pushes her away.* CABOT *stands looking down with fierce triumph*) Ye needn't t've fret, Abbie, I wa'n't aimin' t' kill him. He hain't wuth hangin' fur—not by a hell of a sight! (*More *and more triumphantly*) Seventy-six an' him not thirty yit—an' look whar he be fur thinkin' his Paw was easy! No, by God, I hain't easy! An' him upstairs, I'll raise him t' be like me! (*He turns to leave them*) I'm goin' in an' dance!—sing an' celebrate! (*He walks to the porch—then turns with a great grin*) I don't calc'late it's left in him, but if he gits pesky, Abbie, ye jest sing out. I'll come a-runnin' an' by the Etarnal, I'll put him across my knee an' birch him! Ha-ha-ha! (*He goes into the house laughing. A moment later his loud "whoop" is heard*).

ABBIE. (*tenderly*) Eben. Air ye hurt? (*She tries to kiss him but he pushes her violently away and struggles to a sitting position*).

EBEN. (*gaspingly*) T'hell—with ye!

ABBIE. (*not believing her ears*) It's me, Eben—Abbie—don't ye know me?

EBEN. (*glowering at her with hatred*) Ay-eh—I know ye—now! (*He suddenly breaks down, sobbing weakly*).

ABBIE. (*fearfully*) Eben—what's happened t' ye—why did ye look at me 's if ye hated me?

EBEN. (*violently, between sobs and gasps*) I do hate ye! Ye're a whore—a damn trickin' whore!

ABBIE (*shrinking back horrified*) Eben! Ye don't know what ye're sayin'!

EBEN. (*scrambling to his feet and following her—accusingly*) Ye're nothin' but a stinkin' passel o' lies! Ye've been lyin' t' me every word ye spoke, day an' night, since we fust—done it. Ye've kept sayin' ye loved me. . . .

ABBIE. (*frantically*) I do love ye! (*She takes his hand but he flings hers away*).

EBEN. (*unheeding*) Ye've made a fool o' me—a sick, dumb fool—a-purpose! Ye've been on'y playin' yer sneakin', stealin' game all along—gittin' me t' lie with ye so's ye'd hev a son he'd think was his'n, an' makin' him promise he'd give ye the farm and let me eat dust, if ye did git him a son! (*Staring at her with anguished, bewildered eyes*) They must be a devil livin' in ye! T'ain't human t' be as bad as that be!

ABBIE. (*stunned—dully*) He told yew . . . ?

EBEN. Hain't it true? It hain't no good in yew lyin'.

ABBIE. (*pleadingly*) Eben, listen—ye must listen—it was long ago—afore we done nothin'—yew was scornin' me—goin' t' see Min—when I was lovin' ye—an' I said it t' him t' git vengeance on ye!

EBEN. (*unheedingly. With tortured passion*) I wish ye was dead! I wish I was dead along with ye afore this come! (*Ragingly*) But I'll git my vengeance too! I'll pray Maw t' come back t' help me—t' put her cuss on yew an' him!

ABBIE. (*brokenly*) Don't ye, Eben! Don't ye! (*She throws herself on *her knees before him, weeping)* I didn't mean t' do bad t'ye! Fergive me, won't ye?

EBEN. (*not seeming to hear her—fiercely*) I'll git squar' with the old skunk—an' yew! I'll tell him the truth 'bout the son he's so proud o'! Then I'll leave ye here t' pizen each other—with Maw comin' out o' her grave at nights—an' I'll go t' the gold fields o' Californi-a whar Sim an' Peter be!

ABBIE. (*terrified*) Ye won't—leave me? Ye can't!

EBEN. (*with fierce determination*) I'm a-goin', I tell ye! I'll git rich thar an' come back an' fight him fur the farm he stole—an' I'll kick ye both out in the road—t' beg an' sleep in the woods—an' yer son along with ye—t' starve an' die! (*He is hysterical at the end*).

ABBIE. (*with a shudder—humbly*) He's yewr son, too, Eben.

EBEN. (*torturedly*) I wish he never was born! I wish he'd die this minit! I wish I'd never sot eyes on him! It's him—yew havin' him—a-purpose t' steal—that's changed everythin'!

ABBIE. (*gently*) Did ye believe I loved ye—afore he come?

EBEN. Ay-eh—like a dumb ox!

ABBIE. An' ye don't believe no more?

EBEN. B'lieve a lyin' thief! Ha!

ABBIE. (*shudders—then humbly*) An' did ye r'ally love me afore?

EBEN. (*brokenly*) Ay-eh—an' ye was trickin' me!

ABBIE. An' ye don't love me now!

EBEN. (*violently*) I hate ye, I tell ye!

ABBIE. An' ye're truly goin' West—goin' t' leave me—all account o' him being born?

EBEN. I'm a-goin' in the mornin'—or may God strike me t' hell!

ABBIE. (*after a pause—with a dreadful cold intensity—slowly*) If that's what his comin's done t' me—killin' yewr love—takin' yew away—my on'y joy—the on'y joy I ever knowed—like heaven t' me—purtier'n heaven—then I hate him, too, even if I be his Maw!

EBEN. (*bitterly*) Lies! Ye love him! He'll steal the farm fur ye! (*Brokenly*) But t'ain't the farm so much—not no more—it's yew foolin' me—gittin' me t' love ye—lyin' yew loved me—jest t' git a son t' steal!

ABBIE. (*distractedly*) He won't steal! I'd kill him fust! I do love ye! I'll prove t' ye. . . !

EBEN. (*harshly*) T'aint no use lyin' no more. I'm deaf t' ye! (*He turns away*) I hain't seein' ye agen. Good-by!

ABBIE. (*pale with anguish*) Hain't ye even goin' t' kiss me—not once—arter all we loved?

EBEN. (*in a hard voice*) I hain't wantin' t' kiss ye never agen! I'm wantin' t' forgit I ever sot eyes on ye!

ABBIE. Eben!—ye mustn't—wait a spell—I want t' tell ye. . . .

EBEN. I'm a-goin' in t' git drunk. I'm a-goin' t' dance.

ABBIE. (*clinging to his arm—with passionate earnestness*) If I could make it—'s if he'd never come up between us—if I could prove t' ye I wa'n't schemin' t' steal from ye—so's everythin' could be jest the same with us, lovin' each other jest the same, kissin' an' happy the same's we've been happy afore he come—if I could do it—ye'd love me agen, wouldn't ye? Ye'd kiss me agen? Ye wouldn't never leave me, would ye?

EBEN. (*moved*) I calc'late not. (*Then shaking her hand off his arm—with a bitter smile*) But ye hain't God, be ye?

ABBIE. (*exultantly*) Remember ye've promised! (*Then with strange intensity*) Mebbe I kin take back one thin' God does!

EBEN. (*peering at her*) Ye're gittin' cracked, hain't ye? (*Then going towards door*) I'm a-goin' t' dance.

ABBIE. (*calls after him intensely*) I'll prove t' ye! I'll prove I love ye better'n. . . . (*He goes in the door, not seeming to hear. She remains standing where she is, looking after him—then she finishes desperately*) Better'n everythin' else in the world!

SCENE THREE

Just before dawn in the morning—shows the kitchen and CABOT'*s bedroom. In the kitchen, by the light of a tallow candle on the table,* EBEN *is sitting, his chin propped on his hands, his drawn face blank and expressionless. His carpetbag is on the floor beside him. In the bedroom, dimly lighted by a small whale-oil lamp,* CABOT *lies asleep.* ABBIE *is bending over the cradle, listening, her face full of terror yet with an undercurrent of desperate triumph. Suddenly, she breaks down and sobs, appears about to throw herself on her knees beside the cradle; but the old man turns restlessly, groaning in his sleep, and she controls herself, and, shrinking away from the cradle with a gesture of horror, backs swiftly toward the door in rear and goes out. A moment later she comes into the kitchen and, running to* EBEN, *flings her arms about his neck and kisses him wildly. He hardens himself, he remains unmoved and cold, he keeps his eyes straight ahead.*

ABBIE. (*hysterically*) I done it, Eben! I told ye I'd do it! I've proved I love ye—better'n everythin'—so's ye can't never doubt me no more!

EBEN. (*dully*) Whatever ye done, it hain't no good now.

ABBIE. (*wildly*) Don't ye say that! Kiss me, Eben, won't ye? I need ye t' kiss me arter what I done! I need ye t' say ye love me!

EBEN. (*kisses her without emotion—dully*) That's fur good-by. I'm a-goin' soon.

ABBIE. No! No! Ye won't go—not now!

EBEN. (*going on with his own thoughts*) I been a-thinkin'—an' I hain't goin' t' tell Paw nothin'. I'll leave Maw t' take vengeance on ye. If I told him, the old skunk'd jest be stinkin' mean enuf to take it out on that baby. (*His voice showing emotion in spite of him*) An' I don't want nothin' bad t' happen t' him. He hain't t' blame fur yew. (*He adds with a certain queer pride*) An' he looks like me! An' by God, he's mine! An' some day I'll be a-comin' back an' . . . !

ABBIE. (*too absorbed in her own thoughts to listen to him—pleadingly*) They's no cause fur ye t' go now—they's no sense—it's all the same's it was—they's nothin' come b'tween us now—arter what I done!

EBEN. (*something in her voice arouses him. He stares at her a bit frightenedly*) Ye look mad, Abbie. What did ye do?

ABBIE. I—I killed him, Eben.

EBEN (*amazed*) Ye killed him?

ABBIE. (*dully*) Ay-eh.

EBEN. (*recovering from his astonishment—savagely*) An' serves him right! But we got t' do somethin' quick t' make it look s'if the old skunk'd killed himself when he was drunk. We kin prove by 'em all how drunk he got.

ABBIE. (*wildly*) No! No! Not him! (*Laughing distractedly*) But that's what I ought t' done, hain't it? I oughter killed him instead! Why didn't ye tell me?

EBEN. (*appalled*) Instead? What d'ye mean?

ABBIE. Not him.

EBEN. (*his face grown ghastly*) Not—not that baby!

ABBIE. (*dully*) Ay-eh!

EBEN. (*falls to his knees as if he'd been struck—his voice trembling with horror*) Oh, God A'mighty! A'mighty God! Maw, whar was ye, why didn't ye stop her?

ABBIE. (*simply*) She went back t' her grave that night we fust done it, remember? I hain't felt her about since. (*A pause.* EBEN *hides his head in his hands, trembling all over as if he had the ague. She goes on dully*) I left the piller over his little face. Then he killed himself. He stopped breathin'. (*She begins to weep softly*).

EBEN. (*rage beginning to mingle with grief*) He looked like me. He was mine, damn ye!

ABBIE. (*slowly and brokenly*) I didn't want t' do it. I hated myself fur doin' it. I loved him. He was so purty—dead spit 'n' image o' yew. But I loved yew more—an' yew was goin' away—far off whar I'd never see ye agen, never kiss ye, never feel ye pressed agin me agen—an' ye said ye hated me fur havin' him—ye said ye hated him an' wished he was dead—ye said if it hadn't been fur him comin' it'd be the same's afore between us.

EBEN. (*unable to endure this, springs to his feet in a fury, threatening her, his twitching fingers seeming to reach out for her throat*) Ye lie! I never said—I never dreamed ye'd—I'd cut off my head afore I'd hurt his finger!

ABBIE. (*piteously, sinking on her knees*) Eben, don't ye look at me like that—hatin' me—not after what I done fur ye—fur us—so's we could be happy agen—

EBEN. (*furiously now*) Shut up, or I'll kill ye! I see yer game now—the same old sneakin' trick—ye're aimin' t' blame me fur the murder ye done!

ABBIE. (*moaning—putting her hands over her ears*) Don't ye, Eben! Don't ye! (*She grasps his legs*).

EBEN. (*his mood suddenly changing to horror, shrinks away from her*) Don't ye tech me! Ye're pizen! How could ye—t' murder a pore little critter—Ye must've swapped yer soul t' hell! (*Suddenly raging*) Ha! I kin see why ye done it! Not the lies ye jest told—but 'cause ye wanted t' steal agen—steal the last thin' ye'd left me—my part o' him—no, the hull o' him—ye saw he looked like me—ye knowed he was all mine—an' ye couldn't b'ar it—I know ye! Ye killed him fur bein' mine! (*All this has driven him almost insane. He makes a rush past her for the door—then turns—shaking both fists at her, violently*) But I'll take vengeance now! I'll git the Sheriff! I'll tell him everythin'! Then I'll sing "I'm off to Californi-a!" an' go—gold—Golden Gate—gold sun—fields o' gold in the West! (*This last he half shouts, half croons incoherently, suddenly breaking off passionately*) I'm a-goin' fur the Sheriff t' come an' git ye! I want ye tuk away, locked up from me! I can't stand t' luk at ye! Murderer an' thief 'r not, ye still tempt me! I'll give ye up t' the Sheriff! (*He turns and runs out, around the corner of house, panting and sobbing, and breaks into a swerving sprint down the road*).

ABBIE. (*struggling to her feet, runs to the door, calling after him*) I love ye, Eben! I love ye! (*She stops at the door weakly, swaying, about to fall*) I don't care what ye do—if ye'll on'y love me agen—(*She falls limply to the floor in a faint*).

SCENE FOUR

About an hour later. Same as Scene Three. Shows the kitchen and CABOT'S *bedroom. It is after dawn. The sky is brilliant with the sunrise. In the kitchen,* ABBIE *sits at the table, her body limp and exhausted, her head bowed down over her arms, her face hidden. Upstairs,* CABOT *is still asleep but awakens with a start. He looks toward the window and gives a snort of surprise and irritation—throws back the covers and begins hurriedly pulling on his clothes. Without looking behind him, he begins talking to* ABBIE *whom he supposes beside him.*

CABOT. Thunder 'n' lightin', Abbie! I hain't slept this late in fifty year! Looks 's if the sun was full riz a'most. Must've been the dancin' an' likker. Must be gittin' old. I hope Eben's t' wuk. Ye might've tuk the trouble t' rouse me, Abbie. (*He turns—sees no one there—surprised*) Waal—whar air she? Gittin' vittles, I calc'late. (*He tiptoes to the cradle and peers down—proudly*) Mornin', sonny. Purty's a picter! Sleepin' sound. He don't beller all night like most o' 'em. (*He goes quietly out the door in rear—few moments later enters kitchen—sees* ABBIE*—with satisfaction*) So thar ye be. Ye got any vittles cooked?

ABBIE. (*without moving*) No.

CABOT. (*coming to her, almost sympathetically*) Ye feelin' sick?

ABBIE. No.

CABOT. (*pats her on shoulder. She shudders*) Ye'd best lie down a spell. (*Half jocularly*) Yer son'll be needin' ye soon. He'd ought t' wake up with a gnashin' appetite, the sound way he's sleepin'.

ABBIE. (*shudders—then in a dead voice*) He hain't never goin' t' wake up.

CABOT. (*jokingly*) Takes after me this mornin'. I hain't slept so late in . . .

ABBIE. He's dead.

CABOT. (*stares at her—bewilderedly*) What. . . .

ABBIE. I killed him.

CABOT. (*stepping back from her—aghast*) Air ye drunk—'r crazy—'r . . . !

ABBIE. (*suddenly lifts her head and turns on him—wildly*) I killed him, I tell ye! I smothered him. Go up an' see if ye don't b'lieve me! (CABOT *stares at her a second, then bolts out the rear door, can be heard bounding up the stairs, and rushes into the bedroom and over to the cradle.* ABBIE *has sunk back lifelessly into her former position.* CABOT *puts his hand down on the body in the crib. An expression of fear and horror comes over his face*).

CABOT. (*shrinking away—tremblingly*) God A'mighty! God A'mighty. (*He stumbles out the door—in a short while returns to the kitchen—comes to* ABBIE, *the stunned expression still on his face—hoarsely*) Why did ye do it? Why? (*As she doesn't answer, he grabs her violently by the shoulder and shakes her*) I ax ye why ye done it! Ye'd better tell me 'r . . . !

ABBIE. (*gives him a furious push which sends him staggering back and springs to her feet—with wild rage and hatred*) Don't ye dare tech me! What right hev ye t' question me 'bout him? He wa'n't yewr son! Think I'd have a son by yew? I'd die fust! I hate the sight o' ye an' allus did! It's yew I should've murdered, if I'd had good sense! I hate ye! I love Eben. I did from the fust. An' he was Eben's son—mine an' Eben's—not your'n!

CABOT. (*stands looking at her dazedly—a pause—finding his words with an effort—dully*) That was it—what I felt—pokin' round the corners—while ye lied—holdin' yerself from me—sayin' ye'd a'ready conceived—(*He lapses into crushed silence—then with a strange emotion*) He's dead, sart'n. I felt his heart. Pore little critter! (*He blinks back one tear, wiping his sleeve across his nose*).

ABBIE. (*hysterically*) Don't ye! Don't ye! (*She sobs unrestrainedly*).

CABOT. (*with a concentrated effort that stiffens his body into a rigid line and hardens his face into a stony mask–through his teeth to himself*) I got t' be–like a stone–a rock o' jedgment! (*A pause. He gets complete control over himself–harshly*) If he was Eben's, I be glad he air gone! An' mebbe I suspicioned it all along. I felt they was somethin' onnateral–somewhars–the house got so lonesome–an' cold–drivin' me down t' the barn–t' the beasts o' the field. . . . Ay-eh. I must've suspicioned –somethin'. Ye didn't fool me–not altogether, leastways–I'm too old a bird–growin' ripe on the bough. . . . (*He becomes aware he is wandering, straightens again, looks at* ABBIE *with a cruel grin*) So ye'd liked t' hev murdered me 'stead o' him, would ye? Waal, I'll live to a hundred! I'll live t' see ye hung! I'll deliver ye up t' the jedgment o' God an' the law! I'll git the Sheriff now. (*Starts for the door*).

ABBIE. (*dully*) Ye needn't. Eben's gone fur him.

CABOT. (*amazed*) Eben–gone fur the Sheriff?

ABBIE. Ay-eh.

CABOT. T' inform agen ye?

ABBIE. Ay-eh.

CABOT. (*considers this–a pause–then in a hard voice*) Waal, I'm thankful fur him savin' me the trouble. I'll git t' wuk. (*He goes to the door–then turns–in a voice full of strange emotion*) He'd ought t' been my son, Abbie. Ye'd ought t' loved me. I'm a man. If ye'd loved me, I'd never told no Sheriff on ye no matter what ye did, if they was t' brile me alive!

ABBIE. (*defensively*) They's more to it nor yew know, makes him tell.

CABOT. (*dryly*) Fur yewr sake, I hope they be. (*He goes out–comes around to the gate–stares up at the sky. His control relaxes. For a moment he is old and weary. He murmurs despairingly*) God A'mighty, I be lonesomer'n ever! (*He hears running footsteps from the left, immediately is himself again.* EBEN *runs in, panting exhaustedly, wild-eyed and mad looking. He lurches through the gate.* CABOT *grabs him by the shoulder.* EBEN *stares at him dumbly*) Did ye tell the Sheriff?

EBEN. (*nodding stupidly*) Ay-eh.

CABOT. (*gives him a push away that sends him sprawling–laughing with withering contempt*) Good fur ye! A prime chip o' yer Maw ye be! (*He goes toward the barn, laughing harshly.* EBEN *scrambles to his feet. Suddenly* CABOT *turns–grimly threatening*) Git off this farm when the Sheriff takes her–or, by God, he'll have t' come back an' git me fur murder, too! (*He stalks off.* EBEN *does not appear to have heard him. He runs to the door and comes into the kitchen.* ABBIE *looks up with a cry of anguished joy.* EBEN *stumbles over and throws himself on his knees beside her–sobbing brokenly*).

EBEN. Fergive me!

ABBIE. (*happily*) Eben! (*She kisses him and pulls his head over against her breast*).

EBEN. I love ye! Fergive me!

ABBIE. (*ecstatically*) I'd fergive ye all the sins in hell fur sayin' that! (*She kisses his head, pressing it to her with a fierce passion of possession*).

EBEN. (*brokenly*) But I told the Sheriff. He's comin' fur ye!

ABBIE. I kin b'ar what happens t' me—now!

EBEN. I woke him up. I told him. He says, wait 'til I git dressed. I was waiting. I got to thinkin' o' yew. I got to thinkin' how I'd loved ye. It hurt like somethin' was bustin' in my chest an' head. I got t' cryin'. I knowed sudden I loved ye yet, an' allus would love ye!

ABBIE. (*caressing his hair—tenderly*) My boy, hain't ye?

EBEN. I begun t' run back. I cut across the fields an' through the woods. I thought ye might have time t' run away—with me—an' . . .

ABBIE. (*shaking her head*) I got t' take my punishment—t' pay fur my sin.

EBEN. Then I want t' share it with ye.

ABBIE. Ye didn't do nothin'.

EBEN. I put it in yer head. I wisht he was dead! I as much as urged ye t' do it!

ABBIE. No. It was me alone!

EBEN. I'm as guilty as yew be! He was the child o' our sin.

ABBIE. (*lifting her head as if defying God*) I don't repent that sin! I hain't askin' God t' fergive that!

EBEN. Nor me—but it led up t' the other—an' the murder ye did, ye did 'count o' me—an' it's my murder, too, I'll tell the Sheriff—an' if ye deny it, I'll say we planned it t'gether—an' they'll all b'lieve me, fur they suspicion everythin' we've done, an' it'll seem likely an' true to 'em. An' it is true—way down. I did help ye—somehow.

ABBIE. (*laying her head on his—sobbing*) No! I don't want yew t' suffer!

EBEN. I got t' pay fur my part o' the sin! An' I'd suffer wuss leavin' ye, goin' West, thinkin' o' ye day an' night, bein' out when yew was in—(*Lowering his voice*) 'r bein' alive when yew was dead. (*A pause*) I want t' share with ye, Abbie—prison 'r death 'r hell 'r anythin'! (*He looks into her eyes and forces a trembling smile*) If I'm sharin' with ye, I won't feel lonesome, leastways.

ABBIE. (*weakly*) Eben! I won't let ye! I can't let ye!

EBEN. (*kissing her—tenderly*) Ye can't he'p yerself. I got ye beat fur once!

ABBIE. (*forcing a smile—adoringly*) I hain't beat—s'long's I got ye!

EBEN. (*hears the sound of feet outside*) Ssshh! Listen! They've come t' take us!

ABBIE. No, it's him. Don't give him no chance to fight ye, Eben. Don't say nothin'—no matter what he says. An' I won't neither. (*It is* CABOT. *He comes up from the barn in a great state of excitement and strides into the house and then into the kitchen.* EBEN *is kneeling beside* ABBIE, *his arm around her, hers around him. They stare straight ahead*).

CABOT. (*stares at them, his face hard. A long pause—vindictively*) Ye make a slick pair o' murderin' turtle doves! Ye'd ought t' be both hung on the same limb an' left thar t' swing in the breeze an' rot—a warnin' t' old fools like me t' b'ar their lonesomeness alone—an' fur young fools like ye t' hobble their lust. (*A pause. The excitement returns to his face, his eyes snap, he looks a bit crazy*) I couldn't work today. I couldn't take no interest. T' hell with the farm! I'm leavin' it! I've turned the cows an' other stock loose! I've druv 'em into the woods whar they kin be free! By freein' 'em, I'm freein' myself! I'm quittin' here today! I'll set fire t' house an' barn an' watch 'em burn, an' I'll leave yer Maw t' haunt the ashes, an' I'll will the fields back t' God, so that nothin' human kin never touch 'em! I'll be a-goin' to Californi-a—t' jine Simeon an' Peter—true sons o' mine if they be dumb fools—an' the Cabots'll find Solomon's Mines t'gether! (*He suddenly cuts a mad caper*) Whoop! What was the song they sung? "Oh, Californi-a! That's the land fur me." (*He sings this—then gets on his knees by the floor-board under which the money was hid*) An' I'll sail thar on one o' the finest clippers I kin find! I've got the money! Pity ye didn't know whar this was hidden so's ye could steal. . . . (*He has pulled up the board. He stares—feels—stares again. A pause of dead silence. He slowly turns, slumping into a sitting position on the floor, his eyes like those of a dead fish, his face the sickly green of an attack of nausea. He swallows painfully several times—forces a weak smile at last*) So—ye did steal it!

EBEN. (*emotionlessly*) I swapped it t' Sim an' Peter fur their share o' the farm—t' pay their passage t' Californi-a.

CABOT. (*with one sardonic*) Ha! (*He begins to recover. Gets slowly to his feet—strangely*) I calc'late God give it to 'em—not yew! God's hard, not easy! Mebbe they's easy gold in the West but it hain't God's gold. It hain't fur me. I kin hear His voice warnin' me agen t' be hard an' stay on my farm. I kin see his hand usin' Eben t' steal t' keep me from weakness. I kin feel I be in the palm o' His hand, His fingers guidin' me. (*A pause—then he mutters sadly*) It's a-goin' t' be lonesomer now than ever it war afore—an' I'm gittin' old, Lord—ripe on the bough. . . . (*Then stiffening*) Waal—what d'ye want? God's lonesome, hain't He? God's hard an' lonesome! (*A pause. The Sheriff with two men comes up the road from the left. They move cautiously to the door. The Sheriff knocks on it with the butt of his pistol*).

SHERIFF. Open in the name o' the law! (*They start*).

CABOT. They've come fur ye. (*He goes to the rear door*) Come in,

Jim! (*The three men enter.* CABOT *meets them in doorway*) Jest a minit, Jim. I got 'em safe here. (*The Sheriff nods. He and his companions remain in the doorway*).

EBEN. (*suddenly calls*) I lied this mornin', Jim. I helped her to do it. Ye kin take me, too.

ABBIE. (*brokenly*) No!

CABOT. Take 'em both. (*He comes forward—stares at* EBEN *with a trace of grudging admiration*) Purty good—fur yew! Waal, I got t' round up the stock. Good-by.

EBEN. Good-by.

ABBIE. Good-by. (CABOT *turns and strides past the men—comes out and around the corner of the house, his shoulders squared, his face stony, and stalks grimly toward the barn. In the meantime the Sheriff and men have come into the room*).

SHERIFF. (*embarrassedly*) Waal—we'd best start.

ABBIE. Wait. (*Turns to* EBEN) I love ye, Eben.

EBEN. I love ye, Abbie. (*They kiss. The three men grin and shuffle embarrassedly.* EBEN *takes* ABBIE'S *hand. They go out the door in rear, the men following, and come from the house, walking hand in hand to the gate.* EBEN *stops there and points to the sunrise sky*) Sun's a-rizin'. Purty, hain't it?

ABBIE. Ay-eh. (*They both stand for a moment looking up raptly in attitudes strangely aloof and devout*).

SHERIFF. (*looking around at the farm enviously—to his companion*) It's a jim-dandy farm, no denyin'. Wished I owned it!

CURTAIN 1925

Tennessee [Thomas Lanier] Williams

(1914-)

CHRONOLOGY:

1914 Born on March 26, in Columbus, Mississippi.
1926 Moved to St. Louis.
1938 Was a student at the University of Iowa.
1940 Awarded a Rockefeller Fellowship; *Battle of Angels.*
1945 *The Glass Menagerie* (awarded New York Drama Critics Circle Award).
1946 *Twenty-Seven Wagons Full of Cotton and Other One-Act Plays.*
1947 *A Streetcar Named Desire* (awarded Pulitzer Prize); *You Touched Me!* (with Donald Windham).
1948 *Summer and Smoke; One Arm and Other Stories.*
1950 *The Roman Spring of Mrs. Stone,* a novel.
1951 *The Rose Tattoo.*
1953 *Camino Real.*

1955 *Cat on a Hot Tin Roof* (awarded Pulitzer Prize); *In the Winter of Cities*, poems.
1956 *Baby Doll*, movie scenario.
1958 *Suddenly, Last Summer* (with *Something Unspoken*, under the title *Garden District*).
1959 *Sweet Bird of Youth.*
1960 *Period of Adjustment.*
1961 *The Night of the Iguana.*
1963 *The Milk Train Doesn't Stop Here Anymore.*

BIBLIOGRAPHY:

There is no collected edition of Williams' plays, although most of them are available in inexpensive paperback editions. Two recent book-length studies of him and his writing are Benjamin Nelson's *Tennessee Williams: The Man and His Work* (New York, 1961), and Nancy Tischler's *Tennessee Williams: Rebellious Puritan* (New York, 1961).

The Glass Menagerie

Nobody, not even the rain, has such small hands.
E E CUMMINGS

CHARACTERS

Amanda Wingfield (the mother)
A little woman of great but confused vitality clinging frantically to another time and place. Her characterization must be carefully created, not copied from type. She is not paranoiac, but her life is paranoia. There is much to admire in Amanda, and as much to love and pity as there is to laugh at. Certainly she has endurance and a kind of heroism, and though her foolishness makes her unwittingly cruel at times, there is tenderness in her slight person.

Laura Wingfield (her daughter)
Amanda, having failed to establish contact with reality, continues to live vitally in her illusions, but Laura's situation is even graver. A childhood illness has left her crippled, one leg slightly shorter than the other, and held in a brace. This defect need not be more than suggested on the stage. Stemming from this, Laura's separation increases till she is like a piece of her own glass collection, too exquisitely fragile to move from the shelf.

Tom Wingfield (her son)
And the narrator of the play. A poet with a job in a warehouse. His nature is not remorseless, but to escape from a trap he has to act without pity.

Jim O'Connor (the gentleman caller)
A nice, ordinary, young man.

Scene

AN ALLEY IN ST. LOUIS

PART I. *Preparation for a Gentleman Caller*
PART II. *The Gentleman calls*

Time: Now and the Past

PRODUCTION NOTES

Being a "memory play," The Glass Menagerie *can be presented with unusual freedom of convention. Because of its considerably delicate or tenuous material, atmospheric touches and subtleties of direction play a particularly important part. Expressionism and all other unconventional techniques in drama have only one valid aim, and that is a closer approach to truth. When a play employs unconventional techniques, it is not, or certainly shouldn't be, trying to escape its responsibility of dealing with reality, or interpreting experience, but is actually or should be attempting to find a closer approach, a more penetrating and vivid expression of things as they are. The straight realistic play with its genuine frigidaire and authentic ice-cubes, its characters that speak exactly as its audience speaks, corresponds to the academic landscape and has the same virtue of a photographic likeness. Everyone should know nowadays the unimportance of the photographic in art: that truth, life, or reality is an organic thing which the poetic imagination can represent or suggest, in essence, only through transformation, through changing into other forms than those which were merely present in appearance.*

These remarks are not meant as a preface only to this particular play. They have to do with a conception of a new, plastic theatre which must take the place of the exhausted theatre of realistic conventions if the theatre is to resume vitality as a part of our culture.

the screen device

There is only one important difference between the original and acting version of the play *and that is the* omission *in the latter of the device which I tentatively included in my* original *script. This device was the use of a screen on which were projected magic-lantern slides bearing images or titles. I do not regret the omission of this device from the present Broadway production. The extraordinary power of Miss Taylor's performance made it suitable to have the utmost simplicity in the physical production. But I think it may be interesting to some readers to see how this device was conceived. So I am putting it into the published manuscript. These images and legends, projected from behind, were cast on a section of wall between the front-room and dining-room areas, which should be indistinguishable from the rest when not in use.*

The purpose of this will probably be apparent. It is to give accent to certain values in each scene. Each scene contains a particular point (or several) which is structurally the most important. In an episodic play, such as this, the basic structure or narrative line may be obscured from the audience; the effect may seem fragmentary rather than architectural. This may not be the fault of the play so much as a lack of attention in the audience. The legend or image upon the screen will strengthen the effect of what is merely allusion in the writing and allow the primary point to be made more simply and lightly than if the entire responsibility were on the spoken lines. Aside from this structural value, I think the screen will have a definite emotional appeal, less definable but just as important. An imaginative producer or director may invent many other uses for this device than those indicated in the present script. In fact the possibilities of the device seem much larger to me than the instance of this play can possibly utilize.

the music

Another extra-literary accent in this play is provided by the use of music. A single recurring tune, "The Glass Menagerie," is used to give emotional emphasis to suitable passages. This tune is like circus music, not when you are on the grounds or in the immediate vicinity of the parade, but when you are at some distance and very likely thinking of something else. It seems under those circumstances to continue almost interminably and it weaves in and out of your preoccupied consciousness; then it is the lightest, most delicate music in the world and perhaps the saddest. It expresses the surface vivacity of life with the underlying strain of immutable and inexpressible sorrow. When you look at a piece of delicately spun glass you think of two things: how beautiful it is and how easily it can be broken. Both of those ideas should be woven into the recurring tune, which dips in and out of the play as if it were carried on a wind that changes. It serves as a thread of connection and allusion between the narrator with his separate point in time and space and the subject of his story. Between each episode it returns as reference to the emotion, nostalgia, which is the first condition of the play. It is primarily Laura's music and therefore comes out most clearly when the play focuses upon her and the lovely fragility of glass which is her image.

the lighting

The lighting in the play is not realistic. In keeping with the atmosphere of memory, the stage is dim. Shafts of light are focused on selected areas or actors, sometimes in contradistinction to what is the apparent center. For instance, in the quarrel scene between Tom and Amanda, in which Laura has no active part, the clearest pool of light is on her figure. This is also true of the supper scene, when her silent figure on the sofa should remain the visual center. The light upon Laura should be distinct from the others, having a peculiar pristine clarity such as light used in early religious portraits of female saints or madonnas. A certain correspondence to light in religious paintings, such as El Greco's, where the figures are radiant in atmosphere that is relatively dusky, could be effectively used throughout the play. (It will also permit a more effective use of the screen.) A free, imaginative use of light can be of enormous value in giving a mobile, plastic quality to plays of a more or less static nature.

T. W.

SCENE 1

The Wingfield apartment is in the rear of the building, one of those vast hive-like conglomerations of cellular living-units that flower as warty growths in overcrowded urban centers of lower middle-class population and are symptomatic of the impulse of this largest and fundamentally enslaved section of American society to avoid fluidity and differentiation and to exist and function as one interfused mass of automatism.

The apartment faces an alley and is entered by a fire-escape, a structure whose name is a touch of accidental poetic truth, for all of these huge buildings are always burning with the slow and implacable fires of human desperation. The fire-escape is included in the set—that is, the landing of it and steps descending from it.

The scene is memory and is therefore nonrealistic. Memory takes a lot of poetic license. It omits some details; others are exaggerated, according to the emotional value of the articles it touches, for memory is seated predominantly in the heart. The interior is therefore rather dim and poetic.

At the rise of the curtain, the audience is faced with the dark, grim rear wall of the Wingfield tenement. This building, which runs parallel to the footlights, is flanked on both sides by dark, narrow alleys which run into murky canyons of tangled clotheslines, garbage cans and the sinister lattice-work of neighboring fire-escapes. It is up and down these side alleys that exterior entrances and exits are made, during the play. At the end of TOM'S *opening commentary, the dark tenement wall slowly reveals (by means of a transparency) the interior of the ground floor Wingfield apartment.*

Downstage is the living room, which also serves as a sleeping room for LAURA, *the sofa unfolding to make her bed. Upstage, center, and divided by a wide arch or second proscenium with transparent faded portieres (or second curtain), is the dining room. In an old-fashioned what-not in the living room are seen scores of transparent glass animals. A blown-up photograph of the father hangs on the wall of the living room, facing the audience, to the left of the archway. It is the face of a very handsome young man in a doughboy's First World War cap. He is gallantly smiling, ineluctably smiling, as if to say, "I will be smiling forever."*

The audience hears and sees the opening scene in the dining room through both the transparent fourth wall of the building and the transparent gauze portieres of the dining-room arch. It is during this revealing scene that the fourth wall slowly ascends, out of sight. This transparent exterior wall is not brought down again until the very end of the play, during TOM'S *final speech.*

The narrator is an undisguised convention of the play. He takes whatever license with dramatic convention as is convenient to his purposes.

TOM *enters dressed as a merchant sailor from alley, stage left, and strolls across the front of the stage to the fire-escape. There he stops and lights a cigarette. He addresses the audience.*

TOM. Yes, I have tricks in my pocket, I have things up my sleeve. But I am the opposite of a stage magician. He gives you illusion that has the appearance of truth. I give you truth in the pleasant disguise of illusion.

To begin with, I turn back time. I reverse it to that quaint period, the thirties, when the huge middle class of America was matriculating in a school for the blind. Their eyes had failed them, or they had failed their eyes, and so they were having their fingers pressed forcibly down on the fiery Braille alphabet of a dissolving economy.

In Spain there was revolution. Here there was only shouting and confusion.

In Spain there was Guernica. Here there were disturbances of labor, sometimes pretty violent, in otherwise peaceful cities such as Chicago, Cleveland, Saint Louis . . .

This is the social background of the play.

[MUSIC]

The play is memory.

Being a memory play, it is dimly lighted, it is sentimental, it is not realistic.

In memory everything seems to happen to music. That explains the fiddle in the wings.

I am the narrator of the play, and also a character in it.

The other characters are my mother, Amanda, my sister, Laura, and a gentleman caller who appears in the final scenes.

He is the most realistic character in the play, being an emissary from a world of reality that we were somehow set apart from.

But since I have a poet's weakness for symbols, I am using this character also as a symbol; he is the long delayed but always expected something that we live for.

There is a fifth character in the play who doesn't appear except in this larger-than-life-size photograph over the mantel.

This is our father who left us a long time ago.

He was a telephone man who fell in love with long distances; he gave up his job with the telephone company and skipped the light fantastic out of town . . .

The last we heard of him was a picture post-card from Mazatlan, on the Pacific coast of Mexico, containing a message of two words—

"Hello—Good-bye!" and no address.

I think the rest of the play will explain itself. . . .

[AMANDA's *voice becomes audible through the portieres.*]

[LEGEND ON SCREEN: "OU SONT LES NEIGES"]

[*He divides the portieres and enters the upstage area.*]

[AMANDA *and* LAURA *are seated at a drop-leaf table. Eating is indicated by gestures without food or utensils.* AMANDA *faces the audience.* TOM *and* LAURA *are seated in profile.*]

[*The interior has lit up softly and through the scrim we see* AMANDA *and* LAURA *seated at the table in the upstage area.*]

AMANDA [*calling*]. Tom?

TOM. Yes, Mother.

AMANDA. We can't say grace until you come to the table!

TOM. Coming, Mother. [*He bows slightly and withdraws, reappearing a few moments later in his place at the table.*]

AMANDA [*to her son*]. Honey, don't *push* with your *fingers.* If you have to push with something, the thing to push with is a crust of bread. And chew—chew! Animals have sections in their stomachs which enable them to digest food without mastication, but human beings are supposed to chew their food before they swallow it down. Eat food leisurely, son, and really enjoy it. A well-cooked meal has lots of delicate flavors that have to be held in the mouth for appreciation. So chew your food and give your salivary glands a chance to function!

[TOM *deliberately lays his imaginary fork down and pushes his chair back from the table.*]

TOM. I haven't enjoyed one bite of this dinner because of your constant directions on how to eat it. It's you that makes me rush through meals with your hawk-like attention to every bite I take. Sickening—spoils my appetite—all this discussion of—animal's secretion—salivary glands—mastication!

AMANDA [*lightly*]. Temperament like a Metropolitan star! [*He rises and crosses downstage.*] You're not excused from the table.

TOM. I'm getting a cigarette.

AMANDA. You smoke too much.

[LAURA *rises.*]

LAURA. I'll bring in the blanc mange.

[*He remains standing with his cigarette by the portieres during the following.*]

AMANDA [*rising*]. No, sister, no, sister—you be the lady this time and I'll be the darky.

LAURA. I'm already up.

AMANDA. Resume your seat, little sister—I want you to stay fresh and pretty—for gentlemen callers!

LAURA. I'm not expecting any gentlemen callers.

AMANDA [*crossing out to kitchenette. Airily*]. Sometimes they come when they are least expected! Why, I remember one Sunday afternoon in Blue Mountain—[*Enters kitchenette*]

TOM. I know what's coming!

LAURA. Yes. But let her tell it.

TOM. Again?

LAURA. She loves to tell it.

[AMANDA *returns with bowl of dessert.*]

AMANDA. One Sunday afternoon in Blue Mountain—your mother received—*seventeen!*—gentlemen callers! Why, sometimes there weren't chairs enough to accommodate them all. We had to send the nigger over to bring in folding chairs from the parish house.

TOM [*remaining at portieres*]. How did you entertain those gentlemen callers?

AMANDA. I understood the art of conversation!

TOM. I bet you could talk.

AMANDA. Girls in those days *knew* how to talk, I can tell you.

TOM. Yes?

[IMAGE: AMANDA AS A GIRL ON A PORCH GREETING CALLERS]

AMANDA. They knew how to entertain their gentlemen callers. It wasn't enough for a girl to be possessed of a pretty face and a graceful figure—although I wasn't slighted in either respect. She also needed to have a nimble wit and a tongue to meet all occasions.

TOM. What did you talk about?

AMANDA. Things of importance going on in the world! Never anything coarse or common or vulgar. [*She addresses* TOM *as though he were seated in the vacant chair at the table though he remains by portieres. He plays this scene as though he held the book.*] My callers were gentlemen—all! Among my callers were some of the most prominent young planters of the Mississippi Delta—planters and sons of planters!

[TOM *motions for music and a spot of light on* AMANDA.]

[*Her eyes lift, her face glows, her voice becomes rich and elegiac.*]

[SCREEN LEGEND: "OU SONT LES NEIGES"]

There was young Champ Laughlin who later became vice-president of the Delta Planters Bank.

Hadley Stevenson who was drowned in Moon Lake and left his widow one hundred and fifty thousand in Government bonds.

There were the Cutrere brothers, Wesley and Bates. Bates was one of my bright particular beaux! He got in a quarrel with that wild Wainwright boy. They shot it out on the floor of Moon Lake Casino. Bates was shot through the stomach. Died in the ambulance on his way to Memphis. His widow was also well-provided for, came into eight or ten thousand acres, that's all. She married him on the rebound—never loved her—carried my picture on him the night he died!

And there was that boy that every girl in the Delta had set her cap for! That beautiful, brilliant young Fitzhugh boy from Greene County!

TOM. What did he leave his widow?

AMANDA. He never married! Gracious, you talk as though all of my old admirers had turned up their toes to the daisies!

TOM. Isn't this the first you've mentioned that still survives?

AMANDA. That Fitzhugh boy went North and made a fortune—came to be known as the Wolf of Wall Street! He had the Midas touch, whatever he touched turned to gold!

And I could have been Mrs. Duncan J. Fitzhugh, mind you! But—I picked your *father!*

LAURA [*rising*]. Mother, let me clear the table.

AMANDA. No, dear, you go in front and study your typewriter chart. Or practice your shorthand a little. Stay fresh and pretty!—It's almost time for our gentlemen callers to start arriving. [*She flounces girlishly toward the kitchenette.*] How many do you suppose we're going to entertain this afternoon?

[TOM *throws down the paper and jumps up with a groan.*]

LAURA [*alone in the dining room*]. I don't believe we're going to receive any, Mother.

AMANDA [*reappearing, airily*]. What? No one—not one? You must be joking! [LAURA *nervously echoes her laugh. She slips in a fugitive manner through the half-open portieres and draws them gently behind her. A shaft of very clear light is thrown on her face against the faded tapestry of the curtains.* MUSIC: "THE GLASS MENAGERIE" UNDER FAINTLY. *Lightly*] Not one gentleman caller? It can't be true! There must be a flood, there must have been a tornado!

LAURA. It isn't a flood, it's not a tornado, Mother. I'm just not popular like you were in Blue Mountain. . . . [TOM *utters another groan.* LAURA *glances at him with a faint, apologetic smile. Her voice catching a little*] Mother's afraid I'm going to be an old maid.

THE SCENE DIMS OUT WITH "GLASS MENAGERIE" MUSIC

SCENE 2

"Laura, Haven't You Ever Liked Some Boy?"

On the dark stage the screen is lighted with the image of blue roses.

Gradually LAURA'S *figure becomes apparent and the screen goes out.*

The music subsides.

LAURA *is seated in the delicate ivory chair at the small claw-foot table. She wears a dress of soft violet material for a kimono—her hair tied back from her forehead with a ribbon.*

She is washing and polishing her collection of glass.

AMANDA *appears on the fire-escape steps. At the sound of her ascent,* LAURA *catches her breath, thrusts the bowl of ornaments away and seats herself stiffly before the diagram of the typewriter keyboard as though it held her spellbound.*

Something has happened to AMANDA. *It is written in her face as she climbs to the landing: a look that is grim and hopeless and a little absurd.*

She has on one of those cheap or imitation velvety-looking cloth coats with imitation fur collar. Her hat is five or six years old, one of those dreadful cloche hats that were worn in the late twenties and she is clasping an enormous black patent-leather pocketbook with nickel clasps and initials. This is her full-dress outfit, the one she usually wears to the D.A.R.

Before entering she looks through the door.

She purses her lips, opens her eyes very wide, rolls them upward and shakes her head.

Then she slowly lets herself in the door. Seeing her mother's expression LAURA *touches her lips with a nervous gesture.*

LAURA. Hello, Mother, I was—[*She makes a nervous gesture toward the chart on the wall.* AMANDA *leans against the shut door and stares at* LAURA *with a martyred look.*]

AMANDA. Deception? Deception? [*She slowly removes her hat and gloves, continuing the sweet suffering stare. She lets the hat and gloves fall on the floor—a bit of acting.*]

LAURA [*shakily*]. How was the D.A.R. meeting? [AMANDA *slowly opens her purse and removes a dainty white handkerchief which she shakes out delicately and delicately touches to her lips and nostrils.*] Didn't you go to the D.A.R. meeting, Mother?

AMANDA [*faintly, almost inaudibly*].—No.—No. [*Then more forcibly*] I did not have the strength—to go to the D.A.R. In fact, I did not have the courage! I wanted to find a hole in the ground and hide myself in it forever! [*She crosses slowly to the wall and removes the diagram of the typewriter keyboard. She holds it in front of her for a second, staring at it sweetly and sorrowfully—then bites her lips and tears it in two pieces.*]

LAURA [*faintly*]. Why did you do that, Mother? [AMANDA *repeats the same procedure with the chart of the Gregg Alphabet.*] Why are you—

AMANDA. Why? Why? How old are you, Laura?

LAURA. Mother, you know my age.

AMANDA. I thought that you were an adult; it seems that I was mistaken. [*She crosses slowly to the sofa and sinks down and stares at* LAURA.]

LAURA. Please don't stare at me, Mother.

[AMANDA *closes her eyes and lowers her head. Count ten*]

AMANDA. What are we going to do, what is going to become of us, what is the future?

[*Count ten*]

LAURA. Has something happened, Mother? [AMANDA *draws a long breath and takes out the handkerchief again. Dabbing process*] Mother, has—something happened?

AMANDA. I'll be all right in a minute, I'm just bewildered—[*count five*] —by life. . . .

LAURA. Mother, I wish that you would tell me what's happened!

AMANDA. As you know, I was supposed to be inducted into my office at the D.A.R. this afternoon. [IMAGE: A SWARM OF TYPEWRITERS] But I stopped off at Rubicam's business college to speak to your teachers about your having a cold and ask them what progress they thought you were making down there.

LAURA. Oh. . . .

AMANDA. I went to the typing instructor and introduced myself as your mother. She didn't know who you were. Wingfield, she said. We don't have any such student enrolled at the school!

I assured her she did, that you had been going to classes since early in January.

"I wonder," she said, "if you could be talking about that terribly shy little girl who dropped out of school after only a few days' attendance?"

"No," I said, "Laura, my daughter, has been going to school every day for the past six weeks!"

"Excuse me," she said. She took the attendance book out and there was your name, unmistakably printed, and all the dates you were absent until they decided that you had dropped out of school.

I still said, "No, there must have been some mistake! There must have been some mix-up in the records!"

And she said, "No—I remember her perfectly now. Her hands shook so that she couldn't hit the right keys! The first time we gave a speed-test, she broke down completely—was sick at the stomach and almost had to be carried into the wash-room! After that morning she never showed up any more. We phoned the house but never got any answer"—while I was working at Famous and Barr, I suppose, demonstrating those—Oh!

I felt so weak I could barely keep on my feet!

I had to sit down while they got me a glass of water!

Fifty dollars' tuition, all of our plans—my hopes and ambitions for you—just gone up the spout, just gone up the spout like that.

[LAURA *draws a long breath and gets awkwardly to her feet. She crosses to the victrola and winds it up.*]

What are you doing?

LAURA. Oh! [*She releases the handle and returns to her seat.*]

AMANDA. Laura, where have you been going when you've gone out pretending that you were going to business college?

LAURA. I've just been going out walking.

AMANDA. That's not true.

LAURA. It is. I just went walking.

AMANDA. Walking? Walking? In winter? Deliberately courting pneumonia in that light coat? Where did you walk to, Laura?

LAURA. All sorts of places—mostly in the park.

AMANDA. Even after you'd started catching that cold?

LAURA. It was the lesser of two evils, Mother. [IMAGE: WINTER SCENE IN PARK] I couldn't go back up. I—threw up—on the floor!

AMANDA. From half past seven till after five every day you mean to tell me you walked around in the park, because you wanted to make me think that you were still going to Rubicam's Business College?

LAURA. It wasn't as bad as it sounds. I went inside places to get warmed up.

AMANDA. Inside where?

LAURA. I went in the art museum and the bird-houses at the Zoo. I visited the penguins every day! Sometimes I did without lunch and went to the movies. Lately I've been spending most of my afternoons in the Jewel-box, that big glass house where they raise the tropical flowers.

AMANDA. You did all this to deceive me, just for deception? [LAURA *looks down.*] Why?

LAURA. Mother, when you're disappointed, you get that awful suffering look on your face, like the picture of Jesus' mother in the museum!

AMANDA. Hush!

LAURA. I couldn't face it.

[*Pause. A whisper of strings*]

[LEGEND: "THE CRUST OF HUMILITY"]

AMANDA. [*hopelessly fingering the huge pocketbook*]. So what are we going to do the rest of our lives? Stay home and watch the parades go by? Amuse ourselves with the glass menagerie, darling? Eternally play those worn-out phonograph records your father left as a painful reminder of him?

We won't have a business career—we've given that up because it gave us nervous indigestion! [*Laughs wearily*] What is there left but dependency all our lives? I know so well what becomes of unmarried women who aren't prepared to occupy a position. I've seen such pitiful cases in the South—barely tolerated spinsters living upon the grudging patronage of sister's husband or brother's wife!—stuck away in some little mouse-trap of a room—encouraged by one in-law to visit another—little birdlike women without any nest—eating the crust of humility all their life!

Is that the future that we've mapped out for ourselves?

I swear it's the only alternative I can think of!

It isn't a very pleasant alternative, is it?

Of course—some girls *do marry.*

[LAURA *twists her hands nervously.*]

Haven't you ever liked some boy?

LAURA. Yes. I liked one once. [*Rises*] I came across his picture a while ago.

AMANDA [*with some interest*]. He gave you his picture?

LAURA. No, it's in the year-book.

AMANDA [*disappointed*]. Oh—a high-school boy.

[SCREEN IMAGE: JIM AS HIGH-SCHOOL HERO BEARING A SILVER CUP]

LAURA. Yes. His name was Jim. [LAURA *lifts the heavy annual from the claw-foot table.*] Here he is in *The Pirates of Penzance.*

AMANDA [*absently*]. The what?

LAURA. The operetta the senior class put on. He had a wonderful voice and we sat across the aisle from each other Mondays, Wednesdays and Fridays in the Aud. Here he is with the silver cup for debating! See his grin?

AMANDA [*absently*]. He must have had a jolly disposition.

LAURA. He used to call me—Blue Roses.

[IMAGE: BLUE ROSES]

AMANDA. Why did he call you such a name as that?

LAURA. When I had that attack of pleurosis—he asked me what was the matter when I came back. I said pleurosis—he thought that I said Blue Roses! So that's what he always called me after that. Whenever he saw me, he'd holler, "Hello, Blue Roses!" I didn't care for the girl that he went out with. Emily Meisenbach. Emily was the best-dressed girl at Soldan. She never struck me, though, as being sincere . . . It says in the Personal Section—they're engaged. That's—six years ago! They must be married by now.

AMANDA. Girls that aren't cut out for business careers usually wind up married to some nice man. [*Gets up with a spark of revival*] Sister, that's what you'll do!

[LAURA *utters a startled, doubtful laugh. She reaches quickly for a piece of glass.*]

LAURA. But, Mother—

AMANDA. Yes? [*Crossing to photograph*]

LAURA [*in a tone of frightened apology*]. I'm—crippled!

[IMAGE: SCREEN]

AMANDA. Nonsense! Laura, I've told you never, never to use that word. Why, you're not crippled, you just have a little defect—hardly noticeable, even! When people have some slight disadvantage like that, they cultivate other things to make up for it—develop charm—and vivacity—and—*charm!* That's all you have to do! [*She turns again to the photograph.*] One thing your father had *plenty of*—was *charm!*

[TOM *motions to the fiddle in the wings.*]

THE SCENE FADES OUT WITH MUSIC

SCENE 3

LEGEND ON SCREEN: "AFTER THE FIASCO—"

TOM *speaks from the fire-escape landing.*

TOM. After the fiasco at Rubicam's Business College, the idea of getting a gentleman caller for Laura began to play a more and more important part in Mother's calculations.

It became an obsession. Like some archetype of the universal unconscious, the image of the gentleman caller haunted our small apartment. . . .

[IMAGE: YOUNG MAN AT DOOR WITH FLOWERS]

An evening at home rarely passed without some allusion to this image, this spectre, this hope. . . .

Even when he wasn't mentioned, his presence hung in Mother's preoccupied look and in my sister's frightened, apologetic manner—hung like a sentence passed upon the Wingfields!

Mother was a woman of action as well as words.

She began to take logical steps in the planned direction.

Late that winter and in the early spring—realizing that extra money would be needed to properly feather the nest and plume the bird—she conducted a vigorous campaign on the telephone, roping in subscribers to one of those magazines for matrons called *The Home-maker's Companion,* the type of journal that features the serialized sublimations of ladies of letters who think in terms of delicate cup-like breasts, slim, tapering waists, rich, creamy thighs, eyes like wood-smoke in autumn, fingers that soothe and caress like strains of music, bodies as powerful as Etruscan sculpture.

[SCREEN IMAGE: GLAMOR MAGAZINE COVER]

[AMANDA *enters with phone on long extension cord. She is spotted in the dim stage.*]

AMANDA. Ida Scott? This is Amanda Wingfield!

We *missed* you at the D.A.R. last Monday!

I said to myself: She's probably suffering with that sinus condition! How is that sinus condition?

Horrors! Heaven have mercy!—You're a Christian martyr, yes, that's what you are, a Christian martyr!

Well, I just now happened to notice that your subscription to the *Companion's* about to expire! Yes, it expires with the next issue, honey!—just when that wonderful new serial by Bessie Mae Hopper is getting off to such an exciting start. Oh, honey, it's something that you can't miss! You remember how *Gone With the Wind* took everybody by storm? You simply couldn't go out if you hadn't read it. All everybody *talked* was Scarlett O'Hara. Well, this is a book that critics already compare to *Gone With the Wind.* It's the *Gone With the Wind* of the post-World War generation!—What?—Burning?—Oh, honey, don't let them burn, go take a look in the oven and I'll hold the wire! Heavens—I think she's hung up!

DIM OUT

[LEGEND ON SCREEN: "YOU THINK I'M IN LOVE WITH CONTINENTAL SHOEMAKERS?"]

[*Before the stage is lighted, the violent voices of* TOM *and* AMANDA *are heard.*]

[*They are quarreling behind the portieres. In front of them stands* LAURA *with clenched hands and panicky expression.*]

[*A clear pool of light on her figure throughout this scene*]

TOM. What in Christ's name am I—

AMANDA [*shrilly*]. Don't you use that—

TOM. Supposed to do!

AMANDA. Expression! Not in my—

TOM. Ohhh!

AMANDA. Presence! Have you gone out of your senses?

TOM. I have, that's true, *driven* out!

AMANDA. What is the matter with you, you—big—big—IDIOT!

TOM. Look!—I've got *no thing*, no single thing—

AMANDA. Lower your voice!

TOM. In my life here that I can call my OWN! Everything is—

AMANDA. Stop that shouting!

TOM. Yesterday you confiscated my books! You had the nerve to—

AMANDA. I took that horrible novel back to the library—yes! That hideous book by that insane Mr. Lawrence. [TOM *laughs wildly.*] I cannot control the output of diseased minds or people who cater to them—[TOM *laughs still more wildly.*] BUT I WON'T ALLOW SUCH FILTH BROUGHT INTO MY HOUSE! No, no, no, no, no!

TOM. House, house! Who pays rent on it, who makes a slave of himself to—

AMANDA. [*fairly screeching*]. Don't you DARE to—

TOM. No, no, I mustn't say things! *I've* got to just—

AMANDA. Let me tell you—

TOM. I don't want to hear any more! [*He tears the portieres open. The upstage area is lit with a turgid smoky red glow.*]

[AMANDA'S *hair is in metal curlers and she wears a very old bathrobe, much too large for her slight figure, a relic of the faithless Mr. Wingfield.*]

[*An upright typewriter and a wild disarray of manuscripts is on the drop-leaf table. The quarrel was probably precipitated by* AMANDA'S *interruption of his creative labor. A chair lying overthrown on the floor*]

[*Their gesticulating shadows are cast on the ceiling by the fiery glow.*]

AMANDA. You *will* hear more, you—

TOM. No, I won't hear more, I'm going out!

AMANDA. You come right back in—

TOM. Out, out, out! Because I'm—

AMANDA. Come back here, Tom Wingfield! I'm not through talking to you!

TOM. Oh, go—

LAURA [*desperately*].—Tom!

AMANDA. You're going to listen, and no more insolence from you! I'm at the end of my patience!

[*He comes back toward her.*]

TOM. What do you think I'm at? Aren't I supposed to have any patience to reach the end of, Mother? I know, I know. It seems unimportant to you, what I'm *doing*—what I *want* to do—having a little *difference* between them! You don't think that—

AMANDA. I think you've been doing things that you're ashamed of. That's why you act like this. I don't believe that you go every night to the movies. Nobody goes to the movies night after night. Nobody in their right minds goes to the movies as often as you pretend to. People don't go to the movies at nearly midnight, and movies don't let out at two A.M. Come in stumbling. Muttering to yourself like a maniac! You get three hours' sleep and then go to work. Oh, I can picture the way you're doing down there. Moping, doping, because you're in no condition.

TOM [*wildly*]. No, I'm in no condition!

AMANDA. What right have you got to jeopardize your job? Jeopardize the security of us all? How do you think we'd manage if you were—

TOM. Listen! You think I'm crazy *about* the *warehouse?* [*He bends fiercely toward her slight figure.*] You think I'm in love with the Continental Shoemakers? You think I want to spend fifty-five *years* down there in that—*celotex interior!* with—*fluorescent—tubes!* Look! I'd rather somebody picked up a crowbar and battered out my brains—than go back mornings! I *go!* Every time you come in yelling that God damn "*Rise and Shine!*" "*Rise and Shine!*" I say to myself, "How *lucky dead* people are!" But I get up. I *go!* For sixty-five dollars a month I give up all that I dream of doing and being *ever!* And you say self—*self's* all I ever think of. Why, listen, if self is what I thought of, Mother, I'd be where he is—GONE! [*Pointing to father's picture*] As far as the system of transportation reaches! [*He starts past her. She grabs his arm.*] Don't grab at me, Mother!

AMANDA. Where are you going?

TOM. I'm going to the *movies!*

AMANDA. I don't believe that lie!

TOM [*crouching toward her, overtowering her tiny figure. She backs away, gasping*]. I'm going to opium dens! Yes, opium dens, dens of vice and criminals' hang-outs, Mother. I've joined the Hogan gang. I'm a hired assassin, I carry a tommy-gun in a violin case! I run a string of cat-houses in the Valley! They call me Killer, Killer Wingfield, I'm leading a double-life, a simple, honest warehouse worker by day, by night a dynamic *czar* of the *underworld, Mother.* I go to gambling casinos, I spin away fortunes on the roulette table! I wear a patch over one eye and a false mustache, sometimes I put on green whiskers. On those occasions they call me—*El Diablo!* Oh, I could tell you things to make you sleepless! My enemies plan to dynamite this place. They're going to blow us all sky-high some night! I'll be glad, very happy, and so will you! You'll go up, up on a broomstick, over Blue Mountain with seventeen gentlemen callers! You ugly—babbling old—*witch.* . . . [*He goes through a series of violent, clumsy movements, seizing his overcoat, lunging to the door, pulling it fiercely open. The women watch him, aghast. His arm catches in the sleeve of the coat as he struggles to pull it on. For a moment he is pinioned by the bulky garment. With an outraged groan he tears the coat off again, splitting the shoulder of it, and hurls it across the room. It strikes against the shelf of* LAURA'S *glass collection, there is a tinkle of shattering glass.* LAURA *cries out as if wounded.*]

[MUSIC. LEGEND: "THE GLASS MENAGERIE"]

LAURA [*shrilly*]. *My glass!*—menagerie. . . . [*She covers her face and turns away.*]

[*But* AMANDA *is still stunned and stupefied by the "ugly witch" so that she barely notices this occurrence. Now she recovers her speech.*]

AMANDA [*in an awful voice*]. I won't speak to you—until you apologize! [*She crosses through portieres and draws them together behind her.* TOM *is left with* LAURA. LAURA *clings weakly to the mantel with her face averted.* TOM *stares at her stupidly for a moment. Then he crosses to shelf. Drops awkwardly on his knees to collect the fallen glass, glancing at* LAURA *as if he would speak but couldn't*]

"The Glass Menagerie" steals in as

THE SCENE DIMS OUT

SCENE 4

The interior is dark. Faint light in the alley.

A deep-voiced bell in a church is tolling the hour of five as the scene commences.

TOM *appears at the top of the alley. After each solemn boom of the bell in the tower, he shakes a little noise-maker or rattle as if to express the tiny spasm of man in contrast to the sustained power and dignity of the Almighty. This and the unsteadiness of his advance make it evident that he has been drinking.*

As he climbs the few steps to the fire-escape landing light steals up inside. LAURA *appears in night-dress, observing* TOM'S *empty bed in the front room.*

TOM *fishes in his pockets for door-key, removing a motley assortment of articles in the search, including a perfect shower of movie-ticket stubs and an empty bottle. At last he finds the key, but just as he is about to insert it, it slips from his fingers. He strikes a match and crouches below the door.*

TOM [*bitterly*]. One crack—and it falls through!

[LAURA *opens the door.*]

LAURA. Tom! Tom, what are you doing?

TOM. Looking for a door-key.

LAURA. Where have you been all this time?

TOM. I have been to the movies.

LAURA. All this time at the movies?

TOM. There was a very long program. There was a Garbo picture and a Mickey Mouse and a travelogue and a newsreel and a preview of coming attractions. And there was an organ solo and a collection for the milk-fund—simultaneously—which ended up in a terrible fight between a fat lady and an usher!

LAURA [*innocently*]. Did you have to stay through everything?

TOM. Of course! And, oh, I forgot! There was a big stage show! The headliner on this stage show was Malvolio the Magician. He performed wonderful tricks, many of them, such as pouring water back and forth between pitchers. First it turned to wine and then it turned to beer and then it turned to whiskey. I know it was whiskey it finally turned into because he needed somebody to come up out of the audience to help him, and I came up—both shows! It was Kentucky Straight Bourbon. A very generous fellow, he gave souvenirs. [*He pulls from his back pocket a shimmering rainbow-colored scarf.*] He gave me this. This is his magic scarf. You can have it, Laura. You wave it over a canary cage and you get a bowl of gold-fish. You wave it over the gold-fish bowl and they fly away canaries. . . . But the wonderfullest trick of all was the coffin trick. We nailed him into a coffin and he got out of the coffin without removing one nail. [*He has come inside.*] There is a trick that would come in handy for me—get me out of this 2 by 4 situation! [*Flops onto bed and starts removing shoes*]

LAURA. Tom—Shhh!

TOM. What're you shushing me for?

LAURA. You'll wake up Mother.

TOM. Goody, goody! Pay 'er back for all those "Rise an' Shines." [*Lies down, groaning*] You know it don't take much intelligence to get yourself into a nailed-up coffin, Laura. But who in hell ever got himself out of one without removing one nail?

[*As if in answer, the father's grinning photograph lights up.*]

SCENE DIMS OUT

[*Immediately following: The church bell is heard striking six. At the sixth stroke the alarm clock goes off in* AMANDA'S *room, and after a few moments we hear her calling: "Rise and Shine! Rise and Shine! Laura, go tell your brother to rise and shine!"*]

TOM [*sitting up slowly*]. I'll rise—but I won't shine.

[*The light increases.*]

AMANDA. Laura, tell your brother his coffee is ready.

[LAURA *slips into front room.*]

LAURA. Tom!—It's nearly seven. Don't make Mother nervous. [*He stares at her stupidly. Beseechingly*] Tom, speak to Mother this morning. Make up with her, apologize, speak to her!

TOM. She won't to me. It's her that started not speaking.

LAURA. If you just say you're sorry she'll start speaking.

TOM. Her not speaking—is that such a tragedy?

LAURA. Please—please!

AMANDA [*calling from kitchenette*]. Laura, are you going to do what I asked you to do, or do I have to get dressed and go out myself?

LAURA. Going, going—soon as I get on my coat! [*She pulls on a shapeless felt hat with nervous, jerky movement, pleadingly glancing at* TOM. *Rushes awkwardly for coat. The coat is one of* AMANDA'S, *inaccurately made-over, the sleeves too short for* LAURA.] Butter and what else?

AMANDA [*entering upstage*]. Just butter. Tell them to charge it.

LAURA. Mother, they make such faces when I do that.

AMANDA. Sticks and stones can break our bones, but the expression on Mr. Garfinkel's face won't harm us! Tell your brother his coffee is getting cold.

LAURA [*at door*]. Do what I asked you, will you, will you, Tom?

[*He looks sullenly away.*]

AMANDA. Laura, go now or just don't go at all!

LAURA [*rushing out*]. Going—going! [*A second later she cries out.* TOM *springs up and crosses to door.* AMANDA *rushes anxiously in.* TOM *opens the door.*]

TOM. Laura?

LAURA. I'm all right. I slipped, but I'm all right.

AMANDA [*peering anxiously after her*]. If anyone breaks a leg on those fire-escape steps, the landlord ought to be sued for every cent he possesses! [*She shuts door. Remembers she isn't speaking and returns to other room.*]

[*As* TOM *enters listlessly for his coffee, she turns her back to him and stands rigidly facing the window on the gloomy gray vault of the areaway. Its light on her face with its aged but childish features is cruelly sharp, satirical as a Daumier print.*]

[MUSIC UNDER: "AVE MARIA"]

[TOM *glances sheepishly but sullenly at her averted figure and slumps at the table. The coffee is scalding hot; he sips it and gasps and spits it back in the cup. At his gasp,* AMANDA *catches her breath and half turns. Then catches herself and turns back to window*]

[TOM *blows on his coffee, glancing sidewise at his mother. She clears her throat.* TOM *clears his. He starts to rise. Sinks back down again, scratches his head, clears his throat again.* AMANDA *coughs.* TOM *raises his cup in both hands to blow on it, his eyes staring over the rim of it at his mother for several moments. Then he slowly sets the cup down and awkwardly and hesitantly rises from the chair.*]

TOM [*hoarsely*]. Mother. I—I apologize, Mother. [AMANDA *draws a quick, shuddering breath. Her face works grotesquely. She breaks into childlike tears.*] I'm sorry for what I said, for everything that I said, I didn't mean it.

AMANDA [*sobbingly*]. My devotion has made me a witch and so I make myself hateful to my children!

TOM. *No,* you *don't.*

AMANDA. I worry so much, don't sleep, it makes me nervous!

TOM [*gently*]. I understand that.

AMANDA. I've had to put up a solitary battle all these years. But you're my right-hand bower! Don't fall down, don't fail!

TOM [*gently*]. I try, Mother.

AMANDA [*with great enthusiasm*]. Try and you will SUCCEED! [*The notion makes her breathless.*] Why, you—you're just *full* of natural endowments! Both of my children—they're *unusual* children! Don't you think I know it? I'm so—*proud!* Happy and—feel I've—so much to be thankful for but—Promise me one thing, Son!

TOM. What, Mother?

AMANDA. Promise, son, you'll—never be a drunkard!

TOM [*turns to her grinning*]. I will never be a drunkard, Mother.

AMANDA. That's what frightened me so, that you'd be drinking! Eat a bowl of Purina!

TOM. Just coffee, Mother.

AMANDA. Shredded wheat biscuit?

TOM. No. No, Mother, just coffee.

AMANDA. You can't put in a day's work on an empty stomach. You've got ten minutes—don't gulp! Drinking too-hot liquids makes cancer of the stomach. . . . Put cream in.

TOM. No, thank you.

AMANDA. To cool it.

TOM. No! No, thank you, I want it black.

AMANDA. I know, but it's not good for you. We have to do all that we can to build ourselves up. In these trying times we live in, all that we have to cling to is—each other. . . . That's why it's so important to—Tom, I—I sent out your sister so I could discuss something with you. If you hadn't spoken I would have spoken to you. [*Sits down*]

TOM [*gently*]. What is it, Mother, that you want to discuss?

AMANDA. *Laura!*

[TOM *puts his cup down slowly.*]

[LEGEND ON SCREEN: "LAURA"]

[MUSIC: "THE GLASS MENAGERIE"]

TOM.—Oh.—Laura . . .

AMANDA [*touching his sleeve*]. You know how Laura is. So quiet but—still water runs deep! She notices things and I think she—broods about them. [TOM *looks up.*] A few days ago I came in and she was crying.

TOM. What about?

AMANDA. You.

TOM. Me?

AMANDA. She has an idea that you're not happy here.

TOM. What gave her that idea?

AMANDA. What gives her any idea? However, you do act strangely. I—I'm not criticizing, understand *that!* I know your ambitions do not lie in the warehouse, that like everybody in the whole wide world—you've had to—make sacrifices, but—Tom—Tom—life's not easy, it calls for—Spartan endurance! There's so many things in my heart that I cannot describe to you! I've never told you but I—*loved* your father. . . .

TOM [*gently*]. I know that, Mother.

AMANDA. And you—when I see you taking after his ways! Staying out late—and—well, you *had* been drinking the night you were in that—terrifying condition! Laura says that you hate the apartment and that you go out nights to get away from it! Is that true, Tom?

TOM. No. You say there's so much in your heart that you can't describe to me. That's true of me, too. There's so much in my heart that I can't describe to *you!* So let's respect each other's—

AMANDA. But, why—*why*, Tom—are you always so *restless?* Where do you *go* to, nights?

TOM. I—go to the movies.

AMANDA. Why do you go to the movies so much, Tom?

TOM. I go to the movies because—I like adventure. Adventure is something I don't have much of at work, so I go to the movies.

AMANDA. But, Tom, you go to the movies *entirely* too *much!*

TOM. I like a lot of adventure.

[AMANDA *looks baffled, then hurt. As the familiar inquisition resumes he becomes hard and impatient again.* AMANDA *slips back into her querulous attitude toward him.*]

[IMAGE ON SCREEN: SAILING VESSEL WITH JOLLY ROGER]

AMANDA. Most young men find adventure in their careers.

TOM. Then most young men are not employed in a warehouse.

AMANDA. The world is full of young men employed in warehouses and offices and factories.

TOM. Do all of them find adventure in their careers?

AMANDA. They do or they do without it! Not everybody has a craze for adventure.

TOM. Man is by instinct a lover, a hunter, a fighter, and none of those instincts are given much play at the warehouse!

AMANDA. Man is by instinct! Don't quote instinct to me! Instinct is something that people have got away from. It belongs to animals! Christian adults don't want it!

TOM. What do Christian adults want, then, Mother?

AMANDA. Superior things! Things of the mind and the spirit! Only animals have to satisfy instincts! Surely your aims are somewhat higher than theirs. Than monkeys—pigs—

TOM. I reckon they're not.

AMANDA. You're joking. However, that isn't what I wanted to discuss.

TOM [*rising*]. I haven't much time.

AMANDA [*pushing his shoulders*]. Sit down.

TOM. You want me to punch in red at the warehouse, Mother?

AMANDA. You have five minutes. I want to talk about Laura.

[LEGEND: "PLANS AND PROVISIONS"]

TOM. All right! What about Laura?

AMANDA. We have to be making some plans and provisions for her. She's older than you, two years, and nothing has happened. She just drifts along doing nothing. It frightens me terribly how she just drifts along.

TOM. I guess she's the type that people call home girls.

AMANDA. There's no such type, and if there is, it's a pity! That is unless the home is hers, with a husband!

TOM. What?

AMANDA. Oh, I can see the handwriting on the wall as plain as I see the nose in front of my face! It's terrifying!

More and more you remind me of your father! He was out all hours without explanation—then *left! Good-bye!*

And me with the bag to hold. I saw that letter you got from the Merchant Marine. I know what you're dreaming of. I'm not standing here blindfolded.

Very well, then. Then *do* it!

But not till there's somebody to take your place.

TOM. What do you mean?

AMANDA. I mean that as soon as Laura has got somebody to take care of her, married, a home of her own, independent—why, then you'll be free to go wherever you please, on land, on sea, whichever way the wind blows you!

But until that time you've got to look out for your sister. I don't say me because I'm old and don't matter! I say for your sister because she's young and dependent.

I put her in business college—a dismal failure! Frightened her so it made her sick at the stomach.

I took her over to the Young People's League at the church. Another fiasco. She spoke to nobody, nobody spoke to her. Now all she does is fool with those pieces of glass and play those worn-out records. What kind of a life is that for a girl to lead?

TOM. What can I do about it?

AMANDA. Overcome selfishness!

Self, self, self is all that you ever think of!

[TOM *springs up and crosses to get his coat. It is ugly and bulky. He pulls on a cap with earmuffs.*]

Where is your muffler? Put your wool muffler on!

[*He snatches it angrily from the closet and tosses it around his neck and pulls both ends tight.*]

Tom! I haven't said what I had in mind to ask you.

TOM. I'm too late to—

AMANDA [*catching his arm—very importunately. Then shyly*]. Down at the warehouse, aren't there some—nice young men?

TOM. No!

AMANDA. There *must* be—*some* . . .

TOM. Mother—

[*Gesture*]

AMANDA. Find out one that's clean-living—doesn't drink and—ask him out for sister!

TOM. What?

AMANDA. For *sister!* To *meet!* Get *acquainted!*

TOM [*stamping to door*]. Oh, my *go-osh!*

AMANDA. Will you? [*He opens door. Imploringly*] Will you? [*He starts down.*] Will you? *Will* you, dear?

TOM [*calling back*]. Yes!

[AMANDA *closes the door hesitantly and with a troubled but faintly hopeful expression.*]

[SCREEN IMAGE: GLAMOUR MAGAZINE COVER]

[*Spot* AMANDA *at phone*]

AMANDA. Ella Cartwright? This is Amanda Wingfield!

How are you, honey?

How is that kidney condition?

[*Count five*]

Horrors!

[*Count five*]

You're a Christian martyr, yes, honey, that's what you are, a Christian martyr!

Well, I just now happened to notice in my little red book that your subscription to the *Companion* has just run out! I knew that you wouldn't want to miss out on the wonderful serial starting in this new issue. It's by

Bessie Mae Hopper, the first thing she's written since *Honeymoon for Three.*

Wasn't that a strange and interesting story? Well, this one is even lovelier, I believe. It has a sophisticated, society background. It's all about the horsey set on Long Island!

FADE OUT

SCENE 5

LEGEND ON SCREEN: "ANNUNCIATION." *Fade with music.*

It is early dusk of a spring evening. Supper has just been finished in the Wingfield apartment. AMANDA *and* LAURA *in light-colored dresses are removing dishes from the table, in the upstage area, which is shadowy, their movements formalized almost as a dance or ritual, their moving forms as pale and silent as moths.*

TOM, *in white shirt and trousers, rises from the table and crosses toward the fire-escape.*

AMANDA [*as he passes her*]. Son, will you do me a favor?

TOM. What?

AMANDA. Comb your hair! You look so pretty when your hair is combed! [TOM *slouches on sofa with evening paper. Enormous caption "Franco Triumphs"*] There is only one respect in which I would like you to emulate your father.

TOM. What respect is that?

AMANDA. The care he always took of his appearance. He never allowed himself to look untidy. [*He throws down the paper and crosses to fire-escape.*] Where are you going?

TOM. I'm going out to smoke.

AMANDA. You smoke too much. A pack a day at fifteen cents a pack. How much would that amount to in a month? Thirty times fifteen is how much, Tom? Figure it out and you will be astounded at what you could save. Enough to give you a night-school course in accounting at Washington U! Just think what a wonderful thing that would be for you, Son!

[TOM *is unmoved by the thought.*]

TOM. I'd rather smoke. [*He steps out on landing, letting the screen door slam.*]

AMANDA [*sharply*]. I know! That's the tragedy of it. . . . [*Alone, she turns to look at her husband's picture.*]

[DANCE MUSIC: "ALL THE WORLD IS WAITING FOR THE SUNRISE!"]

TOM [*to the audience*]. Across the alley from us was the Paradise Dance Hall. On evenings in spring the windows and doors were open and the music came outdoors. Sometimes the lights were turned out except for a large glass sphere that hung from the ceiling. It would turn slowly about and filter the dusk with delicate rainbow colors. Then the orchestra played a waltz or a tango, something that had a slow and sensuous rhythm. Couples would come outside, to the relative privacy of the alley. You could see them kissing behind ash-pits and telephone poles.

This was the compensation for lives that passed like mine, without any change or adventure.

Adventure and change were imminent in this year. They were waiting around the corner for all these kids.

Suspended in the mist over Berchtesgaden, caught in the folds of Chamberlain's umbrella—

In Spain there was Guernica!

But here there was only hot swing music and liquor, dance halls, bars, and movies, and sex that hung in the gloom like a chandelier and flooded the world with brief, deceptive rainbows. . . .

All the world was waiting for bombardments!

[AMANDA *turns from the picture and comes outside.*]

AMANDA [*sighing*]. A fire-escape landing's a poor excuse for a porch. [*She spreads a newspaper on a step and sits down, gracefully and demurely as if she were settling into a swing on a Mississippi veranda.*] What are you looking at?

TOM. The moon.

AMANDA. Is there a moon this evening?

TOM. It's rising over Garfinkel's Delicatessen.

AMANDA. So it is! A little silver slipper of a moon. Have you made a wish on it yet?

TOM. Um-hum.

AMANDA. What did you wish for?

TOM. That's a secret.

AMANDA. A secret, huh? Well, I won't tell mine either. I will be just as mysterious as you.

TOM. I bet I can guess what yours is.

AMANDA. Is my head so transparent?

TOM. You're not a sphinx.

AMANDA. No, I don't have secrets. I'll tell you what I wished for on the moon. Success and happiness for my precious children! I wish for that whenever there's a moon, and when there isn't a moon, I wish for it, too.

TOM. I thought perhaps you wished for a gentleman caller.

AMANDA. Why do you say that?

TOM. Don't you remember asking me to fetch one?

AMANDA. I remember suggesting that it would be nice for your sister if you brought home some nice young man from the warehouse. I think that I've made that suggestion more than once.

TOM. Yes, you have made it repeatedly.

AMANDA. Well?

TOM. We are going to have one.

AMANDA. *What?*

TOM. A gentleman caller!

[THE ANNUNCIATION IS CELEBRATED WITH MUSIC.]

[AMANDA *rises.*]

[IMAGE ON SCREEN: CALLER WITH BOUQUET]

AMANDA. You mean you have asked some nice young man to come over?

TOM. Yep. I've asked him to dinner.

AMANDA. You really did?

TOM. I did!

AMANDA. You did, and did he—*accept?*

TOM. He did!

AMANDA. Well, well—well, well! That's—lovely!

TOM. I thought that you would be pleased.

AMANDA. It's definite, then?

TOM. Very definite.

AMANDA. Soon?

TOM. Very soon.

AMANDA. For heaven's sake, stop putting on and tell me some things, will you?

TOM. What things do you want me to tell you?

AMANDA. *Naturally* I would like to know when he's *coming!*

TOM. He's coming tomorrow.

AMANDA. *Tomorrow?*

TOM. Yep. Tomorrow.

AMANDA. But, Tom!

TOM. Yes, Mother?

AMANDA. Tomorrow gives me no time!

TOM. Time for what?

AMANDA. Preparations! Why didn't you phone me at once, as soon as you asked him, the minute that he accepted? Then, don't you see, I could have been getting ready!

TOM. You don't have to make any fuss.

AMANDA. Oh, Tom, Tom, Tom, of course I have to make a fuss! I want things nice, not sloppy! Not thrown together. I'll certainly have to do some fast thinking, won't I?

TOM. I don't see why you have to think at all.

AMANDA. You just don't know. We can't have a gentleman caller in a pig-sty! All my wedding silver has to be polished, the monogrammed table linen ought to be laundered! The windows have to be washed and fresh curtains put up. And how about clothes? We have to *wear* something, don't we?

TOM. Mother, this boy is no one to make a fuss over!

AMANDA. Do you realize he's the first young man we've introduced to your sister?

It's terrible, dreadful, disgraceful that poor little sister has never received a single gentleman caller! Tom, come inside! [*She opens the screen door.*]

TOM. What for?

AMANDA. I want to ask you some things.

TOM. If you're going to make such a fuss, I'll call it off, I'll tell him not to come!

AMANDA. You certainly won't do anything of the kind. Nothing offends people worse than broken engagements. It simply means I'll have to work like a Turk! We won't be brilliant, but we will pass inspection. Come on inside. [TOM *follows, groaning.*] Sit down.

TOM. Any particular place you would like me to sit?

AMANDA. Thank heavens I've got that new sofa! I'm also making payments on a floor lamp I'll have sent out! And put the chintz covers on, they'll brighten things up! Of course I'd hoped to have these walls repapered. . . . What is the young man's name?

TOM. His name is O'Connor.

AMANDA. That, of course, means fish—tomorrow is Friday! I'll have that salmon loaf—with Durkee's dressing! What does he do? He works at the warehouse?

TOM. Of course! How else would I—

AMANDA. Tom, he—doesn't drink?

TOM. Why do you ask me that?

AMANDA. Your father *did!*

TOM. Don't get started on that!

AMANDA. He *does* drink, then?

TOM. Not that I know of!

AMANDA. Make sure, be certain! The last thing I want for my daughter's a boy who drinks!

TOM. Aren't you being a little bit premature? Mr. O'Connor has not yet appeared on the scene!

AMANDA. But will tomorrow. To meet your sister, and what do I know about his character? Nothing! Old maids are better off than wives of drunkards!

TOM. Oh, my God!

AMANDA. Be still!

TOM [*leaning forward to whisper*]. Lots of fellows meet girls whom they don't marry!

AMANDA. Oh, talk sensibly, Tom—and don't be sarcastic! [*She has gotten a hairbrush.*]

TOM. What are you doing?

AMANDA. I'm brushing that cow-lick down!

What is this young man's position at the warehouse?

TOM [*submitting grimly to the brush and the interrogation*]. This young man's position is that of a shipping clerk, Mother.

AMANDA. Sounds to me like a fairly responsible job, the sort of a job *you* would be in if you just had more *get-up*.

What is his salary? Have you any idea?

TOM. I would judge it to be approximately eighty-five dollars a month.

AMANDA. Well—not princely, but—

TOM. Twenty more than I make.

AMANDA. Yes, how well I know! But for a family man, eighty-five dollars a month is not much more than you can just get by on. . . .

TOM. Yes, but Mr. O'Connor is not a family man.

AMANDA. He might be, mightn't he? Some time in the future?

TOM. I see. Plans and provisions.

AMANDA. You are the only young man that I know of who ignores the fact that the future becomes the present, the present the past, and the past turns into everlasting regret if you don't plan for it!

TOM. I will think that over and see what I can make of it.

AMANDA. Don't be supercilious with your mother! Tell me some more about this—what do you call him?

TOM. James D. O'Connor. The D. is for Delaney.

AMANDA. Irish on *both* sides! *Gracious!* And doesn't drink?

TOM. Shall I call him up and ask him right this minute?

AMANDA. The only way to find out about those things is to make discreet inquiries at the proper moment. When I was a girl in Blue Mountain and it was suspected that a young man drank, the girl whose attentions he had been receiving, if any girl *was*, would sometimes speak to the minister of his church, or rather her father would if her father was living, and sort of feel him out on the young man's character. That is the way such things are discreetly handled to keep a young woman from making a tragic mistake!

TOM. Then how did you happen to make a tragic mistake?

AMANDA. That innocent look of your father's had everyone fooled!

He *smiled*—the world was *enchanted!*

No girl can do worse than put herself at the mercy of a handsome appearance!

I hope that Mr. O'Connor is not too good-looking.

TOM. No, he's not too good-looking. He's covered with freckles and hasn't too much of a nose.

AMANDA. He's not right-down homely, though?

TOM. Not right-down homely. Just medium homely, I'd say.

AMANDA. Character's what to look for in a man.

TOM. That's what I've always said, Mother.

AMANDA. You've never said anything of the kind and I suspect you would never give it a thought.

TOM. Don't be so suspicious of me.

AMANDA. At least I hope he's the type that's up and coming.

TOM. I think he really goes in for self-improvement.

AMANDA. What reason have you to think so?

TOM. He goes to night school.

AMANDA [*beaming*]. Splendid! What does he do, I mean study?

TOM. Radio engineering and public speaking!

AMANDA. Then he has visions of being advanced in the world!

Any young man who studies public speaking is aiming to have an executive job some day!

And radio engineering? A thing for the future!

Both of these facts are very illuminating. Those are the sort of things that a mother should know concerning any young man who comes to call on her daughter. Seriously or—not.

TOM. One little warning. He doesn't know about Laura. I didn't let on that we had dark ulterior motives. I just said, why don't you come and have dinner with us? He said okay and that was the whole conversation.

AMANDA. I bet it was! You're eloquent as an oyster.

However, he'll know about Laura when he gets here. When he sees how lovely and sweet and pretty she is, he'll thank his lucky stars he was asked to dinner.

TOM. Mother, you mustn't expect too much of Laura.

AMANDA. What do you mean?

TOM. Laura seems all those things to you and me because she's ours and we love her. We don't even notice she's crippled any more.

AMANDA. Don't say crippled! You know that I never allow that word to be used!

TOM. But face facts, Mother. She is and—that's not all—

AMANDA. What do you mean "not all"?

TOM. Laura is very different from other girls.

AMANDA. I think the difference is all to her advantage.

TOM. Not quite all—in the eyes of others—strangers—she's terribly shy and lives in a world of her own and those things make her seem a little peculiar to people outside the house.

AMANDA. Don't say peculiar.

TOM. Face the facts. She is.

[THE DANCE-HALL MUSIC CHANGES TO A TANGO THAT HAS A MINOR AND SOMEWHAT OMINOUS TONE.]

AMANDA. In what way is she peculiar—may I ask?

TOM [*gently*]. She lives in a world of her own—a world of—little glass ornaments, Mother. . . . [*Gets up.* AMANDA *remains holding brush, look-*

ing at him, troubled.] She plays old phonograph records and—that's about all—[*He glances at himself in the mirror and crosses to door.*]

AMANDA [*sharply*]. Where are you going?

TOM. I'm going to the movies. [*Out screen door*]

AMANDA. Not to the movies, every night to the movies! [*Follows quickly to screen door*] I don't believe you always go to the movies! [*He is gone.* AMANDA *looks worriedly after him for a moment. Then vitality and optimism return and she turns from the door. Crossing to portieres*] Laura! Laura! [LAURA *answers from kitchenette.*]

LAURA. Yes, Mother.

AMANDA. Let those dishes go and come in front! [LAURA *appears with dish towel. Gaily*] Laura, come here and make a wish on the moon.

[SCREEN IMAGE: MOON]

LAURA [*entering*]. Moon—moon?

AMANDA. A little silver slipper of a moon.

Look over your left shoulder, Laura, and make a wish!

[LAURA *looks faintly puzzled as if called out of sleep.* AMANDA *seizes her shoulders and turns her at an angle by the door.*]

Now!

Now, darling, *wish!*

LAURA. What shall I wish for, Mother?

AMANDA [*her voice trembling and her eyes suddenly filling with tears*]. Happiness! Good fortune!

[*The violin rises and the stage dims out.*]

CURTAIN

SCENE 6

IMAGE: HIGH SCHOOL HERO

And so the following evening I brought Jim home to dinner. I had known Jim slightly in high school. In high school Jim was a hero. He had tremendous Irish good nature and vitality with the scrubbed and polished look of white chinaware. He seemed to move in a continual spotlight. He was a star in basketball, captain of the debating club, president of the senior class and the glee club and he sang the male lead in the annual light operas. He was always running or bounding, never just walking. He seemed always at the point of defeating the law of gravity. He was shooting with such velocity through his adolescence that you would logically expect him to arrive at nothing short of the White House by the time he was thirty. But Jim apparently ran into more interference after his graduation from Soldan. His speed had definitely slowed. Six years after he left high school he was holding a job that wasn't much better than mine.

[IMAGE: CLERK]

He was the only one at the warehouse with whom I was on friendly terms. I was valuable to him as someone who could remember his former glory, who had seen him win basketball games and the silver cup in debating. He knew of my secret practice of retiring to a cabinet of the washroom to work on poems when business was slack in the warehouse. He called me Shakespeare. And while the other boys in the warehouse regarded me with suspicious hostility, Jim took a humorous attitude toward me. Gradually his attitude affected the others, their hostility wore off and they also began to smile at me as people smile at an oddly fashioned dog who trots across their path at some distance.

I knew that Jim and Laura had known each other at Soldan, and I had heard Laura speak admiringly of his voice. I didn't know if Jim remembered her or not. In high school Laura had been as unobtrusive as Jim had been astonishing. If he did remember Laura, it was not as my sister, for when I asked him to dinner, he grinned and said, "You know, Shakespeare, I never thought of you as having folks!"

He was about to discover that I did. . . .

[LIGHT UP STAGE]

[LEGEND ON SCREEN: "THE ACCENT OF A COMING FOOT"]

[*Friday evening. It is about five o'clock of a late spring evening which comes "scattering poems in the sky."*]

[*A delicate lemony light is in the Wingfield apartment.*]

AMANDA *has worked like a Turk in preparation for the gentleman caller. The results are astonishing. The new floor lamp with its rose-silk shade is in place, a colored paper lantern conceals the broken light fixture in the ceiling, new billowing white curtains are at the windows, chintz covers are on chairs and sofa, a pair of new sofa pillows make their initial appearance.*]

[*Open boxes and tissue paper are scattered on the floor.*]

[LAURA *stands in the middle with lifted arms while* AMANDA *crouches before her, adjusting the hem of the new dress, devout and ritualistic. The dress is colored and designed by memory. The arrangement of* LAURA's *hair is changed; it is softer and more becoming. A fragile, unearthly prettiness has come out in* LAURA: *she is like a piece of translucent glass touched by light, given a momentary radiance, not actual, not lasting.*]

AMANDA [*impatiently*]. Why are you trembling?

LAURA. Mother, you've made me so nervous!

AMANDA. How have I made you nervous?

LAURA. By all this fuss! You make it seem so important!

AMANDA. I don't understand you, Laura. You couldn't be satisfied with just sitting home, and yet whenever I try to arrange something for you, you seem to resist it.

[*She gets up.*]

Now take a look at yourself.

No, wait! Wait just a moment—I have an idea!

LAURA. What is it now?

[AMANDA *produces two powder puffs which she wraps in handkerchiefs and stuffs in* LAURA'S *bosom.*]

LAURA. Mother, what are you doing?

AMANDA. They call them "Gay Deceivers"!

LAURA. I won't wear them!

AMANDA. You will!

LAURA. Why should I?

AMANDA. Because, to be painfully honest, your chest is flat.

LAURA. You make it seem like we were setting a trap.

AMANDA. All pretty girls are a trap, a pretty trap, and men expect them to be.

[LEGEND: "A PRETTY TRAP"]

Now look at yourself, young lady. This is the prettiest you will ever be! I've got to fix myself now! You're going to be surprised by your mother's appearance! [*She crosses through portieres, humming gaily.*]

[LAURA *moves slowly to the long mirror and stares solemnly at herself.*]

[*A wind blows the white curtains inward in a slow, graceful motion and with a faint, sorrowful sighing.*]

AMANDA [*off stage*]. It isn't dark enough yet. [*She turns slowly before the mirror with a troubled look.*]

[LEGEND ON SCREEN: "THIS IS MY SISTER: CELEBRATE HER WITH STRINGS!" MUSIC]

AMANDA [*laughing, off*]. I'm going to show you something. I'm going to make a spectacular appearance!

LAURA. What is it, Mother?

AMANDA. Possess your soul in patience—you will see!

Something I've resurrected from that old trunk! Styles haven't changed so terribly much after all. . . .

[*She parts the portieres.*]

Now just look at your mother!

[*She wears a girlish frock of yellowed voile with a blue silk sash. She carries a bunch of jonquils—the legend of her youth is nearly revived. Feverishly*]

This is the dress in which I led the cotillion. Won the cakewalk twice at Sunset Hill, wore one spring to the Governor's ball in Jackson!

See how I sashayed around the ballroom, Laura?

[*She raises her skirt and does a mincing step around the room.*]

I wore it on Sundays for my gentlemen callers! I had it on the day I met your father—

I had malaria fever all that spring. The change of climate from East Tennessee to the Delta—weakened resistance—I had a little temperature all the time—not enough to be serious—just enough to make me restless and giddy!—Invitations poured in—parties all over the Delta!—"Stay in bed," said Mother, "you have fever!"—but I just wouldn't.—I took quinine but kept on going, going!—Evenings, dances!—Afternoons, long, long rides! Picnics—lovely!—So lovely, that country in May.—All lacy with dogwood, literally flooded with jonquils!—That was the spring I had the craze for jonquils. Jonquils became an absolute obsession. Mother said, "Honey, there's no more room for jonquils." And still I kept on bringing in more jonquils. Whenever, wherever I saw them, I'd say, "Stop! Stop! I see jonquils!" I made the young men help me gather the jonquils! It was a joke, Amanda and her jonquils! Finally there were no more vases to hold them, every available space was filled with jonquils. No vases to hold them? All right, I'll hold them myself! And then I—[*She stops in front of the picture.* MUSIC] met your father!

Malaria fever and jonquils and then—this—boy. . . .

[*She switches on the rose-colored lamp.*]

I hope they get here before it starts to rain.

[*She crosses upstage and places the jonquils in bowl on table.*]

I gave your brother a little extra change so he and Mr. O'Connor could take the service car home.

LAURA [*with altered look*]. What did you say his name was?

AMANDA. O'Connor.

LAURA. What is his first name?

AMANDA. I don't remember. Oh, yes, I do. It was—Jim!

[LAURA *sways slightly and catches hold of a chair.*]

[LEGEND ON SCREEN: "NOT JIM!"]

LAURA [*faintly*]. Not—Jim!

AMANDA. Yes, that was it, it was Jim! I've never known a Jim that wasn't nice!

[MUSIC: OMINOUS]

LAURA. Are you sure his name is Jim O'Connor?

AMANDA. Yes. Why?

LAURA. Is he the one that Tom used to know in high school?

AMANDA. He didn't say so. I think he just got to know him at the warehouse.

LAURA. There was a Jim O'Connor we both knew in high school—[*Then, with effort*] If that is the one that Tom is bringing to dinner—you'll have to excuse me, I won't come to the table.

AMANDA. What sort of nonsense is this?

LAURA. You asked me once if I'd ever liked a boy. Don't you remember I showed you this boy's picture?

AMANDA. You mean the boy you showed me in the year book?

LAURA. Yes, that boy.

AMANDA. Laura, Laura, were you in love with that boy?

LAURA. I don't know, Mother. All I know is I couldn't sit at the table if it was him!

AMANDA. It won't be him! It isn't the least bit likely. But whether it is or not, you will come to the table. You will not be excused.

LAURA. I'll have to be, Mother.

AMANDA. I don't intend to humor your silliness, Laura. I've had too much from you and your brother, both!

So just sit down and compose yourself till they come. Tom has forgotten his key so you'll have to let them in, when they arrive.

LAURA [*panicky*]. Oh, Mother—*you* answer the door!

AMANDA [*lightly*]. I'll be in the kitchen—busy!

LAURA. Oh, Mother, please answer the door, don't make me do it!

AMANDA [*crossing into kitchenette*]. I've got to fix the dressing for the salmon. Fuss, fuss—silliness—over a gentleman caller!

[*Door swings shut.* LAURA *is left alone.*]

[LEGEND: "TERROR!"]

[*She utters a low moan and turns off the lamp, sits stiffly on the edge of the sofa, knotting her fingers together.*]

[LEGEND ON SCREEN: "THE OPENING OF A DOOR!"]

[TOM *and* JIM *appear on the fire-escape steps and climb to landing. Hearing their approach,* LAURA *rises with a panicky gesture. She retreats to the portieres.*]

[*The doorbell.* LAURA *catches her breath and touches her throat. Low drums*]

AMANDA [*calling*]. Laura, sweetheart! The door!

[LAURA *stares at it without moving.*]

JIM. I think we just beat the rain.

TOM. Uh-huh. [*He rings again, nervously.* JIM *whistles and fishes for a cigarette.*]

AMANDA [*very, very gaily*]. Laura, that is your brother and Mr. O'Connor! Will you let them in, darling?

[LAURA *crosses toward kitchenette door.*]

LAURA [*breathlessly*]. Mother—you go to the door!

[AMANDA *steps out of kitchenette and stares furiously at* LAURA. *She points imperiously at the door.*]

LAURA. Please, please!

AMANDA [*in a fierce whisper*]. What is the matter with you, you silly thing?

LAURA [*desperately*]. Please, you answer it, *please!*

AMANDA. I told you I wasn't going to humor you, Laura. Why have you chosen this moment to lose your mind?

LAURA. Please, please, please, you go!

AMANDA. You'll have to go to the door because I can't!

LAURA [*despairingly*]. I can't either!

AMANDA. *Why?*

LAURA. I'm *sick!*

AMANDA. I'm sick, too—of your nonsense! Why can't you and your brother be normal people? Fantastic whims and behavior!

[TOM *gives a long ring.*]

Preposterous goings on! Can you give me one reason—[*Calls out lyrically*] COMING! JUST ONE SECOND!—why you should be afraid to open a door? Now you answer it, Laura!

LAURA. Oh, oh, oh . . . [*She returns through the portieres. Darts to the victrola and winds it frantically and turns it on*]

AMANDA. Laura Wingfield, you march right to that door!

LAURA. Yes—yes, Mother!

[*A faraway, scratchy rendition of "Dardanella" softens the air and gives her strength to move through it. She slips to the door and draws it cautiously open.*]

[TOM *enters with the caller,* JIM O'CONNOR.]

TOM. Laura, this is Jim. Jim, this is my sister, Laura.

JIM [*stepping inside*]. I didn't know that Shakespeare had a sister!

LAURA [*retreating stiff and trembling from the door*]. How—how do you do?

JIM [*heartily extending his hand*]. Okay!

[LAURA *touches it hesitantly with hers.*]

JIM. Your hand's *cold,* Laura!

LAURA. Yes, well—I've been playing the victrola. . . .

JIM. Must have been playing classical music on it! You ought to play a little hot swing music to warm you up!

LAURA. Excuse me—I haven't finished playing the victrola. . . . [*She turns awkwardly and hurries into the front room. She pauses a second by the victrola. Then catches her breath and darts through the portieres like a frightened deer*]

JIM [*grinning*]. What was the matter?

TOM. Oh—with Laura? Laura is—terribly shy.

JIM. Shy, huh? It's unusual to meet a shy girl nowadays. I don't believe you ever mentioned you had a sister.

TOM. Well, now you know. I have one. Here is the *Post Dispatch.* You want a piece of it?

JIM. Uh-huh.

TOM. What piece? The comics?

JIM. Sports! [*Glances at it*] Ole Dizzy Dean is on his bad behavior.

TOM [*disinterest*]. Yeah? [*Lights cigarette and crosses back to fire-escape door*]

JIM. Where are *you* going?

TOM. I'm going out on the terrace.

JIM [*goes after him*]. You know, Shakespeare—I'm going to sell you a bill of goods!

TOM. What goods?

JIM. A course I'm taking.

TOM. Huh?

JIM. In public speaking! You and me, we're not the warehouse type.

TOM. Thanks—that's good news.

But what has public speaking got to do with it?

JIM. It fits you for—executive positions!

TOM. Awww.

JIM. I tell you it's done a helluva lot for me.

[IMAGE: EXECUTIVE AT DESK]

TOM. In what respect?

JIM. In every! Ask yourself what is the difference between you an' me and men in the office down front? Brains?—No!—Ability?—No! Then what? Just one little thing—

TOM. What is that one little thing?

JIM. Primarily it amounts to—social poise! Being able to square up to people and hold your own on any social level!

AMANDA [*off stage*]. Tom?

TOM. Yes, Mother?

AMANDA. Is that you and Mr. O'Connor?

TOM. Yes, Mother.

AMANDA. Well, you just make yourselves comfortable in there.

TOM. Yes, Mother.

AMANDA. Ask Mr. O'Connor if he would like to wash his hands.

JIM. Aw, no—no—thank you—I took care of that at the warehouse. Tom—

TOM. Yes?

JIM. Mr. Mendoza was speaking to me about you.

TOM. Favorably?

JIM. What do you think?

TOM. Well—

JIM. You're going to be out of a job if you don't wake up.

TOM. I am waking up—

JIM. You show no signs.

TOM. The signs are interior.

[IMAGE ON SCREEN: THE SAILING VESSEL WITH JOLLY ROGER AGAIN]

TOM. I'm planning to change. [*He leans over the rail speaking with quiet exhilaration. The incandescent marquees and signs of the first-run movie houses light his face from across the alley. He looks like a voyager.*] I'm right at the point of committing myself to a future that doesn't include the warehouse and Mr. Mendoza or even a night-school course in public speaking.

JIM. What are you gassing about?

TOM. I'm tired of the movies.

JIM. Movies!

TOM. Yes, movies! Look at them—[*A wave toward the marvels of Grand Avenue*] All of those glamorous people—having adventures—hogging it all, gobbling the whole thing up! You know what happens? People go to the *movies* instead of *moving!* Hollywood characters are supposed to have all the adventures for everybody in America, while everybody in America sits in a dark room and watches them have them! Yes, until there's a war. That's when adventure becomes available to the masses! *Everyone's* dish, not only Gable's! Then the people in the dark room come out of the dark room to have some adventures themselves—Goody, goody! —It's our turn now, to go to the South Sea Island—to make a safari—to be exotic, far-off!—But I'm not patient. I don't want to wait till then. I'm tired of the *movies* and I am *about* to *move!*

JIM [*incredulously*]. Move?

TOM. Yes.

JIM. When?

TOM. Soon!

JIM. Where? Where?

[THEME THREE MUSIC SEEMS TO ANSWER THE QUESTION, WHILE TOM THINKS IT OVER. HE SEARCHES AMONG HIS POCKETS.]

TOM. I'm starting to boil inside. I know I seem dreamy, but inside—well, I'm boiling!—Whenever I pick up a shoe, I shudder a little thinking how short life is and what I am doing!—Whatever that means, I know it doesn't mean shoes—except as something to wear on a traveler's feet! [*Finds paper*] Look—

JIM. What?

TOM. I'm a member.

JIM [*reading*]. The Union of Merchant Seamen.

TOM. I paid my dues this month, instead of the light bill.

JIM. You will regret it when they turn the lights off.

TOM. I won't be here.

JIM. How about your mother?

TOM. I'm like my father. The bastard son of a bastard! See how he grins? And he's been absent going on sixteen years!

JIM. You're just talking, you drip. How does your mother feel about it?

TOM. Shhh!—Here comes Mother! Mother is not acquainted with my plans!

AMANDA [*enters portieres*]. Where are you all?

TOM. On the terrace, Mother.

[*They start inside. She advances to them.* TOM *is distinctly shocked at her appearance. Even* JIM *blinks a little. He is making his first contact with girlish Southern vivacity and in spite of the night-school course in public speaking is somewhat thrown off the beam by the unexpected outlay of social charm.*]

[*Certain responses are attempted by* JIM *but are swept aside by* AMANDA'S *gay laughter and chatter.* TOM *is embarrassed but after the first shock* JIM *reacts very warmly. Grins and chuckles, is altogether won over*]

[IMAGE: AMANDA AS A GIRL]

AMANDA [*coyly smiling, shaking her girlish ringlets*]. Well, well, well, so this is Mr. O'Connor. Introductions entirely unnecessary. I've heard so much about you from my boy. I finally said to him, Tom–good gracious!–why don't you bring this paragon to supper? I'd like to meet this nice young man at the warehouse!–Instead of just hearing him sing your praises so much!

I don't know why my son is so stand-offish–that's not Southern behavior!

Let's sit down and–I think we could stand a little more air in here! Tom, leave the door open. I felt a nice fresh breeze a moment ago. Where has it gone to?

Mmm, so warm already! And not quite summer, even. We're going to burn up when summer really gets started.

However, we're having–we're having a very light supper. I think light things are better fo' this time of year. The same as light clothes are. Light clothes an' light food are what warm weather calls fo'. You know our blood gets so thick during th' winter–it takes a while fo' us to *adjust* ou'selves!–when the season changes . . .

It's come so quick this year. I wasn't prepared. All of a sudden–heavens! Already summer!–I ran to the trunk an' pulled out this light dress–Terribly old! Historical almost! But feels so good–so good an' co-ol, y' know. . . .

TOM. Mother–

AMANDA. Yes, honey?

TOM. How about–supper?

AMANDA. Honey, you go ask Sister if supper is ready! You know that Sister is in full charge of supper!

Tell her you hungry boys are waiting for it.

[*To* JIM]

Have you met Laura?

JIM. She–

AMANDA. Let you in? Oh, good, you've met already! It's rare for a girl as sweet an' pretty as Laura to be domestic! But Laura is, thank heavens, not only pretty but also very domestic. I'm not at all. I never was a bit. I never could make a thing but angel-food cake. Well, in the South we had so many servants. Gone, gone, gone. All vestige of gracious living!

Gone completely! I wasn't prepared for what the future brought me. All of my gentlemen callers were sons of planters and so of course I assumed that I would be married to one and raise my family on a large piece of land with plenty of servants. But man proposes—and woman accepts the proposal!—To vary that old, old saying a little bit—I married no planter! I married a man who worked for the telephone company!—That gallantly smiling gentleman over there! [*Points to the picture*] A telephone man who—fell in love with long-distance!—Now he travels and I don't even know where!—But what am I going on for about my—tribulations?

Tell me yours—I hope you don't have any!

Tom?

TOM [*returning*]. Yes, Mother?

AMANDA. Is supper nearly ready?

TOM. It looks to me like supper is on the table.

AMANDA. Let me look—[*She rises prettily and looks through portieres.*] Oh, lovely!—But where is Sister?

TOM. Laura is not feeling well and she says that she thinks she'd better not come to the table.

AMANDA. What?—Nonsense!—Laura? Oh, Laura!

LAURA [*off stage, faintly*]. Yes, Mother.

AMANDA. You really must come to the table. We won't be seated until you come to the table!

Come in, Mr. O'Connor. You sit over there, and I'll—

Laura? Laura Wingfield!

You're keeping us waiting, honey! We can't say grace until you come to the table!

[*The back door is pushed weakly open and* LAURA *comes in. She is obviously quite faint, her lips trembling, her eyes wide and staring. She moves unsteadily toward the table.*]

[LEGEND: "TERROR"]

[*Outside a summer storm is coming abruptly. The white curtains billow inward at the windows and there is a sorrowful murmur and deep blue dusk.*]

[LAURA *suddenly stumbles—she catches at a chair with a faint moan.*]

TOM. Laura!

AMANDA. Laura!

[*There is a clap of thunder.*]

[LEGEND: "AH!"]

[*Despairingly*]

Why, Laura, you *are* sick, darling! Tom, help your sister into the living room, dear!

Sit in the living room, Laura—rest on the sofa.

Well!

[*To the gentleman caller*]

Standing over the hot stove made her ill!—I told her that it was just too warm this evening, but—

[TOM *comes back in.* LAURA *is on the sofa.*]

Is Laura all right now?

TOM. Yes.

AMANDA. What *is* that? Rain? A nice cool rain has come up!

[*She gives the gentleman caller a frightened look.*]

I think we may—have grace—now . . .

[TOM *looks at her stupidly.*]

Tom, honey—you say grace!

TOM. Oh . . .
"For these and all thy mercies—"

[*They bow their heads,* AMANDA *stealing a nervous glance at* JIM. *In the living room* LAURA, *stretched on the sofa, clenches her hands to her lips, to hold back a shuddering sob.*]

God's Holy Name be praised—

THE SCENE DIMS OUT

SCENE 7

A Souvenir.

Half an hour later. Dinner is just being finished in the upstage area which is concealed by the drawn portieres.

As the curtain rises LAURA *is still huddled upon the sofa, her feet drawn under her, her head resting on a pale blue pillow, her eyes wide and mysteriously watchful. The new floor lamp with its shade of rose-colored silk gives a soft, becoming light to her face, bringing out the fragile, unearthly prettiness which usually escapes attention. There is a steady murmur of rain, but it is slackening and stops soon after the scene begins; the air outside becomes pale and luminous as the moon breaks out.*

A moment after the curtain rises, the lights in both rooms flicker and go out.

JIM. Hey, there, Mr. Light Bulb!

[AMANDA *laughs nervously.*]

[LEGEND: "SUSPENSION OF A PUBLIC SERVICE"]

AMANDA. Where was Moses when the lights went out? Ha-ha. Do you know the answer to that one, Mr. O'Connor?

JIM. No, Ma'am, what's the answer?

AMANDA. In the dark!

[JIM *laughs appreciatively.*]

Everybody sit still. I'll light the candles. Isn't it lucky we have them on the table? Where's a match? Which of you gentlemen can provide a match?

JIM. Here.

AMANDA. Thank you, sir.

JIM. Not at all, Ma'am!

AMANDA. I guess the fuse has burnt out. Mr. O'Connor, can you tell a burnt-out fuse? I know I can't and Tom is a total loss when it comes to mechanics.

[SOUND: GETTING UP: VOICES RECEDE A LITTLE TO KITCHENETTE]

Oh, be careful you don't bump into something. We don't want our gentleman caller to break his neck. Now wouldn't that be a fine howdy-do?

JIM. Ha-ha!

Where is the fuse-box?

AMANDA. Right here next to the stove. Can you see anything?

JIM. Just a minute.

AMANDA. Isn't electricity a mysterious thing?

Wasn't it Benjamin Franklin who tied a key to a kite?

We live in such a mysterious universe, don't we? Some people say that science clears up all the mysteries for us. In my opinion it only creates more!

Have you found it yet?

JIM. No, Ma'am. All these fuses look okay to me.

AMANDA. Tom!

TOM. Yes, Mother?

AMANDA. That light bill I gave you several days ago. The one I told you we got the notices about?

[LEGEND: "HA!"]

TOM. Oh.—Yeah.

AMANDA. You didn't neglect to pay it by any chance?

TOM. Why, I—

AMANDA. Didn't! I might have known it!

JIM. Shakespeare probably wrote a poem on that light bill, Mrs. Wingfield.

AMANDA. I might have known better than to trust him with it! There's such a high price for negligence in this world!

JIM. Maybe the poem will win a ten-dollar prize.

AMANDA. We'll just have to spend the remainder of the evening in the nineteenth century, before Mr. Edison made the Mazda lamp!

JIM. Candlelight is my favorite kind of light.

AMANDA. That shows you're romantic! But that's no excuse for Tom.

Well, we got through dinner. Very considerate of them to let us get through dinner before they plunged us into everlasting darkness, wasn't it, Mr. O'Connor?

JIM. Ha-ha!

AMANDA. Tom, as a penalty for your carelessness you can help me with the dishes.

JIM. Let me give you a hand.

AMANDA. Indeed you will not!

JIM. I ought to be good for something.

AMANDA. Good for something? [*Her tone is rhapsodic.*]

You? Why, Mr. O'Connor, nobody, *nobody's* given me this much entertainment in years—as you have!

JIM. Aw, now, Mrs. Wingfield!

AMANDA. I'm not exaggerating, not one bit! But Sister is all by her lonesome. You go keep her company in the parlor!

I'll give you this lovely old candelabrum that used to be on the altar at the church of the Heavenly Rest. It was melted a little out of shape when the church burnt down. Lightning struck it one spring. Gypsy Jones was holding a revival at the time and he intimated that the church was destroyed because the Episcopalians gave card parties.

JIM. Ha-ha.

AMANDA. And how about you coaxing Sister to drink a little wine? I think it would be good for her! Can you carry both at once?

JIM. Sure. I'm Superman!

AMANDA. Now, Thomas, get into this apron!

[*The door of kitchenette swings closed on* AMANDA*'s gay laughter; the flickering light approaches the portieres.*]

[LAURA *sits up nervously as he enters. Her speech at first is low and breathless from the almost intolerable strain of being alone with a stranger.*]

[THE LEGEND: "I DON'T SUPPOSE YOU REMEMBER ME AT ALL!"]

[*In her first speeches in this scene, before* JIM'S *warmth overcomes her paralyzing shyness,* LAURA'S *voice is thin and breathless as though she has just run up a steep flight of stairs.*]

[JIM'S *attitude is gently humorous. In playing this scene it should be stressed that while the incident is apparently unimportant, it is to* LAURA *the climax of her secret life.*]

JIM. Hello, there, Laura.

LAURA [*faintly*]. Hello. [*She clears her throat.*]

JIM. How are you feeling now? Better?

LAURA. Yes. Yes, thank you.

JIM. This is for you. A little dandelion wine. [*He extends it toward her with extravagant gallantry.*]

LAURA. Thank you.

JIM. Drink it—but don't get drunk!

[*He laughs heartily.* LAURA *takes the glass uncertainly; laughs shyly.*]

Where shall I set the candles?

LAURA. Oh—oh, anywhere . . .

JIM. How about here on the floor? Any objections?

LAURA. No.

JIM. I'll spread a newspaper under to catch the drippings. I like to sit on the floor. Mind if I do?

LAURA. Oh, no.

JIM. Give me a pillow?

LAURA. What?

JIM. A pillow!

LAURA. Oh . . . [*Hands him one quickly*]

JIM. How about you? Don't you like to sit on the floor?

LAURA. Oh—yes.

JIM. Why don't you, then?

LAURA. I—will.

JIM. Take a pillow! [LAURA *does. Sits on the other side of the candelabrum.* JIM *crosses his legs and smiles engagingly at her.*] I can't hardly see you sitting way over there.

LAURA. I can—see you.

JIM. I know, but that's not fair, I'm in the limelight. [LAURA *moves her pillow closer.*] Good! Now I can see you! Comfortable?

LAURA. Yes.

JIM. So am I. Comfortable as a cow! Will you have some gum?

LAURA. No, thank you.

JIM. I think that I will indulge, with your permission. [*Musingly unwraps it and holds it up*] Think of the fortune made by the guy that invented the first piece of chewing gum. Amazing, huh? The Wrigley Building is one of the sights of Chicago.—I saw it summer before last when I went up to the Century of Progress. Did you take in the Century of Progress?

LAURA. No, I didn't.

JIM. Well, it was quite a wonderful exposition. What impressed me most was the Hall of Science. Gives you an idea of what the future will be in America, even more wonderful than the present time is! [*Pause. Smiling at her*] Your brother tells me you're shy. Is that right, Laura?

LAURA. I—don't know.

JIM. I judge you to be an old-fashioned type of girl. Well, I think that's a pretty good type to be. Hope you don't think I'm being too personal—do you?

LAURA [*hastily, out of embarrassment*]. I believe, I *will* take a piece of gum, if you—don't mind. [*Clearing her throat*] Mr. O'Connor, have you—kept up with your singing?

JIM. Singing? Me?

LAURA. Yes. I remember what a beautiful voice you had.

JIM. When did you hear me sing?

[VOICE OFF STAGE IN THE PAUSE]

VOICE [*off stage*].

O blow, ye winds, heigh-ho,
A-roving I will go!
I'm off to my love
With a boxing glove—
Ten thousand miles away!

JIM. You say you've heard me sing?

LAURA. Oh, yes! Yes, very often . . . I—don't suppose—you remember me—at all?

JIM [*smiling doubtfully*]. You know I have an idea I've seen you before. I had that idea soon as you opened the door. It seemed almost like I was about to remember your name. But the name that I started to call you—wasn't a name! And so I stopped myself before I said it.

LAURA. Wasn't it—Blue Roses?

JIM [*springs up. Grinning*]. Blue Roses!—My gosh, yes—Blue Roses!

That's what I had on my tongue when you opened the door!

Isn't it funny what tricks your memory plays? I didn't connect you with high school somehow or other.

But that's where it was; it was high school. I didn't even know you were Shakespeare's sister!

Gosh, I'm sorry.

LAURA. I didn't expect you to. You—barely knew me!

JIM. But we did have a speaking acquaintance, huh?

LAURA. Yes, we—spoke to each other.

JIM. When did you recognize me?

LAURA. Oh, right away!

JIM. Soon as I came in the door?

LAURA. When I heard your name I thought it was probably you. I knew that Tom used to know you a little in high school. So when you came in the door—

Well, then I was—sure.

JIM. Why didn't you *say* something, then?

LAURA [*breathlessly*]. I didn't know what to say, I was—too surprised!

JIM. For goodness' sakes! You know, this sure is funny!

LAURA. Yes! Yes, isn't it, though . . .

JIM. Didn't we have a class in something together?

LAURA. Yes, we did.

JIM. What class was that?

LAURA. It was—singing—Chorus!

JIM. Aw!

LAURA. I sat across the aisle from you in the Aud.

JIM. Aw.

LAURA. Mondays, Wednesdays and Fridays.

JIM. Now I remember—you always came in late.

LAURA. Yes, it was so hard for me, getting upstairs. I had that brace on my leg—it clumped so loud!

JIM. I never heard any clumping.

LAURA [*wincing at the recollection*]. To me it sounded like—thunder!

JIM. Well, well, well, I never even noticed.

LAURA. And everybody was seated before I came in. I had to walk in front of all those people. My seat was in the back row. I had to go clumping all the way up the aisle with everyone watching!

JIM. You shouldn't have been self-conscious.

LAURA. I know, but I was. It was always such a relief when the singing started.

JIM. Aw, yes, I've placed *you* now! I used to call you Blue Roses. How was it that I got started calling you that?

LAURA. I was out of school a little while with pleurosis. When I came back you asked me what was the matter. I said I had pleurosis—you thought I said Blue Roses. That's what you always called me after that!

JIM. I hope you didn't mind.

LAURA. Oh, no—I liked it. You see, I wasn't acquainted with many—people. . . .

JIM. As I remember you sort of stuck by yourself.

LAURA. I—I—never have had much luck at—making friends.

JIM. I don't see why you wouldn't.

LAURA. Well, I—started out badly.

JIM. You mean being—

LAURA. Yes, it sort of—stood between me—

JIM. You shouldn't have let it!

LAURA. I know, but it did, and—

JIM. You were shy with people!

LAURA. I tried not to be but never could—

JIM. Overcome it?

LAURA. No, I—I never could!

JIM. I guess being shy is something you have to work out of kind of gradually.

LAURA [*sorrowfully*]. Yes—I guess it—

JIM. Takes time!

LAURA. Yes—

JIM. People are not so dreadful when you know them. That's what you have to remember! And everybody has problems, not just you, but practically everybody has got some problems.

You think of yourself as having the only problems, as being the only one who is disappointed. But just look around you and you will see lots of people as disappointed as you are. For instance, I hoped when I was going to high school that I would be further along at this time, six years later, than I am now—You remember that wonderful write-up I had in *The Torch?*

LAURA. Yes! [*She rises and crosses to table.*]

JIM. It said I was bound to succeed in anything I went into! [LAURA *returns with the annual.*] Holy Jeez! *The Torch!* [*He accepts it reverently. They smile across it with mutual wonder.* LAURA *crouches beside him and they begin to turn through it.* LAURA'S *shyness is dissolving in his warmth.*]

LAURA. Here you are in *The Pirates of Penzance!*

JIM [*wistfully*]. I sang the baritone lead in that operetta.

LAURA [*raptly*]. So—*beautifully!*

JIM [*protesting*]. Aw—

LAURA. Yes, yes—beautifully—beautifully!

JIM. You heard me?

LAURA. All three times!

JIM. No!

LAURA. Yes!

JIM. All three performances?

LAURA [*looking down*]. Yes.

JIM. Why?

LAURA. I—wanted to ask you to—autograph my program.

JIM. Why didn't you ask me to?

LAURA. You were always surrounded by your own friends so much that I never had a chance to.

JIM. You should have just—

LAURA. Well, I—thought you might think I was—

JIM. Thought I might think you was—what?

LAURA. Oh—

JIM [*with reflective relish*]. I was beleaguered by females in those days.

LAURA. You were terribly popular!

JIM. Yeah—

LAURA. You had such a—friendly way—

JIM. I was spoiled in high school.

LAURA. Everybody—liked you!

JIM. Including you?

LAURA. I—yes, I—I did, too—[*She gently closes the book in her lap.*]

JIM. Well, well, well!—Give me that program, Laura. [*She hands it to him. He signs it with a flourish.*] There you are—better late than never!

LAURA. Oh, I—what a—surprise!

JIM. My signature isn't worth very much right now.

But some day—maybe—it will increase in value!

Being disappointed is one thing and being discouraged is something else. I am disappointed but I am not discouraged.

I'm twenty-three years old.
How old are you?

LAURA. I'll be twenty-four in June.

JIM. That's not old age!

LAURA. No, but–

JIM. You finished high school?

LAURA [*with difficulty*]. I didn't go back.

JIM. You mean you dropped out?

LAURA. I made bad grades in my final examinations. [*She rises and replaces the book and the program. Her voice strained.*] How is–Emily Meisenbach getting along?

JIM. Oh, that kraut-head!

LAURA. Why do you call her that?

JIM. That's what she was.

LAURA. You're not still–going with her?

JIM. I never see her.

LAURA. It said in the Personal Section that you were–engaged!

JIM. I know, but I wasn't impressed by that–propaganda!

LAURA. It wasn't–the truth?

JIM. Only in Emily's optimistic opinion!

LAURA. Oh–

[LEGEND: "WHAT HAVE YOU DONE SINCE HIGH SCHOOL?"]

[JIM *lights a cigarette and leans indolently back on his elbows smiling at* LAURA *with a warmth and charm which lights her inwardly with altar candles. She remains by the table and turns in her hands a piece of glass to cover her tumult.*]

JIM [*after several reflective puffs on a cigarette*]. What have you done since high school? [*She seems not to hear him.*] Huh? [LAURA *looks up.*] I said what have you done since high school, Laura?

LAURA. Nothing much.

JIM. You must have been doing something these six long years.

LAURA. Yes.

JIM. Well, then, such as what?

LAURA. I took a business course at business college–

JIM. How did that work out?

LAURA. Well, not very–well–I had to drop out, it gave me–indigestion– [JIM *laughs gently.*]

JIM. What are you doing now?

LAURA. I don't do anything–much. Oh, please don't think I sit around doing nothing! My glass collection takes up a good deal of time. Glass is something you have to take good care of.

JIM. What did you say–about glass?

LAURA. Collection I said–I have one– [*She clears her throat and turns away again, acutely shy.*]

JIM [*abruptly*]. You know what I judge to be the trouble with you? Inferiority complex! Know what that is? That's what they call it when someone low-rates himself!

I understand it because I had it, too. Although my case was not so aggravated as yours seems to be. I had it until I took up public speaking, developed my voice, and learned that I had an aptitude for science. Before that time I never thought of myself as being outstanding in any way whatsoever!

Now I've never made a regular study of it, but I have a friend who says I can analyze people better than doctors that make a profession of it. I don't claim that to be necessarily true, but I can sure guess a person's psychology, Laura! [*Takes out his gum*] Excuse me, Laura. I always take it out when the flavor is gone. I'll use this scrap of paper to wrap it in. I know how it is to get it stuck on a shoe.

Yep—that's what I judge to be your principal trouble. A lack of confidence in yourself as a person. You don't have the proper amount of faith in yourself. I'm basing that fact on a number of your remarks and also on certain observations I've made. For instance that clumping you thought was so awful in high school. You say that you even dreaded to walk into class. You see what you did? You dropped out of school, you gave up an education because of a clump, which as far as I know was practically nonexistent! A little physical defect is what you have. Hardly noticeable even! Magnified thousands of times by imagination!

You know what my strong advice to you is? Think of yourself as *superior* in some way!

LAURA. In what way would I think?

JIM. Why, man alive, Laura! Just look about you a little. What do you see? A world full of common people! All of 'em born and all of 'em going to die!

Which of them has one-tenth of your good points! Or mine! Or anyone else's, as far as that goes—Gosh!

Everybody excels in some one thing. Some in many!

[*Unconsciously glances at himself in the mirror*]

All you've got to do is discover in *what!*

Take me, for instance.

[*He adjusts his tie at the mirror.*]

My interest happens to lie in electro-dynamics. I'm taking a course in radio engineering at night school, Laura, on top of a fairly responsible job at the warehouse. I'm taking that course and studying public speaking.

LAURA. Ohhhh.

JIM. Because I believe in the future of television!

[*Turning back to her*]

I wish to be ready to go up right along with it. Therefore I'm planning to get in on the ground floor. In fact I've already made the right connections and all that remains is for the industry itself to get under way! Full steam—

[*His eyes are starry.*]

Knowledge—Zzzzzp! *Money*—Zzzzzzp!—*Power!*

That's the cycle democracy is built on!

[*His attitude is convincingly dynamic.* LAURA *stares at him, even her shyness eclipsed in her absolute wonder. He suddenly grins.*]

I guess you think I think a lot of myself!

LAURA. No—o-o-o, I—

JIM. Now how about you? Isn't there something you take more interest in than anything else?

LAURA. Well, I do—as I said—have my—glass collection—

[*A peal of girlish laughter from the kitchen*]

JIM. I'm not right sure I know what you're talking about.

What kind of glass is it?

LAURA. Little articles of it, they're ornaments mostly!

Most of them are little animals made out of glass, the tiniest little animals in the world. Mother calls them a glass menagerie!

Here's an example of one, if you'd like to see it!

This one is one of the oldest. It's nearly thirteen.

[MUSIC: "THE GLASS MENAGERIE"]

[*He stretches out his hand.*]

Oh, be careful—if you breathe, it breaks!

JIM. I'd better not take it. I'm pretty clumsy with things.

LAURA. Go on, I trust you with him!

[*Places it in his palm.*]

There now—you're holding him gently!

Hold him over the light, he loves the light! You see how the light shines through him?

JIM. It sure does shine!

LAURA. I shouldn't be partial, but he is my favorite one.

JIM. What kind of a thing is this one supposed to be?

LAURA. Haven't you noticed the single horn on his forehead?

JIM. A unicorn, huh?

LAURA. Mmmm-hmmm!

JIM. Unicorns, aren't they extinct in the modern world?

LAURA. I know!

JIM. Poor little fellow, he must feel sort of lonesome.

LAURA [*smiling*]. Well, if he does he doesn't complain about it. He stays on a shelf with some horses that don't have horns and all of them seem to get along nicely together.

JIM. How do you know?

LAURA [*lightly*]. I haven't heard any arguments among them!

JIM [*grinning*]. No arguments, huh? Well, that's a pretty good sign! Where shall I set him?

LAURA. Put him on the table. They all like a change of scenery once in a while!

JIM [*stretching*]. Well, well, well, well—
Look how big my shadow is when I stretch!

LAURA. Oh, oh, yes—it stretches across the ceiling!

JIM [*crossing to door*]. I think it's stopped raining. [*Opens fire-escape door*] Where does the music come from?

LAURA. From the Paradise Dance Hall across the alley.

JIM. How about cutting the rug a little, Miss Wingfield?

LAURA. Oh, I—

JIM. Or is your program filled up? Let me have a look at it. [*Grasps imaginary card*] Why, every dance is taken! I'll just have to scratch some out. [WALTZ MUSIC: "LA GOLONDRINA"] Ahhh, a waltz! [*He executes some sweeping turns by himself then holds his arms toward* LAURA.]

LAURA [*breathlessly*]. I—can't dance!

JIM. There you go, that inferiority stuff!

LAURA. I've never danced in my life!

JIM. Come on, try!

LAURA. Oh, but I'd step on you!

JIM. I'm not made out of glass.

LAURA. How—how—how do we start?

JIM. Just leave it to me. You hold your arms out a little.

LAURA. Like this?

JIM. A little bit higher. Right. Now don't tighten up, that's the main thing about it—relax.

LAURA [*laughing breathlessly*]. It's hard not to.

JIM. Okay.

LAURA. I'm afraid you can't budge me.

JIM. What do you bet I can't? [*He swings her into motion.*]

LAURA. Goodness, yes, you can!

JIM. Let yourself go, now, Laura, just let yourself go.

LAURA. I'm—

JIM. Come on!

LAURA. Trying!

JIM. Not so stiff—Easy does it!

LAURA. I know but I'm—

JIM. Loosen th' backbone! There now, that's a lot better.

LAURA. Am I?

JIM. Lots, lots better! [*He moves her about the room in a clumsy waltz.*]

LAURA. Oh, my!

JIM. Ha-ha!

LAURA. Oh, my goodness!

JIM. Ha-ha-ha! [*They suddenly bump into the table.* JIM *stops.*] What did we hit on?

LAURA. Table.

JIM. Did something fall off it? I think–

LAURA. Yes.

JIM. I hope that it wasn't the little glass horse with the horn!

LAURA. Yes.

JIM. Aw, aw, aw. Is it broken?

LAURA. Now it is just like all the other horses.

JIM. It's lost its–

LAURA. Horn!

It doesn't matter. Maybe it's a blessing in disguise.

JIM. You'll never forgive me. I bet that that was your favorite piece of glass.

LAURA. I don't have favorites much. It's no tragedy, Freckles. Glass breaks so easily. No matter how careful you are. The traffic jars the shelves and things fall off them.

JIM. Still I'm awfully sorry that I was the cause.

LAURA [*smiling*]. I'll just imagine he had an operation.

The horn was removed to make him feel less–freakish!

[*They both laugh.*]

Now he will feel more at home with the other horses, the ones that don't have horns . . .

JIM. Ha-ha, that's very funny!

[*Suddenly serious*]

I'm glad to see that you have a sense of humor.

You know–you're–well–very different!

Surprisingly different from anyone else I know!

[*His voice becomes soft and hesitant with a genuine feeling.*]

Do you mind me telling you that?

[LAURA *is abashed beyond speech.*]

I mean it in a nice way . . .

[LAURA *nods shyly, looking away.*]

You make me feel sort of–I don't know how to put it!

I'm usually pretty good at expressing things, but–

This is something that I don't know how to say!

[LAURA *touches her throat and clears it–turns the broken unicorn in her hands.*]

[*Even softer*]

Has anyone ever told you that you were pretty?

[PAUSE: MUSIC]

[LAURA *looks up slowly, with wonder, and shakes her head.*]

Well, you are! In a very different way from anyone else.

And all the nicer because of the difference, too.

[*His voice becomes low and husky.* LAURA *turns away, nearly faint with the novelty of her emotions.*]

I wish that you were my sister. I'd teach you to have some confidence in yourself. The different people are not like other people, but being different is nothing to be ashamed of. Because other people are not such wonderful people. They're one hundred times one thousand. You're one times one! They walk all over the earth. You just stay here. They're common as—weeds, but—you—well, you're—*Blue Roses!*

[IMAGE ON SCREEN: BLUE ROSES]

[MUSIC CHANGES]

LAURA. But blue is wrong for—roses . . .

JIM. It's right for you!—You're—pretty!

LAURA. In what respect am I pretty?

JIM. In all respects—believe me! Your eyes—your hair—are pretty! Your hands are pretty!

[*He catches hold of her hand.*]

You think I'm making this up because I'm invited to dinner and have to be nice. Oh, I could do that! I could put on an act for you, Laura, and say lots of things without being very sincere. But this time I am. I'm talking to you sincerely. I happened to notice you had this inferiority complex that keeps you from feeling comfortable with people. Somebody needs to build your confidence up and make you proud instead of shy and turning away and—blushing—

Somebody—ought to—

Ought to—*kiss* you, Laura!

[*His hand slips slowly up her arm to her shoulder.*]

[MUSIC SWELLS TUMULTUOUSLY.]

[*He suddenly turns her about and kisses her on the lips.*]

[*When he releases her,* LAURA *sinks on the sofa with a bright, dazed look.*]

[JIM *backs away and fishes in his pocket for a cigarette.*]

[LEGEND ON SCREEN: "SOUVENIR"]

Stumble-john!

[*He lights the cigarette, avoiding her look.*]

[*There is a peal of girlish laughter from* AMANDA *in the kitchen.*]

[LAURA *slowly raises and opens her hand. It still contains the little broken glass animal. She looks at it with a tender, bewildered expression.*]

Stumble-john!

I shouldn't have done that— That was way off the beam.

You don't smoke, do you?

[*She looks up, smiling, not hearing the question.*]

[He sits beside her a little gingerly. She looks at him speechlessly—waiting.]

[He coughs decorously and moves a little farther aside as he considers the situation and senses her feelings, dimly, with perturbation.]

[Gently]

Would you—care for a—mint?

[She doesn't seem to hear him but her look grows brighter even.]

Peppermint—Life-Saver?

My pocket's a regular drug store—wherever I go . . .

[He pops a mint in his mouth. Then gulps and decides to make a clean breast of it. He speaks slowly and gingerly.]

Laura, you know, if I had a sister like you, I'd do the same thing as Tom. I'd bring out fellows and—introduce her to them. The right type of boys of a type to—appreciate her.

Only—well—he made a mistake about me.

Maybe I've got no call to be saying this. That may not have been the idea in having me over. But what if it was?

There's nothing wrong about that. The only trouble is that in my case—I'm not in a situation to—do the right thing.

I can't take down your number and say I'll phone.

I can't call up next week and—ask for a date.

I thought I had better explain the situation in case you—misunderstood it and—hurt your feelings. . . .

[Pause]

[Slowly, very slowly, LAURA'S *look changes, her eyes returning slowly from his to the ornament in her palm.]*

[AMANDA *utters another gay laugh in the kitchen.]*

LAURA [*faintly*]. You—won't—call again?

JIM. No, Laura, I can't.

[He rises from the sofa.]

As I was just explaining, I've—got strings on me.

Laura, I've—been going steady!

I go out all the time with a girl named Betty, She's a homegirl like you, and Catholic, and Irish, and in a great many ways we—get along fine.

I met her last summer on a moonlight boat trip up the river to Alton, on the *Majestic*.

Well—right away from the start it was—love!

[LEGEND: LOVE!]

[LAURA *sways slightly forward and grips the arm of the sofa. He fails to notice, now enrapt in his own comfortable being.]*

Being in love has made a new man of me!

[*Leaning stiffly forward, clutching the arm of the sofa,* LAURA *struggles visibly with her storm. But* JIM *is oblivious, she is a long way off.*]

The power of love is really pretty tremendous!

Love is something that—changes the whole world, Laura!

[*The storm abates a little and* LAURA *leans back. He notices her again.*]

It happened that Betty's aunt took sick, she got a wire and had to go to Centralia. So Tom—when he asked me to dinner—I naturally just accepted the invitation, not knowing that you—that he—that I—

[*He stops awkwardly.*]

Huh—I'm a stumble-john!

[*He flops back on the sofa.*]

[*The holy candles in the altar of* LAURA'S *face have been snuffed out. There is a look of almost infinite desolation.*]

[JIM *glances at her uneasily.*]

I wish that you would—say something. [*She bites her lip which was trembling and then bravely smiles. She opens her hand again on the broken glass ornament. Then she gently takes his hand and raises it level with her own. She carefully places the unicorn in the palm of his hand, then pushes his fingers closed upon it.*] What are you—doing that for? You want me to have him?—Laura? [*She nods.*] What for?

LAURA. A—souvenir . . .

[*She rises unsteadily and crouches beside the victrola to wind it up.*]

[LEGEND ON SCREEN: "THINGS HAVE A WAY OF TURNING OUT SO BADLY!"]

[OR IMAGE: "GENTLEMAN CALLER WAVING GOOD-BYE!—GAILY"]

[*At this moment* AMANDA *rushes brightly back in the front room. She bears a pitcher of fruit punch in an old-fashioned cut-glass pitcher and a plate of macaroons. The plate has a gold border and poppies painted on it.*]

AMANDA. Well, well, well! Isn't the air delightful after the shower?

I've made you children a little liquid refreshment.

[*Turns gaily to the gentleman caller*]

Jim, do you know that song about lemonade?

"Lemonade, lemonade
Made in the shade and stirred with a spade—
Good enough for any old maid!"

JIM [*uneasily*]. Ha-ha! No—I never heard it.

AMANDA. Why, Laura! You look so serious!

JIM. We were having a serious conversation.

AMANDA. Good! Now you're better acquainted!

JIM [*uncertainly*]. Ha-ha! Yes.

AMANDA. You modern young people are much more serious-minded than my generation. I was so gay as a girl!

JIM. You haven't changed, Mrs. Wingfield.

AMANDA. Tonight I'm rejuvenated! The gaiety of the occasion, Mr. O'Connor!

[*She tosses her head with a peal of laughter. Spills lemonade*]

Oooo! I'm baptizing myself!

JIM. Here—let me—

AMANDA [*setting the pitcher down*]. There now. I discovered we had some maraschino cherries. I dumped them in, juice and all!

JIM. You shouldn't have gone to that trouble, Mrs. Wingfield.

AMANDA. Trouble, trouble? Why, it was loads of fun!

Didn't you hear me cutting up in the kitchen? I bet your ears were burning! I told Tom how outdone with him I was for keeping you to himself so long a time! He should have brought you over much, much sooner! Well, now that you've found your way, I want you to be a very frequent caller! Not just occasional but all the time.

Oh, we're going to have a lot of gay times together! I see them coming!

Mmm, just breathe that air! So fresh, and the moon's so pretty!

I'll skip back out—I know where my place is when young folks are having a—serious conversation!

JIM. Oh, don't go out, Mrs. Wingfield. The fact of the matter is I've got to be going.

AMANDA. Going, now? You're joking! Why, it's only the shank of the evening, Mr. O'Connor!

JIM. Well, you know how it is.

AMANDA. You mean you're a young workingman and have to keep workingmen's hours. We'll let you off early tonight. But only on the condition that next time you stay later.

What's the best night for you? Isn't Saturday night the best night for you workingmen?

JIM. I have a couple of time-clocks to punch, Mrs. Wingfield. One at morning, another one at night!

AMANDA. My, but you *are* ambitious! You work at night, too?

JIM. No, Ma'am, not work but—Betty! [*He crosses deliberately to pick up his hat. The band at the Paradise Dance Hall goes into a tender waltz.*]

AMANDA. Betty? Betty? Who's—Betty!

[*There is an ominous cracking sound in the sky.*]

JIM. Oh, just a girl. The girl I go steady with! [*He smiles charmingly. The sky falls.*]

[LEGEND: "THE SKY FALLS."]

AMANDA [*a long-drawn exhalation*]. Ohhh . . . Is it a serious romance, Mr. O'Connor?

JIM. We're going to be married the second Sunday in June.

AMANDA. Ohhh—how nice!

Tom didn't mention that you were engaged to be married.

JIM. The cat's not out of the bag at the warehouse yet.

You know how they are. They call you Romeo and stuff like that.

[*He stops at the oval mirror to put on his hat. He carefully shapes the brim and the crown to give a discreetly dashing effect.*]

It's been a wonderful evening, Mrs. Wingfield. I guess this is what they mean by Southern hospitality.

AMANDA. It really wasn't anything at all.

JIM. I hope it don't seem like I'm rushing off. But I promised Betty I'd pick her up at the Wabash depot, an' by the time I get my jalopy down there her train'll be in. Some women are pretty upset if you keep 'em waiting.

AMANDA. Yes, I know— The tyranny of women!

[*Extends her hand*]

Good-bye, Mr. O'Connor.

I wish you luck—and happiness—and success! All three of them, and so does Laura!—Don't you, Laura?

LAURA. Yes!

JIM [*taking her hand*]. Good-bye, Laura. I'm certainly going to treasure that souvenir. And don't you forget the good advice I gave you.

[*Raises his voice to a cheery shout*]

So long, Shakespeare!

Thanks again, ladies— Good night!

[*He grins and ducks jauntily out.*]

[*Still bravely grimacing,* AMANDA *closes the door on the gentleman caller. Then she turns back to the room with a puzzled expression. She and* LAURA *don't dare to face each other.* LAURA *crouches beside the victrola to wind it.*]

AMANDA [*faintly*]. Things have a way of turning out so badly.

I don't believe that I would play the victrola.

Well, well—well—

Our gentleman caller was engaged to be married!

Tom!

TOM [*from back*]. Yes, Mother?

AMANDA. Come in here a minute. I want to tell you something awfully funny.

TOM [*enters with macaroon and a glass of the lemonade*]. Has the gentleman caller gotten away already?

AMANDA. The gentleman caller has made an early departure.

What a wonderful joke you played on us!

TOM. How do you mean?

AMANDA. You didn't mention that he was engaged to be married.

TOM. Jim? Engaged?

AMANDA. That's what he just informed us.

TOM. I'll be jiggered! I didn't know about that.

AMANDA. That seems very peculiar.

TOM. What's peculiar about it?

AMANDA. Didn't you call him your best friend down at the warehouse?

TOM. He is, but how did I know?

AMANDA. It seems extremely peculiar that you wouldn't know your best friend was going to be married!

TOM. The warehouse is where I work, not where I know things about people!

AMANDA. You don't know things anywhere! You live in a dream; you manufacture illusions!

[*He crosses to door.*]

Where are you going?

TOM. I'm going to the movies.

AMANDA. That's right, now that you've had us make such fools of ourselves. The effort, the preparations, all the expense! The new floor lamp, the rug, the clothes for Laura! All for what? To entertain some other girl's fiancé!

Go to the movies, go! Don't think about us, a mother deserted, an unmarried sister who's crippled and has no job! Don't let anything interfere with your selfish pleasure!

Just go, go, go—to the movies!

TOM. All right, I will! The more you shout about my selfishness to me the quicker I'll go, and I won't go to the movies!

AMANDA. Go, then! Then go to the moon—you selfish dreamer!

[TOM *smashes his glass on the floor. He plunges out on the fire-escape, slamming the door.* LAURA *screams—cut by door.*]

[*Dance-hall music up.* TOM *goes to the rail and grips it desperately, lifting his face in the chill white moonlight penetrating the narrow abyss of the alley.*]

[LEGEND ON SCREEN: "AND SO GOOD-BYE . . ."]

[TOM'*s closing speech is timed with the interior pantomine. The interior scene is played as though viewed through soundproof glass.* AMANDA *appears to be making a comforting speech to* LAURA *who is huddled upon the sofa. Now that we cannot hear the mother's speech, her silliness is gone and she has dignity and tragic beauty.* LAURA'*s dark hair hides her face until at the end of the speech she lifts it to smile at her mother.* AMANDA'*s gestures are slow and graceful, almost dance-like, as she comforts the daughter. At the end of her speech she glances a moment at the father's picture—then withdraws through the portieres. At close of* TOM'*s speech,* LAURA *blows out the candles, ending the play.*]

TOM. I didn't go to the moon, I went much further—for time is the longest distance between two places—

Not long after that I was fired for writing a poem on the lid of a shoe-box.

I left Saint Louis. I descended the steps of this fire-escape for a last time and followed, from then on, in my father's footsteps, attempting to find in motion what was lost in space—

I traveled around a great deal. The cities swept about me like dead leaves, leaves that were brightly colored but torn away from the branches.

I would have stopped, but I was pursued by something.

It always came upon me unawares, taking me altogether by surprise. Perhaps it was a familiar bit of music. Perhaps it was only a piece of transparent glass—

Perhaps I am walking along a street at night, in some strange city, before I have found companions. I pass the lighted window of a shop where perfume is sold. The window is filled with pieces of colored glass, tiny transparent bottles in delicate colors, like bits of a shattered rainbow.

Then all at once my sister touches my shoulder. I turn around and look into her eyes . . .

Oh, Laura, Laura, I tried to leave you behind me, but I am more faithful than I intended to be!

I reach for a cigarette, I cross the street, I run into the movies or a bar, I buy a drink, I speak to the nearest stranger—anything that can blow your candles out!

[LAURA *bends over the candles.*]

—for nowadays the world is lit by lightning! Blow out your candles, Laura—and so good-bye. . . .

[*She blows the candles out.*]

THE SCENE DISSOLVES

1945

C H A P T E R
S E V E N

EXPERIMENTATION IN POETRY

The four poets represented in this section—Hart Crane, Archibald MacLeish, Robinson Jeffers, and E. E. Cummings—have in common only a highly individualized experimentalism. Among them are no significant regional, thematic, or personal ties. They are collectively a part of no one school or movement, and they were not in any meaningful sense important influences on one another. They do, however, collectively suggest the eclectic vitality of poetic activity in America. During and following the development of the so-called new poetry—by Robinson and Frost, by the Chicago group and the expatriates, and by others—poetry was flourishing in America in a variety of ways among a variety of poets.

In a sense, to be sure, the four poets are related both to one another and some of the poets we have already discussed who were their contemporaries or predecessors; for all parts of a civilized culture touch all other parts in one way or another. In yet another sense, however, these four in particular—although any one could be replaced by some other poet—do at least demonstrate that modern American poetry has been widely experimental, widely individualized, widely adventuresome. More importantly, all four are simply good poets.

Hart Crane's tragically brief life is in many ways a paradigm of his poetry. Both reflect a tense and continuous oscillation between acceptance and rejection, between a vital affirmation and a turbulent rebellion. Both were cut too short, and both alternate an untidy and impassioned chaos with lengths of ordered beauty. Crane's life and background were not those of the American dream. He hated the mercantilistic Midwestern drabness of his youth; his quarreling parents, who ultimately separated; his rootless wanderings and various menial jobs as clerk, as salesman, as mechanic; his homosexuality. He killed himself at the age of thirty-three. Yet, he loved the tawdry vastness of his America and wanted to understand it and accept it; he wanted to express it.

Crane began writing poetry at the early age of thirteen, repudiated his father's Ohio candy business, rejected college, and eventually settled permanently in New York. Self-taught, he read Laforgue and Rimbaud, Donne and Marlowe, Poe and Melville; and he was soon publishing in the little magazines, which brought him to the attention of writers such as Waldo Frank, Gorham Munson, Allen Tate, and others. In these early poems as well as in those of his first volume, *White Buildings* (1926), the influence of Whitman, and of Eliot and other moderns, was readily apparent, but his logic of metaphor and image, of unconventional diction and syntax, is more suggestive of Emily Dickinson or E. E. Cummings than of Whitman and Eliot. More importantly, perhaps, they suggest only Crane himself, as all good poetry ultimately must suggest its maker alone.

Just how individualized Crane's vision and technique ultimately were became apparent only with the publication of *The Bridge* (1930), his last poem, his masterpiece, which is still, even after all its faults have been listed, (as Oscar Cargill put it) "one of the best of modern times." The most ambitious poem by an American since Eliot's *The Waste Land*—whose "pessimistic" tone, to Crane, needed some kind of affirmative counterpart—*The Bridge* is attempting a modern synthesis of the American experience. Its central symbol is Brooklyn Bridge, an attempt at some kind of unity in diversity, some kind of vision that transcends the vulgarity and commercialism and barbarity of Crane's America. All American history, geography, and industrialism are also used, the *Twentieth-Century Limited* no less than the Mississippi River, Rip Van Winkle and Pocahantas, Columbus and Walt Whitman, the New York subway and Edgar Allan Poe. Only partly successful, uneven in execution if not in its scheme, "difficult" to even the sympathetic and tolerant reader, it nonetheless represents one of America's most ambitious poetic undertakings, an undertaking that has parallels perhaps only in Eliot, Pound's *Cantos*, and Whitman's *Song of Myself*.

When Crane committed suicide in April of 1932 by jumping overboard from a steamer that was returning him from Mexico to America, his alcoholism, his homosexuality, his poverty, his family problems, and his self-doubts all no doubt played a part. An exquisite vision imperfectly executed probably played its part too.

Archibald MacLeish is as unlike Hart Crane as one man can be to another. Wealthy, well-educated, "proper" in every conventional way, and "successful" in all his undertakings (as poet, as soldier, as editor, as statesman, as diplomat, as dramatist, and as educator), MacLeish apparently, in any popular sense, never knew failure. His significance in part resides in his remarkable representativeness of twentieth-century poetic and intellectual tendencies. In, respectively, the 1920's, the '30's, the '40's, and the '50's, we can see in his work clear-cut developments reflecting some of the major interests of each of those decades. Yet, we can also see throughout all those years an integrity and a devotion to his own vision of what the "truth" had to be that somehow transcends the value of his verse as a mere litmus paper to its times.

MacLeish's expatriate years, for example (he lived with his family in Paris between 1923 and 1928), are marked by the associations and influences one would have expected: the French Symbolists, Eliot and Pound, and the masters these last two had themselves turned to. Yet among the several volumes of poetry that he published during those years—*The Happy Marriage* (1924), *The Pot of Earth* (1925), *Streets in the Moon* (1926), *The Hamlet of A. MacLeish* (1928)—are achievements that do much more than reflect the techniques, moods, and subjects of the other expatriates. His "Ars Poetica," for example, from his *Streets in the Moon*, was for years the embodiment par excellence of what the "new poetry" at its best was striving to be. He could also respond to current trends in more than imitative ways, as exemplified in his use of Frazer's *The Golden Bough*, for another example, in his *The Pot of Earth*.

Soon after his return to America in 1928, however, an enlarging social consciousness became predominant in his work—and along with it a new kind of experimentation. In his *New Found Land* (1930) and his *Conquistador* (1932) are glowing American affirmations of what the new world could be at the same time that they point clearly to the disparity between that dream and the actuality. Other work of the 1930's—the anticapitalistic *Frescoes for Mr. Rockefeller's City* (1933); his verse drama *Panic* (1935); the radio dramas *The Fall of the City* (1937) and *Air Raid* (1938)—are all marked by a concern for contemporary events, a deeply felt need for national awakening, and a belief that poetry could again be a variously effective didactic tool.

During most of the 1940's MacLeish was actively engaged in public responsibilities brought on by the war and its aftermath, as a Librarian of Congress, as a director of a governmental agency, as an Assistant Secretary of State, and as a diplomat for cultural missions. Some of the poetry of this period was derisively termed "public" or "patriotic"; and the prose of that time—in such works as the attacks on fellow poets in *The Irresponsibles* (1940), or the exhortations in *A Time to Speak* (1941) and *A Time to Act* (1943)—reveals clearly enough a concern for public affairs at the expense of his poetry.

Appointment in 1949 as Boylston Professor at Harvard, however, heralded a still further development in MacLeish. His powers as a quiet lyricist had again become evident in *ActFive and Other Poems* as early as 1948. The achievement of the 1950's was his renewed imaginative use of classical and Biblical mythology to create effective "modern" metaphors. This direction was clear enough in both *The Trojan Horse* (1952) and *Songs for Eve* (1954). The technique was most successful in the prize-winning verse drama, *J.B.* (1958), a controversial adaptation of the story of Job into a modern situation.

What the 1960's will ultimately reveal of the various talents of this remarkably endowed man cannot, of course, be predicted. His latest volume, *Poetry and Experience* (1961), is a book-length statement of his critical theory. Whatever it brings, the disparity between the achievement of Crane and the achievement of MacLeish is apparent enough.

Neither poet, however, nor even the disparity itself, quite prepares one for the stark and solitary contrast that Robinson Jeffers offers to both. With no real antecedents in American literature, with no real *confrère* among the moderns (although O'Neill is occasionally pointed to), Robinson Jeffers' inexorable nihilism is equally removed from the sensitive ambivalences of Crane and the warm humanism of MacLeish.

Jeffers' background and precocious early learning as well as his virtual forty-year isolation in the great stone house and tower he himself built at Carmel at the base of California's magnificent Monterey peninsula are closely related to his poetry. His ability to read Greek at the age of five, his early wide travels and Continental education, his mastery of several languages by the age of fifteen, his graduation from college at the age of eighteen, his further disparate studies at various universities (in English and medicine, law, forestry, zoology)—do not, to be sure, suggest a career in poetry. Yet, a temperamental pessimism, an addiction to classical and Biblical themes of violence, and a preference for the raw, gaunt grandeurs of natural phenomena in contrast to the inevitable self-destructive stupidities of man are not inconsistent with that background. The long rolling lines of his poetry, with rhythms like those of the California surf itself, are as indigenous to the scenes of his residence as are his favorite symbols: the enduring, immemorial rocks and cliffs of the coast; and the soaring, wild, but inevitably doomed circlings of the hawks.

Jeffers' two earliest volumes are insignificant, but by the end of the 1920's—in *Roan Stallion, Tamar, and Other Poems* (1925), *The Women at Point Sur* (1927), *Poems* (1928), *Cawdor* (1928), and *Dear Judas and Other Poems* (1929)—his techniques and themes were clearly established. Technically, his lines show great flexibility. In some indeterminate but clearly controlled position between free verse and blank verse, his rolling lines give the effect of both expansive luxuriance and a strictly ordered control. His diction and rhythms somehow retain the tones of colloquial speech even as they reveal the intricacies of their music-like structure. In these early volumes too are his bleak, black views of man—his incestuous introversions; his clear, inevitable mortality; his muckish puniness over and against the clean, silent, and enduring works of nature. In the volumes of the 1930's and '40's—in *Thurso's Landing* (1932), *Give Your Heart to the Hawks and Other Poems* (1933), and *The Double Axe and Other Poems* (1948), among others—we see again Jeffers' views of the inevitable doom of man, the need for man to go beyond humanity to the peace of stones and the loneliness of hawks if he is to have significance. The two World Wars, the privations of the depression, the horrors of the Nazis, and the atomic bomb were all equally natural parts of the human slime that still exists and grows worse.

The poet's mastery of the tragic narrative served him well in his free adaptations of classical drama. His various reconstructions of the Greeks in *The Tower Beyond Tragedy* (1924), his sensationally successful *Medea* (1946), and his *The Cretan Woman* (1954)—are a unique and impressive contribution to American poetic drama; however, it is probably in the rolling eloquence of his lines rather than in the nihilism of his views that his lasting significance will be found.

The poetry of E. E. Cummings is not as revolutionary as it looks, even if its look (on the printed page) is the most revolutionary appearing of all modern American poetry. E. E. Cummings is part clown, part Pan—but in the best senses of both those words. He is also perhaps America's purest lyricist. Fresh, naughty, warm, impassioned, he is modern America's closest approximation to Henry David Thoreau, hater of the masses, lover of the intricately unique mysteries of the self. When he died in 1962 America lost one of its most daring and endearing poets.

His literary beginnings would probably not have suggested so. Because of an error of a French military censor, he was suspected of treason and confined during World War I for three months in a detention camp. The literary result, *The Enormous Room* (1922), is one of the best novels to have come from an American in that war. Even in that earliest work, one clearly sees his abhorrence of the brutalizing effects of officialdom; his zany love for the individual, especially the eccentric; and his lifelong conviction that love and war are antithetical.

Although also an occasional playwright and painter, Cummings' real forte was poetry. In it he stands intransigently consistent in his opposition to organized society, to any kind of mass movement or collectivization, to most that is not "me" or "now." His oppostion to these qualities is love—love of all kinds, from the frankly obscene to the quietly lyrical. To the pretentiousness of American militarists, political orators, advertising writers, mass producers, and salesmen of all kinds, he is likely to affirm quietly the "mud-luscious" spring, "when the world is puddle-wonderful."

His verbal and typographical innovations are more than eccentricities; they are organic cues, not unlike musical notations, to suggest how one should see and hear and know. Spaces indicate pauses, the absence of them continuity—"onetwothreefourfive . . . justlikethat." Capital letters are touches of emphasis, parentheses a delicate suspension. His wrenching of syntax and grammar, his refusal to be dictated to by PARTS OF SPEECH (capital letters or not), are similarly organic. How better express the inseparableness of love than "one's not half two. It's two are halves of one:"? What gloss is needed for "my father moved through dooms of love," or "anyone lived in a pretty how town"?

Cummings' work throughout remained remarkably consistent. From the poems in *Tulips and Chimneys* of 1923 through those in *73 Poems* of 1963 we do not have a progression so much as we have a continuum. He never compromised his convictions or succumbed to any cheap exploitation of his technique—all of which is not to contend that his poems have been uniformly successful; they have not been. If, moreover, he has been taken too seriously by some and not seriously enough by others, he nonetheless, with more integrity than most, brought to modern American poetry a grace, a wit, and a unique sensitivity without which modern verse in America would be much poorer than it is.

These qualities may count for more than his innovations in the long run. Even if they do, there is, nevertheless (in this whole viable context of experimentation—represented by Crane and MacLeish and Jeffers as much as by Cummings) clearly an enrichment of the poetic achievement in America. This accomplished experimentation does not detract from, but adds to, the established stature of poets such as Robinson and Frost, Eliot and Stevens. The riches these masters stand above are often glittering riches indeed.

[Harold] Hart Crane

(1899-1932)

CHRONOLOGY:

1899 Born July 21, in Garretsville, Ohio.

1912 Began writing poetry.

1914 Published first poetry in *Bruno's Bohemian.*

1915-17 Visited Cuba, Paris, New York, but returned to Ohio.

1920 Broke with family and returned to New York.

1925 Received financial assistance from Otto Kahn.

1926 *White Buildings: Poems.*

1927-29 Again visited Cuba, England, France.

1930 *The Bridge: A Poem* (awarded the Helen Haire Levison Award from *Poetry*).

1931 Awarded a Guggenheim Fellowship to work in Mexico.

1932 Committed suicide in the Gulf of Mexico by jumping from a steamer returning him to the States.

BIBLIOGRAPHY:

Waldo Frank edited the *Collected Poems of Hart Crane* (New York, 1933, 1946). *The Letters of Hart Crane, 1916-1932* (New York, 1952) was edited by Brom Weber. The best bibliography is by H. D. Rowe, *Hart Crane, a Bibliography* (Denver, 1955).

The book-length critical and biographical studies are Philip Horton's *Hart Crane: The Life of an American Poet* (New York, 1937) and Brom Weber's *Hart Crane: A Biographical and Critical Study* (New York, 1948).

For explications, see Allen Tate, *Sixty American Poets, 1896-1944* (Rev. ed.; Washington, 1954) and Joseph M. Kuntz, *Poetry Explication* (Rev. ed.; Denver, 1962).

Chaplinesque

We make our meek adjustments,
Contented with such random consolations
As the wind deposits
In slithered and too ample pockets.

For we can still love the world, who find
A famished kitten on the step, and know
Recesses for it from the fury of the street,
Or warm torn elbow coverts.

We will sidestep, and to the final smirk
Dally the doom of that inevitable thumb
That slowly chafes its puckered index toward us,
Facing the dull squint with what innocence
And what surprise!

And yet these fine collapses are not lies
More than the pirouettes of any pliant cane;
Our obsequies are, in a way, no enterprise.
We can evade you, and all else but the heart:
What blame to us if the heart live on.

The game enforces smirks; but we have seen
The moon in lonely alleys make
A grail of laughter of an empty ash can,
And through all sound of gaiety and quest
Have heard a kitten in the wilderness. 1926

From *The Bridge*

Proem: To Brooklyn Bridge

How many dawns, chill from his rippling rest
The seagull's wings shall dip and pivot him,
Shedding white rings of tumult, building high
Over the chained bay waters Liberty—

Then, with inviolate curve, forsake our eyes
As apparitional as sails that cross
Some page of figures to be filed away;
—Till elevators drop us from our day . . .

I think of cinemas, panoramic sleights
With multitudes bent toward some flashing scene
Never disclosed, but hastened to again,
Foretold to other eyes on the same screen;

And Thee, across the harbor, silver-paced
As though the sun took step of thee, yet left
Some motion ever unspent in thy stride,—
Implicitly thy freedom staying thee!

Out of some subway scuttle, cell or loft
A bedlamite speeds to thy parapets,
Tilting there momentarily, shrill shirt ballooning,
A jest falls from the speechless caravan.

Down Wall, from girder into street noon leaks,
A rip-tooth of the sky's acetylene;
All afternoon the cloud-flown derricks turn . . .
Thy cables breathe the North Atlantic still.

And obscure as that heaven of the Jews,
Thy guerdon . . . Accolade thou dost bestow
Of anonymity time cannot raise:
Vibrant reprieve and pardon thou dost show.

O harp and altar, of the fury fused,
(How could mere toil align thy choiring strings!)
Terrific threshold of the prophet's pledge,
Prayer of pariah, and the lover's cry,—

Again the traffic lights that skim thy swift
Unfractioned idiom, immaculate sigh of stars,
Beading thy path—condense eternity:
And we have seen night lifted in thine arms.

Under thy shadow by the piers I waited;
Only in darkness is thy shadow clear.
The City's fiery parcels all undone,
Already snow submerges an iron year . . .

O Sleepless as the river under thee,
Vaulting the sea, the prairies' dreaming sod,
Unto us lowliest sometime sweep, descend
And of the curveship lend a myth to God. 1930

From *The Bridge*

Van Winkle

Macadam, gun-gray as the tunny's belt,
Leaps from Far Rockaway to Golden Gate:
Listen! the miles a hurdy-gurdy grinds—
Down gold arpeggios mile on mile unwinds.

Times earlier, when you hurried off to school,
—It is the same hour though a later day—
You walked with Pizarro in a copybook,
And Cortes rode up, reining tautly in—
Firmly as coffee grips the taste,—and away!

There was Priscilla's cheek close in the wind,
And Captain Smith, all beard and certainty,
And Rip Van Winkle, bowing by the way,—
"Is this Sleepy Hollow, friend—?" And he—

And Rip forgot the office hours,
and he forgot the pay;
Van Winkle sweeps a tenement
down town on Avenue A,—

The grind-organ says . . . Remember, remember
The cinder pile at the end of the backyard
Where we stoned the family of young
Garter snakes under . . . And the monoplanes
We launched—with paper wings and twisted
Rubber bands. . . . Recall—
the rapid tongues
That flittered from under the ash heap day
After day whenever your stick discovered
Some sunning inch of unsuspecting fiber—
It flashed back at your thrust, as clean as fire.

And Rip was slowly made aware
that he, Van Winkle, was not here
Nor there. He woke and swore he'd seen Broadway
a Catskill daisy chain in May—

So memory, that strikes a rhyme out of a box,
Or splits a random smell of flowers through glass—
Is it the whip stripped from the lilac tree
One day in spring my father took to me,

Or is it the Sabbatical, unconscious smile
My mother almost brought me once from church
And once only, as I recall—?

It flickered through the snow screen, blindly
It forsook her at the doorway; it was gone
Before I had left the window. It
Did not return with the kiss in the hall.

Macadam, gun-gray as the tunny's belt,
Leaps from Far Rockaway to Golden Gate . . .
Keep hold of that nickel for car-change, Rip,—
Have you got your paper—?
And hurry along, Van Winkle—it's getting late!

1930

From *The Bridge*

The River

[. . . *and past the din and slogans of the year*—]

Stick your patent name on a signboard
brother—all over—going west—young man
Tintex—Japalac—Certain-teed Overalls ads
and lands sakes! under the new playbill ripped
in the guaranteed corner—see Bert Williams what?
Minstrels when you steal a chicken just
save me the wing, for if it isn't
Erie it ain't for miles around a
Mazda—the telegraphic night coming on Thomas

a Ediford—and whistling down the tracks
a headlight rushing with the sound—can you
imagine—while an EXPRESS makes time like
SCIENCE—COMMERCE and the HOLYGHOST
RADIO ROARS IN EVERY HOME WE HAVE THE NORTHPOLE
WALLSTREET AND VIRGINBIRTH WITHOUT STONES OR
WIRES OR EVEN RUNning brooks connecting ears
and no more sermons windows flashing roar
Breathtaking—as you like it . . . eh?

So the 20th Century—so
whizzed the Limited—roared by and left
three men, still hungry on the tracks, ploddingly
watching the tail lights wizen and converge, slipping gimleted and neatly out of sight.

•

[*to those whose addresses are never near*]

The last bear, shot drinking in the Dakotas,
Loped under wires that span the mountain stream.
Keen instruments, strung to a vast precision
Bind town to town and dream to ticking dream.
But some men take their liquor slow—and count
—Though they'll confess no rosary nor clue—
The river's minute by the far brook's year.
Under a world of whistles, wires and steam
Caboose-like they go ruminating through
Ohio, Indiana—blind baggage—
To Cheyenne tagging . . . Maybe Kalamazoo.

Time's renderings, time's blendings they construe
As final reckonings of fire and snow;
Strange bird-wit, like the elemental gist
Of unwalled winds they offer, singing low
My Old Kentucky Home and Casey Jones,
Some Sunny Day. I heard a road-gang chanting so.
And afterwards, who had a colt's eyes—one said,
"Jesus! Oh I remember watermelon days!" And sped
High in a cloud of merriment, recalled
"—And when my Aunt Sally Simpson smiled," he drawled—
"It was almost Louisiana, long ago."
"There's no place like Booneville though, Buddy,"
One said, excising a last burr from his vest,
"—For early trouting." Then peering in the can,
"—But I kept on the tracks." Possessed, resigned,
He trod the fire down pensively and grinned,
Spreading dry shingles of a beard. . . .
                                                            Behind
My father's cannery works I used to see
Rail-squatters ranged in nomad raillery,
The ancient men—wifeless or runaway
Hobo-trekkers that forever search
An empire wilderness of freight and rails.
Each seemed a child, like me, on a loose perch,
Holding to childhood like some termless play.
John, Jake, or Charley, hopping the slow freight
—Memphis to Tallahassee—riding the rods,
Blind fists of nothing, humpty-dumpty clods.

[*but who have touched her, knowing her without name*]

Yet they touch something like a key perhaps.

From pole to pole across the hills, the states
—They know a body under the wide rain;
Youngsters with eyes like fjords, old reprobates
With racetrack jargon,—dotting immensity
They lurk across her, knowing her yonder breast
Snow-silvered, sumac-stained or smoky blue,
Is past the valley-sleepers, south or west.
—As I have trod the rumorous midnights, too.

And past the circuit of the lamp's thin flame
(O Nights that brought me to her body bare!)
Have dreamed beyond the print that bound her name.
Trains sounding the long blizzards out—I heard
Wail into distances I knew were hers.
Papooses crying on the wind's long mane
Screamed redskin dynasties that fled the brain,
—Dead echoes! But I knew her body there,
Time like a serpent down her shoulder, dark,
And space, an eaglet's wing, laid on her hair.

*

[*nor the myths of her fathers . . .*]

Under the Ozarks, domed by Iron Mountain,
The old gods of the rain lie wrapped in pools
Where eyeless fish curvet a sunken fountain
And re-descend with corn from querulous crows.
Such pilferings make up their timeless eatage,
Propitiate them for their timber torn
By iron, iron—always the iron dealt cleavage!
They doze now, below axe and powder horn.

And Pullman breakfasters glide glistening steel
From tunnel into field—iron strides the dew—
Straddles the hill, a dance of wheel on wheel.
You have a half-hour's wait at Siskiyou,
Or stay the night and take the next train through.
Southward, near Cairo passing, you can see
The Ohio merging,—borne down Tennessee;
And if it's summer and the sun's in dusk
Maybe the breeze will lift the River's musk
—As though the waters breathed that you might know
Memphis Johnny, Steamboat Bill, Missouri Joe.
Oh, lean from the window, if the train slows down,
As though you touched hands with some ancient clown,
—A little while gaze absently below
And hum *Deep River* with them while they go.

Yes, turn again and sniff once more—look see,
O Sheriff, Brakeman and Authority—
Hitch up your pants and crunch another quid,
For you, too, feed the River timelessly.
And few evade full measure of their fate;
Always they smile out eerily what they seem.
I could believe he joked at heaven's gate—
Dan Midland—jolted from the cold brake-beam.

Down, down—born pioneers in time's despite,
Grimed tributaries to an ancient flow—
They win no frontier by their wayward plight,
But drift in stillness, as from Jordan's brow.

You will not hear it as the sea; even stone
Is not more hushed by gravity . . . But slow,
As loth to take more tribute—sliding prone
Like the one whose eyes were buried long ago

The River, spreading, flows—and spends your dream.
What are you, lost within this tideless spell?
You are your father's father, and the stream—
A liquid theme that floating niggers swell.

Damp tonnage and alluvial march of days—
Nights turbid, vascular with silted shale
And roots surrendered down of moraine clays:
The Mississippi drinks the farthest dale.

O quarrying passion, undertowed sunlight!
The basalt surface drags a jungle grace
Ochreous and lynx-barred in lengthening might;
Patience! and you shall reach the biding place!

Over De Soto's bones the freighted floors
Throb past the City storied of three thrones.
Down two more turns the Mississippi pours
(Anon tall ironsides up from salt lagoons)

And flows within itself, heaps itself free.
All fades but one thin skyline 'round . . . Ahead
No embrace opens but the stinging sea;
The River lifts itself from its long bed,

Poised wholly on its dream, a mustard glow,
Tortured with history, its one will—flow!
—The Passion spreads in wide tongues, chocked and slow,
Meeting the Gulf, hosannas silently below. 1930

Archibald MacLeish

(1892-)

CHRONOLOGY:

1892 Born May 8, in Glencoe, Illinois.
1915 Graduated from Yale University; *Songs for a Summer Day.*
1915-17 Attended Harvard Law School.
1917-18 Served in the Army.
1917 *Tower of Ivory.*
1919-23 Practiced law in Boston.
1923-28 Lived in France, visiting the Mediterranean and Persia.
1924 *The Happy Marriage and Other Poems.*
1925 *The Pot of Earth.*
1926 *Nobodaddy; Streets in the Moon.*
1928 *The Hamlet of A. MacLeish.*
1929 *Einstein;* travelled the route of Cortez in Mexico.
1930 *New Found Land.*
1932 *Conquistador* (awarded Pulitzer Prize).
1933 *Frescoes for Mr. Rockefeller's City; Poems, 1924-1933.*
1934 *Union Pacific,* ballet.
1935 *Panic,* verse play.
1936 *Public Speech,* poetry.
1937 *The Fall of the City,* verse play.
1938 *Air Raid,* verse play; *Land of the Free,* poems.
1939-44 Librarian of Congress.
1940 *The Irresponsibles: A Declaration,* prose.
1941-42 Served as Director of the Office of Facts and Figures.
1941 *A Time to Speak; The American Cause.*
1942-43 Served as Assistant Director of War Information.
1943 *A Time to Act,* prose.
1944 *The American Story: Ten Broadcasts.*
1944-45 Served as Assistant Secretary of State.
1946 Served as chief American delegate to UNESCO.
1948 *Act Five and Other Poems.*
1949 Appointed Boylston Professor at Harvard University.
1950 *Poetry and Opinion: The Pisan Cantos of Ezra Pound. . . .*
1951 *Freedom Is the Right to Choose . . . ,* prose.
1952 *The Trojan Horse; The Collected Poems, 1917-1952* (awarded Pulitzer Prize).
1953 *The Music Crept by Me upon the Waters.*
1954 *Songs for Eve.*
1958 *J.B.* (awarded Pulitzer Prize).
1961 *Poetry and Experience,* prose.

BIBLIOGRAPHY:

The standard edition through 1952 is *Collected Poems, 1917-1952* (Boston, 1952). Later works have not yet been collected.

There is no book-length study of MacLeish. For bibliography and explications, see Allen Tate, *Sixty American Poets, 1896-1944* (Rev. ed.; Washington, 1954) and Joseph M. Kuntz, *Poetry Explication* (Rev. ed.; Denver, 1962).

Ars Poetica

A poem should be palpable and mute
As a globed fruit,

Dumb
As old medallions to the thumb,

Silent as the sleeve-worn stone
Of casement ledges where the moss has grown—

A poem should be wordless
As the flight of birds.

* * *

A poem should be motionless in time
As the moon climbs,
Leaving, as the moon releases
Twig by twig the night-entangled trees,

Leaving, as the moon behind the winter leaves,
Memory by memory the mind—

A poem should be motionless in time
As the moon climbs

* * *

A poem should be equal to:
Not true

For all the history of grief
An empty doorway and a maple leaf

For love
The leaning grasses and the two lights above the sea—

A poem should not mean
But be 1926

You, Andrew Marvell

And here face down beneath the sun
And here upon earth's noonward height
To feel the always coming on
The always rising of the night:

To feel creep up the curving east
The earthy chill of dusk and slow
Upon those under lands the vast
And ever climbing shadow grow

And strange at Ecbatan the trees
Take leaf by leaf the evening strange
The flooding dark about their knees
The mountains over Persia change

And now at Kermanshah the gate
Dark empty and the withered grass
And through the twilight now the late
Few travelers in the westward pass

And Baghdad darken and the bridge
Across the silent river gone
And through Arabia the edge
Of evening widen. and steal on

And deepen on Palmyra's street
The wheel rut in the ruined stone
And Lebanon fade out and Crete
High through the clouds and overblown

And over Sicily the air
Still flashing with the landward gulls
And loom and slowly disappear
The sails above the shadowy hulls

And Spain go under and the shore
Of Africa the gilded sand
And evening vanish and no more
The low pale light across that land:

Nor now the long light on the sea

And here face downward in the sun
To feel how swift how secretly
The shadow of the night comes on . . .

1930

Immortal Autumn

I speak this poem now with grave and level voice
In praise of autumn of the far-horn-winding fall
I praise the flower-barren fields the clouds the tall
Unanswering branches where the wind makes sullen noise

I praise the fall it is the human season
now
No more the foreign sun does meddle at our earth
Enforce the green and bring the fallow land to birth
Nor winter yet weigh all with silence the pine bough

But now in autumn with the black and outcast crows
Share we the spacious world the whispering year is gone
There is more room to live now the once secret dawn
Comes late by daylight and the dark unguarded goes

Between the mutinous brave burning of the leaves
And winter's covering of our hearts with his deep snow
We are alone there are no evening birds we know
The naked moon the tame stars circle at our eaves

It is the human season on this sterile air
Do words outcarry breath the sound goes on and on.
I hear a dead man's cry from autumn long since gone.

I cry to you beyond upon this bitter air. 1930

"Not Marble nor the Gilded Monuments"

The praisers of women in their proud and beautiful poems
Naming the grave mouth and the hair and the eyes
Boasted those they loved should be forever remembered
These were lies

The words sound but the face in the Istrian sun is forgotten
The poet speaks but to her dead ears no more
The sleek throat is gone—and the breast that was troubled to listen
Shadow from door

Therefore I will not praise your knees nor your fine walking
Telling you men shall remember your name as long
As lips move or breath is spent or the iron of English
Rings from a tongue

I shall say you were young and your arms straight and your mouth
scarlet
I shall say you will die and none will remember you
Your arms change and none remember the swish of your garments
Nor the click of your shoe

Not with my hand's strength not with difficult labor
Springing the obstinate words to the bones of your breast

And the stubborn line to your young stride and the breath to your breathing
And the beat to your haste
Shall I prevail on the hearts of unborn men to remember

(What is a dead girl but a shadowy ghost
Or a dead man's voice but a distant and vain affirmation
Like dream words most)

Therefore I will not speak of the undying glory of women
I will say you were young and straight and your skin fair
And you stood in the door and the sun was a shadow of leaves on your shoulders
And a leaf on your hair

I will not speak of the famous beauty of dead women
I will say the shape of a leaf lay once on your hair
Till the world ends and the eyes are out and the mouths broken
Look! It is there! 1930

Empire Builders

[*The Museum Attendant:*]

This is *The Making of America In Five Panels:*

This is Mister Harriman making America:
Mister-Harriman-is-buying-the-Union-Pacific-at-Seventy:
The Santa Fe is shining on his hair:

This is Commodore Vanderbilt making America:
Mister-Vanderbilt-is-eliminating-the-short-interest-in-Hudson:
Observe the carving on the rocking chair:

This is J. P. Morgan making America:
(The Tennessee Coal is behind to the left of the Steel Company:)
Those in mauve are braces he is wearing:

This is Mister Mellon making America:
Mister-Mellon-is-represented-as-a-symbolical-figure-in-aluminum-
Strewing-bank-stocks-on-a-burnished-stair:

This is the Bruce is the Barton making America:
Mister-Barton-is-selling-us-Doctor's-Deliciousest-Dentifrice:
This is he in beige with the canary:

You have just beheld the makers making America:
This is *The Making of America In Five Panels:*

America lies to the West-South-West of the Switch-Tower:

There is nothing to see of America but land:

[*The Original Document under the Panel paint:*]

"To Thos. Jefferson Esq. his obd't serv't
M. Lewis: captain: detached:
Sir:

Having in mind your repeated commands in this matter:
And the worst half of it done and the streams mapped:

And we here on the back of this beach beholding the
Other ocean—two years gone and the cold

Breaking with rain for the third spring since St. Louis:
The crows at the fish bones on the frozen dunes:

The first cranes going over from south north:
And the river down by a mark of the pole since the morning:

And time near to return: and a ship (Spanish)
Lying in for the salmon: and fearing chance or the

Droughts or the Sioux should deprive you of these discoveries—
Therefore we send by sea in this writing:

Above the
Platte there were long plains and a clay country:
Rim of the sky far off: grass under it:

Dung for the cook fires by the sulphur licks:
After that there were low hills and the sycamores:

And we poled up by the Great Bend in the skiffs:
The honey bees left us after the Osage River:

The wind was west in the evenings and no dew and the
Morning Star larger and whiter than usual—

The winter rattling in the brittle haws:
The second year there was sage and the quail calling:

All that valley is good land by the river:
Three thousand miles and the clay cliffs and

Rue and beargrass by the water banks
And many birds and the brant going over and tracks of

Bear elk wolves martin: the buffalo
Numberless so that the cloud of their dust covers them:

The antelope fording the fall creeks and the mountains and
Grazing lands and the meadow lands and the ground

Sweet and open and well-drained:
We advise you to
Settle troops at the forks and to issue licenses:

Many men will have living on these lands:
There is wealth in the earth for them all and the wood standing

And wild birds on the water where they sleep:
There is stone in the hills for the towns of a great people. . . ."

You have just beheld the Makers making America:
They screwed her scrawny and gaunt with their seven-year panics:
They bought her back on their mortgages old-whore-cheap:
They fattened their bonds at her breasts till the thin blood ran from them:

Men have forgotten how full clear and deep
The Yellowstone moved on the gravel and grass grew
When the land lay waiting for her westward people!

1933

Winter Is Another Country

If the autumn would
End! If the sweet season,
The late light in the tall trees would
End! If the fragrance, the odor of
Fallen apples, dust on the road,
Water somewhere near, the scent of
Water touching me; if this would end
I could endure the absence in the night,
The hands beyond the reach of hands, the name
Called out and never answered with my name:
The image seen but never seen with sight.
I could endure this all
If autumn ended and the cold light came.

1948

Robinson Jeffers

(1887-1962)

CHRONOLOGY:

1887 Born on January 10, in Pittsburgh, Pennsylvania.
1893-99 Visited Europe frequently.
1899-1903 Attended boarding schools in Switzerland and Germany.
1903 Moved to California.
1905 Graduated from Occidental College.
1906-11 Graduate work in English, law, medicine, zoology, and forestry at, variously, the Universities of Southern California and Washington and at Zurich.
1912 *Flagons and Apples,* privately published.
1914 Settled permanently in Carmel, California.
1916 *Californians.*
1924 *Tamar and Other Poems.*
1925 *Roan Stallion, Tamar, and Other Poems.*
1927 *The Women at Point Sur.*
1928 *Poems; An Artist; Cawdor.*
1929 *Dear Judas and Other Poems.*
1930 *Stars; Apology for Bad Dreams.*
1931 *Descend to the Dead.*
1932 *Thurso's Landing.*
1933 *Give Your Heart to the Hawks.*
1934 *Return: An Unpublished Poem.*
1935 *Solstice and Other Poems.*
1936 *Beaks of Eagles.*
1937 *Such Counsels You Gave to Me; Hope Is Not for the Wise: An Unpublished Poem.*
1940 *Two Consolations.*
1941 *Be Angry at the Sun.*
1946 *Medea.*
1948 *The Double Axe and Other Poems.*
1954 *Hungerfield and Other Poems; The Cretan Woman.*
1962 Died January 20, at Carmel, California.

BIBLIOGRAPHY:

There is no collected edition of Jeffers' poems, although the *Selected Poetry* (New York, 1938) is still useful. The Modern Library re-issued *Roan Stallion, Tamar, and Other Poems* (New York, 1935).

The important book-length studies are L. C. Powell, *Robinson Jeffers: The Man and His Work* (Rev. ed.; Pasadena, 1940); Radcliffe Squires, *The Loyalties of Robinson Jeffers* (Ann Arbor, 1956); and Mercedes C. Monjian, *Robinson Jeffers: A Study in Inhumanism* (Pittsburgh, 1958).

For bibliography and explications, see Allen Tate, *Sixty American Poets, 1896-1944* (Rev. ed.; Washington, 1954), and Joseph M. Kuntz, *Poetry Explication* (Rev. ed.; Denver, 1962).

Shine, Perishing Republic

While this America settles in the mould of its vulgarity, heavily
thickening to empire,
And protest, only a bubble in the molten mass, pops and sighs out,
and the mass hardens,

I sadly smiling remember that the flower fades to make fruit, the fruit rots to make earth.
Out of the mother; and through the spring exultances, ripeness and decadence; and home to the mother.

You making haste haste on decay: not blameworthy; life is good, be it stubbornly long or suddenly
A mortal splendor: meteors are not needed less than mountains: shine, perishing republic.

But for my children, I would have them keep their distance from the thickening center; corruption
Never has been compulsory, when the cities lie at the monster's feet there are left the mountains.

And boys, be in nothing so moderate as in love of man, a clever servant, insufferable master.
There is the trap that catches noblest spirits, that caught—they say—God, when he walked on earth. 1925

Boats in a Fog

Sports and gallantries, the stage, the arts, the antics of dancers,
The exuberant voices of music,
Have charm for children but lack nobility; it is bitter earnestness
That makes beauty; the mind
Knows, grown adult.
A sudden fog-drift muffled the ocean,
A throbbing of engines moved in it,
At length, a stone's throw out, between the rocks and the vapor,
One by one moved shadows
Out of the mystery, shadows, fishing-boats, trailing each other,
Following the cliff for guidance,
Holding a difficult path between the peril of the sea-fog
And the foam on the shore granite.
One by one, trailing their leader, six crept by me,
Out of the vapor and into it,
The throb of their engines subdued by the fog, patient and cautious,
Coasting all around the peninsula
Back to the buoys in Monterey harbor. A flight of pelicans
Is nothing lovelier to look at;
The flight of the planets is nothing nobler; all the arts lose virtue
Against the essential reality
Of creatures going about their business among the equally
Earnest elements of nature. 1925

Joy

Though joy is better than sorrow, joy is not great;
Peace is great, strength is great.
Not for joy the stars burn, not for joy the vulture
Spreads her gray sails on the air
Over the mountain; not for joy the worn mountain
Stands, while years like water
Trench his long sides. "I am neither mountain nor bird
Nor star; and I seek joy."
The weakness of your breed: yet at length quietness
Will cover those wistful eyes. 1925

Fire on the Hills

The deer were bounding like blown leaves
Under the smoke in front of the roaring wave of the brushfire;
I thought of the smaller lives that were caught.
Beauty is not always lovely; the fire was beautiful, the terror
Of the deer was beautiful; and when I returned
Down the black slopes after the fire had gone by, an eagle
Was perched on the jag of a burnt pine,
Insolent and gorged, cloaked in the folded storms of his shoulders.
He had come from far off for the good hunting
With fire for his beater to drive the game; the sky was merciless
Blue, and the hills merciless black,
The sombre-feathered great bird sleepily merciless between them.
I thought, painfully, but the whole mind,
The destruction that brings an eagle from heaven is better than mercy. 1932

The Purse-Seine

Our sardine fishermen work at night in the dark of the moon; daylight or moonlight
They could not tell where to spread the net, unable to see the phosphorescence of the shoals of fish.
They work northward from Monterey, coasting Santa Cruz; off New Year's Point or off Pigeon Point
The look-out man will see some lakes of milk-color light on the sea's night-purple; he points, and the helmsman

Turns the dark prow, the motorboat circles the gleaming shoal and drifts out her seine-net. They close the circle
And purse the bottom of the net, then with great labor haul it in.

I cannot tell you
How beautiful the scene is, and a little terrible, then, when the crowded fish
Know they are caught, and wildly beat from one wall to the other of their closing destiny the phosphorescent
Water to a pool of flame, each beautiful slender body sheeted with flame, like a live rocket
A comet's tail wake of clear yellow flame; while outside the narrowing
Floats and cordage of the net great sea-lions come up to watch, sighing in the dark; the vast walls of night
Stand erect to the stars.
Lately I was looking from a night mountain-top
On a wide city, the colored splendor, galaxies of light: how could I help but recall the seine-net
Gathering the luminous fish? I cannot tell you how beautiful the city appeared, and a little terrible.
I thought, We have geared the machines and locked all together into interdependence; we have built the great cities; now
There is no escape. We have gathered vast populations incapable of free survival, insulated
From the strong earth, each person in himself helpless, on all dependent.
The circle is closed, and the net
Is being hauled in. They hardly feel the cords drawing, yet they shine already. The inevitable mass-disasters
Will not come in our time nor in our children's, but we and our children
Must watch the net draw narrower, government take all powers—or revolution, and the new government
Take more than all, add to kept bodies kept souls—or anarchy, the mass-disasters.
These things are Progress;
Do you marvel our verse is troubled or frowning, while it keeps its reason? Or it lets go, lets the mood flow
In the manner of the recent young men into mere hysteria, splintered gleams, crackled laughter. But they are quite wrong.
There is no reason for amazement; surely one always knew that cultures decay, and life's end is death. 1937

The Bloody Sire

It is not bad. Let them play.
Let the guns bark and the bombing-plane
Speak his prodigious blasphemies.
It is not bad, it is high time,
Stark violence is still the sire of all the world's values.

What but the wolf's tooth whittled so fine
The fleet limbs of the antelope?
What but fear winged the birds, and hunger
Jeweled with such eyes the great goshawk's head?
Violence has been the sire of all the world's values.

Who would remember Helen's face
Lacking the terrible halo of spears?
Who formed Christ but Herod and Caesar,
The cruel and bloody victories of Caesar?
Violence, the bloody sire of all the world's values.

Never weep, let them play,
Old violence is not too old to beget new values. 1941

E[dward] E[stlin] Cummings

(1894-1962)

CHRONOLOGY:

1894 Born October 14, in Cambridge, Massachusetts.
1915 Graduated from Harvard University.
1916 Awarded M.A. Degree, Harvard University.
1917 Appeared in *Eight Harvard Poets;* joined the Norton Harjes Ambulance Corp in France; arrested and detained, *La Ferté Macé* detention camp there; released and joined U.S. Army.
1920 Returned to Paris to write and paint.
1922 *The Enormous Room,* novel.
1923 *Tulips and Chimneys.*
1925 *&; XLI Poems* (given *Dial* Award).
1926 *Is 5.*
1927 *Him,* play.
1928 *Christmas Tree.*
1930 A book of poems with no title.
1931 *CLOPW,* drawings; *VV (Viva: Seventy New Poems).*
1933 *Eimi,* travel diary.
1935 *Tom: A Ballet; No Thanks.*
1936 *1/20 (One Over Twenty).*
1940 *50 Poems.*
1944 *1 × 1.*
1945 *Anthropos: The Future of Art.*
1946 *Santa Claus: A Morality Play.*
1950 *Xaipe: 71 Poems.*

1953 *i: six nonlectures.*
1954 *Poems, 1923-1954.*
1958 *95 Poems; e. e. cummings: A Miscellany* (ed. by George James Firmage).
1959 *One Hundred Selected Poems.*
1962 Died September 3, in North Conway, New Hampshire.
1963 *73 Poems.*

BIBLIOGRAPHY:

All but his last two volumes of poems are collected in *Poems, 1923-1952* (New York, 1954). *The Enormous Room* was re-issued with a new introduction by the Modern Library (New York, 1934).

Two book-length studies are Charles Norman, *The Magic Maker: E. E. Cummings* (New York, 1958), and Norman Friedman, *E. E. Cummings: The Art of His Poetry* (New York, 1960).

A useful mimeographed bibliography is Paul Lauter's *E. E. Cummings: Index to First Lines and Bibliography of Works by and about the Poet.* For explications, see Joseph M. Kuntz, *Poetry Explication* (Rev. ed.; Denver, 1962).

Foreword to *Is 5*

On the assumption that my technique is either complicated or original or both, the publishers have politely requested me to write an introduction to this book.

At least my theory of technique, if I have one, is very far from original; nor is it complicated. I can express it in fifteen words, by quoting The Eternal Question And Immortal Answer of burlesk, viz. "Would you hit a woman with a child?—No, I'd hit her with a brick." Like the burlesk comedian, I am abnormally fond of that precision which creates movement.

If a poet is anybody, he is somebody to whom things made matter very little—somebody who is obsessed by Making. Like all obsessions, the Making obsession has disadvantages; for instance, my only interest in making money would be to make it. Fortunately, however, I should prefer to make almost anything else, including locomotives and roses. It is with roses and locomotives (not to mention acrobats Spring electricity Coney Island the 4th of July the eyes of mice and Niagara Falls) that my "poems" are competing.

They are also competing with each other, with elephants, and with El Greco.

Ineluctable preoccupation with The Verb gives a poet one priceless advantage: whereas nonmakers must content themselves with the merely undeniable fact that two times two is four, he rejoices in a purely irresistible truth (to be found, in abbreviated costume, upon the title page of the present volume). 1926

[in Just-]

in Just-
spring   when the world is mud-
luscious the little
lame baloonman

whistles   far   and wee

and eddieandbill come
running from marbles and
piracies and it's
spring

when the world is puddle-wonderful

the queer
old baloonman whistles
far   and   wee
and bettyandisbel come dancing

from hop-scotch and jump-rope and

it's
spring
and
    the

        goat-footed

baloonMan   whistles
far
and
wee

1920

[Buffalo Bill's]

Buffalo Bill's
defunct
        who used to
        ride a watersmooth-silver
                                                  stallion
and break onetwothreefourfive pigeonsjustlikethat
                                                                      Jesus

he was a handsome man
                                        and what i want to know is
how do you like your blueeyed boy
Mister Death

1923

[when god lets my body be]

when god lets my body be

From each brave eye shall sprout a tree
fruit that dangles therefrom

the purpled world will dance upon
Between my lips which did sing

a rose shall beget the spring
that maidens whom passion wastes

will lay between their little breasts
My strong fingers beneath the snow

Into strenuous birds shall go
my love walking in the grass

their wings will touch with her face
and all the while shall my heart be

With the bulge and nuzzle of the sea

1923

[i sing of Olaf glad and big]

i sing of Olaf glad and big
whose warmest heart recoiled at war:
a conscientious object-or

his well-belovéd colonel (trig
westpointer most succinctly bred)
took erring Olaf soon in hand;
but—though an host of overjoyed
noncoms (first knocking on the head
him) do through icy waters roll
that helplessness which others stroke
with brushes recently employed
anent this muddy toiletbowl,
while kindred intellects evoke
allegiance per blunt instruments—
Olaf (being to all intents
a corpse and wanting any rag
upon what God unto him gave)
responds, without getting annoyed
"I will not kiss your f.ing flag"

straightway the silver bird looked grave
(departing hurriedly to shave)

but—though all kinds of officers
(a yearning nation's blueeyed pride)
their passive prey did kick and curse
until for wear their clarion
voices and boots were much the worse,
and egged the firstclassprivates on
his rectum wickedly to tease
by means of skilfully applied
bayonets roasted hot with heat—
Olaf (upon what were once knees)
does almost ceaselessly repeat
"there is some s. I will not eat"

our president, being of which
assertions duly notified
threw the yellowsonofabitch
into a dungeon, where he died

Christ (of His mercy infinite)
i pray to see; and Olaf, too

preponderatingly because
unless statistics lie he was
more brave than me: more blond than you. 1931

[anyone lived in a pretty how town]

anyone lived in a pretty how town
(with up so floating many bells down)
spring summer autumn winter
he sang his didn't he danced his did.

Women and men(both little and small)
cared for anyone not at all
they sowed their isn't they reaped their same
sun moon stars rain

children guessed(but only a few
and down they forgot as up they grew
autumn winter spring summer)
that noone loved him more by more

when by now and tree by leaf
she laughed his joy she cried his grief

bird by snow and stir by still
anyone's any was all to her

someones married their everyones
laughed their cryings and did their dance
(sleep wake hope and then) they
said their nevers they slept their dream

stars rain sun moon
(and only the snow can begin to explain
how children are apt to forget to remember
with up so floating many bells down)

one day anyone died i guess
(and noone stooped to kiss his face)
busy folk buried them side by side
little by little and was by was

all by all and deep by deep
and more by more they dream their sleep
noone and anyone earth by april
wish by spirit and if by yes.

Women and men(both dong and ding)
summer autumn winter spring
reaped their sowing and went their came
sun moon stars rain 1940

[one's not half two. It's two are halves of one:]

one's not half two. It's two are halves of one:
which halves reintegrating,shall occur
no death and any quantity;but than
all numerable mosts the actual more

minds ignorant of stern miraculous
this every truth—beware of heartless them
(given the scalpel,they dissect a kiss;
or,sold the reason,they undream a dream)

one is the song which fiends and angels sing:
all murdering lies by mortals told make two.
Let liars wilt,repaying life they're loaned;
we(by a gift called dying born)must grow

deep in dark least ourselves remembering
love only rides his year.
All lose,whole find 1944

[pity this busy monster,manunkind]

pity this busy monster,manunkind,

not. Progress is a comfortable disease:
your victim(death and life safely beyond)

plays with the bigness of his littleness
—electrons deify one razorblade
into a mountainrange;lenses extend

unwish through curving wherewhen till unwish
returns on its unself.
A world of made
is not a world of born—pity poor flesh

and trees,poor stars and stones,but never this
fine specimen of hypermagical

ultraomnipotence. We doctors know

a hopeless case if—listen: there's a hell
of a good universe next door;let's go 1944

[what if a much of a which of a wind]

what if a much of a which of a wind
gives the truth to summer's lie;
bloodies with dizzying leaves the sun
and yanks immortal stars awry?
Blow king to beggar and queen to seem
(blow friend to fiend:blow space to time)
—when skies are hanged and oceans drowned,
the single secret will still be man

what if a keen of a lean wind flays
screaming hills with sleet and snow:
strangles valleys by ropes of thing
and stifles forests in white ago?
Blow hope to terror;blow seeing to blind
(blow pity to envy and soul to mind)
—whose hearts are mountains,roots are trees,
it's they shall cry hello to the spring

what if a dawn of a doom of a dream
bites this universe in two,

peels forever out of his grave
and sprinkles nowhere with me and you?
Blow soon to never and never to twice
(blow life to isn't:blow death to was)
—all nothing's only our hugest home;
the most who die,the more we live 1944

NEW CONSOLIDATIONS

CHAPTER EIGHT

REPRESENTATIVE NOVELISTS

Thomas Wolfe, John Dos Passos, and John Steinbeck all had spectacular successes—both popular and critical—with single novels. Wolfe's first novel, *Look Homeward, Angel* (1929), Dos Passos's monumental trilogy, *U.S.A.* (composed of *The 42nd Parallel, 1919,* and *The Big Money,* and published collectively in 1937), and Steinbeck's *The Grapes of Wrath* (1939) are generally considered these authors' most successful works. The three novels are refreshingly varied. The Whitmanesque exuberance of Wolfe, the experimental techniques of Dos Passos, and the mythological sociology of Steinbeck have very little in common with one another. However, their short stories—with the possible exception of some of Steinbeck's and Wolfe's short novels—are generally considered inferior to their major novels. To read, therefore, substantial and representative portions of the most highly regarded work of each is to get a fair sample of their worth, although to read the entire novels would admittedly be a more rewarding endeavor.

Look Homeward, Angel constitutes in length about one-third of Wolfe's published writings before his death at the age of thirty-eight. Its sequel, *Of Time and the River,* appeared in 1935; and his other two major novels—*The Web and the Rock* (1939) and *You Can't Go Home Again* (1940)—were both published posthumously. Some early plays, two collections of short stories and novellas, and a book of criticism constitute the major portion of Wolfe's other work. His reputation, however, rests primarily on his four "big" novels—especially the first one.

Look Homeward, Angel is one of modern America's major books. Autobiographical (as all his works were), loose and sprawling (but not without a "form" of its own), it has a vigor, verbiage, and color unique in American fiction. Enormously popular in the 1930's, influential in a way perhaps no book should be, especially appealing to the sensitive and young (which is not to suggest that it is a child's book), it is the first and most successful of Wolfe's novelistic self-definitions, which transcend the personal and become one of the definitions of the American experience itself. Its young hero, Eugene Gant, is clearly Wolfe himself. Its characters and setting in "Altamont" are clearly his own family and acquaintances in his own home town of Asheville, North Carolina. Neither these truths nor the fact that it needed the help of a Scribner editor (Maxwell Perkins) to cut it to a length suitable for publication makes its "finished" imagined experience less valuable. Wolfe's other depictions of self never quite had the happy conjunction of subject and treatment that give to his first novel not only a vibrant involvement with life (which all of his fiction was to have) but also that special, organic grasp of what it means to grow up in America.

The sequel to his first novel, *Of Time and the River,* provoked rather insistent charges against Wolfe's apparent inability to shape his own material or to write about anything but himself. His consequent change of publisher (to Harper's) and the transformation of his hero, Eugene Gant, into George Webber made those charges no less valid than they already were. *The Web and the Rock* probably owes as much to Wolfe's new editor, Edward C. Aswell, as *Of Time and the River* did to Perkins, but George Webber's clear-cut relation to Eugene Gant and the consequent Gant-Webber relation to Wolfe himself make the only accomplishment that matters in Wolfe's books clearly Wolfe's own. The intimations of increased esthetic distance suggested by the fragments Aswell collected and published as *The Hills Beyond* in 1941 do not at all affect the already demonstrated accomplishments of the four major novels. The publication in 1961 of the original versions of five of Wolfe's novellas, *The Short Novels of Thomas Wolfe,* demonstrated an artistic control which many had denied that Wolfe possessed.

Dos Passos's great trilogy, *U.S.A.,* is as much an achievement of method, of technique and style, as it is of subject, of a realized point of view and a demonstrated attitude. Thus, not only is it generally considered the greatest "social novel" yet produced in America but at the same time is also considered an experiment with technique unprecedented in American fiction. The three novels that constitute the trilogy have no hero or heroine, have no plot in the accepted sense of the word, have as subject matter nothing less than "American life" during the first three decades of the twentieth century. The same characters appear and disappear and provide a sort of continuity; they touch one another, affect one another, and in turn are all affected by the events of the time. But narrative as such is subordinate: the events are the determinants that shape the parts to an all-important whole. It is the presentation of event that is novel and effective in the trilogy: event as revealed by the "Newsreels," current happenings often ironically juxtaposed internally as well as strategically related to narrative; event as "Biography," the thumb-nail profiles of prominent men of the time, again judiciously chosen and toned and strategically placed to affect reaction to narrative; and event as seen through "The Camera Eye," subjective and even surrealistic "views" of the created world before us. It was a marvelously original method for Dos Passos's particular subject, and if it depletes itself in this particular endeavor in so far as there is nowhere else for the technique to go, its appropriateness for the thing it does here is unassailable.

Dos Passos's work preceding *U.S.A.* has two high points. His early World War I service, in a French ambulance unit, the Italian Red Cross, and the American Medical Corp, resulted in the same bitter disillusionment and disenchantment that marked so many of his contemporaries. Of his first three novels—*One Man's Initiation* (1920), *Three Soldiers* (1921), and *Streets of Night* (1923)—only the second is in any way remarkable; and even it, as one of the better novels of World War I, suffers in comparison with Hemingway's *A Farewell to Arms.* Dos Passos's next work of fiction, *Manhattan Transfer* (1925), broke new ground and established his fame. In this novel, chronological development and conventional forms are abandoned for abrupt scene-shifting and juxtaposed depiction of milieu. The city itself is more the subject than are its characters. It thus clearly prefigures the "collectivistic" techniques of *U.S.A.*, and there is a thematic prefigurement of the trilogy in its many depictions of crushed and defeated and thwarted metropolitan "lives."

The work following *U.S.A.* has been far less well received. Another trilogy appeared as *District of Columbia* in 1952, composed of *Adventures of a Young Man* (1939), *Number One* (1943), and *The Grand Design* (1949)—a sort of collective indictment of the collectivistic answer to the problems of the time, especially as it related to the New Deal. This indictment is more explicit in his view of American history in *The Ground We Stand On* (1941) and in the many other volumes of personal observations that he wrote later in the 1940's and throughout the 1950's. His latest novel, *Midcentury* (1961), was more favorably received; but there seems to be little expectation that he will match again the achievement of *U.S.A.*

John Steinbeck's major novel of the 1930's, *The Grapes of Wrath* (1939), seems similarly destined. Although he has published many other works of fiction since then (and was awarded the Nobel Prize for Literature in 1962), none of his other work quite measures up to the achievement of his chronicle of the Joads' dust-bowl trek from Oklahoma to California and the conflict there between the Okies and the landowners. Often called "the Twentieth Century's *Uncle Tom's Cabin,*" *The Grapes of Wrath* has come to personify the depression-ridden 1930's in America as no other work in our literature does. The novel's appeal is probably more subtly based, however. Its essay chapters, to be sure, widen the implications beyond the scope of the exclusively narrative ones; and the symbolism works toward the same end. The mythical appeal of the odyssey itself is also part of its achievement. Treks westward (to California and elsewhere) hold somehow a special position in the American imagination, whatever the disillusionments after arrival; and this truth is probably one of the more enduring webs of the novel's various appeals.

Steinbeck's concern for the exploited, the little man—whether the laborer, the *paisano* of Southern California, or the displaced dust-bowl farmers—marks all his major work even as their "simple" lives and uncomplicated, non-abstracted relations to Nature represent, for him, some kind of human ideal. It was not until his fourth book, *Tortilla Flat* (1935), that he achieved any kind of fame or recognition, although he had already introduced the regional folk material of his Southern California background in the connected stories of *The Pastures of Heaven* (1932). His major works were all to follow: *In Dubious Battle* (1936) and its stark picture of some exploited, migratory apple pickers; *Of Mice and Men* (1937) and its theatrically planned depiction of a slow, hulking farmhand whose alert partner must kill him in order to prevent his trial for murder; *The Red Pony* (1937) and its sensitive picture of a child's introduction to the complications of nature; and *The Grapes of Wrath.*

The work immediately following this period seems to have been of less importance. His *The Moon Is Down* (1942) depicts the heroic Norwegian resistance to the Nazi invasion during World War II, and *The Pearl* (1947), set in modern Mexico, resembles a morality play. His return to the material and scenery of the Monterey coast and its "sweet bums" resulted in *Cannery Row* (1945) and its sequel, *Sweet Thursday* (1954). Neither they nor *The Wayward Bus* (1947), depicting the sexual misadventures of a group stranded overnight on the California wayside, shows any advance over the work of the 1940's. Among his nonfiction of the period, the most impressive is clearly his *Sea of Cortez* (1941), in its revelation of his life-long, almost professional interest in marine biology no less than in its picture of his abiding attitudes towards life and art.

One of his most ambitious works, *East of Eden* (1952), a long historical work of the California settlement and semi-autobiographical in its material, provoked mixed critical reaction. *The Short Reign of Pippin IV* (1957), labeled a "fabrication," is an amusing satire of contemporary French politics. His latest novel, *The Winter of Our Discontent* (1961), laid in New England, has been more widely praised than most, but few were willing to equate its achievement with that of *The Grapes of Wrath.*

Although critical ideals sometimes change and what one generation values may well be damned by another, there appears to be little likelihood that the three novels here represented will ever be considered anything less than their creator's best work. Modern American fiction is variously rich. These three novelists, especially in these three novels, constitute a major reason for its being so.

Thomas [Clayton] Wolfe
(1900-1938)

CHRONOLOGY:

1900 Born October 3, in Asheville, North Carolina.

1916-20 Attended University of North Carolina.

1920-24 Attended Harvard University.

1924-30 Was an instructor in English, New York University.

1924 *The Return of Buck Gavin*, play (in *Carolina Folk Plays: Second Series*, ed. by Frederick Koch).

1929 *Look Homeward, Angel.*

1930-31 Awarded a Guggenheim Fellowship and traveled in Europe.

1935 *Of Time and the River; From Death to Morning*, stories.

1936 *The Story of a Novel*, criticism.

1938 Traveled to the West; died September 15, in Baltimore, Maryland.

1939 *The Web and the Rock; A Note on Experts: Dexter Vespasian Joyner.*

1940 *You Can't Go Home Again.*

1941 *The Hills Beyond*, unfinished novel plus stories (ed. by Edward C. Aswell).

1942 *Gentlemen of the Press, A Play.*

1943 *Thomas Wolfe's Letters to His Mother* (ed. by John S. Terry).

1944 *A Stone, A Leaf, A Door: Poems by Thomas Wolfe* (passages from his poetry, arranged by John S. Barnes).

1948 *Mannerhouse: A Play.*

1951 *A Western Journal.*

1954 *The Correspondence of Thomas Wolfe and Homer Andrew Watt* (ed. by Oscar Cargill and Thomas Clark Pollock).

1956 *Letters* (ed. by Elizabeth Nowell).

1961 *The Short Novels of Thomas Wolfe* (ed. by C. Hugh Holman).

BIBLIOGRAPHY:

There is no collected edition of Wolfe's works. All of the major novels, however, are available in inexpensive reprints. *The Thomas Wolfe Reader*, ed. by C. Hugh Holman (New York, 1962), is a generous sampling of his work. Of special importance are the letters mentioned in the Chronology.

Wolfe has attracted much critical attention. Important book-length studies include Herbert J. Muller, *Thomas Wolfe* (Norfolk, Conn., 1947); Floyd C. Watkins, *Thomas Wolfe's Characters* (Norman, Okla., 1957); Elizabeth Nowell, *Thomas Wolfe* (New York, 1960); and Richard Kennedy, *The Window of Memory* (Chapel Hill, 1962). Two collections of essays about Wolfe are Richard Walser, ed., *The Enigma of Thomas Wolfe: Biographical and Critical Selections* (Cambridge, Mass., 1953), and Thomas Clark Pollock and Oscar Cargill, eds., *Thomas Wolfe at Washington Square* (New York, 1954).

For studies of individual novels, see Donna Gerstenberger and George Hendrick, *The American Novel, 1789-1959: A Checklist of Twentieth-Century Criticism* (Denver, 1961); for short stories, Warren S. Walker, *Twentieth-Century Short Story Explication . . .* (Hamden, Conn., 1961), Supplement, 1963; and for a useful casebook, C. Hugh Holman, ed., *The World of Thomas Wolfe* (New York, 1962).

From Letter to His Mother, May, 1923

. . . . .

. . . I know this now: I am inevitable. I sincerely believe the only thing that can stop me now is insanity, disease, or death. The plays I am going to write may not be suited to the tender bellies of old maids, sweet young girls, or Baptist Ministers but they will be true and honest and courageous, and the rest doesn't matter. If my play goes on I want you to be prepared for execrations upon my head. I have stepped on toes right and left—I spared Boston with its nigger-sentimentalists no more than the South, which I love, but which I am nevertheless pounding. I am not interested in writing what our pot-bellied members of the Rotary and Kiwanis call a "good show"—I want to know life and understand it and interpret it without fear or favor. This, I feel is a man's work and worthy of a man's dignity. For life is not made up of sugary, sticky, sickening Edgar A. Guest sentimentality, it is not made up of dishonest optimism, God is *not* always in his Heaven, all is *not* always right with the world. It is not all bad, but it is not all good, it is not all ugly, but it is not all beautiful, it is life, life, life—the only thing that matters. It is savage, cruel, kind, noble, passionate, selfish, generous, stupid, ugly, beautiful, painful, joyous,—it is all these, and more, and it's all these I want to know and, by God, I shall, though they crucify me for it. I will go to the ends of the earth to find it, to understand it, I will know this country when I am through as I know the palm of my hand, and I will put it on paper, and make it true and beautiful.

I will step on toes, I will not hesitate to say what I think of those people who shout "Progress, Progress, Progress"—when what they mean is more Ford automobiles, more Rotary Clubs, more Baptist Ladies Social unions. I will say that "Greater Asheville" does not necessarily mean "100,000 by 1930," that we are not necessarily 4 times as civilized as our grandfathers because we go four times as fast in automobiles, because our buildings are four times as tall. What I shall try to get into their dusty little pint-measure minds is that a full belly, a good automobile, paved streets, and so on, do not make them one whit better or finer,—that there is beauty in this world,—beauty even in this wilderness of ugliness and provincialism that is at present our country, beauty and spirit which will make us men instead of cheap Board of Trade Boosters, and blatant pamphleteers. I shall try to impress upon their little craniums that one does not have to be a "highbrow" or "queer" or "impractical" to know these things, to love them, and to realize they are our common heritage, there for us all to possess and make a part of us. In the name of God, let us learn to be men, not monkies.

When I speak of beauty I do not mean a movie close-up where Susie and Johnnie meet at the end and clinch and all the gum-chewing ladies go home thinking husband is not so good a lover as Valentino. That's cheap and vulgar. I mean everything which is lovely, and noble, and true. It does not have to be sweet, it may be bitter, it does not have to be joyous, it may be sad.

When Spring comes I think of a cool, narrow back yard in North Carolina with green, damp earth, and cherry trees in blossom. I think of a skinny little boy at the top of one of those trees, with the fragrant blooms about him, with the tang of the sap in his nose, looking out on a world of back yards, and building his Castles in Spain. That's beauty, that's romance. I think of an old man in the grip of a terrible disease, who thought he was afraid to die, but who died like a warrior in an epic poem. That's beauty. I think of a boy of twenty-six years heaving his life away, and gasping to regain it, I think of the frightened glare in his eyes and the way he seizes my hands, and cries "What have you come home for." I think of the lie that trembles in my throat. I think of a woman who sits with a face as white and set as if cut from marble, and whose fingers can not be unclasped from his hand. And the boy of eighteen sees and knows for the first time that more than a son is dying, that part of a mother is being buried before her,—life in death, that something which she nursed and loved, something out of her blood, out of her life, is taken away. It's terrible but it's beautiful. I think of the devotion of a woman of frail physique to a father, I think of the daisy meadows on the way to Craggy Mountain, of the birch forests of New Hampshire, of the Mississippi River at Memphis—of all of which I have been a part—and I know there is nothing so commonplace, so dull, that is not touched with nobility and dignity. And I intend to wreak out my soul on paper and express it all. This is what my life means to me: I am at the mercy of this thing and I will do it or die. I never forget; I have never forgotten. I have tried to make myself conscious of the whole of my life since first the baby in the basket became conscious of the warm sunlight on the porch, and saw his sister go up the hill to the girl's school on the corner (the first thing I remember). Slowly out of the world of infant darkness things take shape, the big terrifying faces become familiar,—I recognize my father by his bristly moustache. Then the animal books and the Mother Goose poetry which I memorize before I can read, and recite for the benefit of admiring neighbors every night, holding my book upside down. I become conscious of Santa Claus and send scrawls up the chimney. Then St. Louis. A flight of stairs at the Cincinnati rail road station which must be gone up,—the World's Fair, the Ferris Wheel, Grover at the Inside Inn, the Delmar Gardens where you let me taste beer which I spit out, a ride on a bus-automobile—over the Fair Grounds with Effie —it is raining, raining—the Cascades in the rain—a ride in the scenic railway—scared at the darkness and the hideous faces—eating a peach in the back yard (St. Louis)—I swallow a fly and am sick—and one of my brothers laughs at me. Two little boys who ride tricycles up and down the street—they dress in white and look alike—their father injured or killed in elevator accident (wasn't he)—I "commit a nuisance" on the narrow step of side yard and the policeman sees me and reports me—the smell of tea at the East India House—I'll never forget it—Grover's sickness and death—I am wakened at midnight by Mabel and she says "Grover's on the cooling board." I don't know what a cooling board is but am curious to see. I don't know what death is but have a vague, terrified sensation that something awful has happened—then she takes me in her arms and up the hall.—Disappointed at the cooling board—it's only a table—the brown mole on his neck—the trip home—visitors in the parlor with condolences—Norah Israel was there—Then it gets fairly plain thereafter, and I can trace it step by step.

This is why I think I'm going to be an artist. The things that really mattered sunk in and left their mark. Sometimes only a word—sometimes a peculiar smile—sometimes death—sometimes the smell of dandelions in Spring—once Love. Most people have little more mind than brutes: they live from day to day. I will go everywhere and see everything. I will meet all the people I can. I will think all the thoughts, feel all the emotions I am able, and I will write, write, write. . . .

From *Look Homeward, Angel*

The Return of the Far-Wanderer

This journey to California was Gant's last great voyage. He made it two years after Eliza's return from St. Louis, when he was fifty-six years old. In the great frame was already stirring the chemistry of pain and death. Unspoken and undefined there was in him the knowledge that he was at length caught in the trap of life and fixity, that he was being borne under in this struggle against the terrible will that wanted to own the earth more than to explore it. This was the final flare of the old hunger that had once darkened in the small gray eyes, leading a boy into new lands and toward the soft stone smile of an angel.

And he returned from nine thousand miles of wandering, to the bleak bare prison of the hills on a gray day late in winter.

In the more than eight thousand days and nights of this life with Eliza, how often had he been wakefully, soberly and peripatetically conscious of the world outside him between the hours of one and five A.M.? Wholly, for not more than nineteen nights—one for the birth of Leslie, Eliza's first daughter; one for her death twenty-six months later, cholera infantis; one for the death of Major Tom Pentland, Eliza's father, in May, 1902; one for the birth of Luke; one, on the train westbound to Saint Louis, en route to Grover's death; one for the death in the Playhouse (1893) of Uncle Thaddeus Evans, an aged and devoted Negro; one, with Eliza, in the month of March, 1897, as deathwatch to the corpse of old Major Isaacs; three at the end of the month of July, 1897, when it was thought that Eliza, withered to a white sheeting of skin upon a bone frame, must die of typhoid; again in early April, 1903, for Luke, typhoid death near; one for the death of Greeley Pentland, aged twenty-six, congenital scrofulous tubercular, violinist, Pentlandian punster, petty check-forger, and six weeks' jailbird; three nights, from the eleventh to the fourteenth of January, 1905, by the rheumatic crucifixion of his right side, participant in his own grief, accuser of himself and his God; once in February, 1896, as deathwatch to the remains of Sandy Duncan, aged eleven; once in September, 1895, penitentially alert and shamefast in the City "calaboose"; in a room of the Keeley Institute at Piedmont, North Carolina, June 7, 1896; on March 17, 1906, between Knoxville, Tennessee, and Altamont, at the conclusion of a seven weeks' journey to California.

How looked the home-earth then to Gant the Far-Wanderer? Light crept gayly, melting on the rocky river, the engine smoke streaked out on dawn like a cold breath, the hills were big, but nearer, nearer than he thought. And Altamont lay gray and withered in the hills, a bleak mean wintry dot. He stepped carefully down in squalid Toytown, noting that everything was low, near, and shrunken as he made his Gulliverian entry. He had a roof-and-gulley high conviction; with careful tucked-in elbows he weighted down the heated Toytown street-car, staring painfully at the dirty pasteboard *pebbledash* of the Pisgah Hotel, the brick and board cheap warehouses of Depot Street, the rusty clapboard flimsiness of the Florence (Railway Men's) Hotel, quaking with beef-fed harlotry.

So small, so small, so small, he thought. I never believed it. Even the hills here. I'll soon be sixty.

His sallow face, thin-flanked, was hang-dog and afraid. He stared wistful-sullenly down at the rattan seat as the car screeched round into the switch at the cut and stopped; the motorman, smoke-throated, slid the door back and entered with his handle. He closed the door and sat down yawning.

"Where you been, Mr. Gant?"

"California," said Gant.

"Thought I hadn't seen you," said the motorman.

There was a warm electric smell and one of hot burnt steel.

But two months dead! But two months dead! Ah, Lord! So it's come to this. Merciful God, this fearful, awful, and damnable climate. Death, death! Is it too late? A land of life, a flower land. How clear the green clear sea was. And all the fishes swimming there. Santa Catalina. Those in the East should always go West. How came I here? Down, down—always down, did I know where? Baltimore, Sydney—In God's name, why? The little boat glass-bottomed, so you could look down. She lifted up her skirts as she stepped down. Where now? A pair of pippins.

"Jim Bowles died while you were gone, I reckon," said the motorman.

"What!" howled Gant. "Merciful God!" he clucked mournfully downward. "What did he die of?" he asked.

"Pneumonia," said the motorman. "He was dead four days after he was took down."

"Why, he was a big healthy man in the prime of life," said Gant. "I was talking to him the day before I went away," he lied, convincing himself permanently that this was true. "He looked as if he had never known a day's sickness in his life."

"He went home one Friday night with a chill," said the motorman, "and the next Tuesday he was gone."

There was a crescent humming on the rails. With his thick glove finger he pushed away a clearing in the window-coated ice scurf and looked smokily out on the raw red cut-bank. The other car appeared abruptly at the end of the cut and curved with a skreeking jerk into the switch.

"No, sir," said the motorman, sliding back the door, "you never know who'll go next. Here to-day and gone to-morrow. Hit gits the big 'uns first sometimes."

He closed the door behind him and jerkily opened three notches of juice. The car ground briskly off like a wound toy.

In the prime of life, thought Gant. Myself like that some day. No, for others. Mother almost eighty-six. Eats like a horse, Augusta wrote. Must send her twenty dollars. Now in the cold clay, frozen. Keep till Spring. Rain, rot, rain. Who got the job? Brock or Saul Gudger? Bread out of my mouth. Do me to death—the stranger. Georgia marble, sandstone base, forty dollars.

"A gracious friend from us is gone,
A voice we loved is fled,
But faith and memory lead us on:
He lives; he is not dead."

Four cents a letter. Little enough, God knows, for the work you do. My letters the best. Could have been a writer. Like to draw too. And all of mine! I would have heard if anything—he would have told me. I'll never go that way. All right above the waist. If anything happens it will be down below. Eaten away. Whisky holes through all your guts. Pictures in Cardiac's office of man with cancer. But several doctors have to agree on it. Criminal offense if they don't. But, if worse comes to worst—all that's outside. Get it before it gets up in you. Still live. Old man Haight had a flap in his belly. Ladled it out in a cup. McGuire—damned butcher. But he can do anything. Cut off a piece here, sew it on there.

Made the Hominy man a nose with a piece of shinbone. Couldn't tell it. Ought to be possible. Cut all the strings, tie them up again. While you wait. Sort of job for McGuire—rough and ready. They'll do it some day. After I'm gone. Things standing thus, unknown—but kill you maybe. Bull's too big. Soon now the Spring. You'd die. Not big enough. All bloody in her brain. Full filling fountains of bull-milk. Jupiter and what's-her-name.

But westward now he caught a glimpse of Pisgah and the western range. It was more spacious there. The hills climbed sunward to the sun. There was width to the eye, a smoking sun-hazed amplitude, the world convoluting and opening into the world, hill and plain, into the west. The West for desire, the East for home. To the east the short near mile-away hills reeked protectively above the town. Birdseye, Sunset. A straight plume of smoke coiled thickly from Judge Buck Sevier's smut-white clapboard residence on the decent side of Pisgah Avenue, thin smoke-wisps rose from the nigger shacks in the ravine below. Breakfast. Fried brains and eggs with streaky rashers of limp bacon. Wake, wake, wake, you mountain grills! Sleeps she yet, wrapped dirtily in three old wrappers in stale, airless yellow-shaded cold. The chapped hands sick-sweet glycerined. Gum-headed bottles, hairpins, and the bits of string. No one may enter now. Ashamed.

A paper-carrier, number 7, finished his route on the corner of Vine Street, as the car stopped, turned eastwards now from Pisgah Avenue toward the town core. The boy folded, bent, and flattened the fresh sheets deftly, throwing the block angularly thirty yards upon the porch of Shields the jeweller; it struck the boarding and bounded back with a fresh plop. Then he walked off with fatigued relief into time toward the twentieth century, feeling gratefully the ghost-kiss of absent weight upon his now free but still leaning right shoulder.

About fourteen, thought Gant. That would be Spring of 1864. The mule camp at Harrisburg. Thirty a month and keep. Men stank worse than mules. I was in third bunk on top. Gil in second. Keep your damned dirty hoof out of my mouth. It's bigger than a mule's. That was the man. If it ever lands on you, you bastard, you'll think it is a mule's, said Gil. Then they had it. Mother made us go. Big enough to work, she said. Born at the heart of the world, why here? Twelve miles from Gettysburg. Out of the South they came. Stove-pipe hats they had stolen. No shoes. Give me a drink, son. That was Fitzhugh Lee. After the third day we went over. Devil's Den. Cemetery Ridge. Stinking piles of arms and legs. Some of it done with meat-saws. Is the land richer now? The great barns bigger than the houses. Big eaters, all of us. I hid the cattle in the thicket. Belle Boyd, the Beautiful Rebel Spy. Sentenced to be shot four times. Took the dispatches from his pocket while they danced. Probably a little chippie.

Hog-chitlins and hot cracklin' bread. Must get some. The whole hog or none. Always been a good provider. Little I ever had done for me.

The car still climbing, mounted the flimsy cheap-boarded brown-gray smuttiness of Skyland Avenue.

America's Switzerland. The Beautiful Land of the Sky. Jesus God! Old Bowman said he'll be a rich man some day. Built up all the way to Pasadena. Come on out. Too late now. Think he was in love with her. No matter. Too old. Wants her out there. No fool like—White bellies of the fish. A spring somewhere to wash me through. Clean as a baby once more. New Orleans, the night Jim Corbett knocked out John L. Sullivan. The man who tried to rob me. My clothes and my watch. Five blocks down Canal Street in my nightgown. Two A.M. Threw them all in a heap—watch landed on top. Fight in my room. Town full of crooks and pick-pockets for prize-fight. Make good story. Policeman half hour later. They come out and beg you to come in. Frenchwomen. Creoles. Beautiful Creole heiress. Steamboat race. Captain, they are gaining. I will not be beaten. Out of wood. Use the bacon she said proudly. There was a terrific explosion. He got her as she sank the third time and swam to shore. They powder in front of the window, smacking their lips at you. For old men better maybe. Who gets the business there? Bury them all above ground. Water two feet down. Rots them. Why not? All big jobs. Italy. Carrara and Rome. Yet Brutus is an honor-able man. What's a Creole? French and Spanish. Has she any nigger blood? Ask Cardiac?

The car paused briefly at the car-shed, in sight of its stabled brothers. Then it moved reluctantly past the dynamic atmosphere of the Power and Light Company, wheeling bluntly into the gray frozen ribbon of Hatton Avenue, running gently up hill near its end into the frore silence of the Square.

Ah, Lord! Well do I remember. The old man offered me the whole piece for $1,000 three days after I arrived. Millionaire to-day if—

The car passed the Tuskegee on its eighty-yard climb into the Square. The fat slick worn leather-chairs marshalled between a fresh-rubbed gleaming line of brass spittoons squatted massively on each side of the entry door, before thick sheets of plate-glass that extended almost to the sidewalks with indecent nearness.

Many a fat man's rump upon the leather. Like fish in a glass case. Travelling man's wet chewed cigar, spit-limp on his greasy lips. Staring at all the women. Can't look back long. Gives advantage.

A Negro bellboy sleepily wafted a gray dust-cloth across the leather. Within, before the replenished crackle-dance of the wood-fire, the night-clerk sprawled out in the deep receiving belly of a leather divan.

The car reached the Square, jolted across the netting of north-south lines, and came to a halt on the north side, facing east. Scurfing a patch away from the glazed window, Gant looked out. The Square in the wan-gray frozen morning walled round him with frozen unnatural smallness. He felt suddenly the cramped mean fixity of the Square: this was the one fixed spot in a world that writhed, evolved, and changed constantly in his vision, and he felt a sick green fear, a frozen constriction about his heart because the centre of his life now looked so shrunken. He got very definitely the impression that if he flung out his arms they would strike against the walls of the mean three-and-four-story brickbuilt buildings that flanked the Square raggedly.

Anchored to earth at last, he was hit suddenly by the whole cumulation of sight and movement, of eating, drinking, and acting that had gathered in him for two months. The limitless land, wood, field, hill, prairie, desert, mountain, the coast rushing away below his eyes, the ground that swam before his eyes at stations, the remembered ghosts of gumbo, oysters, huge Frisco seasteaks, tropical fruits swarmed with the infinite life, the ceaseless pullulation of the sea. Here only, in his unreal-reality, this unnatural vision of what he had known for twenty years, did life lose its movement, change, color.

The Square had the horrible concreteness of a dream. At the far southeastern edge he saw his shop: his name painted hugely in dirty scaly white across the brick near the roof: W. O. Gant—Marbles, Tombstones, Cemetery Fixtures. It was like a dream of hell, when a man finds his own name staring at him from the Devil's ledger; like a dream of death, when he who comes as mourner finds himself in the coffin, or as witness to a hanging, the condemned upon the scaffold.

A sleepy Negro employed at the Manor Hotel clambered heavily up and slumped into one of the seats reserved for his race at the back. In a moment he began to snore gently through his blubbered lips.

At the east end of the Square, Big Bill Messler, with his vest half-unbuttoned over his girdled paunch-belly, descended slowly the steps of the City Hall, and moved soundingly off with country leisure along the cold-metallic sidewalk. The fountain, ringed with a thick bracelet of ice, played at quarter-strength a sheening glut of ice-blue water.

Cars droned separately into their focal positions; the carmen stamped their feet and talked smokily together; there was a breath of beginning life. Beside the City Hall, the firemen slept above their wagons: behind the bolted door great hoofs drummed woodenly.

A dray rattled across the east end of the Square before the City Hall, the old horse leaning back cautiously as he sloped down into the dray market by the oblique cobbled passage at the southeast that cut Gant's shop away from the market and "calaboose." As the car moved eastward again, Gant caught an angular view of Niggertown across this passage. The settlement was plumed delicately with a hundred tiny fumes of smoke.

The car sloped swiftly now down Academy Street, turned, as the upper edge of the Negro settlement impinged steeply from the valley upon the white, into Ivy Street, and proceeded north along a street bordered on one side by smutty pebble-dash cottages, and on the other by a grove of lordly oaks, in which the large quaking plaster pile of old Professor Bowman's deserted School for Young Ladies loomed desolately, turning and stopping at the corner, at the top of the Woodson Street hill, by the great wintry, wooden, and deserted barn of the Ivy Hotel. It had never paid.

Gant kneed his heavy bag before him down the passage, depositing it for a moment at the curbing before he descended the hill. The unpaved frozen clay fell steeply and lumpily away. It was steeper, shorter, nearer than he thought. Only the trees looked large. He saw Duncan come out on his porch, shirtsleeved, and pick up the morning paper. Speak to him later. Too long now. As he expected, there was a fat coil of morning smoke above the Scotchman's chimney, but none from his own.

He went down the hill, opening his iron gate softly, and going around to the side entrance by the yard, rather than ascend the steep veranda steps. The grape vines, tough and barren, writhed about the house like sinewy ropes. He entered the sitting-room quietly. There was a strong odor of cold leather. Cold ashes were strewn thinly in the grate. He put his bag down and went back through the wash-room into the kitchen. Eliza, wearing one of his old coats, and a pair of fingerless woollen gloves, poked among the embers of a crawling little fire.

"Well, I'm back," Gant said.

"Why, what on earth!" she cried as he knew she would, becoming flustered and moving her arms indeterminately. He laid his hand clumsily on her shoulder for a moment. They stood awkwardly without movement. Then he seized the oil-can, and drenched the wood with kerosene. The flame roared up out of the stove.

"Mercy, Mr. Gant," cried Eliza, "you'll burn us up!"

But, seizing a handful of cut sticks and the oil-can, he lunged furiously towards the sitting-room.

As the flame shot roaring up from the oiled pine sticks, and he felt the fire-full chimney-throat tremble, he recovered joy. He brought back the width of the desert; the vast yellow serpent of the river, alluvial with the mined accretions of the continent; the rich vision of laden ships, masted above the sea-walls, the world-nostalgic ships, bearing about them the filtered and concentrated odors of the earth, sensual Negroid rum and molasses, tar, ripening guavas, bananas, tangerines, pineapples in the warm holds of tropical boats, as cheap, as profuse, as abundant as the lazy equatorial earth and all its women; the great names of Louisiana, Texas, Arizona, Colorado, California; the blasted fiend-world of the desert, and the terrific boles of trees, tunnelled for the passage of a coach; water that fell from a mountain-top in a smoking noiseless coil, internal boiling lakes flung skywards by the punctual respiration of the earth, the multitudinous torture in form of granite oceans, gouged depthlessly by canyons, and irridescent with the daily chameleon-shift beyond man, beyond nature, of terrific colors, below the un-human iridescence of the sky.

Eliza, still excited, recovering speech, followed him into the sitting-room, holding her chapped gloved hands clasped before her stomach while she talked.

"I was saying to Steve last night, 'It wouldn't surprise me if your papa would come rolling in at any minute now'—I just had a feeling, I don't know what you'd call it," she said, her face plucked inward by the sudden fabrication of legend, "but it's pretty strange when you come to think of it. I was in Garret's the other day ordering some things, some vanilla extract, soda and a pound of coffee when Aleck Carter came up to me. 'Eliza,' he said, 'when's Mr. Gant coming back—I think I may have a job for him?' 'Why, Aleck,' I said, 'I don't much expect him before the first of April.' Well, sir, what do you know—I had no sooner got out on the street—I suppose I must have been thinking of something else, because I remember Emma Aldrich came by and hollered to me and I didn't think to answer her until she had gone on by, so I called out just as big as you please to her, 'Emma!'—the thing flashed over me all of a sudden—I was just as sure of it as I'm standing here—'what do you think? Mr. Gant's on his way back home.' "

Jesus God! thought Gant. It's begun again.

Her memory moved over the ocean-bed of event like a great octopus, blindly but completely feeling its way into every seacave, rill, and estuary, focussed on all she had done, felt and thought, with sucking Pentlandian intentness, for whom the sun shone, or grew dark, rain fell, and mankind came, spoke, and died, shifted for a moment in time out of its void into the Pentlandian core, pattern and heart of purpose.

Meanwhile, as he laid big gleaming lumps of coal upon the wood, he muttered to himself, his mind ordering in a mounting sequence, with balanced and climactic periods, his carefully punctuated rhetoric.

Yes, musty cotton, baled and piled under long sheds of railway sidings; and odorous pine woodlands of the level South, saturated with brown faery light, and broken by the tall straight leafless poles of trees; a woman's leg below an elegantly lifted skirt mounting to a carriage in Canal Street (French or Creole probably); a white arm curved reaching for a window shade, French-olive faces window-glimmering, the Georgia doctor's wife who slept above him going out, the unquenchable fish-filled abundance of the unfenced, blue, slow cat-slapping lazy Pacific; and the river, the all-drinking, yellow, slow-surging snake that drained the continent. His life was like that river, rich with its own deposited and onward-borne agglutinations, fecund with its sedimental accretions, filled exhaustlessly by life in order to be more richly itself, and this life, with the great purpose of a river, he emptied now into the harbor of his house, the sufficient haven of himself, for whom the gnarled vines wove round him thrice, the earth burgeoned with abundant fruit and blossom, the fire burnt madly.

"What have you got for breakfast?" he said to Eliza.

"Why," she said, pursing her lips meditatively, "would you like some eggs?"

"Yes," said he, "with a few rashers of bacon and a couple of pork sausages."

He strode across the dining-room and went up the hall.

"Steve! Ben! Luke! You damned scoundrels!" he yelled. "Get up!"

Their feet thudded almost simultaneously upon the floor.

"Papa's home!" they shrieked.

Mr. Duncan watched butter soak through a new-baked roll. He looked through his curtain angularly down, and saw thick acrid smoke biting heavily into the air above Gant's house.

"He's back," said he, with satisfaction.

So, at the moment looking, Tarkington of the paints said: "W. O.'s back."

Thus came he home, who had put out to land westward, Gant the Far-Wanderer. 1929

John [Roderigo] Dos Passos

(1896-)

CHRONOLOGY:

1896 Born January 14, in Chicago, Illinois.

1912-16 Travelled widely in the states, Mexico, and Europe; attended the Choate School in Connecticut; attended Harvard University.

1917-18 Served in the Norton Harjes Ambulance Service, France; the Italian Red Cross; the American Medical Corp; appeared as a contributor to *Eight Harvard Poets.*

1920 *One Man's Initiation* . . . (reissued as *First Encounter,* 1945).

1921 *Three Soldiers.*

1922 *Rosinante to the Road Again,* travels in Spain; *A Pushcart to the Curb,* verse.

1923 *Streets of Night.*

1925 *Manhattan Transfer.*

1926 *The Garbage Man,* play.

1927 *Orient Express,* travel.

1928 *Airways, Inc.,* play.

1930 *The 42nd Parallel*

1932 *1919.*

1934 *In All Countries,* criticism; *Three Plays* (including the new *Fortune Heights*).

1936 *The Big Money.*

1938 *U.S.A. (The 42nd Parallel; 1919; The Big Money).*

1938 *Journeys Between Wars,* criticism.

1939 *Adventures of a Young Man.*

1941 *The Ground We Stand On*, criticism.
1943 *Number One: A Novel.*
1944 *State of the Nation*, journalism.
1946 *Tour of Duty*, journalism.
1949 *Grand Design.*
1950 *The Prospect Before Us*, journalism.
1951 *Chosen Country.*
1952 *District of Columbia (Adventures of a Young Man, Number One, The Grand Design).*
1956 *The Theme Is Freedom.*
1957 *The Men Who Made the Nation.*
1958 *The Great Days.*
1959 *Prospects of a Golden Age.*
1961 *Midcentury.*
1962 *Mr. Wilson's War.*
1963 *Brazil on the Move; The Head and Heart of Thomas Jefferson.*

BIBLIOGRAPHY:

Although there is no collected edition of Dos Passos's works, both of his trilogies, as well as *Three Soldiers* and *Manhattan Transfer*, are available in inexpensive reprints, as are scattered other novels.

A book-length study of Dos Passos in English is John H. Wren's *John Dos Passos* (New York, 1962), which also contains a good bibliography. For studies of individual novels, see Donna Gerstenberger and George Hendrick, *The American Novel, 1789-1959: A Checklist of Twentieth-Century Criticism* (Denver, 1961).

Preface to *U.S.A.*

The young man walks fast by himself through the crowd that thins into the night streets; feet are tired from hours of walking; eyes greedy for warm curve of faces, answering flicker of eyes, the set of a head, the lift of a shoulder, the way hands spread and clench; blood tingles with wants; mind is a beehive of hopes buzzing and stinging; muscles ache for the knowledge of jobs, for the roadmender's pick and shovel work, the fisherman's knack with a hook when he hauls on the slithery net from the rail of the lurching trawler, the swing of the bridgeman's arm as he slings down the whitehot rivet, the engineer's slow grip wise on the throttle, the dirtfarmer's use of his whole body when, whoaing the mules, he yanks the plow from the furrow. The young man walks by himself searching through the crowd with greedy eyes, greedy ears taut to hear, by himself, alone.

The streets are empty. People have packed into subways, climbed into streetcars and buses; in the stations they've scampered for suburban trains; they've filtered into lodgings and tenements, gone up in elevators into apartmenthouses. In a showwindow two sallow windowdressers in their shirtsleeves are bringing out a dummy girl in a red evening dress, at a corner welders in masks lean into sheets of blue flame repairing a cartrack, a few drunk bums shamble along, a sad streetwalker fidgets under an arclight. From the river comes the deep rumbling whistle of a steamboat leaving dock. A tug hoots far away.

The young man walks by himself, fast but not fast enough, far but not far enough (faces slide out of sight, talk trails into tattered scraps, footsteps tap fainter in alleys); he must catch the last subway, the streetcar, the bus, run up the gangplanks of all the steamboats, register at all the hotels, work in the cities, answer the wantads, learn the trades, take up the jobs, live in all the boardinghouses, sleep in all the beds. One bed is not enough, one job is not enough, one life is not enough. At night, head swimming with wants, he walks by himself alone.

No job, no woman, no house, no city.

Only the ears busy to catch the speech are not alone; the ears are caught tight, linked tight by the tendrils of phrased words, the turn of a joke, the sing-song fade of a story, the gruff fall of a sentence; linking tendrils of speech twine through the city blocks, spread over pavements, grow out along broad parked avenues, speed with the trucks leaving on their long night runs over roaring highways, whisper down sandy byroads past wornout farms, joining up cities and fillingstations, roundhouses, steamboats, planes groping along airways; words call out on mountain pastures, drift slow down rivers widening to the sea and the hushed beaches.

It was not in the long walks through jostling crowds at night that he was less alone, or in the training camp at Allentown, or in the day on the docks at Seattle, or in the empty reek of Washington City hot boyhood summer nights, or in the meal on Market Street, or in the swim off the red rocks at San Diego, or in the bed full of fleas in New Orleans, or in the cold razorwind off the lake, or in the gray faces trembling in the grind of gears in the street under Michigan Avenue, or in the smokers of limited expresstrains, or walking across country, or riding up the dry mountain canyons, or the night without a sleepingbag among frozen beartracks in the Yellowstone, or canoeing Sundays on the Quinnipiac;

but in his mother's words telling about longago, in his father's telling about when I was a boy, in the kidding stories of uncles, in the lies the kids told at school, the hired man's yarns, the tall tales the doughboys told after taps;

it was the speech that clung to the ears, the link that tingled in the blood; U.S.A.

U.S.A. is the slice of a continuent. U.S.A. is a group of holding companies, some aggregations of trade unions, a set of laws bound in calf, a radio network, a chain of moving picture theatres, a column of stockquotations rubbed out and written in by a Western Union boy on a blackboard, a publiclibrary full of old newspapers and dogeared historybooks with protests scrawled on the margins in pencil. U.S.A. is the world's greatest rivervalley fringed with mountains and hills, U.S.A. is a set of bigmouthed officials with too many bankaccounts. U.S.A. is a lot of men buried in their uniforms in Arlington Cemetery. U.S.A. is the letters at the end of an address when you are away from home. But mostly U.S.A. is the speech of the people.

1938

From *1919*

Newsreel XXXIV

WHOLE WORLD IS SHORT OF PLATINUM

Il serait Criminel de Negliger Les Intérêts Français dans les Balkans

KILLS SELF IN CELL

the quotation of United Cigar Stores made this month of $167 per share means $501 per share for the old stock upon which present stockholders are receiving 27% per share as formerly held. Through peace and war it has maintained and increased its dividends

6 TRAPPED ON UPPER FLOOR

How are you goin' to keep 'em down on the farm
After they've seen Paree

If Wall street needed the treaty, which means if the business interests of the country properly desired to know to what extent we are being committed in affairs which do not concern us, why should it take the trouble to corrupt the tagrag and bobtail which forms Mr. Wilson's following in Paris?

ALLIES URGE MAGYAR PEOPLE TO UPSET
BELA KUN REGIME

2 WOMEN MISSING IN BLUEBEARD MYSTERY

Enfin La France Achète les stocks Américains

How are you goin' to keep 'em away from Broadway
Jazzin' around
Paintin' the town

the boulevards during the afternoon presented an unwonted aspect. The café terraces in most cases were deserted and had been cleared of their tables and chairs. At some of the cafés customers were admitted one by one and served by faithful waiters, who, however, had discarded their aprons

YEOMANETTE SHRIEKS FOR FORMER
SUITOR AS SHE SEEKS DEATH
IN DRIVE APARTMENT

DESIRES OF HEDJAZ STIR PARIS CRITICS

in order not prematurely to show their colors a pretense is made of disbanding a few formations; in reality however, these troops are being transferred lock stock and barrel to Kolchak

I.W.W. IN PLOT TO KILL WILSON

Find 10,000 Bags of Decayed Onions

FALL ON STAIRS KILLS WEALTHY CITIZEN

the mistiness of the weather hid the gunboat from sight soon after it left the dock, but the President continued to wave his hat and smile as the boat headed towards the George Washington

OVERTHROW OF SOVIET RULE SURE 1932

From *1919*

The House of Morgan

I commit my soul into the hands of my savior, wrote John Pierpont Morgan in his will, *in full confidence that having redeemed it and washed it in His most precious blood, He will present it faultless before my heavenly father, and I intreat my children to maintain and defend at all hazard and at any cost of personal sacrifice the blessed doctrine of complete atonement for sin through the blood of Jesus Christ once offered and through that alone.*

and into the hands of the House of Morgan represented by his son,

he committed,

when he died in Rome in 1913,

the control of the Morgan interests in New York, Paris and London, four national banks, three trust companies, three life insurance companies, ten railroad systems, three street railway companies, an express company, the International Mercantile Marine,

power,

on the cantilever principle, through interlocking directorates

over eighteen other railroads, U.S. Steel, General Electric, American Tel and Tel, five major industries;

the interwoven cables of the Morgan Stillman Baker combination held credit up like a suspension bridge, thirteen percent of the banking resources of the world.

The first Morgan to make a pool was Joseph Morgan, a hotelkeeper in Hartford Connecticut who organized stagecoach lines and bought up Ætna Life Insurance stock in a time of panic caused by one of the big New York fires in the 1830's;

his son Junius followed in his footsteps, first in the drygoods business, and then as partner to George Peabody, a Massachusetts banker who built up an enormous underwriting and mercantile business in London and became a friend of Queen Victoria;

Junius married the daughter of John Pierpont, a Boston preacher, poet, eccentric, and abolitionist; and their eldest son,

John Pierpont Morgan

arrived in New York to make his fortune

after being trained in England, going to school at Vevey, proving himself a crack mathematician at the University of Göttingen,

a lanky morose young man of twenty,

just in time for the panic of '57.

(war and panics on the stock exchange, bankruptcies, warloans, good growing weather for the House of Morgan.)

When the guns started booming at Fort Sumter, young Morgan turned some money over reselling condemned muskets to the U.S. army and began to make himself felt in the gold room in downtown New York; there was more in trading in gold than in trading in muskets; so much for the Civil War.

During the Franco-Prussian war Junius Morgan floated a huge bond issue for the French government at Tours.

At the same time young Morgan was fighting Jay Cooke and the German-Jew bankers in Frankfort over the funding of the American war debt (he never did like the Germans or the Jews).

The panic of '75 ruined Jay Cooke and made J. Pierpont Morgan the boss croupier of Wall Street; he united with the Philadelphia Drexels and built the Drexel building where for thirty years he sat in his glassedin office, redfaced and insolent, writing at his desk, smoking great black cigars, or, if important issues were involved, playing solitaire in his inner office; he was famous for his few words, Yes or No, and for his way of suddenly blowing up in a visitor's face and for that special gesture of the arm that meant, *What do I get out of it?*

In '77 Junius Morgan retired; J. Pierpont got himself made a member of the board of directors of the New York Central railroad and launched the first *Corsair*. He liked yachting and to have pretty actresses call him Commodore.

He founded the Lying-in Hospital on Stuyvesant Square, and was fond of going into St. George's church and singing a hymn all alone in the afternoon quiet.

In the panic of '93

at no inconsiderable profit to himself

Morgan saved the U.S. Treasury; gold was draining out, the country was ruined, the farmers were howling for a silver standard, Grover Cleveland and his cabinet were walking up and down in the blue room at the White House without being able to come to a decision, in Congress they were making speeches while the gold reserves melted in the Subtreasuries; poor people were starving; Coxey's army was marching to Washington; for a long time Grover Cleveland couldn't bring himself to call in the representative of the Wall Street moneymasters; Morgan sat in his suite at the Arlington smoking cigars and quietly playing solitaire until at last the president sent for him;

he had a plan all ready for stopping the gold hemorrhage.

After that what Morgan said went; when Carnegie sold out he built the Steel Trust.

J. Pierpont Morgan was a bullnecked irascible man with small black magpie's eyes and a growth on his nose; he let his partners work themselves to death over the detailed routine of banking, and sat in his back office smoking black cigars; when there was something to be decided he said Yes or No or just turned his back and went to his solitaire.

Every Christmas his librarian read him Dickens' *A Christmas Carol* from the original manuscript.

He was fond of canarybirds and pekinese dogs and liked to take pretty actresses yachting. Each *Corsair* was a finer vessel than the last.

When he dined with King Edward he sat at His Majesty's right; he ate with the Kaiser tête-à-tête; he liked talking to cardinals or the pope, and never missed a conference of Episcopal bishops;

Rome was his favorite city.

He liked choice cookery and old wines and pretty women and yachting, and going over his collections, now and then picking up a jewelled snuffbox and staring at it with his magpie's eyes.

He made a collection of the autographs of the rulers of France, owned glass cases full of Babylonian tablets, seals, signets, statuettes, busts,

Gallo-Roman bronzes,

Merovingian jewels, miniatures, watches, tapestries, porcelains, cuneiform inscriptions, paintings by all the old masters, Dutch, Italian, Flemish, Spanish,

manuscripts of the gospels and the Apocalypse,

a collection of the works of Jean-Jacques Rousseau,

and the letters of Pliny the Younger.

His collectors bought anything that was expensive or rare or had the glint of empire on it, and he had it brought to him and stared hard at it with his magpie's eyes. Then it was put in a glass case.

The last year of his life he went up the Nile on a dahabiyeh and spent a long time staring at the great columns of the Temple of Karnak.

The panic of 1907 and the death of Harriman, his great opponent in railroad financing, in 1909, had left him the undisputed ruler of Wall Street, most powerful private citizen in the world;

an old man tired of the purple, suffering from gout, he had deigned to go to Washington to answer the questions of the Pujo Committee during the Money Trust Investigation: Yes, I did what seemed to me to be for the best interests of the country.

So admirably was his empire built that his death in 1913 hardly caused a ripple in the exchanges of the world: the purple descended to his son, J. P. Morgan,

who had been trained at Groton and Harvard and by associating with the British ruling class

to be a more constitutional monarch: *J. P. Morgan suggests . . .*

By 1917 the Allies had borrowed one billion, nine-hundred million dollars through the House of Morgan: we went overseas for democracy and the flag;

and by the end of the Peace Conference the phrase *J. P. Morgan suggests* had compulsion over a power of seventyfour billion dollars.

J. P. Morgan is a silent man, not given to public utterances, but during the great steel strike, he wrote Gary: *Heartfelt congratulations on your stand for the open shop, with which I am, as you know, absolutely in accord. I believe American principles of liberty are deeply involved, and must win if we stand firm.*

(Wars and panics on the stock exchange,
machinegunfire and arson,
bankruptcies, warloans,
starvation, lice, cholera and typhus:
good growing weather for the House of Morgan.) 1932

From *1919*

Newsreel XXXV

the Grand Prix de la Victoire, run yesterday for fifty-second time was an event that will long remain in the memories of those present, for never in the history of the classic race has Longchamps presented such a glorious scene

Keep the home fires burning
Till the boys come home

LEVIATHAN UNABLE TO PUT TO SEA

BOLSHEVIKS ABOLISH POSTAGE STAMPS

ARTIST TAKES GAS IN NEW HAVEN

FIND BLOOD ON $1 BILL

While our hearts are yearning

POTASH CAUSE OF BREAK IN PARLEY

MAJOR DIES OF POISONING

TOOK ROACH SALTS BY MISTAKE

riot and robbery developed into the most awful pogrom ever heard of. Within two or three days the Lemberg ghetto was turned into heaps of smoking debris. Eyewitnesses estimate that the Polish soldiers killed more than a thousand jewish men and women and children

LENINE SHOT BY TROTSKY IN DRUNKEN BRAWL

you know where I stand on beer, said Brisbane in seeking assistance

Though the boys are far away
They long for home
There's a silver lining
Through the dark clouds shining

PRESIDENT EVOKES CRY OF THE DEAD

LETTER CLEW TO BOMB OUTRAGE

Emile Deen in the preceding three installments of his interview described the situation between the Royal Dutch and the Standard Oil Company, as being the beginning of a struggle for the control of the markets of the world which was only halted by the war. "The basic factors," he said, "are envy, discontent and suspicion." The extraordinary industrial growth of our nation since the Civil War, the opening up of new territory, the development of resources, the rapid increase in population, all these things have resulted in the creation of many big and sudden fortunes. Is there a mother, father, sweetheart, relative or friend of any one of the two million boys fighting abroad who does not thank God that Wall Street contributed H. P. Davidson to the Red Cross?

BOND THIEF MURDERED

Turn the bright side inside out
Till the boys come home

1932

From *1919*

The Camera Eye (39)

daylight enlarges out of ruddy quiet very faintly throbbing wanes into my sweet darkness broadens red through the warm blood weighting the lids warmsweetly then snaps on

enormously blue yellow pink

today is Paris   pink sunlight hazy on the clouds

against patches of robinsegg a tiny siren hoots shrilly traffic drowsily rumbles clatters over the cobbles taxis squawk the yellow's the comforter through the open window the Louvre emphasizes its sedate architecture of greypink stone between the Seine and the sky

and the certainty of Paris

the towboat shiny green and red chugs against the current towing three black and mahoganyvarnished barges their deckhouse windows have green shutters and lace curtains and pots of geraniums in flower to get under the bridge a fat man in blue had to let the little black stack drop flat to the deck

Paris comes into the room in the servantgirl's eyes the warm bulge of her breasts under the grey smock the smell of chickory in coffee scalded milk and the shine that crunches on the crescent rolls stuck with little dabs of very sweet unsalted butter

in the yellow paperback of the book that halfhides the agreeable countenance of my friend

Paris of 1919

paris-mutuel

roulettewheel that spins round the Tour Eiffel red square white square a million dollars a billion marks a trillion roubles baisse du franc or a mandate for Montmartre

Cirque Médrano the steeplechase gravity of cellos tuning up on the stage at the Salle Gaveau oboes and a triangle la musique s'en fout de moi says the old marchioness jingling with diamonds as she walks out on Stravinski but the red colt took the jumps backwards and we lost all our money

la peinture opposite the Madeleine Cezanne Picasso Modigliani

Nouvelle Athènes

la poesie of manifestos always freshtinted on the kiosks and slogans scrawled in chalk on the urinals L'UNION DES TRAVAILLEURS FERA LA PAIX DU MONDE

revolution round the spinning Eiffel Tower

that burns up our last year's diagrams the dates fly off the calendar we'll make everything new today is the Year I Today is the sunny morning of the first day of spring We gulp our coffee splash water on us jump into our clothes run downstairs step out wideawake into the first morning of the first day of the first year 1932

John [Ernst] Steinbeck
(1902-)

CHRONOLOGY:

1902 Born February 27, in Salinas, California.
1919-25 Attended Stanford University as special student in marine biology.
1925-29 Varied wanderings and jobs —Panama Canal, New York, California—as sailor, newspaperman, bricklayer, caretaker, chemist's assistant, migratory fruitpicker.
1929 *Cup of God: A Life of Henry Morgan, Buccaneer.*
1932 *The Pastures of Heaven,* connected stories.
1933 *To a God Unknown.*
1935 *Tortilla Flat.*
1936 *In Dubious Battle: Saint Katy the Virgin,* story.
1937 *Of Mice and Men* (turned into a prize-winning play); *The Red Pony.*
1938 *Their Blood Is Strong,* nonfiction; *The Long Valley,* stories.
1939 *The Grapes of Wrath* (awarded a Pulitzer Prize).
1941 *The Forgotten Village,* nonfiction; *Sea of Cortez,* nonfiction.
1942 *The Moon Is Down; Bombs Away,* journalism.
1943 *How Edith McGillicudy Met R. L. S.*
1945 *Cannery Row.*
1947 *The Wayward Bus; The Pearl.*
1948 *A Russian Journal* (with Robert Capa).
1950 *Burning Bright* (turned into a play).
1952 *East of Eden.*
1954 *Sweet Thursday.*
1957 *The Short Reign of Pippin IV.*
1958 *Once There Was a War,* journalism.
1961 *The Winter of Our Discontent.*
1962 Awarded the Nobel Prize for Literature; *Travels with Charley.*

BIBLIOGRAPHY:

There is no collected edition of Steinbeck's works, although most of the major novels are available in inexpensive reprints. Pascal Covici edited *The Portable Steinbeck* (with an Introduction by Lewis Garnett) (Rev. ed.; New York, 1946), and Joseph Henry Jackson edited *The Short Novels of John Steinbeck* (New York, 1963).

Three important book-length studies include Harry T. Moore, *The Novels of John Steinbeck: A First Critical Study* (Chicago, 1939); Peter Lisca's *Wide World of John Steinbeck* (New Brunswick, N.J., 1957); and Warren French's *John Steinbeck* (New York, 1961). An important collection is E. W. Tedlock, Jr., and C. V. Wicker, eds., *Steinbeck and His Critics, a Record of Twenty-five Years* (Albuquerque, N.M., 1957).

For studies of individual novels, see Donna Gerstenberger and George Hendrick, *The American Novel, 1789-1959: A Checklist of Twentieth-Century Criticisms* (Denver, 1961); and for the shorter fiction, Warren S. Walker, *Twentieth-Century Short Story Explication . . .* (Hamden, Conn., 1961), Supplement, 1963. Of special interest to students of *The Grapes of Wrath* is Warren French's *A Companion to the Grapes of Wrath* (New York, 1963).

From *The Grapes of Wrath*

CHAPTER SEVEN

In the towns, on the edges of the towns, in fields, in vacant lots, the used-car yards, the wreckers' yards, the garages with blazoned signs—Used Cars, Good Used Cars. Cheap transportation, three trailers. '27 Ford, clean. Checked cars, guaranteed cars. Free radio. Car with 100 gallons of gas free. Come in and look. Used Cars. No overhead.

A lot and a house large enough for a desk and chair and a blue book. Sheaf of contracts, dog-eared, held with paper clips, and a neat pile of unused contracts. Pen—keep it full, keep it working. A sale's been lost 'cause a pen didn't work.

Those sons-of-bitches over there ain't buying. Every yard gets 'em. They're lookers. Spend all their time looking. Don't want to buy no cars; take up your time. Don't give a damn for your time. Over there, them two people—no, with the kids. Get 'em in a car. Start 'em at two hundred and work down. They look good for one and a quarter. Get 'em rolling. Get 'em out in a jalopy. Sock it to 'em! They took our time.

Owners with rolled-up sleeves. Salesmen, neat, deadly, small intent eyes watching for weaknesses.

Watch the woman's face. If the woman likes it we can screw the old man. Start' em on that Cad'. Then you can work 'em down to that '26 Buick. 'F you start on the Buick, they'll go for a Ford. Roll up your sleeves an' get to work. This ain't gonna last forever. Show 'em that Nash while I get the slow leak pumped up on that '25 Dodge. I'll give you a Hymie when I'm ready.

What you want is transportation, ain't it? No baloney for you. Sure the upholstery is shot. Seat cushions ain't turning no wheels over.

Cars lined up, noses forward, rusty noses, flat tires. Parked close together.

Like to get in to see that one? Sure, no trouble. I'll pull her out of the line.

Get 'em under obligation. Make 'em take up your time. Don't let 'em forget they're takin' your time. People are nice, mostly. They hate to put you out. Make 'em put you out, an' then sock it to 'em.

Cars lined up, Model T's, high and snotty, creaking wheel, worn bands. Buicks, Nashes, De Sotos.

Yes, sir. '22 Dodge. Best goddamn car Dodge ever made. Never wear out. Low compression. High compression got lots a sap for a while, but the metal ain't made that'll hold it for long. Plymouths, Rocknes, Stars.

Jesus, where'd that Apperson come from, the Ark? And a Chalmers and a Chandler—ain't made 'em for years. We ain't sellin' cars—rolling junk. Goddamn it, I got to get jalopies. I don't want nothing for more'n twenty-five, thirty bucks. Sell 'em for fifty, seventy-five. That's a good profit. Christ, what cut do you make on a new car? Get jalopies. I can sell 'em fast as I get 'em. Nothing over two hundred fifty. Jim, corral that old bastard on the sidewalk. Don't know his ass from a hole in the ground. Try him on that Apperson. Say, where is that Apperson? Sold? If we don't get some jalopies we got nothing to sell.

Flags, red and white, white and blue—all along the curb. Used Cars. Good Used Cars.

Today's bargain—up on the platform. Never sell it. Makes folks come in, though. If we sold that bargain at that price we'd hardly make a dime. Tell 'em it's jus' sold. Take out that yard battery before you make delivery. Put in that dumb cell. Christ, what they want for six bits? Roll up your sleeves—pitch in. This ain't gonna last. If I had enough jalopies I'd retire in six months.

Listen, Jim, I heard that Chevvy's rear end. Sounds like bustin' bottles. Squirt in a couple quarts of sawdust. Put some in the gears, too. We got to move that lemon for thirty-five dollars. Bastard cheated me on that one. I offer ten an' he jerks me to fifteen, an' then the son-of-a-bitch took the tools out. God Almighty! I wisht I had five hundred jalopies. This ain't gonna last. He don't like the tires? Tell 'im they got ten thousand in 'em, knock off a buck an' a half.

Piles of rusty ruins against the fence, rows of wrecks in back, fenders, grease-black wrecks, blocks lying on the ground and a pig weed growing up through the cylinders. Brake rods, exhausts, piled like snakes. Grease, gasoline.

See if you can't find a spark plug that ain't cracked. Christ, if I had fifty trailers at under a hundred I'd clean up. What the hell is he kickin' about? We sell 'em, but we don't push 'em home for him. That's good! Don't push 'em home. Get that one in the Monthly, I bet. You don't think he's a prospect? Well, kick 'im out. We got too much to do to bother with a guy that can't make up his mind. Take the right front tire off the Graham. Turn that mended side down. The rest looks swell. Got tread an' everything.

Sure! There's fifty thousan' in that ol' heap yet. Keep plenty oil in. So long. Good luck.

Lookin' for a car? What did you have in mind? See anything attracts you? I'm dry. How about a little snort a good stuff? Come on, while your wife's lookin' at that La Salle. You don't want no La Salle. Bearings shot. Uses too much oil. Got a Lincoln '24. There's a car. Run forever. Make her into a truck.

Hot sun on rusted metal. Oil on the ground. People are wandering in, bewildered, needing a car.

Wipe your feet. Don't lean on that car, it's dirty. How do you buy a car? What does it cost? Watch the children, now. I wonder how much for this one? We'll ask. It don't cost money to ask. We can ask, can't we? Can't pay a nickel over seventy-five, or there won't be enough to get to California.

God, if I could only get a hundred jalopies. I don't care if they run or not.

Tires, used, bruised tires, stacked in tall cylinders; tubes, red, gray, hanging like sausages.

Tire patch? Radiator cleaner? Spark intensifier? Drop this little pill in your gas tank and get ten extra miles to the gallon. Just paint it on—you got a new surface for fifty cents. Wipers, fan belts, gaskets? Maybe it's the valve. Get a new valve stem. What can you lose for a nickel?

All right, Joe. You soften 'em up an' shoot 'em in here. I'll close 'em, I'll deal 'em or I'll kill 'em. Don't send in no bums. I want deals.

Yes, sir, step in. You got a buy there. Yes, sir! At eighty bucks you got a buy.

I can't go no higher than fifty. The fella outside says fifty.

Fifty. Fifty? He's nuts. Paid seventy-eight fifty for that little number. Joe, you crazy fool, you tryin' to bust us? Have to can that guy. I might take sixty. Now look here, mister, I ain't got all day. I'm a business man but I ain't out to stick nobody. Got anything to trade?

Got a pair of mules I'll trade.

Mules! Hey, Joe, hear this? This guy wants to trade mules. Didn't nobody tell you this is the machine age? They don't use mules for nothing but glue no more.

Fine big mules—five and seven years old. Maybe we better look around.

Look around! You come in when we're busy, an' take up our time an' then walk out! Joe, did you know you was talkin' to pikers?

I ain't a piker. I got to get a car. We're goin' to California. I got to get a car.

Well, I'm a sucker. Joe says I'm a sucker. Says if I don't quit givin' my shirt away I'll starve to death. Tell you what I'll do—I can get five bucks apiece for them mules for dog feed.

I wouldn't want them to go for dog feed.

Well, maybe I can get ten or seven maybe. Tell you what we'll do. We'll take your mules for twenty. Wagon goes with 'em, don't it? An' you put up fifty, an' you can sign a contract to send the rest at ten dollars a month.

But you said eighty.

Didn't you never hear about carrying charges and insurance? That just boosts her a little. You'll get her all paid up in four-five months. Sign your name right here. We'll take care of ever'thing.

Well, I don't know—

Now, look here. I'm givin' you my shirt, an' you took all this time. I might a made three sales while I been talkin' to you. I'm disgusted. Yeah, sign right there. All right, sir. Joe, fill up the tank for this gentleman. We'll give him gas.

Jesus, Joe, that was a hot one! What'd we give for that jalopy? Thirty bucks—thirty-five wasn't it? I got that team, an' if I can't get seventy-five for that team, I ain't a business man. An' I got fifty cash an' a contract for forty more. Oh, I know they're not all honest, but it'll surprise you how many kick through with the rest. One guy comes through with a hundred two years after I wrote him off. I bet you this guy sends the money. Christ, if I could only get five hundred jalopies! Roll up your sleeves, Joe. Go out an' soften 'em an' send 'em in to me. You get twenty on that last deal. You ain't doing bad.

Limp flags in the afternoon sun. Today's Bargain. '29 Ford pickup, runs good.

What do you want for fifty bucks—a Zephyr?

Horsehair curling out of seat cushions, fenders battered and hammered back. Bumpers torn loose and hanging. Fancy Ford roadster with little colored lights at fender guide, at radiator cap, and three behind. Mud aprons, and a big die on the gear-shift lever. Pretty girl on tire cover, painted in color and named Cora. Afternoon sun on the dusty windshields.

Christ, I ain't had time to go out an' eat! Joe, send a kid for a hamburger.

Spattering roar of ancient engines.

There's a dumb-bunny lookin' at that Chrysler. Find out if he got any jack in his jeans. Some a these farm boys is sneaky. Soften 'em up an' roll 'em in to me, Joe. You're doin' good.

Sure, we sold it. Guarantee? We guaranteed it to be an automobile. We didn't guarantee to wet-nurse it. Now listen here, you—you bought a car, an' now you're squawkin'. I don't give a damn if you don't make payments. We ain't got your paper. We turn that over to the finance company. They'll get after you, not us. We don't hold no paper. Yeah? Well you jus' get tough an' I'll call a cop. No, we did not switch the tires. Run 'im outa here, Joe. He bought a car, an' now he ain't satisfied. How'd you think if I bought a steak an' et half an' try to bring it back? We're runnin' a business, not a charity ward. Can ya imagine that guy, Joe? Say—looka there! Got a Elk's tooth! Run over there. Let 'em glance over that '36 Pontiac. Yeah.

Square noses, round noses, rusty noses, shovel noses, and the long curves of streamlines, and the flat surfaces before streamlining. Bargains Today. Old monsters with deep upholstery—you can cut her into a truck easy. Two-wheel trailers, axles rusty in the hard afternoon sun. Used Cars. Good Used Cars. Clean, runs good. Don't pump oil.

Christ, look at 'er! Somebody took nice care of 'er.

Cadillacs, La Salles, Buicks, Plymouths, Packards, Chevvies, Fords,

Pontiacs. Row on row, headlights glinting in the afternoon sun. Good Used Cars.

Soften 'em up, Joe. Jesus, I wisht I had a thousand jalopies! Get 'em ready to deal, an' I'll close 'em.

Goin' to California? Here's jus' what you need. Looks shot, but they's thousan's of miles in her.

Lined up side by side. Good Used Cars. Bargains. Clean, runs good.

CHAPTER EIGHT

The sky grayed among the stars, and the pale, late quarter-moon was insubstantial and thin. Tom Joad and the preacher walked quickly along a road that was only wheel tracks and beaten caterpillar tracks through a cotton field. Only the unbalanced sky showed the approach of dawn, no horizon to the west, and a line to the east. The two men walked in silence and smelled the dust their feet kicked into the air.

"I hope you're dead sure of the way," Jim Casy said. "I'd hate to have the dawn come and us be way to hell an' gone somewhere." The cotton field scurried with waking life, the quick flutter of morning birds feeding on the ground, the scamper over the clods of disturbed rabbits. The quiet thudding of the men's feet in the dust, the squeak of crushed clods under their shoes, sounded against the secret noises of the dawn.

Tom said, "I could shut my eyes an' walk right there. On'y way I can go wrong is think about her. Jus' forget about her, an' I'll go right there. Hell, man, I was born right aroun' in here. I run aroun' here when I was a kid. They's a tree over there—look, you can jus' make it out. Well, once my old man hung up a dead coyote in that tree. Hung there till it was all sort of melted, an' then dropped off. Dried up, like. Jesus, I hope Ma's cookin' somepin. My belly's caved."

"Me too," said Casy. "Like a little eatin' tobacca? Keeps ya from gettin' too hungry. Been better if we didn' start so damn early. Better if it was light." He paused to gnaw off a piece of plug. "I was sleepin' nice."

"That crazy Muley done it," said Tom. "He got me clear jumpy. Wakes me up an says, ' 'By, Tom. I'm goin' on. I got places to go.' An' he says, 'Better get goin' too, so's you'll be offa this lan when the light comes.' He's gettin' screwy as a gopher, livin' like he does. You'd think Injuns was after him. Think he's nuts?"

"Well, I dunno. You seen that car come las' night when we had a little fire. You seen how the house was smashed. They's somepin purty mean goin' on. 'Course Muley's crazy, all right. Creepin' aroun' like a coyote; that's boun' to make him crazy. He'll kill somebody purty soon an' they'll run him down with dogs. I can see it like a prophecy. He'll get worse an' worse. Wouldn' come along with us, you say?"

"No," said Joad. "I think he's scared to see people now. Wonder he come up to us. We'll be at Uncle John's place by sunrise." They walked along in silence for a time, and the late owls flew over toward the barns, the hollow trees, the tank houses, where they hid from daylight. The eastern sky grew fairer and it was possible to see the cotton plants and the graying earth. "Damn' if I know how they're all sleepin' at Uncle John's. He on'y got one room an' a cookin' leanto, an' a little bit of a barn. Must be a mob there now."

The preacher said, "I don't recollect that John had a fambly. Just a lone man, ain't he? I don't recollect much about him."

"Lonest goddamn man in the world," said Joad. "Crazy kind of son-of-a-bitch, too—somepin like Muley, on'y worse in some ways. Might see 'im anywheres—at Shawnee, drunk, or visitin' a widow twenty miles away, or workin' his place with a lantern. Crazy. Ever'body thought he wouldn't live long. A lone man like that don't live long. But Uncle John's older'n Pa. Jus' gets stringier an' meaner ever' year. Meaner'n Grampa."

"Look a the light comin'," said the preacher. "Silvery-like. Didn' John never have no fambly?"

"Well, yes, he did, an' that'll show you the kind a fella he is—set in his ways. Pa tells about it. Uncle John, he had a young wife. Married four months. She was in a family way, too, an' one night she gets a pain in her stomick, an' she says, 'You better go for a doctor.' Well, John, he's settin' there, an' he says, 'You just got a stomickache. You et too much. Take a dose a pain killer. You crowd up ya stomick an' ya get a stomickache,' he says. Nex' noon she's outa her head, an' she dies at about four in the afternoon."

"What was it?" Casy asked. "Poisoned from somepin she et?"

"No, somepin jus' bust in her. Ap—appendick or somepin. Well, Uncle John, he's always been a easy-goin' fella, an' he takes it hard. Takes it for a sin. For a long time he won't have nothin' to say to nobody. Just walks aroun' like he don't see nothin', an' he prays some. Took 'im two years to come out of it, an' then he ain't the same. Sort of wild. Made a damn nuisance of hisself. Ever' time one of us kids got worms or a gut-ache Uncle John brings a doctor out. Pa finally tol' him he got to stop. Kids all the time gettin' a gutache. He figures it's his fault his woman died. Funny fella. He's all the time makin' it up to somebody—givin' kids stuff, droppin' a sack a meal on somebody's porch. Give away about ever'thing he got, an' still he ain't very happy. Gets walkin' around alone at night sometimes. He's a good farmer, though. Keeps his lan' nice."

"Poor fella," said the preacher. "Poor lonely fella. Did he go to church much when his woman died?"

"No, he didn'. Never wanted to get close to folks. Wanted to be off alone. I never seen a kid that wasn't crazy about him. He'd come to our house in the night sometimes, an' we knowed he come 'cause jus' as sure as he come there'd be a pack a gum in the bed right beside ever' one of us. We thought he was Jesus Christ Awmighty."

The preacher walked along, head down. He didn't answer. And the light of the coming morning made his forehead seem to shine, and his hands, swinging beside him, flicked into the light and out again.

Tom was silent too, as though he had said too intimate a thing and was ashamed. He quickened his pace and the preacher kept step. They could see a little into gray distance ahead now. A snake wriggled slowly from the cotton rows into the road. Tom stopped short of it and peered. "Gopher snake," he said. "Let him go." They walked around the snake and went on their way. A little color came into the eastern sky, and almost immediately the lonely dawn light crept over the land. Green appeared on the cotton plants and the earth was gray-brown. The faces of the men lost their grayish shine. Joad's face seemed to darken with the growing light. "This is the good time," Joad said softly. "When I was a kid I used to get up an' walk around by myself when it was like this. What's that ahead?"

A committee of dogs had met in the road, in honor of a bitch. Five males, shepherd mongrels, collie mongrels, dogs whose breeds had been blurred by a freedom of social life, were engaged in complimenting the bitch. For each dog sniffed daintily and then stalked to a cotton plant on stiff legs, raised a hind foot ceremoniously and wetted, then went back to smell. Joad and the preacher stopped to watch, and suddenly Joad laughed joyously. "By God!" he said. "By God!" Now all dogs met and hackles rose, and they all growled and stood stiffly, each waiting for the others to start a fight. One dog mounted and, now that it was accomplished, the others gave way and watched with interest, and their tongues were out, and their tongues dripped. The two men walked on. "By God!" Joad said. "I think that up-dog is our Flash. I thought he'd be dead. Come, Flash!" He laughed again. "What the hell, if somebody called me, I wouldn't hear him neither. 'Minds me of a story they tell about Willy Feeley when he was a young fella. Willy was bashful, awful bashful. Well, one day he takes a heifer over to Graves' bull. Ever'body was out but Elsie Graves, and Elsie wasn't bashful at all. Willy, he stood there turnin' red an' he couldn't even talk. Elsie says, 'I know what you come for; the bull's out in back a the barn.' Well, they took the heifer out there an' Willy an' Elsie sat on the fence to watch. Purty soon Willy got feelin' purty fly. Elsie looks over an' says, like she don't know, 'What's a matter, Willy?' Willy's so randy he can't hardly set still. 'By God,' he says, 'by God, I wisht I was a-doin' that!' Elsie says, 'Why not, Willy? It's your heifer.' "

The preacher laughed softly. "You know," he said, "it's a nice thing not bein' a preacher no more. Nobody use' ta tell stories when I was there, or if they did I couldn' laugh. An' I couldn' cuss. Now I cuss all I want, any time I want, an' it does a fella good to cuss if he wants to."

A redness grew up out of the eastern horizon, and on the ground birds began to chirp, sharply. "Look!" said Joad. "Right ahead. That's Uncle John's tank. Can't see the win'mill, but there's his tank. See it against the sky?" He speeded his walk. "I wonder if all the folks are there." The hulk of the tank stood above a rise. Joad, hurrying, raised a cloud of dust about his knees. "I wonder if Ma—" They saw the tank legs now, and the house, a square little box, unpainted and bare, and the barn, low-roofed and huddled. Smoke was rising from the tin chimney of the house. In the yard was a litter, piled furniture, the blades and motor of the windmill, bedsteads, chairs, tables. "Holy Christ, they're fixin' to go!" Joad said. A truck stood in the yard, a truck with high sides, but a strange truck, for while the front of it was a sedan, the top had been cut off in the middle and the truck bed fitted on. And as they drew near, the men could hear pounding from the yard, and as the rim of the blinding sun came up over the horizon, it fell on the truck, and they saw a man and the flash of his hammer as it rose and fell. And the sun flashed on the windows of the house. The weathered boards were bright. Two red chickens on the ground flamed with reflected light.

"Don't yell," said Tom. "Let's creep up on 'em, like," and he walked so fast that the dust rose as high as his waist. And then he came to the edge of the cotton field. Now they were in the yard proper, earth beaten hard, shiny hard, and a few dusty crawling weeds on the ground. And Joad slowed as though he feared to go on. The preacher, watching him, slowed to match his step. Tom sauntered forward, sidled embarrassedly toward the truck. It was a Hudson Super-Six sedan, and the top had been ripped in two with a cold chisel. Old Tom Joad stood in the truck bed and he was nailing on the top rails of the truck sides. His grizzled, bearded face was low over his work, and a bunch of six-penny nails stuck out of his mouth. He set a nail and his hammer thundered it in. From the house came the clash of a lid on the stove and the wail of a child. Joad sidled up to the truck bed and leaned against it. And his father looked at him and did not see him. His father set another nail and drove it in. A flock of pigeons started from the deck of the tank house and flew around and settled again and strutted to the edge to look over; white pigeons and blue pigeons and grays, with iridescent wings.

Joad hooked his fingers over the lowest bar of the truck side. He looked up at the aging, graying man on the truck. He wet his thick lips with his tongue, and he said softly, "Pa."

"What do you want?" old Tom mumbled around his mouthful of nails. He wore a black, dirty slouch hat and a blue work shirt over which was a buttonless vest; his jeans were held up by a wide harness-leather belt with a big square brass buckle, leather and metal polished from years of wearing; and his shoes were cracked and the soles swollen and boat-shaped from years of sun and wet and dust. The sleeves of his shirt were tight on his forearms, held down by the bulging powerful muscles.

Stomach and hips were lean, and legs, short, heavy, and strong. His face, squared by a bristling pepper and salt beard, was all drawn down to the forceful chin, a chin thrust out and built out by the stubble beard which was not so grayed on the chin, and gave weight and force to its thrust. Over old Tom's unwhiskered cheek bones the skin was as brown as meerschaum, and wrinkled in rays around his eye-corners from squinting. His eyes were brown, black-coffee brown, and he thrust his head forward when he looked at a thing, for his bright dark eyes were failing. His lips, from which the big nails protruded, were thin and red.

He held his hammer suspended in the air, about to drive a set nail, and he looked over the truck side at Tom, looked resentful at being interrupted. And then his chin drove forward and his eyes looked at Tom's face, and then gradually his brain became aware of what he saw. The hammer dropped slowly to his side, and with his left hand he took the nails from his mouth. And he said wonderingly, as though he told himself the fact, "It's Tommy—" And then, still informing himself, "It's Tommy come home." His mouth opened again, and a look of fear came into his eyes. "Tommy," he said softly, "you ain't busted out? You ain't got to hide?" He listened tensely.

"Naw," said Tom. "I'm paroled. I'm free. I got my papers." He gripped the lower bars of the truck side and looked up.

Old Tom laid his hammer gently on the floor and put his nails in his pocket. He swung his leg over the side and dropped lithely to the ground, but once beside his son he seemed embarrassed and strange. "Tommy," he said, "we are goin' to California. But we was gonna write you a letter an' tell you." And he said, incredulously, "But you're back. You can go with us. You can go!" The lid of a coffee pot slammed in the house. Old Tom looked over his shoulder. "Le's supprise 'em," he said, and his eyes shone with excitement. "Your ma got a bad feelin' she ain't never gonna see you no more. She got that quiet look like when somebody died. Almost she don't want to go to California, fear she'll never see you no more." A stove lid clashed in the house again. "Le's supprise 'em," old Tom repeated. "Le's go in like you never been away. Le's jus' see what your ma says." At last he touched Tom, but touched him on the shoulder, timidly, and instantly took his hand away. He looked at Jim Casy.

Tom said, "You remember the preacher, Pa. He come along with me."

"He been in prison too?"

"No, I met 'im on the road. He been away."

Pa shook hands gravely. "You're welcome here, sir."

Casy said, "Glad to be here. It's a thing to see when a boy comes home. It's a thing to see."

"Home," Pa said.

"To his folks," the preacher amended quickly. "We stayed at the other place last night."

Pa's chin thrust out, and he looked back down the road for a moment. Then he turned to Tom. "How'll we do her?" he began excitedly. "S'pose I go in an' say, 'Here's some fellas want some breakfast,' or how'd it be if you jus' come in an' stood there till she seen you? How'd that be?" His face was alive with excitement.

"Don't le's give her no shock," said Tom. "Don't le's scare her none."

Two rangy shepherd dogs trotted up pleasantly, until they caught the scent of strangers, and then they backed cautiously away, watchful, their tails moving slowly and tentatively in the air, but their eyes and noses quick for animosity or danger. One of them, stretching his neck, edged forward, ready to run, and little by little he approached Tom's legs and sniffed loudly at them. Then he backed away and watched Pa for some kind of signal. The other pup was not so brave. He looked about for something that could honorably divert his attention, saw a red chicken go mincing by, and ran at it. There was the squawk of an outraged hen, a burst of red feathers, and the hen ran off, flapping stubby wings for speed. The pup looked proudly back at the men, and then flopped down in the dust and beat its tail contentedly on the ground.

"Come on," said Pa, "come on in now. She got to see you. I got to see her face when she sees you. Come on. She'll yell breakfast in a minute. I heard her slap the salt pork in the pan a good time ago." He led the way across the fine-dusted ground. There was no porch on this house, just a step and then the door; a chopping block beside the door, its surface matted and soft from years of chopping. The graining in the sheathing wood was high, for the dust had cut down the softer wood. The smell of burning willow was in the air, and, as the three men neared the door, the smell of frying side-meat and the smell of high brown biscuits and the sharp smell of coffee rolling in the pot. Pa stepped up into the open doorway and stood there blocking it with his wide short body. He said, "Ma, there's a coupla fellas jus' come along the road, an' they wonder if we could spare a bite."

Tom heard his mother's voice, the remembered cool, calm drawl, friendly and humble. "Let 'em come," she said. "We got a'plenty. Tell 'em they got to wash their han's. The bread is done. I'm jus' takin' up the side-meat now." And the sizzle of the angry grease came from the stove.

Pa stepped inside, clearing the door, and Tom looked in at his mother. She was lifting the curling slices of pork from the frying pan. The oven door was open, and a great pan of high brown biscuits stood waiting there. She looked out the door, but the sun was behind Tom, and she saw only a dark figure outlined by the bright yellow sunlight. She nodded pleasantly. "Come in," she said. "Jus' lucky I made plenty bread this morning."

Tom stood looking in. Ma was heavy, but not fat; thick with child-bearing and work. She wore a loose Mother Hubbard of gray cloth in which there had once been colored flowers, but the color was washed out now, so that the small flowered pattern was only a little lighter gray than the background. The dress came down to her ankles, and her strong, broad, bare feet moved quickly and deftly over the floor. Her thin, steel-gray hair was gathered in a sparse wispy knot at the back of her head. Strong, freckled arms were bare to the elbow, and her hands were chubby and delicate, like those of a plump little girl. She looked out into the sunshine. Her full face was not soft; it was controlled, kindly. Her hazel eyes seemed to have experienced all possible tragedy and to have mounted pain and suffering like steps into a high calm and a superhuman understanding. She seemed to know, to accept, to welcome her position, the citadel of the family, the strong place that could not be taken. And since old Tom and the children could not know hurt or fear unless she acknowledged hurt and fear, she had practiced denying them in herself. And since, when a joyful thing happened, they looked to see whether joy was on her, it was her habit to build up laughter out of inadequate materials. But better than joy was calm. Imperturbability could be depended upon. And from her great and humble position in the family she had taken dignity and a clean calm beauty. From her position as healer, her hands had grown sure and cool and quiet; from her position as arbiter she had become as remote and faultless in judgment as a goddess. She seemed to know that if she swayed the family shook, and if she ever really deeply wavered or despaired the family would fall, the family will to function would be gone.

She looked out into the sunny yard, at the dark figure of a man. Pa stood near by, shaking with excitement. "Come in," he cried. "Come right in, mister." And Tom a little shamefacedly stepped over the doorsill.

She looked up pleasantly from the frying pan. And then her hand sank slowly to her side and the fork clattered to the wooden floor. Her eyes opened wide, and the pupils dilated. She breathed heavily through her open mouth. She closed her eyes. "Thank God," she said. "Oh, thank God!" And suddenly her face was worried. "Tommy, you ain't wanted? You didn' bust loose?"

"No, Ma. Parole. I got the papers here." He touched his breast.

She moved toward him lithely, soundlessly in her bare feet, and her face was full of wonder. Her small hand felt his arm, felt the soundness of his muscles. And then her fingers went up to his cheek as a blind man's fingers might. And her joy was nearly like sorrow. Tom pulled his underlip between his teeth and bit it. Her eyes went wonderingly to his bitten lip, and she saw the little line of blood against his teeth and the trickle of blood down his lip. Then she knew, and her control came back, and her hand dropped. Her breath came out explosively. "Well!" she cried. "We come mighty near to goin' without ya. An' we was wonderin' how in the worl' you could ever find us." She picked up the fork and combed the boiling grease and brought out a dark curl of crisp pork. And she set the pot of tumbling coffee on the back of the stove.

Old Tom giggled, "Fooled ya, huh, Ma? We aimed to fool ya, and we done it. Jus' stood there like a hammered sheep. Wisht Grampa'd been here to see. Looked like somebody'd beat ya between the eyes with a sledge. Grampa would a whacked 'imself so hard he'd a throwed his hip out—like he done when he seen Al take a shot at that grea' big airship the army got. Tommy, it come over one day, half a mile big, an' Al gets the thirty-thirty and blazes away at her. Grampa yells, 'Don't shoot no fledglin's, Al; wait till a growed-up one goes over,' an' then he whacked 'imself an' throwed his hip out."

Ma chuckled and took down a heap of tin plates from a shelf.

Tom asked, "Where is Grampa? I ain't seen the ol' devil."

Ma stacked the plates on the kitchen table and piled cups beside them. She said confidentially, "Oh, him an' Granma sleeps in the barn. They got to get up so much in the night. They was stumblin' over the little fellas."

Pa broke in, "Yeah, ever' night Grampa'd get mad. Tumble over Winfield, an' Winfield'd yell, an' Grampa'd get mad an' wet his drawers, an' that'd make him madder, an' purty soon ever'body in the house'd be yellin' their head off." His words tumbled out between chuckles. "Oh, we had lively times. One night when ever'body was yellin' an' a-cussin', your brother Al, he's a smart aleck now, he says, 'Goddamn it, Grampa, why don't you run off an' be a pirate?' Well, that made Grampa so goddamn mad he went for his gun. Al had ta sleep out in the fiel' that night. But now Granma an' Grampa both sleeps in the barn."

Ma said, "They can jus' get up an' step outside when they feel like it. Pa, run on out an' tell 'em Tommy's home. Grampa's a favorite of him."

"A course," said Pa. "I should of did it before." He went out the door and crossed the yard, swinging his hands high.

Tom watched him go, and then his mother's voice called his attention. She was pouring coffee. She did not look at him. "Tommy," she said hesitantly, timidly.

"Yeah?" His timidity was set off by hers, a curious embarrassment. Each one knew the other was shy, and became more shy in the knowledge.

"Tommy, I got to ask you—you ain't mad?"

"Mad, Ma?"

"You ain't poisoned mad? You don't hate nobody? They didn' do nothin' in that jail to rot you out with crazy mad?"

He looked sidewise at her, studied her, and his eyes seemed to ask how she could know such things. "No-o-o," he said. "I was for a little while. But I ain't proud like some fellas. I let stuff run off'n me. What's a matter, Ma?"

Now she was looking at him, her mouth open, as though to hear better, her eyes digging to know better. Her face looked for the answer that is always concealed in language. She said in confusion, "I knowed Purty Boy Floyd. I knowed his ma. They was good folks. He was full a hell, sure, like a good boy oughta be." She paused and then her words poured out. "I don' know all like this—but I know it. He done a little bad thing a' they hurt 'im, caught 'im an' hurt him so he was mad, an' the nex' bad thing he done was mad, an' they hurt 'im again. An' purty soon he was mean-mad. They shot at him like a varmint, an' he shot back, an' then they run him like a coyote, an' him a-snappin' an' a-snarlin', mean as a lobo. An' he was mad. He wasn't no boy or no man no more, he was jus' a walkin' chunk a mean-mad. But the folks that knowed him didn' hurt 'im. He wasn' mad at them. Finally they run him down an' killed 'im. No matter how they say it in the paper how he was bad—that's how it was." She paused and she licked her dry lips, and her whole face was an aching question. "I got to know, Tommy. Did they hurt you so much? Did they make you mad like that?"

Tom's heavy lips were pulled tight over his teeth. He looked down at his big flat hands. "No," he said. "I ain't like that." He paused and studied the broken nails, which were ridged like clam shells. "All the time in stir I kep' away from stuff like that. I ain' so mad."

She sighed, "Thank God!" under her breath.

He looked up quickly. "Ma, when I seen what they done to our house—"

She came near to him then, and stood close; and she said passionately, "Tommy, don't you go fightin' 'em alone. They'll hunt you down like a coyote. Tommy, I got to thinkin' an' dreamin' an' wonderin'. They say there's a hun'erd thousand of us shoved out. If we was all mad the same way, Tommy—they wouldn't hunt nobody down—" She stopped.

Tommy, looking at her, gradually drooped his eyelids, until just a short glitter showed through his lashes. "Many folks feel that way?" he demanded.

"I don' know. They're jus' kinda stunned. Walk aroun' like they was half asleep."

From outside and across the yard came an ancient creaking bleat. "Pu-raise Gawd fur vittory! Pu-raise Gawd fur vittory!"

Tom turned his head and grinned. "Granma finally heard I'm home. Ma," he said, "you never was like this before!"

Her face hardened and her eyes grew cold. "I never had my house pushed over," she said. "I never had my fambly stuck out on the road. I never had to sell—ever'thing—Here they come now." She moved back to the stove and dumped the big pan of bulbous biscuits on two tin plates. She shook flour into the deep grease to make gravy, and her hand was white with flour. For a moment Tom watched her, and then he went to the door.

Across the yard came four people. Grampa was ahead, a lean, ragged, quick old man, jumping with quick steps and favoring his right leg—the side that came out of joint. He was buttoning his fly as he came, and his old hands were having trouble finding the buttons, for he had buttoned the top button into the second buttonhole, and that threw the whole sequence off. He wore dark ragged pants and a torn blue shirt, open all the way down, and showing long gray underwear, also unbuttoned. His lean white chest, fuzzed with white hair, was visible through the opening in his underwear. He gave up the fly and left it open and fumbled with the underwear buttons, then gave the whole thing up and hitched his brown suspenders. His was a lean excitable face with little bright eyes as evil as a frantic child's eyes. A cantankerous, complaining, mischievous, laughing face. He fought and argued, told dirty stories. He was as lecherous as always. Vicious and cruel and impatient, like a frantic child, and the whole structure overlaid with amusement. He drank too much when he could get it, ate too much when it was there, talked too much all the time.

Behind him hobbled Granma, who had survived only because she was as mean as her husband. She had held her own with a shrill ferocious religiosity that was as lecherous and as savage as anything Grampa could offer. Once, after a meeting, while she was still speaking in tongues, she fired both barrels of a shotgun at her husband, ripping one of his buttocks nearly off, and after that he admired her and did not try to torture her as children torture bugs. As she walked she hiked her Mother Hubbard up to her knees, and she bleated her shrill terrible war cry: "Pu-raise Gawd fur vittory."

Granma and Grampa raced each other to get across the broad yard. They fought over everything, and loved and needed the fighting.

Behind them, moving slowly and evenly, but keeping up, came Pa and Noah—Noah the first-born, tall and strange, walking always with a wondering look on his face, calm and puzzled. He had never been angry in his life. He looked in wonder at angry people, wonder and uneasiness, as normal people look at the insane. Noah moved slowly, spoke seldom, and then so slowly that people who did not know him often thought him stupid. He was not stupid, but he was strange. He had little pride, no sexual urges. He worked and slept in a curious rhythm that nevertheless sufficed him. He was fond of his folks, but never showed it in any way. Although an observer could not have told why, Noah left the impression of being misshapen, his head or his body or his legs or his mind; but no misshapen member could be recalled. Pa thought he knew why Noah was strange, but Pa was ashamed, and never told. For on the night when Noah was born, Pa, frightened at the spreading thighs, alone in the house, and horrified at the screaming wretch his wife had become, went mad with apprehension. Using his hands, his strong fingers for forceps, he had pulled and twisted the baby. The midwife, arriving late, had found the baby's head pulled out of shape, its neck stretched, its body warped; and she had pushed the head back and molded the body with her hands. But Pa always remembered, and was ashamed. And he was kinder to Noah than to the others. In Noah's broad face, eyes too far apart, and long fragile jaw, Pa thought he saw the twisted, warped skull of the baby. Noah could do all that was required of him, could read and write, could work and figure, but he didn't seem to care; there was a listlessness in him toward things people wanted and needed. He lived in a strange silent house and looked out of it through calm eyes. He was a stranger to all the world, but he was not lonely.

The four came across the yard, and Grampa demanded, "Where is he? Goddamn it, where is he?" And his fingers fumbled for his pants button, and forgot and strayed into his pocket. And then he saw Tom standing in the door. Grampa stopped and he stopped the others. His little eyes glittered with malice. "Lookut him," he said. "A jailbird. Ain't been no Joads in jail for a hell of a time." His mind jumped. "Got no right to put 'im in jail. He done just what I'd do. Sons-a-bitches got no right." His mind jumped again. "An' ol' Turnbull, stinkin' skunk, braggin' how he'll shoot ya when ya come out. Says he got Hatfield blood. Well, I sent word to him. I says, 'Don't mess around with no Joad. Maybe I got McCoy blood for all I know.' I says, 'You lay your sights anywheres near Tommy an' I'll take it an' I'll ram it up your ass,' I says. Scairt 'im, too."

Granma, not following the conversation, bleated, "Pu-raise Gawd fur vittory."

Grampa walked up and slapped Tom on the chest, and his eyes grinned with affection and pride. "How are ya, Tommy?"

"O.K." said Tom. "How ya keepin' yaself?"

"Full a piss an' vinegar," said Grampa. His mind jumped. "Jus' like I said, they ain't a gonna keep no Joad in jail. I says, 'Tommy'll come a-bustin' outa that jail like a bull through a corral fence.' An' you done it. Get outa my way, I'm hungry." He crowded past, sat down, loaded his plate with pork and two big biscuits and poured the thick gravy over the whole mess, and before the others could get in, Grampa's mouth was full.

Tom grinned affectionately at him. "Ain't he a heller?" he said. And Grampa's mouth was so full that he couldn't even splutter, but his mean little eyes smiled, and he nodded his head violently.

Granma said proudly, "A wicketer, cussin'er man never lived. He's goin' to hell on a poker, praise Gawd! Wants to drive the truck!" she said spitefully. "Well, he ain't goin' ta."

Grampa choked, and a mouthful of paste sprayed into his lap, and he coughed weakly.

Granma smiled up at Tom. "Messy, ain't he?" she observed brightly.

Noah stood on the step, and he faced Tom, and his wide-set eyes seemed to look around him. His face had little expression. Tom said, "How ya, Noah?"

"Fine," said Noah. "How a' you?" That was all, but it was a comfortable thing.

Ma waved the flies away from the bowl of gravy. "We ain't got room to set down," she said. "Jus' get yaself a plate an' set down wherever ya can. Out in the yard or someplace."

Suddenly Tom said, "Hey! Where's the preacher? He was right here. Where'd he go?"

Pa said, "I seen him, but he's gone."

And Granma raised a shrill voice, "Preacher? You got a preacher? Go git him. We'll have a grace." She pointed at Grampa. "Too late for him—he's et. Go git the preacher."

Tom stepped out on the porch. "Hey, Jim! Jim Casy!" he called. He walked out in the yard. "Oh, Casy!" The preacher emerged from under the tank, sat up, and then stood up and moved toward the house. Tom asked, "What was you doin', hidin'?"

"Well, no. But a fella shouldn' butt his head in where a fambly got fambly stuff. I was jus' settin' a-thinkin'."

"Come on in an' eat," said Tom. "Granma wants a grace."

"But I ain't a preacher no more," Casy protested.

"Aw, come on. Give her a grace. Don't do you no harm, an' she likes 'em." They walked into the kitchen together.

Ma said quietly, "You're welcome."

And Pa said, "You're welcome. Have some breakfast."

"Grace fust," Granma clamored. "Grace fust."

Grampa focused his eyes fiercely until he recognized Casy. "Oh, that preacher," he said. "Oh, he's all right. I always liked him since I seen him—" He winked so lecherously that Granma thought he had spoken and retorted, "Shutup, you sinful ol' goat."

Casy ran his fingers through his hair nervously. "I got to tell you, I ain't a preacher no more. If me jus' bein' glad to be here an' bein' thankful for people that's kind and generous, if that's enough—why, I'll say that kinda grace. But I ain't a preacher no more."

"Say her," said Granma. "An' get in a word about us goin' to California." The preacher bowed his head, and the others bowed their heads. Ma folded her hands over her stomach and bowed her head. Granma bowed so low that her nose was nearly in her plate of biscuit and gravy. Tom, leaning against the wall, a plate in his hand, bowed stiffly, and Grampa bowed his head sidewise, so that he could keep one mean and merry eye on the preacher. And on the preacher's face there was a look not of prayer, but of thought; and in his tone not supplication, but conjecture.

"I been thinkin'," he said. "I been in the hills, thinkin', almost you might say like Jesus went into the wilderness to think His way out of a mess of troubles."

"Pu-raise Gawd!" Granma said, and the preacher glanced over at her in surprise.

"Seems like Jesus got all messed up with troubles, and He couldn't figure nothin' out, an' He got to feelin' what the hell good is it all, an' what's the use fightin' an' figurin'. Got tired, got good an' tired, an' His sperit all wore out. Jus' about come to the conclusion, the hell with it. An' so He went off into the wilderness."

"A—men," Granma bleated. So many years she had timed her responses to the pauses. And it was so many years since she had listened to or wondered at the words used.

"I ain't sayin' I'm like Jesus," the preacher went on. "But I got tired like Him, an' I got mixed up like Him, an' I went into the wilderness like Him, without no campin' stuff. Nighttime I'd lay on my back an' look up at the stars; morning I'd set an' watch the sun come up; midday I'd look out from a hill at the rollin' dry country; evenin' I'd foller the sun down. Sometimes I'd pray like I always done. On'y I couldn' figure what I was prayin' to or for. There was the hills, an' there was me, an' we wasn't separate no more. We was one thing. An' that one thing was holy."

"Hallelujah," said Granma, and she rocked a little, back and forth, trying to catch hold of an ecstasy.

"An' I got thinkin', on'y it wasn't thinkin', it was deeper down than thinkin'. I got thinkin' how we was holy when we was one thing, an' mankin' was holy when it was one thing. An' it on'y got unholy when one mis'able little fella got the bit in his teeth an' run off his own way, kickin' an' draggin' an' fightin'. Fella like that bust the holiness. But when they're all workin' together, not one fella for another fella, but one fella kind of harnessed to the whole shebang—that's right, that's holy. An' then I got thinkin' I don't even know what I mean by holy." He paused, but the bowed heads stayed down, for they had been trained like dogs to rise at the "amen" signal. "I can't say no grace like I use' ta say. I'm glad of the holiness of breakfast. I'm glad there's love here. That's all." The heads stayed down. The preacher looked around. "I've got your breakfast cold," he said; and then he remembered. "Amen," he said, and all the heads rose up.

"A—men," said Granma, and she fell to her breakfast, and broke down the soggy biscuits with her hard old toothless gums. Tom ate quickly, and Pa crammed his mouth. There was no talk until the food was gone, the coffee drunk; only the crunch of chewed food and the slup of coffee cooled in transit to the tongue. Ma watched the preacher as he ate, and her eyes were questioning, probing and understanding. She watched him as though he were suddenly a spirit, not human any more, a voice out of the ground.

The men finished and put down their plates, and drained the last of their coffee; and then the men went out, Pa and the preacher and Noah and Grampa and Tom, and they walked over to the truck, avoiding the litter of furniture, the wooden bedsteads, the windmill machinery, the old plow. They walked to the truck and stood beside it. They touched the new pine side-boards.

Tom opened the hood and looked at the big greasy engine. And Pa came up beside him. He said, "Your brother Al looked her over before we bought her. He says she's all right."

"What's he know? He's just a squirt," said Tom.

"He worked for a company. Drove truck last year. He knows quite a little. Smart aleck like he is. He knows. He can tinker an engine, Al can."

Tom asked, "Where's he now?"

"Well," said Pa, "he's a-billygoatin' aroun' the country. Tom-cattin' hisself to death. Smart-aleck sixteen-year-older, an' his nuts is just a-eggin' him on. He don't think of nothin' but girls and engines. A plain smart aleck. Ain't been in nights for a week."

Grampa, fumbling with his chest, had succeeded in buttoning the buttons of his blue shirt into the buttonholes of his underwear. His fingers felt that something was wrong, but did not care enough to find out. His fingers went down to try to figure out the intricacies of the buttoning of his fly. "I was worse," he said happily. "I was much worse. I was a heller, you might say. Why, they was a camp meetin' right in Sallisaw when I was a young fella a little bit older'n Al. He's just a squirt, an' punkin soft. But I was older. An' we was to this here camp meetin'. Five hundred folks there, an' a proper sprinklin' of young heifers."

"You look like a heller yet, Grampa," said Tom.

"Well, I am, kinda. But I ain't nowheres near the fella I was. Jus' let me get out to California where I can pick me an orange when I want it. Or grapes. There's a thing I ain't never had enough of. Gonna get me a whole big bunch a grapes off a bush, or whatever, an' I'm gonna squash 'em on my face an' let 'em run offen my chin."

Tom asked, "Where's Uncle John? Where's Rosasharn? Where's Ruthie an' Winfield? Nobody said nothin' about them yet."

Pa said, "Nobody asked. John gone to Sallisaw with a load a stuff to sell: pump, tools, chickens, an' all the stuff we brung over. Took Ruthie an' Winfield with 'im. Went 'fore daylight."

"Funny I never saw him," said Tom.

"Well, you come down from the highway, didn' you? He took the back way, by Cowlington. An' Rosasharn, she's nestin' with Connie's folks. By God! You don't even know Rosasharn's married to Connie Rivers. You 'member Connie. Nice young fella. An' Rosasharn's due 'bout three-four-five months now. Swellin' up right now. Looks fine."

"Jesus!" said Tom. "Rosasharn was just a little kid. An' now she's gonna have a baby. So damn much happens in four years if you're away. When ya think to start out west, Pa?"

"Well, we got to take this stuff in an' sell it. If Al gets back from his squirtin' aroun', I figgered he could load the truck an' take all of it in, an' maybe we could start out tomorra or day after. We ain't got so much money, an' a fella says it's damn near two thousan' miles to California. Quicker we get started, surer it is we get there. Money's a-dribblin' out all the time. You got any money?"

"On'y a couple dollars. How'd you get money?"

"Well," said Pa, "we sol' all the stuff at our place, an' the whole bunch of us chopped cotton, even Grampa."

"Sure did," said Grampa.

"We put ever'thing together—two hundred dollars. We give seventy-five for this here truck, an' me an' Al cut her in two an' built on this here back. Al was gonna grind the valves, but he's too busy messin' aroun' to get down to her. We'll have maybe a hunderd an' fifty when we start. Damn ol' tires on this here truck ain't gonna go far. Got a couple of wore out spares. Pick stuff up along the road, I guess."

The sun, driving straight down, stung with its rays. The shadows of the truck bed were dark bars on the ground, and the truck smelled of hot oil and oilcloth and paint. The few chickens had left the yard to hide in the tool shed from the sun. In the sty the pigs lay panting, close to the fence where a thin shadow fell, and they complained shrilly now and then. The two dogs were stretched in the red dust under the truck, panting, their dripping tongues covered with dust. Pa pulled his hat low over his eyes and squatted down on his hams. And, as though this were his natural position of thought and observation, he surveyed Tom critically, the new but aging cap, the suit, and the new shoes.

"Did you spen' your money for them clothes?" he asked. "Them clothes are jus' gonna be a nuisance to ya."

"They give 'em to me," said Tom. "When I come out they give 'em to me." He took off his cap and looked at it with some admiration, then wiped his forehead with it and put it on rakishly and pulled at the visor.

Pa observed, "Them's a nice-lookin' pair a shoes they give ya."

"Yeah," Joad agreed. "Purty for nice, but they ain't no shoes to go walkin' aroun' in on a hot day." He squatted beside his father.

Noah said slowly, "Maybe if you got them side-boards all true on, we could load up this stuff. Load her up so maybe if Al comes in—"

"I can drive her, if that's what you want," Tom said. "I drove truck at McAlester."

"Good," said Pa, and then his eyes stared down the road. "If I ain't mistaken, there's a young smart aleck draggin' his tail home right now," he said. "Looks purty wore out, too."

Tom and the preacher looked up the road. And randy Al, seeing he was being noticed, threw back his shoulders, and he came into the yard with a swaying strut like that of a rooster about to crow. Cockily, he walked close before he recognized Tom; and when he did, his boasting face changed, and admiration and veneration shone in his eyes, and his swagger fell away. His stiff jeans, with the bottoms turned up eight inches to show his heeled boots, his three-inch belt with copper figures on it, even the red arm bands on his blue shirt and the rakish angle of his Stetson hat could not build him up to his brother's stature; for his brother had killed a man, and no one would ever forget it. Al knew that even he had inspired some admiration among boys of his own age because his brother had killed a man. He had heard in Sallisaw how he was pointed out: "That's Al Joad. His brother killed a fella with a shovel."

And now Al, moving humbly near, saw that his brother was not a swaggerer as he had supposed. Al saw the dark brooding eyes of his brother, and the prison calm, the smooth hard face trained to indicate nothing to a prison guard, neither resistance nor slavishness. And instantly Al changed. Unconsciously he became like his brother, and his handsome face brooded, and his shoulders relaxed. He hadn't remembered how Tom was.

Tom said, "Hello, Al. Jesus, you're growin' like a bean! I wouldn't of knowed you."

Al, his hand ready if Tom should want to shake it, grinned self-consciously. Tom stuck out his hand and Al's hand jerked out to meet it. And there was liking between these two. "They tell me you're a good hand with a truck," said Tom.

And Al, sensing that his brother would not like a boaster, said, "I don't know nothin' much about it."

Pa said, "Been smart-alecking aroun' the country. You look wore out. Well, you got to take a load of stuff into Sallisaw to sell."

Al looked at his brother Tom. "Care to ride in?" he said as casually as he could.

"No, I can't," said Tom. "I'll help aroun' here. We'll be—together on the road."

Al tried to control his question. "Did—did you bust out? Of jail?"

"No," said Tom. "I got paroled."

"Oh." And Al was a little disappointed. 1939

CHAPTER NINE

REPRESENTATIVE MODERN AMERICAN ESSAYS

The essay as a form in modern America has become increasingly specialized; it has nevertheless not lost its vibrancy. If today we are not likely to give much thought to the essay as essay, if instead we are likely to think of it in terms of its subject matter (politics, or economics, international affairs, literature, atomic science), or of form (parody, invective, satire, imaginary dialogue, etc.), or even of format (newspaper column, book review, periodical section)—it does not thereby follow that significant essay writing is not being done. On the contrary, expository writing on affairs of the moment (literary, political, sociological) is probably more widespread than has ever been the case in the past. That the greater part of such writing is worth no more than the attention of the moment is perhaps also true. But there is and has been in modern America significant writing that is neither short story, poem, play, nor novel; writing that has a style of its own, a "voice" and technique and influence of its own; writing, in short, that in some of its parts may well prove to be as enduring a record of its time as that part of literature we too exclusively term "creative."

The ten selections here collected are designed to give a sampling of that complex and varied voice. They have little else in common with one another. They are somewhat arbitrarily organized. They follow no strict chronological progression, and their topical arrangements follow the loosest of patterns. They are all, however, with one or two exceptions, concerned with the complex subject of American literature. Even those few that are not have felicities of style or expression, of technique or of vision, or of intrinsic relation to other works of importance to American literature which make them appropriate companions to the rest.

The following section is not a selection of formal modern American literary criticism. Even though the last two or three decades of this century have often been called an age of criticism with good reason, criticism as such is not often and never necessarily literature. Consequently, there is no section of pure literary criticism in this volume, although there is literary criticism throughout it, in the letters, essays, manifestoes, diaries, speeches, proclamations, prefaces, introductions, and explications accompanying the other writings of most of modern America's major authors represented in this anthology. There is literary criticism in this section too, but only when there are also virtues of style, of humor, or of imagination. The selection, although an arbitrary one, presents a wide sampling and an appropriate introduction to the varieties of expository "literary" writing in modern America.

The first two selections, by H. L. Mencken and James Baldwin, have nothing overtly to do with the subject of American literature, although each author affected the American literature of his time in several memorable ways. Mencken, the bumptious, boisterous iconoclast, was the scourge of upholders of Victorian gentility and of any kind of entrenched orthodoxy—religious, political, moral, or literary. He set the "tone" of the second and third decades of the new century as no other one man could have. His thirty-five-year association with the Baltimore *Evening Sun*, his influential position on *The Smart Set*, his co-founding (with George Jean Nathan) of *The American Mercury*, and his many, many books provided ample platforms from which to attack the *booboisie*, his famous neologism for anyone holding a conventional or entrenched position, especially those from the so-called "Bible Belt," another of his neologisms. His platforms were also evaluations for and revolutionary encouragement to the then new writers, as diverse as Dreiser, Masters, Sandburg, O'Neill, Willa Cather, and Sinclair Lewis. His real forte was his vivid, vigorous style—a talent related to the scholarly achievement of his monumental *The American Language* (1919) which, with its various revisions and supplements, is the basic, pioneering study of our native American language. The essay here reprinted, "The Husbandman," is characteristic Mencken invective at fever pitch.

In tone and mood James Baldwin is as far removed from Mencken as one man could be from another. A talented young Harlem Negro, his fiction and essays are among the most effective of any his race has produced in America. Although caught up in the various civil rights battles of the late 1950's and early '60's and thus a vigorous spokesman for racial equality in its broadest sense, he has always been a good deal more than a polemicist. His understanding of the American mind has few contemporary parallels of whatever race. And his account of a winter in a small French village among people who had never before seen a Negro reveals that accompanying sensitivity in one of its most memorable moods. A special virtue of all of Baldwin's best writing, both fictional and expository, is its ability to leave the reader with a much more profound understanding of self than he had before he began reading. "Stranger in the Village," though its setting is far and remote, is a prime example of this special Baldwinian talent.

The two essays which follow are literary history and criticism—but with a difference. Leslie Fiedler and Lionel Trilling are two of our most controversial yet widely read literary critics. They both have produced significant fiction of their own. They both are reputable scholars and Professors of English. They are both lucid, vigorous stylists. Yet their literary criticism is not like one another's at all, as the two essays here demonstrate. Fiedler is the cantankerous, individualistic, but always sensitive and brilliant "thesis maker" about large areas of American literature. A certain belligerence of tone often puts the reader off at first—until he sees the evidence begin to fall neatly in place and discovers refutation far more difficult to make than he would have supposed. Trilling's tone is almost the exact opposite. "Sweet reasonableness" and quiet but prodigious learning are characteristic of almost all his prose. "That certainly seems to be the way it has to be," the thoughtful reader is likely to say to himself. Yet, the end result is often as sweeping, as brilliant, and as original as that produced by any modern American critic. Together they exemplify the prose of modern American criticism at its most effective.

E. B. White and Joseph Wood Krutch are birds of an entirely different feather. The two examples given here exemplify the uses of fantasy to suggest the modern significances of one nineteenth-century American worthy—the recluse of Walden Pond, Henry David Thoreau. Elwyn Brooks White, the *New Yorker's* famous essayist, is probably modern America's closest parallel to Thoreau, whose influence on White has been acknowledged by the writer many times and is, at any rate, everywhere apparent in his works. The example given here is only one of the many essays he has written on the visitor to Walden Pond. White's voice, however, is neither Thoreau's nor any other's except his own, and the wide range of subjects described by his brilliant and witty pen is probably the most inclusive among modern essayists.

Joseph Wood Krutch is an amateur naturalist. For many years he was also a Professor of Dramatic Literature at Columbia University, dramatic critic for *The Nation*, editor, scholar, and biographer of, among others, Poe, Samuel Johnson, and Thoreau. He is the author of a good history of the modern American theater. His assessment of contemporary values in *The Modern Temper* (1929), as extended and revised somewhat in *The Measure of Man* (1954), takes nothing less than the whole human condition as its subject. His imaginary dialogue between George Bernard Shaw and Thoreau would probably have pleased the participants as much at it does the reader.

James Thurber deserves a section of his own. He has probably made more modern Americans laugh than any other one writer, but he has also caused many to think. The seriousness underlying his comedy is, of course, what gives it its worth. He has an artist's understanding of American prose rhythms, and although as dexterous as any in handling what E. B. White once called "the bronco-like ability" of the English language to unseat the unwary, he has never condescended to the merely verbal frivolities so often engaged in by lesser comics. He is alternately tender and tough, but the significant absurdity rarely escapes him. Underneath it all is an intelligence of heart which sees the warm necessity for puncturing human follies. Although he has practiced parody, satire, and even invective, he is probably at his best with various kinds of fantasy, especially when illustrated with his deceptively simple line drawings. The fantasies venture into the macabre from time to time, but the startling absurdity, more often than not, is the inexplicable everyday behavior, the commonplace predicaments, of the average individual.

The last three selections are diverse examples of what has come to be known as the *New Yorker* school. To be sure, both E. B. White and Thurber have the same associations, but those two writers have somehow risen above, or at least established themselves sufficiently outside the coterie, as to have escaped the limitations of any so easily named grouping. This assertion in no way denigrates the achievement of the *New Yorker* magazine, for any disinterested examination of both the essay and humor in modern America would inevitably lead to the files of that magazine which, since its founding by Harold Ross in 1925, has exercised an influence on the humorous essay unequalled by any other American periodical. It is still one of the most viable forces in modern American literary circles, and the diversity of ways in which its humor is significant (even outside White and Thurber) is well enough demonstrated by the selections given here from the pens of Wolcott Gibbs, Leo Rosten, and Peter De Vries. These three writers have little else in common with one another, and their various deflations of different kinds of pretentiousness provide an appropriate cap to the selections which follow in this section and which, in small scope, suggest the larger scope of the essay in general in modern American literature.

H[enry] L[ouis] Mencken

(1880-1956)

Born in Baltimore and graduated from the Baltimore Polytechnic Institute in 1896, H. L. Mencken's first newspaper job was with that city's *Morning Herald*, on which he was successively reporter, city editor, and editor. In 1906 he began a thirty-five year association with the Baltimore *Evening Sun*, as foreign correspondent, editor, and columnist. His national reputation first came through his literary criticism on *The*

Smart Set which, with George Jean Nathan, he edited from 1914 to 1923, when he and Nathan left *The Smart Set* and founded *The American Mercury,* which they edited until 1933. Among his many, many books are a study of Shaw's plays (1905) and one on Nietzche's philosophy (1908). His reputation was first made with a collection of miscellaneous critical essays in *A Book of Burlesques* (1916) and *A Book of Prejudices* (1917), the latter of which continued through six series (1919-1927). His monumental *The American Language* first appeared in 1919, but was successively revised in 1921, 1923, and 1936; and Supplements appeared in 1945 and 1948. Among his significant later writings is his three-volume autobiography (1940, 1941, 1943). The best one-volume sampling of his work is probably *A Mencken Chrestomathy* (1949).

The Husbandman

Let the farmer, so far as I am concerned, be damned forevermore. To Hell with him, and bad luck to him. He is a tedious fraud and ignoramus, a cheap rogue and hypocrite, the eternal Jack of the human pack. He deserves all that he ever suffers under our economic system, and more. Any city man, not insane, who sheds tears for him is shedding tears of the crocodile.

No more grasping, selfish and dishonest mammal, indeed, is known to students of the *Anthropoidea.* When the going is good for him he robs the rest of us up to the extreme limit of our endurance; when the going is bad he comes bawling for help out of the public till. Has anyone ever heard of a farmer making any sacrifice of his own interests, however slight, to the common good? Has anyone ever heard of a farmer practising or advocating any political idea that was not alsolutely self-seeking—that was not, in fact, deliberately designed to loot the rest of us to his gain? Greenbackism, free silver, the government guarantee of prices, bonuses, all the complex fiscal imbecilities of the cow State John Baptists—these are the contributions of the virtuous husbandmen to American political theory. There has never been a time, in good seasons or bad, when his hands were not itching for more; there has never been a time when he was not ready to support any charlatan, however grotesque, who promised to get it for him. Only one issue ever fetches him, and that is the issue of his own profit. He must be promised something definite and valuable, to be paid to him alone, or he is off after some other mountebank. He simply cannot imagine himself as a citizen of a commonwealth, in duty bound to give as well as take; he can imagine himself only as getting all and giving nothing.

Yet we are asked to venerate this prehensile moron as the *Ur*-burgher, the citizen *par excellence,* the foundation-stone of the state! And why? Because he produces something that all of us must have—that we must get somehow on penalty of death. And how do we get it from him? By submitting helplessly to his unconscionable blackmailing—by paying him, not under any rule of reason, but in proportion to his roguery and incompetence, and hence to the direness of our need. I doubt that the human race, as a whole, would submit to that sort of high-jacking, year in and year out, from any other necessary class of men. But the farmers carry it on incessantly, without challenge or reprisal, and the only thing that keeps them from reducing us, at intervals, to actual famine is their own imbecile knavery. They are all willing and eager to pillage us by starving us, but they can't do it because they can't resist attempts to swindle each other. Recall, for example, the case of the cotton-growers in the South. Back in the 1920s they agreed among themselves to cut down the cotton acreage in order to inflate the price—and instantly every party to the agreement began planting *more* cotton in order to profit by the abstinence of his neighbors. That abstinence being wholly imaginary, the price of cotton fell instead of going up—and then the entire pack of scoundrels began demanding assistance from the national treasury—in brief, began demanding that the rest of us indemnify them for the failure of their plot to blackmail us.

The same demand is made sempiternally by the wheat farmers of the Middle West. It is the theory of the zanies who perform at Washington that a grower of wheat devotes himself to that banal art in a philanthropic and patriotic spirit—that he plants and harvests his crop in order that the folks of the cities may not go without bread. It is the plain fact that he raises wheat because it takes less labor than any other crop—because it enables him, after working no more than sixty days a year, to loaf the rest of the twelve months. If wheat-raising could be taken out of the hands of such lazy *fellahin* and organized as the production of iron or cement is organized, the price might be reduced by two-thirds, and still leave a large profit for *entrepreneurs*. But what would become of the farmers? Well, what rational man gives a hoot? If wheat went to $10 a bushel tomorrow, and all the workmen of the cities became slaves in name as well as in fact, no farmer in this grand land of freedom would consent voluntarily to a reduction of as much as ⅛ of a cent a bushel. "The greatest wolves," said E. W. Howe, a graduate of the farm, "are the farmers who bring produce to town to sell." Wolves? Let us not insult *Canis lupus*. I move the substitution of *Hyæna hyæna*.

Meanwhile, how much truth is in the common theory that the husbandman is harassed and looted by our economic system, that the men of the cities prey upon him—specifically, that he is the chronic victim of such devices as the tariff, railroad regulation, and the banking system? So far as I can make out, there is none whatever. The net effect of our present banking system is that the money accumulated by the cities is used to finance the farmers, and that they employ it to blackmail the cities. As for the tariff, is it a fact that it damages the farmer, or benefits him? Let us turn for light to the worst tariff act ever heard of in human history: that of 1922. It put a duty of 30 cents a bushel on wheat, and so barred out Canadian wheat, and gave the American farmer a vast and unfair advantage. For months running the difference in the price of wheat on the two sides of the American-Canadian border—wheat raised on farms not a mile apart—ran from 25 to 30 cents a bushel. Danish butter was barred out by a duty of 8 cents a pound—and the American farmer pocketed the 8 cents. Potatoes carried a duty of 50 cents a hundredweight—and the potato-growers of Maine, eager to mop up, raised such an enormous crop that the market was glutted, and they went bankrupt, and began bawling for government aid. High duties were put, too, upon meats, upon cheese, upon wool—in brief, upon practically everything that the farmer produced. But his profits were taken from him by even higher duties upon manufactured goods, and by high freight rates. Were they, indeed? There was, in fact, no duty at all upon many of the things he consumed. There was no duty, for example, upon shoes. The duty upon woolen goods gave a smaller advantage to the manufacturer than the duty on wool gave to the farmer. So with the duty on cotton goods. Automobiles were cheaper in the United States than anywhere else on earth. So were all agricultural implements. So were groceries. So were fertilizers.

But here I come to the brink of an abyss of statistics, and had better haul up. The enlightened reader is invited to investigate them for himself; they will bring him, I believe, some surprises. They by no means exhaust the case against the consecrated husbandman. I have said that the only political idea he can grasp is one which promises him a direct profit. It is, alas, not quite true: he can also grasp one which has the sole effect of annoying and damaging his enemy, the city man. The same mountebanks who get to Washington by promising to augment his gains and make good his losses devote whatever time is left over from that enterprise to saddling the rest of us with oppressive and idiotic laws, all hatched on the farm. There, where the cows low through the still night, and the jug of Peruna stands behind the stove, and bathing begins, as at Biarritz, with the vernal equinox—there is the reservoir of all the nonsensical legislation which makes the United States a buffoon among the great nations. It was among country Methodists, practitioners of a theology degraded almost to the level of voodooism, that Prohibition was invented, and it was by country Methodists, nine-tenths of them actual followers of the plow, that it was fastened upon the rest of us, to the damage of our bank accounts, our dignity and our viscera. What lay under it, and under all the other crazy enactments of its category, was no more and no less than the yokel's congenital and incurable hatred of the city man—his simian rage against everyone who, as he sees it, is having a better time than he is.

The same animus is visible in innumerable other moral statutes, all ardently supported by the peasantry. For example, the Mann Act. The aim of this amazing law, of course, is not to put down adultery; it is simply to put down that variety of adultery which is most agreeable. What got it upon the books was the constant gabble in the rural newspapers about the byzantine debaucheries of urban antinomians—rich stockbrokers who frequented Atlantic City from Friday to Monday, movie actors who traveled about the country with beautiful wenches, and so on. Such aphrodisiacal tales, read beside the kitchen-stove by hinds condemned to monogamous misery with stupid, unclean and ill-natured wives, naturally aroused in them a vast detestation of errant cockneys, and this detestation eventually rolled up enough force to attract the attention of the quacks who make laws at Washington. The result was the Mann Act. Since then a number of the cow States have passed Mann Acts of their own, usually forbidding the use of automobiles "for immoral purposes." But there is nowhere a law forbidding the use of cow-stables, hay-ricks and other such familiar rustic ateliers of sin. That is to say, there is nowhere a law forbidding yokels to drag virgins into infamy by the crude technic practised since Tertiary times on the farms; there are only laws forbidding city youths to do it according to the refined technic of the great Babylons.

Such are the sweet-smelling and altruistic agronomists whose sorrows are the *Leitmotiv* of our politics, whose welfare is alleged to be the chief end of democratic statecraft, whose patriotism is the so-called bulwark of this so-called Republic.

1924

James Baldwin

(1924-   )

Except for an extended stay in Europe, mostly in Paris, James Baldwin's major place of residence has been Harlem, in New York City, the place of his birth. His first major work of fiction was *Go Tell It on the Mountain* (1953). *Notes of a Native Son* appeared in 1955, and *Giovanni's Room* in 1956. Two works appeared in 1961, *Another Country*, a novel, and *Nobody Knows My Name: More Notes of a Native Son*. His latest book is *The Fire Next Time* (1963).

Stranger in the Village

From all available evidence no black man had ever set foot in this tiny Swiss village before I came. I was told before arriving that I would probably be a "sight" for the village; I took this to mean that people of my complexion were rarely seen in Switzerland, and also that city people are always something of a "sight" outside of the city. It did not occur to me—possibly because I am an American—that there could be people anywhere who had never seen a Negro.

It is a fact that cannot be explained on the basis of the inaccessibility of the village. The village is very high, but it is only four hours from Milan and three hours from Lausanne. It is true that it is virtually unknown. Few people making plans for a holiday would elect to come here. On the other hand, the villagers are able, presumably, to come and go as they please—which they do: to another town at the foot of the mountain, with a population of approximately five thousand, the nearest place to see a movie or go to the bank. In the village there is no movie house, no bank, no library, no theater; very few radios, one jeep, one station wagon; and, at the moment, one typewriter, mine, an invention which the woman next door to me here had never seen. There are about six hundred people living here, all Catholic—I conclude this from the fact that the Catholic church is open all year round, whereas the Protestant chapel, set off on a hill a little removed from the village, is open only in the summertime when the tourists arrive. There are four or five hotels, all closed now, and four or five *bistros,* of which, however, only two do any business during the winter. These two do not do a great deal, for life in the village seems to end around nine or ten o'clock. There are a few stores, butcher, baker, *épicerie,* a hardware store, and a money-changer—who cannot change travelers' checks, but must send them down to the bank, an operation which takes two or three days. There is something called the *Ballet Haus,* closed in the winter and used for God knows what, certainly not ballet, during the summer. There seems to be only one schoolhouse in the village, and this for the quite young children; I suppose this to mean that their older brothers and sisters at some point descend from these mountains in order to complete their education—possibly, again, to the town just below. The landscape is absolutely forbidding, mountains towering on all four sides, ice and snow as far as the eye can reach. In this white wilderness, men and women and children move all day, carrying washing, wood, buckets of milk or water, sometimes skiing on Sunday afternoons. All week long boys and young men are to be seen shoveling snow off the rooftops, or dragging wood down from the forest in sleds.

The village's only real attraction, which explains the tourist season, is the hot spring water. A disquietingly high proportion of these tourists are cripples, or semi-cripples, who come year after year—from other parts of Switzerland, usually—to take the waters. This lends the village, at the height of the season, a rather terrifying air of sanctity, as though it were a lesser Lourdes. There is often something beautiful, there is always something awful, in the spectacle of a person who has lost one of his faculties, a faculty he never questioned until it was gone, and who struggles to recover it. Yet people remain people, on crutches or indeed on deathbeds; and wherever I passed, the first summer I was here, among the native villagers or among the lame, a wind passed with me—of astonishment, curiosity, amusement, and outrage. That first summer I stayed two weeks and never intended to return. But I did return in the winter, to work; the village offers, obviously, no distractions whatever and has the further advantage of being extremely cheap. Now it is winter again, a year later, and I am here again. Everyone in the village knows my name, though they scarcely ever use it, knows that I come from America—though, this, apparently, they will never really believe: black men come from Africa—and everyone knows that I am the friend of the son of a woman who was born here, and that I am staying in their chalet. But I remain as much a stranger today as I was the first day I arrived, and the children shout *Neger! Neger!* as I walk along the streets.

It must be admitted that in the beginning I was far too shocked to have any real reaction. In so far as I reacted at all, I reacted by trying to be pleasant—it being a great part of the American Negro's education (long before he goes to school) that he must make people "like" him. This smile-and-the-world-smiles-with-you routine worked about as well in this situation as it had in the situation for which it was designed, which is to say that it did not work at all. No one, after all, can be liked whose human weight and complexity cannot be, or has not been, admitted. My smile was simply another unheard-of phenomenon which allowed them to see my teeth—they did not, really, see my smile and I began to think that, should I take to snarling, no one would notice any difference. All of the physical characteristics of the Negro which had caused me, in America, a very different and almost forgotten pain were nothing less than miraculous—or infernal—in the eyes of the village people. Some thought my hair was the color of tar, that it had the texture of wire, or the texture of cotton. It was jocularly suggested that I might let it all grow long and make myself a winter coat. If I sat in the sun for more than five minutes some daring creature was certain to come along and gingerly put his fingers on my hair, as though he were afraid of an electric shock, or put his hand on my hand, astonished that the color did not rub off. In all of this, in which it must be conceded there was the charm of genuine wonder and in which there was certainly no element of intentional unkindness, there was yet no suggestion that I was human: I was simply a living wonder.

I knew that they did not mean to be unkind, and I know it now; it is necessary, nevertheless, for me to repeat this to myself each time that I walk out of the chalet. The children who shout *Neger!* have no way of knowing the echoes this sound raises in me. They are brimming with good humor and the more daring swell with pride when I stop to speak with them. Just the same, there are days when I cannot pause and smile, when I have no heart to play with them; when, indeed, I mutter sourly to myself, exactly as I muttered on the streets of a city these children have never seen, when I was no bigger than these children are now: *Your* mother *was a nigger.* Joyce is right about history being a nightmare—but it may be the nightmare from which no one *can* awaken. People are trapped in history and history is trapped in them.

There is a custom in the village—I am told it is repeated in many villages—of "buying" African natives for the purpose of converting them to Christianity. There stands in the church all year round a small box with a slot for money, decorated with a black figurine, and into this box the villagers drop their francs. During the *carnaval* which precedes Lent, two village children have their faces blackened—out of which bloodless darkness their blue eyes shine like ice—and fantastic horsehair wigs are placed on their blond heads; thus disguised, they solicit among the villagers for money for the missionaries in Africa. Between the box in the church and the blackened children, the village "bought" last year six or eight African natives. This was reported to me with pride by the wife of one of the *bistro* owners and I was careful to express astonishment and pleasure at the solicitude shown by the village for the souls of black folk. The *bistro* owner's wife beamed with a pleasure far more genuine than my own and seemed to feel that I might now breathe more easily concerning the souls of at least six of my kinsmen.

I tried not to think of these so lately baptized kinsmen, of the price paid for them, or the peculiar price they themselves would pay, and said nothing about my father, who having taken his own conversion too literally never, at bottom, forgave the white world (which he described as heathen) for having saddled him with a Christ in whom, to judge at least from their treatment of him, they themselves no longer believed. I thought of white men arriving for the first time in an African village, strangers there, as I am a stranger here, and tried to imagine the astounded populace touching their hair and marveling at the color of their skin. But there is a great difference between being the first white man to be seen by Africans and being the first black man to be seen by whites. The white man takes the astonishment as tribute, for he arrives to conquer and to convert the natives, whose inferiority in relation to himself is not even to be questioned; whereas I, without a thought of conquest, find myself among a people whose culture controls me, has even, in a sense, created me, people who have cost me more in anguish and rage than they will ever know, who yet do not even know of my existence. The astonishment with which I might have greeted them, should they have stumbled into my African village a few hundred years ago, might have rejoiced their hearts. But the astonishment with which they greet me today can only poison mine.

And this is so despite everything I may do to feel differently, despite my friendly conversations with the *bistro* owner's wife, despite their three-year-old son who has at last become my friend, despite the *saluts* and *bonsoirs* which I exchange with people as I walk, despite the fact that I know that no individual can be taken to task for what history is doing, or has done. I say that the culture of these people controls me—but they can scarcely be held responsible for European culture. America comes out of Europe, but these people have never seen America, nor have most of them seen more of Europe than the hamlet at the foot of their mountain. Yet they move with an authority which I shall never have; and they regard me, quite rightly, not only as a stranger in their village but as a suspect latecomer, bearing no credentials, to everything they have—however unconsciously—inherited.

For this village, even were it incomparably more remote and incredibly more primitive, is the West, the West onto which I have been so strangely grafted. These people cannot be, from the point of view of power, strangers anywhere in the world; they have made the modern world, in effect, even if they do not know it. The most illiterate among them is related, in a way that I am not, to Dante, Shakespeare, Michelangelo, Aeschylus, Da Vinci, Rembrandt, and Racine; the cathedral at Chartres says something to them which it cannot say to me, as indeed would New York's Empire State Building, should anyone here ever see it. Out of their hymns and dances come Beethoven and Bach. Go back a few centuries and they are in their full glory—but I am in Africa, watching the conquerors arrive.

The rage of the disesteemed is personally fruitless, but it is also absolutely inevitable; this rage, so generally discounted, so little understood even among the people whose daily bread it is, is one of the things that makes history. Rage can only with difficulty, and never entirely, be brought under the domination of the intelligence and is therefore not susceptible to any arguments whatever. This is a fact which ordinary representatives of the *Herrenvolk*, having never felt this rage and being unable to imagine it, quite fail to understand. Also, rage cannot be hidden, it can only be dissembled. This dissembling deludes the thoughtless, and strengthens rage and adds, to rage, contempt. There are, no doubt, as many ways of coping with the resulting complex of tensions as there are black men in the world, but no black man can hope ever to be entirely liberated from this internal warfare—rage, dissembling, and contempt having inevitably accompanied his first realization of the power of white men. What is crucial here is that, since white men represent in the black man's world so heavy a weight, white men have for black men a reality which is far from being reciprocal; and hence all black men have toward all white men an attitude which is designed, really, either to rob the white man of the jewel of his naïveté, or else to make it cost him dear.

The black man insists, by whatever means he finds at his disposal, that the white man cease to regard him as an exotic rarity and recognize him as a human being. This is a very charged and difficult moment, for there is a great deal of will power involved in the white man's naïveté. Most people are not naturally reflective any more than they are naturally malicious, and the white man prefers to keep the black man at a certain human remove because it is easier for him thus to preserve his simplicity and avoid being called to account for crimes committed by his forefathers, or his neighbors. He is inescapably aware, nevertheless, that he is in a better position in the world than black men are, nor can he quite put to death the suspicion that he is hated by black men therefore. He does not wish to be hated, neither does he wish to change places, and at this point in his uneasiness he can scarcely avoid having recourse to those legends which white men have created about black men, the most usual effect of which is that the white man finds himself enmeshed, so to speak, in his own language which describes hell, as well as the attributes which lead one to hell, as being as black as night.

Every legend, moreover, contains its residuum of truth, and the root function of language is to control the universe by describing it. It is of quite considerable significance that black men remain, in the imagination, and in overwhelming numbers in fact, beyond the disciplines of salvation; and this despite the fact that the West has been "buying" African natives for centuries. There is, I should hazard, an instantaneous necessity to be divorced from this so visibly unsaved stranger, in whose heart, moreover, one cannot guess what dreams of vengeance are being nourished; and, at the same time, there are few things on earth more attractive than the idea of the unspeakable liberty which is allowed the unredeemed. When, beneath the black mask, a human being begins to make himself felt one cannot escape a certain awful wonder as to what kind of human being it is. What one's imagination makes of other people is dictated, of course, by the laws of one's own personality and it is one of the ironies of black-white relations that, by means of what the white man imagines the black man to be, the black man is enabled to know who the white man is.

I have said, for example, that I am as much a stranger in this village today as I was the first summer I arrived, but this is not quite true. The villagers wonder less about the texture of my hair than they did then, and wonder rather more about me. And the fact that their wonder now exists on another level is reflected in their attitudes and in their eyes. There are the children who make those delightful, hilarious sometimes astonishingly grave overtures of friendship in the unpredictable fashion of children; other children, having been taught that the devil is a black man, scream in genuine anguish as I approach. Some of the older women never pass without a friendly greeting, never pass, indeed, if it seems that they will be able to engage me in conversation; other women look down or look away or rather contemptuously smirk. Some of the men drink with me and suggest that I learn how to ski—partly, I gather, because they cannot imagine what I would look like on skis—and want to know if I am married, and ask questions about my *métier*. But some of the men have accused *le sale nègre*—behind my back—of stealing wood and there is already in the eyes of some of them that peculiar, intent, paranoiac malevolence which one sometimes surprises in the eyes of American white men when, out walking with their Sunday girl, they see a Negro male approach.

There is a dreadful abyss between the streets of this village and the streets of the city in which I was born, between the children who shout *Neger!* today and those who shouted *Nigger!* yesterday—the abyss is experience, the American experience. The syllable hurled behind me today expresses, above all, wonder: I am a stranger here. But I am not a stranger in America and the same syllable riding on the American air expresses the war my presence has occasioned in the American soul.

For this village brings home to me this fact: that there was a day, and not really a very distant day, when Americans were scarcely Americans at all but discontented Europeans, facing a great unconquered continent and strolling, say, into a marketplace and seeing black men for the first time. The shock this spectacle afforded is suggested, surely, by the promptness with which they decided that these black men were not really men but cattle. It is true that the necessity on the part of the settlers of the New World of reconciling their moral assumptions with the fact—and the necessity—of slavery enhanced immensely the charm of this idea, and it is also true that this idea expresses, with a truly American bluntness, the attitude which to varying extents all masters have had toward all slaves.

But between all former slaves and slave-owners and the drama which begins for Americans over three hundred years ago at Jamestown, there are at least two differences to be observed. The American Negro slave could not suppose, for one thing, as slaves in past epochs had supposed and often done, that he would ever be able to wrest the power from his master's hands. This was a supposition which the modern era, which was to bring about such vast changes in the aims and dimensions of power, put to death; it only begins, in unprecedented fashion, and with dreadful implications, to be resurrected today. But even had this supposition persisted with undiminished force, the American Negro slave could not have used it to lend his condition dignity, for the reason that this supposition rests on another: that the slave in exile yet remains related to his past, has some means—if only in memory—of revering and sustaining the forms of his former life, is able, in short, to maintain his identity.

This was not the case with the American Negro slave. He is unique among the black men of the world in that his past was taken from him, almost literally, at one blow. One wonders what on earth the first slave found to say to the first dark child he bore. I am told that there are Haitians able to trace their ancestry back to African kings, but any American Negro wishing to go back so far will find his journey through time abruptly arrested by the signature on the bill of sale which served as the entrance paper for his ancestor. At the time—to say nothing of the circumstances—of the enslavement of the captive black man who was to become the American Negro, there was not the remotest possibility that he would ever take power from his master's hands. There was no reason to suppose that his situation would ever change, nor was there, shortly, anything to indicate that his situation had ever been different. It was his necessity, in the words of E. Franklin Frazier, to find a "motive for living under American culture or die." The identity of the American Negro comes out of this extreme situation, and the evolution of this identity was a source of the most intolerable anxiety in the minds and the lives of his masters.

For the history of the American Negro is unique also in this: that the question of his humanity, and of his rights therefore as a human being, became a burning one for several generations of Americans, so burning a question that it ultimately became one of those used to divide the nation. It is out of this argument that the venom of the epithet *Nigger!* is derived. It is an argument which Europe has never had, and hence Europe quite sincerely fails to understand how or why the argument arose in the first place, why its effects are so frequently disastrous and always so unpredictable, why it refuses until today to be entirely settled. Europe's black possessions remained—and do remain—in Europe's colonies, at which remove they represented no threat whatever to European identity. If they posed any problem at all for the European conscience, it was a problem which remained comfortingly abstract: in effect, the black man, *as a man*, did not exist for Europe. But in America, even as a slave, he was an inescapable part of the general social fabric and no American could escape having an attitude toward him. Americans attempt until today to make an abstraction of the Negro, but the very nature of these abstractions reveals the tremendous effects the presence of the Negro has had on the American character.

When one considers the history of the Negro in America it is of the greatest importance to recognize that the moral beliefs of a person, or a people, are never really as tenuous as life—which is not moral—very often causes them to appear; these create for them a frame of reference and a necessary hope, the hope being that when life has done its worst they will be enabled to rise above themselves and to triumph over life. Life would scarcely be bearable if this hope did not exist. Again, even when the worst has been said, to betray a belief is not by any means to have put oneself beyond its power; the betrayal of a belief is not the same thing as ceasing to believe. If this were not so there would be no moral standards in the world at all. Yet one must also recognize that morality is based on ideas and that all ideas are dangerous—dangerous because ideas can only lead to action and where the action leads no man can say. And dangerous in this respect: that confronted with the impossibility of remaining faithful to one's beliefs, and the equal impossibility of becoming free of them, one can be driven to the most inhuman excesses. The ideas on which American beliefs are based are not, though Americans often seem to think so, ideas which originated in America. They came out of Europe. And the establishment of democracy on the American continent was scarcely as radical a break with the past as was the necessity, which Americans faced, of broadening this concept to include black men.

This was, literally, a hard necessity. It was impossible, for one thing, for Americans to abandon their beliefs, not only because these beliefs alone seemed able to justify the sacrifices they had endured and the blood that they had spilled, but also because these beliefs afforded them their only bulwark against a moral chaos as absolute as the physical chaos of the continent it was their destiny to conquer. But in the situation in which Americans found themselves, these beliefs threatened an idea which, whether or not one likes to think so, is the very warp and woof of the heritage of the West, the idea of white supremacy.

Americans have made themselves notorious by the shrillness and the brutality with which they have insisted on this idea, but they did not invent it; and it has escaped the world's notice that those very excesses of which Americans have been guilty imply a certain, unprecedented uneasiness over the idea's life and power, if not, indeed, the idea's validity. The idea of white supremacy rests simply on the fact that white men are the creators of civilization (the present civilization, which is the only one that matters; all previous civilizations are simply "contributions" to our own) and are therefore civilization's guardians and defenders. Thus it was impossible for Americans to accept the black man as one of themselves, for to do so was to jeopardize their status as white men. But not so to accept him was to deny his human reality, his human weight and complexity, and the strain of denying the overwhelmingly undeniable forced Americans into rationalizations so fantastic that they approached the pathological.

At the root of the American Negro problem is the necessity of the American white man to find a way of living with the Negro in order to be able to live with himself. And the history of this problem can be reduced to the means used by Americans—lynch law and law, segregation and legal acceptance, terrorization and concession—either to come to terms with this necessity, or to find a way around it, or (most usually) to find a way of doing both these things at once. The resulting spectacle, at once foolish and dreadful, led someone to make the quite accurate observation that "the Negro-in-America is a form of insanity which overtakes white men."

In this long battle, a battle by no means finished, the unforeseeable effects of which will be felt by many future generations, the white man's motive was the protection of his identity; the black man was motivated by the need to establish an identity. And despite the terrorization which the Negro in America endured and endures sporadically until today, despite the cruel and totally inescapable ambivalence of his status in his country, the battle for his identity has long ago been won. He is not a visitor to the West, but a citizen there, an American; as American as the Americans who despise him, the Americans who fear him, the Americans who love him—the Americans who became less than themselves, or rose to be greater than themselves by virtue of the fact that the challenge he represented was inescapable. He is perhaps the only black man in the world whose relationship to white men is more terrible, more subtle, and more meaningful than the relationship of bitter possessed to uncertain possessor. His survival depended, and his development depends, on his ability to turn his peculiar status in the Western world to his own advantage and, it may be, to the very great advantage of that world. It remains for him to fashion out of his experience that which will give him sustenance, and a voice.

The cathedral at Chartres, I have said, says something to the people of this village which it cannot say to me; but it is important to understand that this cathedral says something to me which it cannot say to them. Perhaps they are struck by the power of the spires, the glory of the windows; but they have known God, after all, longer than I have known him, and in a different way, and I am terrified by the slippery bottomless well to be found in the crypt, down which heretics were hurled to death, and by the obscene, inescapable gargoyles jutting out of the stone and seeming to say that God and the devil can never be divorced. I doubt that the villagers think of the devil when they face a cathedral because they have never been identified with the devil. But I must accept the status which myth, if nothing else, gives me in the West before I can hope to change the myth.

Yet, if the American Negro has arrived at his identity by virtue of the absoluteness of his estrangement from his past, American white men still nourish the illusion that there is some means of recovering the European innocence, of returning to a state in which black men do not exist. This is one of the greatest errors Americans can make. The identity they fought so hard to protect has, by virtue of that battle, undergone a change: Americans are as unlike any other white people in the world as it is possible to be. I do not think, for example, that it is too much to suggest that the American vision of the world—which allows so little reality, generally speaking, for any of the darker forces in human life, which tends until today to paint moral issues in glaring black and white —owes a great deal to the battle waged by Americans to maintain between themselves and black men a human separation which could not be bridged. It is only now beginning to be borne in on us—very faintly, it must be admitted, very slowly, and very much against our will—that this vision of the world is dangerously inaccurate, and perfectly useless. For it protects our moral high-mindedness at the terrible expense of weakening our grasp of reality. People who shut their eyes to reality simply invite their own destruction, and anyone who insists on remaining in a state of innocence long after that innocence is dead turns himself into a monster.

The time has come to realize that the interracial drama acted out on the American continent has not only created a new black man, it has created a new white man, too. No road whatever will lead Americans back to the simplicity of this European village where white men still have the luxury of looking on me as a stranger. I am not, really, a stranger any longer for any American alive. One of the things that distinguishes Americans from other people is that no other people has ever been so deeply involved in the lives of black men, and vice versa. This fact faced, with all its implications, it can be seen that the history of the American Negro problem is not merely shameful, it is also something of an achievement. For even when the worst has been said, it must also be added that the perpetual challenge posed by this problem was always, somehow, perpetually met. It is precisely this black-white experience which may prove of indispensable value to us in the world we face today. This world is white no longer, and it will never be white again.

1953

Leslie Fiedler

(1917-)

Leslie Fielder was associated with the English Department of Montana State University for many years, although he was born in Newark, New Jersey. He is now a Professor of English at the State University of New York, Buffalo. His first book, *An End to Innocence* (1955), included essays on Whittaker Chambers, Alger Hiss, and Senator McCarthy, in addition to literary studies, including the much discussed "Come Back to the Raft Ag'in, Huck Honey!" *Love and Death in the American Novel* appeared in 1959, and the essays of *No! In Thunder* in 1960. His two most recent books include a collection of short stories, *Pull Down Vanity and Other Stories* (1962), and a novel, *The Second Stone* (1963).

No! In Thunder

That the practice of any art at any time is essentially a moral activity I have always believed; indeed, I do not know how to begin to make a book or talk about one without moral commitment. Yet for a long time I tried to keep this secret from myself as well as from others, since in the critical world in which I grew up, a "moralistic approach" to literature was considered not only indecent but faintly comic. Most of my best literary friends, at any rate, considered it strategically advisable to speak of novels and poems *purely* (the adverb is theirs) in terms of diction, structure and point of view, remaining safely inside the realm of the formal. But an author's choice of—or a critic's preference for—one point of view, or type of diction, or kind of structure, or even his emphasis on one of these elements at the expense of the others, involves a judgment of the experience he is rendering; and such a judgment is, implicitly at least, a moral one.

One of the special strengths of modern fiction has been its awareness of the moral dimension of form; and the seminal greatness of Flaubert lies in his willingness to entrust judgment primarily to style: to transform style, in effect, from a social grace to a tool of ethical analysis. The author of *Madame Bovary* seldom comments directly on the social concerns which most deeply vex him; he has, indeed, an almost fanatic resolve *not* to admonish or preach, but his style is his surrogate in this regard. And his style judges—judges Emma and Homais, the clichés of Romanticism and Revolution, the formlessness and falsity of bourgeois life. By the same token, that style judges and condemns, as all serious style continues to judge and condemn, the literature of the market place and those misguided books dedicated to anti-style.

There are, of course, certain counterfeits of style, quite unlike Flaubert's, which are symptoms of the decay of their world rather than judgments of it; for there can be no neutrality in the area of technique. The form of a book represents either a moral critique of man and society, or a moral surrender. The pseudo-styles—which are called, a little misleadingly, "naturalist" and which have been practiced from the time of Émile Zola to that of James Jones—have represented such capitulations before the collapse of discrimination and sensitivity in the world around them; even as earlier Scott's manly carelessness and Dickens' hasty improvisations represented a retreat from moral engagement, and the ecstatic schoolgirl anti-style of Jack Kerouac projects a more recent sort of cowardice. Such writers as Zola, Jones and Kerouac are guilty not only of moral weakness but of hypocrisy as well, for they proffer their sloppiness and their submission to the decay of language as tokens of their sincerity and belongingness. To seem "one of the boys" is especially an American temptation, eternally offered and eternally accepted. But it is not only the principled anti-stylists, populist or Beat, who stand condemned in the court of high art for flagrant immorality, an immorality of form which all their avowed (and guilt-compelled) dedication to quite moral ideas and causes cannot mitigate. Those responsible for books like *Exodus,* or *Advise and Consent,* or whatever improbable contender is currently fighting its way up the best-seller lists, must also be adjudged guilty; since ignorance is no excuse, and good will merely aggravates the crime.

In the realm of fiction, to be inept, whether unwittingly or on purpose, is the single unforgivable sin. To be inept is to lie; and for this, time and the critics grant no pardon. Yet the contemporary audience forgives the liar in art, even adulates him. It knows he is lying, but it needs his lies. In our Do-It-Yourself Age, when no one can really do anything for himself unless provided a kit and instructions, men are plagued by the failure of self-deceit itself, afflicted with a fatal incapacity to believe themselves happy. If happiness is, as Swift insisted, the faculty of being well-deceived, most men can no longer achieve it on their own. They must be lied to every day, and they are willing to pay well for the service.

Our culture is organized around the satisfaction of this demand, and the moral artist, who is the truthteller, is subject (not invariably, but with distressing frequency) to one of two indignities, the first of which is called success, the second failure. Either he is admired, like Faulkner, for the wrong reasons: bought and unread because he is a living "classic" (in the United States, everything is speeded up to a bewildering tempo), his works posthumous before he is laid in the grave; or he is even more enthusiastically bought and *mis*read—like Pasternak, whose *Doctor Zhivago* became the very symbol of being one up on the Russians, or like Nabokov and D. H. Lawrence, the happy authors of once-banned books! Or the moral artist may be condemned out of hand, like Pasternak in Russia or Lawrence in the United States (until only the other day).

The customary charge leveled at the serious writer, until he is ripe for the even more deadly one of being a classic, is that of having written a dirty book. The Russians apparently believe this of all successful American writers who do not sympathize with Soviet objectives; but ironically, the charge is also believed in America of many of the same authors. It is, indeed, part of what has almost assumed the status of a ritual—the standard initiation of the truthteller into the culture of his country, inflicted at the moment when his truth still hurts. One is not startled, perhaps, to discover that Walt Whitman was once called "the dirtiest beast of the age," but it is a little disconcerting to learn that Hawthorne's *The Scarlet Letter* was accused of representing "the beginning of the era of French immorality" in American letters.

Yet it will not do to ignore the difference in the level of hysteria with which such charges were leveled at serious art one hundred years ago and that with which they were made of the first great books in the "modern" tradition at the point when the first of the Great Wars was about to begin. Whatever offense great art has always given and given with particular effect in America seems to have been compounded when, in what is still called, after nearly fifty years, "modern art," that offense was confessed in nonconventional form. Apparently the common man can more easily forgive an attack on home and mother than a flagrant disregard for harmony, or punctuation, or representation. Perhaps it is simply because technical offenses are less easy to overlook or to cancel out by misreading.

I have a clear memory of myself at fourteen or fifteen, struggling for an education in the public libraries of Newark, New Jersey, and having to fight to get Joyce's *A Portrait of the Artist as a Young Man* out of a locked room where it was kept with other dangerous material. Proust's *Remembrance of Things Past* was on the open shelves, but it was no easy matter to get it past the vigilance of a certain librarian who, in her spare time, went through the photography magazines stamping all female nudes three times with the official library stamp (to keep, I suppose, the minds of adolescents pure) and who regarded me as a special challenge. This experience has always seemed to me an archetypal one, my personal myth of The Intellectual Life as Moral Combat; for certainly (to a temperament for which, and in a time when, struggle seemed as necessary as eating) the library became for me an arena in which my morality was pitted against theirs in a war to end all wars! It was not dirty books I was after, I wanted to protest; it was. . . . But I did not know how to explain what it was I sought.

Only a long time afterward did I realize that I had been completely misled by the rationalizations of the guardians of the library, that it was not really the "dirtiness," the frank sexuality, of certain novels that irked the censors, but something quite different. Best sellers—in our country at least—have always been books which exploit sex as far as (and a little farther than) contemporary taboos will permit. From *The Monks of Monk Hall* to *Peyton Place* or the latest paperback by Richard S. Prather, the really popular book has talked of sex on the level of broad suggestion; it has spoken the last common language bearing on the last link (as Moravia has argued) between us and the world of nature. It seems to me now that what must be insisted upon is that even a good book can be a popular success if it can be thought of as dirty, like Nabokov's *Lolita* and Faulkner's *Sanctuary*.

No, the problem of the nonacceptance of serious fiction lies elsewhere: in the fact that *to fulfill its essential moral obligation, such fiction must be negative.* There is a dim sense of this in the popular mind, reflected in the over-the-bridge-table charge that certain great books, whatever their merits, are too "morbid" and responded to by the publishers' defensive assurances on the book jackets: "But beneath the shattering events of that book . . . lies a passionate affirmation" or "This is a book of great themes, of life, death and regeneration, of the dignity and triumph of man." Like the more particular religious reassurances of another age, these vaguely pious assertions are rooted in a profound distrust of art itself; and before them I am moved to resentment and anger. I can never read one without remembering a favorite anecdote of my old teacher, William Ellery Leonard, about how, one night in an inn, he had to share a bed with a man whom he had never met before. He felt no qualms until his bedmate kneeled down beside the bed to pray. "At that point," he liked to say, "I grabbed my wallet and ran!" So I before the book whose jacket assures me that the author is committed to affirmation, or love, or a belief in the dignity of man.

Insofar as a work of art is, as art, successful, it performs a negative critical function; for the irony of art in the human situation lies in this: that man—or better, some men—are capable of achieving in works of art a coherence, a unity, a balance, a satisfaction of conflicting impulses which they cannot (but which they desperately long to) achieve in love, family relations, politics. Yet works of art are *about* love, family relations, politics, etc.; and to the degree that these radically imperfect human activities are represented in a perfectly articulated form, they are revealed in all their intolerable inadequacy. The image of man in art, however magnificently portrayed—indeed, precisely when it is most magnificently portrayed—is the image of a failure. There is no way out.

The self-conscious writer, realizing this irony, feels a demand to make explicit the essentially negative view of man implicit in his work insofar as it is art at all. He is driven to make his avowed attitudes and allegiances congruous with the meaning that his techniques cannot help declaring. Especially in recent times, when the obligations of self-consciousness are imposed on us with a rigor unheard of in the past, the writer becomes aware that his Muse is more like the *Daimon* of Socrates (who appeared only to say *No!*) or the God of Job than like any of those white-draped Ladies of the genteel mythologists. The spirit which speaks to him conveys no reassurances or positive revelations; only the terrible message that what his best friends—in newspaper offices, or the pulpit, or Congress—have been, like Job's, telling him is "the thing which is not right." And that spirit addresses him from the whirlwind, directing his attention from himself to those absurd beasts, the Behemoth and the Leviathan.

Demonic, terrible and negative: this is the Modern Muse—"Bluff'd not a bit by drain-pipe, gasometers, artificial fertilizers," as Walt Whitman had the wit to see; but in his euphoric, comic vision the sense of terror is dissipated. It is to such a writer as James Joyce (who chose for his slogan the device of Satan himself: *Non serviam,* "I will not obey!") or to Henrik Ibsen (whose final words were "On the contrary . . .") or to Whitman's contemporary, Herman Melville, that we must turn for the decisive clue. The secret motto of *Moby Dick* was, Melville once confided: "I baptize you not in the name of the Father, the Son and the Holy Ghost, but in the name of the Devil." Even better, perhaps, because less theatrically gothic, is the phrase Melville attributes to Bartleby the Scrivener, his portrait of the writer in the modern world—a phrase in which there is already implicit Bartleby's insanity and death: "I would prefer not to." Most explicit of all is the comment in a letter to Hawthorne, in which Melville pretends to describe the essence of his beloved contemporary's art, while in fact revealing the deepest sources of his own:

> There is the grand truth about Nathaniel Hawthorne. He says No! in thunder; but the Devil himself cannot make him say *yes.* For all men who say *yes,* lie; and all men who say *no*—why, they are in the happy condition of judicious, unincumbered travellers in Europe; they cross the frontiers into Eternity with nothing but a carpetbag,—that is to say, the Ego.

It pays to be clear about the nature of the "No! in thunder," which is quite different from certain lesser *no's* in which a thriving trade is always done: the *no* in newsprint, for instance, and the *no* on manifestoes and petitions. A play written in the 1950s about the Salem witch trials, or a novel of the same period celebrating the revolt of the Maccabees, despite their allegorical intentions, are cheats, exploitations of the pseudo-*no.* Even the attack on slavery in Twain's post-Civil War *Huckleberry Finn*—or, for that matter, in Mrs. Stowe's pre-Civil War *Uncle Tom's Cabin*—like an anti-McCarthyite fiction in the recent past or an excoriation of segregation right now, carry with them a certain air of presumptive self-satisfaction, an assurance of being justified by the future. They are Easy No's, merely disguised *yes's,* in varying degrees sentimental and righteous; they are *yes's* by anticipation, tomorrow's *yes's.* The "No! in thunder" remains a *no* forever; like the *no* implicit in the whole work of the Marquis de Sade, or the deeper *no* of *Huckleberry Finn*—Huck's *no* to womankind, the family and organized society, which remains to this very day a *no.*

The "No! in thunder" is never partisan; it infuriates Our Side as well as Theirs, reveals that all Sides are one, insofar as they are all yea-sayers and hence all liars. There is some evidence that the Hard No is being spoken when the writer seems a traitor to those whom he loves and who have conditioned his very way of responding to the world. When the writer says of precisely the cause that is dearest to him what is always and everywhere the truth about all causes—that it has been imperfectly conceived and inadequately represented, and that it is bound to be betrayed, consciously or unconsciously, by its leading spokesmen—we know that he is approaching an art of real seriousness if not of actual greatness. The thrill we all sense but hesitate to define for ourselves—the thrill of confronting a commitment to truth which transcends all partial allegiances—comes when Dante turns on Florence, Molière on the moderate man, de Sade on reason, Shaw on the socialists, Tolstoy on the reformers, Joyce on Ireland, Faulkner on the South, Graham Greene on the Catholics, Pasternak on the Russians and Abraham Cahan or Nathanael West on the Jews. What people, what party, what church needs an enemy when it has a great writer in its ranks?

Unless he bites the hand that feeds him, the writer cannot live; and this those who would prefer him dead (so they can erect statues of him) can never understand. I remember Faulkner's coming once, rather improbably, to Missoula, Montana, and getting engaged in conversation with a lady Montanan, who cried out at one point, "Why can't So-and-so write a novel that would do for this part of the world what you've done for Mississippi? He *loves* Montana so!" To which Faulkner, of course, answered (maybe I only dreamed it; it all seems so pat), "To write well about some place, you've got to *hate* it." A pause, and then, "The way a man hates his own wife." But this is scandalous in a way with which the righteous cannot seem to come to terms. Not only the Great Audience but also, and even especially, the Little Elite Audiences demand of the writer its disavowal in the name of a kind of loyalty which is for him death. The first attack on me as a critic ever to appear was launched because I had made some rather drastic qualifying remarks about, I think, Thomas Mann—a small god, at any rate, of the avant-garde church to which I was presumably applying for admission. "Aid and comfort to the enemy" was the implicit charge; but this charge the sayer of the Hard No must be willing to face; for he knows that the writer who rejects the negative obligation perishes even as he pleases, perishes though he please only a handful of the very best people—those, for instance, whom he has begun by admiring and whom he never ceases to admire.

It has not always been necessary for the writer to be aware of his denial; his work will do it for him anyhow, if it is honest work. Indeed, at certain periods in the past, it seemed almost better that the writer deceive himself as well as his contemporary audience about his intent: that Dickens, for example, believe himself to be glorifying the purity of woman and the simple heart of the child, while giving us in fact his mad, black-and-white nightmares, in which things live the life of men, and men perform with the lifeless rigidity of things. In the same way, Dostoevsky could think himself the apostle of a revived orthodoxy, and Samuel Richardson considered his essential task the defense of bourgeois virtue. But these days the writer cannot afford to lose for an instant his sense of himself in opposition to the world; let him pretend, however briefly, that his *no* is a *yes,* and he will end up writing *A Fable* or *The Town,* travesties of his own best work.

Naturally, not all writers in our time accept the negative obligation; and, indeed, its rejection separates the purveyor of commodity-fiction from the serious artist in the novel. There are certain pseudo-novels which are, in fact, transitional stages on the way to becoming movies or substitutes for going to the movies; and these books are obliged to be cheerful, positive, affirmative: to sustain the belief in endurance, piety, hard work and a deliberately maintained, blessed stupidity. Here is the giveaway! Nothing can, after all, be wholly positive; and even the most affirmative of subnovels (say, *Marjorie Morningstar*) must end by denying something: dirt, disorder, eccentricity, non-conformism, skepticism, intelligence—in short, the negative obligation itself! Conversely, the nay-saying writer is not wholly negative; he is in favor of one thing by definition: telling the truth (*Madame Bovary* will do as the counterexample) and accepting the tragic implications of that truth, the vision of an eternal gap between imagined order and actual chaos.

But it is not enough, in our time, for the serious writer to confess *in general* the inevitable discrepancy between dream and fact, between the best man can imagine and the best he can achieve. The artist must be willing specifically to comment on the defeat of a particular dream. The anti-artist, on the other hand, incurs only the most general obligation; despite the particulars in which he apparently deals, he is in fact composing parables, pseudo-myths, to express not wonder and terror but sentimental reassurance. What life refuses, the anti-artist grants: the dying catcher hits a three bagger, and everyone loves him; the coward, at the last moment, finds the courage to fight the segregationist and his hired thugs; the girl in the office takes off her glasses and wins the heart of the boss's playboy son. That these are prefabricated, masturbatory dreams almost everyone (including, I suspect, the authors) would be prepared to admit, yet they do not stir in most of us the moral indignation we feel at the distribution of other habit-forming drugs.They seem more benign than marijuana, which is banned, or tranquilizers, which may soon be sharply regulated; because we accept the fantasies they promote as finally truer than those born of "pot" or happiness pills. Assuring us that man is OK, that men are OK, that we are all—despite our mistakes and the machinations of others—OK, they feed into (at least they do not contradict) the last widely held *Weltanschauung* of the West: the progressive and optimistic, rational and kindly dogma of liberal humanism.

Yet, as some of us are rather disturbedly aware, many if not most of the eminent writers of the twentieth century have found themselves in conflict with this dogma, not always *despite* its nobility, but often because of it. The fact that such otherwise ill-assorted writers as Shaw, Joyce, Faulkner, Yeats, Pound, Eliot, Wyndham Lewis and Samuel Beckett are arrayed against the liberal tradition indicates that it represents for our age the belief against which the serious artist must define himself, the official "Yea!" to which he must say his private "Nay!" As earlier poets had to say "Nay!" to the fifth-century Greeks' belief that their world was really explicable in terms of the Homeric gods, or the Christians' assumption that their society was Christian, or the Enlightenment's conviction that its passion and politics were finally rational, so the artist today must deny the liberal view of the possibilities of man. But liberalism is essentially different from earlier official faiths, religious or secular, in that its ideal is "openness" rather than orthodoxy; and the writer striving toward the Hard No is likely to discover that his most ardent denial is met with a disconcerting "Yes, yes, though all the same . . ." or "I don't finally agree with you, of course, but still . . ."

Nietzsche's assertion that God is dead once shook half the world, and Ibsen's attack on marriage left northern Europe trembling, but they find us merely confused or indifferent—or, as we say when confusion and indifference reach their highest pitch, "tolerant." Only an assault on tolerance itself is able to stir us as Goethe's assault on the ban against suicide once stirred his readers. The very advocacy of adultery, which from the time of the troubadours to that of D. H. Lawrence possessed an almost magic potency to provoke, has now become fashionable and meaningless. The recent redemption of *Lady Chatterley's Lover* in the courts represents not a triumph of literary taste over taboo but a failure of the moral imagination; and Lillian Smith can suggest in her novel *One Hour*, an essentially middlebrow book, that an Episcopalian priest's moment of vision and truth comes when he is in bed with his friend's wife. Who can *épater la bourgeoisie* when the bourgeoisie regards even the grossest scandal as a test of its capacity for understanding and forgiveness?

Yet there is finally a liberal view of man, to deny which is to risk blasphemy: an image of the human situation which persists very like a dogma beneath the undogmatic "openness" of which contemporary society is so proud. This view sees man as the product of a perhaps unplanned but rationally ordered and rationally explicable universe, a product which science can explain, even as it can explain the world which conditions him. The first fictionists who accepted this view of man thought of themselves as protoscientists and of their books as scientific reports on how vice and virtue are produced in the great laboratory of society. Such books, with their blend of rationalism, determinism and quasi-scientific objectivity, were variously hailed when they appeared as examples of Realism, Naturalism, Verism, etc.; and whatever the inadequacy of their styles, they performed in the beginning the essential function of art, the negative one of provocation and scandal. Novelists like Zola and de

Maupassant—in America, even so belated a representative of the school as Dreiser—horrified the genteel by exposing the self-delusions of sentimental Christianity. They soon fell victim to the fallacy of imitative form (realism-naturalism did not *have* to eschew style, as the example of Flaubert should have made clear) and profferred anti-style as evidence of their honesty. But even their very bad writing served temporarily a good cause, exposing the pretensions of academic rhetoric.

Purveyors of the old realistic article still circulate among us (James T. Farrell, for instance, and Nelson Algren), but they tell no truths that are not clichés, and they give no valuable offense. Indeed, they have become indistinguishable from the producers of chic Italian movies and from TV entertainers like Paddy Chayefsky—second-rate artists, purveyors of the scandal of the day before yesterday. The day is gone when the tradition of realism-naturalism was so deeply accepted as *the* mode of serious literature that a mannered and artificial stylist like Hemingway, or an exploiter of backwoods rhetoric and gothic nightmare like Faulkner, had to pretend to be a "naturalist" in order to seem respectable. In the first place, realism-naturalism has become an academy itself, sustaining a triumphant orthodoxy instead of challenging one; and meanwhile, certain contraband, smuggled into the presumably objective laboratory report from the beginning, has come to seem more and more essential: political propaganda, heavy-handed symbolism, righteous pornography and sentimentality.

The latter two especially have assumed a disheartening importance in the standard subforms of post-realism, first clearly defined in the United States in the 1930s: the Popular Front Novel, on the one hand, and Regionalist or Protest Pornography on the other. John Steinbeck is the father of the first, having established in *The Grapes of Wrath* the prototype of the pious tract disguised as a sociological report, in which the cruel exploiters of labor are contrasted with simple and kindly men who give candy to children, and women of the people who offer their swollen breasts to the starving unemployed. Erskine Caldwell is the founder of the other, having created in *Tobacco Road* a genre capable of providing all the forbidden thrills of a peep show together with the conscientious satisfactions of deploring the state of the (more exotic) poor. It is hard to remember that Caldwell was considered a serious "proletarian" writer before he became a paperback best seller; one reads with surprise the accounts of his current reception in places like Turkey, where he is still regarded as a pattern for "village literature." In this country, his example has occasioned lately only such bootleg high-school literature as Grace Metalious' *Peyton Place.*

Steinbeck's prototype, however, continues to provide inspiration for the prevailing upper middlebrow form of our time: the serious pseudo-novel as practiced by certain not-quite-first-rate authors, committed equally to social conscience and success, and sure that these are not mutually exclusive goals. There is scarcely a moment these days when such authors of the Sentimental Liberal Protest Novel as Irwin Shaw, John Hersey, Budd Schulberg and James Michener are not fighting for slots on the list of best sellers; since in our time left-of-center politics has become, by virtue of converting all its political content to sentiment, the reigning belief of the educated middle classes. In our genteel age, the class struggle has been translated from a confrontation of workers and bosses on the barricades to a contest between certain invisible or remote exploiters and all the rest of us—a contest in which more tears are shed than blood. The writer dedicated to portraying that struggle is no longer the man in the work shirt rolled to the elbow and open at the neck, but the man ashamed of his gray flannel suit—the searcher out and defender of Victims. For the image of man which possesses the genteel conscience is the image of the Victim: the snubbed Jew, the oppressed Negro, the starving Chinese, the atom-scarred Japanese, the betrayed Hungarian, the misunderstood paraplegic. For each Victim there is an appropriate book, a last indignity: *Gentlemen's Agreement, The Wall, The Bridge at Andau, The Last Pebble, One Hour*. Even the War Novel is recast in the prevailing form, captured, like *The Young Lions,* for piety, protest, and self-pity. In the end, we are left with the sense that wars are fought and armies organized (in representative platoons, with all minorities duly represented) so that the persecuted Jew or tormented Italian can shame his fellows by proving his unforeseen valor in the end.

Having only a single theme, of a rather simple-minded sort, the Sentimental Protestors are driven to eke it out, to conceal its stereotypical bareness with up-to-date details and topical references. Their eyes are constantly on the headlines; and before the ink is dry, Michener and Hersey are already embarked for the scene of the latest indignity—or at least racing for their typewriters! It is a somewhat comic contest, with the whole reading world breathlessly waiting to discover who will get Little Rock first, who the Puerto Ricans. But what is the ersatz morality which sustains the protest fictionists, from Hersey-Shaw to Jones-Algren, from the soft-sell defenders of the dark-skinned peoples to the tough apologists for maximum security prisoners and minor hoods? It is the theory that the "Little Man" must be defended against the great and powerful merely because he is little and "wants only to be let alone." Little! Surely no more degrading label has ever been invented for the exploited, none which has so combined pathos and condescension: the little Jew, the little shopkeeper, the little mixed-up kid, the bewildered little pusher of dope, the little pimp trying to establish himself against the competition of the big operators. . . . Against so abject a surrender to sentiment, one wants to cry out in the terrible words of the Old Testament, "Thou shalt not honor the poor man in his cause." But who could be heard over the voices of those storming their book counters for copies of *Exodus* and *Hawaii*?

What, then, of serious literature in our time? What counter-image of man does it proffer? Not, as so often in the past, an image of man struggling (and failing) to fulfill some revealed or inherited view of himself and his destiny; but of man learning that it is the struggle itself which is his definition. In a time when answers are the business of professional answer men (cheats and delusions carefully rehearsed before the show is put on the air), we have been forced to learn that our humanity is dependent not on the answers we hope for but on the questions we are able to ask. Like Job, we are granted no response except from the apparition which tells us it is time to be still, time to know that man is he who asks what man is. And like Melville's "unincumbered travellers," we must be prepared to leave our Encyclopedia Britannicas and Oxford English Dictionaries behind us, to cross the frontiers of Eternity with no baggage except the Ego. This the most serious writers of our day have taught us, insisting that we endure uncertainty, not as a stage on the way to knowledge, but as our essential condition. Now we see as through a glass darkly. There is no "then."

This view of man opens into a world not of melodrama but of ambiguity, not of the polemical but of the problematical. Saul Bellow's *The Victim*, for instance, will survive *Focus, Gentlemen's Agreement, The Professor's Umbrella* and all the other earnest and humane tracts on anti-Semitism because, despite its title, it is not a protest novel at all. In Bellow's view, both Jew and gentile are simultaneously Victim and Victimizer; he renders their mutual torment in terms of their common desire to discover what it means to be human, their common need to *be* what is human. Our Jewishness or gentileness, Bellow leaves us feeling, is *given;* our humanity is what we must achieve. There is no more room for sentimentality in such a travesty of the liberal Jewish novel than there is in Robert Penn Warren's similar recasting of the political novel, or Malamud's of the novel about baseball, or James Baldwin's of the standard Negro novel, or Mary McCarthy's of fictional protests against the restriction of academic freedom. Reading, say, *All the King's Men,* one need only think of *The Last Hurrah* or *Advise and Consent*—or picking up *The Natural,* one need only recall Mark Harris' *Bang the Drum Slowly*—to realize how we ordinarily lust to be lied to, and how seldom we are granted the privilege of hearing the truth.

Ambiguity is the first resource of the serious novelist, tempted like all the rest of us to clichés of simplicity; but to say that the good novel is ambiguous is not to say that it is difficult and confused (this is optional), merely to insist that it is *about* moral ambiguity and that it cannot betray its theme. I distrust the writer who claims to know black and white, left from right, Hip from Square, Them from Us—no matter which of the sides he chooses. And I distrust especially the characters in whom he embodies his presumable insights. The protagonists of the best recent books are not self-righteous, long-suffering, diminished prigs, who want only to live in peace and are sure they know what peace is. From the most sympathetic to the least, they are troublemakers like their authors, who will not let the world rest until it acknowledges that they exist. We have by now quite a gallery of such types, including Joyce's insufferable Stephen, too stiff-necked to grant his mother's deathbed wish; Kafka's K., guilty as charged though no one knows quite what the charge is; Nathanael West's Miss Lonelyhearts, trying in vain to be the Christ in whom he does not believe; Ralph Ellison's Invisible Man, vainly striving to escape the myth of his color; and Faulkner's Popeye, counterfeiting manhood with a bloody corncob.

The contemporary novel through which such characters stalk—bringing harm to those around them, even as they court destruction for themselves—is terror-ridden, dreadful; but it is not humorless. In the midst of Faulkner's grimmest book, *Sanctuary*, a couple of rustics play out a humorous scene in a whorehouse. West's bleakest novel is his funniest, *A Cool Million*, whose title comes from the "Old Saying": "John D. Rockefeller would give a cool million to have a stomach like yours." Kafka, we are told, used to laugh until the tears ran down his cheeks, reading aloud from *Amerika*. Joyce, one sometimes feels, would do anything for a laugh, and Beckett has thought of some things to do which even his master could not imagine; Bellow can be a clown; Mary McCarthy insists on compelling our titters in the midst of our deepest shame; and the British "Angries" have us guffawing like a pack of fools. In this sense, Mark Twain is the true ancestor of the modern writer, and his *Pudd'nhead Wilson* a storehouse of the sort of humor which is not dated by changes of fashion. "*October* 12, *the Discovery*. It was wonderful to find America, but it would have been more wonderful to miss it." This is our kind of joke, proper to a world in which we may all die laughing —as we like to say.

Such humor is not incompatible with negation, or even terror, for it is not party or factional humor, with which the *in's* satirize the *out's*, and the "normal" put the eccentric in their places. It is total humor, through which men laugh not at their foibles but at their essential selves. The vision of man shared by our greatest writers involves an appreciation of his absurdity, and the protagonists of our greatest books are finally neither comic nor tragic but absurd. To the modern writer, the distinction between comedy and tragedy seems as forced and irrelevant as that between hallucination and reality; his world partakes of both, and he would be hard put to it to say where one ends and the other begins. The conventional definitions of the comic and the tragic strike him as simplifications, falsifications of human life, appropriate to a less complex time. To insist that we regard man, even for the space of three acts or five, as *either* horrible or funny; to require us, through four or five hundred pages, *either* to laugh or to cry we find offensive in an age when we can scarcely conceive of wanting to do one without the other. For us, the great works of the past are those which occupy an intermediate position between comedy and tragedy: the *Bacchae* of Euripides, the *Misanthrope* of Molière, Shakespeare's *Measure for Measure,* Ibsen's *An Enemy of the People,* Twain's *Pudd'nhead Wilson* and Melville's *The Confidence Man.* And the writers of our own time whom we most admire—West, Faulkner and Beckett, among others—pursue a third genre, which suggests that the ludicrous is the source of pity and terror, and that pity and terror themselves are the heart of the ludicrous.

The vision of the truly contemporary writer is that of a world not only absurd but also chaotic and fragmentary. He tries in his work to find techniques for representing a universe in which our perceptions overlap but do not coincide, in which we share chiefly a sense of loneliness: our alienation from whatever things finally are, as well as from other men's awareness of those things and of us. Rapid shifts in point of view; dislocations of syntax and logic; a vividness more like hallucination than photography; the use of parody and slapstick at moments of great seriousness; the exploitation of puns and of the vaudeville of dreams—these experiments characterize much of the best work of recent decades, from Joyce's *Ulysses* through Djuna Barnes' *Nightwood* to Wright Morris' *Field of Vision,* whose winning of the National Book Award so incensed the guardians of middlebrow standards. At the present moment, Morris is almost alone in the United States in his continuing devotion to the themes and techniques of the negative novel. (There is, to be sure, the young novelist John Barth, strangely ignored.) For we have been suffering a general loss of nerve, or a waning of talent, which has persuaded writers of such different origins and generations as Hemingway, Faulkner, Saul Bellow and Mary McMarthy to pursue affirmation in the place of art—disconcerted, perhaps, as they pass from being ignored to relative degrees of fame and victimized by a perverse sort of *noblesse oblige.*

The unearned euphoria of *Henderson, the Rain King;* the shapeless piety of *A Fable;* the sentimental self-indulgence of *Across the River and into the Trees;* the maudlin falsity of *The Town;* the heavy-handed symbolism and religiosity of *The Old Man and the Sea,* destined from its inception for the pages of *Life*—such failures make over and over the point that the contemporary American writer can abjure negativism only if he is willing to sacrifice truth and art. For major novelists and minor, the pursuit of the positive means stylistic suicide. Language itself decays, and dialogue becomes travesty; character, stereotype; insight, sentiment. The Nobel Prize speech destined for high-school anthologies requires quite another talent from that demanded by the novel; and the abstract praise of love requires another voice from that which cries *No!* to the most noble temptations, the most defensible lies.

Yet one must not forget, in the face of their recent decline, the successes of Bellow and Hemingway and Faulkner: the terrible impact of *The Victim, The Sun Also Rises* and *The Sound and the Fury.* The last, in particular, remains the exemplary American novel, perhaps the greatest work of fiction produced in the United States in the twentieth century. And it is no accident that its title comes from the bleakest passage in Shakespeare, or that its action begins inside the mind of an idiot. The point is insisted upon bluntly, almost too obviously: life is a tale told by an idiot, full of sound and fury, signifying nothing. Here is the ultimate negation, the Hard No pressed as far as it will go. Yet "nothing" is not quite Faulkner's last word, only the next to the last. In the end, the negativist is no nihilist, for he affirms the void. Having endured a vision of the meaninglessness of existence, he retreats neither into self-pity and aggrieved silence nor into a realm of beautiful lies. He chooses, rather, to render the absurdity which he perceives, to know it and make it known. To know and to render, however, mean to give form; and to give form is to provide the possibility of delight—a delight which does not deny horror but lives at its intolerable heart. 1960

Lionel Trilling

(1905-)

Born in New York City and a recipient of three degrees from Columbia University, Lionel Trilling joined the English faculty of his alma mater in 1931 and has been associated with that institution ever since. He is an advisory editor of both the influential *Kenyon Review* and the *Partisan Review.* Two early biographies are *Matthew Arnold* (1939) and *E. M. Forster* (1943). His sociological novel of the 1930's, *The Middle of the Journey,* appeared in 1947. His most important critical essays to date are collected in *The Liberal Imagination* (1950), *The Opposing Self* (1955), and *A Gathering of Fugitives* (1956). *Freud and the Crisis of Our Culture* appeared in 1955.

Reality in America

I

It is possible to say of V. L. Parrington that with his *Main Currents in American Thought* he has had an influence on our conception of American culture which is not equaled by that of any other writer of the last two decades. His ideas are now the accepted ones wherever the college course in American literature is given by a teacher who conceives himself to be opposed to the genteel and the academic and in alliance with the vigorous and the actual. And whenever the liberal historian of America finds occasion to take account of the national literature, as nowadays he feels it proper to do, it is Parrington who is his standard and guide. Parrington's ideas are the more firmly established because they do not have to be imposed—the teacher or the critic who presents them is likely to find that his task is merely to make articulate for his audience what it has always believed, for Parrington formulated in a classic way the suppositions about our culture which are held by the American middle class so far as that class is at all liberal in its social thought and so far as it begins to understand that literature has anything to do with society.

Parrington was not a great mind; he was not a precise thinker or, except when measured by the low eminences that were about him, an impressive one. Separate Parrington from his informing idea of the economic and social determination of thought and what is left is a simple intelligence, notable for its generosity and enthusiasm but certainly not for its accuracy or originality. Take him even with his idea and he is, once its direction is established, rather too predictable to be continuously interesting; and, indeed, what we dignify with the name of economic and social determinism amounts in his use of it to not much more than the demonstration that most writers incline to stick to their own social class. But his best virtue was real and important—he had what we like to think of as the saving salt of the American mind, the lively sense of the practical, workaday world, of the welter of ordinary undistinguished things and people, of the tangible, quirky, unrefined elements of life. He knew what so many literary historians do not know, that emotions and ideas are the sparks that fly when the mind meets difficulties.

Yet he had after all but a limited sense of what constitutes a difficulty. Whenever he was confronted with a work of art that was complex, personal and not literal, that was not, as it were, a public document, Parrington was at a loss. Difficulties that were complicated by personality or that were expressed in the language of successful art did not seem quite real to him and he was inclined to treat them as aberrations, which is one way of saying what everybody admits, that the weakest part of Parrington's talent was his aesthetic judgment. His admirers and disciples like to imply that his errors of aesthetic judgment are merely lapses of taste, but this is not so. Despite such mistakes as his notorious praise of Cabell, to whom in a remarkable passage he compares Melville, Parrington's taste was by no means bad. His errors are the errors of understanding which arise from his assumptions about the nature of reality.

Parrington does not often deal with abstract philosophical ideas, but whenever he approaches a work of art we are made aware of the metaphysics on which his aesthetics is based. There exists, he believes, a thing called *reality;* it is one and immutable, it is wholly external, it is irreducible. Men's minds may waver, but reality is always reliable, always the same, always easily to be known. And the artist's relation to reality he conceives as a simple one. Reality being fixed and given, the artist has but to let it pass through him, he is the lens in the first diagram of an elementary book on optics: Fig. 1, Reality; Fig. 2, Artist; Fig. 1′, Work of Art. Figs. 1 and 1′ are normally in virtual correspondence with each other. Sometimes the artist spoils this ideal relation by "turning away from" reality. This results in certain fantastic works, unreal and ultimately useless. It does not occur to Parrington that there is any other relation possible between the artist and reality than his passage of reality through the transparent artist; he meets evidence of imagination and creativeness with a settled hostility the expression of which suggests that he regards them as the natural enemies of democracy.

In this view of things, reality, although it is always reliable, is always rather sober-sided, even grim. Parrington, a genial and enthusiastic man, can understand how the generosity of man's hopes and desires may leap beyond reality; he admires will in the degree that he suspects mind. To an excess of desire and energy which blinds a man to the limitations of reality he can indeed be very tender. This is one of the many meanings he gives to *romance* or *romanticism,* and in spite of himself it appeals to something in his own nature. The praise of Cabell is Parrington's response not only to Cabell's elegance—for Parrington loved elegance—but also to Cabell's insistence on the part which a beneficent self-deception may and even should play in the disappointing fact-bound life of man, particularly in the private and erotic part of his life.[1]

The second volume of *Main Currents* is called *The Romantic Revolution in America* and it is natural to expect that the word romantic should appear in it frequently. So it does, more frequently than one can count, and seldom with the same meaning, seldom with the sense that the word, although scandalously vague as it has been used by the literary historians, is still full of complicated but not wholly pointless ideas, that it involves many contrary but definable things; all too often Parrington uses the word romantic with the word romance close at hand, meaning *a* romance, in the sense that *Graustark* or *Treasure Island* is a romance, as though it signified chiefly a gay disregard of the limitations of everyday fact. Romance is refusing to heed the counsels of experience (p. iii); it is ebullience (p. iv); it is utopianism (p. iv); it is individualism (p. vi); it is self-deception (p. 59)—"romantic faith . . . in the beneficent processes of trade and industry" (as held, we inevitably ask,

[1] See, for example, how Parrington accounts for the "idealizing mind"—Melville's—by the discrepancy between "a wife in her morning kimono" and "the Helen of his dreams." Vol. II, p. 259.

by the romantic Adam Smith?); it is the love of the picturesque (p. 49); it is the dislike of innovation (p. 50) but also the love of change (p. iv); it is the sentimental (p. 192); it is patriotism, and then it is cheap (p. 235). It may be used to denote what is not classical, but chiefly it means that which ignores reality (pp. ix, 136, 143, 147, and *passim*); it is not critical (pp. 225, 235), although in speaking of Cooper and Melville, Parrington admits that criticism can sometimes spring from romanticism.

Whenever a man with whose ideas he disagrees wins from Parrington a reluctant measure of respect, the word romantic is likely to appear. He does not admire Henry Clay, yet something in Clay is not be to despised—his romanticism, although Clay's romanticism is made equivalent with his inability to "come to grips with reality." Romanticism is thus, in most of its significations, the venial sin of *Main Currents;* like carnal passion in the *Inferno*, it evokes not blame but tender sorrow. But it can also be the great and saving virtue which Parrington recognizes. It is ascribed to the transcendental reformers he so much admires; it is said to mark two of his most cherished heroes, Jefferson and Emerson: "they were both romantics and their idealism was only a different expression of a common spirit." Parrington held, we may say, at least two different views of romanticism which suggest two different views of reality. Sometimes he speaks of reality in an honorific way, meaning the substantial stuff of life, the ineluctable facts with which the mind must cope, but sometimes he speaks of it pejoratively and means the world of established social forms; and he speaks of realism in two ways: sometimes as the power of dealing intelligently with fact, sometimes as a cold and conservative resistance of idealism.

Just as for Parrington there is a saving grace and a venial sin, there is also a deadly sin, and this is turning away from reality, not in the excess of generous feeling, but in what he believes to be a deficiency of feeling, as with Hawthorne, or out of what amounts to sinful pride, as with Henry James. He tells us that there was too much realism in Hawthorne to allow him to give his faith to the transcendental reformers: "he was too much of a realist to change fashions in creeds"; "he remained cold to the revolutionary criticism that was eager to pull down the old temples to make room for nobler." It is this cold realism, keeping Hawthorne apart from his enthusiastic contemporaries, that alienates Parrington's sympathy—"Eager souls, mystics and revolutionaries, may propose to refashion the world in accordance with their dreams; but evil remains, and so long as it lurks in the secret places of the heart, utopia is only the shadow of a dream. And so while the Concord thinkers were proclaiming man to be the indubitable child of God, Hawthorne was critically examining the question of evil as it appeared in the light of his own experience. It was the central fascinating problem of his intellectual life, and in pursuit of a solution he probed curiously into the hidden, furtive recesses of the soul." Parrington's disapproval of the enterprise is unmistakable.

Now we might wonder whether Hawthorne's questioning of the naïve and often eccentric faiths of the transcendental reformers was not, on the face of it, a public service. But Parrington implies that it contributes nothing to democracy, and even that it stands in the way of the realization of democracy. If democracy depends wholly on a fighting faith, I suppose he is right. Yet society is after all something that exists at the moment as well as in the future, and if one man wants to probe curiously into the hidden furtive recesses of the contemporary soul, a broad democracy and especially one devoted to reality should allow him to do so without despising him. If what Hawthorne did was certainly nothing to build a party on, we ought perhaps to forgive him when we remember that he was only one man and that the future of mankind did not depend upon him alone. But this very fact serves only to irritate Parrington; he is put out by Hawthorne's loneliness and believes that part of Hawthorne's insufficiency as a writer comes from his failure to get around and meet people. Hawthorne could not, he tells us, establish contact with the "Yankee reality," and was scarcely aware of the "substantial world of Puritan reality that Samuel Sewall knew."

To turn from reality might mean to turn to romance, but Parrington tells us that Hawthorne was romantic "only in a narrow and very special sense." He was not interested in the world of, as it were, practical romance, in the Salem of the clipper ships; from this he turned away to create "a romance of ethics." This is not an illuminating phrase but it is a catching one, and it might be taken to mean that Hawthorne was in the tradition of, say, Shakespeare; but we quickly learn that, no, Hawthorne had entered a barren field, for although he himself lived in the present and had all the future to mold, he preferred to find many of his subjects in the past. We learn too that his romance of ethics is not admirable because it requires the hard, fine pressing of ideas, and we are told that "a romantic uninterested in adventure and afraid of sex is likely to become somewhat graveled for matter." In short, Hawthorne's mind was a thin one, and Parrington puts in evidence his use of allegory and symbol and the very severity and precision of his art to prove that he suffered from a sadly limited intellect, for so much fancy and so much art could scarcely be needed unless the writer were trying to exploit to the utmost the few poor ideas that he had.

Hawthorne, then, was "forever dealing with shadows, and he knew that he was dealing with shadows." Perhaps so, but shadows are also part of reality and one would not want a world without shadows, it would not even be a "real" world. But we must get beyond Parrington's metaphor. The fact is that Hawthorne was dealing beautifully with realities, with substantial things. The man who could raise those brilliant and serious doubts about the nature and possibility of moral perfection, the man who could keep himself aloof from the "Yankee reality" and who could dissent from the orthodoxies of dissent and tell us so much about the nature of moral zeal, is of course dealing exactly with reality.

Parrington's characteristic weakness as a historian is suggested by his title, for the culture of a nation is not truly figured in the image of the current. A culture is not a flow, nor even a confluence; the form of its existence is struggle, or at least debate—it is nothing if not a dialectic. And in any culture there are likely to be certain artists who contain a large part of the dialectic within themselves, their meaning and power lying in their contradictions; they contain within themselves, it may be said, the very essence of the culture, and the sign of this is that they do not submit to serve the ends of any one ideological group or tendency. It is a significant circumstance of American culture, and one which is susceptible of explanation, that an unusually large proportion of its notable writers of the nineteenth century were such repositories of the dialectic of their times—they contained both the yes and the no of their culture, and by that token they were prophetic of the future. Parrington said that he had not set up shop as a literary critic; but if a literary critic is simply a reader who has the ability to understand literature and to convey to others what he understands, it is not exactly a matter of free choice whether or not a cultural historian shall be a literary critic, nor is it open to him to let his virtuous political and social opinions do duty for percipience. To throw out Poe because he cannot be conveniently fitted into a theory of American culture, to speak of him as a biological sport and as a mind apart from the main current, to find his gloom to be merely personal and eccentric, "only the atrabilious wretchedness of a dipsomaniac," as Hawthorne's was "no more than the skeptical questioning of life by a nature that knew no fierce storms," to judge Melville's response to American life to be less noble than that of Bryant or of Greeley, to speak of Henry James as an escapist, as an artist similar to Whistler, a man characteristically afraid of stress—this is not merely to be mistaken in aesthetic judgment; rather it is to examine without attention and from the point of view of a limited and essentially arrogant conception of reality the documents which are in some respects the most suggestive testimony to what America was and is, and of course to get no answer from them.

Parrington lies twenty years behind us, and in the intervening time there has developed a body of opinion which is aware of his inadequacies and of the inadequacies of his coadjutors and disciples, who make up what might be called the literary academicism of liberalism. Yet Parrington still stands at the center of American thought about American culture because, as I say, he expresses the chronic American belief that there exists an opposition between reality and mind and that one must enlist oneself in the party of reality.

1940

II

This belief in the incompatibility of mind and reality is exemplified by the doctrinaire indulgence which liberal intellectuals have always displayed toward Theodore Dreiser, an indulgence which becomes the worthier of remark when it is contrasted with the liberal severity toward Henry James. Dreiser and James: with that juxtaposition we are immediately at the dark and bloody crossroads where literature and politics meet. One does not go there gladly, but nowadays it is not exactly a matter of free choice whether one does or does not go. As for the particular juxtaposition itself, it is inevitable and it has at the present moment far more significance than the juxtaposition which once used to be made between James and Whitman. It is not hard to contrive factitious oppositions between James and Whitman, but the real difference between them is the difference between the moral mind, with its awareness of tragedy, irony, and multitudinous distinctions, and the transcendental mind, with its passionate sense of the oneness of multiplicity. James and Whitman are unlike not in quality but in kind, and in their very opposition they serve to complement each other. But the difference between James and Dreiser is not of kind, for both men addressed themselves to virtually the same social and moral fact. The difference here is one of quality, and perhaps nothing is more typical of American liberalism than the way it has responded to the respective qualities of the two men.

Few critics, I suppose, no matter what their political disposition, have ever been wholly blind to James's great gifts, or even to the grandiose moral intention of these gifts. And few critics have ever been wholly blind to Dreiser's great faults. But by liberal critics James is traditionally put to the ultimate question: of what use, of what actual political use, are his gifts and their intention? Granted that James was devoted to an extraordinary moral perceptiveness, granted too that moral perceptiveness has something to do with politics and the social life, of what possible practical value in our world of impending disaster can James's work be? And James's style, his characters, his subjects, and even his own social origin and the manner of his personal life are adduced to show that his work cannot endure the question. To James no quarter is given by American criticism in its political and liberal aspect. But in the same degree that liberal criticism is moved by political considerations to treat James with severity, it treats Dreiser with the most sympathetic indulgence. Dreiser's literary faults, it gives us to understand, are essentially social and political virtues. It was Parrington who established the formula for the liberal criticism of Dreiser by calling him a "peasant": when Dreiser thinks stupidly, it is because he has the slow stubbornness of a peasant; when he writes badly, it is because he is impatient of the sterile literary gentility of the bourgeoisie. It is as if wit, and flexibility of mind, and perception, and knowledge were to be equated with aristocracy and political reaction, while dullness and stupidity must naturally suggest a virtuous democracy, as in the old plays.

The liberal judgment of Dreiser and James goes back of politics, goes back to the cultural assumptions that make politics. We are still haunted by a kind of political fear of the intellect which Tocqueville observed in us more than a century ago. American intellectuals, when they are being consciously American or political, are remarkably quick to suggest that an art which is marked by perception and knowledge, although all very well in its way, can never get us through gross dangers and difficulties. And their misgivings become the more intense when intellect works in art as it ideally should, when its processes are vivacious and interesting and brilliant. It is then that we like to confront it with the gross dangers and difficulties and to challenge it to save us at once from disaster. When intellect in art is awkward or dull we do not put it to the test of ultimate or immediate practicality. No liberal critic asks the question of Dreiser whether *his* moral preoccupations are going to be useful in confronting the disasters that threaten us. And it is a judgment on the proper nature of mind, rather than any actual political meaning that might be drawn from the works of the two men, which accounts for the unequal justice they have received from the progressive critics. If it could be conclusively demonstrated—by, say, documents in James's handwriting—that James explicitly intended his books to be understood as pleas for co-operatives, labor unions, better housing, and more equitable taxation, the American critic in his liberal and progressive character would still be worried by James because his work shows so many of the electric qualities of mind. And if something like the opposite were proved of Dreiser, it would be brushed aside—as his doctrinaire anti-Semitism has in fact been brushed aside—because his books have the awkwardness, the chaos, the heaviness which we associate with "reality." In the American metaphysic, reality is always material reality, hard, resistant, unformed, impenetrable, and unpleasant. And that mind is alone felt to be trustworthy which most resembles this reality by most nearly reproducing the sensations it affords.

In *The Rise of American Civilization,* Professor Beard uses a significant phrase when, in the course of an ironic account of James's career, he implies that we have the clue to the irrelevance of that career when we know that James was "a whole generation removed from the odors of the shop." Of a piece with this, and in itself even more significant, is the comment which Granville Hicks makes in *The Great Tradition* when he deals with James's stories about artists and remarks that such artists as James portrays, so concerned for their art and their integrity in art, do not really exist: "After all, who has ever known such artists? Where are the Hugh Verekers, the Mark Ambients, the Neil Paradays, the Overts, Limberts, Dencombes, Delavoys?" This question, as Mr. Hicks admits, had occurred to James himself, but what answer had James given to it? "If the life about us for the last thirty years refused warrant for these examples," he said in the preface to volume XII of the New York Edition, "then so much the worse for that life. . . . There are decencies that in the name of the general self-respect we must take for granted, there's a rudimentary intellectual honor to which we must, in the interest of civilization, at least pretend." And to this Mr. Hicks, shocked beyond argument, makes this reply, which would be astonishing had we not heard it before: "But this is the purest romanticism, this writing about what ought to be rather than what is!"

The "odors of the shop" are real, and to those who breathe them they guarantee a sense of vitality from which James is debarred. The idea of intellectual honor is not real, and to that chimera James was devoted. He betrayed the reality of what is in the interests of what ought to be. Dare we trust him? The question, we remember, is asked by men who themselves have elaborate transactions with what ought to be. Professor Beard spoke in the name of a growing, developing, and improving America. Mr. Hicks, when he wrote *The Great Tradition,* was in general sympathy with a nominally radical movement. But James's own transaction with what ought to be is suspect because it is carried on through what I have called the electrical qualities of mind, through a complex and rapid imagination and with a kind of authoritative immediacy. Mr. Hicks knows that Dreiser is "clumsy" and "stupid" and "bewildered" and "crude in his statement of materialistic monism"; he knows that Dreiser in his personal life—which is in point because James's personal life is always supposed to be so much in point—was not quite emancipated from "his boyhood longing for crass material success," showing "again and again a desire for the ostentatious luxury of the successful business man." But Dreiser is to be accepted and forgiven because his faults are the sad, lovable, honorable faults of reality itself, or of America itself—huge, inchoate, struggling toward expression, caught between the dream of raw power and the dream of morality.

"The liability in what Santayana called the genteel tradition was due to its being the product of mind apart from experience. Dreiser gave us the stuff of our common experience, not as it was hoped to be by any idealizing theorist, but as it actually was in its crudity." The author of this statement certainly cannot be accused of any lack of feeling for mind as Henry James represents it; nor can Mr. Matthiessen be thought of as a follower of Parrington—indeed, in the preface to *American Renaissance* he has framed one of the sharpest and most cogent criticisms of Parrington's method. Yet Mr. Matthiessen, writing in the *New York Times Book Review* about Dreiser's posthumous novel, *The Bulwark,* accepts the liberal cliché which opposes crude experience to mind and establishes Dreiser's value by implying that the mind which Dreiser's crude experience is presumed to confront and refute is the mind of gentility.

This implied amalgamation of mind with gentility is the rationale of the long indulgence of Dreiser, which is extended even to the style of his prose. Everyone is aware that Dreiser's prose style is full of roughness and ungainliness, and the critics who admire Dreiser tell us it does not matter. Of course it does not matter. No reader with a right sense of style would suppose that it does matter, and he might even find it a virtue. But it has been taken for granted that the ungainliness of Dreiser's style is the only possible objection to be made to it, and that whoever finds in it any fault at all wants a prettified genteel style (and is objecting to the ungainliness of reality itself). For instance, Edwin Berry Burgum, in a leaflet on Dreiser put out by the Book Find Club, tells us that Dreiser was one of those who used—or, as Mr. Burgum says, utilized—"the diction of the Middle West, pretty much as it was spoken, rich in colloquialism and frank in the simplicity and directness of the pioneer tradition," and that this diction took the place of "the literary English, formal and bookish, of New England provincialism that was closer to the aristocratic spirit of the mother country than to the tang of everyday life in the new West." This is mere fantasy. Hawthorne, Thoreau, and Emerson were for the most part remarkably colloquial—they wrote, that is, much as they spoke; their prose was specifically American in quality, and, except for occasional lapses, quite direct and simple. It is Dreiser who lacks the sense of colloquial diction—that of the Middle West or any other. If we are to talk of bookishness, it is Dreiser who is bookish; he is precisely literary in the bad sense; he is full of flowers of rhetoric and shines with paste gems; at hundreds of points his diction is not only genteel but fancy. It is he who speaks of "a scene more distingué than this," or of a woman "artistic in form and feature," or of a man who, although "strong, reserved, aggressive, with an air of wealth and experience, was *soi-disant* and not particularly eager to stay at home." Colloquialism held no real charm for him and his natural tendency is always toward the "fine":

> . . . . Moralists come and go; religionists fulminate and declare the pronouncements of God as to this; but Aphrodite still reigns. Embowered in the festal depths of the spring, set above her altars of porphyry, chalcedony, ivory and gold, see her smile the smile that is at once the texture and essence of delight, the glory and despair of the world! Dream on, oh Buddha, asleep on your lotus leaf, of an undisturbed Nirvana! Sweat, oh Jesus, your last agonizing drops over an unregenerate world! In the forests of Pan still ring the cries of the worshippers of Aphrodite! From her altars the incense of adoration ever rises! And see, the new red grapes dripping where votive hands new-press them!

Charles Jackson, the novelist, telling us in the same leaflet that Dreiser's style does not matter, remarks on how much still comes to us when we have lost by translation the stylistic brilliance of Thomas Mann or the Russians or Balzac. He is in part right. And he is right too when he says that a certain kind of conscious, supervised artistry is not appropriate to the novel of large dimensions. Yet the fact is that the great novelists have usually written very good prose, and what comes through even a bad translation is exactly the power of mind that made the well-hung sentence of the original text. In literature style is so little the mere clothing of thought—need it be insisted on at this late date?—that we may say that from the earth of the novelist's prose spring his characters, his ideas, and even his story itself.[2]

To the extent that Dreiser's style is defensible, his thought is also defensible. That is, when he thinks like a novelist, he is worth following—when by means of his rough and ungainly but no doubt cumulatively effective style he creates rough, ungainly, but effective characters and events. But when he thinks like, as we say, a philosopher, he is likely to be not only foolish but vulgar. He thinks as the modern crowd thinks when it decides to think: religion and morality are nonsense, "religionists" and moralists are fakes, tradition is a fraud, what is man but matter and impulses, mysterious "chemisms," what value has life anyway? "What, cooking, eating, coition, job holding, growing, aging, losing, winning, in so changeful and passing a scene as this, important? Bunk! It is some form of titillating illusion with about as much import to the superior forces that bring it all about as the functions and gyrations of a fly. No more. And maybe less." Thus Dreiser at sixty. And yet there is for him always the vulgarly saving suspicion that maybe, when all is said and done, there is Something Behind It All. It is much to the point of his intellectual vulgarity that Dreiser's anti-Semitism was not merely a social prejudice but an idea, a way of dealing with difficulties.

No one, I suppose, has ever represented Dreiser as a masterly intellect.

[2] The latest defense of Dreiser's style, that in the chapter on Dreiser in the *Literary History of the United States,* is worth noting: "Forgetful of the integrity and power of Dreiser's whole work, many critics have been distracted into a condemnation of his style. He was, like Twain and Whitman, an organic artist; he wrote what he knew—what he was. His many colloquialisms were part of the coinage of his time, and his sentimental and romantic passages were written in the language of the educational system and the popular literature of his formative years. In his style, as in his material, he was a child of his time, of his class. Self-educated, a type or model of the artist of plebeian origin in America, his language, like his subject matter, is not marked by internal inconsistencies." No doubt Dreiser was an organic artist in the sense that he wrote what he knew and what he was, but so, I suppose, is every artist; the question for criticism comes down to *what* he knew and *what* he was. That he was a child of his time and class is also true, but this can be said of everyone without exception; the question for criticism is how he transcended the imposed limitations of his time and class. As for the defense made on the ground of his particular class, it can only be said that liberal thought has come to a strange pass when it assumes that a plebeian origin is accountable for a writer's faults through all his intellectual life.

It is even commonplace to say that his ideas are inconsistent or inadequate. But once that admission has been made, his ideas are hustled out of sight while his "reality" and great brooding pity are spoken of. (His pity is to be questioned: pity is to be judged by kind, not amount, and Dreiser's pity—*Jennie Gerhardt* provides the only exception—is either destructive of its object or it is self-pity.) Why has no liberal critic ever brought Dreiser's ideas to the bar of political practicality, asking what use is to be made of Dreiser's dim, awkward speculation, of his self-justification, of his lust for "beauty" and "sex" and "living" and "life itself," and of the showy nihilism which always seems to him so grand a gesture in the direction of profundity? We live, understandably enough, with the sense of urgency; our clock, like Baudelaire's, has had the hands removed and bears the legend, "It is later than you think." But with us it is always a little too late for mind, yet never too late for honest stupidity; always a little too late for understanding, never too late for righteous, bewildered wrath; always too late for thought, never too late for naïve moralizing. We seem to like to condemn our finest but not our worst qualities by pitting them against the exigency of time.

But sometimes time is not quite so exigent as to justify all our own exigency, and in the case of Dreiser time has allowed his deficiencies to reach their logical, and fatal, conclusion. In *The Bulwark* Dreiser's characteristic ideas come full circle, and the simple, didactic life history of Solon Barnes, a Quaker business man, affirms a simple Christian faith, and a kind of practical mysticism, and the virtues of self-abnegation and self-restraint, and the belief in and submission to the hidden purposes of higher powers, those "superior forces that bring it all about"—once, in Dreiser's opinion, so brutally indifferent, now somehow benign. This is not the first occasion on which Dreiser has shown a tenderness toward religion and a responsiveness to mysticism. *Jennie Gerhardt* and the figure of the Reverend Duncan McMillan in *An American Tragedy* are forecasts of the avowals of *The Bulwark*, and Dreiser's lively interest in power of any sort led him to take account of the power implicit in the cruder forms of mystical performance. Yet these rifts in his nearly monolithic materialism cannot quite prepare us for the blank pietism of *The Bulwark*, not after we have remembered how salient in Dreiser's work has been the long surly rage against the "religionists" and the "moralists," the men who have presumed to believe that life can be given any law at all and who have dared to suppose that will or mind or faith can shape the savage and beautiful entity that Dreiser liked to call "life itself." Now for Dreiser the law may indeed be given, and it is wholly simple—the safe conduct of the personal life requires only that we follow the Inner Light according to the regimen of the Society of Friends, or according to some other godly rule. And now the smiling Aphrodite set above her altars of porphyry, chalcedony, ivory, and gold is quite forgotten, and we are told that the sad joy of cosmic acceptance goes hand in hand with sexual abstinence.

Dreiser's mood of "acceptance" in the last years of his life is not, as a personal experience, to be submitted to the tests of intellectual validity. It consists of a sensation of cosmic understanding, of an overarching sense of unity with the world in its apparent evil as well as in its obvious good. It is no more to be quarreled with, or reasoned with, than love itself—indeed, it is a kind of love, not so much of the world as of oneself in the world. Perhaps it is either the cessation of desire or the perfect balance of desires. It is what used often to be meant by "peace," and up through the nineteenth century a good many people understood its meaning. If it was Dreiser's own emotion at the end of his life, who would not be happy that he had achieved it? I am not even sure that our civilization would not be the better for more of us knowing and desiring this emotion of grave felicity. Yet granting the personal validity of the emotion, Dreiser's exposition of it fails, and is, moreover, offensive. Mr. Matthiessen has warned us of the attack that will be made on the doctrine of *The Bulwark* by "those who believe that any renewal of Christianity marks a new 'failure of nerve.'" But Dreiser's religious avowal is not a failure of nerve—it is a failure of mind and heart. We have only to set his book beside any work in which mind and heart are made to serve religion to know this at once. Ivan Karamazov's giving back his ticket of admission to the "harmony" of the universe suggests that *The Bulwark* is not morally adequate, for we dare not, as its hero does, blandly "accept" the suffering of others; and the Book of Job tells us that it does not include enough in its exploration of the problem of evil, and is not stern enough. I have said that Dreiser's religious affirmation was offensive; the offense lies in the vulgar ease of its formulation, as well as in the comfortable untroubled way in which Dreiser moved from nihilism to pietism.[3]

The Bulwark is the fruit of Dreiser's old age, but if we speak of it as a failure of thought and feeling, we cannot suppose that with age Dreiser weakened in mind and heart. The weakness was always there. And in a sense it is not Dreiser who failed but a whole way of dealing with ideas, a way in which we have all been in some degree involved. Our liberal, progressive culture tolerated Dreiser's vulgar materialism with its huge negation, its simple cry of "Bunk!," feeling that perhaps it was not quite

[3] This ease and comfortableness seem to mark contemporary religious conversions. Religion nowadays has the appearance of what the ideal modern house has been called, "a machine for living," and seemingly one makes up one's mind to acquire and use it not with spiritual struggle but only with a growing sense of its practicability and convenience. Compare *The Seven Storey Mountain*, which Monsignor Sheen calls "a twentieth-century form of the *Confessions* of St. Augustine," with the old, the as it were original, *Confessions* of St. Augustine.

intellectually adequate but certainly very *strong*, certainly very *real*. And now, almost as a natural consequence, it has been given, and is not unwilling to take, Dreiser's pietistic religion in all its inadequacy.

Dreiser, of course, was firmer than the intellectual culture that accepted him. He *meant* his ideas, at least so far as a man can mean ideas who is incapable of following them to their consequences. But we, when it came to his ideas, talked about his great brooding pity and shrugged the ideas off. We are still doing it. Robert Elias, the biographer of Dreiser, tells us that "it is part of the logic of [Dreiser's] life that he should have completed *The Bulwark* at the same time that he joined the Communists." Just what kind of logic this is we learn from Mr. Elias's further statement. "When he supported left-wing movements and finally, last year, joined the Communist Party, he did so not because he had examined the details of the party line and found them satisfactory, but because he agreed with a general program that represented a means for establishing his cherished goal of greater equality among men." Whether or not Dreiser was following the logic of his own life, he was certainly following the logic of the liberal criticism that accepted him so undiscriminatingly as one of the great, significant expressions of its spirit. This is the liberal criticism, in the direct line of Parrington, which establishes the social responsibility of the writer and then goes on to say that, apart from his duty of resembling reality as much as possible, he is not really responsible for anything, not even for his ideas. The scope of reality being what it is, ideas are held to be mere "details," and, what is more, to be details which, if attended to, have the effect of diminishing reality. But ideals are different from ideas; in the liberal criticism which descends from Parrington ideals consort happily with reality and they urge us to deal impatiently with ideas—a "cherished goal" forbids that we stop to consider how we reach it, or if we may not destroy it in trying to reach it the wrong way.

1946

E[lwyn] B[rooks] White

(1899-   )

E. B. White was born in Mount Vernon, New York, and attended Cornell University. After newspaper work in Seattle, a trip as a mess boy on a ship bound for Alaska, and some advertising work in New York City, he joined the staff of the *New Yorker*, where he held a variety of positions for eleven years. He later moved to Maine and conducted the "One Man's Meat" department for *Harper's* from 1938-43, but he continued to contribute to the *New Yorker*, and still does. Among his many early books are *The Lady Is Cold* (1929, poems); *Is Sex Necessary?* (1929, with James Thurber); *Alice Through the Cellophane* (1933); and *Quo Vadimus?* (1938). With his wife he compiled *A Subtreasury of American Humor* in 1942. Then came *One Man's Meat* (1942), *The Wild Flag* (1946), *Here Is New York* (1949), *The Second Tree from the Corner* (1953), and *The Points of My Compass* (1962). Two of his highly acclaimed children's books are *Stuart Little* (1945) and *Charlotte's Web* (1952).

Walden

Miss Nims, take a letter to Henry David Thoreau. Dear Henry: I thought of you the other afternoon as I was approaching Concord doing fifty on Route 62. That is a high speed at which to hold a philosopher in one's mind, but in this century we are a nimble bunch.

On one of the lawns in the outskirts of the village a woman was cutting the grass with a motorized lawn mower. What made me think of you was that the machine had rather got away from her, although she was game enough, and in the brief glimpse I had of the scene it appeared to me that the lawn was mowing the lady. She kept a tight grip on the handles, which throbbed violently with every explosion of the one-cylinder motor, and as she sheered around bushes and lurched along at a reluctant trot behind her impetuous servant, she looked like a puppy who had grabbed something that was too much for him. Concord hasn't changed much, Henry; the farm implements and the animals still have the upper hand.

I may as well admit that I was journeying to Concord with the deliberate intention of visiting your woods; for although I have never knelt at the grave of a philosopher nor placed wreaths on moldy poets, and have often gone a mile out of my way to avoid some place of historical interest, I have always wanted to see Walden Pond. The account which you left of your sojourn there is, you will be amused to learn, a document of increasing pertinence; each year it seems to gain a little headway, as the world loses ground. We may all be transcendental yet, whether we like it or not. As our common complexities increase, any tale of individual simplicity (and yours is the best written and the cockiest) acquires a new fascination; as our goods accumulate, but not our well-being, your report of an existence without material adornment takes on a certain awkward credibility.

My purpose in going to Walden Pond, like yours, was not to live cheaply or to live dearly there, but to transact some private business with the fewest obstacles. Approaching Concord, doing forty, doing forty-five, doing fifty, the steering wheel held snug in my palms, the highway held grimly in my vision, the crown of the road now serving me (on the right-hand curves), now defeating me (on the lefthand curves), I began to rouse myself from the stupefaction which a day's motor journey induces.

It was a delicious evening, Henry, when the whole body is one sense, and imbibes delight through every pore, if I may coin a phrase. Fields were richly brown where the harrow, drawn by the stripped Ford, had lately sunk its teeth; pastures were green; and overhead the sky had that same everlasting great look which you will find on Page 144 of the Oxford pocket edition. I could feel the road entering me, through tire, wheel, spring, and cushion; shall I not have intelligence with earth too? Am I not partly leaves and vegetable mold myself?—a man of infinite horsepower, yet partly leaves.

Stay with me on 62 and it will take you into Concord. As I say, it was a delicious evening. The snake had come forth to die in a bloody S on the highway, the wheel upon its head, its bowels flat now and exposed. The turtle had come up too to cross the road and die in the attempt, its hard shell smashed under the rubber blow, its intestinal yearning (for the other side of the road) forever squashed. There was a sign by the wayside which announced that the road had a "cotton surface." You wouldn't know what that is, but neither, for that matter, did I. There is a cryptic ingredient in many of our modern improvements—we are awed and pleased without knowing quite what we are enjoying. It is something to be traveling on a road with a cotton surface.

The civilization round Concord to-day is an odd distillation of city, village, farm, and manor. The houses, yards, fields look not quite suburban, not quite rural. Under the bronze beech and the blue spruce of the departed baron grazes the milch goat of the heirs. Under the porte-cochère stands the reconditioned station wagon; under the grape arbor sit the puppies for sale. (But why do men degenerate ever? What makes families run out?)

It was June and everywhere June was publishing her immemorial stanza; in the lilacs, in the syringa, in the freshly edged paths and the sweetness of moist beloved gardens, and the little wire wickets that preserve the tulips' front. Farmers were already moving the fruits of their toil into their yards, arranging the rhubarb, the asparagus, the strictly fresh eggs on the painted stands under the little shed roofs with the patent shingles. And though it was almost a hundred years since you had taken your ax and started cutting out your home on Walden Pond, I was interested to observe that the philosophical spirit was still alive in Massachusetts: in the center of a vacant lot some boys were assembling the framework of a rude shelter, their whole mind and skill concentrated in the rather inauspicious helter-skeleton of studs and rafters. They too were escaping from town, to live naturally, in a rich blend of savagery and philosophy.

That evening, after supper at the inn, I strolled out into the twilight to dream my shapeless transcendental dreams and see that the car was locked up for the night (first open the right front door, then reach over, straining, and pull up the handles of the left rear and the left front till you hear the click, then the handle of the right rear, then shut the right front but open it again, remembering that the key is still in the ignition switch, remove the key, shut the right front again with a bang, push the tiny keyhole cover to one side, insert key, turn, and withdraw). It is what we all do, Henry. It is called locking the car. It is said to confuse thieves and keep them from making off with the laprobe. Four doors to lock behind one robe. The driver himself never uses a laprobe, the free movement of his legs being vital to the operation of the vehicle; so that when he locks the car it is a pure and unselfish act. I have in my life gained very little essential heat from laprobes, yet I have ever been at pains to lock them up.

The evening was full of sounds, some of which would have stirred your memory. The robins still love the elms of New England villages at sundown. There is enough of the thrush in them to make song inevitable at the end of day, and enough of the tramp to make them hang round the dwellings of men. A robin, like many another American, dearly loves a white house with green blinds. Concord is still full of them.

Your fellow-townsmen were stirring abroad—not many afoot, most of them in their cars; and the sound which they made in Concord at evening was a rustling and a whispering. The sound lacks steadfastness and is wholly unlike that of a train. A train, as you know who lived so near the Fitchburg line, whistles once or twice sadly and is gone, trailing a memory in smoke, soothing to ear and mind. Automobiles, skirting a village green, are like flies that have gained the inner ear—they buzz, cease, pause, start, shift, stop, halt, brake, and the whole effect is a nervous polytone curiously disturbing.

As I wandered along, the toc toc of ping pong balls drifted from an attic window. In front of the Reuben Brown house a Buick was drawn up. At the wheel, motionless, his hat upon his head, a man sat, listening to Amos and Andy on the radio (it is a drama of many scenes and without an end). The deep voice of Andrew Brown, emerging from the car, although it originated more than two hundred miles away, was unstrained by distance. When you used to sit on the shore of your pond on Sunday morning, listening to the church bells of Acton and Concord, you were aware of the excellent filter of the intervening atmosphere. Science has attended to that, and sound now maintains its intensity without regard for distance. Properly sponsored, it goes on forever.

A fire engine, out for a trial spin, roared past Emerson's house, hot with readiness for public duty. Over the barn roofs the martins dipped and chittered. A swarthy daughter of an asparagus grower, in culottes, shirt, and bandanna, pedalled past on her bicycle. It was indeed a delicious evening, and I returned to the inn (I believe it was your house once) to rock with the old ladies on the concrete veranda.

Next morning early I started afoot for Walden, out Main Street and down Thoreau, past the depot and the Minuteman Chevrolet Company. The morning was fresh, and in a bean field along the way I flushed an agriculturalist, quietly studying his beans. Thoreau Street soon joined Number 126, an artery of the State. We number our highways nowadays, our speed being so great we can remember little of their quality or character and are lucky to remember their number. (Men have an indistinct notion that if they keep up this activity long enough all will at length ride somewhere, in next to no time.) Your pond is on 126.

I knew I must be nearing your woodland retreat when the Golden Pheasant lunchroom came into view—Sealtest ice cream, toasted sandwiches, hot frankfurters, waffles, tonics, and lunches. Were I the proprietor, I should add rice, Indian meal, and molasses—just for old time's sake. The Pheasant, incidentally, is for sale: a chance for some nature lover who wishes to set himself up beside a pond in the Concord atmosphere and live deliberately, fronting only the essential facts of life on Number 126. Beyond the Pheasant was a place called Walden Breezes, an oasis whose porch pillars were made of old green shutters sawed into lengths. On the porch was a distorting mirror, to give the traveler a comical image of himself, who had miraculously learned to gaze in an ordinary glass without smiling. Behind the Breezes, in a sun-parched clearing, dwelt your philosophical descendants in their trailers, each trailer the size of your hut, but all grouped together for the sake of congeniality. Trailer people leave the city, as you did, to discover solitude and in any weather, at any hour of the day or night, to improve the nick of time; but they soon collect in villages and get bogged deeper in the mud than ever. The camp behind Walden Breezes was just rousing itself to the morning. The ground was packed hard under the heel, and the sun came through the clearing to bake the soil and enlarge the wry smell of cramped housekeeping. Cushman's bakery truck had stopped to deliver an early basket of rolls. A camp dog, seeing me in the road, barked petulantly. A man emerged from one of the trailers and set forth with a bucket to draw water from some forest tap.

Leaving the highway I turned off into the woods toward the pond, which was apparent through the foliage. The floor of the forest was strewn with dried old oak leaves and *Transcripts*. From beneath the flattened popcorn wrapper (*granum explosum*) peeped the frail violet. I followed a footpath and descended to the water's edge. The pond lay clear and blue in the morning light, as you have seen it so many times. In the shallows a man's waterlogged shirt undulated gently. A few flies came out to greet me and convoy me to your cove, past the No Bathing signs on which the fellows and the girls had scrawled their names. I felt strangely excited suddenly to be snooping around your premises, tiptoeing along watchfully, as though not to tread by mistake upon the intervening century. Before I got to the cove I heard something which seemed to me quite wonderful: I heard your frog, a full, clear *troonk*, guiding me, still hoarse and solemn, bridging the years as the robins had bridged them in the sweetness of the village evening. But he soon quit, and I came on a couple of young boys throwing stones at him.

Your front yard is marked by a bronze tablet set in a stone. Four small granite posts, a few feet away, show where the house was. On top of the tablet was a pair of faded blue bathing trunks with a white stripe. Back of it is a pile of stones, a sort of cairn, left by your visitors as a tribute I suppose. It is a rather ugly little heap of stones, Henry. In fact the hillside itself seems faded, browbeaten; a few tall skinny pines, bare of lower limbs, a smattering of young maples in suitable green, some birches and oaks, and a number of trees felled by the last big wind. It was from the bole of one of these fallen pines, torn up by the roots, that I extracted the stone which I added to the cairn—a sentimental act in which I was interrupted by a small terrier from a nearby picnic group, who confronted me and wanted to know about the stone.

I sat down for a while on one of the posts of your house to listen to the bluebottles and the dragon flies. The invaded glade sprawled shabby and mean at my feet, but the flies were tuned to the old vibration. There were the remains of a fire in your ruins, but I doubt that it was yours; also two beer bottles trodden into the soil and become part of earth. A young oak had taken root in your house, and two or three ferns, unrolling like the ticklers at a banquet. The only other furnishings were a DuBarry pattern sheet, a page torn from a picture magazine, and some crusts in wax paper.

Before I quit I walked clear round the pond and found the place where you used to sit on the northeast side to get the sun in the fall, and the beach where you got sand for scrubbing your floor. On the eastern side of the pond, where the highway borders it, the State has built dressing rooms for swimmers, a float with diving towers, drinking fountains of porcelain, and rowboats for hire. The pond is in fact a State Preserve, and carries a twenty-dollar fine for picking wild flowers, a decree signed in all solemnity by your fellow-citizens Walter C. Wardwell, Erson B. Barlow, and Nathaniel I. Bowditch. There was a smell of creosote where they had been building a wide wooden stairway to the road and the parking area. Swimmers and boaters were arriving; bodies plunged vigorously into the water and emerged wet and beautiful in the bright air. As I left, a boatload of town boys were splashing about in mid-pond, kidding and fooling, the young fellows singing at the tops of their lungs in a wild chorus:

Amer-ica, Amer-i-ca, God shed his grace on thee,
And crown thy good with brotherhood
From sea to shi-ning sea!

I walked back to town along the railroad, following your custom. The rails were expanding noisily in the hot sun, and on the slope of the roadbed the wild grape and the blackberry sent up their creepers to the track.

The expense of my brief sojourn in Concord was:

Canvas shoes	$1.95	
Baseball bat	.25	gifts to take back to a boy
Left-handed fielder's glove	1.25	
Hotel and meals	4.25	
In all	$7.70	

As you see, this amount was almost what you spent for food for eight months. I cannot defend the shoes or the expenditure for shelter and food: they reveal a meanness and grossness in my nature which you would find contemptible. The baseball equipment, however, is the kind of impediment with which you were never on even terms. You must remember that the house where you practiced the sort of economy which I respect was haunted only by mice and squirrels. You never had to cope with a shortstop.

1939

Joseph Wood Krutch

(1893-)

Joseph Wood Krutch was born in Knoxville, Tennessee, educated at Vanderbilt and Columbia Universities, and for many years was both a Professor of English at Columbia and drama critic for *The Nation*. He now lives in Tucson, Arizona. Aside from *American Drama Since 1918* (1939; rev. 1957), he has written biographies of Poe (1926), Samuel Johnson (1944), and Thoreau (1948). His *The Modern Temper* (1929) was partly extended in *The Measure of Man* (1954). *Human Nature and the Human Condition* appeared in 1959. His meditative essays on nature and man's relation to the universe appear in such volumes as *The Desert Year* (1952), *The Great Chain of Life* (1956), and *The Forgotten Peninsula* (1961).

G.B.S. Enters Heaven(?)

SCENE: *The after-world. Thoreau is seated quietly on a pumpkin. To Mozartian strains the ectoplasmic form of Bernard Shaw is taking shape. Before it has become recognizable he begins to speak.*

Shaw (triumphantly): I talk, therefore I am. But let no one seize this occasion to tell me that I was wrong about Eternity. With my usual perceptiveness I realized it before anyone else had the gumption to do so; with my usual frankness I admit it at once. The truth of the matter is that simple honesty has always been my chief distinction though no doubt the angelic hosts will take up the babble about my paradoxes and my brilliance, instead.

Nevertheless, I am disappointed. I had hoped that the Life Force had used me up. What I want is to be thrown into the dustbin. If necessary I will consent to spend a few eons in the contemplation and ecstasy appropriate to an ancient. But on all the Dominions, Principalities, and Powers I hereby serve notice. I will *not* explain anything further to them or to anyone else. Besides, it ought to be evident to the meanest intelligence not befuddled by romantic nonsense about Music, Beauty, and the other excuses for parasitic idleness that what the angels really need is an honest day's work—something which will give them the sense of being used for a noble purpose. *(He is struck by a sudden doubt.)* The atmosphere here is distressingly suggestive of the third act of "Man and Superman"—*(to Thoreau)* this isn't by any chance Hell, is it?

Thoreau: I have never taken the trouble to ask. Whatever it is, it suits me very well. One world at a time, you know.

Shaw: A surprisingly sensible remark. It is what the churches forgot when they made the simple common sense of Jesus an excuse for shirking their responsibilities. You must be that American backwoodsman who caught a glimpse of the truth and then lost sight of it among the trees. Marx would have made a man of you.

Thoreau: I never doubted that I was one—except perhaps when I saw too many men about me. This Marx, I suppose, was one of those reformers who would have too benevolently insisted upon doing for me what I had much rather do for myself.

Shaw: Marx was the greatest mind between John Bunyan and me. Of course, he was wrong about many simple things, the real nature of rent for example. What is even more important, he never made it clear that there is no contradiction whatever between economic determinism and Lamarckian free will. Thus, the only trouble with the poor is poverty, while at the same time the only trouble with the poor and the rich alike is their failure to realize that man can make of himself whatever he has the will to become. But I explained all that in plays which Shakespeare would have written if he had not, unfortunately, been born brainless. Nevertheless, I owe much to Marx, and because I have no foolish pride in the fact that the Life Force happened to make me its chosen instrument, I acknowledge the debt.

Thoreau: I find that I got along very well without him. He could not have told me how to spend an afternoon. That, like every other really important thing, I had to learn for myself, not from my elders or my contemporaries, from whom I never heard one sensible piece of advice. Since the seventeenth century there have been no really manly writers in the line of Homer and Shakespeare. They all use words like "determinism" and "evolutionary"—words which have a paralysis in their tails. As for rent, I know well enough what *that* is. It is the tribute one man pays to another for doing for him what he would have better done for himself—build a house, for example. To what a sorry pass has this division of labor led us! The mass of men slavishly do things not worth doing in order to escape the opportunity of leading their own lives. Every man for himself, say I! Even the devil won't want the hindmost.

Shaw: Would you tear down the Brooklyn Bridge and let every man carry his own plank? That is the only logical alternative to Communism.

Thoreau: I did not know that there was a Brooklyn Bridge. But it does not surprise me. No doubt there will some day be an Atlantic Bridge and a Pacific Bridge too. But it will not be a good thing. How many dismal days will have been spent in slavery just to pay for what most would be better without! As for carrying your own plank, I can easily imagine a man worse employed. Besides, most men need do nothing of the sort. They would be better off staying on their own side of the river.

Shaw: You almost persuade me to go on all fours. Even Voltaire—despite his dirty little mind—saw that this is what all the babble about simplicity would logically come down to. Man can go up or he can go down. The Life Force says "Go Up." For my part I am with it. What you call simplicity is only the inefficient, romanticized. Life is a great deal simpler with bridges and sewers than without them. They help free men for nobler work.

Thoreau: I have not often seen them engaged upon any. Noble is not the term I should apply to what I saw of men's daily labors when I was so unfortunate as to visit New York or Boston. They seemed busier—and busy to less purpose—than Minot, the farmer of Concord. For all I know the Indian before the white man came may have known better than either how to live. I was a writer, and I learned more from woodchucks and snapping turtles than I did from my most civilized neighbors.

Shaw: The ghosts of dead ideas still haunt the regions of the blest! I would never have dreamed that even Hell could be so far behind the times. But writers have always been half sage, half fool. They do not even know which side their bread is buttered on. Most of them have some silly hankering after anarchy instead of realizing that the only hope for any kind of artist is a society so thoroughly organized and regimented that he can always earn a living by three hours of brainless, robot labor like machine-tending and then have twice that long left over to write his books and paint his pictures. Until Socialism has achieved that for him he will remain the begging, borrowing, stealing, self-pitying parasite he is at present.

Thoreau: Three hours of robot labor per day would be more than I could stand, and it is far more than I had to force myself to perform. Besides, and as I would have known, I was dead long before this utopia of yours could come about. I remember an acquaintance who devoted himself to accumulating money in the hope of getting enough to enable him to become a poet. I told him that he should have gone up to the garret at once. That is what I did. If other men were sensible they would do the same.

Shaw: Like nearly every other artist who has ever lived, you were a parasite and not ashamed to be one. You took advantage of a security and a stability which others had established. A world full of Thoreaus is unthinkable.

Thoreau: There is no danger of that; there were never even two. As for taking advantage of the society I found, I did it exactly as I took advantage of the sun and rain, the earth and water. How I should have conducted my life on some other planet I do not know, but I think I would have managed. God sent me into a peculiar world, and I took my principal business to be to live in it—be it good or bad. That was at least a better way of spending my time than dreaming of different and impossible ones. I consider myself remarkably fortunate, and I was certainly remarkably happy.

Shaw: Are you so besotted as to think *that* important? Happiness and Beauty are by-products. I was too busy to ask whether or not I was happy. That must mean that I was.

Thoreau: On the contrary, it must mean that you died without ever knowing that you had lived. I feared I might do that but I escaped it.

Shaw: I very much doubt that you did. One must live before one can know that one has. Contemplation will be for those who have grown older than Methuselah. Three score and ten is too short a span to be wasted in idleness. Come to think of it, four score and thirteen is not so very much longer. But I did make a beginning.

Thoreau: I died at forty-five. One year would have been enough. But ten thousand would not have been too many.

Shaw: You are more extraordinary than I thought. I doubt if any man before you was ever so wrong twice in two successive sentences. One year would not have been enough because as the world grows more complicated, there are more and more things that must be learned. Ten thousand would have been too many because if the Life Force is to satisfy her passion for improvement she cannot permit the earth to become too cluttered with her discarded experiments.

Thoreau: He who has not learned all that is really important by the time he is twenty will never learn it. Even I forgot much that I had known very well in my youth.

Shaw: You were merely putting away childish things and had not the wit to know that dreams are well exchanged for realities.

Thoreau: And do you really think that you really know what the most important realities really are? From all you have said so far I doubt that you do.

Shaw: I know that growth and change are real. I know that neither human life nor human society is what it will become. As Nietzsche—another of Life's unsuccessful attempts to create me—proclaimed, "Man is something which must be surpassed."

Thoreau: If man could once understand the unspeakable truth about himself and the equally unspeakable truth about the world of nature in which he lives then there would be no need for him to surpass either himself or it.

Shaw: All my doubts are resolved! Only in Hell could a man utter such blasphemies against the Holy Ghost—an old name for the Life Force—and not be incontinently blasted. But I solemnly warn the Prince of Darkness that I have no intention of spending Eternity in happiness and contentment. I will *not* become a romantic lover or a musical amateur. Even in the infernal regions there must be a borough council in need of a clerk. And if this Choctaw here is a typical specimen of the citizenry, then the affairs of hell must be in a hellish state. *(He rushes vigorously off left to a flourish of trombones. Thoreau remains exactly where he was—on a pumpkin.)*

1952

James [Grover] Thurber

(1894-1961)

Born in Columbus, Ohio, and educated at Ohio State University, James Thurber worked briefly for the State Department in Washington and Paris before engaging in newspaper work on, successively, the Columbus *Dispatch* (1920-24), the Chicago *Tribune* in Paris (1924-25), and the New York *Evening Post* (1925-27). He had begun contributing to the *New Yorker* in 1926, and the next year he became a member of its staff. Although he soon resigned that position, he continued as a featured contributor until his death. Among his many books are his collaborations with E. B. White, *Is Sex Necessary?* (1929); *The Owl in the Attic and Other Perplexities* (1931); *The Seal in the Bedroom and Other Predicaments* (1932); his semi-autobiographical *My Life and Hard Times* (1933); *The Middle-Aged Man on the Flying Trapeze* (1935); *Let Your Mind Alone* (1937); *Fables for Our Times* (1940, 1956); *Men, Women and Dogs* (1943); *The Thurber Carnival* (1945); *The Beast in Me and Other Animals* (1949); *Thurber's Dogs* (1955); and *Alarms and Diversions* (1957). His dramatic collaboration with Elliot Nugent, *The Male Animal* (1940), was successful on Broadway and is still widely played around the country. Three of his children's books are *The White Deer* (1945), *The Thirteen Clocks* (1950), and *The Wonderful O* (1957). Not long before he died he wrote his memoirs of the *New Yorker*'s founder and first editor, in *The Years with Ross* (1957).

The Unicorn in the Garden

JAMES THURBER

Once upon a sunny morning a man who sat in a breakfast nook looked up from his scrambled eggs to see a white unicorn with a golden horn quietly cropping the roses in the garden. The man went up to the bedroom where his wife was still asleep and woke her. "There's a unicorn in the garden," he said. "Eating roses." She opened one unfriendly eye and looked at him. "The unicorn is a mythical beast," she said, and turned her back on him. The man walked slowly downstairs and out into the garden. The unicorn was still there; he was now browsing among the tulips. "Here, unicorn," said the man, and he pulled up a lily and gave it to him. The unicorn ate it gravely. With a high heart, because there was a unicorn in his garden, the man went upstairs and roused his wife again. "The unicorn," he said, "ate a lily." His wife sat up in bed and looked at him, coldly. "You are a booby," she said, "and I am going to have you put in the booby-hatch." The man, who had never liked the words "booby" and "booby-hatch," and who liked them even less on a shining morning when there was a unicorn in the garden, thought for a moment. "We'll see about that," he said. He walked over to the door. "He has a golden horn in the middle of his forehead," he told her. Then he went back to the garden to watch the unicorn; but the unicorn had gone away. The man sat down among the roses and went to sleep.

As soon as the husband had gone out of the house, the wife got up and dressed as fast as she could. She was very excited and there was a gloat in her eye. She telephoned the police and she telephoned a psychiatrist; she told them to hurry to her house and bring a strait-jacket. When the police and the psychiatrist arrived they sat down in chairs and looked at her, with great interest. "My husband," she said, "saw a unicorn this morning." The police looked at the psychiatrist and the psychiatrist looked at the police. "He told me it ate a lily," she said. The psychiatrist looked at the police and the police looked at the psychiatrist. "He told me it had a golden horn in the middle of its forehead," she said. At a solemn signal from the psychiatrist, the police leaped from their chairs and seized the wife. They had a hard time subduing her, for she put up a terrific struggle, but they finally subdued her. Just as they got her into the strait-jacket, the husband came back into the house.

"Did you tell your wife you saw a unicorn?" asked the police. "Of course not," said the husband. "The unicorn is a mythical beast." "That's all I wanted to know," said the psychiatrist. "Take her away. I'm sorry, sir, but your wife is as crazy as a jay bird." So they took her away, cursing and screaming, and shut her up in an institution. The husband lived happily ever after.

Moral: Don't count your boobies until they are hatched. 1939

Reprinted by permission. Copyright © 1939 The New Yorker Magazine, Inc.

Wolcott Gibbs

(1902-1958)

Wolcott Gibbs' entire professional career was marked by close association with the *New Yorker* magazine in the city of his birth. His literary criticism, his short stories, his parodies, and his reporting all appeared there. He was also one of its best known drama critics. Part of his *Bed of Neuroses* (1937) was incorporated into *More in Sorrow* (1958), his last book. His one play, *Season in the Sun* (1950), contains a thinly disguised portrait of Harold Ross.

The Factory and the Attic

Small women in funny hats keep asking me how to tell a good short story from a bad one. For years, they complain, they have been reading such wholly disparate publications as *Scribner's* and the *Saturday Evening Post,* miserably unable to determine what is Art and what is Tripe. At the time they came to me most of these women had arrived at some arbitrary solution of their own. One pinched little thing admitted that she had come to the point of judging literature purely on the basis of its nuisance value: that is, a story must be regarded as important only if it bored her to the edge of madness. Another defined significant stories as those dealing with persons who would have been intolerable to her socially. (She was particularly impressed by one about a rural spinster with an unconquerable desire to go walking in the rain with no clothes on.) Still another reserved her approval for narratives in which nothing much ever seemed to happen. Curiously enough, this defeatist point of view was quite general; almost all the ladies assumed that literature, to be worthy of their admiration, must also make them unhappy. Unfortunately, I am not able to deny this theory altogether, since some moments of pain are inseparable from real culture, but it seems to me that any sound philosophy of criticism must go somewhat deeper. There are, in fact, almost infinite ramifications to be considered. Anxious to avoid the drain on my time caused by these endless appeals, in this article I have prepared a few tests for separating the sheep of modern fiction from its gilded and elegant goats.

The first point to be considered in judging the merits of any story is, of course, the plot, and here, for purposes of comparison, I shall outline two which seem representative of the best and worst in magazine prose. The first is called "Even the Least of These, Thy Sparrows," and runs somewhat as follows:

Hector Le Boutillier, scion of an old Kentucky family, is wounded at Belleau Wood while attempting to bring back a wounded private, a colored man, from behind the German lines. When Hector stumbles into the trench with the wounded man on his back, his comrades are horrified to observe that his face has been almost entirely obliterated by a burst of shrapnel. He is rushed at once to a base hospital, where he is placed under the care of a surgeon famous for his work in plastic surgery. Unfortunately, the damage wrought by the shell is so complete that the surgeon is unable to tell what Hector looked like before he was hit, and obviously it would be absurd to equip him with a meaningless and irrelevant face made up out of the doctor's head. The United States Medical Corps, however, rises to the occasion and a cable is dispatched to the Le Boutilliers in America asking them for recent and characteristic photographs of Hector. Through some error in the cable office, Hector's name is transmitted as "Richard," which chances to be the name of a ne'er-do-well younger brother, who unknown to his family has deserted from the Allied armies and become a German spy. It is his photograph which reaches the surgeon, and when Hector leaves the operating-room he is wearing Richard's face. The story then leaps to the end of the war and to America, where the Le Boutilliers' home town has been wiped out by a passing earthquake, so that there is nobody to recognize Hector (even as Richard) upon his return. Before the war, however, Richard had become engaged to an old-fashioned girl who lived in the Greenwich Village section of New York, where she seems to have been a little out of her element. Richard's actual intentions toward her had been far from honorable, but the war started too soon, and he drew a blank.

Upon his return to America, Hector (in Richard's face) wanders around for a while trying to forget the loss of his rather extensive family, and eventually comes to the very city where the girl, whose name was Smyrna Phelps, is living. Finally, at a batik pull, they meet and Smyrna naturally supposes that Hector is Richard (on account of the face). She is so preposterously glad to see him that Hector, believing his brother dead, decides not to disillusion her. In a short time, too, he discovers that he has come to love her. They are married and are living quite happily in Montclair when the real Richard comes back to New York in search of Smyrna. Eventually he traces her to Montclair, and there is an extremely trying scene in which Richard accuses Hector of lifting both his face and his girl. At the end of it Hector promises to go away, leaving Smyrna to the real Richard, although she has discovered what a bounder he is. This looks pretty bad, but just as Hector is packing his bag to go away, a state trooper who had been in Richard's company abroad comes in and shoots him for being a German spy. This, of course, settles everything, and Smyrna contributes to the felicity of the moment by discovering that she is going to have a baby.

The other story, which can be summarized rather more briefly, is called "Meg" and the plot, disregarding some of its profounder psychological undertones, goes something like this:

At the age of fifteen Meg was seduced by the president of the First National Bank, who was old enough not only to be her father, but also to make it seem like a pretty good trick. For some reason, doubtless professional, he elected to stage this idyll in a safe-deposit vault, and consequently Meg grew up with a horror of being shut up in anything. By the time she was sixteen, even houses had become intolerable to her, and she began to sleep out in the fields beyond the village. Eventually she gave up all contact with the villagers. Once a month she trudged into town for supplies, a bent and tragic figure, wrapped in an atrocity of rags, muttering endlessly to herself. She began to drink, too, and under its influence her behavior grew even more *outré*; she took to stopping young girls on the streets and warning them against bankers.

Inevitably this came to the ears of the matrons of the town, and at last (ironically enough, at the instigation of the banker's wife) Meg was arrested as a public nuisance and sentenced to a month in jail. She never served it. No sooner had the steel door of the cell closed behind her than Meg fell to the floor, dead. At the inquest the doctor said she died of fear. She thought they'd deposited her in a bank.

Although the discerning reader can have no real doubt about the comparative merits of these samples, it might be well to examine the technical considerations which are involved. By any enlightened standards it is apparent that "Even the Least of These, Thy Sparrows" belongs emphatically among the goats. We are struck at once by the author's basic insincerity—by his use of the most palpable literary tricks, and especially by his persistent overplay of coincidence. We are quite ready to accept one, and the mistake by which Hector was made to look like his brother seems both plausible and ingenious. From this point, however, we become involved in a welter of fortuitous circumstance. We are asked not only to believe that Hector's whole family was wiped out by an earthquake (in Kentucky, where they are extremely rare), that by pure chance he encountered his brother's fiancée in a city as large as New York, but also that Richard's old companion, the trooper, appeared at so critical a juncture of the story. In this connection, it seems to me that "Sparrows" exhibits another serious flaw in that, since both brothers looked precisely alike, it was just as probable that he would have shot one as the other.

Altogether we find that this story is an almost perfect example of commercial prose at its worst, written with an eye on the movies, and with no discernible relation to actual contemporary life.

"Meg," on the other hand, is a little gem of morbid psychology, moving with majestic inevitability from its tragic inception to its even more tragic dénouement. The setting is simple, even drab; the plot has none of the feverish activity, the insane complexity, which are so apparent in "Sparrows," and the protagonists, Meg and the banker, are not, as were Hector and Richard, actuated by any preposterous nobility or even more preposterous villainy. They are people very like you and me, and their behavior is doubtless what yours or mine would be if we were either a girl who had been enticed into a vault by a banker or a banker who had simultaneous access both to a girl and a vault.

For all these reasons it should be abundantly clear that "Sparrows" and "Meg" represent the poles of modern fiction. To be doubly sure, however, let us examine the styles in which they are written. First let us consider "Sparrows"—specifically the scene in which Hector relinquishes Smyrna to his brother. A few paragraphs will do:

> Over the mantel there was a clock and to Hector it seemed that presently the ticking of the clock resolved itself into words. " 'Vengeance is mine,' saith the Lord." This over and over until at last the bright hatred went out of his soul and he knew a curious peace. And again "Blessed are the meek, for they shall inherit the earth." And at last Hector turned from the window and it seemed to the two watching him that there was a light, lambent and unearthly, on his face. He put his hand on the doorknob and smiled at them.
>
> "I am going," he said gently, "away."
>
> And while they stood transfixed the door opened and closed and he was gone.
>
> "Hector," cried Smyrna, but the room gave her back only the sound of her own voice and the slow and fatal ticking of the clock.

The passage from "Meg" describes her last journey from the hut in the fields to the village and goes as follows:

> Meg walked slowly along the muddy road. It was hot and ragged children ran out of the farmhouses that bordered the road and threw stones at her. When one of the stones hit her Meg would turn around in the road, and the children would run screaming back into the houses, afraid of her tall, pale madness. Meg did not know they were stones. She thought they were half-dollars and that the children were bankers. Once she caught one of the children and broke its neck. That made her laugh.
>
> "I guess that will learn you to get tough with me, Mr. James Waldemar," she said.

I see no reason for further comment. If any of my readers are still unable to distinguish between the produce of the factory and attic, with a clear conscience I leave them in Montclair, with Hector and Smyrna. The rest of you, imperturbably cultured, can follow me over the hill and down into despair and death with Meg.

1937

Leo [Calvin] Rosten

[Leonard Q. Ross]

(1908-)

Although he was born in Poland, most of Leo Rosten's life has been spent in America, which is now his home. As a political scientist, teacher, research worker, editor, and humorist, he has made varied contributions to the intellectual life of America. One of his best known is his *Hollywood: The Movie Colony, the Movie Makers* (1941). *The Washington Correspondents* (1937) is an analysis of news gathering in the capital. He also wrote *A Guide to the Religions of America* (1955), but his most widely read book was undoubtedly *The Education of H*Y*M*A*N K*A*P*L*A*N* (1937), a fictional account of a New York night school for immigrant adults. It first appeared in the *New Yorker;* and both it and its continuation, *The Return of H*Y*M*A*N K*A*P*L*A*N* (1959), were written under the pseudonymn of "Leonard Q. Ross."

O K★A★P★L★A★N! MY K★A★P★L★A★N!

Mr. Parkhill was not surprised when the first three students to participate in Recitation and Speech practice delivered eloquent orations on "Abraham Lincoln," "Little George and the Sherry Tree," and "Wonderful U. S.," respectively. For the activities of the month of February had injected a patriotic fervor into the beginners' grade, an *amor patriae* which would last well into March. There was a simple enough reason for this phenomenon: Mr. Robinson, principal of the school, did not allow either Lincoln's or Washington's Birthday to pass without appropriate ceremonies. On each occasion the whole student body would crowd into Franklin Hall, the largest of the five rooms occupied by the school, to commemorate the nativity of one of the two great Americans.

At the Lincoln assembly, Mr. Robinson always gave a long eulogy entitled "The Great Emancipator." ("His name is inscribed on the immortal roll of history, in flaming letters of eternal gold!") A "prize" student from the graduating class delivered a carefully corrected speech on "Lincoln and the Civil War"—a rather short speech. Then Miss Higby recited "O Captain! My Captain!" to an audience which listened with reverently bated breath.

For the Washington convocation, the order of things was much the same. Mr. Robinson's address was entitled "The Father of His Country." ("First in war, first in peace, and first in the hearts of his countrymen—his name burns in the hearts of true Americans, each letter a glowing ember, a symbol of his glorious achievement!") The prize student's speech was on "Washington and the American Revolution." And Miss Higby recited "My Country, 'Tis of Thee." (Miss Higby often remarked that it was a sad commentary on our native bards that there was no poem as *perfectly* appropriate for Washington as "O Captain! My Captain!" was for Lincoln.)

The result of these patriotic rites was that for weeks afterward, each year, the faculty would be deluged with compositions on Lincoln or Washington, speeches on Washington or Lincoln, even little poems on Lincoln or Washington. Night after night, the classrooms echoed with the hallowed phrases "1776," "Father of His Country," "The Great Emancipator," "The Civil War," "Honest Abe," "Valley Forge." Mr. Parkhill found it a nerve-sapping ordeal. He thought of this annual period as "the Ides of February and March."

"I will spik ona Garibaldi," announced Miss Caravello, the fourth student to face the class.

Mr. Parkhill felt a surge of gratitude within him. It was, however, short-lived.

"Garibaldi—joosta lak Washington! Firsta da war, firsta da peace, firsta da heartsa da countrymens!"

In the middle of the front row, Mr. Hyman Kaplan printed his name aimlessly for the dozenth time on a large sheet of foolscap, and sighed. Mr. Kaplan had been sighing, quite audibly, throughout each of the successive historico-patriotic declamations. Mr. Parkhill felt a distinct sense of comradeship with Mr. Kaplan.

"Hisa name burns, lak Mist' Principal say. Da 'g,' da 'a,' da 'r,' da 'i' . . ." Miss Caravello articulated the letters with gusto. Mr. Norman Bloom sharpened his pencil. Miss Schneiderman stared into space, vacantly. Mrs. Moskowitz rounded out the latest of a lengthy series of yawns. Mr. Parkhill frowned.

"Hooray Washington! Viva Garibaldi!"

In a fine Latin flush, Miss Caravello resumed her seat. Mr. Kaplan sighed again, rather more publicly. E ★ N ★ N ★ U ★ I was stamped on Mr. Kaplan's features.

"Corrections, please," Mr. Parkhill announced, trying to be as cheery as possible.

The zest of competition animated the class for a few brief moments. Miss Mitnick began the discussion, commenting on Miss Caravello's failure to distinguish between the past and present tenses of verbs, and her habit of affixing mellifluous "a"s to prosaic Anglo-Saxon words. Mr. Pinsky suggested, with a certain impatience, that it was "foist ***in*** war, foist ***in*** peace, foist ***in*** the hots his countryman."

"How you can comparink a Judge Vashington mit a Gary Baldy?" Mr. Kaplan remarked with icy scorn. "Ha!"

Mr. Parkhill quickly spread oil on the troubled nationalistic waters. To avoid an open clash (Miss Caravello had long ago allied herself with the Mitnick forces in the Kaplan-Mitnick vendetta), and in an effort to introduce a more stimulating note into Recitation and Speech, Mr. Parkhill said, "Er—suppose *you* speak next, Mr. Kaplan." Mr. Parkhill had learned to respect the catalytic effect of Mr. Kaplan's performances, oral or written.

Mr. Kaplan's ever-incipient smile burst into full bloom. He advanced to the front of the room, stuffing crayons into his pocket. Then he buttoned his coat with delicate propriety, made a little bow to Mr. Parkhill, and began, "Ladies an' gantleman, faller-students, an' Mr. Pockheel." He paused for the very fraction of a moment, as if permitting the class to steel itself; then, in a dramatic voice, he cried, "JUDGE VASHINGTON, ABRAM LINCOHEN, AN' JAKE POPPER!"

The class was galvanized out of its lassitude. Other students, less adventurous students, might undertake comments on Lincoln *or* Washington, but only Mr. Kaplan had the vision and the fortitude to encompass Lincoln *and* Washington—to say nothing of "Jake Popper."

"Er—Mr. Kaplan," suggested Mr. Parkhill anxiously. "It's *George* Washington, not 'Judge.' And Abra*ham* Lin*coln*, not 'Ab*ram* Lin*cohen*.' Please try it again." (Mr. Parkhill could think of nothing relevant to say in regard to "Jake Popper.")

"*Jaw*DGE VASHINGTON, ABRA*ham* LIN*collen*, AN' JAKE POPPER!" Mr. Kaplan repeated, with renewed ardor. "Is dat right, Mr. Pockheel?"

Mr. Parkhill decided it might be best to let well enough alone. "It's—er—*better*."

"Hau Kay! So foist abot Jawdge Vashington. He vas a fine man. Ectually Fodder fromm His Contry, like dey say. Ve hoid awreddy, fromm planty students, all abot his movvellous didds. How, by beink even a leetle boy, he chopped don de cherries so he could enswer, 'I cannot tell lies, Papa. I did it mit mine leetle hatchik!' But ve shouldn't forgat dat Vashington vas a beeg ravolutionist! He vas fightink for Friddom, against de Kink Ingland, Kink Jawdge Number Tree, dat tarrible autocrap who—"

" 'Auto*crat*!' " Mr. Parkhill put in, but too late.

"—who vas puddink stemps on *tea* even, so it tasted bed, an' Jawdge Vashington trew de tea in Boston Hobber, drassed op like a Hindian. So vas de Ravolution!"

The class, Mr. Parkhill could not help observing, hung on Mr. Kaplan's every word, entranced by his historiography.

"Jawdge Vashington vas a hero. A foist-cless hero! In de meedle de coldest vedder he crossed de ice in a lettle boat, he should cetch de Bridish an' de missionaries—"

" '*Mercen*aries,' Mr. Kaplan, '*mer*cenaries'!"

"—foolink arond, not mit deir minds on de var!" Mr. Kaplan, having finished the sentence, said, "Podden me, '*Moisinaries*' I mant!" and, with scarcely a break in his stride, continued. "So efter de Ravolution de pipple said, 'Jawdge Vashington, you our hero an' lidder! Ve elactink you Prazident!' So he vas elacted Prazident U.S.—anonymously!"

Mr. Parkhill's " 'Unanimously!' " was lost in Mr. Kaplan's next words.

"An' like Mr. Robinson said, 'In Vashington's name is itch ladder like a coal, boinink ot his gloryous achivmants!' "

Mr. Kaplan ended the peroration with a joyous sweep of the arm.

"Mr. Kaplan!" Mr. Parkhill took the occasion to interrupt firmly. "You *must* speak more slowly, and—er—more carefully. You are making too many mistakes, far too many. It is *very* difficult to correct your English." Mr. Parkhill was aware that "Abraham Lincollen an' Jake Popper" were still to come.

Mr. Kaplan's face fell as he recognized the necessity of smothering the divine fire which flamed within him. "I'll try mine bast," he said. In a gentler mood, he continued. "Vell, I said a lot fine tings abot Jawdge Vashington. But enyho, is Abraham Lincollen more *close* to me. Dat Abraham Lincollen! Vat a sveet man. Vat a fine cherecter. Vat a hot—like *gold!* Look!" Mr. Kaplan pointed dramatically to the lithograph of the Great Emancipator which hung on the back wall; the heads of the students turned. "Look on his face! Look his ice, so sad mit fillink. Look his mot, so full goodness. Look de high forehat—dat's showink smotness, *brains!*" Mr. Kaplan's invidious glance toward Miss Caravello left no doubt that this high quality was missing in "Gary Baldy." "Look de honest axpression! I esk, is it a *vunder* dey vas callink him 'Honest Abie'?"

" 'Honest Abe!' " Mr. Parkhill exclaimed with some desperation, but Mr. Kaplan, carried away by the full, rich sweep of his passion, had soared on.

"No, it's no vunder. He vas a poor boy, a vood-chopper, a rail-splinter like dey say. But he made de Tsivil Var! Oh my, den vas tarrible times! Shoodink, killink, de Naut Site U. S. A. aganst de Sot Site U. S. A. Black neegers aganst vhite, brodder fightink brodder, de Blues mit de Grays. An' who von? *Who?* Ha! Abraham Lincollen von, netcherally! So he made de neegers should be like vhite. Ufcawss, Lincollen didn't change de *collars*," Mr. Kaplan foot-noted with scholarly discretion. "Dey vas still *black*. But *free* black, not slafe black. Den"—Mr. Kaplan's voice took on a pontifical note—"Lincollen gave ot de Mancipation Prockilmation. Dat vas, dat all men are born an' created *in de same vay!* So he vas killed."

Exhausted by this mighty passage, Mr. Kaplan paused. Mrs. Moskowitz chose the opportunity to force down a yawn.

"Vell, vat's got all dis to do mit Jake Popper?" Mr. Kaplan asked suddenly. He had taken the question out of the very mouths of Miss Mitnick Mr. Bloom, *et al:* It was a triumph of prescience. "Vell, Jake Popper also a fine man, mit a hot like gold. Ve called him 'Honest Jake.' Ufcawss, Jake Popper vasn't a beeg soldier; he didn't make Velley Fudges or free slafes. Jake Popper had a dalicatessen store." (The modest shrug which accompanied this sentence made it live and breathe: "Jake Popper had a dalicatessen store.") "An' in his store could even poor pipple mitout money, alvays gat somting to eat—if dey vas honest. Jake Popper did a tremandous beeg business—on cradit. An' averybody loved him.

"Vun day vas 'Honest Jake' fillink bed. He had hot an' cold vaves on de body by de same time; vat ve call a fivver. So averybody said, 'Jake, lay don in bad, rast.' But did Jake Popper lay don in bad, rast? No! He stayed in store, day an' night. He said, 'I got to tink abot mine *customers!*' Dat's de kind high sanse *duty* he had!"

Whether from throat strain or emotion, a husky tone crept into Mr. Kaplan's voice at this point.

"Den de doctor came an' said, 'Popper, you got bronxitis!' So Jake vent in bad. An' he got voise an' voise. So de doctor insulted odder doctors—"

" '*Con*sulted' other—"

"—an' dey took him in Mont Sinai Hospital. He had double demonia! So dere vas spacial noises, an' fromm all kinds maditzins de bast, an' an oxen tant, he should be able to breed. Even blood confusions dey gave him!"

" '*Trans*fusions,' Mr. Kaplan!" It was no use. Mr. Kaplan, like a spirited steed, was far ahead.

"An' dey shot him in de arm, he should fallink aslip. Dey gave him *epidemics*." Mr. Parkhill estimated his speed and made no protest. "An' efter a vhile, 'Honest Jake' Popper pest avay."

Mr. Kaplan's face was bathed in reverence, suffused with a lofty dignity. Mrs. Moskowitz yawned no more; she was shaking her head sadly, back and forth, back and forth. (Mrs. Moskowitz wore her heart on her sleeve.)

"So in Jake Popper's honor I made dis leettle spitch. An' I vant also to say for him somting like 'O Ceptin! My Ceptin!'—dat Miss Higby said abot Abraham Lincollen. I got fromm her de voids." Mr. Kaplan took a piece of paper out of an inner vest pocket, drew his head up high, and, as Mr. Parkhill held his breath, read:

> "O hot! hot! hot!
> O de bliddink drops ra
> Dere on de dack
> Jake Popper lies,
> Fallink cold an' dad!"

Celestial wings fluttered over the beginners' grade of the American Night Preparatory School for Adults, whispering of the grandeur that was Popper.

"Isn't dat beauriful?" Mr. Kaplan mused softly, with the detachment of the true artist. "My!"

Mr. Parkhill was just about to call for corrections when Mr. Kaplan said, "Vun ting more I should say, so de cless shouldn't fill *too* bed abot Jake Popper. It's awreddy nine yiss since he pest avay!"

Mrs. Moskowitz shot Mr. Kaplan a furious look: her tender emotions had been cruelly exploited.

"An' *I* didn't go to de funeral!" On this strange note, Mr. Kaplan took his seat.

The class hummed, protesting against this anticlimax which left so much to the imagination.

"Why you didn't?" cried Mr. Bloom, with a knowing nod to the Misses Mitnick and Caravello.

Mr. Kaplan's face was a study in sufferance. "Becawss de funeral vas in de meedle of de veek," he sighed. "An' I said to minesalf, 'Keplen, you in America, so tink like de *Americans* tink!' So I tought, an' I didn't go. Becawss I tought of dat *dip* American idea, *'Business before pleasure!'*"

1937

Peter De Vries

(1910-)

Born in Chicago, educated at Michigan's Calvin College and Northwestern University, and an editor for a while of *Poetry,* Peter De Vries's fame is a result of his humorous fiction. His first novel was *But Who Wakes the Bugler?* (1940). He joined the editorial staff of the *New Yorker* in 1944, the same year in which his *Angels Can't Do Better* appeared. His work since then includes *No, But I Saw the Movie* (1952), *Tunnel of Love* (1954), *Comfort Me with Apples* (1956), *The Mackerel Plaza* (1958), *The Tents of Wickedness* (1959), and *Through the Fields of Clover* (1961).

Requiem for a Noun, or Intruder in the Dusk

PETER DE VRIES

The cold Brussels sprout rolled off the page of the book I was reading and lay inert and defunctive in my lap. Turning my head with a leisure at least three-fourths impotent rage, I saw him standing there holding the toy with which he had catapulted the vegetable, or rather the reverse, the toy first then the fat insolent fist clutching it and then above that the bland defiant face beneath the shock of black hair like tangible gas. It, the toy, was one of those cardboard funnels with a trigger near

Reprinted by permission. Copyright © 1950 The New Yorker Magazine, Inc.

the point for firing a small celluloid ball. Letting the cold Brussels sprout lie there in my lap for him to absorb or anyhow apprehend rebuke from, I took a pull at a Scotch highball I had had in my hand and then set it down on the end table beside me.

"So instead of losing the shooter which would have been a mercy you had to lose the ball," I said, fixing with a stern eye what I had fathered out of all sentient and biding dust; remembering with that retroactive memory by which we count chimes seconds and even minutes after they have struck (recapitulate, even, the very grinding of the bowels of the clock before and during and after) the cunning furtive click, clicks rather, which perception should have told me then already were not the trigger plied but the icebox opened. "Even a boy of five going on six should have more respect for his father if not for food," I said, now picking the cold Brussels sprout out of my lap and setting it—not dropping it, setting it—in an ashtray; thinking how across the wax bland treachery of the kitchen linoleum were now in all likelihood distributed the remnants of string beans and cold potatoes and maybe even tapioca. "You're no son of mine."

I took up the thread of the book again or tried to: the weft of legitimate kinship that was intricate enough without the obbligato of that dark other: the sixteenths and thirty-seconds and even sixty-fourths of dishonoring cousinships brewed out of the violable blood by the ineffaceable errant lusts. Then I heard another click; a faint metallic rejoinder that this time was neither the trigger nor the icebox but the front door opened and then shut. Through the window I saw him picking his way over the season's soiled and sun-frayed vestiges of snow like shreds of rotted lace, the cheap upended toy cone in one hand and a child's cardboard suitcase in the other, toward the road.

I dropped the book and went out after him who had forgotten not only that I was in shirtsleeves but that my braces hung down over my flanks in twin festoons. "Where are you going?" I called, my voice expostulant and forlorn on the warm numb air. Then I caught it: caught it in the succinct outrage of the suitcase and the prim churning rear and marching heels as well: I had said he was no son of mine, and so he was leaving a house not only where he was not wanted but where he did not even belong.

"I see," I said in that shocked clarity with which we perceive the truth instantaneous and entire out of the very astonishment that refuses to acknowledge it. "Just as you now cannot be sure of any roof you belong more than half under, you figure there is no housetop from which you might not as well begin to shout it. Is that it?"

Something was trying to tell me something. Watching him turn off on the road—and that not only with the ostensible declaration of vagabondage but already its very assumption, attaining as though with a single footfall the very apotheosis of wandering just as with a single shutting of a door he had that of renunciation and farewell—watching him turn off on it, the road, in the direction of the Permisangs', our nearest neighbors, I thought *Wait; no; what I said was not enough for him to leave the house on; it must have been the blurted inscrutable chance confirmation of something he already knew, and was half able to assess, either out of the blown facts of boyhood or pure male divination or both.*

"What is it you know?" I said springing forward over the delicate squalor of the snow and falling in beside the boy. "Does any man come to the house to see your mother when I'm away, that you know of?" Thinking *We are mocked, first by the old mammalian snare, then, snared, by the final unilaterality of all flesh to which birth is given; not only not knowing when we may be cuckolded, but not even sure that in the veins of the very bantling we dandle does not flow the miscreant sniggering wayward blood.*

"I get it now," I said, catching in the undeviating face just as I had in the prim back and marching heels the steady articulation of disdain. "Cuckoldry is something of which the victim may be as guilty as the wrong-doers. That's what you're thinking? That by letting in this taint upon our heritage I am as accountable as she or they who have been its actual avatars. More. Though the foe may survive, the sleeping sentinel must be shot. Is that it?"

"You talk funny."

Mother-and-daughter blood conspires in the old mammalian office. Father-and-son blood vies in the ancient phallic enmity. I caught him by the arm and we scuffled in the snow. "I will be heard," I said, holding him now as though we might be dancing, my voice intimate and furious against the furious sibilance of our feet in the snow. Thinking how revelation had had to be inherent in the very vegetable scraps to which venery was probably that instant contriving to abandon me, the cold boiled despair of whatever already featureless suburban Wednesday, Thursday or Saturday supper the shot green was the remainder. "I see another thing," I panted, cursing my helplessness to curse whoever it was had given him blood and wind. Thinking *He's glad; glad to credit what is always secretly fostered and fermented out of the vats of childhood fantasy anyway (for all childhood must conceive a substitute for the father that has conceived it (finding that other inconceivable?);* thinking *He is walking in a nursery fairy tale to find the king his sire.* "Just as I said to you 'You're no son of mine' so now you answer back 'Neither are you any father to me.' "

The scherzo of violence ended as abruptly as it had begun. He broke away and walked on, after retrieving the toy he had dropped and adjusting his grip on the suitcase which he had not, this time faster and more urgently.

The last light was seeping out of the shabby sky, after the hemorrhage of sunset. High in the west where the fierce constellations soon would wheel, the evening star in single bombast burned and burned. The boy passed the Permisangs' without going in, then passed the Kellers'. Maybe he's heading for the McCullums', I thought, but he passed their house too. Then he, we, neared the Jelliff's. He's got to be going there, his search will end there, I thought. Because that was the last house this side of the tracks. And because *something was trying to tell me something.*

"Were you maybe thinking of what you heard said about Mrs. Jelliff and me having relations in Spuyten Duyvil?" I said in rapid frantic speculation. "But they were talking about mutual kin—nothing else." The boy said nothing. But I had sensed it instant and complete: the boy felt that, whatever of offense his mother may or may not have given, his father had given provocation; and out of the old embattled malehood, it was the hairy ineluctable Him whose guilt and shame he was going to hold preponderant. *Because now I remembered.*

"So it's Mrs. Jelliff—Sue Jelliff—and me you have got this all mixed up with," I said, figuring he must, in that fat sly nocturnal stealth that took him creeping up and down the stairs to listen when he should have been in bed, certainly have heard his mother exclaiming to his father behind that bedroom door it had been vain to close since it was not sound-proof: "I saw you. I saw that with Sue. There may not be anything between you but you'd like there to be! Maybe there is at that!"

Now like a dentist forced to ruin sound enamel to reach decayed I had to risk telling him what he did not know to keep what he assuredly did in relative control.

"This is what happened on the night in question," I said. "It was under the mistletoe, during the Holidays, at the Jelliffs'. Wait! I will be heard out! See your father as he is, but see him in no baser light. He has his arms around his neighbor's wife. It is evening, in the heat and huddled spiced felicity of the year's end, under the mistletoe (where as well as anywhere else the thirsting and exasperated flesh might be visited by the futile pangs and jets of later lust, the omnivorous aches of fifty and forty and even thirty-five to seize what may be the last of the allotted lips). Your father seems to prolong beyond its usual moment's span that custom's usufruct. Only for an instant, but in that instant letting trickle through the fissures of appearance what your mother and probably Rudy Jelliff too saw as an earnest of a flood that would have devoured that house and one four doors away."

A moon hung over the eastern roofs like a phantasmal bladder. Somewhere an icicle crashed and splintered, fruits of the day's thaw.

"So now I've got it straight," I said. "Just as through some nameless father your mother has cuckolded me (you think), so through one of

Rudy Jelliff's five sons I have probably cuckolded him. Which would give you at least a half brother under that roof where under ours you have none at all. So you balance out one miscreance with another, and find your rightful kin in our poor weft of all the teeming random bonded sentient dust."

Shifting the grip, the boy walked on past the Jelliffs'. Before him—the tracks; and beyond that—the other side of the tracks. And now out of whatever reserve capacity for astonished incredulity may yet have remained I prepared to face this last and ultimate outrage. But he didn't cross. Along our own side of the tracks ran a road which the boy turned left on. He paused before a lighted house near the corner, a white cottage with a shingle in the window which I knew from familiarity to read, "Viola Pruett, Piano Lessons," and which, like a violently unscrambled pattern on a screen, now came to focus.

Memory adumbrates just as expectation recalls. The name on the shingle made audible to listening recollection the last words of the boy's mother as she'd left, which had fallen short then of the threshold of hearing. ". . . Pruett," I remembered now. "He's going to have supper and stay with Buzzie Pruett overnight. . . . Can take a few things with him in that little suitcase of his. If Mrs. Pruett phones about it, just say I'll take him over when I get back," I recalled now in that chime-counting recapitulation of retroactive memory—better than which I could not have been expected to do. Because the eternal Who-instructs might have got through to the whiskey-drinking husband or might have got through to the reader immersed in that prose vertiginous intoxicant and unique, but not to both.

"So that's it," I said. "You couldn't wait till you were taken much less till it was time but had to sneak off by yourself and that not cross-lots but up the road I've told you a hundred times to keep off even the shoulder of."

The boy had stopped and now appeared to hesitate before the house. He turned around at last, switched the toy and the suitcase in his hands, and started back in the direction he had come.

"What are you going back for now?" I asked.

"More stuff to take in this suitcase," he said. "I was going to just sleep at the Pruetts' overnight, but now I'm going to ask them to let me stay there for good."

1950

CHAPTER TEN

REPRESENTATIVE LATER POETS

The three poets represented in this section—Marianne Moore, William Carlos Williams, and John Crowe Ransom—might easily have appeared earlier in this anthology. They were born in the 1890's, and each has significant ties with the early movements of the new poetry and criticism—Marianne Moore, with T. S. Eliot, *Poetry* magazine, and *The Egoist;* William Carlos Williams, with Ezra Pound and the first volume of *Des Imagistes;* and John Crowe Ransom, with the *Fugitive* group at Vanderbilt University in Nashville, Tennessee, and as a major contributor to *I'll Take My Stand.* They might also be viewed as precursors of or continuators of the writers represented in the section "Experimentation in Poetry," for these three poets are also highly individualized, adventuresome, and experimental. However, their major recognition came relatively late in the new century, with Miss Moore's *Collected Poems* in 1952, with Williams' first volume of *Paterson* in 1946, and with Ransom's *Selected Poems* in 1945, although they all had done significant work earlier. Williams' first volume appeared in 1909, and the other two poets', only a decade later, in 1919.

Although Marianne Moore had published in both *Poetry* and *The Egoist* as early as 1915, her first volume, *Poems,* was published (without her knowledge) in 1921 by two friends of the Imagist movement, Hilda Doolittle and Robert McAlmon. Her remarkable career was foreshadowed by little in her earlier life: birth in St. Louis, Missouri; an education at Bryn Mawr College; a stint of teaching stenography at the United States Indian School at Carlisle, Pennsylvania; a job with the New York Public Library; and the editorship of *Dial* magazine for the four years before its demise in 1929. Her permanent move to Brooklyn soon thereafter, in spite of the splendid precedent of Whitman, hardly presaged more.

One has, however, only to turn to one of her very early poems, "Poetry" (first published in *Observations*, 1924, and revised and expanded in *Selected Poems,* 1935), for two since-famous lines that predict as well as any what her poetry was to be. Poets, she there says, must be "literalists of the imagination"; they must "present/for inspection, imaginary gardens with real toads in them." And this, indeed, is what Marianne Moore has continually been and done. The Brooklyn Dodgers, elephants, snails, swans, steam rollers, and unicorns, among other things, have all been successful subjects for her disciplined pen. Her extension of Imagism is uniquely her own, and her poetic line, although having the effect of free verse, is characteristically carefully measured and balanced. Suddenly discovered rhymes reveal intricately designed patterns wherein syllables, lines, and stanzas are all under strict and exquisite control.

T. S. Eliot early recognized Miss Moore's talent, and in the Introduction he wrote for her 1935 volume, he called her "the most accomplished poetess in the English-speaking world today." The world soon caught up. The volumes following *Selected Poems–The Pangolin and Other Verse* (1936), *What Are Years?* (1941), and *Nevertheless* (1944)–culminated in *Collected Poems* (1952), which won her not only the Pulitzer Prize, but also the National Book Award for Poetry and the Bollingen Award. Her complete translation of La Fontaine's Fables appeared in 1954, a collection of essays in 1955, *Like a Bulwark* in 1956, and *O To Be a Dragon* in 1959.

William Carlos Williams, M.D., also had some Imagistic backgrounds and affinities. He received his medical degree in 1906 from the University of Pennsylvania where he met Pound, and he renewed his association with Pound in Europe, where he had gone to study pediatrics. He did not remain in Europe, however, and the general medical practice he set up (in 1909) in Rutherford, New Jersey (and its Manhattan-Passaic-Paterson surroundings), was to result in a life-long "professional" medical career every bit as successful as his concomitant careers as poet, novelist, short-story writer, playwright, and essayist. Like Wallace Stevens, the successful insurance executive who was more importantly a poet, Williams is better known as a writer than as a doctor, and, among the various literary genres he successfully practiced, better known as a poet than anything else.

His prose, however, should not be underestimated. In both the novel and the short-story form he has some significant accomplishments, and were his poetry less prolific or persuasive, his fiction would probably be better known than it is. In such novels as *A Voyage to Pangany* (1928), *White Mule* (1937), *White Mule: Part II* (1940), and *The Build Up* (1952), he clearly caught, as one critic has put it, "the forms and pressures of inchoate modern life." In his shorter fiction, collected in such volumes as *The Knife of the Times and Other Stories* (1932) or *Life Along the Passaic River* (1938), his acquired discipline as a poet is turned easily to the intricacies required in successful modern short-story writing. A characteristic later play, *A Dream of Love*, was produced in New York in 1949. Among his notable nonfiction are such volumes as *In the American Grain* (1924), a highly stylized study of our cultural origins, and his *Autobiography* (1951), an excellent source of biographical data and an informative account of the exciting world in which Williams lived.

His earliest poetry, in such volumes as *Poems* (1909) and *The Tempers* (1913), clearly reveals his ties with the Imagists. And the good Imagistic adjectives–short, hard, precise, informal, and colloquial–were applicable to many of the poems in those volumes as well as to most of those which followed in *Collected Poems, 1921-31* (1934). There was also a difference as he began to find his true voice: a seemingly objective statement of simple and ordinary things; a flat, matter-of-fact, conversational tone with an avoidance of emotional heightening; but also (as George Whicher has pointed out) "extreme rapidity of pace, a dramatic juxtaposition of images, a startling succession of sensations," and thus both a bold tension and an inexorable release as the thing seen moves toward objective and meaningful definition. The subject may well be as commonplace as the white chicken beside the red wheelbarrow or the plums in the icebox, but what the reader ultimately sees is a good deal more.

Williams' most ambitious poem is *Paterson* (published in four books between 1946 and 1951), and capped with a sort of coda, in Book V, published some years later in 1958. Here Paterson is not only the city which gives the poem its name, but the human mind (both male and female) of the city beside the river (time), as it erodes, is rebuilt, and speaks, through the language of events from the time of its Indian origins to the highly industrialized city of the present, which Williams thoroughly knew through his long medical practice there. History, fancy, alien chronicles, personal reminiscences, letters, love poems, stories–all are incorporated into a historical moment that becomes an ultimate reality. Some consider *Paterson* to be the twentieth century's closest parallel to Whitman's *Leaves of Grass.* Whatever posterity's final judgment may be, this particular work will have to be viewed as one of modern American poetry's most ambitious attempts, just as Williams himself will have to be viewed as one of its most indefatigable writers.

The truism that a little bit of poetry can be as important as a great deal of it is well demonstrated by the slender volume that constitutes John Crowe Ransom's total poetic output–especially when it is contrasted to William Carlos Williams'. However, Ransom, like Williams, also has had distinguished "other" careers, as critic, as educator, and as editor; but it is probably his poetry that should be held in highest regard.

If Williams' poetry obscured to some extent the achievement of his fiction, it can perhaps be similarly observed of Ransom that the fame of his critical essays has to some extent obscured the achievement of his poetry. As one of the most prominent of the Southern Agrarians, he was actively associated with the Vanderbilt University "Fugitive" group and was one of the leading contributors to the famous symposium, *I'll Take My Stand* (1930). In that volume as well as in *God Without Thunder* (of the same year), the stable virtues of an agrarian culture are advocated over those of an industrial one which too often admires science and technology to the point of abstracting and thus violently reducing the rich potential of the human experience. His critical essays—in such volumes as *The World's Body* (1938) and *The New Criticism* (1941), and as editor and editorialist in the *Kenyon Review*—are among the most influential by any modern American critic. The argument is always for the need of poetry, of art, to represent the fullness, the "body," the totality of the human possibilities. This ideological position is always supported by the most knowledgeable technical detail and thus always lucid and clean but with no sacrifices to over-simplification or distortion.

When he published his *Selected Poems* in 1945, he included only forty-two, most of them extensively revised, from the volumes that had preceded it. When these were reprinted in *Poems and Essays* a decade later (1955), only two additional poems had been added. Small though this output is, his poetry has always been highly regarded for its judicious avoidance of sentimentality, its wit and irony, its classical adherence to form. His always precise diction sometimes reveals a stringent quaintness which somehow allows him (seemingly at the same time) both to evoke and denigrate pathos. Excessive feeling is likely to be joined to bemused comment, precarious imbalance to firm control, a Southern richness of texture to a rigidly classical form.

Art "wants us to enjoy life, to taste and reflect as we drink," Ransom said in *The World's Body*. To taste and reflect is not an ignoble end for poetry, when what is tasted and reflected upon is "life." This is the case with the poetry of John Crowe Ransom, as it is with that of Marianne Moore and William Carlos Williams, as, indeed, it is with that of any good poet. Both the flavor of experience and the intellectual "savor" caught by these three American poets are distinctive.

Marianne (Craig) Moore

(1887-   )

CHRONOLOGY:

1887 Born November 14, in St. Louis, Missouri.

1909 Graduated from Bryn Mawr.

1910 Completed a year's study of "business" subjects at the Metzger Institute, in Carlisle, Pennsylvania.

1910-14 Taught in the Indian School, Carlisle.
1915 First poems appeared in *Poetry* and *The Egoist.*
1921 *Poems* (arranged for by "H.D." and others).
1924 *Observations* (a reprint of first volume, with additions, given the *Dial* Award).
1925-29 Was Acting Editor, the *Dial.*
1935 *Selected Poems* (with introduction by T. S. Eliot).
1936 *The Pangolin and Other Verse.*
1941 *What Are Years?*
1944 *Nevertheless.*
1945 *Rock Crystal: A Christmas Tale* (translated from the German of Adalbert Stifter).
1952 *Collected Poems* (awarded Pulitzer Prize, National Book Award, and Bollingen Award).
1954 *The Fables of La Fontaine,* trans.
1955 *Predilections,* criticism.
1956 *Like a Bulwark.*
1959 *O To Be a Dragon.*
1961 *A Marianne Moore Reader.*

BIBLIOGRAPHY:

Marianne Moore's poetry beyond the 1952 volume has not been collected, and the material in *A Marianne Moore Reader* (New York, 1961) contains both old and new.

There is no book-length study of her work or her life, but among the important numerous short studies are T. S. Eliot's "Introduction" to her *Selected Poems* (New York, 1935); Kenneth Burke, "Motives and Motifs in the Poetry of Marianne Moore," *Accent,* LX (1942), 157-169; and Randall Jarrell, "Thoughts About Marianne Moore," *Partisan Review,* XIX (1952), 687-700. *The Quarterly Review of Literature,* IV (1948) is a special Marianne Moore issue.

The most complete bibliography is that compiled by Eugene P. Sheehy and Kenneth A. Lohf, "The Achievement of Marianne Moore: A Bibliography," *Bulletin of the New York Public Library,* LXII (March-May, 1958), 131-149 ff. For explications, see Joseph M. Kuntz, *Poetry Explication* (Rev. ed.; Denver, 1962).

Poetry

I, too, dislike it: there are things that are important beyond all this
   fiddle.
 Reading it, however, with a perfect contempt for it, one discovers
   in
 it after all, a place for the genuine.
   Hands that can grasp, eyes
   that can dilate, hair that can rise
     if it must, these things are important not because a

high-sounding interpretation can be put upon them but because
   they are
 useful. When they become so derivative as to become unintelligible,
 the same thing may be said for all of us, that we
   do not admire what
   we cannot understand: the bat
     holding on upside down or in quest of something to

eat, elephants pushing, a wild horse taking a roll, a tireless wolf
under
a tree, the immovable critic twitching his skin like a horse that
feels a flea, the base-
ball fan, the statistician—
nor is it valid
to discriminate against "business documents and

school-books"; all these phenomena are important. One must make
a distinction
however: when dragged into prominence by half poets, the result
is not poetry,
nor till the poets among us can be
"literalists of
the imagination"—above
insolence and triviality and can present

for inspection, "imaginary gardens with real toads in them," shall
we have
it. In the meantime, if you demand on the one hand,
the raw material of poetry in
all its rawness and
that which is on the other hand
genuine, you are interested in poetry. 1921

To a Steam Roller

The illustration
is nothing to you without the application.
You lack half wit. You crush all the particles down
into close conformity, and then walk back and forth on them.

Sparkling chips of rock
are crushed down to the level of the parent block.
Were not "impersonal judgment in aesthetic
matters, a metaphysical impossibility," you

might fairly achieve
it. As for butterflies, I can hardly conceive
of one's attending upon you, but to question
the congruence of the complement is vain, if it exists. 1924

To a Snail

If "compression is the first grace of style,"
you have it. Contractility is a virtue
as modesty is a virtue.
It is not the acquisition of any one thing
that is able to adorn,
or the incidental quality that occurs
as a concomitant of something well said,
that we value in style,
but the principle that is hid:
in the absence of feet, "a method of conclusions";
"a knowledge of principles,"
in the curious phenomenon of your occipital horn.

1924

The Mind Is an Enchanting Thing

is an enchanted thing
    like the glaze on a
katydid-wing
        subdivided by sun
        till the nettings are legion.
Like Gieseking playing Scarlatti;

like the apteryx-awl
    as a beak, or the
kiwi's rain-shawl
        of haired feathers, the mind
        feeling its way as though blind,
walks along with its eyes on the ground.

It has memory's ear
    that can hear without
having to hear.
        Like the gyroscope's fall,
        truly unequivocal
because trued by regnant certainty,

it is a power of
    strong enchantment. It
is like the dove-

neck animated by
sun; it is memory's eye;
it's conscientious inconsistency.

It tears off the veil; tears
the temptation, the
mist the heart wears,
from its eyes,—if the heart
has a face; it takes apart
dejection. It's fire in the dove-neck's

iridescence; in the
inconsistencies
of Scarlatti.
Unconfusion submits
its confusion to proof; it's
not a Herod's oath that cannot change.

1944

William Carlos Williams

(1883-1963)

CHRONOLOGY:

1883 Born September 17, in Rutherford, New Jersey.
1906-09 Did graduate study in New York City and Europe.
1909 *Poems;* set up permanent medical practice in Rutherford, New Jersey.
1913 *The Tempers.*
1917 *A Book of Poems, Al Que Quiere!*
1920 *Kora in Hell: Improvisations.*
1921 *Sour Grapes: A Book of Poems.*
1923 *Spring and All: Go Go; The Great American Novel,* criticism.
1925 *In the American Grain,* essays.
1926 Given the *Dial* Award for service to American literature.
1928 *A Voyage to Pagany,* novel.
1931 Given the Guarantors' Prize by *Poetry.*
1932 *The Knife of the Times and Other Stories; A Novelette and Other Prose.*
1934 *Collected Poems, 1921-1931* (with introduction by Wallace Stevens).
1935 *An Early Martyr and Other Poems.*
1936 *Adam and Eve & the City.*
1937 *White Mule,* novel.
1938 *The Complete Collected Poems; Life Along the Passaic River,* stories.
1940 *In the Money: White Mule, Part II,* novel.
1941 *The Broken Span.*
1944 *The Wedge.*
1946 *Paterson.*
1948 *Paterson, Book II* (given the Loines Award); *A Dream of Love,* verse play; *The Clouds.*
1949 *Paterson, Book III* (given the National Book Award); *The Pink Church.*
1950 *The Collected Later Poems of William Carlos Williams; Make Light of It,* stories.
1951 *Paterson, Book IV; The Auto-*

biography of William Carlos Williams; The Collected Earlier Poems of William Carlos Williams.

1952 *The Build-Up,* novel.

1954 *The Desert Music, and Other Poems; Selected Essays.*

1955 *Journey to Love.*

1956 *John Marin* (with Duncan Phillips and others).

1957 *The Selected Letters of William Carlos Williams* (ed. by John C. Thirlwall); *The Past Recaptured; Sappho.*

1958 *Many Loves,* play; *Paterson, Book V.*

1963 Died March 4, at Rutherford, New Jersey.

BIBLIOGRAPHY:

Except for his very latest work, the poetry of Williams is adequately collected in *The Collected Earlier Poems* . . . and *The Collected Later Poems* . . . (see Chronology). *Selected Essays, Selected Letters,* and the *Autobiography* are also listed there.

The single full-length study is Vivienne Koch, *William Carlos Williams* (Norfolk, Conn., 1950), but both the *Briarcliff Quarterly,* III (October, 1946) and *Perspective,* VI (Autumn-Winter, 1953), are special issues on Williams. Especially interesting is Edith Heal, ed., *I Wanted to Write a Poem: The Autobiography of the Works of a Poet* (Boston, 1958), a list of all of Williams' publications to that date with his comment on each work.

For explications of the poetry, see Joseph M. Kuntz, *Poetry Explication* (Rev. ed.; Denver, 1962). For studies of his novels, see Donna Gerstenberger and George Hendrick, *The American Novel, 1789-1959* . . . (Denver, 1961); for his short stories, Warren S. Walker, *Twentieth-Century Short Story Explication* . . . (Hamden, Conn., 1961), Supplement, 1963.

Danse Russe

If I when my wife is sleeping
and the baby and Kathleen
are sleeping
and the sun is a flame-white disc
in silken mists
above shining trees,—
if I in my north room
dance naked, grotesquely
before my mirror
waving my shirt round my head
and singing softly to myself:
"I am lonely, lonely.
I was born to be lonely,
I am best so!"
If I admire my arms, my face
my shoulders, flanks, buttocks
against the yellow drawn shades,—

Who shall say I am not
the happy genius of my household? 1917

Tract

I will teach you my townspeople
how to perform a funeral—
for you have it over a troop
of artists—
unless one should scour the world—
you have the ground sense necessary.

See! the hearse leads.
I begin with a design for a hearse.
For Christ's sake not black—
nor white either—and not polished!
Let it be weathered—like a farm wagon—
with gilt wheels (this could be
applied fresh at small expense)
or no wheels at all:
a rough dray to drag over the ground.

Knock the glass out!
My God—glass, my townspeople!
For what purpose? It is for the dead
to look out or for us to see
how well he is housed or to see
the flowers or the lack of them—
or what?
To keep the rain and snow from him?
He will have a heavier rain soon:
pebbles and dirt and what not.
Let there be no glass—
and no upholstery! phew!
and no little brass rollers
and small easy wheels on the bottom—
my townspeople what are you thinking of!

A rough plain hearse then
with gilt wheels and no top at all.
On this the coffin lies
by its own weight.

No wreaths please—
especially no hot-house flowers.

Some common memento is better,
something he prized and is known by:
his old clothes—a few books perhaps—
God knows what! You realize
how we are about these things,
my townspeople—
something will be found—anything—
even flowers if he had come to that.
So much for the hearse.

For heaven's sake though see to the driver!
Take off the silk hat! In fact
that's no place at all for him
up there unceremoniously
dragging our friend out to his own dignity!
Bring him down—bring him down!
Low and inconspicuous! I'd not have him ride
on the wagon at all—damn him—
the undertaker's understrapper!
Let him hold the reins
and walk at the side
and inconspicuously too!

Then briefly as to yourselves:
Walk behind—as they do in France,
seventh class, or if you ride
Hell take curtains! Go with some show
of inconvenience; sit openly—
to the weather as to grief.
Or do you think you can shut grief in?
What—from us? We who have perhaps
nothing to lose? Share with us
share with us—it will be money
in your pockets.

Go now
I think you are ready. 1920

The Red Wheelbarrow

so much depends
upon

a red wheel
barrow

glazed with rain
water

beside the white
chickens. 1923

This Is Just to Say

I have eaten
the plums
that were in
the icebox

and which
you were probably
saving
for breakfast.

Forgive me
they were delicious
so sweet
and so cold 1934

John Crowe Ransom

(1888-)

CHRONOLOGY:

1888 Born on April 30, in Pulaski, Tennessee.

1909 Graduated from Vanderbilt University.

1909-13 Was a Rhodes Scholar, Christ Church College, Oxford.

1914-37 Was a Professor of English, Vanderbilt University.

1919 *Poems About God.*

1922-25 Was an editor of the *Fugitive*.
1924 *Chills and Fever; Grace After Meat* (London).
1927 *Two Gentlemen in Bonds.*
1930 *God Without Thunder*, criticism; contributor to *I'll Take My Stand.*
1931-32 Was a Guggenheim Fellow at Exeter, England.
1937-58 Was Carnegie Professor of English, Kenyon College, editor (1938-1961) *Kenyon Review.*
1938 *The World's Body.*
1941 *The New Criticism.*
1945 *Selected Poems.*
1951 Edited *The Keyon Critics;* received the Bollingen Award.
1955 *Poems and Essays.*
1958 Awarded the Brandeis University Gold Medal.
1963 Awarded National Book Award for *Selected Poems.*
1964 *Selected Poems*, revised and enlarged.

BIBLIOGRAPHY:

Poems and Essays (New York, 1955) contains two poems in addition to those in *The Selected Poems* (New York, 1945) and the uncollected criticism. A revised and enlarged edition of *Selected Poems* (New York, 1964) is available.

There is no book-length study of Ransom, but the "Homage to John Crowe Ransom" issue of the *Sewanee Review,* LVIII (1948) is a good introduction and contains a check list of his work.

For explications of individual poems, see Joseph M. Kuntz, *Poetry Explication* (Rev. ed.; Denver, 1962).

Bells for John Whiteside's Daughter

There was such speed in her little body,
And such lightness in her footfall,
It is no wonder that her brown study
Astonishes us all.

Her wars were bruited in our high window.
We looked among orchard trees and beyond
Where she took arms against her shadow,
Or harried unto the pond

The lazy geese, like a snow cloud
Dripping their snow on the green grass,
Tricking and stopping, sleepy and proud,
Who cried in goose, Alas,

For the tireless heart within the little
Lady with rod that made them rise
From their noon apple-dreams and scuttle
Goose-fashion under the skies!

But now go the bells, and we are ready,
In one house we are sternly stopped
To say we are vexed at her brown study,
Lying so primly propped. 1924

Here Lies a Lady

Here lies a lady of beauty and high degree.
Of chills and fever she died, of fever and chills,
The delight of her husband, her aunts, an infant of three,
And of medicos marvelling sweetly on her ills.

For either she burned, and her confident eyes would blaze,
And her fingers fly in a manner to puzzle their heads—
What was she making? Why, nothing; she sat in a maze
Of old scraps of laces, snipped into curious shreds—

Or this would pass, and the light of her fire decline
Till she lay discouraged and cold as a thin stalk white and blown,
And would not open her eyes, to kisses, to wine;
The sixth of these states was her last; the cold settled down.

Sweet ladies, long may ye bloom, and toughly I hope ye may thole,
But was she not lucky? In flowers and lace and mourning,
In love and great honour we bade God rest her soul
After six little spaces of chill, and six of burning. 1924

Blue Girls

Twirling your blue skirts, traveling the sward
Under the towers of your seminary,
Go listen to your teachers old and contrary
Without believing a word.

Tie the white fillets then about your lustrous hair
And think no more of what will come to pass
Than bluebirds that go walking on the grass
And chattering on the air.

Practice your beauty, blue girls, before it fail;
And I will cry with my loud lips and publish
Beauty which all our power shall never establish,
It is so frail.

For I could tell you a story which is true:
I know a lady with a terrible tongue,
Blear eyes fallen from blue,
All her perfections tarnished—yet it is not long
Since she was lovelier than any of you. 1927

CHAPTER ELEVEN

THE SOUTHERN ACHIEVEMENT IN FICTION

It is in a way a disservice to give a regional label to the fiction of Robert Penn Warren, Katherine Anne Porter, and William Faulkner. Although they are all Southerners and their fiction has Southern locales, its achievement transcends mere regional worth—or even nationalistic worth, for that matter—and forms, in some of its aspects, the most highly regarded fiction produced in America. The American South was the most active literary region in America during some stretches of the twentieth century, and its writers would certainly constitute the most impressive list to come from any single region of modern America. Although such a list would be impressive enough in the field of poetry and drama (containing John Crowe Ransom, Conrad Aiken, John Peale Bishop, Lizette Wood Reese, John Gould Fletcher, Allen Tate, Randall Jarrell, Paul Green, Lillian Hellman, and Tennessee Williams), a list of its writers of fiction would be even more distinguished—with Thomas Wolfe, Elizabeth Madox Roberts, Ellen Glasgow, Erskine Caldwell, James Branch Cabell, Eudora Welty, Stark Young, Truman Capote, William Styron, Flannery O'Connor, and Shirley Ann Grau, among others. Warren, Porter, and Faulkner are a central part of this group, but if they are representatives of the so-called Southern Renaissance, they are also representatives of the modern literary achievement in America. In the field of fiction, some of their work represents that achievement at its very best.

Robert Penn Warren, the youngest of these three, is also the most versatile. A native of Guthrie, Kentucky, a student of John Crowe Ransom's at Vanderbilt, an undergraduate contributor to the *Fugitive*, one of the agrarians represented in *I'll Take My Stand*, a Rhodes Scholar at Oxford, an educator, an editor, a critic—Warren is also, of the three, the only successful poet, in addition to his achievement as a writer of fiction. In fact, his fiction came relatively late in his career.

Although he had written a biography in 1929, *John Brown: The Making of a Martyr,* and published a volume of verse in 1935, *Thirty-six Poems,* fame probably first came, aside from his association with the Southern agrarians, through his editorship of the influential *Southern Review,* which he founded at Louisiana State University with Cleanth Brooks, and in which were continued many of the policies associated with the Nashville group. The two also edited *Understanding Poetry* (1938) and *Understanding Fiction* (1943)—college-level text books which, with their "New Critical" insistence upon formal analyses and techniques, revolutionized the teaching of literature in American colleges and universities. Warren was later to teach at both Minnesota and Yale, and important volumes of criticism, essays, and poetry have all continued to appear; but with the publication of his third novel, *All the King's Men* (1946), his fiction came to be seen as perhaps his richest achievement.

The two novels which preceded it—*Night Rider* (1939) and *At Heaven's Gate* (1943)—although suggested by, respectively, the Kentucky Tobacco War of 1904 and the career of Luke Lea, a corrupt Tennessee politician, are both examinations of the inadequacies of Eden, that is, tests of "innocence," which came to be one of his major themes. Perhaps its finest realization, in his long fiction, is in *All the King's Men,* the most popular of his novels, winner of a Pulitzer prize, and basis for a powerful motion picture (for which Warren also wrote the scenario). Ostensibly the story of Willie Stark, a Southern politician (and at least partly based on the life of Huey P. Long), it depicts the inevitable corruption resulting from too simple an idea of "political good." Actually, Willie Stark mirrors the somewhat too stringent and inflexible idealism of Jack Burden, protagonist-narrator and real hero of the novel. "Blackberry Winter," the story reprinted here, appeared the same year and is another test of innocence.

Among the novels which followed—*World Enough and Time* (1950), *Band of Angels* (1955), *The Cave* (1959), *Wilderness* (1961), and *The Flood* (1964)—*The Cave* and *The Flood* are probably the most ambitious. Although the former is an avowedly "philosophical" novel, it has violence for its subject (a mine cave-in in the Appalachians); and both effectively join a poetic feeling for words to a rare respect for form in a way that marks Warren's best fiction. His *Brother to Dragons, A Tale in Verse and Voices* (1953) also deserves mention. Two important pamphlets—*Segregation: The Inner Conflict in the South* (1956) and *The Legacy of the Civil War* (1961) reveal his perceptive understanding of the temper of his time. His *Selected Essays* appeared in 1958.

It was Warren himself, incidentally, as one of his many "other" selves (this time as critic), who best helped explain the curious achievement of Katherine Anne Porter, a writer possibly without parallel in American literature, in view of her paucity of output as contrasted with her remarkable reputation. With the exception of her very recent and only full-length novel, *Ship of Fools* (1962), which was her first new fiction in twenty years, her entire creative corpus includes only five novellas and three slim volumes of short stories. Yet her work is well known to discriminating readers of modern American literature; it has been enormously influential; and it has the curious distinction (again with the exception of her late novel) of having elicited almost universal praise.

Warren considered her keen sense of irony a major reason for her success—an irony which consistently rejects the simple and ready-made and demands instead the complex and human. Her magnificently controlled style is also relevant here. It is sensitive, both subtle and supple, and yet stringently mannered, clearly a "voice" of her own in a way matched only by the masters of fiction. Her complete dedication and absorption are evident on every page of her work. Indeed, as she herself has said, writing is the central meaning and pattern of her life.

All of these virtues were apparent in her very earliest work, *Flowering Judas,* a volume of six stories, published in 1930, when she was forty years old. Expanded to include four more stories five years later, *Flowering Judas and Other Stories* (1935) made her reputation. Her five novelettes—*Hacienda* (1934), *Noon Wine* (1937), *Old Mortality* and *Pale Horse, Pale Rider* (1939), and *No Safe Harbor* (1941)—are equally accomplished, although *Pale Horse, Pale Rider,* an unforgettable portrait of a girl's tragic discovery of self, is perhaps the favorite of most readers. Her last collection of short fiction, *The Leaning Tower and Other Stories,* appeared in 1944. The locales of her fiction reflect her life in the South, in California, in Mexico, in Colorado, in France, and New York—and all with an appropriate and heightened sense of "place." Distance is always apparent also—the distance between the thing seen and the imaginative control of the artist, so that subject has less importance than the artistic vision, exquisitely blended though they both always are in Miss Porter's work.

Although the long-awaited *Ship of Fools,* a highly metaphorical account of a sea-voyage from Mexico to Germany during the 1930's, was widely praised and a best seller for months, some critics considered it not among her best works. She collected her essays in *The Days Before* in 1952, and she has also translated some stories from the French and Spanish.

It is, however, William Faulkner who towers over this group, as he towers over most areas of modern American literature. His is probably the most prodigious literary imagination in America since the death of Henry James, and there are some who consider him the greatest novelist America has yet produced. Whatever posterity's ultimate judgment may be, in range, in technical dexterity, and in the number of different solid achievements, no other modern writer of fiction in America appears today to be his superior. Yet the "world" of the major part of this achievement is a mythical county in northern Mississippi, comprising, its creator once slyly said, 2,400 square miles, with a precise population of 6,298 Whites and 9,313 Negroes. "Yoknapatawpha County, Mississippi, William Faulkner sole owner and proprietor," a modest-enough statement accompanying a map he once drew of his mythical county, tags the very center of this remarkable creative achievement.

Yoknapatawpha County in actuality, of course, is the entire universe; but it is also America at its most diverse and most self-conscious: it is the American South, especially that little postage-stamp area of Northern Mississippi that Faulkner knew so well. The score of books that both created and contained this world appeared in a remarkable series of fits and starts. The first great series appeared in four short years: *Sartoris* and *The Sound and the Fury* in 1929; *As I Lay Dying*, in 1930; *Sanctuary*, in 1931; and *Light in August*, in 1932. An inconsequential volume of poetry, *The Marble Faun* (1924), and two relatively unimportant novels had appeared previously, *Soldier's Pay* (1926) and *Mosquitoes* (1927). An important collection of short stories is also of these years, *These Thirteen* (1931).

Had Faulkner written no more than these, he probably still would have had a permanent and prominent place in the history of modern American literature. *Sartoris*, the first of the Yoknapatawpha saga, began to develop the themes which run through his greatest work. In a world somewhat surprisingly like that of *The Waste Land* or *The Sun Also Rises*, however dissimilar the respective locales, it depicts a restless, returned young Southern soldier, burned out by the ravages of war, "craving violence," as one critic has put it, "as a kind of substitute for meaning." The novel that followed, *The Sound and the Fury*, was his first great novel and is still considered by many as his finest. It focusses on the death of a world in the fall of a family, the aristocratic Compsons, as retold by the three Compson brothers, the idiot Benjy, the acute and sensitive suicide Quentin, and the greedy, petty-minded Jason. It is a difficult work, and what Cleanth Brooks has called "the audacity of its technique" (the first part is told from the point of view of the idiot Benjy) has made of it a kind of critical *cause célèbre*. *As I Lay Dying*, another picture of a Southern family, but this time poor whites, is a riotous, macabre and yet heroic comedy of the trials and tribulations of Addie Bundren's husband and five children and their "odyssey" to Jefferson with Addie's dead body. However, tenderness and sensitivity are as much a part of its conception and execution as its comedy, Faulkner's encompassing dual vision as much at work here as it is with his picture of the magnificent and "positive" Negress Dilsey in *The Sound and the Fury*. *Sanctuary*, partly set in a Memphis brothel and the most notorious of his novels, has in recent years gained increasing respect. *Light in August*, the last and in some ways the peak of the early group, spins out the timeless fates of the crucified mulatto Joe Christmas, the passively bovine Lena Grove, and all of the outrageous discrepancy—both comic and tragic—in between.

The next big addition to the Yoknapatawpha saga dates roughly from *Absalom, Absalom!* in 1936 through *Go Down, Moses, and Other Stories* in 1942. In between appeared *The Unvanquished* (1938), *The Wild Palms* (1939), and *The Hamlet* (1940). Both *Absalom, Absalom!* and *The Unvanquished* return to the Southern past, the first through young Quentin Compson's reconstruction of Thomas Sutpen and his "doomed baronial dream," the second through the Sartorises during the time of the Civil War. *The Wild Palms* is a bold joining of two seemingly disparate and distinct novellas, chapter by chapter, so that the meaning of one becomes involved with the meaning of the other. In *The Hamlet* he completed the first volume of what was later to be a trilogy of the Snopes family—with *The Town* (1957) and *The Mansion* (1959). In *Go Down, Moses,* right in the center of his career, he reveals, in a group of interrelated stories, perhaps his most profound understanding of the relationship between Negro and White, in Isaac McCaslin, whom Irving Howe calls "the moral hero of the Yoknapatawpha saga"; in Lucus Beauchamp, one of his greatest Negro characters; and in "The Bear," the novella-length tale that recounts the initiation of young Ike McCaslin into manhood and his discovery and renunciation of the legacy of his forefathers.

Faulkner's own legacy of the next few years—*Intruder in the Dust* (1948), *Knight's Gambit* (1949), *Requiem for a Nun* (1951), and *A Fable* (1954)—is generally considered the weakest of his "major" periods, although his *Collected Stories* (1950), like those of Hemingway and Fitzgerald, reveal him to be a master of short fiction as well as of long. In "Dry September," "A Rose for Emily," or "There Was a Queen" is testimony enough to his accomplishment in the short-story form.

The work of his last period was marked by the completed Snopes trilogy and (in 1962) *The Reivers,* published the year he died. His Snopes trilogy—in its depiction of the rise, the flourishing, and the demise of Flem Snopes and all its accumulative and accompanying comic-tragic ramifications—is regarded by some critics as one of his major achievements, and with the nostalgic *The Reivers* he left an appropriate farewell to Yoknapatawpha.

Little has been said here about the problems and delights of Faulkner's difficult style, the range of myth and history encompassed by his work, the technical experiments that mark his different achievements, or the mine of contemporary ideas it both catches and judges. The reader can perhaps best discover these for himself. Suffice it to suggest that he should enter Faulkner's world with the same deference and respect he would give the language, the habits and mores, the characteristic manners and modes of a culturally rich and respected foreign country. If he does so, he is likely to discover a world rich in variety and meaning—a world, moreover, that ultimately but inexorably extends the reader's understanding of himself and his own world.

Faulkner, no less than Robert Penn Warren and Katherine Anne Porter, wrote of the American South, but they did not write for the South alone. The best of their work, especially Faulkner's and Porter's, may prove as lasting as any work produced in modern America.

Robert Penn Warren

(1905-)

CHRONOLOGY:

1905 Born on April 24, in Guthrie, Kentucky.
1921-25 Attended Vanderbilt University, and contributed to the *Fugitive*.
1927 Received M.A. degree from University of California, and studied at Yale.
1929 *John Brown: The Making of a Martyr*.
1930 Awarded a B.Litt. by Oxford, where he was a Rhodes Scholar; contributed to *I'll Take My Stand*.
1935-42 Professor of English at Louisiana State University and an editor of the *Southern Review*.
1935 *Thirty-six Poems*.
1938 Edited *Understanding Poetry* (with Cleanth Brooks).
1939 Guggenheim Fellow; *Night Rider*.
1942-50 Was a Professor of English, University of Minnesota.
1942 *Eleven Poems on the Same Theme*.
1943 *At Heaven's Gate;* edited *Understanding Fiction* (with Cleanth Brooks).
1944 *Selected Poems, 1923-1943*.
1946 "Blackberry Winter," story; *All the King's Men* (awarded Pulitzer Prize).
1947 *The Circus in the Attic and Other Stories;* Guggenheim Fellow.
1950 *World Enough and Time*.
1951 Became associated with Yale University; *William Faulkner and His South*.
1953 *Brother to Dragons: A Tale in Verse and Voices*.
1955 *Band of Angels*.
1956 *Segregation, the Inner Conflict in the South*.
1957 *Promises: Poems, 1954-1956*, awarded Pulitzer Prize and National Book Award.
1958 *Selected Essays*.
1959 *The Cave*.
1960 *You, Emperors, and Others: Poems 1957-1960*.
1961 *Wilderness; The Legacy of the Civil War*.
1964 *The Flood*.

BIBLIOGRAPHY:

There is no collected edition of Warren's work, although most of the important fiction is available in inexpensive reprints.

Two book-length studies are those by Leonard Casper (New York, 1960) and by Charles H. Bohner (New York, 1964). *Modern Fiction Studies*, VI (Spring, 1960), is a special Warren issue and contains a check list of studies about him and individual works of fiction. For explications of individual poems, see Joseph Kuntz, *Poetry Explication* (Rev. ed.; Denver, 1962).

Blackberry Winter

It was getting into June and past eight o'clock in the morning, but there was a fire—even if it wasn't a big fire, just a fire of chunks—on the hearth of the big stone fireplace in the living room. I was standing on the hearth, almost into the chimney, hunched over the fire, working my bare toes slowly on the warm stone. I relished the heat which made the skin of my bare legs warp and creep and tingle, even as I called to my mother, who was somewhere back in the dining room or kitchen, and said: "But, it's June, I don't have to put them on!"

"You put them on if you are going out," she called.

I tried to assess the degree of authority and conviction in the tone, but at that distance it was hard to decide. I tried to analyze the tone, and then I thought what a fool I had been to start out the back door and let her see that I was barefoot. If I had gone out the front door or the side door she would never have known, not till dinner time anyway, and by then the day would have been half gone and I would have been all over the farm to see what the storm had done and down to the creek to see the flood. But it had never crossed my mind that they would try to stop you from going barefoot in June, no matter if there had been a gully-washer and a cold spell.

Nobody had ever tried to stop me in June as long as I could remember, and when you are nine years old, what you remember seems forever; for you remember everything and everything is important and stands big and full and fills up Time and is so solid that you can walk around and around it like a tree and look at it. You are aware that time passes, that there is a movement in time, but that is not what Time is. Time is not a movement, a flowing, a wind then, but is, rather, a kind of climate in which things are, and when a thing happens it begins to live and keeps on living and stands solid in Time like the tree that you can walk around. And if there is a movement, the movement is not Time itself, any more than a breeze is climate, and all the breeze does is to shake a little the leaves on the tree which is alive and solid. When you are nine, you know that there are things that you don't know, but you know that when you know something you know it. You know how a thing has been and you know that you can go barefoot in June. You do not understand that voice from back in the kitchen which says that you cannot go barefoot outdoors and run to see what has happened and rub your feet over the wet shivery grass and make the perfect mark of your foot in the smooth, creamy, red mud and then muse upon it as though you had suddenly come upon that single mark on the glistening auroral beach of the world. You have never seen a beach, but you have read the book and how the footprint was there.

The voice had said what it had said, and I looked savagely at the black stockings and the strong, scuffed brown shoes which I had brought from my closet as far as the hearth rug. I called once more, "But it's June," and waited.

"It's June," the voice replied from far away, "but it's blackberry winter."

I had lifted my head to reply to that, to make one more test of what was in that tone, when I happened to see the man.

The fireplace in the living room was at the end; for the stone chimney was built, as in so many of the farmhouses in Tennessee, at the end of a gable, and there was a window on each side of the chimney. Out of the window on the north side of the fireplace I could see the man. When I saw the man I did not call out what I had intended, but, engrossed by the strangeness of the sight, watched him, still far off, come along the path by the edge of the woods.

What was strange was that there should be a man there at all. That path went along the yard fence, between the fence and the woods which came right down to the yard, and then on back past the chicken runs and on by the woods until it was lost to sight where the woods bulged out and cut off the back field. There the path disappeared into the woods. It led on back, I knew, through the woods and to the swamp, skirted the swamp where the big trees gave way to sycamores and water oaks and willows and tangled cane, and then led on to the river. Nobody ever went back there except people who wanted to gig frogs in the swamp or to fish in the river or to hunt in the woods, and those people, if they didn't have a standing permission from my father, always stopped to ask permission to cross the farm. But the man whom I now saw wasn't, I could tell even at that distance, a sportsman. And what would a sportsman have been doing down there after a storm? Besides, he was coming from the river, and nobody had gone down there that morning. I knew that for a fact, because if anybody had passed, certainly if a stranger had passed, the dogs would have made a racket and would have been out on him. But this man was coming up from the river and had come up through the woods. I suddenly had a vision of him moving up the grassy path in the woods, in the green twilight under the big trees, not making any sound on the path, while now and then, like drops off the eaves, a big drop of water would fall from a leaf or bough and strike a stiff oak leaf lower down with a small, hollow sound like a drop of water hitting tin. That sound, in the silence of the woods, would be very significant.

When you are a boy and stand in the stillness of woods, which can be so still that your heart almost stops beating and makes you want to stand there in the green twilight until you feel your very feet sinking into and clutching the earth like roots and your body breathing slow through its pores like the leaves—when you stand there and wait for the next drop to drop with its small, flat sound to a lower leaf, that sound seems to measure out something, to put an end to something, to begin something, and you cannot wait for it to happen and are afraid it will not happen, and then when it has happened, you are waiting again, almost afraid.

But the man whom I saw coming through the woods in my mind's eye did not pause and wait, growing into the ground and breathing with the enormous, soundless breathing of the leaves. Instead, I saw him moving in the green twilight inside my head as he was moving at that very moment along the path by the edge of the woods, coming toward the house. He was moving steadily, but not fast, with his shoulders hunched a little and his head thrust forward, like a man who has come a long way and has a long way to go. I shut my eyes for a couple of seconds, thinking that when I opened them he would not be there at all. There was no place for him to have come from, and there was no reason for him to come where he was coming, toward our house. But I opened my eyes, and there he was, and he was coming steadily along the side of the woods. He was not yet even with the back chicken yard.

"Mama," I called.

"You put them on," the voice said.

"There's a man coming," I called, "out back."

She did not reply to that, and I guessed that she had gone to the kitchen window to look. She would be looking at the man and wondering who he was and what he wanted, the way you always do in the country, and if I went back there now she would not notice right off whether or not I was barefoot. So I went back to the kitchen.

She was standing by the window. "I don't recognize him," she said, not looking around at me.

"Where could he be coming from?" I asked.

"I don't know," she said.

"What would he be doing down at the river? At night? In the storm?"

She studied the figure out the window, then said, "Oh, I reckon maybe he cut across from the Dunbar place."

That was, I realized, a perfectly rational explanation. He had not been down at the river in the storm, at night. He had come over this morning. You could cut across from the Dunbar place if you didn't mind breaking through a lot of elder and sassafras and blackberry bushes which had about taken over the old cross path, which nobody ever used any more. That satisfied me for a moment, but only for a moment. "Mama," I asked, "what would he be doing over at the Dunbar place last night?"

Then she looked at me, and I knew I had made a mistake, for she was looking at my bare feet. "You haven't got your shoes on," she said.

But I was saved by the dogs. That instant there was a bark which I recognized as Sam, the collie, and then a heavier, churning kind of bark which was Bully, and I saw a streak of white as Bully tore round the corner of the back porch and headed out for the man. Bully was a big, bone-white bull dog, the kind of dog that they used to call a farm bull dog but that you don't see any more, heavy chested and heavy headed, but with pretty long legs. He could take a fence as light as a hound. He had just cleared the white paling fence toward the woods when my mother ran out to the back porch and began calling, "Here you, Bully! Here you!"

Bully stopped in the path, waiting for the man, but he gave a few more of those deep, gargling, savage barks that reminded you of something down a stone-lined well. The red clay mud, I saw, was splashed up over his white chest and looked exciting, like blood.

The man, however, had not stopped walking even when Bully took the fence and started at him. He had kept right on coming. All he had done was to switch a little paper parcel which he carried from the right hand to the left, and then reach into his pants pocket to get something. Then I saw the glitter and knew that he had a knife in his hand, probably the kind of mean knife just made for devilment and nothing else, with a blade as long as the blade of a frog-sticker, which will snap out ready when you press a button in the handle. That knife must have had a button in the handle, or else how could he have had the blade out glittering so quick and with just one hand?

Pulling his knife against the dogs was a funny thing to do, for Bully was a big, powerful brute and fast, and Sam was all right. If those dogs had meant business, they might have knocked him down and ripped him before he got a stroke in. He ought to have picked up a heavy stick, something to take a swipe at them with and something which they could see and respect when they came at him. But he apparently did not know much about dogs. He just held the knife blade close against the right leg, low down, and kept on moving down the path.

Then my mother had called, and Bully had stopped. So the man let the blade of the knife snap back into the handle, and dropped it into his pocket, and kept on coming. Many women would have been afraid with the strange man who they knew had that knife in his pocket. That is, if they were alone in the house with nobody but a nine-year-old boy. And my mother was alone, for my father had gone off, and Dellie, the cook, was down at her cabin because she wasn't feeling well. But my mother wasn't afraid. She wasn't a big woman, but she was clear and brisk about everything she did and looked everybody and everything right in the eye from her own blue eyes in her tanned face. She had been the first woman in the county to ride a horse astride (that was back when she was a girl and long before I was born), and I have seen her snatch up a pump gun and go out and knock a chicken hawk out of the air like a busted skeet when he came over her chicken yard. She was a steady and self-reliant woman, and when I think of her now after all the years she has been dead, I think of her brown hands, not big, but somewhat square for a woman's hands, with square-cut nails. They looked, as a matter of fact, more like a young boy's hands than a grown woman's. But back then it never crossed my mind that she would ever be dead.

She stood on the back porch and watched the man enter the back gate, where the dogs (Bully had leaped back into the yard) were dancing and muttering and giving sidelong glances back to my mother to see if she meant what she had said. The man walked right by the dogs, almost brushing them, and didn't pay them any attention. I could see now that he wore old khaki pants, and a dark wool coat with stripes in it, and a gray felt hat. He had on a gray shirt with blue stripes in it, and no tie. But I could see a tie, blue and reddish, sticking in his side coat-pocket. Everything was wrong about what he wore. He ought to have been wearing blue jeans or overalls, and a straw hat or an old black felt hat, and the coat, granting that he might have been wearing a wool coat and not a jumper, ought not to have had those stripes. Those clothes, despite the fact that they were old enough and dirty enough for any tramp, didn't belong there in our back yard, coming down the path, in Middle Tennessee, miles away from any big town, and even a mile off the pike.

When he got almost to the steps, without having said anything, my mother, very matter-of-factly, said, "Good morning."

"Good morning," he said, and stopped and looked her over. He did not take off his hat, and under the brim you could see the perfectly unmemorable face, which wasn't old and wasn't young, or thick or thin. It was grayish and covered with about three days of stubble. The eyes were a kind of nondescript, muddy hazel, or something like that, rather bloodshot. His teeth, when he opened his mouth, showed yellow and uneven. A couple of them had been knocked out. You knew that they had been knocked out, because there was a scar, not very old, there on the lower lip just beneath the gap.

"Are you hunting work?" my mother asked him.

"Yes," he said—not "yes, mam"—and still did not take off his hat.

"I don't know about my husband, for he isn't here," she said, and didn't mind a bit telling the tramp, or whoever he was, with the mean knife in his pocket, that no man was around, "but I can give you a few things to do. The storm has drowned a lot of my chicks. Three coops of them. You can gather them up and bury them. Bury them deep so the dogs won't get at them. In the woods. And fix the coops the wind blew over. And down yonder beyond that pen by the edge of the woods are some drowned poults. They got out and I couldn't get them in. Even after it started to rain hard. Poults haven't got any sense."

"What are them things—poults?" he demanded, and spat on the brick walk. He rubbed his foot over the spot, and I saw that he wore a black, pointed-toe low shoe, all cracked and broken. It was a crazy kind of shoe to be wearing in the country.

"Oh, they're young turkeys," my mother was saying. "And they haven't got any sense. I oughtn't to try to raise them around here with so many chickens, anyway. They don't thrive near chickens, even in separate pens. And I won't give up my chickens." Then she stopped herself and resumed briskly on the note of business. "When you finish that, you can fix my flower beds. A lot of trash and mud and gravel has washed down. Maybe you can save some of my flowers if you are careful."

"Flowers," the man said, in a low, impersonal voice which seemed to have a wealth of meaning, but a meaning which I could not fathom. As I think back on it, it probably was not pure contempt. Rather, it was a kind of impersonal and distant marveling that he should be on the verge of grubbing in a flower bed. He said the word, and then looked off across the yard.

"Yes, flowers," my mother replied with some asperity, as though she would have nothing said or implied against flowers. "And they were very fine this year." Then she stopped and looked at the man. "Are you hungry?" she demanded.

"Yeah," he said.

"I'll fix you something," she said, "before you get started." She turned to me. "Show him where he can wash up," she commanded, and went into the house.

I took the man to the end of the porch where a pump was and where a couple of wash pans sat on a low shelf for people to use before they went into the house. I stood there while he laid down his little parcel wrapped in newspaper and took off his hat and looked around for a nail to hang it on. He poured the water and plunged his hands into it. They were big hands, and strong looking, but they did not have the creases and the earth-color of the hands of men who work outdoors. But they were dirty, with black dirt ground into the skin and under the nails. After he had washed his hands, he poured another basin of water and washed his face. He dried his face, and with the towel still dangling in his grasp, stepped over to the mirror on the house wall. He rubbed one hand over the stubble on his face. Then he carefully inspected his face, turning first one side and then the other, and stepped back and settled his striped coat down on his shoulders. He had the movements of a man who has just dressed up to go to church or a party—the way he settled his coat and smoothed it and scanned himself in the mirror.

Then he caught my glance on him. He glared at me for an instant out of the bloodshot eyes, then demanded in a low, harsh voice, "What you looking at?"

"Nothing," I managed to say, and stepped back a step from him.

He flung the towel down, crumpled, on the shelf, and went toward the kitchen door and entered without knocking.

My mother said something to him which I could not catch. I started to go in again, then thought about my bare feet, and decided to go back of the chicken yard, where the man would have to come to pick up the dead chicks. I hung around behind the chicken house until he came out.

He moved across the chicken yard with a fastidious, not quite finicking motion, looking down at the curdled mud flecked with bits of chicken-droppings. The mud curled up over the soles of his black shoes. I stood back from him some six feet and watched him pick up the first of the drowned chicks. He held it up by one foot and inspected it.

There is nothing deader looking than a drowned chick. The feet curl in that feeble, empty way which back when I was a boy, even if I was a country boy who did not mind hog-killing or frog-gigging, made me feel hollow in the stomach. Instead of looking plump and fluffy, the body is stringy and limp with the fluff plastered to it, and the neck is long and loose like a little string of rag. And the eyes have that bluish membrane over them which makes you think of a very old man who is sick about to die.

The man stood there and inspected the chick. Then he looked all around as though he didn't know what to do with it.

"There's a great big old basket in the shed," I said, and pointed to the shed attached to the chicken house.

He inspected me as though he had just discovered my presence, and moved toward the shed.

"There's a spade there, too," I added.

He got the basket and began to pick up the other chicks, picking each one up slowly by a foot and then flinging it into the basket with a nasty, snapping motion. Now and then he would look at me out of the blood-shot eyes. Every time he seemed on the verge of saying something, but he did not. Perhaps he was building up to say something to me, but I did not wait that long. His way of looking at me made me so uncomfortable that I left the chicken yard.

Besides, I had just remembered that the creek was in flood, over the bridge, and that people were down there watching it. So I cut across the farm toward the creek. When I got to the big tobacco field I saw that it had not suffered much. The land lay right and not many tobacco plants had washed out of the ground. But I knew that a lot of tobacco round the country had been washed right out. My father had said so at breakfast.

My father was down at the bridge. When I came out of the gap in the osage hedge into the road, I saw him sitting on his mare over the heads of the other men who were standing around, admiring the flood. The creek was big here, even in low water; for only a couple of miles away it ran into the river, and when a real flood came, the red water got over the pike where it dipped down to the bridge, which was an iron bridge, and high over the floor and even the side railings of the bridge. Only the upper iron work would show, with the water boiling and frothing red and white around it. That creek rose so fast and so heavy because a few miles back it came down out of the hills, where the gorges filled up with water in no time when a rain came. The creek ran in a deep bed with limestone bluffs along both sides until it got within three quarters of a mile of the bridge, and when it came out from between those bluffs in flood it was boiling and hissing and steaming like water from a fire hose.

Whenever there was a flood, people from half the county would come down to see the sight. After a gully-washer there would not be any work to do anyway. If it didn't ruin your crop, you couldn't plow and you felt like taking a holiday to celebrate. If it did ruin your crop, there wasn't anything to do except to try to take your mind off the mortgage, if you were rich enough to have a mortgage, and if you couldn't afford a mortgage you needed something to take your mind off how hungry you would be by Christmas. So people would come down to the bridge and look at the flood. It made something different from the run of days.

There would not be much talking after the first few minutes of trying to guess how high the water was this time. The men and kids just stood around, or sat their horses or mules, as the case might be, or stood up in the wagon beds. They looked at the strangeness of the flood for an hour or two, and then somebody would say that he had better be getting on home to dinner and would start walking down the gray, puddled limestone pike, or would touch heel to his mount and start off. Everybody always knew what it would be like when he got down to the bridge, but people always came. It was like church or a funeral. They always came, that is, if it was summer and the flood unexpected. Nobody ever came down in winter to see high water.

When I came out of the gap in the bodock hedge, I saw the crowd, perhaps fifteen or twenty men and a lot of kids, and saw my father sitting his mare, Nellie Gray. He was a tall, limber man and carried himself well. I was always proud to see him sit a horse, he was so quiet and straight, and when I stepped through the gap of the hedge that morning, the first thing that happened was, I remember, the warm feeling I always had when I saw him up on a horse, just sitting. I did not go toward him, but skirted the crowd on the far side, to get a look at the creek. For one thing, I was not sure what he would say about the fact that I was barefoot. But the first thing I knew, I heard his voice calling, "Seth!"

I went toward him, moving apologetically past the men, who bent their large, red or thin, sallow faces above me. I knew some of the men, and knew their names, but because those I knew were there in a crowd, mixed with the strange faces, they seemed foreign to me, and not friendly. I did not look up at my father until I was almost within touching distance of his heel. Then I looked up and tried to read his face, to see if he was angry about my being barefoot. Before I could decide anything from that impassive, high-boned face, he had leaned over and reached a hand to me. "Grab on," he commanded.

I grabbed on and gave a little jump, and he said, "Up-see-daisy!" and whisked me, light as a feather, up to the pommel of his McClellan saddle.

"You can see better up here," he said, slid back on the cantle a little to make me more comfortable, and then, looking over my head at the swollen, tumbling water, seemed to forget all about me. But his right hand was laid on my side, just above my thigh, to steady me.

I was sitting there as quiet as I could, feeling the faint stir of my father's chest against my shoulders as it rose and fell with his breath, when I saw the cow. At first, looking up the creek, I thought it was just another big piece of driftwood steaming down the creek in the ruck of water, but all at once a pretty good-size boy who had climbed part way up a telephone pole by the pike so that he could see better yelled out, "Golly-damn, look at that-air cow!"

Everybody looked. It was a cow all right, but it might just as well have been driftwood; for it was dead as a chunk, rolling and rolling down the creek, appearing and disappearing, feet up or head up, it didn't matter which.

The cow started up the talk again. Somebody wondered whether it would hit one of the clear places under the top girder of the bridge and get through or whether it would get tangled in the drift and trash that had piled against the upright girders and braces. Somebody remembered how about ten years before so much driftwood had piled up on the bridge that it was knocked off its foundations. Then the cow hit. It hit the edge of the drift against one of the girders, and hung there. For a few seconds it seemed as though it might tear loose, but then we saw that it was really caught. It bobbed and heaved on its side there in a slow, grinding, uneasy fashion. It had a yoke around its neck, the kind made out of a forked limb to keep a jumper behind fence.

"She shore jumped one fence," one of the men said.

And another: "Well, she done jumped her last one, fer a fack."

Then they began to wonder about whose cow it might be. They decided it must belong to Milt Alley. They said that he had a cow that was a jumper, and kept her in a fenced-in piece of ground up the creek. I had never seen Milt Alley, but I knew who he was. He was a squatter and lived up the hills a way, on a shirt-tail patch of set-on-edge land, in a cabin. He was pore white trash. He had lots of children. I had seen the children at school, when they came. They were thin-faced, with straight, sticky-looking, dough-colored hair, and they smelled something like old sour buttermilk, not because they drank so much buttermilk but because that is the sort of smell which children out of those cabins tend to have. The big Alley boy drew dirty pictures and showed them to the little boys at school.

That was Milt Alley's cow. It looked like the kind of cow he would have, a scrawny, old, sway-backed cow, with a yoke around her neck. I wondered if Milt Alley had another cow.

"Poppa," I said, "do you think Milt Alley has got another cow?"

"You say 'Mr. Alley,' " my father said quietly.

"Do you think he has?"

"No telling," my father said.

Then a big gangly boy, about fifteen, who was sitting on a scraggly little old mule with a piece of croker sack thrown across the saw-tooth spine, and who had been staring at the cow, suddenly said to nobody in particular, "Reckin anybody ever et drownt cow?"

He was the kind of boy who might just as well as not have been the son of Milt Alley, with his faded and patched overalls ragged at the bottom of the pants and the mud-stiff brogans hanging off his skinny, bare ankles at the level of the mule's belly. He had said what he did, and then looked embarrassed and sullen when all the eyes swung at him. He hadn't meant to say it, I am pretty sure now. He would have been too proud to say it, just as Milt Alley would have been too proud. He had just been thinking out loud, and the words had popped out.

There was an old man standing there on the pike, an old man with a white beard. "Son," he said to the embarrassed and sullen boy on the mule, "you live long enough and you'll find a man will eat anything when the time comes."

"Time gonna come fer some folks this year," another man said.

"Son," the old man said, "in my time I et things a man don't like to think on. I was a sojer and I rode with Gin'l Forrest, and them things we et when the time come. I tell you. I et meat what got up and run when you taken out yore knife to cut a slice to put on the fire. You had to knock it down with a carbene butt, it was so active. That-air meat would jump like a bullfrog, it was so full of skippers."

But nobody was listening to the old man. The boy on the mule turned his sullen sharp face from him, dug a heel into the side of the mule and went off up the pike with a motion which made you think that any second you would hear mule bones clashing inside that lank and scrofulous hide.

"Cy Dundee's boy," a man said, and nodded toward the figure going up the pike on the mule.

"Reckin Cy Dundee's young-uns seen times they'd settle fer drownt cow," another man said.

The old man with the beard peered at them both from his weak, slow eyes, first at one and then at the other. "Live long enough," he said, "and a man will settle for what he kin git."

Then there was silence again, with the people looking at the red, foam-flecked water.

My father lifted the bridle rein in his left hand, and the mare turned and walked around the group and up the pike. We rode on up to our big gate, where my father dismounted to open it and let me myself ride Nellie Gray through. When he got to the lane that led off from the drive about two hundred yards from our house, my father said, "Grab on." I grabbed on, and he let me down to the ground. "I'm going to ride down and look at my corn," he said. "You go on." He took the lane, and I stood there on the drive and watched him ride off. He was wearing cowhide boots and an old hunting coat, and I thought that that made him look very military, like a picture. That and the way he rode.

I did not go to the house. Instead, I went by the vegetable garden and crossed behind the stables, and headed down for Dellie's cabin. I wanted to go down and play with Jebb, who was Dellie's little boy about two years older than I was. Besides, I was cold. I shivered as I walked, and I had gooseflesh. The mud which crawled up between my toes with every step I took was like ice. Dellie would have a fire, but she wouldn't make me put on shoes and stockings.

Dellie's cabin was of logs, with one side, because it was on a slope, set on limestone chunks, with a little porch attached to it, and had a little white-washed fence around it and a gate with plow-points on a wire to clink when somebody came in, and had two big white oaks in the yard and some flowers and a nice privy in the back with some honeysuckle growing over it. Dellie and Old Jebb, who was Jebb's father and who lived with Dellie and had lived with her for twenty-five years even if they never had got married, were careful to keep everything nice around their cabin. They had the name all over the community for being clean and clever Negroes. Dellie and Jebb were what they used to call "white-folks' niggers." There was a big difference between their cabin and the other two cabins farther down where the other tenants lived. My father kept the other cabins weatherproof, but he couldn't undertake to go down and pick up after the litter they strewed. They didn't take the trouble to have a vegetable patch like Dellie and Jebb or to make preserves from wild plum, and jelly from crab apple the way Dellie did. They were shiftless, and my father was always threatening to get shed of them. But he never did. When they finally left, they just up and left on their own, for no reason, to go and be shiftless somewhere else. Then some more came. But meanwhile they lived down there, Matt Rawson and his family, and Sid Turner and his, and I played with their children all over the farm when they weren't working. But when I wasn't around they were mean sometimes to Little Jebb. That was because the other tenants down there were jealous of Dellie and Jebb.

I was so cold that I ran the last fifty yards to Dellie's gate. As soon as I had entered the yard, I saw that the storm had been hard on Dellie's flowers. The yard was, as I have said, on a slight slope, and the water running across had gutted the flower beds and washed out all the good black woods-earth which Dellie had brought in. What little grass there was in the yard was plastered sparsely down on the ground, the way the drainage water had left it. It reminded me of the way the fluff was plastered down on the skin of the drowned chicks that the strange man had been picking up, up in my mother's chicken yard.

I took a few steps up the path to the cabin, and then I saw that the drainage water had washed a lot of trash and filth out from under Dellie's house. Up toward the porch, the ground was not clean any more. Old pieces of rag, two or three rusted cans, pieces of rotten rope, some hunks of old dog dung, broken glass, old paper, and all sorts of things like that had washed out from under Dellie's house to foul her clean yard. It looked just as bad as the yards of the other cabins, or worse. It was worse, as a matter of fact, because it was a surprise. I had never thought of all that filth being under Dellie's house. It was not anything against Dellie that the stuff had been under the cabin. Trash will get under any house. But I did not think of that when I saw the foulness which had washed out on the ground which Dellie sometimes used to sweep with a twig broom to make nice and clean.

I picked my way past the filth, being careful not to get my bare feet on it, and mounted to Dellie's door. When I knocked, I heard her voice telling me to come in.

It was dark inside the cabin, after the daylight, but I could make out Dellie piled up in bed under a quilt, and Little Jebb crouched by the hearth, where a low fire simmered. "Howdy," I said to Dellie, "how you feeling?"

Her big eyes, the whites surprising and glaring in the black face, fixed on me as I stood there, but she did not reply. It did not look like Dellie, or act like Dellie, who would grumble and bustle around our kitchen, talking to herself, scolding me or Little Jebb, clanking pans, making all sorts of unnecessary noises and mutterings like an old-fashioned black steam thrasher engine when it has got up an extra head of steam and keeps popping the governor and rumbling and shaking on its wheels. But now Dellie just lay up there on the bed, under the patch-work quilt, and turned the black face, which I scarcely recognized, and the glaring white eyes to me.

"How you feeling?" I repeated.

"I'se sick," the voice said croakingly out of the strange black face which was not attached to Dellie's big, squat body, but stuck out from under a pile of tangled bedclothes. Then the voice added: "Mighty sick."

"I'm sorry," I managed to say.

The eyes remained fixed on me for a moment, then they left me and the head rolled back on the pillow. "Sorry," the voice said, in a flat way which wasn't question or statement of anything. It was just the empty word put into the air with no meaning or expression, to float off like a feather or a puff of smoke, while the big eyes, with the whites like the peeled white of hard-boiled eggs, stared at the ceiling.

"Dellie," I said after a minute, "there's a tramp up at the house. He's got a knife."

She was not listening. She closed her eyes.

I tiptoed over to the hearth where Jebb was and crouched beside him. We began to talk in low voices. I was asking him to get out his train and play train. Old Jebb had put spool wheels on three cigar boxes and put wire links between the boxes to make a train for Jebb. The box that was the locomotive had the top closed and a length of broom stick for a smoke stack. Jebb didn't want to get the train out, but I told him I would go home if he didn't. So he got out the train, and the colored rocks, and fossils of crinoid stems, and other junk he used for the load, and we began to push it around, talking the way we thought trainmen talked, making a chuck-chucking sound under the breath for the noise of the locomotive and now and then uttering low, cautious toots for the whistle. We got so interested in playing train that the toots got louder. Then, before he thought, Jebb gave a good, loud *toot-toot*, blowing for a crossing.

"Come here," the voice said from the bed.

Jebb got up slow from his hands and knees, giving me a sudden, naked, inimical look.

"Come here!" the voice said.

Jebb went to the bed. Dellie propped herself weakly up on one arm, muttering, "Come closer."

Jebb stood closer.

"Last thing I do, I'm gonna do it," Dellie said. "Done tole you to be quiet."

Then she slapped him. It was an awful slap, more awful for the kind of weakness which it came from and brought to focus. I had seen her slap Jebb before, but the slapping had always been the kind of easy slap you would expect from a good-natured, grumbling Negro woman like Dellie. But this was different. It was awful. It was so awful that Jebb didn't make a sound. The tears just popped out and ran down his face, and his breath came sharp, like gasps.

Dellie fell back. "Cain't even be sick," she said to the ceiling. "Git sick and they won't even let you lay. They tromp all over you. Cain't even be sick." Then she closed her eyes.

I went out of the room. I almost ran getting to the door, and I did run across the porch and down the steps and across the yard, not caring whether or not I stepped on the filth which had washed out from under the cabin. I ran almost all the way home. Then I thought about my mother catching me with the bare feet. So I went down to the stables.

I heard a noise in the crib, and opened the door. There was Big Jebb, sitting on an old nail keg, shelling corn into a bushel basket. I went in, pulling the door shut behind me, and crouched on the floor near him. I crouched there for a couple of minutes before either of us spoke, and watched him shelling the corn.

He had very big hands, knotted and grayish at the joints, with calloused palms which seemed to be streaked with rust with the rust coming up between the fingers to show from the back. His hands were so strong and tough that he could take a big ear of corn and rip the grains right off the cob with the palm of his hand, all in one motion, like a machine. "Work long as me," he would say, "and the good Lawd'll give you a hand lak cass-ion won't nuthin' hurt." And his hands did look like cast iron, old cast iron streaked with rust.

He was an old man, up in his seventies, thirty years or more older than Dellie, but he was strong as a bull. He was a squat sort of man, heavy in the shoulders, with remarkably long arms, the kind of build they say the river natives have on the Congo from paddling so much in their boats. He had a round bullet-head, set on powerful shoulders. His skin was very black, and the thin hair on his head was now grizzled like tufts of old cotton batting. He had small eyes and a flat nose, not big, and the kindest and wisest old face in the world, the blunt, sad, wise face of an old animal peering tolerantly out on the goings-on of the merely human creatures before him. He was a good man, and I loved him next to my mother and father. I crouched there on the floor of the crib and watched him shell corn with the rusty cast-iron hands, while he looked down at me out of the little eyes set in the blunt face.

"Dellie says she's might sick," I said.

"Yeah," he said.

"What's she sick from?"

"Woman-mizry," he said.

"What's woman-mizry?"

"Hit comes on 'em," he said. "Hit just comes on 'em when the time comes."

"What is it?"

"Hit is the change," he said. "Hit is the change of life and time."

"What changes?"

"You too young to know."

"Tell me."

"Time come and you find out everything."

I knew that there was no use in asking him any more. When I asked him things and he said that, I always knew that he would not tell me. So I continued to crouch there and watch him. Now that I had sat there a little while, I was cold again.

"What you shiver fer?" he asked me.

"I'm cold. I'm cold because it's blackberry winter," I said.

"Maybe 'tis and maybe 'tain't," he said.

"My mother says it is."

"Ain't sayen Miss Sallie doan know and ain't sayen she do. But folks doan know everthing."

"Why isn't it blackberry winter?"

"Too late fer blackberry winter. Blackberries done bloomed."

"She said it was."

"Blackberry winter just a leetle cold spell. Hit come and then hit go away, and hit is growed summer of a sudden lak a gunshot. Ain't no tellen hit will go way this time."

"It's June," I said.

"June," he replied with great contempt. "That what folks say. What June mean? Maybe hit is come cold to stay."

"Why?"

"Cause this-here old yearth is tahrd. Hit is tahrd and ain't gonna perduce. Lawd let hit come rain one time forty days and forty nights, 'cause He was tahrd of sinful folks. Maybe this-here old yearth say to the Lawd, Lawd, I done plum tahrd, Lawd, lemme rest. And Lawd say, Yearth, you done yore best, you give 'em cawn and you give 'em taters, and all they think on is they gut, and, Yearth, you kin take a rest."

"What will happen?"

"Folks will eat up everthing. The yearth won't perduce no more. Folks cut down all the trees and burn 'em 'cause they cold, and the yearth won't grow no more. I been tellen 'em. I been tellen folks. Sayen, maybe this year, hit is the time. But they doan listen to me, how the yearth is tahrd. Maybe this year they find out."

"Will everything die?"

"Everthing and everbody, hit will be so."

"This year?"

"Ain't no tellen. Maybe this year."

"My mother said it is blackberry winter," I said confidently, and got up.

"Ain't sayen nuthin' agin Miss Sallie," he said.

I went to the door of the crib. I was really cold now. Running, I had got up a sweat and now I was worse.

I hung on the door, looking at Jebb, who was shelling corn again.

"There's a tramp came to the house," I said. I had almost forgotten the tramp.

"Yeah."

"He came by the back way. What was he doing down there in the storm?"

"They comes and they goes," he said, "and ain't no tellen."

"He had a mean knife."

"The good ones and the bad ones, they comes and they goes. Storm or sun, light or dark. They is folks and they comes and they goes lak folks."

I hung on the door, shivering.

He studied me a moment, then said, "You git on to the house. You ketch yore death. Then what yore mammy say?"

I hesitated.

"You git," he said.

When I came to the back yard, I saw that my father was standing by the back porch and the tramp was walking toward him. They began talking before I reached them, but I got there just as my father was saying, "I'm sorry, but I haven't got any work. I got all the hands on the place I need now. I won't need any extra until wheat thrashing."

The stranger made no reply, just looked at my father.

My father took out his leather coin purse, and got out a half-dollar. He held it toward the man. "This is for half a day," he said.

The man looked at the coin, and then at my father, making no motion to take the money. But that was the right amount. A dollar a day was what you paid them back in 1910. And the man hadn't even worked half a day.

Then the man reached out and took the coin. He dropped it into the right side pocket of his coat. Then he said, very slowly and without feeling: "I didn't want to work on your ——— farm."

He used the word which they would have frailed me to death for using.

I looked at my father's face and it was streaked white under the sunburn. Then he said, "Get off this place. Get off this place or I won't be responsible."

The man dropped his right hand into his pants pocket. It was the pocket where he kept the knife. I was just about to yell to my father about the knife when the hand came back out with nothing in it. The man gave a kind of twisted grin, showing where the teeth had been knocked out above the new scar. I thought that instant how maybe he had tried before to pull a knife on somebody else and had got his teeth knocked out.

So now he just gave that twisted, sickish grin out of the unmemorable, grayish face, and then spat on the brick path. The glob landed just about six inches from the toe of my father's right boot. My father looked down at it, and so did I. I thought that if the glob had hit my father's boot something would have happened. I looked down and saw the bright glob, and on one side of it my father's strong cowhide boots, with the brass eyelets and the leather thongs, heavy boots splashed with good red mud and set solid on the bricks, and on the other side the pointed-toe, broken, black shoes, on which the mud looked so sad and out of place. Then I saw one of the black shoes move a little, just a twitch first, then a real step backward.

The man moved in a quarter circle to the end of the porch, with my father's steady gaze upon him all the while. At the end of the porch, the man reached up to the shelf where the wash pans were to get his little newspaper-wrapped parcel. Then he disappeared around the corner of the house and my father mounted the porch and went into the kitchen without a word.

I followed around the house to see what the man would do. I wasn't afraid of him now, no matter if he did have the knife. When I got around in front, I saw him going out the yard gate and starting up the drive toward the pike. So I ran to catch up with him. He was sixty yards or so up the drive before I caught up.

I did not walk right up even with him at first, but trailed him, the way a kid will, about seven or eight feet behind, now and then running two or three steps in order to hold my place against his longer stride. When I first came up behind him, he turned to give me a look, just a meaningless look, and then fixed his eyes up the drive and kept on walking.

When we had got around the bend in the drive which cut the house from sight, and were going along by the edge of the woods, I decided to come up even with him. I ran a few steps, and was by his side, or almost, but some feet off to the right. I walked along in this position for a while, and he never noticed me. I walked along until we got within sight of the big gate that let on the pike.

Then I said: "Where did you come from?"

He looked at me then with a look which seemed almost surprised that I was there. Then he said, "It ain't none of yore business."

We went on another fifty feet.

Then I said, "Where are you going?"

He stopped, studied me dispassionately for a moment, then suddenly took a step toward me and leaned his face down at me. The lips jerked back, but not in any grin, to show where the teeth were knocked out and to make the scar on the lower lip come white with the tension.

He said: "Stop following me. You don't stop following me and I cut yore throat, you little son-of-a-bitch."

Then he went on to the gate, and up the pike.

That was thirty-five years ago. Since that time my father and mother have died. I was still a boy, but a big boy, when my father got cut on the blade of a mowing machine and died of lockjaw. My mother sold the place and went to town to live with her sister. But she never took hold after my father's death, and she died within three years, right in middle life. My aunt always said, "Sallie just died of a broken heart, she was so devoted." Dellie is dead, too, but she died, I heard, quite a long time after we sold the farm.

As for Little Jebb, he grew up to be a mean and ficey Negro. He killed another Negro in a fight and got sent to the penitentiary, where he is yet, the last I heard tell. He probably grew up to be mean and ficey from just being picked on so much by the children of the other tenants, who were jealous of Jebb and Dellie for being thrifty and clever and being white-folks' niggers.

Old Jebb lived forever. I saw him ten years ago and he was about a hundred then, and not looking much different. He was living in town then, on relief—that was back in the Depression—when I went to see him. He said to me:. "Too strong to die. When I was a young feller just comen on and seen how things wuz, I prayed the Lawd. I said, O, Lawd, gimme strength and meke me strong fer to do and to in-dure. The Lawd hearkened to my prayer. He give me strength. I was in-duren proud fer being strong and me much man. The Lawd give me my prayer and my strength. But now He done gone off and fergot me and left me alone with my strength. A man doan know what to pray fer, and him mortal."

Jebb is probably living yet, as far as I know.

That is what has happened since the morning when the tramp leaned his face down at me and showed his teeth and said: "Stop following me. You don't stop following me and I cut yore throat, you little son-of-a-bitch." That was what he said, for me not to follow him. But I did follow him, all the years.

1947

Katherine Anne Porter

(1890-)

CHRONOLOGY:

1890 Born on May 15, in Indian Creek, Texas.
1922 Stories began to appear in literary magazines.
1930 *Flowering Judas.*
1931 Guggenheim Fellow.
1934 *Hacienda.*
1935 *Flowering Judas and Other Stories.*
1937 *Noon Wine.*
1938 Guggenheim Fellow.
1939 *Pale Horse, Pale Rider* (including also *Noon Wine* and *Old Mortality*).
1941 *No Safe Harbor.*
1944 *The Leaning Tower and Other Stories.*
1952 *The Days Before,* essays.
1962 *Ship of Fools.*

BIBLIOGRAPHY:

There is no collected edition of Katherine Anne Porter's work, but both *Flowering Judas and Other Stories* and *Pale Horse, Pale Rider* are available in Modern Library editions.

Two important critical articles are Robert Penn Warren's "Katherine Anne Porter (Irony with a Center,)" *Kenyon Review,* IV (1942), and J. W. Johnson's "Another Look at Katherine Anne Porter," *Virginia Quarterly Review,* XXXVI (1960). Also helpful is E. Schwartz' *Katherine Anne Porter: A Critical Bibliography* (New York, 1957).

For explications of her stories, see Warren S. Walker's *Twentieth-Century Short Story Explication . . .* (Hamden, Conn., 1961), Supplement, 1963.

Introduction to *Flowering Judas and Other Stories*

It is just ten years since this collection of short stories first appeared. They are literally first fruits, for they were written and published in order of their present arrangement in this volume, which contains the first story I ever finished. Looking at them again, it is possible still to say that I do not repent of them; if they were not yet written, I should have to write them still. They were done with intention and in firm faith, though I had no plan for their future and no notion of what their meaning might be to such readers as they would find. To any speculations from interested sources as to why there were not more of them, I can answer simply and truthfully that I was not one of those who could flourish in the conditions of the past two decades. They are fragments of a much larger plan which I am still engaged in carrying out, and they are what I was then able to achieve in the way of order and form and statement in a period of grotesque dislocations in a whole society when the world was heaving in the sickness of a millennial change. They were first published by what seems still merely a lucky accident, and their survival through this crowded and slowly darkening decade is the sort of fate no one, least of all myself, could be expected to predict or even to hope for.

We none of us flourished in those times, artists or not, for art, like the human life of which it is the truest voice, thrives best by daylight in a green and growing world. For myself, and I was not alone, all the conscious and recollected years of my life have been lived to this day under the heavy threat of world catastrophe, and most of the energies of my mind and spirit have been spent in the effort to grasp the meaning of those threats, to trace them to their sources and to understand the logic of this majestic and terrible failure of the life of man in the Western world. In the face of such shape and weight of present misfortune, the voice of the individual artist may seem perhaps of no more consequence than the whirring of a cricket in the grass; but the arts do live continuously, and they live literally by faith; their names and their shapes and their uses and their basic meanings survive unchanged in all that matters through times of interruption, diminishment, neglect; they outlive governments and creeds and the societies, even the very civilizations that produced them. They cannot be destroyed altogether because they represent the substance of faith and the only reality. They are what we find again when the ruins are cleared away. And even the smallest and most incomplete offering at this time can be a proud act in defense of that faith.

KATHERINE ANNE PORTER

June 21, 1940

Flowering Judas

Braggioni sits heaped upon the edge of a straight-backed chair much too small for him, and sings to Laura in a furry, mournful voice. Laura has begun to find reasons for avoiding her own house until the latest possible moment, for Braggioni is there almost every night. No matter how late she is, he will be sitting there with a surly, waiting expression, pulling at his kinky yellow hair, thumbing the strings of his guitar, snarling a tune under his breath. Lupe the Indian maid meets Laura at the door, and says with a flicker of a glance towards the upper room, "He waits."

Laura wishes to lie down, she is tired of her hairpins and the feel of her long tight sleeves, but she says to him, "Have you a new song for me this evening?" If he says yes, she asks him to sing it. If he says no, she remembers his favorite one, and asks him to sing it again. Lupe brings her a cup of chocolate and a plate of rice, and Laura eats at the small table under the lamp, first inviting Braggioni, whose answer is always the same: "I have eaten, and besides, chocolate thickens the voice."

Laura says, "Sing, then," and Braggioni heaves himself into song. He scratches the guitar familiarly as though it were a pet animal, and sings passionately off key, taking the high notes in a prolonged painful squeal. Laura, who haunts the markets listening to the ballad singers, and stops every day to hear the blind boy playing his reed-flute in Sixteenth of September Street, listens to Braggioni with pitiless courtesy, because she dares not smile at his miserable performance. Nobody dares to smile at him. Braggioni is cruel to everyone, with a kind of specialized insolence, but he is so vain of his talents, and so sensitive to slights, it would require a cruelty and vanity greater than his own to lay a finger on the vast cureless wound of his self-esteem. It would require courage, too, for it is dangerous to offend him, and nobody has this courage.

Braggioni loves himself with such tenderness and amplitude and eternal charity that his followers—for he is a leader of men, a skilled revolutionist, and his skin has been punctured in honorable warfare—warm themselves in the reflected glow, and say to each other: "He has a real nobility, a love of humanity raised above mere personal affections." The excess of this self-love has flowed out, inconveniently for her, over Laura, who, with so many others, owes her comfortable situation and her salary to him. When he is in a very good humor, he tells her, "I am tempted to forgive you for being a *gringa. Gringita!*" and Laura, burning, imagines herself leaning forward suddenly, and with a sound back-handed slap wiping the suety smile from his face. If he notices her eyes at these moments he gives no sign.

She knows what Braggioni would offer her, and she must resist tenaciously without appearing to resist, and if she could avoid it she would not admit even to herself the slow drift of his intention. During these long evenings which have spoiled a long month for her, she sits in her deep chair with an open book on her knees, resting her eyes on the consoling rigidity of the printed page when the sight and sound of Braggioni singing threaten to identify themselves with all her remembered afflictions and to add their weight to her uneasy premonitions of the future. The gluttonous bulk of Braggioni has become a symbol of her many disillusions, for a revolutionist should be lean, animated by heroic faith, a vessel of abstract virtues. This is nonsense, she knows it now and is ashamed of it. Revolution must have leaders, and leadership is a career for energetic men. She is, her comrades tell her, full of romantic error, for what she defines as cynicism in them is merely "a developed sense of reality." She is almost too willing to say, "I am wrong, I suppose I don't really understand the principles," and afterward she makes a secret truce with herself, determined not to surrender her will to such expedient logic. But she cannot help feeling that she has been betrayed irreparably by the disunion between her way of living and her feeling of what life should be, and at times she is almost contented to rest in this sense of grievance as a private store of consolation. Sometimes she wishes to run away, but she stays. Now she longs to fly out of this room, down the narrow stairs, and into the street where the houses lean together like conspirators under a single mottled lamp, and leave Braggioni singing to himself.

Instead she looks at Braggioni, frankly and clearly, like a good child who understands the rules of behavior. Her knees cling together under sound blue serge, and her round white collar is not purposely nun-like. She wears the uniform of an idea, and has renounced vanities. She was born Roman Catholic, and in spite of her fear of being seen by someone who might make a scandal of it, she slips now and again into some crumbling little church, kneels on the chilly stone, and says a Hail Mary on the gold rosary she bought in Tehuantepec. It is no good and she ends by examining the altar with its tinsel flowers and ragged brocades, and feels tender about the battered doll-shape of some male saint whose white, lace-trimmed drawers hang limply around his ankles below the hieratic dignity of his velvet robe. She has encased herself in a set of principles derived from her early training, leaving no detail of gesture or of personal taste untouched, and for this reason she will not wear lace made on machines. This is her private heresy, for in her special group the machine is sacred, and will be the salvation of the workers. She loves fine lace, and there is a tiny edge of fluted cobweb on this collar, which is one of twenty precisely alike, folded in blue tissue paper in the upper drawer of her clothes chest.

Braggioni catches her glance solidly as if he had been waiting for it, leans forward, balancing his paunch between his spread knees, and sings with tremendous emphasis, weighing his words. He has, the song relates, no father and no mother, nor even a friend to console him; lonely as a wave of the sea he comes and goes, lonely as a wave. His mouth opens round and yearns sideways, his balloon cheeks grow oily with the labor of song. He bulges marvelously in his expensive garments. Over his lavender collar, crushed upon a purple necktie, held by a diamond hoop: over his ammunition belt of tooled leather worked in silver, buckled cruelly around his gasping middle: over the tops of his glossy yellow shoes Braggioni swells with ominous ripeness, his mauve silk hose stretched taut, his ankles bound with the stout leather thongs of his shoes.

When he stretches his eyelids at Laura she notes again that his eyes are the true tawny yellow cat's eyes. He is rich, not in money, he tells her, but in power, and this power brings with it the blameless ownership of things, and the right to indulge his love of small luxuries. "I have a taste for the elegant refinements," he said once, flourishing a yellow silk handkerchief before her nose. "Smell that? It is Jockey Club, imported from New York." Nonetheless he is wounded by life. He will say so presently. "It is true everything turns to dust in the hand, to gall on the tongue." He sighs and his leather belt creaks like a saddle girth. "I am disappointed in everything as it comes. Everything." He shakes his head. "You, poor thing, you will be disappointed too. You are born for it. We are more alike than you realize in some things. Wait and see. Some day you will remember what I have told you, you will know that Braggioni was your friend."

Laura feels a slow chill, a purely physical sense of danger, a warning in her blood that violence, mutilation, a shocking death, wait for her with lessening patience. She has translated this fear into something homely, immediate, and sometimes hesitates before crossing the street. "My personal fate is nothing, except as the testimony of a mental attitude," she reminds herself, quoting from some forgotten philosophic primer, and is sensible enough to add, "Anyhow, I shall not be killed by an automobile if I can help it."

"It may be true I am as corrupt, in another way, as Braggioni," she thinks in spite of herself, "as callous, as incomplete," and if this is so, any kind of death seems preferable. Still she sits quietly, she does not run. Where could she go? Uninvited she has promised herself to this place; she can no longer imagine herself as living in another country, and there is no pleasure in remembering her life before she came here.

Precisely what is the nature of this devotion, its true motives, and what are its obligations? Laura cannot say. She spends part of her days in Xochimilco, near by, teaching Indian children to say in English, "The cat is on the mat." When she appears in the classroom they crowd about her with smiles on their wise, innocent, clay-colored faces, crying, "Good morning, my titcher!" in immaculate voices, and they make of her desk a fresh garden of flowers every day.

During her leisure she goes to union meetings and listens to busy important voices quarreling over tactics, methods, internal politics. She visits the prisoners of her own political faith in their cells, where they entertain themselves with counting cockroaches, repenting of their indiscretions, composing their memoirs, writing out manifestoes and plans for their comrades who are still walking about free, hands in pockets, sniffing fresh air. Laura brings them food and cigarettes and a little money, and she brings messages disguised in equivocal phrases from the men outside who dare not set foot in the prison for fear of disappearing into the cells kept empty for them. If the prisoners confuse night and day, and complain, "Dear little Laura, time doesn't pass in this infernal hole, and I won't know when it is time to sleep unless I have a reminder," she brings them their favorite narcotics, and says in a tone that does not wound them with pity, "Tonight will really be night for you," and though her Spanish amuses them, they find her comforting, useful. If they lose patience and all faith, and curse the slowness of their friends in coming to their rescue with money and influence, they trust her not to repeat everything, and if she inquires, "Where do you think we can find money, or influence?" they are certain to answer, "Well, there is Braggioni, why doesn't he do something?"

She smuggles letters from headquarters to men hiding from firing squads in back streets in mildewed houses, where they sit in tumbled beds and talk bitterly as if all Mexico were at their heels, when Laura knows positively they might appear at the band concert in the Alameda on Sunday morning, and no one would notice them. But Braggioni says, "Let them sweat a little. The next time they may be careful. It is very restful to have them out of the way for a while." She is not afraid to knock on any door in any street after midnight, and enter in the darkness, and say to one of these men who is really in danger: "They will be looking for you—seriously—tomorrow morning after six. Here is some money from Vicente. Go to Vera Cruz and wait."

She borrows money from the Roumanian agitator to give to his bitter enemy the Polish agitator. The favor of Braggioni is their disputed territory, and Braggioni holds the balance nicely, for he can use them both. The Polish agitator talks love to her over café tables, hoping to exploit what he believes is her secret sentimental preference for him, and he gives her misinformation which he begs her to repeat as the solemn truth to certain persons. The Roumanian is more adroit. He is generous with his money in all good causes, and lies to her with an air of ingenuous candor, as if he were her good friend and confidant. She never repeats anything they may say. Braggioni never asks questions. He has other ways to discover all that he wishes to know about them.

Nobody touches her, but all praise her gray eyes, and the soft, round under lip which promises gayety, yet is always grave, nearly always firmly closed: and they cannot understand why she is in Mexico. She walks back and forth on her errands, with puzzled eyebrows, carrying her little folder of drawings and music and school papers. No dancer dances more beautifully than Laura walks, and she inspires some amusing, unexpected ardors, which cause little gossip, because nothing comes of them. A young captain who had been a soldier in Zapata's army attempted, during a horseback ride near Cuernavaca, to express his desire for her with the noble simplicity befitting a rude folk-hero: but gently, because he was gentle. This gentleness was his defeat, for when he alighted, and removed her foot from the stirrup, and essayed to draw her down into his arms, her horse, ordinarily a tame one, shied fiercely, reared and plunged away. The young hero's horse careered blindly after his stable-mate, and the hero did not return to the hotel until rather late that evening. At breakfast he came to her table in full charro dress, gray buckskin jacket and trousers with strings of silver buttons down the leg, and he was in a humorous, careless mood. "May I sit with you?" and "You are a wonderful rider. I was terrified that you might be thrown and dragged. I should never have forgiven myself. But I cannot admire you enough for your riding!"

"I learned to ride in Arizona," said Laura.

"If you will ride with me again this morning, I promise you a horse that will not shy with you," he said. But Laura remembered that she must return to Mexico City at noon.

Next morning the children made a celebration and spent their playtime writing on the blackboard, "We lov ar ticher," and with tinted chalks they drew wreaths of flowers around the words. The young hero wrote her a letter: "I am a very foolish, wasteful, impulsive man. I should have first said I love you, and then you would not have run away. But you shall see me again." Laura thought, "I must send him a box of colored crayons," but she was trying to forgive herself for having spurred her horse at the wrong moment.

A brown, shock-haired youth came and stood in her patio one night and sang like a lost soul for two hours, but Laura could think of nothing to do about it. The moonlight spread a wash of gauzy silver over the clear spaces of the garden, and the shadows were cobalt blue. The scarlet blossoms of the Judas tree were dull purple and the names of the colors repeated themselves automatically in her mind, while she watched not the boy, but his shadow, fallen like a dark garment across the fountain rim, trailing in the water. Lupe came silently and whispered expert counsel in her ear: "If you will throw him one little flower, he will sing another song or two and go away." Laura threw the flower, and he sang a last song and went away with the flower tucked in the band of his hat. Lupe said, "He is one of the organizers of the Typographers Union, and before that he sold corridos in the Merced market, and before that, he came from Guanajuato, where I was born. I would not trust any man, but I trust least those from Guanajuato."

She did not tell Laura that he would be back again the next night, and the next, nor that he would follow her at a certain fixed distance around the Merced market, through the Zócolo, up Francisco I. Madero Avenue, and so along the Paseo de la Reforma to Chapultepec Park, and into the Philosopher's Footpath, still with that flower withering in his hat, and an indivisible attention in his eyes.

Now Laura is accustomed to him, it means nothing except that he is nineteen years old and is observing a convention with all propriety, as though it were founded on a law of nature, which in the end it might well prove to be. He is beginning to write poems which he prints on a wooden press, and he leaves them stuck like handbills in her door. She is pleasantly disturbed by the abstract, unhurried watchfulness of his black eyes which will in time turn easily towards another object. She tells herself that throwing the flower was a mistake, for she is twenty-two years old and knows better; but she refuses to regret it, and persuades herself that her negation of all external events as they occur is a sign that she is gradually perfecting herself in the stoicism she strives to cultivate against that disaster she fears, though she cannot name it.

She is not at home in the world. Every day she teaches children who remain strangers to her, though she loves their tender round hands and their charming opportunist savagery. She knocks at unfamiliar doors not knowing whether a friend or a stranger shall answer, and even if a known face emerges from the sour gloom of that unknown interior, still it is the face of a stranger. No matter what this stranger says to her, nor what her message to him, the very cells of her flesh reject knowledge and kinship in one monotonous word. No. No. No. She draws her strength from this one holy talismanic word which does not suffer her to be led into evil. Denying everything, she may walk anywhere in safety, she looks at everything without amazement.

No, repeats this firm unchanging voice of her blood; and she looks at Braggioni without amazement. He is a great man, he wishes to impress this simple girl who covers her great round breasts with thick dark cloth, and who hides long, invaluably beautiful legs under a heavy skirt. She is almost thin except for the incomprehensible fullness of her breasts, like a nursing mother's, and Braggioni, who considers himself a judge of women, speculates again on the puzzle of her notorious virginity, and takes the liberty of speech which she permits without a sign of modesty, indeed, without any sort of sign, which is disconcerting.

"You think you are so cold, *gringita!* Wait and see. You will surprise yourself some day! May I be there to advise you!" He stretches his eyelids at her, and his ill-humored cat's eyes waver in a separate glance for the two points of light marking the opposite ends of a smoothly drawn path between the swollen curve of her breasts. He is not put off by that blue serge, nor by her resolutely fixed gaze. There is all the time in the world. His cheeks are bellying with the wind of song. "O girl with the dark eyes," he sings, and reconsiders. "But yours are not dark. I can change all that. O girl with the green eyes, you have stolen my heart away!" then his mind wanders to the song, and Laura feels the weight of his attention being shifted elsewhere. Singing thus, he seems harmless, he is quite harmless, there is nothing to do but sit patiently and say "No," when the moment comes. She draws a full breath, and her mind wanders also, but not far. She dares not wander too far.

Not for nothing has Braggioni taken pains to be a good revolutionist and a professional lover of humanity. He will never die of it. He has the malice, the cleverness, the wickedness, the sharpness of wit, the hardness of heart, stipulated for loving the world profitably. *He will never die of it.* He will live to see himself kicked out from his feeding trough by other hungry world-saviors. Traditionally he must sing in spite of his life which drives him to bloodshed, he tells Laura, for his father was a Tuscany peasant who drifted to Yucatan and married a Maya woman: a woman of race, an aristocrat. They gave him the love and knowledge of music, thus: and under the rip of his thumbnail, the strings of the instrument complain like exposed nerves.

Once he was called Delgadito by all the girls and married women who ran after him; he was so scrawny all his bones showed under his thin cotton clothing, and he could squeeze his emptiness to the very backbone with his two hands. He was a poet and the revolution was only a dream then; too many women loved him and sapped away his youth, and he could never find enough to eat anywhere, anywhere! Now he is a leader of men, crafty men who whisper in his ear, hungry men who wait for hours outside his office for a word with him, emaciated men with wild faces who waylay him at the street gate with a timid, "Comrade, let me tell you . . ." and they blow the foul breath from their empty stomachs in his face.

He is always sympathetic. He gives them handfuls of small coins from his own pocket, he promises them work, there will be demonstrations, they must join the unions and attend the meetings, above all they must be on the watch for spies. They are closer to him than his own brothers, without them he can do nothing—until tomorrow, comrade!

Until tomorrow. "They are stupid, they are lazy, they are treacherous, they would cut my throat for nothing," he says to Laura. He has good food and abundant drink, he hires an automobile and drives in the Paseo on Sunday morning, and enjoys plenty of sleep in a soft bed beside a wife who dares not disturb him; and he sits pampering his bones in easy billows of fat, singing to Laura, who knows and thinks these things about him. When he was fifteen, he tried to drown himself because he loved a girl, his first love, and she laughed at him. "A thousand women have paid for that," and his tight little mouth turns down at the corners. Now he perfumes his hair with Jockey Club, and confides to Laura: "One woman is really as good as another for me, in the dark. I prefer them all."

His wife organizes unions among the girls in the cigarette factories, and walks in picket lines, and even speaks at meetings in the evening. But she cannot be brought to acknowledge the benefits of true liberty. "I tell her I must have my freedom, net. She does not understand my point of view." Laura has heard this many times. Braggioni scratches the guitar and meditates. "She is an instinctively virtuous woman, pure gold, no doubt of that. If she were not, I should lock her up, and she knows it."

His wife, who works so hard for the good of the factory girls, employs part of her leisure lying on the floor weeping because there are so many women in the world, and only one husband for her, and she never knows where nor when to look for him. He told her: "Unless you can learn to cry when I am not here, I must go away for good." That day he went away and took a room at the Hotel Madrid.

It is this month of separation for the sake of higher principles that has been spoiled not only for Mrs. Braggioni, whose sense of reality is beyond criticism, but for Laura, who feels herself bogged in a nightmare. Tonight Laura envies Mrs. Braggioni, who is alone, and free to weep as much as she pleases about a concrete wrong. Laura has just come from a visit to the prison, and she is waiting for tomorrow with a bitter anxiety as if tomorrow may not come, but time may be caught immovably in this hour, with herself transfixed, Braggioni singing on forever, and Eugenio's body not yet discovered by the guard.

Braggioni says: "Are you going to sleep?" Almost before she can shake her head, he begins telling her about the May-day disturbances coming on in Morelia, for the Catholics hold a festival in honor of the Blessed Virgin, and the Socialists celebrate their martyrs on that day. "There will be two independent processions, starting from either end of town, and they will march until they meet, and the rest depends . . ." He asks her to oil and load his pistols. Standing up, he unbuckles his ammunition belt, and spreads it laden across her knees. Laura sits with the shells slipping through the cleaning cloth dipped in oil, and he says again he cannot understand why she works so hard for the revolutionary idea unless she loves some man who is in it. "Are you not in love with someone?" "No," says Laura. "And no one is in love with you?" "No." "Then it is your own fault. No woman need go begging. Why, what is the matter with you? The legless beggar woman in the Alameda has a perfectly faithful lover. Did you know that?"

Laura peers down the pistol barrel and says nothing, but a long, slow faintness rises and subsides in her; Braggioni curves his swollen fingers around the throat of the guitar and softly smothers the music out of it, and when she hears him again he seems to have forgotten her, and is speaking in the hypnotic voice he uses when talking in small rooms to a listening, close-gathered crowd. Some day this world, now seemingly so composed and eternal, to the edges of every sea shall be merely a tangle of gaping trenches, of crashing walls and broken bodies. Everything must be torn from its accustomed place where it has rotted for centuries, hurled skyward and distributed, cast down again clean as rain, without separate identity. Nothing shall survive that the stiffened hands of poverty have created for the rich and no one shall be left alive except the elect spirits destined to procreate a new world cleansed of cruelty and injustice, ruled by benevolent anarchy: "Pistols are good, I love them, cannon are even better, but in the end I pin my faith to good dynamite," he concludes, and strokes the pistol lying in her hands. "Once I dreamed of destroying this city, in case it offered resistance to General Ortíz, but it fell into his hands like an overripe pear."

He is made restless by his own words, rises and stands waiting. Laura holds up the belt to him: "Put that on, and go kill somebody in Morelia, and you will be happier," she says softly. The presence of death in the room makes her bold. "Today, I found Eugenio going into a stupor. He refused to allow me to call the prison doctor. He had taken all the tablets I brought him yesterday. He said he took them because he was bored."

"He is a fool, and his death is his own business," says Braggioni, fastening his belt carefully.

"I told him if he had waited only a little while longer, you would have got him set free," says Laura. "He said he did not want to wait."

"He is a fool and we are well rid of him," says Braggioni, reaching for his hat.

He goes away. Laura knows his mood has changed, she will not see him any more for a while. He will send word when he needs her to go on errands into strange streets, to speak to the strange faces that will appear, like clay masks with the power of human speech, to mutter their thanks to Braggioni for his help. Now she is free, and she thinks, I must run while there is time. But she does not go.

Braggioni enters his own house where for a month his wife has spent many hours every night weeping and tangling her hair upon her pillow. She is weeping now, and she weeps more at the sight of him, the cause of all her sorrows. He looks about the room. Nothing is changed, the smells are good and familiar, he is well acquainted with the woman who comes toward him with no reproach except grief on her face. He says to her tenderly: "You are so good, please don't cry any more, you dear good creature." She says, "Are you tired, my angel? Sit here and I will wash your feet." She brings a bowl of water, and kneeling, unlaces his shoes, and when from her knees she raises her sad eyes under her blackened lids, he is sorry for everything, and bursts into tears. "Ah, yes, I am hungry, I am tired, let us eat something together," he says, between sobs. His wife leans her head on his arm and says, "Forgive me!" and this time he is refreshed by the solemn, endless rain of her tears.

Laura takes off her serge dress and puts on a white linen nightgown and goes to bed. She turns her head a little to one side, and lying still, reminds herself that it is time to sleep. Numbers tick in her brain like little clocks, soundless doors close of themselves around her. If you would sleep, you must not remember anything, the children will say tomorrow, good morning, my teacher, the poor prisoners who come every day bringing flowers to their jailor. 1-2-3-4-5—it is monstrous to confuse love with revolution, night with day, life with death—ah, Eugenio!

The tolling of the midnight bell is a signal, but what does it mean? Get up, Laura, and follow me: come out of your sleep, out of your bed, out of this strange house. What are you doing in this house? Without a word, without fear she rose and reached for Eugenio's hand, but he eluded her with a sharp, sly smile and drifted away. This is not all, you shall see—Murderer, he said, follow me, I will show you a new country, but it is far away and we must hurry. No, said Laura, not unless you take my hand, no; and she clung first to the stair rail, and then to the topmost branch of the Judas tree that bent down slowly and set her upon the earth, and then to the rocky ledge of a cliff, and then to the jagged wave of a sea that was not water but a desert of crumbling stone. Where are you taking me, she asked in wonder but without fear. To death, and it is a long way off, and we must hurry, said Eugenio. No, said Laura, not unless you take my hand. Then eat these flowers, poor prisoner, said Eugenio in a voice of pity, take and eat: and from the Judas tree he stripped the warm bleeding flowers, and held them to her lips. She saw that his hand was fleshless, a cluster of small white petrified branches, and his eye sockets were without light, but she ate the flowers greedily for they satisfied both hunger and thirst. Murderer! said Eugenio, and Cannibal! This is my body and my blood. Laura cried No! and at the sound of her own voice, she awoke trembling, and was afraid to sleep again.

1930

William Faulkner

(1897-1962)

CHRONOLOGY:

1897 Born September 25, in New Albany, Mississippi.
1904 Moved to Oxford, Mississippi, where he spent the major part of the rest of his life.
1918 Enlisted in the Canadian Royal Flying Corp.
1919 Returned to Oxford; published a poem in *The New Republic.*
1923 Lived briefly in New York; became a good friend of Stark Young.
1924 *The Marble Faun,* poems.
1925 Lived briefly in New Orleans; became acquainted with Sherwood Anderson.
1925-26 Made walking tour of France and Germany.
1926 *Soldier's Pay.*
1927 *Mosquitoes.*
1929 *Sartoris* (began Yoknapatawpha saga); *The Sound and the Fury.*
1930 *As I Lay Dying.*
1931 *Sanctuary; These 13,* stories; *Idyll in the Desert,* story.
1932 *Salamagundi,* essays and poetry; *This Earth, a Poem; Miss Zilphia Gant,* story; *Light in August.*
1933 *A Green Bough,* poems.
1934 *Doctor Martino and Other Stories.*
1935 *Pylon.*
1936 *Absalom, Absalom!;* began some intermittant screen-writing in Hollywood.
1938 *The Unvanquished.*
1939 *The Wild Palms* (including the interrelated *The Old Man).*
1940 *The Hamlet* (first volume of the Snopes trilogy).
1942 *Go Down, Moses, and Other Stories.*
1948 *Intruder in the Dust.*
1949 *Knight's Gambit.*
1950 *Notes on a Horsethief,* story; *Collected Stories* (awarded National Book Award); awarded Nobel Prize for Literature.
1951 *Requiem for a Nun* (sequel to *Sanctuary*).
1953 *Mirrors of Chartres Street.*
1954 *A Fable.*
1955 *Big Woods,* stories.
1956 *Faulkner at Nagano* (ed. Robert A. Jelliffe), talks in Japan.
1957 *The Town* (second volume of Snopes trilogy).
1958 *William Faulkner: New Orleans Sketches* (ed. by Carvel Collins).
1959 *The Mansion* (third volume of Snopes trilogy); *Faulkner in thė University* (ed. by F. L. Gwynn and J. L. Blotner), talks at the University of Virginia.
1962 *The Reivers;* died on July 6, in Oxford, Mississippi.

BIBLIOGRAPHY:

Although there is no collected edition, all of Faulkner's major novels are now in print, and most of them are available in inexpensive reprints. A pioneering anthology, the *Viking Portable Faulkner,* ed. by Malcolm Cowely (New York, 1946), is still useful. A recent collection is *Selected Short Stories* (New York, 1961).

Book-length critical and biographical studies are numerous and uneven Among the most important, perhaps are Irving Howe, *William Faulkner. A Critical Study* (New York, 1952 rev. 1961); William Van O'Connor *The Tangled Fire of William Faulkner* (Minneapolis, 1954); H. H. Waggoner, *William Faulkner: From Jefferson to the World* (Lexington, Ky.

1959); Olga Vickery, *The Novels of William Faulkner* (Baton Rouge, La., 1960); Lawrance Thompson, *William Faulkner* (New York, 1963). The indispensable collection of critical essays is Frederick Hoffman and Olga Vickery, eds., *Three Decades of Faulkner Criticism* (East Lansing, 1960) and its full bibliography broken down into studies of individual works. The most complete listing is James B. Meriwether, *William Faulkner: A Check List* (Princeton, 1957). A recent specialized compilation is Robert W. Kirk and Marvin Klotz, *Faulkner's People: A Complete Guide and Index to Characters in the Fiction of William Faulkner* (Berkeley, 1963).

For the most recent explications of his stories, see Warren S. Walker, *Twentieth-Century Short Story Explication . . .* (Hamden, Conn., 1961), Supplement, 1963.

Faulkner's Nobel Prize Award Speech, Stockholm, December 10, 1950

I feel that this award was not made to me as a man but to my work—a life's work in the agony and sweat of the human spirit, not for glory and least of all for profit, but to create out of the materials of the human spirit something which did not exist before. So this award is only mine in trust. It will not be difficult to find a dedication for the money part of it commensurate with the purpose and significance of its origin. But I would like to do the same with the acclaim too, by using this moment as a pinnacle from which I might be listened to by the young men and women already dedicated to the same anguish and travail, among whom is already that one who will some day stand here where I am standing.

Our tragedy today is a general and universal physical fear so long sustained by now that we can even bear it. There are no longer problems of the spirit. There is only the question: When will I be blown up? Because of this, the young man or woman writing today has forgotten the problems of the human heart in conflict with itself which alone can make good writing because only that is worth writing about, worth the agony and the sweat.

He must learn them again. He must teach himself that the basest of all things is to be afraid; and, teaching himself that, forget it forever, leaving no room in his workshop for anything but the old verities and truths of the heart, the old universal truths lacking which any story is ephemeral and doomed—love and honor and pity and pride and compassion and sacrifice. Until he does so, he labors under a curse. He writes not of love but of lust, of defeats in which nobody loses anything of value, of victories without hope and, worst of all, without pity or compassion. His griefs grieve on no universal bones, leaving no scars. He writes not of the heart but of the glands.

Until he relearns these things, he will write as though he stood alone and watched the end of man. I decline to accept the end of man. It is easy enough to say that man is immortal simply because he will endure; that when the last ding-dong of doom has clanged and faded from the last worthless rock hanging tideless in the last red and dying evening, that even then there will still be one more sound: that of his puny inexhaustible voice, still talking. I refuse to accept this. I believe that man will not merely endure: he will prevail. He is immortal, not because he alone among creatures has an inexhaustible voice but because he has a soul, a spirit capable of compassion and sacrifice and endurance. The poet's, the writer's, duty is to write about these things. It is his privilege to help man endure by lifting his heart, by reminding him of the courage and honor and hope and pride and compassion and pity and sacrifice which have been the glory of his past. The poet's voice need not merely be the record of man, it can be one of the props, the pillars to help him endure and prevail.

A Rose for Emily

– 1 –

When Miss Emily Grierson died, our whole town went to her funeral: the men through a sort of respectful affection for a fallen monument, the women mostly out of curiosity to see the inside of her house, which no one save an old manservant—a combined gardener and cook—had seen in at least ten years.

It was a big, squarish frame house that had once been white, decorated with cupolas and spires and scrolled balconies in the heavily lightsome style of the seventies, set on what had once been our most select street. But garages and cotton gins had encroached and obliterated even the august names of that neighborhood; only Miss Emily's house was left, lifting its stubborn and coquettish decay above the cotton wagons and the gasoline pumps—an eyesore among eyesores. And now Miss Emily had gone to join the representatives of those august names where they lay in the cedar-bemused cemetery among the ranked and anonymous graves of Union and Confederate soldiers who fell at the battle of Jefferson.

Alive, Miss Emily had been a tradition, a duty, and a care; a sort of hereditary obligation upon the town, dating from that day in 1894 when Colonel Sartoris, the mayor—he who fathered the edict that no Negro woman should appear on the streets without an apron—remitted her taxes, the dispensation dating from the death of her father on into perpetuity. Not that Miss Emily would have accepted charity. Colonel Sartoris invented an involved tale to the effect that Miss Emily's father had loaned money to the town, which the town, as a matter of business, preferred this way of repaying. Only a man of Colonel Sartoris' generation and thought could have invented it, and only a woman could have believed it.

When the next generation, with its more modern ideas, became mayors and aldermen, this arrangement created some little dissatisfaction. On the first of the year they mailed her a tax notice. February came, and there was no reply. They wrote her a formal letter, asking her to call at the sheriff's office at her convenience. A week later the mayor wrote her himself, offering to call or to send his car for her, and received in reply a note on paper of an archaic shape, in a thin, flowing calligraphy in faded ink, to the effect that she no longer went out at all. The tax notice was also enclosed, without comment.

They called a special meeting of the Board of Aldermen. A deputation waited upon her, knocked at the door through which no visitor had passed since she ceased giving china-painting lessons eight or ten years earlier. They were admitted by the old Negro into a dim hall from which a stairway mounted into still more shadow. It smelled of dust and disuse—a close, dank smell. The Negro led them into the parlor. It was furnished in heavy, leather-covered furniture. When the Negro opened the blinds of one window, they could see that the leather was cracked; and when they sat down, a faint dust rose sluggishly about their thighs, spinning with slow motes in the single sun-ray. On a tarnished gilt easel before the fireplace stood a crayon portrait of Miss Emily's father.

They rose when she entered—a small, fat woman in black, with a thin gold chain descending to her waist and vanishing into her belt, leaning on an ebony cane with a tarnished gold head. Her skeleton was small and spare; perhaps that was why what would have been merely plumpness in another was obesity in her. She looked bloated, like a body long submerged in motionless water, and of that pallid hue. Her eyes, lost in the fatty ridges of her face, looked like two small pieces of coal pressed into a lump of dough as they moved from one face to another while the visitors stated their errand.

She did not ask them to sit. She just stood in the door and listened quietly until the spokesman came to a stumbling halt. Then they could hear the invisible watch ticking at the end of the gold chain.

Her voice was dry and cold. "I have no taxes in Jefferson. Colonel Sartoris explained it to me. Perhaps one of you can gain access to the city records and satisfy yourselves."

"But we have. We are the city authorities, Miss Emily. Didn't you get a notice from the sheriff, signed by him?"

"I received a paper, yes," Miss Emily said. "Perhaps he considers himself the sheriff . . . I have no taxes in Jefferson."

"But there is nothing on the books to show that, you see. We must go by the—"

"See Colonel Sartoris. I have no taxes in Jefferson."

"But, Miss Emily—"

"See Colonel Sartoris." (Colonel Sartoris had been dead almost ten years.) "I have no taxes in Jefferson. Tobe!" The Negro appeared. "Show these gentlemen out."

– 2 –

So she vanquished them, horse and foot, just as she had vanquished their fathers thirty years before about the smell. That was two years after her father's death and a short time after her sweetheart—the one we believed would marry her—had deserted her. After her father's death she went out very little; after her sweetheart went away, people hardly saw her at all. A few of the ladies had the temerity to call, but were not received, and the only sign of life about the place was the Negro man—a young man then—going in and out with a market basket.

"Just as if a man—any man—could keep a kitchen properly," the ladies said; so they were not surprised when the smell developed. It was another link between the gross, teeming world and the high and mighty Griersons.

A neighbor, a woman, complained to the mayor, Judge Stevens, eighty years old.

"But what will you have me do about it, madam?" he said.

"Why, send her word to stop it," the woman said. "Isn't there a law?"

"I'm sure that won't be necessary," Judge Stevens said. "It's probably just a snake or a rat that nigger of hers killed in the yard. I'll speak to him about it."

The next day he received two more complaints, one from a man who came in diffident deprecation. "We really must do something about it, Judge. I'd be the last one in the world to bother Miss Emily, but we've got to do something." That night the Board of Aldermen met—three graybeards and one younger man, a member of the rising generation.

"It's simple enough," he said. "Send her word to have her place cleaned up. Give her a certain time to do it in, and if she don't . . ."

"Dammit, sir," Judge Stevens said, "will you accuse a lady to her face of smelling bad?"

So the next night, after midnight, four men crossed Miss Emily's lawn and slunk about the house like burglars, sniffing along the base of the brickwork and at the cellar openings while one of them performed a regular sowing motion with his hand out of a sack slung from his shoulder. They broke open the cellar door and sprinkled lime there, and in all the outbuildings. As they recrossed the lawn, a window that had been dark was lighted and Miss Emily sat in it, the light behind her, and her upright torso motionless as that of an idol. They crept quietly across the lawn and into the shadow of the locusts that lined the street. After a week or two the smell went away.

That was when people had begun to feel really sorry for her. People in our town, remembering how old lady Wyatt, her great-aunt, had gone completely crazy at last, believed that the Griersons held themselves a little too high for what they really were. None of the young men were quite good enough for Miss Emily and such. We had long thought of them as a tableau, Miss Emily a slender figure in white in the background, her father a spraddled silhouette in the foreground, his back to her and clutching a horsewhip, the two of them framed by the back-flung front door. So when she got to be thirty and was still single, we were not pleased exactly, but vindicated; even with insanity in the family she wouldn't have turned down all of her chances if they had really materialized.

When her father died, it got about that the house was all that was left to her; and in a way, people were glad. At last they could pity Miss Emily. Being left alone, and a pauper, she had become humanized. Now she too would know the old thrill and the old despair of a penny more or less.

The day after his death all the ladies prepared to call at the house and offer condolence and aid, as is our custom. Miss Emily met them at the door, dressed as usual and with no trace of grief on her face. She told them that her father was not dead. She did that for three days, with the ministers calling on her, and the doctors, trying to persuade her to let them dispose of the body. Just as they were about to resort to law and force, she broke down, and they buried her father quickly.

We did not say she was crazy then. We believed she had to do that. We remembered all the young men her father had driven away, and we knew that with nothing left, she would have to cling to that which had robbed her, as people will.

– 3 –

She was sick for a long time. When we saw her again, her hair was cut short, making her look like a girl, with a vague resemblance to those angels in colored church windows—sort of tragic and serene.

The town had just let the contracts for paving the sidewalks, and in the summer after her father's death they began the work. The construction company came with niggers and mules and machinery, and a foreman named Homer Barron, a Yankee—a big, dark, ready man, with a big voice and eyes lighter than his face. The little boys would follow in groups to hear him cuss the niggers, and the niggers singing in time to the rise and fall of picks. Pretty soon he knew everybody in town. Whenever you heard a lot of laughing anywhere about the square, Homer Barron would be in the center of the group. Presently we began to see him and Miss Emily on Sunday afternoons driving in the yellow-wheeled buggy and the matched team of bays from the livery stable.

At first we were glad that Miss Emily would have an interest, because the ladies all said, "Of course a Grierson would not think seriously of a Northerner, a day laborer." But there were still others, older people, who said that even grief could not cause a real lady to forget *noblesse oblige*—without calling it *noblesse oblige*. They just said, "Poor Emily. Her kinsfolk should come to her." She had some kin in Alabama; but years ago her father had fallen out with them over the estate of old lady Wyatt, the crazy woman, and there was no communication between the two families. They had not even been represented at the funeral.

And as soon as the old people said, "Poor Emily," the whispering began. "Do you suppose it's really so?" they said to one another. "Of course it is. What else could . . ." This behind their hands; rustling of craned silk and satin behind jalousies closed upon the sun of Sunday afternoon as the thin, swift clop-clop-clop of the matched team passed: "Poor Emily."

She carried her head high enough—even when we believed that she was fallen. It was as if she demanded more than ever the recognition of her dignity as the last Grierson; as if it had wanted that touch of earthiness to reaffirm her imperviousness. Like when she bought the rat poison, the arsenic. That was over a year after they had begun to say "Poor Emily," and while the two female cousins were visiting her.

"I want some poison," she said to the druggist. She was over thirty then, still a slight woman, though thinner than usual, with cold, haughty black eyes in a face the flesh of which was strained across the temples and about the eye-sockets as you imagine a lighthouse-keeper's face ought to look. "I want some poison," she said.

"Yes, Miss Emily. What kind? For rats and such? I'd recom—"

"I want the best you have. I don't care what kind."

The druggist named several. "They'll kill anything up to an elephant. But what you want is—"

"Arsenic," Miss Emily said. "Is that a good one?"

"Is . . . arsenic? Yes, ma'am. But what you want—"

"I want arsenic."

The druggist looked down at her. She looked back at him, erect, her face like a strained flag. "Why, of course," the druggist said. "If that's what you want. But the law requires you to tell what you are going to use it for."

Miss Emily just stared at him, her head tilted back in order to look him eye for eye, until he looked away and went and got the arsenic and wrapped it up. The Negro delivery boy brought her the package; the druggist didn't come back. When she opened the package at home there was written on the box, under the skull and bones: "For rats."

—4—

So the next day we all said, "She will kill herself"; and we said it would be the best thing. When she had first begun to be seen with Homer Barron, we had said, "She will marry him." Then we said, "She will persuade him yet," because Homer himself had remarked—he liked men, and it was known that he drank with the younger men in the Elks' Club—that he was not a marrying man. Later we said, "Poor Emily" behind the jalousies as they passed on Sunday afternoon in the glittering buggy, Miss Emily with her head high and Homer Barron with his hat cocked and a cigar in his teeth, reins and whip in a yellow glove.

Then some of the ladies began to say that it was a disgrace to the town and a bad example to the young people. The men did not want to interfere, but at last the ladies forced the Baptist minister—Miss Emily's people were Episcopal—to call upon her. He would never divulge what happened during that interview, but he refused to go back again. The next Sunday they again drove about the streets, and the following day the minister's wife wrote to Miss Emily's relations in Alabama.

So she had blood-kin under her roof again and we sat back to watch developments. At first nothing happened. Then we were sure that they were to be married. We learned that Miss Emily had been to the jeweler's and ordered a man's toilet set in silver, with the letters H. B. on each piece. Two days later we learned that she had bought a complete outfit of men's clothing, including a nightshirt, and we said, "They are married." We were really glad. We were glad because the two female cousins were even more Grierson than Miss Emily had ever been.

So we were not surprised when Homer Barron—the streets had been finished some time since—was gone. We were a little disappointed that there was not a public blowing-off, but we believed that he had gone on to prepare for Miss Emily's coming, or to give her a chance to get rid of the cousins. (By that time it was a cabal, and we were all Miss Emily's allies to help circumvent the cousins.) Sure enough, after another week they departed. And, as we had expected all along, within three days Homer Barron was back in town. A neighbor saw the Negro man admit him at the kitchen door at dusk one evening.

And that was the last we saw of Homer Barron. And of Miss Emily for some time. The Negro man went in and out with the market basket, but the front door remained closed. Now and then we would see her at a window for a moment, as the men did that night when they sprinkled the lime, but for almost six months she did not appear on the streets. Then we knew that this was to be expected too; as if that quality of her father which had thwarted her woman's life so many times had been too virulent and too furious to die.

When we next saw Miss Emily, she had grown fat and her hair was turning gray. During the next few years it grew grayer and grayer until it attained an even pepper-and-salt iron-gray, when it ceased turning. Up to the day of her death at seventy-four it was still that vigorous iron-gray, like the hair of an active man.

From that time on her front door remained closed, save for a period of six or seven years, when she was about forty, during which she gave lessons in china-painting. She fitted up a studio in one of the downstairs rooms, where the daughters and grand-daughters of Colonel Sartoris' contemporaries were sent to her with the same regularity and in the same spirit that they were sent to church on Sundays with a twenty-five-cent piece for the collection plate. Meanwhile her taxes had been remitted.

Then the newer generation became the backbone and the spirit of the town, and the painting pupils grew up and fell away and did not send their children to her with boxes of color and tedious brushes and pictures cut from the ladies' magazines. The front door closed upon the last one and remained closed for good. When the town got free postal delivery, Miss Emily alone refused to let them fasten the metal numbers above her door and attach a mailbox to it. She would not listen to them.

Daily, monthly, yearly we watched the Negro grow grayer and more stooped, going in and out with the market basket. Each December we sent her a tax notice, which would be returned by the post office a week later, unclaimed. Now and then we would see her in one of the downstairs windows—she had evidently shut up the top floor of the house—like the craven torso of an idol in a niche, looking or not looking at us, we could never tell which. Thus she passed from generation to generation—dear, inescapable, impervious, tranquil, and perverse.

And so she died. Fell ill in the house filled with dust and shadows, with only a doddering Negro man to wait on her. We did not even know she was sick; we had long since given up trying to get any information from the Negro. He talked to no one, probably not even to her, for his voice had grown harsh and rusty, as if from disuse.

She died in one of the downstairs rooms, in a heavy walnut bed with a curtain, her gray head propped on a pillow yellow and moldy with age and lack of sunlight.

–5–

The Negro met the first of the ladies at the front door and let them in, with their hushed, sibilant voices and their quick, curious glances, and then he disappeared. He walked right through the house and out the back and was not seen again.

The two female cousins came at once. They held the funeral on the second day, with the town coming to look at Miss Emily beneath a mass of bought flowers, with the crayon face of her father musing profoundly above the bier and the ladies sibilant and macabre; and the very old men

—some in their brushed Confederate uniforms—on the porch and the lawn, talking of Miss Emily as if she had been a contemporary of theirs, believing that they had danced with her and courted her perhaps, confusing time with its mathematical progression, as the old do, to whom all the past is not a diminishing road but, instead, a huge meadow which no winter ever quite touches, divided from them now by the narrow bottleneck of the most recent decade of years.

Already we knew that there was one room in that region above stairs which no one had seen in forty years, and which would have to be forced. They waited until Miss Emily was decently in the ground before they opened it.

The violence of breaking down the door seemed to fill this room with pervading dust. A thin, acrid pall as of the tomb seemed to lie everywhere upon this room decked and furnished as for a bridal: upon the valance curtains of faded rose color, upon the rose-shaded lights, upon the dressing table, upon the delicate array of crystal and the man's toilet things backed with tarnished silver, silver so tarnished that the monogram was obscured. Among them lay a collar and tie, as if they had just been removed, which, lifted, left upon the surface a pale crescent in the dust. Upon a chair hung the suit, carefully folded; beneath it the two mute shoes and the discarded socks.

The man himself lay in the bed.

For a long while we just stood there, looking down at the profound and fleshless grin. The body had apparently once lain in the attitude of an embrace, but now the long sleep that outlasts love, that conquers even the grimace of love, had cuckolded him. What was left of him, rotted beneath what was left of the nightshirt, had become inextricable from the bed in which he lay; and upon him and upon the pillow beside him lay that even coating of the patient and biding dust.

Then we noticed that in the second pillow was the indentation of a head. One of us lifted something from it, and leaning forward, that faint and invisible dust dry and acrid in the nostrils, we saw a long strand of iron-gray hair.

1930

AT MID-CENTURY

CHAPTER TWELVE

RECENT POETRY

This last section of poetry is by intention more a sampling of recent American poetry than of poets. What follows is fourteen "modern" American poems, all completely products of the twentieth century. This of course is not an assertion of some hiatus between these specific poems and the past; their creators all have their roots, influences, and ties. But their subject matter, their techniques, their particular poetic patterns would probably not have occurred at any other time in history or at any other place.

Most of the poems here are relatively well known, even if the poets, to various degrees, are not. They thus allow the reader to come face to face with a sampling of completed poetic fact—poetic fact that is already widely esteemed but much too recent to be given any reliable and judicious "place" in the complex structure of modern American literature. With these poems the reader can see one concrete artistic result of that multiplicity of forces constituting American literary activity during the first three or four decades of this century. Whatever the ultimate place, worth, and significance assigned to these poems, at the moment they appear to provide an unusually effective cap to many of the strains of American poetry we have already seen developing. More important perhaps is that they give the reader an opportunity for individualized, unfettered critical judgment, a "test," as it were, of the standards of taste and performance instilled by the earlier literature of modern America.

To generalize about the poets themselves is less easy and perhaps less important. Although they were all born during a single thirteen-year period—the period (1904-1917) that covered probably the most zestful and energetic aspects of the new poetry movement—their reputations (with the exception of Eberhart's) are usually dated from the 1940's. Most of them thus have at least a kind of common heritage: childhood or adolescence during the Roaring Twenties, college or job hunting during the depression-ridden 1930's, and actual (or emotional) involvement in World War II. Their poetry, however, reveals little of this common heritage, for they are a disparate group, both in background and training. Among them are soldiers, a conscientious objector, a businessman, lecturers, teachers, editors, critics, and essayists. They come from no single part of the country. They collectively represent no new movement or school.

They are presented here simply as six American poets—four of whom are still active, still producing (at least at the time of this writing)—with relatively fluid, non-crystallized reputations. Their importance is in their poetry—and the kind of attention and standards readers bring to it.

Robert [Traill Spence] Lowell, [Jr.]
(1917-   )

A member of the famous literary Lowells (James Russell was his great grandfather's brother, Amy his cousin), Robert Lowell was born in Boston, educated at St. Mark's School, Harvard, and Kenyon. Something of a New England maverick, he served time in jail during World War II as a conscientious objector, although he had twice previously tried to enlist and had been rejected. He has been a Consultant in Poetry at the Library of Congress and taught at both Boston University and Kenyon College. His first volume of verse was *Land of Unlikeness* (1944); and his second, *Lord Weary's Castle* (1946), won a Pulitzer Prize. *The Mills of the Kavanaughs* appeared in 1951, and *Life Studies,* autobiography in prose and verse, appeared in 1959. *Imitations* (1961) contains translations and adaptions of verse from other languages.

Mr. Edwards and the Spider

I saw the spiders marching through the air,
Swimming from tree to tree that mildewed day
  In latter August when the hay
  Came creaking to the barn. But where
    The wind is westerly,
Where gnarled November makes the spiders fly
Into the apparitions of the sky,
They purpose nothing but their ease and die
Urgently beating east to sunrise and the sea;

What are we in the hands of the great God?
It was in vain you set up thorn and briar
  In battle array against the fire
  And treason crackling in your blood;

For the wild thorns grow tame
And will do nothing to oppose the flame;
Your lacerations tell the losing game
You play against a sickness past your cure.
How will the hands be strong? How will the heart endure?

A very little thing, a little worm,
Or hourglass-blazoned spider, it is said,
Can kill a tiger. Will the dead
Hold up his mirror and affirm
To the four winds the smell
And flash of his authority? It's well
If God who holds you to the pit of hell,
Much as one holds a spider, will destroy,
Baffle and dissipate your soul. As a small boy

On Windsor Marsh, I saw the spider die
When thrown into the bowels of fierce fire:
There's no long struggle, no desire
To get up on its feet and fly—
It stretches out its feet
And dies. This is the sinner's last retreat;
Yes, and no strength exerted on the heat
Then sinews the abolished will, when sick
And full of burning, it will whistle on a brick.

But who can plumb the sinking of that soul?
Josiah Hawley, picture yourself cast
Into a brick-kiln where the blast
Fans your quick vitals to a coal—
If measured by a glass,
How long would it seem burning! Let there pass
A minute, ten, ten trillion; but the blaze
Is infinite, eternal: this is death,
To die and know it. This is the Black Widow, death.

1944

After the Surprising Conversions

September twenty-second, Sir: today
I answer. In the latter part of May,
Hard on our Lord's Ascension, it began
To be more sensible. A gentleman
Of more than common understanding, strict

In morals, pious in behavior, kicked
Against our goad. A man of some renown,
An useful, honored person in the town,
He came of melancholy parents; prone
To secret spells, for years they kept alone–
His uncle, I believe, was killed of it:
Good people, but of too much or little wit.
I preached one Sabbath on a text from Kings;
He showed concernment for his soul. Some things
In his experience were hopeful. He
Would sit and watch the wind knocking a tree
And praise this countryside our Lord has made.
Once when a poor man's heifer died, he laid
A shilling on the doorsill; though a thirst
For loving shook him like a snake, he durst
Not entertain much hope of his estate
In heaven. Once we saw him sitting late
Behind his attic window by a light
That guttered on his Bible; through that night
He meditated terror, and he seemed
Beyond advice or reason, for he dreamed
That he was called to trumpet Judgment Day
To Concord. In the latter part of May
He cut his throat. And though the coroner
Judged him delirious, soon a noisome stir
Palsied our village. At Jehovah's nod
Satan seemed more let loose amongst us: God
Abandoned us to Satan, and he pressed
Us hard, until we thought we could not rest
Till we had done with life. Content was gone.
All the good work was quashed. We were undone.
The breath of God had carried out a planned
And sensible withdrawal from this land;
The multitude, once unconcerned with doubt,
Once neither callous, curious nor devout,
Jumped at broad noon, as though some peddler groaned
At it in its familiar twang: "My friend,
Cut your own throat. Cut your own throat. Now! Now!"
September twenty-second, Sir, the bough
Cracks with the unpicked apples, and at dawn
The small-mouth bass breaks water, gorged with spawn.

1946

Words for Hart Crane

"When the Pulitzers showered on some dope
or screw who flushed our dry mouths out with soap,
few people would consider why I took
to stalking sailors, and scattered Uncle Sam's
phoney gold-plated laurels to the birds.
Because I knew my Whitman like a book,
stranger in America, tell my country: I,
Catullus redivivus, once the rage
of the Village and Paris, used to play my role
of homosexual, wolfing the stray lambs
who hungered by the Place de la Concorde.
My profit was a pocket with a hole.
Who asks for me, the Shelley of my age,
must lay his heart out for my bed and board."

1959

Karl [Jay] Shapiro
(1913-)

The first three volumes of Shapiro's verse appeared while he was with the army in the South Pacific—*Person, Place and Thing* (1942), *The Place for Love* (1943), and the Pulitzer Prize-winning *V-Letter and Other Poems* (1944); and his *Essay on Rime* (1945), a disquisition in verse, was written while he was there. He was born in Baltimore and educated at the University of Virginia and Johns Hopkins, at which he later taught. His earliest volume, *Poems*, appeared in 1935, but he collected none of the verse in it in his *Poems, 1940-1953* (1953). He was editor of *Poetry* from 1950 to 1956, then moved to the University of Nebraska and the editorship of *The Schooner* (formerly *The Prairie Schooner*). He was also for a while a Consultant in Poetry at the Library of Congress. *Beyond Criticism* (1953) is a volume of prose. Other volumes are *Trial of a Poet and Other Poems* (1947) and *Poems of a Jew* (1958).

Auto Wreck

Its quick soft silver bell beating, beating,
And down the dark one ruby flare
Pulsing out red light like an artery,
The ambulance at top speed floating down
Past beacons and illuminated clocks
Wings in a heavy curve, dips down,

And brakes speed, entering the crowd.
The doors leap open, emptying light;
Stretchers are laid out, the mangled lifted
And stowed into the little hospital.
Then the bell, breaking the hush, tolls once,
And the ambulance with its terrible cargo
Rocking, slightly rocking, moves away,
As the doors, an afterthought, are closed.

We are deranged, walking among the cops
Who sweep glass and are large and composed.
One is still making notes under the light.
One with a bucket douches ponds of blood
Into the street and gutter.
One hangs lanterns on the wrecks that cling,
Empty husks of locusts, to iron poles.

Our throats were tight as tourniquets,
Our feet were bound with splints, but now,
Like convalescents intimate and gauche,
We speak through sickly smiles and warn
With the stubborn saw of common sense,
The grim joke and the banal resolution.
The traffic moves around with care,
But we remain, touching a wound
That opens to our richest horror.

Already old, the question Who shall die?
Becomes unspoken Who is innocent?
For death in war is done by hands;
Suicide has cause and stillbirth, logic;
And cancer, simple as a flower, blooms.
But this invites the occult mind,
Cancels our physics with a sneer,
And spatters all we knew of denouement
Across the expedient and wicked stones. 1942

Drug Store

I do remember an apothecary,
And hereabouts 'a dwells

It baffles the foreigner like an idiom,
And he is right to adopt it as a form

Less serious than the living-room or bar;
  For it disestablishes the café,
Is a collective, and on basic country.

Not that it praises hygiene and corrupts
The ice-cream parlor and the tobacconist's
Is it a center; but that the attractive symbols
  Watch over puberty and leer
Like rubber bottles waiting for sick-use.

Youth comes to jingle nickels and crack wise;
The baseball scores are his, the magazines
Devoted to lust, the jazz, the Coca-Cola,
  The lending-library of love's latest.
He is the customer; he is heroized.

And every nook and cranny of the flesh
Is spoken to by packages with wiles.
"Buy me, buy me," they whimper and cajole;
  The hectic range of lipstick pouts,
Revealing the wicked and the simple mouth.

With scarcely any evasion in their eye
They smoke, undress their girls, exact a stance;
But only for a moment. The clock goes round;
  Crude fellowships are made and lost;
They slump in booths like rags, not even drunk.

1942

Randall Jarrell

(1914-1966)

Like Shapiro, Randall Jarrell was also a teacher and critic, and he too was in World War II, when his first significant verse appeared, in *Blood for a Stranger* (1942). Later volumes of the 1940's were *Little Friend, Little Friend* (1945) and *Losses* (1948). During the next decade he published *The Seven-League Crutches* (1951), *Selected Poems* (1955), and *The Woman at the Washington Zoo* (1960) which received the National Book Award for poetry. He was born in Nashville, Tennessee, and educated at Vanderbilt. He has taught in the English departments of several universities, and is now Professor of English at the University of North Carolina at Greensboro. His academic novel, *Pictures from an Institution* (1954), was widely popular. Jarrell also served as Consultant in Poetry to the Library of Congress, and his best essays are collected in *Poetry and the Age* (1953), and *A Sad Heart at the Supermarket* (1961).

The Death of the Ball Turret Gunner

From my mother's sleep I fell into the State,
And I hunched in its belly till my wet fur froze.
Six miles from earth, loosed from its dream of life,
I woke to black flak and the nightmare fighters.
When I died they washed me out of the turret with a hose.

1945

The Orient Express

One looks from the train
Almost as one looked as a child. In the sunlight
What I see still seems to me plain,
I am safe; but at evening
As the lands darken, a questioning
Precariousness comes over everything.

Once after a day of rain
I lay longing to be cold; and after a while
I was cold again, and hunched shivering
Under the quilt's many colors, gray
With the dull ending of the winter day.
Outside me there were a few shapes
Of chairs and tables, things from a primer;
Outside the window
There were the chairs and tables of the world. . . .
I saw that the world
That had seemed to me the plain
Gray mask of all that was strange
Behind it—of all that *was*—was all.

But it is beyond belief.
One thinks, "Behind everything
An unforced joy, an unwilling
Sadness (a willing sadness, a forced joy)
Moves changelessly"; one looks from the train
And there is something, the same thing
Behind everything: all these little villages,
A passing woman, a field of grain,
The man who says good-bye to his wife—
A path through a wood full of lives, and the train

Passing, after all unchangeable
And not now ever to stop, like a heart—

It is like any other work of art.
It is and never can be changed.
Behind everything there is always
The unknown unwanted life. 1951

Richard Eberhart

(1904-)

The oldest of this group of poets, Richard Eberhart has also had the most varied career, including tutoring the son of the King of Siam. Born in Austin, Minnesota, he was educated at Dartmouth and Cambridge University in England. His first volume was *A Bravery of Earth* (1930), and while teaching at St. Mark's School in Massachusetts, he published *Reading the Spirit* and *Song and Idea* (1942). He was then, variously, a naval officer during World War II, a vice-president of a wax company in Boston, a member of President Eisenhower's Advisory Committee on the Arts for the National Cultural Center in Washington, a member of the National Institute of Arts and Letters, a Consultant in Poetry to the Library of Congress, and, in 1962, corecipient (with John Hall Wheelock) of the Bollingen Prize for Poetry. Among his many volumes of verse are *Poems, New and Selected* (1944), *Burr Oaks* (1947), *Brotherhood of Men* (1949), *An Herb Basket* (1950), *Selected Poems* (1951), *The Visionary Farms* (1952), *Great Praises* (1957), *Collected Poems, 1930-1960* (1960), and *Collected Verse Plays* (1962).

The Groundhog

In June, amid the golden fields,
I saw a groundhog lying dead.
Dead lay he; my senses shook,
And mind outshot our naked frailty.
There lowly in the vigorous summer
His form began its senseless change,
And made my senses waver dim
Seeing nature ferocious in him.
Inspecting close his maggots' might
And seething cauldron of his being,
Half with loathing, half with a strange love,
I poked him with an angry stick.
The fever arose, became a flame
And Vigour circumscribed the skies,

Immense energy in the sun,
And through my frame a sunless trembling.
My stick had done nor good nor harm.
Then stood I silent in the day
Watching the object, as before;
And kept my reverence for knowledge
Trying for control, to be still,
To quell the passion of the blood;
Until I had bent down on my knees
Praying for joy in the sight of decay.
And so I left; and I returned
In Autumn strict of eye, to see
The sap gone out of the groundhog,
But the bony sodden hulk remained.
But the year had lost its meaning,
And in intellectual chains
I lost both love and loathing,
Mured up in the wall of wisdom.
Another summer took the fields again
Massive and burning, full of life,
But when I chanced upon the spot
There was only a little hair left,
And bones bleaching in the sunlight
Beautiful as architecture;
I watched them like a geometer,
And cut a walking stick from a birch.
It has been three years, now.
There is no sign of the groundhog.
I stood there in the whirling summer,
My hand capped a withered heart,
And thought of China and of Greece,
Of Alexander in his tent;
Of Montaigne in his tower,
Of Saint Theresa in her wild lament.

1936

Richard Wilbur

(1921-)

Born in New York City, Richard Wilbur was educated at Amherst and Harvard. He was in the army during World War II, and he has taught at Harvard, Wellesley, and Wesleyan University in Connecticut. His first volume was *The Beautiful Changes and Other Poems* (1947). This was followed by *Ceremony and Other Poems* (1950), *A Bestiary* (1955), *Things of This World* (1956, awarded a Pulitzer Prize), *Poems, 1943-1956* (1957), and *Advice to a Prophet and Other Poems* (1961). In 1954 he was awarded the Prix de Rome of the American Academy of Arts and Letters. He is a translator of Molière's *Le Misanthrope* (1955) and a song writer for the musical dramatization of *Candide* (1957).

Juggler

A ball will bounce, but less and less. It's not
A light-hearted thing, resents its own resilience.
Falling is what it loves, and the earth falls
So in our hearts from brilliance,
Settles and is forgot.
It takes a sky-blue juggler with five red balls

To shake our gravity up. Whee, in the air
The balls roll round, wheel on his wheeling hands,
Learning the ways of lightness, alter to spheres
Grazing his finger ends,
Cling to their courses there,
Swinging a small heaven about his ears.

But a heaven is easier made of nothing at all
Than the earth regained, and still and sole within
The spin of worlds, with a gesture sure and noble
He reels that heaven in,
Landing it ball by ball,
And trades it all for a broom, a plate, a table.

Oh, on his toe the table is turning, the broom's
Balancing up on his nose, and the plate whirls
On the tip of the broom! Damn, what a show, we cry:
The boys stamp, and the girls
Shriek, and the drum booms
And all comes down, and he bows and says good-bye.

If the juggler is tired now, if the broom stands
In the dust again, if the table starts to drop
Through the daily dark again, and though the plate
Lies flat on the table top,
For him we batter our hands
Who has won for once over the world's weight.

1949

Museum Piece

The good gray guardians of art
Patrol the halls on spongy shoes,
Impartially protective, though
Perhaps suspicious of Toulouse.

Here dozes one against the wall,
Disposed upon a funeral chair.
A Degas dancer pirouettes
Upon the parting of his hair.

See how she spins! The grace is there,
But strain as well is plain to see.
Degas loved the two together:
Beauty joined to energy.

Edgar Degas purchased once
A fine El Greco, which he kept
Against the wall beside his bed
To hang his pants on while he slept.   1950

Exeunt

Piecemeal the summer dies;
At the field's edge a daisy lives alone;
A last shawl of burning lies
On a gray field-stone.

All cries are thin and terse;
The field has droned the summer's final mass;
A cricket like a dwindled hearse
Crawls from the dry grass.   1956

Theodore Roethke

(1908-1963)

A Pulitzer Prize was awarded Theodore Roethke's first extended collection of his verse, *The Waking, Poems 1933-1953* (1953). This had been preceded by *Open House* (1941), *The Lost Son and Other Poems* (1948), and *Praise to the End!* (1951). He was born in Saginaw, Michigan, and was educated at the state university. He has taught at Lafayette College, Pennsylvania State, Bennington College, and the University of Washington. *Words for the Wind* (1958) won him the Bollingen Prize for that year, and *I am! Says the Lamb* appeared in 1961, and *Far Field* in 1964.

Dolor

I have known the inexorable sadness of pencils,
Neat in their boxes, dolor of pad and paper-weight,
All the misery of manila folders and mucilage,
Desolation in immaculate public places,
Lonely reception room, lavatory, switchboard,
The unalterable pathos of basin and pitcher,
Ritual of multigraph, paper-clip, comma,
Endless duplication of lives and objects.
And I have seen dust from the walls of institutions,
Finer than flour, alive, more dangerous than silica,
Sift, almost invisible, through long afternoons of tedium,
Dripping a fine film on nails and delicate eyebrows,
Glazing the pale hair, the duplicate gray standard faces.

1943

Night Crow

When I saw that clumsy crow
Flap from a wasted tree,
A shape in the mind rose up:
Over the gulfs of dream
Flew a tremendous bird
Further and further away
Into a moonless black,
Deep in the brain, far back.

1944

Old Florist

That hump of a man bunching chrysanthemums
Or pinching-back asters, or planting azaleas,
Tamping and stamping dirt into pots,—
How he could flick and pick
Rotten leaves or yellowy petals,
Or scoop out a weed close to flourishing roots,
Or make the dust buzz with a light spray,
Or drown a bug in one spit of tobacco juice,
Or fan life into wilted sweet-peas with his hat,
Or stand all night watering roses, his feet blue in rubber boots.

1948

CHAPTER THIRTEEN

RECENT FICTION

Recent fiction in America, like recent poetry, is too near us to be judiciously judged; however, a handful of names so stand out that they permit a kind of generalization that is not possible about recent poets. Wright Morris, William Styron, James Baldwin, Ralph Ellison, Herbert Gold, Flannery O'Connor, Bernard Malamud, and John Cheever are among them. They make up, with the three writers whose fiction is here represented—that of J. F. Powers, Saul Bellow, and John Updike—at least a kind of homogeneous achievement. They are much too close, to be sure, to be discernible products of any new "schools" of fiction or the clear-cut representatives of any "new directions." They are, moreover, in their subject matter and background as various and diverse as any other heterogeneous collection of Americans.

But there is in their fiction a similarity. They appear to have a common concern for *form* that is characteristic of no other group of American writers otherwise as large and diverse as this group is. They are collectively knowledgeable about their craft in a way probably without precedent in American fiction. They have dropped the pose of anti-intellectualism. Most of them are college trained. They show, sometimes much too self-consciously, an acquaintance with the whole range of American and foreign literatures. As a consequence, their mastery of the problems of style, of structure, of the uses of symbols, and of narrative techniques is likely to be a highly accomplished one. "Story," for them, could never be separated from expression. Their commitments—whether philosophical, religious, or political—are likely to be far less dogmatic than those of many of their predecessors.

The startling omission from this group (if not from these generalizations) and the one writer of the 1950's whose fiction was probably held in the highest esteem, both with the critics and the public, is J. D. Salinger. His *Catcher in the Rye* (1951), Holden Caufield's Huck Finn-like odyssey among the labyrinthian ways of modern Manhattan, was the most highly praised novel of the decade. His complicated chronicle of the Glass family—recounted partly in *Nine Stories* (1953), *Franny and Zooey* (1961), and *Raise High the Roofbeams, Carpenters; and Seymour: an Introduction* (1963)—made clear that his was an ambitious and dedicated talent.

His fiction, no less than that of the three writers collected here, was clearly fiction of the 1950's. J. F. Powers, Saul Bellow, and John Updike are nonetheless refreshingly individual—unlike one another and collectively unlike Salinger—in characteristic subject matter, in tone, and in technique. To read a representative story from each is to meet the fiction of the 1950's at its best. They provide, like recent American poetry, a cap to the literature of America which preceded theirs—and one of the most hopeful promises for the American literature of the future.

J(ames) F(arl) Powers

(1917-)

Although his output has been small, J. F. Powers's stories of the Catholic clergy—like the short fiction of Katherine Anne Porter—have received wide approval. He was born in Jacksonville, Illinois, educated at Northwestern, and was for a time a bookstore clerk in Chicago. He has taught at Marquette University. His three books are *Prince of Darkness and Other Stories* (1947), *The Presence of Grace* (1956), and *Morte d'Urban* (1962).

The Valiant Woman

They had come to the dessert in a dinner that was a shambles. "Well, John," Father Nulty said, turning away from Mrs. Stoner and to Father Firman, long gone silent at his own table. "You've got the bishop coming for confirmations next week."

"Yes," Mrs. Stoner cut in, "and for dinner. And if he don't eat any more than he did last year—"

Father Firman, in a rare moment, faced it. "Mrs. Stoner, the bishop is not well. You know that."

"And after I fixed that fine dinner and all." Mrs. Stoner pouted in Father Nulty's direction.

"I wouldn't feel bad about it, Mrs. Stoner," Father Nulty said. "He never eats much anywhere."

"It's funny. And that new Mrs. Allers said he ate just fine when he was there," Mrs. Stoner argued, and then spit out, "but she's a damned liar!"

Father Nulty, unsettled but trying not to show it, said, "Who's Mrs. Allers?"

"She's at Holy Cross," Mrs. Stoner said.

"She's the housekeeper," Father Firman added, thinking Mrs. Stoner made it sound as though Mrs. Allers were the pastor there.

"I swear I don't know what to do about the dinner this year," Mrs. Stoner said.

Father Firman moaned. "Just do as you've always done, Mrs. Stoner."

"Huh! And have it all to throw out! Is that any way to do?"

"Is there any dessert?" Father Firman asked coldly.

Mrs. Stoner leaped up from the table and bolted into the kitchen, mumbling. She came back with a birthday cake. She plunged it in the center of the table. She found a big wooden match in her apron pocket and thrust it at Father Firman.

"I don't like this bishop," she said. "I never did. And the way he went and cut poor Ellen Kennedy out of Father Doolin's will!"

She went back into the kitchen.

"Didn't they talk a lot of filth about Doolin and the housekeeper?" Father Nulty asked.

"I should think they did," Father Firman said. "All because he took her to the movies on Sunday night. After he died and the bishop cut her out of the will, though I hear he gives her a pension privately, they talked about the bishop."

"I don't like this bishop at all," Mrs. Stoner said, appearing with a cake knife. "Bishop Doran—there was the man!"

"We know," Father Firman said. "All man and all priest."

"He did know real estate," Father Nulty said.

Father Firman struck the match.

"Not on the chair!" Mrs. Stoner cried, too late.

Father Firman set the candle burning—it was suspiciously large and yellow, like a blessed one, but he could not be sure. They watched the fluttering flame.

"I'm forgetting the lights!" Mrs. Stoner said, and got up to turn them off. She went into the kitchen again.

The priests had a moment of silence in the candlelight.

"Happy birthday, John," Father Nulty said softly. "Is it fifty-nine you are?"

"As if you didn't know, Frank," Father Firman said, "and you the same but one."

Father Nulty smiled, the old gold of his incisors shining in the flickering light, his collar whiter in the dark, and raised his glass of water, which would have been wine or better in the bygone days, and toasted Father Firman.

"Many of 'em, John."

"Blow it out," Mrs. Stoner said, returning to the room. She waited by the light switch for Father Firman to blow out the candle.

Mrs. Stoner, who ate no desserts, began to clear the dishes into the kitchen, and the priests, finishing their cake and coffee in a hurry, went to sit in the study.

Father Nulty offered a cigar.

"John?"

"My ulcers, Frank."

"Ah, well, you're better off." Father Nulty lit the cigar and crossed his long black legs. "Fish Frawley has got him a Filipino, John. Did you hear?"

Father Firman leaned forward, interested. "He got rid of the woman he had?"

"He did. It seems she snooped."

"Snooped, eh?"

"She did. And gossiped. Fish introduced two town boys to her, said, 'Would you think these boys were my nephews?' That's all, and the next week the paper had it that his two nephews were visiting him from Erie. After that, he let her believe he was going East to see his parents, though both are dead. The paper carried the story. Fish returned and made a sermon out of it. Then he got the Filipino."

Father Firman squirmed with pleasure in his chair. "That's like Fish, Frank. He can do that." He stared at the tips of his fingers bleakly. "You could never get a Filipino to come to a place like this."

"Probably not," Father Nulty said. "Fish is pretty close to Minneapolis. Ah, say, do you remember the trick he played on us all in Marmion Hall!"

"That I'll not forget!" Father Firman's eyes remembered. "Getting up New Year's morning and finding the toilet seats all painted!"

"*Happy Circumcision!* Hah!" Father Nulty had a coughing fit.

When he had got himself together again, a mosquito came and sat on his wrist. He watched it a moment before bringing his heavy hand down. He raised his hand slowly, viewed the dead mosquito, and sent it spinning with a plunk of his middle finger.

"Only the female bites," he said.

"I didn't know that," Father Firman said.

"Ah, yes . . ."

Mrs. Stoner entered the study and sat down with some sewing—Father Firman's black socks.

She smiled pleasantly at Father Nulty. "And what do you think of the atom bomb, Father?"

"Not much," Father Nulty said.

Mrs. Stoner had stopped smiling. Father Firman yawned.

Mrs. Stoner served up another: "Did you read about this communist convert, Father?"

"He's been in the Church before," Father Nulty said, "and so it's not a conversion, Mrs. Stoner."

"No? Well, I already got him down on my list of Monsignor's converts."

"It's better than a conversion, Mrs. Stoner, for there is more rejoicing in heaven over the return of . . . uh, he that was lost, Mrs. Stoner, is found.

"And that congresswoman, Father?"

"Yes. A convert—she."

"And Henry Ford's grandson, Father. I got him down."

"Yes, to be sure."

Father Firman yawned, this time audibly, and held his jaw.

"But he's one only by marriage, Father," Mrs. Stoner said. "I always say you got to watch those kind."

"Indeed you do, but a convert nonetheless, Mrs. Stoner. Remember, Cardinal Newman himself was one."

Mrs. Stoner was unimpressed. "I see where Henry Ford's making steering wheels out of soybeans, Father."

"I didn't see that."

"I read it in the *Reader's Digest* or some place."

"Yes, well . . ." Father Nulty rose and held his hand out to Father Firman. "John," he said. "It's been good."

"I heard Hirohito's next," Mrs. Stoner said, returning to converts.

"Let's wait and see, Mrs. Stoner," Father Nulty said.

The priests walked to the door.

"You know where I live, John."

"Yes. Come again, Frank. Good night."

Father Firman watched Father Nulty go down the walk to his car at the curb. He hooked the screen door and turned off the porch light. He hesitated at the foot of the stairs, suddenly moved to go to bed. But he went back into the study.

"Phew!" Mrs. Stoner said. "I thought he'd never go. Here it is after eight o'clock."

Father Firman sat down in his rocking chair. "I don't see him often," he said.

"I give up!" Mrs. Stoner exclaimed, flinging the holey socks upon the horsehair sofa. "I'd swear you had a nail in your shoe."

"I told you I looked."

"Well, you ought to look again. And cut your toenails, why don't you? Haven't I got enough to do?"

Father Firman scratched in his coat pocket for a pill, found one, swallowed it. He let his head sink back against the chair and closed his eyes. He could hear her moving about the room, making the preparations; and how he knew them—the fumbling in the drawer for a pencil with a point, the rip of the page from his daily calendar, and finally the leg of the card table sliding up against his leg.

He opened his eyes. She yanked the floor lamp alongside the table, setting the bead fringe tinkling on the shade, and pulled up her chair on the other side. She sat down and smiled at him for the first time that day. Now she was happy.

She swept up the cards and began to shuffle with the abandoned virtuosity of an old river-boat gambler, standing them on end, fanning them out, whirling them through her fingers, dancing them halfway up her arms, cracking the whip over them. At last they lay before him tamed into a neat deck.

"Cut?"

"Go ahead," he said. She liked to go first.

She gave him her faint, avenging smile and drew a card, cast it aside for another which he thought must be an ace from the way she clutched it face down.

She was getting all the cards, as usual, and would have been invincible if she had possessed his restraint and if her cunning had been of a higher order. He knew a few things about leading and lying back that she would never learn. Her strategy was attack, forever attack, with one baffling departure: she might sacrifice certain tricks as expendable if only she could have the last ones, the heartbreaking ones, if she could slap them down one after another, shatteringly.

She played for blood, no bones about it, but for her there was no other way; it was her nature, as it was the lion's, and for this reason he found her ferocity pardonable, more a defect of the flesh, venial, while his own trouble was all in the will, mortal. He did not sweat and pray over each card as she must, but he did keep an eye out for reneging and demanded a cut now and then just to aggravate her, and he was always secretly hoping for aces.

With one card left in her hand, the telltale trick coming next, she delayed playing it, showing him first the smile, the preview of defeat. She laid it on the table—so! She held one more trump than he had reasoned possible. Had she palmed it from somewhere? No, she would not go that far; that would not be fair, was worse than reneging, which so easily and often happened accidentally, and she believed in being fair. Besides he had been watching her.

God smote the vines with hail, the sycamore trees with frost, and offered up the flocks to the lightning—but Mrs. Stoner! What a cross Father Firman had from God in Mrs. Stoner! There were other housekeepers as bad, no doubt, walking the rectories of the world, yes, but . . . yes. He could name one and maybe two priests who were worse off. One, maybe two. Cronin. His craggly blonde of sixty—take her, with her everlasting banging on the grand piano, the gift of the pastor; her proud talk about the goiter operation at the Mayo Brothers', also a gift; her honking the parish Buick at passing strange priests because they were all in the game together. She was worse. She was something to keep the home fires burning. Yes sir. And Cronin said she was not a bad person really, but what was he? He was quite a freak himself.

For that matter, could anyone say that Mrs. Stoner was a bad person? No. He could not say it himself, and he was no freak. She had her points, Mrs. Stoner. She was clean. And though she cooked poorly, could not play the organ, would not take up the collection in an emergency, and went to card parties, and told all—even so, she was clean. She washed everything. Sometimes her underwear hung down beneath her dress like a paratrooper's pants, but it and everything she touched was clean. She washed constantly. She was clean.

She had her other points, to be sure—her faults, you might say. She snooped—no mistake about it—but it was not snooping for snooping's sake; she had a reason. She did other things, always with a reason. She overcharged on rosaries and prayer books, but that was for the sake of the poor. She censored the pamphlet rack, but that was to prevent scandal. She pried into the baptismal and matrimonial records, but there was no other way if Father was out, and in this way she had once uncovered a bastard and flushed him out of the rectory, but that was the perverted decency of the times. She held her nose over bad marriages in the presence of the victims, but that was her sorrow and came from having her husband buried in a mine. And he had caught her telling a bewildered young couple that there was only one good reason for their wanting to enter into a mixed marriage—the child had to have a name, and that—that was what?

She hid his books, kept him from smoking, picked his friends (usually the pastors of her colleagues), bawled out people for calling after dark, had no humor, except at cards, and then it was grim, very grim, and she sat hatchet-faced every morning at Mass. But she went to Mass, which was all that kept the church from being empty some mornings. She did annoying things all day long. She said annoying things into the night. She said she had given him the best years of her life. Had she? Perhaps—for the miner had her only a year. It was too bad, sinfully bad, when he thought of it like that. But all talk of best years and life was nonsense. He had to consider the heart of the matter, the essence. The essence was that housekeepers were hard to get, harder to get than ushers, than willing workers, than organists, than secretaries—yes, harder to get than assistants or vocations.

And she was a *saver*—saved money, saved electricity, saved string, bags, sugar, saved—him. That's what she did. That's what she said she did, and she was right, in a way. In a way, she was usually right. In fact, she was always right—in a way. And you could never get a Filipino to come way out here and live. Not a young one anyway, and he had never seen an old one. Not a Filipino. They liked to dress up and live.

Should he let it drop about Fish having one, just to throw a scare into her, let her know he was doing some thinking? No. It would be a perfect cue for the one about a man needing a woman to look after him. He was not up to that again, not tonight.

Now she was doing what she liked most of all. She was making a grand slam, playing it out card for card, though it was in the bag, prolonging what would have been cut short out of mercy in gentle company. Father Firman knew the agony of losing.

She slashed down the last card, a miserable deuce trump, and did in the hapless king of hearts he had been saving.

"Skunked you!"

She was awful in victory. Here was the bitter end of their long day together, the final murderous hour in which all they wanted to say—all he wouldn't and all she couldn't—came out in the cards. Whoever won at honeymoon won the day, slept on the other's scalp, and God alone had to help the loser.

"We've been at it long enough, Mrs. Stoner," he said, seeing her assembling the cards for another round.

"Had enough, huh!"

Father Firman grumbled something.

"No?"

"Yes."

She pulled the table away and left it against the wall for the next time. She went out of the study carrying the socks, content and clucking. He closed his eyes after her and began to get under way in the rocking chair, the nightly trip to nowhere. He could hear her brewing a cup of tea in the kitchen and conversing with the cat. She made her way up the stairs, carrying the tea, followed by the cat, purring.

He waited, rocking out to sea, until she would be sure to be through in the bathroom. Then he got up and locked the front door (she looked after the back door) and loosened his collar going upstairs.

In the bathroom he mixed a glass of antiseptic, always afraid of pyorrhea, and gargled to ward off pharyngitis.

When he turned on the light in his room, the moths and beetles began to batter against the screens, the light insects humming. . . .

Yes, and she had the guest room. How did she come to get that? Why wasn't she in the back room, in her proper place? He knew, if he cared to remember. The screen in the back room—it let in mosquitoes, and if it didn't do that she'd love to sleep back there, Father, looking out at the steeple and the blessed cross on top, Father, if it just weren't for the screen, Father. Very well, Mrs. Stoner, I'll get it fixed or fix it myself. Oh, could you now, Father? I could, Mrs. Stoner, and I will. In the meantime you take the guest room. Yes, Father, and thank you, Father, the house ringing with amenities then. Years ago, all that. She was a pie-faced girl then, not really a girl perhaps, but not too old to marry again.

But she never had. In fact, he could not remember that she had even tried for a husband since coming to the rectory, but, of course, he could be wrong, not knowing how they went about it. God! God save us! Had she got her wires crossed and mistaken him all these years for *that?* *That!* Him! Suffering God! No. That was going too far. That was getting morbid. No. He must not think of that again, ever. No.

But just the same she had got the guest room and she had it yet. Well, did it matter? Nobody ever came to see him any more, nobody to stay overnight anyway, nobody to stay very long . . . not any more. He knew how they laughed at him. He had heard Frank humming all right—before he saw how serious and sad the situation was and took pity—humming, "Wedding Bells Are Breaking Up That Old Gang of Mine." But then they'd always laughed at him for something—for not being an athlete, for wearing glasses, for having kidney trouble . . . and mail coming addressed to Rev. and Mrs. Stoner.

Removing his shirt, he bent over the table to read the volume left open from last night. He read, translating easily, "Eisdem licet cum illis . . . Clerics are allowed to reside only with women about whom there can be no suspicion, either because of a natural bond (as mother, sister, aunt) or of advanced age, combined in both cases with good repute."

Last night he had read it, and many nights before, each time as though this time to find what was missing, to find what obviously was not in the paragraph, his problem considered, a way out. She was not mother, not sister, not aunt, and *advanced age* was a relative term (why, she was younger than he was) and so, eureka, she did not meet the letter of the law—but, alas, how she fulfilled the spirit! And besides it would be a slimy way of handling it after all her years of service. He could not afford to pension her off, either.

He slammed the book shut. He slapped himself fiercely on the back missing the wily mosquito, and whirled to find it. He took a magazine and folded it into a swatter. Then he saw it—oh, the preternatural cunning of it!—poised in the beard of St. Joseph on the bookcase. He could not hit it there. He teased it away, wanting it to light on the wall, but it knew his thoughts and flew high away. He swung wildly, hoping to stun it, missed, swung back, catching St. Joseph across the neck. The statute fell to the floor and broke.

Mrs. Stoner was panting in the hall outside his door.

"What is it!"

"Mosquitoes!"

"What is it, Father? Are you hurt?"

"Mosquitoes—damn it! And only the female bites!"

Mrs. Stoner, after a moment, said, "Shame on you, Father. She needs the blood for her eggs."

He dropped the magazine and lunged at the mosquito with his bare hand.

She went back to her room, saying, "Pshaw, I thought it was burglars murdering you in your bed."

He lunged again.

1951

Saul Bellow

(1915-)

Although born in Quebec, Saul Bellow was brought up in Chicago, to which he moved at the age of nine. He has taught at various schools and colleges and is presently connected with the University of Chicago. His first two novels—*Dangling Man* (1944) and *The Victim* (1947)—were both carefully constructed, highly introspective works. His first fame, however, came with *The Adventures of Augie March* (1953), a modern picaresque novel set in the Chicago of the depression years. It won the National Book Award for that year, but many consider the novella, *Seize the Day* (1956), his best work. *Henderson the Rain King* appeared in 1959, and *Herzog*, a novel about a college teacher, in 1964.

A Father-to-Be

The strangest notions had a way of forcing themselves into Rogin's mind. Just thirty-one and passable-looking, with short black hair, small eyes, but a high, open forehead, he was a research chemist, and his mind was generally serious and dependable. But on a snowy Sunday evening while this stocky man, buttoned to the chin in a Burberry coat and walking in his preposterous gait—feet turned outward—was going toward the subway, he fell into a peculiar state.

He was on his way to have supper with his fiancée. She had phoned him a short while ago and said, "You'd better pick up a few things on the way."

"What do we need?"

"Some roast beef, for one thing. I bought a quarter of a pound coming home from my aunt's."

"Why a quarter of a pound, Joan?" said Rogin, deeply annoyed. "That's just about enough for one good sandwich."

"So you have to stop at a delicatessen. I had no more money."

He was about to ask, "What happened to the thirty dollars I gave you on Wednesday?" but he knew that would not be right.

"I had to give Phyllis money for the cleaning woman," said Joan.

Phyllis, Joan's cousin, was a young divorcée, extremely wealthy. The two women shared an apartment.

"Roast beef," he said, "and what else?"

"Some shampoo, sweetheart. We've used up all the shampoo. And hurry, darling, I've missed you all day."

"And I've missed you," said Rogin, but to tell the truth he had been worrying most of the time. He had a younger brother whom he was putting through college. And his mother, whose annuity wasn't quite enough in these days of inflation and high taxes, needed money, too. Joan had debts he was helping her to pay, for she wasn't working. She was looking for something suitable to do. Beautiful, well educated, aristocratic in her attitude, she couldn't clerk in a dime store; she couldn't model clothes (Rogin thought this made girls vain and stiff, and he didn't want her to); she couldn't be a waitress or a cashier. What could she be? Well, something would turn up, and meantime Rogin hesitated to complain. He paid her bills—the dentist, the department store, the osteopath, the doctor, the psychiatrist. At Christmas, Rogin almost went mad. Joan bought him a velvet smoking jacket with frog fasteners, a beautiful pipe, and a pouch. She bought Phyllis a garnet brooch, an Italian silk umbrella, and a gold cigarette holder. For other friends, she bought Dutch pewter and Swedish glassware. Before she was through, she had spent five hundred dollars of Rogin's money. He loved her too much to show his suffering. He believed she had a far better nature than his. She didn't worry about money. She had a marvelous character, always cheerful, and she really didn't need a psychiatrist at all. She went to one because Phyllis did and it made her curious. She tried too much to keep up with her cousin, whose father had made millions in the rug business.

While the woman in the drugstore was wrapping the shampoo bottle, a clear idea suddenly arose in Rogin's thoughts: Money surrounds you in life as the earth does in death. Super-imposition is the universal law. Who is free? No one is free. Who has no burdens? Everyone is under pressure. The very rocks, the waters of the earth, beasts, men, children —everyone has some weight to carry. This idea was extremely clear to him at first. Soon it became rather vague, but it had a great effect nevertheless, as if someone had given him a valuable gift. (Not like the velvet smoking jacket he couldn't bring himself to wear, or the pipe it choked him to smoke.) The notion that all were under pressure and affliction, instead of saddening him, had the opposite influence. It put him in a wonderful mood. It was extraordinary how happy he became and, in addition, clear-sighted. His eyes all at once were opened to what was around him. He saw with delight how the druggist and the woman who wrapped the shampoo bottle were smiling and flirting, how the lines of worry in her face went over into lines of cheer and the druggist's receding gums did not hinder his kidding and friendliness. And in the delicatessen, also, it was amazing how much Rogin noted and what happiness it gave him simply to be there.

Delicatessens on Sunday night, when all other stores are shut, will overcharge you ferociously, and Rogin would normally have been on guard, but he was not tonight, or scarcely so. Smells of pickle, sausage, mustard, and smoked fish overjoyed him. He pitied the people who would buy the chicken salad and chopped herring; they could do it only because their sight was too dim to see what they were getting—the fat flakes of pepper on the chicken, the soppy herring, mostly vinegar-soaked stale bread. Who would buy them? Late risers, people living alone, waking up in the darkness of the afternoon, finding their refrigerators empty, or people whose gaze was turned inward. The roast beef looked not bad, and Rogin ordered a pound.

While the storekeeper was slicing the meat, he yelled at a Puerto Rican kid who was reaching for a bag of chocolate cookies, "Hey, you want to pull me down the whole display on yourself? You, *chico*, wait a half a minute." This storekeeper, though he looked like one of Pancho Villa's bandits, the kind that smeared their enemies with syrup and staked them down on anthills, a man with toadlike eyes and stout hands made to clasp pistols hung around his belly, was not so bad. He was a New York man, thought Rogin—who was from Albany himself—a New York man toughened by every abuse of the city, trained to suspect everyone. But in his own realm, on the board behind the counter, there was justice. Even clemency.

The Puerto Rican kid wore a complete cowboy outfit—a green hat with white braid, guns, chaps, spurs, boots, and gauntlets—but he couldn't speak any English. Rogin unhooked the cellophane bag of hard circular cookies and gave it to him. The boy tore the cellophane with his teeth and began to chew one of those dry chocolate discs. Rogin recognized his state—the energetic dream of childhood. Once, he, too, had found these dry biscuits delicious. It would have bored him now to eat one.

What else would Joan like? Rogin thought fondly. Some strawberries? "Give me some frozen strawberries. No, raspberries, she likes those better. And heavy cream. And some rolls, cream cheese, and some of those rubber-looking gherkins."

"What rubber?"

"Those, deep green, with eyes. Some ice cream might be in order, too."

He tried to think of a compliment, a good comparison, an endearment, for Joan when she'd open the door. What about her complexion? There was really nothing to compare her sweet, small, daring, shapely, timid, defiant, loving face to. How difficult she was, and how beautiful!

As Rogin went down into the stony, odorous, metallic, captive air of the subway, he was diverted by an unusual confession made by a man to his friend. These were two very tall men, shapeless in their winter clothes, as if their coats concealed suits of chain mail.

"So, how long have you known me?" said one.

"Twelve years."

"Well, I have an admission to make," he said. "I've decided that I might as well. For years I've been a heavy drinker. You didn't know. Practically an alcoholic."

But his friend was not surprised, and he answered immediately, "Yes, I did know."

"You knew? Impossible! How could you?"

Why, thought Rogin, as if it could be a secret! Look at that long, austere, alcohol-washed face, that drink-ruined nose, the skin by his ears like turkey wattles, and those whiskey-saddened eyes.

"Well, I did know, though."

"You couldn't have. I can't believe it." He was upset, and his friend didn't seem to want to soothe him. "But it's all right now," he said. "I've been going to a doctor and taking pills, a new revolutionary Danish discovery. It's a miracle. I'm beginning to believe they can cure you of anything and everything. You can't beat the Danes in science. They do everything. They turned a man into a woman."

"That isn't how they stop you from drinking, is it?"

"No. I hope not. This is only like aspirin. It's super-aspirin. They call it the aspirin of the future. But if you use it, you have to stop drinking."

Rogin's illuminated mind asked of itself while the human tides of the subway swayed back and forth, and cars linked and transparent like fish bladders raced under the streets: How come he thought nobody would know what everybody couldn't help knowing? And, as a chemist, he asked himself what kind of compound this new Danish drug might be, and started thinking about various inventions of his own, synthetic albumen, a cigarette that lit itself, a cheaper motor fuel. Ye gods, but he needed money! As never before. What was to be done? His mother was growing more and more difficult. On Friday night, she had neglected to cut up his meat for him, and he was hurt. She had sat at the table motionless, with her long-suffering face, severe, and let him cut his own meat, a thing she almost never did. She had always spoiled him and made his brother envy him. But what she expected now! Oh, Lord, how he had to pay, and it had never even occurred to him formerly that these things might have a price.

Seated, one of the passengers, Rogin recovered his calm, happy, even clairvoyant state of mind. To think of money was to think as the world wanted you to think; then you'd never be your own master. When people said they wouldn't do something for love or money, they meant that love and money were opposite passions and one the enemy of the other. He went on to reflect how little people knew about this, how they slept through life, how small a light the light of consciousness was. Rogin's clean, snub-nosed face shone while his heart was torn with joy at these deeper thoughts of our ignorance. You might take this drunkard as an example, who for long years thought his closest friends never suspected he drank. Rogin looked up and down the aisle for this remarkable knightly symbol, but he was gone.

However, there was no lack of things to see. There was a small girl with a new white muff; into the muff a doll's head was sewn, and the child was happy and affectionately vain of it, while her old man, stout and grim, with a huge scowling nose, kept picking her up and resettling her in the seat, as if he were trying to change her into something else. Then another child, led by her mother, boarded the car, and this other child carried the very same doll-faced muff, and this greatly annoyed both parents. The woman, who looked like a difficult, contentious woman, took her daughter away. It seemed to Rogin that each child was in love with its own muff and didn't even see the other, but it was one of his foibles to think he understood the hearts of little children.

A foreign family next engaged his attention. They looked like Central Americans to him. On one side the mother, quite old, dark-faced, white-haired, and worn out; on the other a son with the whitened, porous hands of a dishwasher. But what was the dwarf who sat between them—a son or a daughter? The hair was long and wavy and the cheeks smooth, but the shirt and tie were masculine. The overcoat was feminine, but the shoes—the shoes were a puzzle. A pair of brown oxfords with an outer seam like a man's, but Baby Louis heels like a woman's—a plain toe like a man's, but a strap across the instep like a woman's. No stockings. That didn't help much. The dwarf's fingers were beringed, but without a wedding band. There were small grim dents in the cheeks. The eyes were puffy and concealed, but Rogin did not doubt that they could reveal strange things if they chose and that this was a creature of remarkable understanding. He had for many years owned De la Mare's *Memoirs of a Midget*. Now he took a resolve; he would read it. As soon as he had decided, he was free from his consuming curiosity as to the dwarf's sex and was able to look at the person who sat beside him.

Thoughts very often grow fertile in the subway, because of the motion, the great company, the subtlety of the rider's state as he rattles under streets and rivers, under the foundations of great buildings, and Rogin's mind had already been strangely stimulated. Clasping the bag of groceries from which there rose odors of bread and pickle spice, he was following a train of reflections, first about the chemistry of sex determination, the X and Y chromosomes, hereditary linkages, the uterus, afterward about his brother as a tax exemption. He recalled two dreams of the night before. In one, an undertaker had offered to cut his hair, and he had refused. In another, he had been carrying a woman on his head. Sad dreams, both! Very sad! Which was the woman—Joan or Mother? And the undertaker—his lawyer? He gave a deep sigh, and by force of habit began to put together his synthetic albumen that was to revolutionize the entire egg industry.

Meanwhile, he had not interrupted his examination of the passengers and had fallen into a study of the man next to him. This was a man whom he had never in his life seen before but with whom he now suddenly felt linked through all existence. He was middle-aged, sturdy, with clear skin and blue eyes. His hands were clean, well formed, but Rogin did not approve of them. The coat he wore was a fairly expensive blue check such as Rogin would never have chosen for himself. He would not have worn blue suède shoes, either, or such a faultless hat, a cumbersome felt animal of a hat encircled by a high, fat ribbon. There are all kinds of dandies, not all of them are of the flaunting kind; some are dandies of respectability, and Rogin's fellow passenger was one of these. His straight-nosed profile was handsome, yet he had betrayed his gift, for he was flat-looking. But in his flat way he seemed to warn people that he wanted no difficulties with them, he wanted nothing to do with them. Wearing such blue suède shoes, he could not afford to have people treading on his feet, and he seemed to draw about himself a circle of privilege, notifying all others to mind their own business and let him read his paper. He was holding a *Tribune*, and perhaps it would be overstatement to say that he was reading. He was holding it.

His clear skin and blue eyes, his straight and purely Roman nose—even the way he sat—all strongly suggested one person to Rogin: Joan. He tried to escape the comparison, but it couldn't be helped. This man not only looked like Joan's father, whom Rogin detested; he looked like Joan herself. Forty years hence, a son of hers, provided she had one, might be like this. A son of hers? Of such a son, he himself, Rogin, would be the father. Lacking in dominant traits as compared with Joan, his heritage would not appear. Probably the children would resemble her. Yes, think forty years ahead, and a man like this, who sat by him knee to knee in the hurtling car among their fellow creatures, unconscious participants in a sort of great carnival of transit—such a man would carry forward what had been Rogin.

This was why he felt bound to him through all existence. What were forty years reckoned against eternity! Forty years were gone, and he was gazing at his own son. Here he was. Rogin was frightened and moved. "My son! My son!" he said to himself, and the pity of it almost made him burst into tears. The holy and frightful work of the masters of life and death brought this about. We were their instruments. We worked toward ends we thought were our own. But no! The whole thing was so unjust. To suffer, to labor, to toil and force your way through the spikes of life, to crawl through its darkest caverns, to push through the worst, to struggle under the weight of economy, to make money—only to become the father of a fourth-rate man of the world like this, so flat-looking, with his ordinary, clean, rosy, uninteresting, self-satisfied, fundamentally bourgeois face. What a curse to have a dull son! A son like this, who could never understand his father. They had absolutely nothing, but nothing, in common, he and this neat, chubby, blue-eyed man. He was so pleased, thought Rogin, with all he owned and all he did and all he was that he could hardly unfasten his lip. Look at that lip, sticking up at the tip like a little thorn or egg tooth. He wouldn't give anyone the time of day. Would this perhaps be general forty years from now? Would personalities be chillier as the world aged and grew colder? The inhumanity of the next generation incensed Rogin. Father and son had no sign to make to each other. Terrible! Inhuman! What a vision of existence it gave him. Man's personal aims were nothing, illusion. The life force occupied each of us in turn in its progress toward its own fulfillment, trampling on our individual humanity, using us for its own ends like mere dinosaurs or bees, exploiting love heartlessly, making us engage in the social process, labor, struggle for money, and submit to the law of pressure, the universal law of layers, superimposition!

What the blazes am I getting into? Rogin thought. To be the father of a throwback to *her* father. The image of this white-haired, gross, peevish old man with his ugly selfish blue eyes revolted Rogin. This was how his grandson would look. Joan, with whom Rogin was now more and more displeased, could not help that. For her, it was inevitable. But did it have to be inevitable for him? Well, then, Rogin, you fool, don't be a damned instrument. Get out of the way!

But it was too late for this, because he had already experienced the sensation of sitting next to his own son, his son and Joan's. He kept staring at him, waiting for him to say something, but the presumptive son remained coldly silent though he must have been aware of Rogin's scrutiny. They even got out at the same stop—Sheridan Square. When they stepped to the platform, the man, without even looking at Rogin, went away in a different direction in his detestable blue-checked coat, with his rosy, nasty face.

The whole thing upset Rogin very badly. When he approached Joan's door and heard Phyllis's little dog Henri barking even before he could knock, his face was very tense. "I won't be used," he declared to himself. "I have my own right to exist." Joan had better watch out. She had a light way of bypassing grave questions he had given earnest thought to. She always assumed no really disturbing thing would happen. He could not afford the luxury of such a carefree, debonair attitude himself, because he had to work hard and earn money so that disturbing things would *not* happen. Well, at the moment this situation could not be helped, and he really did not mind the money if he could feel that she was not necessarily the mother of such a son as his subway son or entirely the daughter of that awful, obscene father of hers. After all,

Rogin was not himself so much like either of his parents, and quite different from his brother.

Joan came to the door, wearing one of Phyllis's expensive housecoats. It suited her very well. At first sight of her happy face, Rogin was brushed by the shadow of resemblance; the touch of it was extremely light, almost figmentary, but it made his flesh tremble.

She began to kiss him, saying, "Oh, my baby. You're covered with snow. Why didn't you wear your hat? It's all over its little head"—her favorite third-person endearment.

"Well, let me put down this bag of stuff. Let me take off my coat," grumbled Rogin, and escaped from her embrace. Why couldn't she wait making up to him? "It's so hot in here. My face is burning. Why do you keep the place at this temperature? And that damned dog keeps barking. If you didn't keep it cooped up, it wouldn't be so spoiled and noisy. Why doesn't anybody ever walk him?"

"Oh, it's not really so hot here! You've just come in from the cold. Don't you think this housecoat fits me better than Phyllis? Especially across the hips. She thinks so, too. She may sell it to me."

"I hope not," Rogin almost exclaimed.

She brought a towel to dry the melting snow from his short black hair. The flurry of rubbing excited Henri intolerably, and Joan locked him up in the bedroom, where he jumped persistently against the door with a rhythmic sound of claws on the wood.

Joan said, "Did you bring the shampoo?"

"Here it is."

"Then I'll wash your hair before dinner. Come."

"I don't want it washed."

"Oh, come on," she said, laughing.

Her lack of consciousness of guilt amazed him. He did not see how it could be. And the carpeted, furnished, lamplit, curtained room seemed to stand against his vision. So that he felt accusing and angry, his spirit sore and bitter, but it did not seem fitting to say why. Indeed, he began to worry lest the reason for it all slip away from him.

They took off his coat and his shirt in the bathroom, and she filled the sink. Rogin was full of his troubled emotions; now that his chest was bare he could feel them even more distinctly inside, and he said to himself, I'll have a thing or two to tell her pretty soon. I'm not letting them get away with it. "Do you think," he was going to tell her, "that I alone was made to carry the burden of the whole world on me? Do you think I was born just to be taken advantage of and sacrificed? Do you think I'm just a natural resource, like a coal mine, or oil well, or fishery, or the like? Remember, that I'm a man is no reason why I should be loaded down. I have a soul in me no bigger or stronger than yours.

"Take away the externals, like the muscles, deeper voice, and so forth, and what remains? A pair of spirits, practically alike. So why shouldn't there also be equality? I can't always be the strong one."

"Sit here," said Joan, bringing up a kitchen stool to the sink. "Your hair's gotten all matted."

He sat with his breast against the cool enamel, his chin on the edge of the basin, the green, hot, radiant water reflecting the glass and the tile, and the sweet, cool, fragrant juice of the shampoo poured on his head. She began to wash him.

"You have the healthiest-looking scalp," she said. "It's all pink."

He answered, "Well, it should be white. There must be something wrong with me."

"But there's absolutely nothing wrong with you," she said, and pressed against him from behind, surrounding him, pouring the water gently over him until it seemed to him that the water came from within him, it was the warm fluid of his own secret loving spirit overflowing into the sink, green and foaming, and the words he had rehearsed he forgot, and his anger at his son-to-be disappeared altogether, and he sighed, and said to her from the water-filled hollow of the sink, "You always have such wonderful ideas, Joan. You know? You have a kind of instinct, a regular gift."

1947

John [Hoyer] Updike

(1932-)

Although still in his thirties, John Updike has already produced two volumes of poetry, two collections of short stories, and three impressive novels. He was born in Shillington, Pennsylvania, educated at Harvard, and began his writing career on the staff of the *New Yorker* magazine. His first volume, *The Carpentered Hen* (1957), was a selection of verse. The next year appeared his first novel, *The Poorhouse Fair. Rabbit, Run* (1960) and *The Centaur* (1963) followed in short order. Two collections of short stories are *The Same Door* (1959) and *Pigeon Feathers and Other Stories* (1962). *Telephone Poles and Other Poems* appeared in 1963.

A & P

In walks these three girls in nothing but bathing suits. I'm in the third checkout slot, with my back to the door, so I don't see them until they're over by the bread. The one that caught my eye first was the one in the plaid green two-piece. She was a chunky kid, with a good tan and a sweet broad soft-looking can with those two crescents of white just under it, where the sun never seems to hit, at the top of the backs of her legs. I stood there with my hand on a box of HiHo crackers trying to remember if I rang it up or not. I ring it up again and the customer starts giving me hell. She's one of these cash-register-watchers, a witch about fifty with rouge on her cheekbones and no eyebrows, and I know it made her day to trip me up. She'd been watching cash registers for fifty years and probably never seen a mistake before.

By the time I got her feathers smoothed and her goodies into a bag—she gives me a little snort in passing, if she'd been born at the right time they would have burned her over in Salem—by the time I get her on her way the girls had circled around the bread and were coming back, without a pushcart, back my way along the counters, in the aisle between the checkouts and the Special bins. They didn't even have shoes on. There was this chunky one, with the two-piece—it was bright green and the seams on the bra were still sharp and her belly was still pretty pale so I guessed she just got it (the suit)—there was this one, with one of those chubby berry-faces, the lips all bunched together under her nose, this one, and a tall one, with black hair that hadn't quite frizzed right, and one of these sunburns right across under the eyes, and a chin that was too long—you know, the kind of girl other girls think is very "striking" and "attractive" but never quite makes it, as they very well know, which is why they like her so much—and then the third one, that wasn't quite so tall. She was the queen. She kind of led them, the other two peeking around and making their shoulders round. She didn't look around, not this queen, she just walked straight on slowly, on these long white prima-donna legs. She came down a little hard on her heels, as if she didn't walk in her bare feet that much, putting down her heels and then letting the weight move along to her toes as if she was testing the floor with every step, putting a little deliberate extra action into it. You never know for sure how girls' minds work (do you really think it's a mind in there or just a little buzz like a bee in a glass jar?) but you got the idea she had talked the other two into coming in here with her, and now she was showing them how to do it, walk slow and hold yourself straight.

She had on a kind of dirty-pink—beige maybe, I don't know—bathing suit with a little nubble all over it and, what got me, the straps were down. They were off her shoulders looped loose around the cool tops of her arms, and I guess as a result the suit had slipped a little on her, so all around the top of the cloth there was this shining rim. If it hadn't been there you wouldn't have known there could have been anything whiter than those shoulders. With the straps pushed off, there was nothing between the top of the suit and the top of her head except just *her*, this clean bare plane of the top of her chest down from the shoulder bones like a dented sheet of metal tilted in the light. I mean, it was more than pretty.

She had sort of oaky hair that the sun and salt had bleached, done up in a bun that was unravelling, and a kind of prim face. Walking into the A & P with your straps down, I suppose it's the only kind of face you *can* have. She held her head so high her neck, coming up out of those white shoulders, looked kind of stretched, but I didn't mind. The longer her neck was, the more of her there was.

She must have felt in the corner of her eye me and over my shoulder Stokesie in the second slot watching, but she didn't tip. Not this queen. She kept her eyes moving across the racks, and stopped, and turned so slow it made my stomach rub the inside of my apron, and buzzed to the other two, who kind of huddled against her for relief, and then they all three of them went up the cat-and-dog-food-breakfast-cereal-macaroni-rice-raisins-seasonings-spreads-spaghetti-soft-drinks-crackers-and-cookies aisle. From the third slot I look straight up this aisle to the meat counter, and I watched them all the way. The fat one with the tan sort of fumbled with the cookies, but on second thought she put the package back. The sheep pushing their carts down the aisle—the girls were walking against the usual traffic (not that we have one-way signs or anything)—were pretty hilarious. You could see them, when Queenie's white shoulders dawned on them, kind of jerk, or hop, or hiccup, but their eyes snapped back to their own baskets and on they pushed. I bet you could set off dynamite in an A & P and the people would by and large keep reaching and checking oatmeal off their lists and muttering "Let me see, there was a third thing, began with A, asparagus, no, ah, yes, applesauce!" or whatever it is they do mutter. But there was no doubt, this jiggled them. A few houseslaves in pin curlers even look around after pushing their carts past to make sure what they had seen was correct.

You know, it's one thing to have a girl in a bathing suit down on the beach, where what with the glare nobody can look at each other much anyway, and another thing in the cool of the A & P, under the fluorescent lights, against all those stacked packages, with her feet paddling along naked over our checker-board green-and-cream rubber-tile floor.

"Oh Daddy," Stokesie said beside me. "I feel so faint."

"Darling," I said. "Hold me tight." Stokesie's married, with two babies chalked up on his fuselage already, but as far as I can tell that's the only difference. He's twenty-two, and I was nineteen this April.

"Is it done?" he asks, the responsible married man finding his voice. I forgot to say he thinks he's going to be manager some sunny day, maybe in 1990 when it's called the Great Alexandrov and Petrooshki Tea Company or something.

What he meant was, our town is five miles from a beach, with a big summer colony out on the Point, but we're right in the middle of town, and the women generally put on a shirt or shorts or something before they get out of the car into the street. And anyway these are usually women with six children and varicose veins mapping their legs and nobody, including them, could care less. As I say, we're right in the middle of town, and if you stand at our front doors you can see two banks and the Congregational church and the newspaper store and three real-estate offices and about twenty-seven old freeloaders tearing up Central Street because the sewer broke again. It's not as if we're on the Cape; we're north of Boston and there's people in this town haven't seen the ocean for twenty years.

The girls had reached the meat counter and were asking McMahon something. He pointed, they pointed, and they shuffled out of sight behind a pyramid of Diet Delight peaches. All that was left for us to see was old McMahon patting his mouth and looking after them sizing up their joints. Poor kids, I began to feel sorry for them, they couldn't help it.

Now here comes the sad part of the story, at least my family says it's sad, but I don't think it's so sad myself. The store's pretty empty, it being Thursday afternoon, so there was nothing much to do except lean on the register and wait for the girls to show up again. The whole store was like a pinball machine and I didn't know which tunnel they'd come out of. After a while they come around out of the far aisle, around the light bulbs, records at discount of the Caribbean Six or Tony Martin Sings or some such gunk you wonder they waste the wax on, sixpacks of candy bars, and plastic toys done up in cellophane that fall apart when a kid looks at them anyway. Around they come, Queenie still leading the way, and holding a little gray jar in her hand. Slots Three through Seven are unmanned and I could see her wondering between Stokes and me, but Stokesie with his usual luck draws an old party in baggy gray pants who stumbles up with four giant cans of pineapple juice (what do these bums *do* with all that pineapple juice? I've often asked myself) so the girls come to me. Queenie puts down the jar and I take it into my fingers icy cold. Kingfish Fancy Herring Snacks in Pure Sour Cream: 49¢. Now her hands are empty, not a ring or a bracelet, bare as God made them, and I wonder where the money's coming from. Still with that prim look she lifts a folded dollar bill out of the hollow at the center of her nubbled pink top. The jar went heavy in my hand. Really, I thought that was so cute.

Then everybody's luck begins to run out. Lengel comes in from haggling with a truck full of cabbages on the lot and is about to scuttle into that door marked MANAGER behind which he hides all day when the girls touch his eye. Lengel's pretty dreary, teaches Sunday school and the rest, but he doesn't miss that much. He comes over and says, "Girls, this isn't the beach."

Queenie blushes, though maybe it's just a brush of sunburn I was noticing for the first time, now that she was so close. "My mother asked me to pick up a jar of herring snacks." Her voice kind of startled me, the way voices do when you see the people first, coming out so flat and dumb yet kind of tony, too, the way it ticked over "pick up" and "snacks." All of a sudden I slid right down her voice into her living room. Her father and the other men were standing around in ice-cream coats and bow ties and the women were in sandals picking up herring snacks on toothpicks off a big glass plate and they were all holding drinks the color of water with olives and sprigs of mint in them. When my parents have somebody over they get lemonade and if it's a real racy affair Schlitz in tall glasses with "They'll Do It Every Time" cartoons stencilled on.

"That's all right," Lengel said. "But this isn't the beach." His repeating this struck me as funny, as if it had just occurred to him, and he had been thinking all these years the A & P was a great big dune and he was the head lifeguard. He didn't like my smiling—as I say he doesn't miss much—but he concentrates on giving the girls that sad Sunday-school-superintendent stare.

Queenie's blush is no sunburn now, and the plump one in plaid, that I liked better from the back—a really sweet can—pipes up, "We weren't doing any shopping. We just came in for the one thing."

"That makes no difference," Lengel tells her, and I could see from the way his eyes went that he hadn't noticed she was wearing a two-piece before. "We want you decently dressed when you come in here."

"We *are* decent," Queenie says suddenly, her lower lip pushing, getting sore now that she remembers her place, a place from which the crowd that runs the A & P must look pretty crummy. Fancy Herring Snacks flashed in her very blue eyes.

"Girls, I don't want to argue with you. After this come in here with your shoulders covered. It's our policy." He turns his back. That's policy for you. Policy is what the kingpins want. What the others want is juvenile delinquency.

All this while, the customers had been showing up with their carts but, you know, sheep, seeing a scene, they had all bunched up on Stokesie, who shook open a paper bag as gently as peeling a peach, not wanting to miss a word. I could feel in the silence everybody getting nervous, most of all Lengel, who asks me, "Sammy, have you rung up this purchase?"

I thought and said "No" but it wasn't about that I was thinking. I go through the punches, 4, 9, GROC, TOT—it's more complicated than you think, and after you do it often enough, it begins to make a little song, that you hear words to, in my case "Hello (*bing*) there, you (*gung*) hap-py *pee*-pul (*splat*)!"—the *splat* being the drawer flying out. I uncrease the bill, tenderly as you may imagine, it just having come from between the two smoothest scoops of vanilla I had ever known were there, and pass a half and a penny into her narrow pink palm, and nestle the herrings in a bag and twist its neck and hand it over, all the time thinking.

The girls, and who'd blame them, are in a hurry to get out, so I say "I quit" to Lengel quick enough for them to hear, hoping they'll stop and watch me, their unsuspected hero. They keep right on going, into the electric eye; the door flies open and they flicker across the lot to their car, Queenie and Plaid and Big Tall Goony-Goony (not that as raw material she was so bad), leaving me with Lengel and a kink in his eyebrow.

"Did you say something, Sammy?"

"I said I quit."

"I thought you did."

"You didn't have to embarrass them."

"It was they who were embarrassing us."

I started to say something that came out "Fiddle-de-doo." It's a saying of my grandmother's, and I know she would have been pleased.

"I don't think you know what you're saying," Lengel said.

"I know you don't," I said. "But I do." I pull the bow at the back of my apron and start shrugging it off my shoulders. A couple customers that had been heading for my slot begin to knock against each other, like scared pigs in a chute.

Lengel sighs and begins to look very patient and old and gray. He's been a friend of my parents for years. "Sammy, you don't want to do this to your Mom and Dad," he tells me. It's true, I don't. But it seems to me that once you begin a gesture it's fatal not to go through with it. I fold the apron, "Sammy" stitched in red on the pocket, and put it on the counter, and drop the bow tie on top of it. The bow tie is theirs, if you've ever wondered. "You'll feel this for the rest of your life," Lengel says, and I know that's true, too, but remembering how he made that pretty girl blush makes me so scrunchy inside I punch the No Sale tab and the machine whirs "pee-pul" and the drawer splats out. One advantage to this scene taking place in summer, I can follow this up with a clean exit, there's no fumbling around getting your coat and galoshes, I just saunter into the electric eye in my white shirt that my mother ironed the night before, and the door heaves itself open, and outside the sunshine is skating around on the asphalt.

I look around for my girls, but they're gone, of course. There wasn't anybody but some young married screaming with her children about some candy they didn't get by the door of a powder-blue Falcon station wagon. Looking back in the big windows, over the bags of peat moss and aluminum lawn furniture stacked on the pavement, I could see Lengel in my place in the slot, checking the sheep through. His face was dark gray and his back stiff, as if he'd just had an injection of iron, and my stomach kind of fell as I felt how hard the world was going to be to me hereafter.

1961

A SELECTED BIBLIOGRAPHY

GENERAL BIBLIOGRAPHICAL REFERENCES:

The academic journals—*Abstracts of English Studies, American Literature, American Quarterly, The Journal of Aesthetics and Arts Criticism, Modern Fiction Studies, PMLA,* and *Twentieth-Century Literature*—all carry current or annual bibliographies of studies of American Literature. Other standard sources follow:

Altick, Richard, and Andrew Wright. *Selected Bibliography for the Study of English and American Literature,* 1960.

Gohdes, Clarence. *Bibliographical Guide to the Study of the Literature of the United States,* 1959; rev. ed., 1963.

Johnson, Merle D. *American First Editions,* 4th ed., 1942.

Jones, Howard Mumford. *Guide to American Literature and Its Backgrounds Since 1890,* 1953; rev. ed., 1964.

Jones, Joseph, and others. *American Literary Manuscripts,* 1961.

Leary, Lewis G. *Articles on American Literature, 1900-1950,* 1954.

———. *Contemporary Literary Scholarship: A Critical Review,* 1958.

Millett, F. B. *Contemporary American Authors: A Critical Survey and 219 Bio-Bibliographies,* 1940.

Quinn, A. H. *The Literature of the American People,* 1951.

Spiller, Robert E., and others. *Literary History of the United States,* Vol. II, 3rd ed., rev., 1964.

Taylor, W. F. *A History of American Letters,* 1935; rev. ed., 1960.

Woodress, James. *Dissertations in American Literature, 1891-1955,* 1957; *Supplement, 1956-1961,* 1962.

———. ed., *Annual Review of American Literary Scholarship* (for 1963), 1965.

GENERAL BIOGRAPHICAL REFERENCES:

Cowley, Malcolm, ed. *Writers at Work: The Paris Review Interviews,* 1958; . . . *Second Series,* with an Introduction by Van Wyck Brooks, 1963.

Hart, James D. *The Oxford Companion to American Literature,* 3rd ed., 1956.

Herzberg, Max J., ed. *The Reader's Encyclopedia of American Literature,* 1962.

Johnson, Allen, and Dumas Malone. *The Dictionary of American Biography,* 20 Vols., 1928-1937; *Supplement I,* 1944; *Supplement II,* 1958.

Kaplin, Louis. *A Bibliography of American Autobiographies,* 1961.

Kunitz, Stanley, and Howard Haycraft. *Twentieth Century Authors,* 1942; *First Supplement,* 1955.

Who Was Who in America, 1897-1950, 1950.

Who's Who, 1951——.

SPECIAL STUDIES AND HISTORIES:

Aaron, Daniel. *Writers on the Left: Episodes in American Literary Communism*, 1961.

Aldrich, John. *In Search of Heresy: American Literature in an Age of Conformity*, 1956.

Allen, Frederick. *Only Yesterday: An Informal History of the Nineteen-Twenties*, 1931, 1946, 1959.

———. *Since Yesterday: The Nineteen-Thirties in America*. 1940.

The American Year Book, 1919-1950, 1911-1951.

Boynton, Percy H. *Some Contemporary Americans*, 1924.

Bradbury, John M. *Renaissance in the South: A Critical History of the Literature, 1920-1960*, 1963.

Brooks, Van Wyck. *Opinions of Oliver Allston*, 1941.

———. *The Confident Years, 1885-1915*, 1952.

Burtis, Mary Elizabeth, and Paul S. Wood. *Recent American Literature*, 1961.

Cargill, Oscar. *Intellectual America: Ideas on the March*, 1941, 1959.

Commager, Henry S. *The American Mind: An Interpretation of American Thought and Character Since the 1880's*, 1950, 1959.

Cowley, Malcolm, ed. *After the Genteel Tradition*, 1937.

———. *Exile's Return: A Narrative of Ideas*, 1934; rev. ed., 1951.

———. *The Literary Situation*, 1954.

Duffey, Bernard. *The Chicago Renaissance in American Letters*, 1954.

Fadiman, Clifton, ed. *I Believe: The Personal Philosophies of Certain Eminent Men and Women of Our Time*, 1939.

Fishman, Solomon. *The Disinherited of Art: Writer and Background*, 1953.

Frohock, Wilbur M. *Strangers to This Ground: Cultural Diversity in Contemporary American Writing*, 1961.

Gurko, Leo. *The Angry Decade*, 1947.

Hoffmann, Frederick J. *Freudianism and the Literary Mind*, 2nd. ed., 1959.

———. *The Twenties*, 1955; rev. ed., 1962.

Kazin, Alfred. *On Native Grounds*, 1942, 1955.

Knight, Grant C. *The Strenuous Age in American Literature, 1900-1910*, 1954.

Krutch, Joseph Wood. *The Modern Temper*, 1929.

Loggins, V. *I Hear America: Literature in the United States Since 1900*, 1937.

Lynn, Kenneth S. *The Dream of Success: A Study of the Modern American Imagination*, 1955.

MacLeish, Archibald. *America Was Promises*, 1939.

———. *The Irresponsibles*, 1940.

McWilliams, C. *The New Regionalism in American Literature*, 1930.

Morris, Lloyd R. *Postscript to Yesterday: American: The Last Fifty Years*, 1947.

Parkinson, Thomas, ed. *A Casebook on the Beat*, 1961.

Rubin, Louis D., Jr., and Robert D. Jacobs, eds. *Southern Renascence: The Literature of the Modern South*, 1953.

———. *South: Modern Southern Literature in Its Cultural Setting*, 1961.

Spiller, Robert, and others, eds. *The Literary History of the United States*, Vol. II, 1948; 1963.

———, ed. *A Time of Harvest: American Literature, 1910-1960*, 1962.

Straumann, Heinrich. *American Literature in the Twentieth Century*, 1951.

Thorp, Willard. *American Writing in the Twentieth Century*, 1960.

University of Minnesota Pamphlets on American Writers. [A series of forty-eight biographical, bibliographical, and critical introductions to major American writers.]

Whipple, T. K. *Spokesmen: Modern Writers and American Life*, 1928.

Wilson, Edmund. *The Shock of Recognition*, Vol. II, 1955.

———. *The Shores of Light: A Literary Chronicle of the Twenties and Thirties*, 1952; 1920-1950, 1956.

CRITICISM:

Beaver, Harold, ed. *American Critical Essays: Twentieth Century,* 1959.
Bowman, J. C., ed. *Contemporary American Criticism,* 1926.
Brooks, Van Wyck. *Sketches in Criticism,* 1932.
Brown, Clarence, ed. *The Achievement of American Criticism, Part IV,* 1954.
Calverton, V. F. *The New Grounds of Criticism,* 1930.
Daiches, David. *Critical Approaches to Literature,* 1956.
Elton, William. *A Guide to the New Criticism,* 1951.
Foster, Richard. *The New Romantics: A Reappraisal of the New Criticism,* 1962.
Frailberg, Louis. *Psychoanalysis and American Literary Criticism,* 1960.
Glicksberg, C. I., ed. *American Literary Criticism: 1900-1950,* 1951.
Hyman, Stanley Edgar. *The Armed Vision: A Study in the Methods of Modern Literary Criticism,* 1947.
Jones, H. M. *The Theory of American Literature,* 1948.
La Drière, J. C. *Directions in Contemporary Criticism and Literary Scholarship,* 1953.
McKean, Keith F. *The Moral Measure of Literature,* 1961.
Muller, Herbert. *Science and Criticism: The Humanist Tradition,* 1943.
O'Connor, W. Van. *An Age of Criticism: 1900-1950,* 1952.
Oldsey, Bernard, and Arthur O. Lewis, eds. *Vision and Revisions in Modern Literary Criticism,* 1962.
Santayana, George. *The Genteel Tradition at Bay,* 1931.
Stallman, R. W., ed. *Critiques and Essays in Criticism, 1920-1948,* 1949.
———. *The Critic's Notebook,* 1950.
Stovall, Floyd, ed. *The Development of American Literary Criticism,* 1955.
Sutton, Walter. *Modern American Criticism,* 1963.
West, R. B., Jr., ed. *Essays in Modern Literary Criticism,* 1952.
Zabel, M. D., ed. *Literary Opinion in America,* 3rd ed., 1962.

DRAMA:

Bander, Robert G. *Playwrights of the Modern American Theatre from O'Neill to Inge,* 1958.
Blum, Daniel, ed. *A Pictorial History of the American Theatre, 1900-1956,* 4th ed., 1956.
Boyd, Alice K. *The Interchange of Plays Between London and New York,* 1948.
Downer, Alan S. *Fifty Years of American Drama, 1900-1950,* 1951.
———. *Recent American Drama,* 1961.
Dusenbury, Winifred L. *The Themes of Loneliness in Modern American Drama,* 1960.
Flanagan, Hallie. *Arena,* 1940.
Gagey, Edmond M. *Revolution in American Drama,* 1947.
Gassner, John. *The Theatre in Our Times,* 1954.
———. *Form and Idea in the Modern Theatre,* 1956.
Hewitt, Barnard. *Theatre U.S.A. 1688 to 1957,* 1959.
Hughes, Glenn. *A History of the American Theatre, 1700-1950,* 1951.
Kinne, Wisner P. *George Pierce Baker and the American Theatre,* 1954.
Krutch, Joseph Wood. *The American Drama Since 1918: An Informal History,* rev. ed., 1957.
Macgowan, Kenneth. *Footlights Across America,* 1929.
Miller, Jordan Y., ed. *American Dramatic Literature: Ten Modern Plays in Historical Perspective,* 1961.
Morehouse, Ward. *Matinee Tomorrow: Fifty Years of Our Theatre,* 1949.
Quinn, Arthur H. *A History of the American Drama from the Civil War to the Present Day,* rev. ed., 1945.
Sievers, W. David. *Freud on Broadway: A History of Psychoanalysis and the American Drama,* 1955.

Smith, Cecil M. *Musical Comedy in America,* 1950.

Sper, Felix. *From Native Roots: A Panorama of Our Regional Drama,* 1948.

Weales, Gerald. *American Drama Since World War II,* 1962.

Weingarten, Joseph A. *Modern American Playwrights, 1918-1948,* 2 Vols., 1946-1947.

FICTION:

Åhnebrink, Lars. *The Beginnings of Naturalism in American Fiction,* 1950.

Aldridge, John W. *After the Lost Generation: A Critical Study of the Writers of Two Wars,* 1951.

———, ed. *Critiques and Essays on Modern Fiction, 1920-1951,* 1952.

Anderson, Carl L. *The Swedish Acceptance of American Literature,* 1957.

Balakian, Nona, and Charles Simmons, eds. *The Creative Present: Notes on Contemporary American Fiction,* 1963.

Beach, Joseph W. *American Fiction: 1920-1940,* 1941.

———. *The Twentieth Century Novel: Studies in Technique,* 1932.

Brooks, Cleanth, and R. P. Warren, eds. *Understanding Fiction,* 2nd ed., 1959.

Dickinson, A. T., Jr. *American Historical Fiction,* 1958.

Eisinger, C. E. *Fiction of the Forties,* 1963.

Fiedler, Leslie. *Love and Death in the American Novel,* 1960.

Friedman, Melvin. *Stream of Consciousness: A Study in Literary Method,* 1955.

Frohock, W. M. *The Novel of Violence in America: 1920-1950,* 1950.

Gardiner, H. C. *Fifty Years of the American Novel,* 1951.

Geismar, Maxwell. *American Moderns: From Rebellion to Conformity,* 1958.

———. *The Last of the Provincials,* 1947.

———. *Rebels and Ancestors: The American Novel: 1890-1915,* 1953.

———. *Writers in Crisis,* 1942.

Gelfant, Blanche. *The American City Novel,* 1954.

Gerstenberger, Donna, and George Henrick. *The American Novel, 1789-1959: A Checklist of Twentieth-Century Criticism,* 1961.

Glasgow, Ellen. *A Certain Measure: An Interpretation of Prose Fiction.*

Hassan, Ihab. *Radical Innocence: The Contemporary American Novel,* 1961.

Hatcher, Harlan. *Creating the Modern American Novel,* 1935.

Hartwick, Harry. *The Foreground of American Fiction,* 1934.

Hoffman, F. J. *The Modern Novel in America: 1900-1950,* rev. ed., 1956.

Howe, Irving. *Politics and the Novel,* 1957.

Kazin, Alfred. *The Inmost Leaf,* 1955.

Levin, Harry. *Symbolism and Fiction,* 1956.

Litz, Walton, ed. *Modern American Fiction: Essays in Criticism,* 1963.

Ludwig, Jack. *Recent American Novelists,* 1962.

Malin, Irving. *New American Gothic,* 1962.

Michaud, R. *The American Novel Today,* 1928.

Miller, James E., ed. *Myth and Method: Modern Theories of Fiction,* 1960.

Mizener, Arthur. *The Sense of Life in the Modern Novel,* 1964.

Muller, Herbert. *Modern Fiction,* 1937.

Munson, G. B. *Style and Form in American Prose,* 1929.

O'Connor, W. Van, ed. *Forms of Modern Fiction,* 1948.

———, ed. *Seven Modern American Novelists: An Introduction,* 1964.

Quinn, A. H. *American Fiction: An Historical and Critical Survey,* 1936.

Rideout, Walter. *The Radical Novel in the United States: 1900-1954,* 1956.

Rose, Lisle A. *A Survey of American Economic Fiction, 1902-1909,* 1938.

Simonini, R. C., Jr., ed. *Southern*

Writers: Appraisals in Our Time, 1964.

Smith, Thelma M., and Ward Miner. *Transatlantic Migration: The Contemporary American Novel in France,* 1955.

Springer, Anne M. *The American Novel in Germany,* 1960.

Stallman, R. W. *The Houses that James Built and Other Literary Studies,* 1961.

Thurston, Jarvis, and others, eds. *Short Fiction Criticism: A Checklist of Interpretation Since 1925 of Stories and Novelettes—1800-1958,* 1960.

Van Doren, Carl, ed. *Modern American Prose,* 1934.

Waldmeir, Joseph, ed. *Recent American Fiction: Some Critical Views,* 1963.

Walker, Warren S. *Twentieth-Century Short Story Explication: Interpretations, 1900-1960 Inclusive, of Short Fiction Since 1880,* 1961; *Supplement,* 1963.

West, R. B., Jr. *The Short Story in America: 1900-1950,* 1952.

Wright, Austin M. *The American Short Story in the Twenties,* 1962.

POETRY:

Beach, Joseph W. *Obsessive Images: Symbolism in the Poetry of the 1930's and 1940's,* 1960.

Bogan, Louise. *Achievement in American Poetry, 1900-1950,* 1951.

Bradbury, John M. *The Fugitives: A Critical Account,* 1958.

Brooks, Cleanth, and R. P. Warren, eds. *Understanding Poetry,* 1938.

Cambon, Glauco. *Recent American Poetry,* 1962.

Coffman, S. K. *Imagism: A Chapter for the History of Modern Poetry,* 1951.

Colum, Mary. *From These Roots,* rev. ed., 1945.

Cowan, Louise. *The Fugitive Group: A Literary History,* 1959.

Daiches, David. *Poetry and the Modern World,* 1940.

Drew, Elizabeth. *Discovering Poetry,* 1933.

Elliott, G. P. *Fifteen Modern American Poets,* 1956.

Granger's Index to Poetry, 4th ed., 1953.

Gregory, Horace, and Marya Zaturenska. *A History of American Poetry: 1900-1940,* 1946.

Hughes, Glenn. *Imagism and the Imagists,* 1931.

Irish, Wynot R. *The Modern American Muse . . . 1900-1925,* 1950.

Jarrell, Randall. *Poetry and the Age,* 1953.

Krieger, Murray. *The New Apologists for Poetry,* 1956.

Kreymborg, Alfred. *Our Singing Strength,* 1929.

Kuntz, Joseph M. *Poetry Explication,* rev. ed., 1962.

Lowell, Amy. *Tendencies in Modern American Poetry,* 1921.

MacLeish, Archibald. *Poetry and Experience,* 1961.

Miller, James E., Jr., and others. *Start with the Sun: Studies in Cosmic Poetry,* 1960.

O'Connor, W. Van. *Sense and Sensibility in Modern Poetry,* 1948.

Rittenhouse, Jessie B. *The Younger American Poets,* 1906.

Rosenthal, M. L. *The Modern Poets: A Critical Introduction,* 1960.

Shapiro, Karl. *A Bibliography of Modern Prosody,* 1948.

———. *In Defense of Ignorance,* 1960.

Skelton, Robert. *The Poetic Pattern,* 1956.

Tate, Allen. *Sixty American Poets, 1896-1944,* rev. ed., 1954.

Unger, Leonard. *The Man in the Name: Essays on the Experience of Poetry,* 1956.

Untermeyer, Louis. *American Poetry Since 1900,* 1923.

Waggoner, H. H. *The Heel of Elohim: Science and Values in Modern American Poetry,* 1950.

Wells, H. W. *New Poets from Old: A Study in Literary Genetics,* 1940.

INDEX

AUTHORS, TITLES, AND FIRST LINES OF POEMS

Numbers in parentheses refer to a discussion of an author in the text. All other numbers indicate selections quoted.